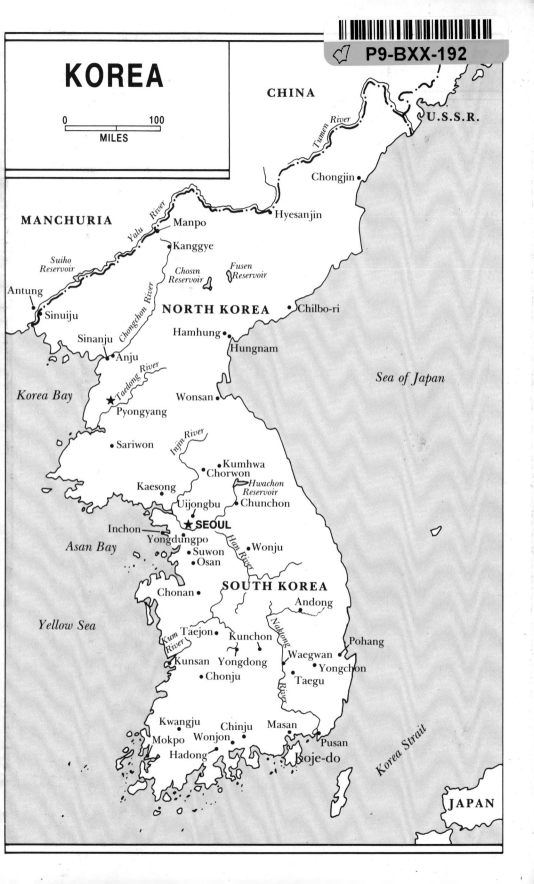

KOREA

0 |———————| 100
MILES

CHINA

U.S.S.R.

Tumen River

Chongjin •

MANCHURIA

Yalu River

Manpo •

Hyesanjin •

• Kanggye

Suiho Reservoir

Chosin Reservoir

Fusen Reservoir

Antung •

• Chilbo-ri

NORTH KOREA

Sinuiju •

Chongchon River

Sinanju •

Hamhung •

Anju •

Hungnam •

Taedong River

Korea Bay

★ Pyongyang

Wonsan •

Sea of Japan

• Sariwon

Imjin River

• Kumhwa
• Chorwon

Kaesong •

Hwachon Reservoir

Uijongbu •

• Chunchon

Inchon —

★ SEOUL

Yongdungpo

Han River

Asan Bay

• Suwon
• Osan

• Wonju

Chonan •

SOUTH KOREA

Andong •

Yellow Sea

Kum River

Taejon •

Kunchon •

Nakdong

Pohang •

Kunsan •

Yongdong

Waegwan •

• Yongchon

• Chonju

Taegu •

River

Kwangju •

Chinju •

Masan •

Mokpo •

Wonjon •

Pusan •

Hadong •

Boje-do

Korea Strait

JAPAN

IN MORTAL COMBAT

BY JOHN TOLAND

Fiction
OCCUPATION
GODS OF WAR

Nonfiction
IN MORTAL COMBAT
INFAMY
NO MAN'S LAND
HITLER: THE PICTORIAL DOCUMENTARY OF HIS LIFE
ADOLF HITLER
THE RISING SUN
THE LAST HUNDRED DAYS
BUT NOT IN SHAME
THE DILLINGER DAYS
BATTLE: THE STORY OF THE BULGE
SHIPS IN THE SKY

IN MORTAL
COMBAT

KOREA, 1950–1953

JOHN TOLAND

William Morrow and Company, Inc.
New York

Library of Congress Cataloguing-in-Publication Data

Toland, John.
    In mortal combat / John Toland.
        p.   cm.
    Includes bibliographical references and index.
    ISBN 0-688-10079-1
    1. Korean War.—1950–1953.   I. Title.
DS918.T658   1991
951.904′2—dc20   91-9320
                                                                                  CIP

Printed in the United States of America

First Edition

1 2 3 4 5 6 7 8 9 10

BOOK DESIGN AND MAPS BY JEFFREY L. WARD GDS

To all those who were there

Preface

Why a history of the Korean War? After two cataclysmic world conflicts it appeared to be lackluster in global importance and dramatic interest. At the time I shared the popular dislike of this war. Drained by World War II, I, like so many Americans, blocked out the three tedious years of this struggle. Our interests were in our own recovery and that of Europe, not dangerous involvement in the Orient.

After reading numerous accounts and interviewing many participants in the United States, Great Britain, Korea, Japan, Taiwan and the People's Republic of China, I came to understand that this war was unique in our history. Acting quickly, in an effort to stop world communism, President Harry Truman had entered the conflict without declaring war, calling it a police action. He persuaded the reluctant United Nations to approve his action, and fifteen nations joined America in battling North Korea and China. Four million human beings, half of them civilians, died in a brutal contest marked by atrocities on both sides, raging up and down a peninsula the size of Utah.

For the first year a series of disastrous American defeats preceded outstanding victories such as MacArthur's surprise amphibious landing at Inchon. Then, with peace in sight, Truman insisted on voluntary repatriation of all prisoners of war, and for the next two years men fought and died in vast numbers, with little exchange of terrain, while the negotiations dragged on.

This phase of the war has usually been dealt with briefly, but in fact, another fierce war was going on within the prison camps of both sides. Here again were high drama and high stakes. During this frustrating period some American leaders wanted to use atomic weapons, and there was fear that a nuclear holocaust would result.

When an armistice was finally signed in 1953, none of the issues that started the war had been settled. It left only a legacy of hate and division, and today ten million Korean people are still separated from their families by a demilitarized zone vigilantly protected by both sides.

The first war America never won, the Korean War left the United States politically embittered. It also accelerated European rearmament and boosted military budgets, and established the dangerous precedent of a president conducting an undeclared war without constitutional sanction under the guise of a police action.

This book is an attempt to throw light on numerous controversial matters. Was Truman correct in believing that the Soviet Union and Communist China conspired to start the war? Are recent historians right in asserting that America instigated the war, using the South Koreans as puppets? Was Truman's insistence on voluntary repatriation of prisoners of war valid? Were the persistent Communist claims that the United States had waged biological warfare true? Or had captured American fliers been brainwashed into confessing they had dropped infected bombs? And, finally, was the war worth fighting?

The Korean War was a memorable saga of human tragedy and courage replete with heroes on both sides, an unforgettable epic of world consequence. I hope my efforts here make amends for my lack of vision in 1950–53.

Contents

Preface   7
List of Maps   13

Prologue: Tools of History   15

PART ONE: SEVEN DAYS IN JUNE   21
  1. A Time of War (June 24–25, 1950)   23
  2. "We've Got to Stop the Sons-of-Bitches No Matter
    What!" (June 25–26)   33
  3. "There Goes the Bridge!" (June 27–28)   43
  4. "Our Forces Will Not Last a Day" (June 28–30)   55

PART TWO: IN DUBIOUS BATTLE   69
  5. "Here, Have Some Earth to Eat" (June 30–July 10)   71
  6. The Fall of Taejon (July 12–21)   91
  7. A Private Takes Command (July 19–31)   108
  8. "General, This Is Complete Chaos and Desolation!"
    (July 11–August 13)   124

PART THREE: THE PUSAN PERIMETER   147
  9. The Battle of the Naktong River (August 14–23)   149
 10. "This Is an Impossible Situation" (August 31–
    September 7)   161
 11. Inchon (August 21–September 15)   175

PART FOUR: THE ROAD BACK   189
 12. "It's a Piece of Cake!" (September 15–19)   191

13. Crossing Two Rivers (September 16–22)   204
14. The Fall of Seoul (September 23–29)   214

PART FIVE: THE CHINESE PUZZLE   231
15. Across the 38th Parallel (September 29–October 15)   233
16. "Many, Many Chinese Are Coming!" (October 14–26)   243
17. The Death March (Late October–November 8)   255
18. Mao Sets a Trap (October 26–November 17)   265
19. Even Victors Are by Victory Undone
    (November 6–26)   276

PART SIX: THE CHOSIN RESERVOIR   287
20. Trapped (November 27–28)   289
21. Chaos on Two Fronts (November 28–29)   304
22. "You Don't Have the Chance of a Snowball in Hell!"
    (November 28–29)   312
23. Bloody Retreat: Running the Gauntlets
    (November 30–December 1)   320
24. "We're Going Out Like Marines"(December 1–4)   339

PART SEVEN: ATTACK AND COUNTERATTACK   353
25. The Breakout (December 5–11)   355
26. "Your Dad Has Had an Accident" (December 11–29)   367
27. The Third Chinese Campaign (December 31, 1950–
    January 20, 1951)   380
28. "The Old Man Will Get Us Out" (January 24–
    February 20)   394
29. Ridgway in Action (Late February–April 5)   408

PART EIGHT: "THE BATTLE IS JOINED"   427
30. "Jeannie, We're Going Home at Last" (April 6–25)   429
31. Prisoners of War (April 25–Early May)   449
32. The Last Chinese Campaign (May 1–30)   457

PART NINE: THE ROCKY ROAD TO PEACE   467
33. The Negotiations Begin (May 31–August 23)   469
34. "An Utterly Useless War" (Early August–
    November 26)   483
35. "I Agree with Ridgway's Stand" (Late November 1951–
    Early February 1952)   492

PART TEN: WAR IN THE PRISON CAMPS   505
36. Friend or Foe? (February 7–Late February)   507
37. "An Unholy Mess" (February–April 28)   516
38. "I Was Forced to Be a Tool of These Warmongers,
    Made to Drop Germ Bombs" (May 23–
    September 28)   532

Contents

PART ELEVEN: WAR AND PEACE   545
   39. "Can Ike Win the War?" (October 3, 1952–
      April 1, 1953)   547
   40. The Rhee Rebellion (February–June 20)   559
   41. A Time of Peace (July 8–September 6, 1953)   573

Epilogue   590

Acknowledgments   597

Notes   600

Index   611

List of Maps

THE FAR EAST   ENDPAPERS

KOREA   ENDPAPERS

THE NORTH KOREAN ADVANCE   49

ADVANCE OF THE NORTH KOREAN
4TH DIVISION   84

THE NORTH KOREAN 30TH DIVISION
CROSSES THE KUM RIVER   95

THE FALL OF TAEJON   102

THE PUSAN PERIMETER   128

THE FIRST NAKTONG COUNTER-
OFFENSIVE   154

INCHON LANDINGS   194

THE ADVANCE FROM INCHON AND
THE RETAKING OF SEOUL   194

MACARTHUR'S ADVANCE BY
OCTOBER 24, 1950   247

CHOSIN RESERVOIR AND CHINESE

    ATTACKS   294

TASK FORCE FAITH'S BREAKOUT

    ATTEMPT   295

THE THIRD CHINESE OFFENSIVE   412

THE FOURTH CHINESE OFFENSIVE   412

THE FIFTH CHINESE OFFENSIVE   413

THE SIXTH CHINESE OFFENSIVE   413

U.N. LINE, JULY 7, 1951   443

PROLOGUE

Tools of History

1.

Korea's long and checkered history has been determined by its location at the crossroads of East Asia. Local wars for power were the rule until finally, in the seventh century B.C., the kingdom of Silla gained control with the help of the neighboring Chinese, who managed to impose their Confucian system of social relationships on the Korean people. They also bequeathed a rich legacy of ethics, arts and literature that endured for thousands of years despite numerous invasions by barbarians and visitations by Westerners.

When they arrived in the middle of the nineteenth century to trade, these Westerners failed to understand the Confucian father-son relationship between China and Korea and assumed Korea was a vassal state. The Japanese, however, understood and were determined to make this strategic peninsula part of the growing Japanese empire. In 1910, they annexed Korea and with ruthless force turned it into a semiindustrialized Japanese colony. A school system was established which created an efficient work force and turned many of the brightest young Koreans into officers of the Japanese army. Several attempts at rebellion were crushed, and soon after Pearl Harbor Day, the Japanese converted Korea into an important military base.

The peninsula of Korea, jutting from northeast Asia towards Japan,

15

was mountainous, with only about twenty percent of the land arable. It was perhaps their topography and hardy life that made Koreans different from the Chinese and Japanese. They took pride in their physical endurance, reacted violently to challenge and could be both sweetnatured and aggressive. Yet even under the most adverse circumstances they retained a sense of humor. They were often called the Irish of the Orient.

After thirty-three years of being exploited by the Japanese, Korean patriots finally got encouragement from the outside world. In 1943, Roosevelt, Churchill and Chiang Kai-shek stated in the Cairo Declaration that they were determined "Korea shall become free and independent." But Roosevelt told Stalin, at Yalta, that it would take twenty to thirty years before Korea would be ready for complete independence. After the surrender of the Japanese, President Truman suggested that the Soviets receive the surrender of those Japanese forces north of the 38th parallel and that the Americans receive the surrender of those to the south. This seemingly innocuous agreement not only ended the Koreans' long-cherished dream of independence, but it also turned a homogenous people into implacable enemies.

The rigid parallel stretched across the country, arbitrarily—the antithesis of a "natural" boundary. The American zone contained only about forty-two percent of the land but two thirds of the total population of thirty million; it was primarily a farming area and furnished food to the North. The Soviet zone was rich in mineral deposits and provided most of the manufactured goods needed by the South. It also possessed the country's only petroleum processing and cement plants, and its hydroelectric works, built by the Japanese, were among the best in the world. Consequently, the South depended largely on the North for its electric power.

The ending of World War II brought an inevitable shift in the balance of international power, with the Soviets and Americans no longer allies but bitter foes in a suicidial ideological conflict. Unfortunately for the Koreans, their country was one of the prizes. The selection of the 38th parallel as the unnatural boundary between North and South incited Koreans on both sides. The Soviets acted quickly and sealed the border at the 38th, cutting off almost all traffic into and out of North Korea.

Now, suddenly, there were two Koreas. President Truman, in an about-face after his agreement with the Russians, angrily announced in July 1946 that Korea was "an ideological battleground on which our entire success in Asia depends." Secretary of State George Marshall tried in vain the following spring to come to terms with the Russians, and in September, the United States laid the issue before the United Nations. The UN General Assembly voted for an all-Korea election and named a nine-nation UN Temporary Commission on Korea (UNTCOK) to supervise it. All foreign troops would then be withdrawn after a legal government was formed. The Soviets, however, not only opposed general elections but refused to permit UN observers to enter North Korea. Instead, they proposed that all foreign troops be withdrawn from Korea in early 1948. On May 10, over ninety-two percent of the registered voters in South Korea elected representatives to a National Assembly. On August 15, Syngman Rhee was elected the first President of the Republic of Korea.

A courageous patriot, an uncompromising anti-Communist, the seventy-five-year old Rhee was also a feisty autocrat. He had been tortured by the Japanese and exiled to America in December, 1904. There he became an ardent Methodist. He also graduated from Princeton. He was a favorite of the Americans, but many Koreans felt he had lost touch with his country during his long absence. He had even married a foreigner, an Austrian.

The Communists in North Korea responded by forming the Democratic People's Republic of Korea, with twenty-eight-year-old Kim Il-sung as premier. Trained in Moscow during World War II, and a prominent partisan fighter in Manchuria during the China civil war, he was one of the few Koreans to embrace both Chinese and Soviet communism. Shrewd and opportunistic, he had clawed his way to the top, eliminating rivals with the help of the Soviets. To many North Koreans he was a charismatic figure. Described by some Americans as ill-educated and loutish, he was, nevertheless, a man to be taken seriously.

The Soviets promptly recognized the Kim government and promised to withdraw all Soviet troops by the end of 1948. The Americans would have liked to do the same, but the new South Korean Army was not yet trained or equipped. Two years later there were still some 16,000 American soldiers in Korea.

There were now two Korean governments, each claiming jurisdiction over the whole country. Behind Kim Il-sung in the North was the Soviet Union; behind Rhee in the South were the United States and UNTCOK. Korea had become a pawn in the great chess match between the United States and the USSR. "Had the United States and the Soviet Union been willing to take a chance on a truly democratic all-Korea election by all parties," observed historian Bevin Alexander, "then neither a right-wing South Korea nor a Communist North Korea would have developed."

On the last day of June, 1949, the last American troops departed Korea, leaving behind only the U.S. Military Advisory Group to the Republic of Korea (KMAG): about five hundred officers and men whose mission was to complete the instruction of the South Korean military force. Theirs was an apparently hopeless task. Truman and his chiefs

of staff wanted the ROK (Republic of Korea) troops to be sturdy enough
to repel any Communist attack but not strong enough to launch an attack
on the North. That was why tanks, heavy guns and aircraft were not left
for Rhee's infant ground forces.

Two hostile forces began digging defenses along the 38th parallel,
each determined to have all of Korea. Border clashes broke out early in
1950. There were rumors of an impending invasion of South Korea;
and in one week alone, March 3–10, there were eighteen armed incidents
along the parallel and twenty-nine attacks by Communist guerrillas
throughout South Korea. Then suddenly, in May, both military incidents
and guerrilla raids dropped off sharply. Was it the calm before the
storm?

The Chinese Communist observers north of the Yalu River had
recently won the bloody civil war against Chiang Kai-shek's Nationalist
(Kuomintang) Army, and had established the People's Republic of China
with its capital in Peking. Now the PRC was preparing to invade the
Chinese island province of Taiwan (Formosa, to Westerners) where
Chiang Kai-shek and the remnants of the Kuomintang had sought refuge. Once Taiwan was seized, the reunification of all China under one
government would be completed. But the Chinese Communists wanted
no trouble with the United States, which had abandoned Chiang Kai-
shek when it was clear he was losing the war. At the same time, Mao felt
he owed a debt to the many North Korean Communists who had fought
so gallantly in the civil war. Already some 16,000 North Korean soldiers
who had enlisted in the Chinese People's Liberation Army had been sent
home. In the spring of 1950, Mao returned 12,000 more veterans of
the Chinese People's Liberation Army to form two divisions of the Korean People's Army. In addition to these divisions, the 1st and 4th divisions of the Korean People's Army each had one regiment of other
PLA veterans. These combat-hardened North Koreans made up about
one third of the KPA.

By early June Premier Kim Il-sung, who was also commander in
chief of the KPA, had eight full divisions and two at half strength, all
trained by high-ranking Soviet military advisers. Although the Russians
had removed their troops, they had left behind a considerable amount
of equipment, including mortars, howitzers, self-propelled guns, antitank guns, and 150 T-34 tanks. Kim's ground forces totaled 150,000, of
which 89,000 were trained combat troops.

In the South, opposing these Communist forces, were about 65,000
partially trained ROK combat troops armed only with M-1 rifles, carbines, mortars, howitzers, and ineffective bazookas. They had no medium artillery and no recoilless rifles, and their pitiful air force consisted
of twenty-two training and liaison planes. On June 11, 1950, only one
regiment of the four ROK divisions near the border was in defensive

position, and more than a third of these troops were at home helping with the harvest. The other regiments were in reserve ten to thirty miles to the rear.

2.

That same day, twenty-four North Korean officers crowded into the office of the chief of operations, Lieutenant General Yu Suncheol, in Pyongyang, capital of North Korea. They were surprised when Kim Il-sung's deputy commander in chief, Marshal Choe Yong-gun, entered with Lim Rae, former vice-commander of cultural affairs. Lim had been a member of a military observation mission sent to Moscow in 1948, but on his return he had been fired from the army for misconduct. He was smiling broadly when introduced as a representative of the Korean Workers' party with the rank of major general.

The chief of operations, General Yu, began to speak. The room grew tense. He said that the People's Army had so far conducted only minor combat exercises. "But now all divisions will be utilized in a major maneuver. It will be the largest and most significant one since the inauguration of our Korean People's Army, and as such it calls for perfection." He did not know how long it would last. Everyone should have enough underwear and socks for several weeks and take only essential belongings. "The coming 'exercise' is a top-secret matter, so you must not talk about it to your friends, wives or relatives."

Marshal Choe then announced that the exercise would be held at two places simultaneously. Those present would be on the staff of II Corps, commanded by the chief of operations, whose vice-commander was to be Major General Lim. Lim rose, smiling with oily confidence. First he obsequiously praised Kim Il-sung for turning the Korean People's Army into a great modern force. "This is to be an *exercise* in name," he said, "but we commanders and staff members should display the fullest devotion and indomitable spirit, armed with high political consciousness."

On June 12, just before dawn, three generals in dress uniforms and twenty senior officers were loaded into two jeeps and a dozen trucks carrying military equipment. The sky was clear as they left the capital and headed south.

Six days later the officers got definite word of the invasion. Their Soviet military adviser, Colonel Dorquinn of the engineering department, had written operation orders, in Russian, to all engineer battalions attached to infantry divisions. The Minister of Defense ordered Major Ju Yeong-bok, who was fluent in Russian, to translate the contents into Korean.

"By June 23," he wrote, "all engineer battalions are requested to

clear minefields laid by the enemy in front of their respective divisions."
The battalions were to be maintained in perfect combat readiness and
provide adequate technical support for the advance of their divisions.
The engineers were also to facilitate river-crossing operations. Their
locations and routes of advance were listed, along with the plan for
deploying and advancing seven infantry divisions and tank regiments.

Never before had the Korean People's Army drafted a plan for
massive maneuvers on a national scale. Such a grand undertaking as this
could only have been conceived by the professional senior advisers from
the Soviet army who had already been assigned to the high command
of the KPA. All intelligence in both South and North Korea—especially
on military matters—was collected and cleared through Moscow.

Several months ago the chief adviser had been replaced by a lieutenant general who brought with him many combat specialists. A war
was about to begin.

3.

On June 18, at Rhee's invitation, John Foster Dulles, a consultant to
Secretary of State Dean Acheson, came to Seoul. He visited the 38th
parallel and was moved by an appeal from Brigadier General Yu Jai-
hung, commander of the ROK 7th Division, for more American aid.
Impressed by what he had learned at the parallel and by President Rhee's
ardent protest that America was letting him down, Dulles promised the
Korean National Assembly the next morning: "You are not alone. You
will never be alone so long as you continue to play worthily your part
in the great design of human freedom." Most observers looked on these
words as spontaneous, but they had, in fact, been drafted in Washington
as an expression of American policy toward Korea.

Dulles's words were comforting to Rhee, but even he had no sus-
picion that American aid would be needed so soon.

PART I

SEVEN DAYS IN JUNE

CHAPTER 1

A Time of War
(June 24–25, 1950)

1.

On the murky night of June 24, 1950, Soviet 122-mm howitzers, 76-mm guns, and self-propelled guns were already emplaced along the 38th parallel. One hundred fifty Russian-built T-34 tanks were cautiously moving forward to their final attack positions along with some 90,000 combat troops, all trained by Soviet military advisers. The Korean People's Army was poised for its surprise invasion of the South.

On the other side of the 38th parallel, four understrength Republic of Korea divisions and one regiment were on the front lines. For months there had been warnings of a major invasion. But rumors and alarms had come so often that most of those up front imagined this was going to be another uneventful night. Enlisted ROK soldiers from farming villages had recently been given fifteen-day leaves to help their families with the crops. Already outnumbered, the ROK front line that night was dangerously depleted.

The cry of "wolf" had come so often that some frontline commanders were in Seoul celebrating the grand opening of the officers' club at ROK Army headquarters. Also present were most of the ranking officers of the Ministry of National Defense. It was a gala affair and later reminded some Americans of the military parties in Honolulu on the eve of the Pearl Harbor attack. They too had been on a Saturday night.

At the officers' club, many Americans were present, including the

American ambassador, John J. Muccio. Born in Italy, he had served in Latin America and was popular at parties where—a fifty-year-old bachelor with an eye for the ladies—he enjoyed singing Spanish love songs. He was not large but gave the impression of being so with a huge head atop broad shoulders. His jet black hair had scarcely a streak of gray, and the bow tie he invariably sported added to his dapper appearance.

He was born for the post in Seoul, according to his first secretary, Harold Noble. "The Republic of Korea was so new, it had so much to learn, it was bound to make so many mistakes, and its officials were so thin-skinned in their personal and national pride, that Muccio's relaxed calmness and sympathy were ideal. He genuinely liked Koreans and most Koreans genuinely admired, liked and respected him."

Unfortunately the most important man in South Korea, President Rhee, was repelled by his familiarity and joviality, disparagingly referring to him in private as "that fellow Muccio," even though he was aware that the ambassador was also dedicated, efficient and intelligent.

On that evening of June 24, the buoyant bachelor was, as usual, the life of the party. Also present were a number of KMAG officers. These Americans had been organizing and training the ROK Army for the past two years. Their commander, Major General William Roberts, shared the general feeling of confidence in the ability of the green ROK Army to repel any North Korean attack. But the man Roberts deemed most essential to his command, Captain James Hausman, was by no means so sanguine. Regarded by Roberts as the father of the ROK Army, Hausman should have had the rank of a full colonel.

In a futile attempt to get him a promotion, General Roberts had written a friend in the adjutant general's department: "He is an organizer of the first water; he is tactful and quite a persuader. He moves Brigades and Divisions around, organizes the Secretary of War's office, organizes the General Staff and tells them what and how to do it, but still he is not a Regular Officer because his educational requirements are short."

Hausman was only thirty-two and had already served sixteen years in the army. When his mother died, he had enlisted as a private, using his brother's birth certificate because he was underage. He had fought in World II as a captain and was wounded in the Battle of the Bulge. In 1948 he was sent to Korea. Although he knew nothing about the country or its people and had little formal education, he soon realized that if he started the job of training ROK troops, he couldn't help them if he thought like an American. Within a year of close work with the ROKs, he understood their abilities and limitations and, unlike most Americans, realized that they could become excellent soldiers with proper training and equipment. Hausman now held the most important assignment in KMAG: he was not only the adviser to the ROK chief of staff but was also the American officer President Rhee chiefly relied on for counsel.

It was dark by the time Reverend Larry Zellers of the American Methodist Mission in Kaesong, the ancient capital of Korea, drove up to his home, a few miles from the 38th parallel. He had been warned by a neighbor, a KMAG officer, Captain Joseph Darrigo, not to head north into his driveway with lights on. He ignored this advice; moreover, there had been no sign of military activity in town, so he assumed it would be another uneventful night.

Like Zellers, few in South Korea went to bed with any fear that by dawn their lives would be disrupted by a bitter civil war. In Tokyo, General Douglas MacArthur, supreme commander of the Far East Command, was soundly asleep in his bed at the United States embassy. For two years he had been warning Washington of a possible North Korean thrust, but there had been no alarms from Seoul.

In Washington it was near noon, and President Harry S. Truman's busy day had been taken up by far more important matters than Korea: the increasing Communist threat in Europe and the fate of the fledgling North Atlantic Treaty Organization.

By midnight scattered but heavy rain was falling along the 38th parallel. All was quiet on the long front—except for a slight mysterious rumbling a few miles north of the parallel, as trucks and tanks moved up slowly to the final attack positions. Kim Il-sung's seven divisions had successfully completed their secret movement to the edge of the parallel along with an armored brigade, a separate infantry regiment, a motorcycle regiment, and the Border Constabulary Brigade—an elite, internal security force trained and supervised by Soviet officers. These 80,000 men were now in place alongside 10,000 others already positioned along the parallel. Yet another 10,000 were in reserve.

Half of this force and most of the Russian T-34 tanks were concentrated in a forty-mile arc on the west end of the peninsula. This was to be the main attack on Seoul and would follow the Uijongbu Corridor, the ancient invasion route to Seoul. One of the first targets would be Kaesong, home of Zellers and Darrigo. A few miles away, North Koreans were quietly re-laying railroad tracks they had torn up long ago. Infantrymen began loading into a long train for a highly organized attack on the old capital.

Although Commander in Chief Kim Il-sung had fought in the Soviet army, neither he nor his deputy, Marshal Choe Yong-gun, had experience beyond a battalion level and had to rely on Russian advisers. In late 1948 the USSR announced that all its armed forces had left Korea, but Kim had refused to allow a United Nations commission to enter North Korea to verify this claim. According to U.S. Army intelligence reports, some three thousand Russians still instructed and supervised the Korean People's Army, with as many as fifteen Soviet officers advising each infantry division. Other reports indicated that Premier Kim received weekly instructions from Russian ambassador Terenty F. Shtykov, a colonel general, who had formerly commanded all Soviet occupation forces.

2.

The South Korean defenders were caught completely by surprise. The only frontline American adviser, Captain Joseph Darrigo, Reverend Zeller's neighbor, was wakened at daybreak. As he jumped out of bed, shell fragments hit his house at the northeast end of Kaesong. He pulled on his pants and darted down the stairs, shoes and shirt in hand. Small-arms fire rattled against the house. Darrigo and a houseboy jumped into a jeep. Although they met no enemy troops, Darrigo knew from the volume of fire that a heavy attack was under way.

As he reached the circle at the center of town, he was shocked to see North Korean soldiers unloading from a long train at the station. There must have been two or three battalions, perhaps an entire regiment! As troops from the train advanced into town, Darrigo stepped on the gas and raced south toward the headquarters of the ROK 1st Division located just across the Imjin River at Munsan.

All along the front bombardments wakened ROK soldiers. Yet in the confusion and lack of communications, each isolated group imagined it was being hit by just another raid.

The telephone jangle roused Captain Hausman about four-thirty A.M. He hurriedly dressed, and in a few minutes he was at KMAG-ROK headquarters. Soon the ROK chief of staff arrived. An imposing sight, Major General Chae Byong-duk weighed almost three hundred pounds and more than deserved his nickname of Fat. He ordered the 2nd Division, already on its way to Seoul from Taejon, to launch a coordinated attack with the 7th Division, located at Uijongbu some twelve air miles north of Seoul. However, Brigadier General Yu Jai-hung, commander of the 7th Division, didn't even know the whereabouts of all his units. He had been roused by a phone call from his intelligence officer. "Commander, the enemy are shelling along our whole front!" Yu ordered him to issue an emergency call to all officers. But it was Sunday morning and a third of his troops were on leave. He had two regiments on the line, some 4,000 men; and his third regiment was south of Seoul. It was a miserable situation. He'd have only about a quarter of his strength to stop the enemy. He remembered meeting Mr. Dulles at the 38th parallel just a week ago and telling him how desperately they needed help from America. Since Dulles had been understanding, Yu felt sure that America was going to come to their aid. But *when*?

Although rain was pouring down along most of the parallel, there were only light, occasional showers in Seoul. First reports of the fighting were coming into KMAG headquarters, but they were considered too fragmentary for relaying to the American embassy.

Colonel Paik Sun-yup, the twenty-nine-year-old commander of the 1st ROK Division, in town on temporary leave for supplementary training, was wakened at seven by his G3 (operations officer) and told that Kaesong had fallen. An affable, talented officer, Paik was highly regarded by the Americans, who called him "Whitey," since *paik* in Korean means white. He dressed and hurried to the street. There were no taxis, so he flagged down a jeep and ordered the driver to take him to ROK Army headquarters.

He rushed into Fat Chae's office.

"Do you think it's all right for me to get back to my unit?"

"What are you talking about?" exclaimed Chae angrily. "You've *got* to get back there!"

Paik ran to the American compound and pounded on the door of his senior adviser, Lieutenant Colonel Lloyd Rockwell, who had spent the night in town. He had a car. "War has come! The North Koreans, they've taken Kaesong!"

Rockwell was surprised, but in a short time the two were at the home of the commander of the 11th Regiment. From there Paik telephoned division headquarters and ordered the 11th Regiment and other units to fall back to defensive positions near Munsan, a village just south of the Imjin River. Then he and Rockwell raced north to Munsan, where they met Captain Darrigo, who told them what had happened at Kaesong. Two of Paik's regiments, the 11th and 13th, were by now engaged in bitter fighting on the near side of the river. After making a reconnaissance, both Paik and Rockwell agreed they should blow up the bridge—the only one for miles, despite the fact that the 12th Regiment had not yet withdrawn across it. An engineer activated the detonation plunger, but nothing happened. The detonating cord was cut. Despite this setback, Paik's men on the south side of the river kept firing so steadily that the North Koreans could not cross the bridge. Neither could Paik's exhausted 12th Regiment.

At the same time, some fifteen miles to the east two North Korean infantry divisions, the 4th and 3rd, supported by tanks of the 105th Armored Brigade, were heading south for Uijongbu, only twenty miles from Seoul, along two roads. The 1st Regiment of the 7th ROK Division had been hit so hard by the initial attack that a desperate message was sent to the minister of defense in Seoul. Key points had fallen and immediate reinforcements were required.

Farther east, in Chunchon, a company of the 6th ROK Division was in reserve. The commander, Captain Rhee Dai-yong, was on the way to the library when he heard artillery. But he thought nothing of it until a messenger told him it was a real attack and that he didn't have time to change from khakis to combat wear. Forty of his 116 men were on weekend pass, so he sent a truck to bring them back to the base. With those men on hand, also in khakis, Rhee headed north to battle.

Up river some thirteen miles, Whitey Paik's 13th Regiment was battered but still holding. It had no antitank weapons. The Americans had left only small 2.36-inch bazookas, whose rounds were bouncing as harmlessly off the Russian-made tanks as Ping-Pong balls. Already ninety men had volunteered for suicide attacks. Some, carrying high explosives, threw themselves under the treads, some rushed forward with satchel or pole charges, while others leaped on top of tanks trying desperately to open hatches and drop in grenades. Few tanks were destroyed, but the enemy was slowed down and, though almost outflanked, the northern line held.

Later that morning at the North Korean forward GHQ, the news was good. The enemy was fleeing in such confusion that important bridges weren't even being blown up. The 2nd KPA Division reported that all regiments were moving ahead without delay, having covered five kilometers during the past hour. One Soviet colonel was so impressed he exclaimed, "You fellows are faster than the Soviet army!"

At ten A.M. command headquarters was ordered to move forward. Soon a motor convoy wound its way westward, past the serene waters of Lake Hwachonho. They moved without interruption to a village just five kilometers from the parallel. By then the two Russian colonels had left, having confirmed the execution of the offensive they had planned.

Major Ju, the North Korean translator, was jolted upon learning that the first broadcasts from Pyongyang stated that Rhee's corrupt forces had started the war by seizing cities and towns north of the parallel. The broadcasts went on to announce that the Korean People's Army was now on the counteroffensive, liberating towns by the dozen. A true Communist, Ju felt, would not spread such a blatant lie.

3.

In Seoul it was not until eight A.M. that Ambassador Muccio, none the worse for his late partying at the officers' club, received a call from his deputy and learned that several ROK units along the front were under attack. During the five-minute walk from his residence to the chancery in the Bando Building, he met Jack James of United Press, who looked as if he had been up most of the night. "What are you doing stirring at this time of the morning?" asked James.

"Oh, we've had some disturbing reports about activities on the 38th parallel. You might want to look into them."

This was not the first James had heard of a possible North Korean attack that Sunday morning, but an Army intelligence officer had assured him it was just another rumor. He now rushed into the embassy pressroom to telephone contacts for confirmation of the story. No other reporter was awake to compete with him and it would be a sensational scoop if true. He queried officers at ROK headquarters, then returned to the embassy to check with Muccio's assistant, who believed it was the major attack they'd been expecting but urged James to be cautious. When James learned that the ambassador had sent a first flash to Washington just after nine, he told a military specialist, "If it's good enough for you to file, it's good enough for me."

James hurriedly drafted his cable and added the cautionary note that his information was still "fragmentary." (He did not know then that the Muccio message had ended with the forthright observation: "It would appear from the nature of the attack and the manner it was launched, that it constitutes an all-out offensive against the Republic of Korea.") James hurried by jeep three blocks to the international cable facilities of the Ministry of Communications and dispatched his report at urgent rates. Moments after the message was typed out, it was received in San Francisco and relayed to UP headquarters in New York.

In Tokyo, MacArthur's chief of staff, Major General Edward Almond, was at his office early that Sunday morning to finish work postponed by the past week's conferences with Defense Secretary Louis Johnson and General Omar Bradley. Twenty minutes after his arrival at the Dai Ichi Building, he was interrupted by a report from KMAG that there had been a "border incident" at the 38th parallel. In the next three hours he got six more reports on "incidents" stretching across the parallel. It was obvious that Kim Il-sung had launched a major attack, and Almond ordered a duty officer to inform MacArthur.

The ringing of the telephone in the general's bedroom at the American embassy wakened him. After hearing that the North Koreans had struck with great force, he had "an uncanny feeling of nightmare." Nine years ago on a Sunday morning, at the same hour, a telephone with the same note of urgency had roused him in his penthouse atop the Manila Hotel. "It was the same fell note of the war cry that was again ringing

in my ears, I told myself. Not again! I must still be asleep and dreaming."
Then he heard the crisp, cool voice of his chief of staff, "Any orders,
General?"

How, MacArthur asked himself, could the United States have allowed such a deplorable situation to develop? In 1945 America had been
the strongest military power in the world. "But in the short space of five
years this power had been frittered away in a bankruptcy of positive and
courageous leadership toward any long-range objectives. Again I asked
myself, 'What is United States policy in Asia?' And the appalling thought
came, 'The United States has no definite policy in Asia.' "

American weakness in the Pacific was enticing the Communists to
take action, he thought, as he paced the room. Now his country, which
had presided over the birth of the new republic, had a moral obligation
to help. But with what? Despite MacArthur's warning, the Joint Chiefs
of Staff had stripped him to four divisions. Each division had three
regiments, but most regiments were reduced by a battalion and most
battalions by a company.

At the Tokyo bureau of the Associated Press, Bill Jorden was on
duty. He'd brought a book to read, since it was rare that anything happened on a Sunday. Suddenly the wires began clicking. New York was
saying that UP had reported North Korean troops moving south.

Jorden called O.H.P. King in Seoul but was told he was at a picnic.
Finally Jorden located King, who said, "I can't believe this. I'm sure I
would have heard about it."

Jorden cabled New York: "Have contacted King. Relayed message
on UP story. He is doubtful but checking." Back in Seoul, King soon
found out the shit had hit the fan. The picnic was over.

In the capital of North Korea, the Home Affairs Bureau of the People's
Republic of Korea was proclaiming over the radio that the troops of the
South Korean puppet regime had launched a surprise invasion along
the whole front of the 38th parallel at dawn. Therefore, the Security
Army of the People's Republic had been ordered to repulse the enemy.
"At this moment, our Security Army is putting up stiff counteroperations
against the enemy."

Song Jeung-taik, a college sophomore majoring in Korean literature,
was watching a soccer game in Pyongyang when he heard this announcement. His father had died in jail for opposing the Japanese, and
he was not at all enthusiastic about the Communist regime. He didn't
believe what he heard. Neither did most of his friends.

Keyes Beech of the Chicago *Daily News* was enjoying a swim at a
beach south of Tokyo. The city was hot and humid, but here it was
pleasantly warm. While he was taking a shower, the phone rang. It was

Larry Tighe in Tokyo. "You'd better get your duff up here fast," he said. "The North Koreans have invaded South Korea."

"How do you know the South didn't invade the North?" replied Beech. Syngman Rhee had always wanted to do that. Beech, a thirty-seven-year-old veteran of the war in the Pacific, had a deserved reputation as a cautious observer, flinty and witheringly honest.

"What the hell difference does it make?" said Tighe. "There's a war on and there's a plane leaving Haneda for Kimpo in forty-five minutes."

With his hand on the horn, Beech made it to the airport with time to spare. Of course, the plane was delayed for an hour—as usual. Rush and wait. There were not as many correspondents as he had thought he would find. Among them was a newly arrived woman reporter for the New York *Herald Tribune*, Marguerite Higgins.

She brought with her a reputation for using her good looks to get a story. Beech could vouch for the looks. She certainly had a street-urchin charm. She was small and pert and radiated the confidence that she was as good as—if not better than—any male competition.

4.

The first news of the attack didn't reach American officials in the United States until 10:04 A.M. Korean time. In Washington it was only 9:04 Saturday night when the UP called W. Bradley Connors, a public affairs officer of the State Department, requesting confirmation of the dispatch from Jack James, who had met Ambassador Muccio on the street in Seoul that morning.

Connors phoned the deputy undersecretary of state, Dean Rusk, who was dining with Joseph Alsop, the noted journalist. Rusk told Connors to telephone Ambassador Muccio at once for information. He himself was getting over to the State Department. Connors tried to phone Muccio, but to his dismay learned that all radiotelephone circuits to Korea had just closed. Connors would have to send a cable.

By chance, Secretary of the Army Frank Pace, Jr., was also at Alsop's. He left immediately for the Pentagon, where he phoned Secretary of Defense Louis Johnson at home. Johnson, who had heard the news from his staff, was amazed. He had just returned from Japan, where the intelligence briefings he'd attended had given no indication that a North Korean assault was imminent. Johnson told Secretary of the Army Pace to act temporarily for the Defense Department, since the Army's interest in Korea was great. Secretary Johnson, who had been under attack from the Army for cutting down national defense, felt he could do nothing and, exhausted by his long trip, went to bed. Pace set to work putting communications together and trying to get

organized so he could give President Truman a reasonable account of
what had happened.

At the State Department the cable from Muccio finally arrived, two
hours after it had been dispatched. It had gone through Tokyo, where,
for some reason, it had been delayed. Finally, at 1:15 P.M., the decoded
message was delivered to Connors at the State Department. Within minutes it was relayed to Secretary Pace at the Pentagon. Two copies were
sent to the White House, but President Truman was at his home in
Independence, Missouri.

Pace rushed to the State Department, where he briefly discussed
the problem with Rusk and the assistant secretary of state, John D.
Hickerson. Hickerson, in turn, called Dean Acheson at his farm in Maryland. He read his chief the report from Muccio, recommending that
they try to call a meeting of the Security Council of the UN.

"Go ahead," said Acheson. "Do everything to get them all together
tomorrow. I'll telephone the President and tell him about this, and if he
agrees with it, all is well, and we'll go ahead." If the president had any
different idea, they could cancel the meeting. But Hickerson was to act
at once.

That morning Truman had dedicated an airport in Baltimore and
then flown aboard the *Independence* to Kansas City. He planned to have
a pleasant weekend with his family and take care of some domestic
business, such as ordering a new roof for the farmhouse. At 9:20, Missouri time, the telephone rang. It was Acheson. "Mr. President," he said
gravely, "I have very serious news. The North Koreans have invaded
South Korea."

"I must get back to the capital," said Truman.

Acheson didn't think it was necessary. "It's not advisable to take the
risk of a night flight." It might even panic the nation and the world. He
said he had authorized Hickerson to arrange an emergency meeting of
the UN Security Council. Did the president approve?

He did. Acheson then suggested that, with Secretary of Defense
Johnson and General Bradley out of town (he didn't know they had
already arrived from the Far East), it might be useful if the president
authorized the secretary of state to assume major responsibility to take
charge. Again Truman agreed. He hung up and told the family there
was a serious crisis. Large Bulgarian armies were massed along the borders of Yugoslavia, which had broken with Stalin; Iran and Turkey were
threatened by powerful Russian forces; a huge Soviet garrison was stationed in East Germany; and the Russians were obviously behind the
attack on South Korea.

This, he feared, was the opening round of World War III.

CHAPTER 2

"We've Got to Stop the Sons-of-Bitches No Matter What!"

(June 25–26)

1.

In Seoul, it was late Sunday morning, June 25. Occasional Yak fighters buzzed over the city, and one group bombed the railroad station. The sight of enemy planes and the antiaircraft fire were terrifying, and the phones of government officers were constantly ringing. Hastily assembled senior officials waited anxiously in their offices for a Cabinet meeting. President Rhee saw some of these men informally at his official residence, but the Cabinet was not summoned. The Kyungmudai, as the building was called, was a private world with its own secretarial staff and a special police force which was reporting dire news from Japanese broadcasts based on rumors, or from a station controlled by Communists. More accurate information was available from Rhee's own minister of defense or from Chief of Staff Fat Chae, but the president, agitated by a Yak strafing just behind his residence, seemed to place more reliance on the purveyors of bad news.

There was no panic at the American embassy. Everyone had confidence in the combat spirit and effectiveness of the ROK troops. The troops seemed to be holding their own. Even so, an afternoon party for teachers from Illinois Tech was canceled. By noon there were so many calls from worried members of the American mission who had been sitting home listening to antiaircraft fire that Ambassador Muccio instructed the English-language radio station, WVTP, to broadcast an announcement to the American community. "There is no reason for alarm. As yet it cannot be determined whether the Northern Communists intend to precipitate all-out warfare."

When James Lee, a college student, first heard of the attack, he was getting his hair cut. They'll never get into Seoul, he thought, and told the barber to continue. But in the afternoon he got a call from a friend urging him to come to the campus at once. They had to protect the school. When Lee arrived he and his classmates were given mops and brooms to fend off the enemy.

The C-54 carrying Keyes Beech and other American correspondents to Korea didn't leave from Japan until five P.M. At last they were off to another war! But as they reached Oshima, the volcanic island off Honshu, the pilot said he'd been ordered to return. Their destination, Kimpo Airfield near Seoul, was being strafed by two Yaks who had hit a gasoline dump and a grounded C-54.

A civilian information official in Seoul phoned a top embassy officer to ask about the Yak attack. "This thing is serious," was the indignant answer. "They strafed an *American* plane. That's destruction of *American* property!" At the same time KMAG was releasing another public report on the fighting. The ROK Army had lost the entire area east of Kaesong and west of the Imjin River, while a North Korean tank regiment with supporting infantry was only twenty-five miles northwest of Seoul and approaching Uijongbu. This did not jibe with information other KMAG officers were giving to correspondents that the drive had been "virtually stopped that afternoon." Ridiculously optimistic reports were also coming from the ROK National Defense Ministry.

Nor was MacArthur concerned. As he strode up and down in his office at the Dai Ichi Building, corncob pipe gripped between his teeth, he was telling John Foster Dulles, resting from his trip to Korea, "This is probably only a reconnaissance in force. If Washington only will not hobble me, I can handle it with one hand tied behind my back."

Dulles was not reassured, for he still remembered what he had seen and heard at the 38th parallel; nor could he forget Syngman Rhee, whose impassioned patriotism had impressed him deeply. He wrote on his ever-present yellow drafting pad a message to Acheson and Rusk:

TO SIT BY WHILE KOREA IS OVERRUN BY UNPROVOKED ARMED
ATTACK WOULD START A DISASTROUS CHAIN OF EVENTS LEADING
MOST PROBABLY TO WORLD WAR.

Muccio was also cabling Washington. He told of the air attacks on Kimpo and the Seoul airstrip. Two hours later the minister of defense came to the American embassy and told Muccio that the president wanted to see him. Muccio found the Kyungmudai in a state of alarm.

When it was apparent that the president was determined to remain in Seoul, the ambassador went to Mrs. Rhee and said it was advisable to leave the capital.

Muccio was driven back to the embassy, where he found an argument between those who felt that all dependents should be evacuated soon and those who supported Muccio's decision to wait. Hausman protested vigorously when the ambassador insisted that dependents remain to give moral support to the Koreans. "Mr. Ambassador," said the outspoken captain, "I cannot do my job, nor can other advisers do their jobs, wondering whether their families are going to be killed. They've got to go." The controversy raged on. Finally, upon hearing that enemy tanks were in Uijongbu, Muccio gave in and at midnight ordered all American women and children evacuated.

While this evacuation was taking place, President Rhee was so alarmed by the situation that he telephoned MacArthur—even though it was three A.M., June 26. An aide answered and asked Rhee to call later. He angrily exclaimed, "American citizens in Korea will die one by one while you keep the general asleep in peace!"

Madame Rhee was so shocked that she placed her palm over the mouthpiece of the telephone. Her husband was trembling with rage. "Our people are dying," he said to her. "And they don't want to wake up the general!"

The aide, apparently moved by Rhee's words, said he would rouse MacArthur. A few minutes later Rhee blurted out to the general, "Had your country been a little more concerned about us, we would not have come to this! We've warned you many times. Now you must save Korea!"

MacArthur promised he would send ten Mustangs, thirty-six 105-mm howitzers, thirty-five 155-mm howitzers and many bazookas at once.

Reassured, Rhee phoned Dr. John Chang, his ambassador in Washington. "Ambassador Chang," he said, his voice trembling with anger, "you will see President Truman immediately. Say to him this. 'The enemy is at our threshold! Whatever has happened to the twenty-million-dollar arms [appropriation] the U.S. Congress approved and you signed?' "

2.

The Sunday morning papers in America paid little attention to Korea. The headlines concerned the crash of a Northwest DC-4 into Lake Michigan. On page 20 of *The New York Times*, under the heading of "Washington Holds Russia to Account," were comments from the State Department accusing the USSR of inspiring the attack on South Korea.

Secretary of Defense Johnson told the press that the Soviet Union was the "one country which might take an aggressive role and bring on war with the United States." But there was nothing to worry about. Our battle plans were signed and sealed for just such a sneak attack.

At the joint meeting in the State Department it was agreed that MacArthur's headquarters should be advised of certain possible courses of action, such as the assigning to it of operational control of all U.S. military activities in Korea.

At two P.M. an emergency meeting of the Security Council of the UN began in an atmosphere of tension and subdued excitement. Was the Cold War going to turn into a hot one? Ever since the surrender of Germany, when the Soviets placed under military rule the territories on its western and southwestern borders from the Baltic to Iran, tension between East and West had increased. The Soviet encroachments had continued so determinedly that President Truman asked a joint session of Congress for authority and funds to assist beleaguered Greece and Turkey. This became known as the Truman Doctrine, and was aided by a major Soviet mistake when, in 1948, Stalin put such pressure on Yugoslavia that it led to a break between the two Communist dictatorships. Thereupon Truman infuriated Stalin by discreetly sending economic aid to Tito. The Berlin Blockade, that same year, heightened the rivalry between the two ideologies, and by now there were so many troubled areas in both Europe and Asia that brushfire hostilities could touch off a third world war, this one to be fought with both sides possessing atom bombs, since Russia had exploded its first nuclear device nine months earlier.

Upon entering the meeting place, the American delegate to the Security Council, Ernest Gross, was delighted to see that the seat for Jakob Malik, the Soviet representative, was empty. It was an unbelievable stroke of luck! Six months earlier the Soviet Union had boycotted all UN meetings because Chiang Kai-shek's Nationalist China was still represented. But why were the Soviets absent now?

Soon after the meeting started, Secretary-General Trygve Lie declared that he was convinced the North Koreans had violated the charter of the United Nations. He cited the report of the UN commission in Korea. "I consider it the clear duty of the Security Council," he concluded, "to take steps necessary to re-establish peace and security in that area."

Next, Gross reviewed the past efforts to reach a peaceful solution in Korea and then read aloud the American resolution: North Korea should be ordered to cease hostilities and withdraw its troops to the 38th parallel.

At 4:15 P.M. the Security Council recessed to deliberate in closed session. In less than one hour the delegates agreed to accept the American resolution, with a few minor changes. The council reconvened and in fifteen minutes adopted the revised resolution unanimously, except for the abstention of Yugoslavia.

That afternoon, radio broadcasters were interrupting regular programs to report the invasion of South Korea. Many listeners, reminded of the interrupted Sunday programs on Pearl Harbor Day, were convinced the USSR was behind the attack. According to a Gallup poll six months earlier, seventy-five percent believed the Soviets were conniving to become "the ruling power of the world." Failure of the free world to intervene against Soviet intervention in Korea would only encourage the Soviets to continue their aggression and bring on World War III.

The first press reports from the Soviet Union gave no hint that its delegate to the UN Security Council had failed to make an appearance. While faithfully reporting the North Korean version of an attack by the South, the Soviet press also printed objective Reuters, France Presse and AP communiqués. For once Russian readers were given a choice. *Pravda*, to the amazement of Westerners in Moscow, also included the full text of the American resolution at the UN meeting. And although condemning the UN Security Council action, *Pravda* did so in mild terms.

In Missouri the Truman family was acting as though it were an ordinary Sunday. When the phone rang, Margaret answered. "Daddy," she said, "it's Dean Acheson and he says it's important."

"Mr. President, the news is bad. The attack is in force all along the parallel."

Truman flared. "Dean," he exclaimed, "we've got to stop the sons-of-bitches no matter what!"

Acheson agreed, and said an emergency meeting of the Security Council was about to start.

Truman asked Acheson to assemble the service secretaries and the chiefs of staff to start working on recommendations. "I'm returning to Washington immediately."

Reporters at the airport noticed that Truman was "stern faced," and his wife had the same look of calm seriousness they had noticed when she learned of Roosevelt's death. Truman urged the reporters not to exaggerate the seriousness of the attack. "Don't make it alarmist." Privately, one of Truman's aides was telling an interviewer, "The boss is going to hit those fellows hard."

On the three-hour trip to Washington, Truman thought about the past. "I remembered how each time that the democracies failed to act it had encouraged the aggressors to keep going ahead. Communism was acting in Korea just as Hitler, Mussolini, and the Japanese had acted ten, fifteen, and twenty years earlier. . . . If this was allowed to go unchallenged, it would mean a third world war. . . . It was also clear to me that the foundations and the principles of the United Nations were at stake unless this unprovoked attack on Korea could be stopped."

What Truman and Acheson did not know was that Stalin was playing a deceptive game in Korea. His main purpose in fostering the invasion was to draw American manpower, weapons and dollars away from Europe, where the infant NATO was struggling to reach its full strength.

From the plane, Truman sent a message to Acheson asking him and his immediate advisers, as well as the top defense chiefs, to join him for a dinner conference. Acheson and Secretary of Defense Johnson met the president at the airport. They went directly to Blair House, where the Trumans were temporarily housed across the street from the White House. Among those present were General Hoyt Vandenberg of the Air Force, General J. Lawton "Joe" Collins of the Army and Admiral Forrest Sherman of the Navy. Truman requested there be no discussion of business until the meal was over. When they had eaten, the mahogany table was cleared to become a conference table. Truman asked the secretary of state to read the first report Muccio had sent from Seoul.

Truman was advised to evacuate Americans from the Seoul area, instruct MacArthur to air-drop supplies including ammunition and weapons, and move the Seventh Fleet from the Philippines to a position between Formosa and the mainland of China. The president promised to adopt these recommendations. Truman's prompt decision to send military help to Korea surprised many Westerners, as well as Stalin. It seemed a sharp departure from the president's policy of accenting the American role in Europe at the expense of that in Asia.

Truman's instinctive reaction when he heard from Acheson was deeply rooted in American experience and tradition. Calculated policy was instantly overridden by the debt owed to an infant country, whose people America had persuaded to travel the path of democracy.

3.

As Truman's plane was nearing Washington, it was already early Monday morning in Pyongyang, a clear, hot summer day with a slight wind blowing from the north. Since there were no radios or newspapers in the dormitories of the Chongjin Medical College, the students had heard nothing of the war. At nine-thirty A.M., about two hundred students and faculty were summoned to the south end of the soccer field to hear an important message that would be broadcast by Marshal Premier Kim Il-sung.

They sang patriotic songs until ordered to be silent. Then came the well-known voice of their hero over the loudspeakers: "Dear brothers and sisters!" began Kim. "Great danger threatens our motherland and its people! What is needed to liquidate this menace? . . . Under the banner of the Korean People's Democratic Republic, we must complete the unification of the motherland and create a single, independent, democratic state! The war which we are forced to wage is a just war for the unification and independence of the motherland and for freedom and democracy!"

Rhee, he said, had sought to make Koreans "the colonial slaves of American imperialism." He called upon guerrillas in the South to hit the enemy from the rear, disrupt communications, destroy roads and bridges. All citizens of the South were to disobey the Rhee regime. Workers were to strike; farmers were to refuse food to the enemy; and intellectuals were to engage in political propaganda and stir up mass uprisings.

"History tells us that people who resolutely fight for freedom and independence," he concluded, "must be victorious. The time has come to unify our country. . . . Forward!"

A dozen North Korean Yaks, made in the USSR, suddenly swooped low, instilling nineteen-year-old Chung Dong-hua and the other students with hatred for the enemy. It never dawned on him or the other students that North Korea might be the aggressor in this new war.

In Seoul there was a moment of jubilation that morning at ROK Army headquarters when it was incorrectly reported that the 7th Division had made a surprise attack on the KPA in Tongduchon, twelve miles north of Uijongbu. The report said that 1,580 enemy troops had been killed and 58 tanks destroyed. Then came realistic news that tanks of the 3rd North Korean Division were already rushing down upon Uijongbu.

General Lee Hyung-koon's 2nd ROK Division had at last reached Seoul from the south, but he felt Fat Chae's order to join in the 7th Division counterattack would be futile. Instead he kept two battalions northeast of Uijongbu to defend the city.

Chae was so furious that he pulled out his pistol and threatened to shoot Lee. But Captain Hausman agreed with Lee and thought he should be given more time to assemble his units. Lee and Chae were long-standing antagonists. Although Chae had been senior to Lee in the Japanese army, the latter had been given the first serial number for ROK officers—10001. Chae had had to accept 10002.

With the front lines crumbling, the 2nd Division became the only defense of Uijongbu and the direct road to Seoul. But Lee's two battalions, with their ineffective bazookas, were unable to stop the Russian T-34s.

The tanks burst through the lines of the two ROK battalions and entered the city. Behind them KPA infantry surged into the ROK lines, and before long the remnants of Lee's two battalions were fleeing into the hills. There were no organized units to send to Uijongbu, and it was obvious that Seoul would soon be under attack. Although there was no panic in the city, the main highway south was jammed with anxious men, women and children carrying bundles on their backs and heads. Some men led oxen.

Radio Seoul, Station HLKA, was now in the hands of the ROK Army. The staff was still on duty, but only programs approved by the military were allowed to be broadcast. The government, hoping to keep the people calm so the highways and railroads wouldn't be jammed by panicky refugees, sent out confident bulletins throughout the day. A reassuring message from Ambassador Muccio was repeated several times. "We have been through a stirring twenty-four hours," he said. But the ROK Army was acquitting itself well and its position at dawn was stronger than it had been at twilight the day before. "I am confident that the righteous cause of the liberty-loving citizens of the independent Republic of Korea will prevail."

He didn't report that American women and children, including the Hausman family and Reverend Zeller's wife, were already aboard the Norwegian fertilizer ship *Reinholt*. Although there were accommodations for only 12, nevertheless 682 passengers were jammed aboard before the ship left Inchon harbor.

Back in Seoul the situation had become so grim that Muccio phoned General Almond in Tokyo: Send enough transport planes to Kimpo at dawn to evacuate two hundred embassy personnel to Japan. During the day the ambassador had visited Rhee to inform him of developments; but Muccio had not been told that the president had already ordered two trains for evacuating himself and other government officials before dawn. "The one thing that I had over Rhee that stood me in good stead the next few months," Muccio recalled, "was that he had left Seoul before I did."

Americans wakened on Monday morning, June 26, to find newspapers at last truly concerned over the crisis in Korea. "This country is committed to repel the aggressor by every reason of prestige in Asia and of moral obligation to the Koreans," editorialized the *Washington Post*. The *New York Times* was even firmer. "Thus far we have temporized and improvised. Our time for that ran out when North Korean tanks crossed the border. We can lose half a world at this point if we lose heart."

It was another hot day in Washington. At the Oval Office, Truman was pointing at Korea on a globe that stood under George Washington's portrait. "This is the Greece of the Far East," he said grimly to an aide. "If we are tough enough now, there won't be any next step."

When Senator Tom Connally of Texas, chairman of the Foreign Relations Committee, talked to him late that morning, Truman was not afraid of Soviet reactions. "I'm not going to tremble like a psychopath before the Russians and I'm not going to surrender our rights or the

rights of the South Koreans." Did Connally think he had the authority
to send United States forces to Korea without approval of the Congress?

"If a burglar breaks into your house, you can shoot him without
going down to the police station and getting permission," replied the
Texas senator. "You might run into a long debate in Congress which
would tie your hands completely. You have the right to do it as Commander-in-Chief and under the UN Charter."

Truman consulted Acheson and just before noon issued his first
formal statement on Korea. "Willful disregard of the obligation to keep
the peace cannot be tolerated by nations that support the United Nations
Charter."

At the same time Republicans in the Senate were attacking the Democrats for their hesitation. "It is the way of appeasement," said Styles
Bridges of New Hampshire. The president should call Russia's bluff. "I
believe the Cominform is too crafty to risk a full-scale armed conflict
with the free world."

"Time is of the essence," said William Knowland of California. "We
must constantly keep in mind that Holland was overrun by Nazi Germany
in five days and Denmark in two."

Despite his recent advice to Truman, Connally urged patience. "We
have set up the United Nations, and when it decides upon the course
that ought to be pursued, we will then be in a better position to judge
our responsibility and what we should do than we are today."

Knowland sarcastically wondered what the United States would do
if the Soviets returned to the UN Security Council with a veto. "Does
the senator from Texas believe that we should sit back and twiddle our
thumbs and do nothing?" Despite the flare-ups, it was evident, said
Arthur Krock in *The New York Times*, that "the President will have firm
bipartisan support for any form of policy that is linked to national policy."

Even while Connally and Knowland were jousting, ROK ambassador
Chang was at the White House pleading desperately for aid to his beleaguered country. Truman tried to encourage the weeping, distraught
Korean. "Hold fast," he said. "Help is on the way." But Chang was not
reassured, nor was Truman's confidence shared by reporters. Some
thought Korea was going to be written off, since the risks of military
intervention were too great. James Reston of *The New York Times* reported
that a feeling of apathetic fatalism was engulfing the capital. "There are
some officials here who argue that Korea, established by the United
Nations and attacked without provocation, furnishes the best possible
moral basis for challenging the Communist campaign of aggression. But
the majority seems to believe that it would be unwise to choose a battleground and a time more favorable to the Communists than to the Western nations."

Truman met with his advisers that evening. Acheson dominated the proceedings, proposing a step-up in military action with an "all-out order" to air and naval forces to "offer fullest possible support" to the ROK Army, as well as specific orders to the Seventh Fleet to prevent an attack on Formosa. Truman went further. For the past five years, he said, he had done everything possible to prevent this kind of crisis. Now they had to do everything they could for the Koreans. "What is developing in Korea seems to me like a repetition on a larger scale of what happened in Berlin. The Reds are probing for weaknesses in our armor. We must meet their threat without getting embroiled in a worldwide war."

He told Secretary of Defense Johnson to call MacArthur on the scrambler. "Tell him in person what my instructions are." He was to support the Republic of Korea with the air and naval elements of his command. "But only south of the 38th parallel."

All recommendations were approved by Truman's advisers, including Secretary Johnson, and the meeting broke up with a feeling of confidence. Truman earnestly remarked to Acheson, "I've been President a little over five years, and I've spent five years to avoid making a decision like the one I've had to make tonight. What I want you to know is that this is not a decision just for Korea. It is a decision for the United Nations itself."

It was a decision that surprised many observers of the Washington scene who did not understand the close relationship of Truman and Acheson, the first of the Cold Warriors. They were an odd couple: Truman the feisty ex-haberdasher from a small town in Missouri who washed his own socks in the sink every night, Acheson the upper-class diplomat out of Harvard who spoke and wrote elegantly. Truman, an orderly, forthright man, was trusting Acheson to conduct foreign affairs; and Acheson, who looked upon Truman as "my President," was serving him loyally and with the highest respect. Together this odd couple was making history.

CHAPTER 3

"There Goes the Bridge!"
(June 27–28)

1.

While Senators Knowland and Connally were wrangling in the Senate, in Seoul Defense Minister Shin was knocking at President Rhee's bedroom door. It was two A.M., June 27, and Mrs. Rhee felt something ominous must have happened. "Your Excellency," said Shin excitedly, "we must leave Seoul!"

"No!" exclaimed Rhee angrily. "Defend Seoul to the death! I will not leave!" He slammed the door. A few minutes later a police officer arrived. He handed the president a report: tanks had reached the outskirts of the city. This time Rhee dressed hastily, unaware that the report was a ruse. Meeting with his advisers, he agreed to evacuate the capital. A former prime minister urged them to go south of the Han River and then blow up the bridge. This would not only keep the People's Army from crossing but would force the ROK troops in the capital to fight.

They decided to evacuate government officials of high rank and their families on a special seven A.M. train. Lower officials would leave on a second train an hour later. The president and his party packed and at about four A.M. were driven through the dark streets to the railroad station where the special train was waiting. Soon it had crossed the Han River and was on its way to Taejon.

Foreign Minister Ben Limb and two other officials were bound for the American embassy to tell Muccio they were not satisfied with the decision of Rhee's Cabinet meeting to evacuate Seoul. They found the parking lot of the embassy ablaze with burning classified documents. The halls inside were cluttered with suitcases and bundles. U.S. Marines were using thorium bombs to destroy coding machines, and the energetic security officer personally smashed the switchboard with a sledgehammer. What should they do? asked Limb of Muccio, who was calm. Muccio would make no definite recommendation but assured them he was not going to leave Seoul.

The ambassador was faced with a hard choice. If he let his people be caught by the North Koreans, he'd be severely criticized. But if he sent them out too early, he'd also be censured. At about five A.M. Muccio, a man of action, decided to evacuate everyone except himself and several volunteers. An hour later he cabled the State Department that Rhee and most of his Cabinet had departed. "I propose remain in Seoul with limited volunteer staff until bitter end." But he was ordered to join Rhee, "before safe departure becomes impossible."

There was near panic at the railroad station, and the seven A.M. train for cabinet members was jammed, with many clinging to the tops of the coaches. There were few ranking members aboard. Most of them had been delayed by wives who insisted on bringing along domestic possessions.

ROK officials as well as ordinary citizens were frantically trying to flee. Those who had missed the first train were on hand for the eight o'clock special, but the stationmaster refused to dispatch it, since he had no orders. Nor could anyone locate the transportation minister. Leaflets from North Korean planes were falling in the streets, calling on South Korea to surrender. Defense Minister Shin feared the soldiers would not fight if they knew their government had fled. He was also worried about the millions of people who would jam the main Han River bridge. And so a broadcast went out at ten A.M. declaring that the government was still in control and had *not* left the city. The effect was dramatic. Relative order was restored and many returned home reassured.

But the head of public information was incensed to hear such a lie. He telephoned Shin in protest. The minister of defense promised to correct the report and at eleven A.M. HLKA announced that part of the government *had* left Seoul, although some, including the vice-president, had remained; but there was no functioning government.

At 11:40 A.M. Rhee's train arrived in Taegu, a city 150 air miles southeast of Seoul. As he stepped onto the platform he looked haggard. "I've made a lifetime mistake," he said. His advisers tried to calm him, but he was adamant. He had to get back. Within the hour the train headed north. Mrs. Rhee, concerned over his condition, offered him tea, but he ignored her and gazed fixedly out the window. "As soon as we reach Suwon," he muttered, "we'll be able to get back to Seoul by car."

When the train reached Taejon on its return trip, Rhee was informed by the transportation minister that Seoul had fallen to the Reds. Rhee and his party moved into the stationmaster's office for a brief rest; there the president learned from Muccio's assistant that the UN had passed a resolution condemning North Korea and President Truman was going to send military forces. With utter gloom turned to optimism, Rhee decided to make Taejon, the sixth city of South Korea, his temporary capital.

Muccio had already informed other foreign diplomats that Americans were being evacuated by air. The French chargé d' affaires had sent his wife and children out with the American women; but since many French citizens, particularly Catholic priests, refused to leave, he decided to stay. The British minister, Captain Vyvyan Holt, a bachelor, also declined to go. When Bishop Patrick Byrne, the Catholic Apostolic Delegate in Korea, learned that all remaining Americans were to be taken by bus to Kimpo Airfield, he summoned his secretary, Father William Booth, and told him to arrange the evacuation of all foreign priests. He himself was staying. He had been a prisoner in Japan during World War II and wasn't afraid of the North Koreans.

The Irish-American Byrne informed Muccio, "It is my duty to remain." Father Booth reported back that all arrangements had been made—and that he had received permission from his superior, Monsignor Carroll, to stay with the bishop. Byrne, a tall, slight man with gray hair and merry, gray-blue eyes, said nothing but shook Booth's hand. Neither knew that other foreign Catholic priests in the area were also to follow their example. The Protestant ministers were all leaving— except for Larry Zellers and five other Methodist missionaries cut off in Kaesong.

Muccio packed some belongings at his home, then drove to KMAG headquarters, where he learned that a group of fifteen officers representing MacArthur was arriving at Suwon airfield at about six P.M. It was finally time for him to leave Seoul.

Seated around the big velvet-covered table in ROK Army headquarters were ten men—the General Staff, four Cabinet ministers and Captain Hausman. As usual, Chief of Staff Fat Chae sat at the head of the table. "We must fight to the end!" pleaded Defense Minister Shin. "Let's pledge to that!"

"Wait a minute," said Captain Hausman. He told his driver to go to his house nearby. "Up in my bedroom closet is a bottle of whiskey. Bring it."

A few minutes later they were drinking a pledge of fight to the end and die if necessary. They decided to set up headquarters in Sihung, halfway between Seoul and Suwon. As everyone was leaving, Chae drew out his revolver and laid it on the table.

About two-thirty P.M. the little convoy—without Chae—crossed the Han River bridge. The convoy's radio picked up a message from MacArthur ordering KMAG to "repair to your former location." Limited U.S. naval forces would soon arrive. Momentous decisions were in the offing. "Be of good cheer." Hausman knew this meant, "Get the hell back to your headquarters!" and ordered a Korean demolitions engineer to remove the dynamite that had been planted on the bridge.

Then Hausman remembered Fat Chae sitting with his .45 on the table. He ordered the driver to rush to headquarters and prayed he'd get there before Chae blew out his brains. He raced up the stairs to the office. Chae was sitting at the table, the gun still there. Hausman told him of the message from MacArthur. When Hausman left the room, he had a thousand things to do. One of the first was to see that the Korean people heard the news from Tokyo. At about four-thirty P.M. HLKA broadcast that a combat command post of MacArthur's headquarters was being established in Seoul. The Americans had promised that air force planes would directly participate in the fighting tomorrow morning. "The national defense forces will resolutely hold their present positions." The broadcast was repeated every ten minutes between intervals of military music. The people didn't know what to think, but the magic name MacArthur had its effect.

North of Seoul, the Korean People's Army was converging on the city. Remnants of ROK units were falling back, some in complete disorder, some fighting stubbornly. There were no antitank mines and few antipersonnel mines left, but one hastily formed group under the commander of the ROK engineer school destroyed, with demolitions and pole charges, four tanks at a bridge several miles north of Seoul.

While almost everyone was trying to get out of Korea, Muccio's viceconsul, Harold Noble, had been desperately trying to get there from Tokyo. At last he left Japan early that morning, but the C-54 was held up en route and didn't land at Kimpo until two P.M. Noble, from a missionary family in Korea, would never forget the sight that met his eyes at the airport. Two hundred men were anxiously waiting to get on the plane he was leaving so they could get to the safety of Tokyo. Fleeing unshaven U.S. Marines, who looked like pirates in their variegated headgear, were dumping nonessentials from their baggage, leaving open suitcases scattered on the tarmac.

Second Secretary Tom Cory told Noble, inaccurately, that Seoul was taken and the North Koreans had crossed the Han and were in Yongdungpo, the big industrial suburb of Seoul. "If you want to stay alive, get back on the plane!"

"But where is Muccio? I must join him," insisted Noble, who had previously worked in Army intelligence.

"He's disappeared and no one knows what's happened to him."

Noble was determined to join Rhee's government until he got instructions. "Where's the government?"

"There's no government to join! It's collapsed!"

Noble was shaken but stubborn. He hadn't come all the way from Tokyo to turn tail. At the same time, there was no use in getting shot. He approached the embassy security officer. "What about Muccio?"

"Oh, he's holed up in his house, and if you want to be a prisoner you can join him."

Just then a Navy CPO, Al Emsley, drove up in a jeep with a trailer piled high with baggage. Did Noble want a ride to Pusan? Noble said he'd go as far as Suwon. If KMAG wasn't there, he'd continue south. A Marine gave Emsley and Noble a carbine, a .45 and extra clips, since they'd have to go through Yongdungpo, which was reported occupied by North Koreans.

As they drove through the suburb, the key to road and rail travel south, Noble held his carbine ready to fire. The streets were empty, ominously quiet, but the group saw no one, and in a few minutes they were safely through the city. As they neared Suwon, Noble asked Emsley to drive to the airport where KMAG was supposed to be located. If there was any semblance of government, he would join it. Otherwise he'd continue on to Pusan. As they approached the airport, a Mercury raced towards them, Muccio at the wheel. With him were two assistants. Noble waved frantically. Both cars stopped and Noble ran up to Muccio.

"Where the hell do you think you're going?" asked the ambassador brusquely. "Japan?"

"No, I'm reporting for duty."

"Oh, get in," he said.

After setting up joint headquarters for the ROK and American commands at an agricultural college about two miles west of Suwon, Muccio and Noble headed for the airfield to meet the American commander, General John H. Church. Rain was softly falling as they neared the short landing strip. The two wandered around the field, querying KMAG officers who were waiting to be evacuated to Japan. Suddenly a message came from ROK Army headquarters in Seoul. All KMAG officers and men at the airfield were to saddle up and get back to Seoul. Never had Noble seen a more dispirited group.

At about six P.M. Noble and Muccio could hear a plane coming into the landing strip from the west. The C-47 carrying the Church party drew up beside them. Muccio led the party to the agricultural college, where dinner was served. Then offices for Church and the embassy were set up in the same small wooden building where they had dined, a shabby structure with little furniture. Church kept insisting on going to Seoul so he could look over the situation, but Muccio said it would be impossible in the dark. At best, Church would get lost; at worst, captured or killed.

In Taejon to the south, Muccio's assistant, Ernest Drumright, had caught up with Rhee at his summer cottage. The president was in a bad mood. He sarcastically inveighed against the lack of American military support, particularly after Dulles's recent promise that the United States would never abandon Korea. Well, where were the American troops? The whole defeat, he claimed, came because of unfulfilled American promises.

All this was unfair and Drumright knew it, but he kept quiet until the tirade ended. Unlike Muccio, he was dogmatic and ill at ease. He said simply that he was at the president's service, would do whatever he could, and left. After a long wait he was able to communicate with Seoul. The smashed embassy switchboard had finally been fixed. KMAG colonel W.H.S. Wright, still at ROK Army headquarters, reported that Church and Muccio were now at Suwon. Drumright hurried to the home of the provincial governor, where Rhee and his wife had moved. Rhee was in a much better mood, particularly on hearing MacArthur's message, "Be of good cheer."

"I want to go back to Seoul!" Rhee kept repeating as Drumright told of Church's arrival. By now many civilian government leaders had appeared and were milling around the governor's house, exchanging gossip and passing on the latest rumors.

Drumright told Rhee that President Truman had ordered MacArthur to give naval and air support to Korea south of the 38th parallel. American planes were already knocking out enemy tanks and blasting transportation north of Seoul. Clasping his hands in prayer, the delighted Rhee exclaimed he must go on the radio and encourage his people! This was quickly arranged, and soon Rhee was speaking over Taejon radio, the first time his voice had been heard by the people since the invasion.

At Kimpo Airfield, a few miles west of Seoul, two planes were burning at the end of the strip. A C-54 was circling overhead. Four American correspondents pressed their faces to the Plexiglas windows. Below they could see Americans frantically waving bedsheets and pillowcases, a signal that Kimpo was still in friendly hands.

The plane landed, but its motors still roared. The correspondents —Keyes Beech of the Chicago *Daily News*, Marguerite Higgins of the New York *Herald Tribune*, Burton Crane of *The New York Times* and Frank

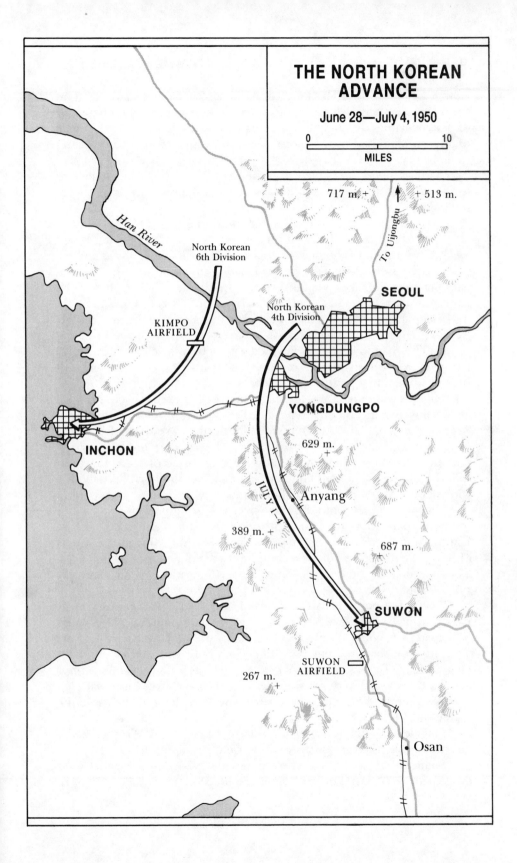

THE NORTH KOREAN
ADVANCE

June 28—July 4, 1950

0   10
MILES

717 m. +   + 513 m.

Han River

North Korean
6th Division

North Korean
4th Division

To Uijongbu

SEOUL

KIMPO
AIRFIELD

YONGDUNGPO

629 m.
+

INCHON

Anyang

389 m. +

687 m.

JULY 1–4

SUWON

267 m.
+

SUWON
AIRFIELD

Osan

Gibney of *Time*—disembarked. Gibney had tried to dissuade Higgins from coming along. Korea was no place for a woman. Aware that some of her colleagues disliked her for being pushy, she felt she was the equal of any man and had proved herself in Europe. For her Korea was more than a story. It was a crusade.

As passengers scrambled into the plane, the crew chief motioned the four correspondents to get back aboard. The answer was, "We're staying."

"You're crazy," said the chief, slamming the door behind them.

Once the plane had roared off, there was an uncanny quiet. Beech looked around and thought, "So this is what it's like when we run."

Nearby were three GI trucks loaded with abandoned trunks and bags. The parking area was filled with more than two dozen abandoned American cars. Some had a key in the ignition. Gibney and Crane got into a jeep. Higgins liberated a Studebaker, and Beech took a new Dodge. At about eight o'clock the three cars started off northward towards the action. The road to Seoul was jammed with refugees fleeing in the other direction. Careening trucks camouflaged with branches endangered ROK soldiers in jeeps and on horseback.

Higgins was moved and terrified to have the crowds cheer and wave as the tiny American convoy passed. Koreans' confidence in anything American was pathetic. Beech honked his horn and yelled foolish words of encouragement as the rain resumed. "The poor fools didn't know that we were merely four correspondents, and one of us a woman at that. I laughed like a loon and kept my hand on the horn. I was giddy with elation. Was I not a symbol of democracy?"

They turned left onto the Han River bridge, a high-level steel-and-concrete span, unaware that the bridge was still planted with TNT. Hausman's order had been ignored. There was no panic in the streets of Seoul. People were quietly moving south as soldiers passed in trucks, jeeps, old taxis, ancient buses and trolleys. Alongside moved columns of singing soldiers.

The correspondents were directed to KMAG headquarters, near ROK Army headquarters, a gloomy, gray-stone building. They were informed by Colonel Wright that the enemy was only twelve miles away. The situation was fluid but hopeful. "The South Koreans have a pathological fear of tanks. That is part of the reason for all this retreating."

As the correspondents were leaving, General Fat Chae waddled towards them. "We fightin' hard now," he told them. "Things gettin' better."

Maggie Higgins was assigned quarters in Colonel Wright's headquarters, while the three men were housed with a deputy.

Soon after the exhausted correspondents crawled into cots they were awakened by a KMAG officer who was buttoning his trousers. "They're in the city! Head for Suwon!" Someone running down the hall shouted derisively, "*KMAG*—Kiss My Ass Good-bye!"

Beech, Crane and Gibney hastily dressed, collected their typewriters and bags. An American major told them enemy tanks were approaching the Han River bridge. "If I were you," he advised, "I would head there too. If you hurry, you'll still have time to make it."

With Crane at the wheel of a jeep, the three men went toward the bridge through blackened streets. Everyone was fleeing that way. Crane's driving on the left side to make better time made Beech nervous. Mortar bursts were landing nearby.

As they approached the bridge, they saw Captain Hausman just ahead. And a few minutes in front of him was General Chae, who had already crossed the river. Maggie Higgins was in a jeep following Colonel Wright, and both vehicles were a minute behind Beech and his two companions.

As the street narrowed onto the bridge, the Beech jeep was caught in a mass of refugees, ox carts, and bicycles. He, Crane, and Gibney left their vehicle and walked forward to see what was wrong, then returned in frustration. The rumble of guns was louder. The end of the bridge —and safety—was only a hundred yards away. Crane savagely shook the wheel. "If we hadn't stopped at headquarters, we would be across by now."

It had been Beech's idea, and he was angry enough at himself. "This isn't the time to think about what we did but what the hell we are going to do now," he said irritably. Gibney, sitting next to the driver, said nothing. Suddenly the sky was illuminated by a huge sheet of orange flame.

The whole world was exploding in front of them. Beech saw a truckload of soldiers rise eerily in the air. His own jeep was hurled back fifteen feet.

Seconds after Hausman's jeep crossed the bridge there had been a tremendous explosion. His ears rang as the jeep leaped into the air. It flopped down with a crash but didn't overturn. Hausman thought it might be an artillery shell and kept racing south.

The bridge had broken in half. Across the great gap behind Hausman, the three correspondents stood dazed on the northern half. "I'm hit," said Crane in a matter-of-fact voice. "I can't see. There's blood in my eyes."

Gibney, his glasses smashed, was also bleeding. Beech was thinking, What a beautiful shot! Those tanks must have had the bridge zeroed in.

But it wasn't artillery or tank fire. Someone had panicked and dynamited the bridge. The dead and dying were strewn over the broken span. Cars and people had plunged into the river, seventy-five feet below. Some refugees were jumping into the water, thinking it was safer there.

"There'll be another round," said Beech. "Let's get out of here." Several minutes passed. Nothing happened, but the bridge was burning. The injured were crying for help. Beech circled around the truck wreckage and its dead. Leaning over the jagged edge of the bridge, he looked down on the black waters. There was no way out by jeep.

Crane, bleeding badly, couldn't see. Beech got an undershirt out of his baggage to bind Crane's head. He also got his typewriter. This was going to be one hell of a story—if he only lived to write it. The three weary correspondents slowly headed back towards Seoul, wondering what had happened to Maggie. Beech felt defeated, washed out. Early that evening they had been congratulating each other on finding they had a scoop on the stand of Seoul. Now Seoul had fallen on top of them.

They decided to return to KMAG headquarters. If they were going to be captured, the best place for it was in an American area. Beech hoped Maggie was still there.

When Maggie and her driver saw a sheet of orange flame tear the sky, her driver shouted, "There goes the bridge!" He turned the jeep around and they raced back to KMAG headquarters. Colonel Wright's jeep followed. In darkness punctuated by shellbursts they found staff officers collecting men. Wright was disgusted. "The South Koreans blew up that bridge without even bothering to give us warning," he explained to Maggie. "And too soon." Most of the city was still in ROK hands.

Maggie could feel tension increasing, but Wright, with quiet authority, said, "Now listen everybody. Nobody is going to go hightailing off by himself. We're all in this together." They would find an alternative route out of Seoul, perhaps a rail bridge, and then they could save their vehicles. A convoy of some sixty jeeps, trucks and weapons carriers soon left with headlights ablaze, looking in vain for a rail span. They finally stopped. Maggie was concerned about her three comrades.

"Oh, they got out in plenty of time," said the operations officer. "They're probably in Suwon right now scooping you."

She pictured the three of them cozily settled, banging out their stories. She was determined to get across the river, even if she had to swim. Colonel Wright noticed her gloomy air. "What's the matter, kid? Afraid you won't get your story out?" She said nothing. "Look, stick by this radio truck and we'll try to send out a message for you if you keep it short." She sat morosely in the jeep waiting for dawn.

When the first light of Wednesday, June 28, appeared, Maggie came to life. She put her typewriter on the hood of the jeep and began typing furiously. Lines of refugees were passing and many gasped to see the young American in a navy blue skirt and flowered blouse banging away in the haze.

* * *

Beech, Crane and Gibney were also still on the wrong side of the Han.
They had spent the night at KMAG headquarters. A Korean corporal
said he knew a way to get across and they prepared to leave. Gibney
pulled out his naval intelligence card and burned it. "Just in case we
don't make it." Burton Crane reached for his wallet. He had served with
the OSS in China and he also burned his card. Beech felt out of it. He
had Marine Corps identification from the last war. There was no need
to destroy it.

The sky was turning gray as they set out in two jeeps along the
northern bank of the Han, heading upstream. Just over the hill behind
them came the boom of heavy guns. Finally they found a bridge over a
tributary, not the Han itself, but that too was broken. Hundreds of white-
clad Koreans were wading across. An ROK soldier with Gibney in the
first jeep plunged his vehicle into the water and made it to the other
side. The second jeep, driven by Beech, got stuck midstream and was
sinking relentlessly into the mud. But a group of Koreans lifted it and
carried it to the other side, with Beech still in the driver's seat.

They headed for the Han itself and found the bank crowded with
Koreans also hoping to get across to safety. It was too deep to wade; a
few rowboats and rafts were serving as ferries. Across the river they saw
a large, empty raft. A young ROK soldier and Gibney went to fetch it
in a rowboat while Crane and Beech waited on the shore. Beech was
feeling much better. "I hate to say this, Burton," he said, "but this is the
first time I've felt alive since Iwo Jima."

"I know what you mean."

2.

In Washington it was time for dinner. June 27th had been another hectic
day for the president. That morning he had met with his vice-president
and fourteen congressmen—nine Democrats and five Republicans. Taking his seat next to Acheson, he asked the secretary of state to present
a summary of the Korean crisis. The military situation was desperate
and many nations were concerned that the United States might not take
strong enough measures to repel the invaders. And unopposed aggression, said Acheson, would certainly lead to World War III.

When Acheson finished, Truman exclaimed, "I have ordered
United States air and sea forces to give the Korean government troops
cover and support." Truman invited questions and discussion. There
was no criticism of the actions taken by the president.

As the congressmen filed out of the White House meeting, they
were besieged by reporters who had just been handed copies of Truman's

statement, which not only demanded action against North Korea but warned the Chinese Communists not to attack Formosa. "I think it is a damned good action," said Senator Bridges. Senator H. Alexander Smith, another Republican, from New Jersey, was equally pleased, and an unidentified participant told James Reston of *The New York Times*, "The president's decision has untied a thousand knots." The correspondent of the Chicago *Tribune* noticed that Truman was "grinning broadly" as he walked across the street to Blair House for lunch. Yet his advisers "wore long faces."

The impact on official Washington of the president's statement was vividly expressed by Joseph Harsch of the *Christian Science Monitor*: He had lived and worked in and out of this city for twenty years, and never before had he felt such a sense of relief and unity pass through the capital. The most curious thing was the contrast with the gloom of the day before, based on the wide belief that Truman would miss the boat and do something idle or specious. "I have never seen such a large part of Washington so nearly satisfied with a decision of the government." There was also a rise in the stock market.

That afternoon there was a dramatic meeting of the UN Security Council. Many feared that Ambassador Malik, the representative of the Soviet Union, would attend. The night before both Charles "Chip" Bohlen and George Kennan had assured Truman that Malik would not appear. These two experts on the USSR pointed out that the cumbersome bureaucracy in Moscow was not equipped to make such quick decisions.

When Malik appeared at the Stockholm Restaurant for lunch, Secretary-General Lie asked him to come to the meeting that afternoon. It would be in the best interests of the Soviet Union. "No," answered the Russian, "I will not go there." Upon hearing this, Ernest Gross heaved a sigh of relief. As he and Lie drove to Lake Success, the American reprimanded him, as an old friend, for trying to convince Malik to come. "Trygve, can you imagine what would have happened if he *had* accepted your invitation?" For the first time in recorded history, thought Gross, a world organization had voted to use force to stop armed aggression. "Lucky or not, it was a considerable victory for Harry Truman."

In London, Prime Minister Attlee read Truman's resolution to the House of Commons. "This [the North Korean attack] is naked aggression," he observed, "and must be checked." He said the British representative at the UN Security Council had been instructed to support the American resolution. At the Security Council meeting, only Yugoslavia opposed the decision, and never before had Harry Truman been so popular in America.

CHAPTER 4

"Our Forces Will Not Last a Day"
(June 28–30)

1.

Colonel Park Ki-byung had been ordered by Fat Chae to defend Seoul to the death with his 4th Regiment. But after the Han bridge was blown, he ordered his men to withdraw to the river and collect boats and empty oil drums. Park had only 50 men with him when, at first light on the 28th, he reached the Han at the still-intact railroad crossing just upstream of the destroyed bridge. On the beach he found 250 of his men waiting. They had constructed rafts and found a small fishing boat. Park gave the order to cross, and as they made their way across the river, they passed the floating bodies of those who had fallen from the bridge. When they reached the southern bank, Park began organizing the remnants of his regiment.

It was still cloudy, and air cover from Japan seemed impossible. Then came a break in the skies, and a small American reconnaissance plane appeared. The pilot's report was encouraging, and at seven-thirty A.M. twelve B-26's took off from Japan to bomb railway yards near the 38th parallel, the first U.S. air sortie of the war.

At the Apostolic Delegation, Bishop Patrick Byrne, the American Mary-knoller, ordered all gates and doors opened to the Communists. At about eleven, shooting broke out. Half an hour later, men in civilian clothes and red armbands poured in and stripped the place of everything movable. The bishop collected the vestments and sacred vessels and sent for the nearest Korean pastor to take them to safety. He arrived with a pushcart and several Catholic boys, but the intruders forbade them to remove anything.

"Why not?" asked the priest. "Aren't we all under the People's government now? These things belong to us as much as they belong to you."

The looters had no answer and the priest left with his treasures. As the scavenging continued, Bishop Byrne protested.

"You believe in heaven, don't you?" said one looter.

"Certainly."

"That's good. You'll soon be going there."

The reports coming into General Church's headquarters at Suwon announced the collapse of Seoul. But Ambassador Muccio's energetic first secretary, Noble, was not satisfied. He persuaded two of Church's operations officers to go north with him to the new ROK Army headquarters at the Sihung Infantry School south of Yongdungpo, where they could get a more accurate estimate of the situation. Their jeep slowly forced its way against the stream of refugees coming south. Thousands of beaten, exhausted ROK soldiers were mixed in the mob, but many waved at the Americans and cheered. Noble was impressed that most of them carried their weapons, defeated but not stampeding to the rear. Civilians also cheered and clapped as the jeep passed. The American uniform still symbolized ultimate victory.

Four or five thousand soldiers were standing or sitting in orderly rows on the parade grounds of the infantry school. Officers and noncoms were creating new formations. The commandant of the military academy, Major General Kim Hong-il, was taking it upon himself to reorganize the scattered army, remnants of four divisions from the north. He didn't know where the 1st Division was, and two others—the 6th and 8th—reportedly were still fighting in the east.

Noble asked what was going on at the Han River. General Kim was not sure. He did know that a few ROK troops were trying to hold the rail span just east of the Han bridge. Noble suggested to his companions that they continue upstream along the south bank of the river. From a rise at the outskirts of Yongdungpo they could see Seoul. All seemed peaceful except for the boom of a distant gun. As they neared the southern approaches of the two Han bridges, an armored car appeared. Fortunately it was South Korean. A lieutenant informed them he was conducting a reconnaissance along the south side of the river. Kimpo Airfield was not in enemy hands, as rumored, and no North Koreans were across the river near the bridges. He thought they could find General Yu, commander of the 7th Division, at the railroad station at the southern end of the undamaged railroad span.

They walked toward the bridge. The station was exposed to fire from the other side, and they approached it cautiously. No Korean soldiers could be seen, but as they entered the station, they were challenged by a sentry. Then Noble saw General Yu sitting at a desk.

He explained that he was holding the railroad span with about 400 men. He would do his best to slow the enemy with one antitank gun and one machine gun. But he had nothing with which to blow the bridge. He begged them to send explosives from Suwon. He also expected reinforcements from General Kim at the infantry school. Please, he begged the two Americans, send planes to bomb and strafe the north banks.

By one P.M. Colonel Whitey Paik was assembling the remnants of his battered 1st Division on the north bank of the Han across from the infantry school. As they were crossing by ferry and small boats, U.S. planes roared overhead and began dropping bombs on them. Some of the men shouted angrily. Why in hell were the Americans bombing them? Paik too was angry but to calm the men shouted that it was a good thing. "The Americans are here! They are finally in the war! Now we have hope!"

After having been rowed across the Han, harassed by heavy but inaccurate rifle fire, Maggie Higgins was walking across a mountain trail to Suwon in a long, single file of soldiers and refugees that included the ROK minister of the interior. Higgins was determined not to give any trouble and marched close to the head of the column. Hearing a steady drone, she looked up to see silvery U.S. fighter planes diving on Seoul. "My heart pounded with excitement—this must be the part of the 'momentous event' mentioned in MacArthur's message." The realization that American air power was in the war hit everybody at the same time. The Koreans around her screamed and yelled joyfully. Women from a nearby village rushed out to grasp her hand and point to the sky with ecstasy.

Ambassador Muccio was about to board a plane to visit Rhee when Yaks strafed the Suwon airstrip. He took cover and emerged unharmed, covered with mud, with one trouser leg torn and bloodied. He arrived at Taejon at about two-fifteen P.M. in tatters but, as usual, radiating confidence. He went directly to President Rhee's quarters. Mrs. Rhee thought he looked as if he had just crawled out of a trash can. His only instruction from the State Department had been, "Act boldly." And so he took it upon himself to tell Rhee that substantial American help was on the way—even though he didn't actually know what Truman's decision would be. His mud-spattered clothes only accented his passionate plea to have faith. They must—and could—fight to victory!

Risking his career, Muccio swore that the United States had decided
to go all out for South Korea. American naval and air forces would stop
military supplies coming down across the 38th parallel. This was a joint
Korean-American effort. Some things could be done better by Koreans,
other things better by the Americans. Later Muccio took Rhee aside to
reveal a secret message from MacArthur. He would be in Suwon the
next morning to determine what help should be given in the war against
the Communists, and had requested that the president meet him there.

This invitation meant more to Rhee than all of Muccio's words of
hope. Nothing, he said, could keep him from Suwon.

2.

President Truman had already called for aid to South Korea. On the
afternoon of June 28 he went public, addressing a convention of the
American Newspaper Guild, with four networks broadcasting his words
to the nation while the Voice of America was beaming them overseas.
He called the North Korean invasion "an example of the danger to which
underdeveloped areas particularly are exposed," and pointed out that
his vigorous actions against aggression were just a "shield" for "the great
constructive task of peace."

From both home and abroad enthusiastic support came to the White
House. "There is only one way out of such situations as this," declared
former president Hoover. "That is to win. To win we must have unity
of purpose and action." *The New York Times* called Truman's decision "a
momentous and courageous act," but the London *Daily Worker* described
his actions as "the adventurist, ruthless, aggressive imperialist operations
of Wall Street for domination of all Asia and the Pacific."

The French ambassador called Truman to say his decision and the
action of the Security Council had been "very well received by the government and by the people." Nicaragua, Colombia, the Dominican Republic, the Philippines, Canada and the Council of the Organization of
American States all praised Truman. But the reaction in Russia was
puzzling. The Sunday edition of *Pravda* had not even mentioned the
war in Korea, but the next day two TASS dispatches from Pyongyang
quoted communiqués from North Korea claiming that South Korea had
initiated the attack. The tempo of protest was raised the next morning
by accusing the United States of "direct aggression against the Korean
People's Democratic Republic and the Chinese People's Republic."

In Peking, forty-six Chinese Communist leaders had heard Foreign
Minister Chou En-lai respond forcefully to Truman's announcement
while Washington was just waking up. Chou called the decision of Truman "armed aggression against the territory of China . . . a blatant violation of the United Nations Charter." He accused the Americans of

ordering the "Korean puppet army of Syngman Rhee" to attack North Korea. And this attack was, in turn, just a "fabricated pretext" for U.S. aggression against Taiwan, Korea, Indochina, and the Phillippines—another step in the "secret plans of American imperialism to seize all of Asia." After Chou's speech there was "a vigorous discussion" during which Mao called Truman a hypocrite. "People of China and peoples of the world, arise!" he shouted. "Defeat every provocation of American imperialism!"

Although most of the reaction in Congress to Truman's announcement was favorable, Republican Senator Robert Taft of Ohio protested vehemently. "If the incident is permitted to go by without protest, at least from this body, we would have finally terminated for all time the right of Congress to declare war, which is granted to Congress alone by the Constitution of the United States."

Despite the feeling of euphoria at the White House, Acheson warned Truman that the apparent unanimity of support for his policy might not last. "The President, mistaking my purpose, which was to prepare for criticism and hard sledding," recalled Acheson, "insisted that we could not back out of the course upon which we had started. He was unmoved by, indeed unmindful of, the effect upon his or his party's political fortunes of action that he thought was right and in the best interest of the country, broadly conceived."

3.

At 8 o'clock on the morning of July 29, Ambassador Muccio called on Rhee at his residence in Taegu to find the president "in a terrible state." Madame Rhee was also extremely nervous. During the night both had received a flock of lurid tales of the situation in Seoul. It was obvious the Americans were doing nothing to aid Korea! After an extremely disagreeable hour and five minutes, they all departed for the airfield.

In Tokyo, rain and clouds surrounded Haneda Airport at dawn, and MacArthur's aides decided the flight should be postponed. "We go," said the general simply. It was still overcast and rainy when the *Bataan*, MacArthur's B-34, took off later that morning.

While Muccio and Rhee were preparing to leave Taegu for Suwon in separate planes, B-29's were successfully laying their five-hundred-pound bombs across Kimpo Airfield while two other B-29's were bombing the main Seoul railroad station. Unfortunately, no one had forwarded an ROK request to blow up the railroad bridge, and it was still intact. Defending it with only a small group of determined ROK soldiers seemed a hopeless task. The beaches all along the northern banks of the Han River were crowded with North Koreans preparing to come across.

Colonel Whitey Paik had finally managed to get some of his surviving 3,000 men across the Han. An equal number had been left behind on the north bank as Paik led the way through the rice paddies above Kimpo. There was some machine-gun fire from the east, but no casualties. Near the infantry school he came across Lieutenant Ray May, a KMAG adviser. Exhausted and hungry, Whitey asked for something to eat. May had nothing. "How about sugar?" May found some. Revitalized, Paik asked what was going on. May told him that the counterattack near Uijongbu had failed. But there was hope. The Americans were coming. The air force had already been committed, but as yet there were no ground forces. Then Paik went up to General Kim Hong-il, commandant of the infantry school, and told about being fired on from Kimpo Airfield. The general asked Paik why he didn't counterattack. "General Kim," explained Paik patiently, "I'm still waiting for my troops to assemble here."

As the *Bataan* neared Korea, MacArthur strode down the aisle to tell his air chief, Lieutenant General George Stratemeyer, that if they couldn't bomb targets above the 38th parallel, North Korea would have a distinct advantage. Was he authorized to hit north of the parallel? No, said MacArthur's close friend and senior aide, Major General Courtney Whitney, who was nearby. But MacArthur told Stratemeyer to make plans to bomb the Communist airbase, then looked back at Whitney. "And now you find something in the orders that will protect me and stand up in a court-martial."

Four Mustangs were escorting the *Bataan*. But as they approached Suwon a Yak dived down and shot at the unarmed transport. An aide shouted, "Mayday!" Everyone ducked but MacArthur. He rushed to a window. "Our fighter is closing in on him," the general reported. "We will get him cold!"

Earnest Hoberecht of UP was thinking, "I hope MacArthur doesn't take too many chances; I don't want him trying to make a hero out of me."

They landed through clouds of oil smoke rising from two transports that had been bombed and strafed a few minutes earlier. Because there could be another attack any minute, they all hustled out of the *Bataan*. Keyes Beech, who had just escaped from Seoul one jump ahead of the Communists, greeted MacArthur. "General, I'm glad to see you here."

"Glad to be here."

The fear and panic Beech had witnessed among Koreans and Americans the past few days vanished.

Within fifteen minutes the MacArthur party was at the temporary headquarters of General Church. MacArthur listened to a military briefing by Church, Captain Hausman and other officers. From time to time MacArthur, pointing the stem of his pipe for emphasis, would ask a question. Church had not intended for any Korean to speak, but both

Muccio and Noble had persuaded him to let Chief of Staff Fat Chae give the Korean point of view, since it was the Koreans who had been fighting. Chae's English was limited, so he spoke through an interpreter, the breaks giving the impression of uncertainty and lack of clarity. When he asked what Chae's operational plans were for the future, the answer was, "I shall collect a million men and fight the war." MacArthur turned to Almond and said, "I am not impressed."

It was obvious to everyone that MacArthur was impatient. He slapped his knee and said, "Let's go to the front and have a look." Several tried to dissuade him from such a risky venture. Enemy tanks and spearheads were already slicing through the thin Korean lines and could be across the Han any minute. Moreover, enemy planes were bombing and strafing almost at will.

MacArthur replied quietly, "The only way to judge a fight is to see the troops in action. Let's go." The MacArthur party set off for the Han in an ancient American sedan and several jeeps. Their progress was slowed by the mass of retreating, exhausted troops. It appeared that the ROKs were in complete and disorganized flight, for the Americans knew nothing of the vigorous efforts to reorganize the survivors of the first assaults. When the convoy neared the banks of the Han, MacArthur pointed the stem of his pipe at a hill. Turning to his chief of staff, General Almond, he said, "What do you say we push up there, Ned?" The convoy ground up the dusty hill. All got out and climbed to the top. It was a dramatic sight—Seoul burning and smoking. Reporters and cameramen massed themselves around MacArthur, taking pictures from every angle as shells were whistling overhead. The others flopped to the ground, but MacArthur was oblivious to the explosions as he stared at the scene of devastation. Captain Hausman was impressed by his disregard for danger. It was not bravado. He simply stood erectly, completely composed. Awed by the image of MacArthur, the others stopped flinching at each explosion.

Seoul was a sight MacArthur would never forget. "Below me, and streaming by both sides of the hill, were the retreating, panting columns of disorganized troops, the drab colors of their weaving lines interspersed here and there with the bright red crosses of ambulances filled with broken, groaning men. The sky was resonant with shrieking missiles of death, and everywhere were the stench and utter desolation of a stricken battlefield." He was shocked by what he saw. "In that brief interval on the blood-soaked hill, I formulated my plans. They were desperate plans indeed, but I could see no other way except to accept a defeat which would include not only Korea but all of continental Asia." Air and naval support alone could not stop the enemy. He would have to throw his occupation soldiers into the breach. "It would be desperate, but it was my only chance."

As he stood on the mound he reminded his intelligence officer,

General Charles A. Willoughby, of Napoleon at Ratisbon. After studying the intact railroad bridge through field glasses, he said, "Take it out!" Then he went down the hill and climbed into the sedan.

Despite Hausman's warning, MacArthur insisted on going forward to visit an old friend, General Kim Chong-kap, whose division was along the river. "I'm up here to see," was his terse comment. "Let's go."

MacArthur asked Kim how things were going. "Well, we're here," he said, pointing out his defenses. "I think we can do all right. We can hold here."

"When are you going to withdraw?"

"We are not going to withdraw! Not unless we are ordered to. We are going to stand and fight to the last man if necessary."

Hausman felt that this was precisely what MacArthur had come up front to hear.

When MacArthur arrived at Suwon, Rhee was waiting outside of Church's headquarters at the agricultural college. Rhee and MacArthur had met before World War I, when Rhee was a student in America and MacArthur was serving in the War Department. By now they were close friends who admired each other. MacArthur put both hands on the president's shoulders. The president embraced MacArthur emotionally, then exclaimed, "General, you are stepping on rice bean sprouts!"

"Mr. President, I didn't know," said the general, moving aside apologetically. "I'm sorry." Somehow this restored Rhee's good nature, and when he later told his wife about MacArthur's apology he was smiling happily.

The two men conferred in private for an hour, with MacArthur promising all possible aid. When the general learned that Rhee and Muccio had come separately in two L-5's, he suggested they go back in a single Beechcraft. The two of them climbed into this plane, and before they could fasten seat belts it began rolling down the runway. Halfway down the strip, the plane jerked into a quick turnabout. A crewman opened the door and shouted, "Jump for it! Take cover!" A Yak was heading towards them.

Grabbing Rhee's hand, the pilot helped him run to a nearby rice paddy. The president and Muccio flung themselves down. "You'd better stay here," said the pilot, "until I see what condition the plane is in."

Rhee got up, dirty but grinning. When the pilot reported it might be some time before the plane was ready, Muccio suggested they go back to Taejon in the car he'd left on the edge of the strip the day before.

Maggie Higgins was crouched by the side of the Suwon airstrip, typing a story of MacArthur's visit, when the general himself approached in his famous crushed gold-braid hat and summer khakis. Recognizing Higgins, he said, "Hello," and asked if she'd like a lift back to Tokyo. She gladly accepted; it meant she could get her story out quickly.

Fifteen minutes later the *Bataan*, which two hours earlier had survived an attack by four Yaks, took off. Everyone on MacArthur's staff heaved a sigh of relief as they passed beyond the range of the North Korean planes, but the general was already in his cabin writing a complete report of the military situation. Before they landed he talked frankly to Higgins. The South Koreans badly needed an injection of American strength. "Give me two American divisions and I can hold Korea." Now he had a job to do. "The moment I reach Tokyo, I shall send President Truman my recommendation for the immediate dispatch of American divisions to Korea. But I have no idea whether he will accept my recommendations."

The *Bataan* touched down at Haneda at 10:15 P.M.

4.

In Washington, 9:15 that same Thursday morning, the news agency stories on the crisis were far more optimistic than MacArthur's report. Lindesay Parrott of *The New York Times* wrote, "The last twenty-four hours have been the brightest for the South Korean Republic since the invading Communists broke into Seoul." More accurate information had already reached the Department of Defense from MacArthur's headquarters: it was doubtful that the Han River line could be held. Just before noon, Secretary of Defense Johnson phoned Truman that the situation was so grave there should be another meeting of his advisers that afternoon. As yet there was no recommendation for commitment of U.S. ground combat troops.

At four P.M., an hour before his scheduled meeting, the president held a press conference. When asked, "Are we or are we not at war?" he retorted, "We are not at war."

"Would it be possible to call this a police action under the United Nations?"

"Yes, that is exactly what it amounts to," said Truman—a police action taken to help the UN repel a bunch of bandits.

At five P.M., the National Security Council met at the White House for forty-five minutes. The Joint Chiefs of Staff recommended that combat troops be committed in Korea, but their primary purpose would be to protect the evacuation of American citizens—not to take offensive action.

Truman was particularly concerned about the Soviet reaction; but Acheson assured him that his expert, George Kennan, was convinced that the Russians intended "to keep out of the business themselves in every way, but to embroil us to the maximum with their Korean and Chinese satellites."

"That means," said Truman, "that the Soviets are going to let the Chinese and North Koreans do their fighting for them."

The meeting ended with Truman's approval of the recommendations from his military advisers. These men were confident that their decisions were sufficient to contain the crisis in Korea.

On the morning of the last day in June, a plane landed at Suwon with a special passenger, Brigadier General Chung Il-kwon. He had been Fat Chae's deputy chief of staff until the previous March, when he had been sent to the infantry school at Fort Benning, Georgia. On the day of the attack he was in Hawaii awaiting transportation to Korea. When General MacArthur learned this, he sent a plane to bring him to Korea at once, for he considered Chung one of the best—if not *the* best—of ROK officers.

As Chung stepped from the plane, Chae, who regarded him as his protégé, said, "Welcome home!" and they embraced. They were driven in a jeep toward the Han so that Chung could assess the situation from the same hill MacArthur had climbed the day before. As Chung stared in shock at the sight of burning Seoul, shells began exploding nearby. "Red bastard!" shouted Chae every time a shell landed. They stood ignoring the danger, both emotionally shaken. On the way back to Suwon, the chief of staff kept falling asleep and Chung had to grasp him tightly to keep him from falling out of the jeep.

5.

While Chae and Chung were surveying Seoul, an urgent cable from MacArthur arrived at the Pentagon at three A.M., June 30. The ROK army was in confusion; supplies and equipment were abandoned or lost. Without artillery, mortars, and antitank guns, the most the South Koreans could hope to accomplish would be to slow the advance of the enemy. The ROK Army was incapable of united action, and there was grave danger of a further breakthrough.

Army Chief of Staff General J. Lawton Collins was promptly informed. He hurried to the Pentagon, where he and General Bradley could talk with MacArthur over the telecon circuits to Tokyo. At 3:40 A.M. the teleconference began. Instead of being transmitted by voice, questions and answers were flashed on screens. The eerie quality about this historic silent meeting became etched in Collins's memory. "The air was fraught with tension as we assembled in the middle of the night in the Army's darkened telecon room."

MacArthur repeated his latest recommendation that a U.S. regimental combat team be immediately committed to the forward battle area. He also wanted authorization to strengthen that combat spearhead so it could launch a counteroffensive. All the men at the Pentagon appeared outwardly calm but, realizing the import of the discussion, spoke instinctively with hushed voices as the questions, numbered serially, appeared on the screen. In Tokyo, MacArthur and six of his principal staff officers were equally tense.

Collins explained that the president, at yesterday's National Security Council meeting, had shown reluctance to commit combat troops. When no response to this was received from Tokyo, Collins took this to mean that MacArthur stood by his emphatic plea for a decision "without delay." After consulting with his staff, Collins sent this answer: "I will proceed immediately through Secretary of the Army to request Presidential approval your proposal to move one RCT [regimental combat team] into forward combat area. Will advise you soon as possible, perhaps within half hour."

Again Collins received no acknowledgment, and since time was critical, he did not attempt to secure the concurrence of the other members of the Joint Chiefs. He left the conference room while his staff continued the telecon with items of less importance. He telephoned Secretary Pace at his home, giving him the gist of MacArthur's report and the urgent request for a regiment.

At 4:57 A.M. Pace called the president at Blair House. Truman, already up and shaved, picked up the receiver beside his bed. He listened for a minute, then said, "Inform General MacArthur immediately that the use of one regimental combat team is approved." These words, delivered briskly, were potent. Truman had boldly taken a risky step that could lead to another world war.

Minutes later Collins was signaling Tokyo: "Your recommendation to move one Regimental Combat Team to combat area is approved. You will be advised later as to further buildup."

"Acknowledged," replied MacArthur. "Is there anything further now?" Then came the final words to MacArthur: "Everyone here delighted your prompt action in personally securing firsthand view of situation. Congratulations and best wishes. We have full confidence in you and your command."

6.

By the time Fat Chae and Chung Il-kwon returned to the Suwon headquarters, it was dark. Chung found a message summoning him to Taejon to see President Rhee. Still exhausted by his plane trips and the hours he had spent with Chae, he set off for Taejon in a jeep.

Maggie Higgins was already back in Suwon. Things were even worse than yesterday. Colonels and majors from Tokyo were bustling around, hanging on to information they imagined was secret. Some American journalists felt they were being treated like Red agents. She found Keyes Beech and Tom Lambert of AP worried about the danger of attack.

"We've got the jeep all set in case there's trouble," said Beech. "And there's a place in it for you."

She hoped this meant she'd won at least one ally among the male reporters. She and the two men stayed outside the conference room, hoping to pick up information from those streaming in and out. Suddenly the doors of the conference room opened and she could hear the thump of running feet as someone exclaimed in a piercing voice, "Head for the airfield!"

Why? wondered the three correspondents. They jumped up and ran inside. No one would answer any questions. Noticing an elderly colonel racing for the door, Maggie blocked his way. "Why, if there isn't something wrong, don't we all take the road south to Taejon?"

"We're surrounded!" shouted the colonel and pushed past her.

The place was a shambles. Everyone was looking for a vehicle. She heard someone cry, "The Reds are down the road!" And someone else replied, "No, they're at the airfield!"

"We're going to defend the airstrip!" yelled a KMAG major.

Beech checked his carbine clip. "My God," said Beech to himself, "do they really think this handful of men can hold the airstrip?" In the darkness the three correspondents jammed themselves into a jeep. A sergeant rode shotgun. All Higgins had was her typewriter and toothbrush.

At the airfield, the KMAG major organized a perimeter defense with about sixty men. Maggie watched as mines were laid and machine guns set up. Still no evacuation planes appeared, and suddenly the rumor spread that the brass had bugged-out to Taejon.

"So we're not surrounded at all!" said Higgins to Beech. "This is a fine way to find out!"

Then they learned that almost everyone, including General Church, was already racing through the torrential night rain to the south. The three correspondents followed the soggy parade.

General Chung was nearing Taejon. On the long trip he had thought of the future facing his old mentor. Most Americans had never appreciated Chae. To them he seemed a mountain of fat, and his pudgy face looked lethargic. They didn't realize he was a man of energy and ability. Chung himself was the son of a handsome, flamboyant man who was an interpreter for the Czarist army. When Chung was old enough he had been sent by the Japanese to the Tokyo military academy and had afterwards graduated at the top of his class. He served in the Japanese army during World War II and, when peace came, enlisted in the ROK Army, becoming Chae's deputy chief of staff in 1948.

At about ten P.M. Chung reached Taejon and reported to President Rhee. "I'm sorry for being late," he said. "From now on I shall do my best to help the chief of staff."

"It's so good to have General Chung here," said Rhee warmly. "General MacArthur also mentioned you to me. According to reports I understand that our national forces have formed a defense line along the south bank of the Han River." He paused. "How long do you think we can hold the line?"

Chung knew that if he spoke the truth it might shock Rhee, but he couldn't say something optimistic just to please the elderly president. He hardened his heart and said, "Mr. President, if the North Communist army starts another attack, our forces will not last one day."

Rhee's face fell. "What will happen to the civilians left in Seoul?" he lamented. "What kind of operational plans do you have for the future?"

"Frankly, the best plan would be to maintain the Han River defense line. That would be the standard operational plan. But it's not possible. Therefore, we must first preserve troop power."

"Does that mean you would withdraw troops from the Han River to preserve as many men as possible?"

"Yes, that is correct. That is the primary objective."

Rhee handed Chung a piece of paper—his appointment as chief of staff. Chung was stunned. He had come to help Chae and now he had to bring him bad news. He left Rhee and soon was knocking at the door of Chae's office. He found the huge man sprawled out on a chair, fast asleep. Chung forced himself to wake him.

Chae smiled. "Oh, you're here." Already told by Rhee that he was to be displaced, he did not know who would succeed him. "What did the president tell you?"

Chung reluctantly handed him the order. "I was coming here to help you as your deputy. But I received this appointment. I'm sorry."

Tears flowed down Chae's face, tears of joy. "So General Chung is my replacement!" He affectionately patted Chung's shoulder. He knew it was the end of his own army career. But he was being replaced by someone he trusted. And he knew the invaluable Captain Hausman also held Chung in high esteem, since Chung was a fine administrator who knew how to get along with people.

7.

At nine-thirty Friday morning, the last day of June, Truman summoned to the Cabinet Room of the White House the same group he had met five days before at Blair House. He told them that he had agreed to send a regiment to Korea, and thought he had done the right thing. Then he asked for comments. Everyone approved.

The president asked for their advice on the use of additional troops. He was inclined to accept Chiang Kai-shek's offer of the day before to send 33,000 Chinese Nationalist troops to Korea within five days. It would certainly be a timely and important contribution. But he asked them to consider carefully places where trouble might break out. What, for instance, would Mao Tse-tung do? What might the Russians do in the Balkans, in Iran, in Germany?

Acheson felt that the appearance of Chinese troops from Formosa might convince Mao to enter the conflict so they could damage the generalissimo's troops and reduce his ability to defend himself if the Reds decided to invade Formosa. Collins added that the 33,000 men offered had little modern equipment and would be as helpless as Rhee's troops against North Korean tanks.

Truman bowed to this position and agreed to decline Chiang's offer politely. Then he told his listeners he had decided that General MacArthur should be given full authority to use all the troops under his command. During a meeting that lasted only half an hour, a crucial decision had been made. Truman had taken a major, risky step. In his brisk manner he had committed combat forces without a declaration of war, one of the few times this had occurred in American history.

Less than an hour later, Truman was briefing congressional leaders. There were seven Democrats, seven Republicans and House speaker Sam Rayburn. Truman reviewed the decisions he had made during the week before, announcing that he had just ordered American ground troops to the defense of the Republic of Korea.

There was a long, tense silence. Only one protest came, from a Republican—Senator Kenneth S. Wherry of Nebraska, the minority floor leader. The president should have first consulted Congress before sending ground soldiers into combat. Truman replied that there had been no time because of the desperate situation. A prompt decision had to be made. Wherry interrupted but was cut off by Republican representative Dewey Short of Missouri who said he believed he was speaking for almost everyone in Congress when he stated that the nation was indebted to the president for his forceful leadership in this crisis.

Despite a few niggling attacks, both houses of Congress expressed overwhelming support for Truman's forthright action. The editorial comment of The New York Times was enthusiastic: "There is something dramatic and decisive about the use of ground troops, partly because throughout history they have been the symbol as well as the primary instrument of war, and partly because ground troops mean the physical occupation of terrain. To stop short of the necessary measures would be folly."

At 1:22 A.M. precisely, on June 30, the orders had been sent to MacArthur. America was in.

PART II

IN DUBIOUS BATTLE

CHAPTER 5

"Here, Have Some Earth to Eat"
(June 30–July 10)

1.

After six days of war, the ROK Army was collapsing and the capital, Seoul, had been abandoned by Rhee and his government. The North Koreans, spearheaded by Russian-made tanks, appeared unstoppable, and the Republic of Korea seemed doomed. But a feisty little man from Missouri had decided to risk his reputation because it was the right thing to do. Hadn't America encouraged South Korea to stand up against the Reds of the North? How could the United States, the champion of democracy, now abandon the infant Republic of Korea, even with its limitations and mistakes?

Harry Truman's decision was courageous but could not have come at a worse time. The state of the U.S. military was deplorable, partially because of Truman's dislike of spending public money and his contempt for generals and admirals. Despite his own tough, Cold War policy of containing communism, he had already cut the Pentagon budget by one third. Instead, money was being spent on foreign aid to nations pressed by the Soviets.

By 1948, the outstanding U.S. World War II ground forces of almost one hundred well-equipped and well-trained divisions had been drastically reduced. The Marine Corps of 480,000, for instance, had been cut to 86,000 men. The situation worsened when Louis Johnson, a millionaire lawyer from West Virginia, succeeded James Forrestal as secretary of defense in 1949. Within weeks he cut the Army to nine divisions. When the Russians shocked the world a few months later with completion of an atom bomb, Johnson and Truman refused to take it seriously, labeling it a "laboratory accident." Two months later came another shock—the decisive victory of Mao's troops over Chiang Kai-shek's Kuomintang.

These two events convinced Secretary of State Acheson that a "different world" had arrived and it was time to rearm; but when Kim Il-sung's troops surged across the 38th parallel, the U.S. Army was still in sad shape. Although a peacetime draft had filled the ranks with 300,000 men, many of them were disgusted and even hostile. They were poorly trained and equipped. Not a single new 3.5 bazooka had been sent to Korea by June 25, 1950. "We were, in short," concluded the outspoken General Matthew Ridgway, "in a state of shameful unreadiness."

Truman's decision to send ground troops to Korea was reinforced by the support of the United Nations. Australia, Canada, New Zealand, the Netherlands, and the United Kingdom all promised military contingents.

There was little criticism of Truman in America, since almost everyone agreed that the war represented a new Soviet policy of military expansion in both Europe and Asia. This misconception was followed by another: that the Chinese Communists were junior partners in this conspiracy for world conquest.

Both Kennan and Bohlen had tried to convince President Truman that the Russians were much too weak for such a grand design. The scarcity of news about the war in the Soviet press indicated that Stalin had been caught by surprise and was meditating on what to do. It was true, concluded Kennan and Bohlen, that the Soviets had given Kim Il-sung arms and that Stalin's military advisers had devised the campaign, but rather than world conquest, their purpose was, according to the two Soviet experts, only to shift American attention away from Europe.

The misconception concerning Chinese partnership with North Korea was also founded on faulty intelligence. In reality there was only a strong Communist bond between the two countries. But Mao appeared to have no intention of becoming seriously involved in North Korea's civil war with South Korea since his chief objectives were to rebuild China after its own bitter civil war, and to put an end to Chiang Kai-shek by seizing Taiwan. Truman's decision to send the Seventh Fleet to the defense of Taiwan had already caused such concern in Peking that troops were being readied for the defense of their own border with North Korea along the Yalu River.

Two days before the war started, the military commission of the Central Committee of the CPC (Communist Party of China) had issued an order to demobilize a million men from the People's Liberation Army so they could go home and work for the country's welfare. As they were preparing to leave, the war broke out. At first Mao thought it was simply a Korean civil war which had nothing to do with China. But when Truman officially announced he was supporting Rhee to the hilt, the leaders of the CPC realized the situation was critical and *did* concern China. Mao was so incensed that on the last day of June he charged that the puppet Rhee had started the war at the instigation of the American government. He immediately canceled the order to demobilize the million soldiers and sent additional units into Manchuria in case the Americans approached the Yalu River. Despite his anger and indignation, he was determined not to get involved in armed conflict with America.

Like many peasants from Hunan Province, Mao had been influenced by the Chu culture and tended to be arrogant, aggressive, and prompt to settle a dispute by force. He never went abroad, like Chou En-lai, his trusted right hand, who came from an intellectual Confucian family. Consequently, he never had the broad perspective of those like Chou and Teng Hsaio-ping (now Deng Xiaoping) who had seen the outside world. He was self-taught and had become a brilliant practitioner of ancient political maneuvering. In 1950 he was lean after the ravages of years of tuberculosis, but somehow he remained charged with energy.

Neither Truman nor Acheson had realized the true significance of the crucial meeting between Mao and Stalin in late 1949, resulting two months later in their mutual-assistance alliance. This treaty in a sense only accented the sharp differences between the two countries. Stalin had secretly supported Chiang Kai-shek even after the Americans had dropped him, because the Soviet leader instinctively distrusted other Communist revolutions. He feared that Mao could become another Tito, and he was convinced it was more profitable to deal with weak, so-called democracies than with burgeoning Communist regimes.

There had been so many arguments during the Stalin-Mao 1949–1950 meeting that it was only upon Mao's insistence that a treaty had been signed. Mao called in Chou En-lai, who simply refused to leave Moscow until this was done. Stalin finally grudgingly agreed to Chou's insistence that, if one of them was invaded, the other would "aid immediately with an all-out effort."

During these talks the Soviets treated their guests scornfully. One night they invited the entire Chinese delegation to see the ballet *The Red Poppy*, which portrayed the Chinese people in such a deprecatory manner that only one stony-faced Chinese appeared in the theater box.

Relations between the two countries had deteriorated immediately after the surrender of Japan, when Soviet troops arrived in Manchuria to dismantle all the factories built during the Japanese occupation and cart them off to Russia. An American commission estimated that stockpiles of food and equipment that the Soviet Union removed amounted to $858 million, and that the total cost of wanton destruction caused by Soviet troops in Manchuria came to over $2 billion.

When the alliance treaty between China and the Soviets was finally signed in early 1950, there were no smiling faces. Although the Soviets did agree to loan China $300 million to help rebuild their country, this was only one tenth of the amount Mao wanted, and the one percent interest was an insult, since the USSR had recently loaned Poland $450 million at no interest at all.

To those on the inside, it was obvious that Stalin had despised and distrusted Mao ever since the mid-1920's, when he became convinced that Mao was a Trotskyite. And Mao, despite his pact with Moscow, distrusted his rival's bellicose attitude towards the West. Mao's dislike of Stalin was also personal. When his second wife, Ho Tzu-chien, had visited Moscow during World War II, she was held prisoner in an insane asylum for several years. This monstrous loss of face for Mao was a humiliation that still rankled.

So the Truman-Acheson conviction that North Korea was only the cat's-paw of a Sino-Soviet conspiracy was completely fallacious. China had contributed only two divisions, composed entirely of North Koreans; and, although the Soviets had masterminded the invasion and provided considerable military equipment, they were contemplating little future help.

2.

At two-thirty A.M., on the 1st of July, it was pitch black and still pouring when vice-consul Noble reached the outskirts of Taejon. He found Muccio's small wooden house, where the ambassador was talking to several assistants and Walter Simmons, the seasoned Chicago *Tribune* correspondent whom he trusted. The ambassador appeared weary, depressed and irritable. The telephone rang. It was President Rhee. "Mr. Noble has just come in from Suwon," said Muccio. "I'll send him over. There are some things I want him to tell you which I'd rather not discuss over the telephone."

Muccio explained to Noble that General Church had called him to say the whole party had left Suwon because the situation was hopeless. Noble was to wait until Church arrived and then evacuate the embassy group by car to the southwest. Most important was the need to convince President Rhee that he must abandon Taejon. The government had to be in a safe place, but most of the ministers would not leave unless Rhee set an example. Their departure would also get rid of the large group of politicians and influential private citizens who had tagged along after Rhee and were now causing panic by spreading ugly rumors that implied that almost every minister and high-ranking army officer was a secret Communist.

It was still raining when Noble set off on his mission. It was three A.M. before he found the large two-story Japanese-Western residence. The president and his wife, looking exhausted, were waiting anxiously. After briefly describing what he had seen at Suwon and the Han River, Noble passed on the ambassador's recommendation to withdraw further south.

The elderly Rhee angrily refused to leave, and Mrs. Rhee supported him. "There's no chance of victory," said the president. With Communist tanks in Suwon, nothing could stop the advance south. And if the North Koreans reached Taejon and killed him, so be it. "I would rather die in Taejon than humiliate myself by further flight." Mrs. Rhee vowed to stay and die with her husband.

Noble argued that the president had no right to follow his individual preference. His duty was to the people of Korea. If he died, the republic died. They argued for almost an hour. At last Noble felt his arguments were weakening the president's resolve and he could see that Mrs. Rhee was willing to leave. At this point Defense Minister Shin and the new chief of staff, General Chung, appeared. Both supported Noble. But Rhee still vowed he would never leave Taejon while Muccio and the American embassy were in danger. Noble assured him that Muccio was planning to leave as soon as he talked to General Church. The embassy party would catch up to them.

The tireless Noble dashed back to Muccio's to find that Church had just arrived with electrifying news: President Truman had ordered U.S. ground troops into Korea! The first elements of the 24th Division would be flown into Taejon within a few days. Everyone rejoiced. One American division would knock those North Koreans on their asses! Muccio was so delighted he said Noble must tell Rhee there was now no need for anyone to leave Taejon.

Noble was embarrassed. After pleading with Rhee and his wife for an exhausting hour, he had to go back and say it was all a mistake! Muccio agreed that he himself should bring the good news, and hurried off, only to learn that the Rhees were already on their way south.

After a harrowing drive, Maggie Higgins and her three fellow correspondents finally arrived in Taejon, soaked to the skin. They drove to the main government building to find the frail General Church in the conference room sitting alone at a long table. Higgins was shivering.

"You may be interested to know," Church said calmly, "that two companies of American troops were airlifted into southern Korea this morning."

She thought, Here we go again—America's at war. She didn't know it was a United Nations action. "Don't you think it's too late?"

"Certainly not. It will be different when the Americans get here. We'll have people we can rely on. To tell you the truth, we've been having a pretty rough time with the South Korean troops. We can't put backbone into them. We have no way of knowing whether the South Korean reports are accurate or just wild rumor." There were still no Communist troops near Suwon; their nightmare trip in the jeep had been unnecessary.

After Church revealed that the first Americans would be deployed north of Taejon and should arrive in a few hours, Higgins asked, "How long will it be before we can mount an offensive?"

"Oh, two weeks or so—maybe a month."

"But suppose the Russkies intervene?" asked Beech.

"If they intervene, we'll hurl them back."

The correspondents now had two great stories: the wild flight from Suwon and the arrival of U.S. troops. Both Maggie and Lambert had immediate deadlines, so they rushed to the office of the U.S. Information Service. Because there was no time to write their stories, both had to dictate their pieces, something Higgins had never done before. There was no one in Tokyo she could give her story to, but Lambert convinced AP to help her. After she had dictated three paragraphs, Barbara Brines, wife of the Tokyo bureau manager, interrupted. "That's all we can take, Marguerite." Higgins phoned the Tokyo Press Club and convinced a fellow correspondent to take the entire story. Frustrated, she slashed the Suwon affair to two paragraphs and crammed the rest of the story into six more. She and Lambert then hitched a ride back to Muccio's with a well-dressed Korean officer who spoke English well. Tom clapped him on the shoulder. "Hey, Buster, do you fight in this man's army?"

"Well," was the polite answer, "I plan to."

Tom clapped him on the shoulder again. "And what do you do?"

"I've just been appointed chief of staff of the Korean Army. My name is Major General Chung Il-kwon."

After dropping them off at Muccio's, the urbane General Chung continued to the headquarters of the ROK Army, where he discussed the military situation with Fat Chae. By this time Noble had managed to get a few hours' sleep and called on General Church to tell him what he had seen the day before along the Han River. He explained what General Yu was trying to do and then went into the next office to check with the ROK commander. To his surprise he found that Chae had been replaced by Chung, and both of these men wanted to talk with General Church about the commitment of U.S. troops and plans for the future. But they had been treated so coolly by some of the American officers that they didn't know how to reach Church.

Noble, never one to be stopped by protocol, simply opened the door that joined the two rooms and announced that the Korean generals wanted to talk to General Church. "It was extraordinary at this stage of the war," Noble recalled, "that the ranking American officer in Korea constantly had to be nudged into even talking with the men who were running the ROK Army."

There was no rest for the zealous vice-consul. Noble was now instructed by Muccio to chase after the Rhees. Undoubtedly the president, learning of the changed situation, would return to Taejon. Noble was to persuade him to stay away for several days until all the politicians and rumormongers were out of town. Noble set off with a colleague and the senior embassy interpreter in two cars, a sedan which he drove and a jeep, in case of emergency, driven by a Korean. They were heading into unknown territory where even good roads were badly marked.

While General Church was discussing the military situation with Chung and Chae, the enemy was crossing the Han River despite bitter resistance by remnants of the ROK 1st and 7th divisions. Of the entire ROK Army, only these two ROK divisions were pulling back in good order, and almost half of the original 98,000 troops were killed, captured or missing.

In Seoul the conquerors were treating children to rides on their tanks and convincing some citizens that true democracy had arrived to rescue them from the corrupt Rhee regime. At first, North Korean correspondent Kim Sin-gyu noticed that the people were frightened. But one told him, "We'd heard the North Korean Communist soldiers were a monstrous rabble with the horns of devils and red faces. But we can see they're the same as us. The soldiers are young and brave and handsome."

At the same time thousands of former government and city officials, as well as affluent private citizens, were being arrested. Some were immediately executed as traitors, while others, who could be useful, were removed to the north. Young men were also being rounded up to fight for the unification of Korea in a volunteer corps. Some were enthusiastic, but most had to be forced.

3.

American help had already arrived from Japan in the form of Task Force Smith, 406 men from the 1st Battalion, 21st Infantry Regiment, 24th Infantry Division. Each man had 120 rounds of .30-caliber rifle ammunition and two days of C-Rations. With them came two 75-mm recoilless guns, two 4.2-inch mortars and some 2.36-inch bazookas— which had already proved worthless against the Soviet tanks. The task force was cheered by crowds waving flags. It was like a holiday. At the station Korean bands gave the troops a rousing welcome as they were loaded into a train for Taejon.

When the train reached there twelve hours later, Lieutenant Colonel Charles Bradley Smith, a West Pointer, was escorted to General Church's headquarters. Smith had fought in the Pacific, but only a third of his officers had any combat experience. Half of his noncoms were veterans of World War II, but not all of them had been in combat. As for the enlisted men, most were twenty years old or under. Smith himself was thirty-four. He was of medium height, his body was strong and compact, and his face open and friendly.

Church pointed to a place on the map. "We have a little action up here. All we need is some men up there who won't run when they see tanks. We're going to move you up to support the ROKs."

Smith suggested he look over the ground while his men bivouacked. He and his key officers headed up the rough road through hordes of retreating ROK soldiers and refugees. He found an excellent infantry position near Osan commanding both the highway and the railroad almost all the eight miles to Suwon. This, he decided, was where Task Force Smith would make its stand. He returned to the Taejon airstrip and that night General Church ordered him to bring his troops north by train.

Noble chased the presidential party through mud over the mountainous area of the west coast and finally caught up with the Rhees in Pusan. On the way to their quarters he met his fellow vice-consul, Gregory Henderson. A Brahmin from Harvard, Henderson was appalled at Noble's buccaneer appearance—open khaki shirt and field dress with a pistol ostentatiously belted at his waist. Henderson agreed to accompany Noble into the provincial governor's residence, where the Rhees were staying. "I had the momentary impression," Henderson recalled, "that in Harold Noble a bird of prey had come wheeling in on some final moment of his quarry. He had zeroed in at once on his presidential victims."

The two sat in a reception room until the Rhees entered. Rhee was gracious but nervous and worried. He admitted he had been angry at Noble upon learning that the American embassy was still in Taejon, but he'd had time to think it over and realized that Noble had acted in good faith. Now he had to get back to Taejon with Muccio and the others. What would his people think if he lived comfortably in Pusan while the rest of the government was near the battlefront?

Noble passed on Muccio's message. It was vitally important to get the political camp followers out of Taejon. This made sense, and Rhee agreed to wait a few days. Urging him to do nothing until they heard from Muccio, Noble telephoned the ambassador, who informed him that

General Dean, commander of the 24th Division, had arrived and did not want Rhee in the midst of a fluid tactical situation. When it was safe, the president could return.

Major General William Dean, a six-footer with a bristling crew cut, was trying to get a picture of what was happening from Church. He revealed that Task Force Smith was to take up positions at a road crossing at Ansong and at Pyongtaek on the main Seoul–Pusan highway. Theoretically these positions blocked the two roads down which the enemy was likely to come. There was only about one company per road to hold them back, but nothing better could be done.

The next afternoon, July 4, General Dean learned that Colonel Smith was going to reconnoiter north of Osan. He ordered Brigadier General George Barth, acting commander of the division artillery, to jeep up to Pyongtaek and tell Smith "to take up those good positions near Osan you told General Church about." This decision made more sense than trying to hold farther south, as some staff officers were suggesting.

Barth located Smith, who went forward late in the afternoon to look at the position for his last stand. Just after midnight the infantry and artillery of the task force moved out of Pyongtaek in commandeered Korean trucks driven by GIs, since the local drivers had refused to go north. It was only twelve miles to Osan, but because of the crowds of refugees, the Americans needed two and a half hours to get there under blackout conditions.

During the day the correspondents had also moved up to Pyongtaek to see the first fighting of American troops. The greatest battle so far had occurred between Higgins and Homer Bigart, who both represented the New York *Herald Tribune*.

Bigart was a quiet man, highly respected for his reporting in World War II. Idolized by the younger correspondents, who strove to imitate him, he radiated competence. Regarding himself as the senior correspondent for the *Herald Tribune*, he saw no reason for Higgins to stay in Korea. He told her to get back to Tokyo and take over the bureau. In a chilly encounter, she refused and he telephoned New York to ask that she be removed at once. Although many of the war correspondents disliked Higgins for her brashness, those at Pyongtaek had seen her in action and were sympathetic. "They can't fire you," Beech told her. "You're doing a good job."

That night at the little house in Pyongtaek where the correspondents were quartered, Maggie approached Carl Mydans, the noted photographer-reporter of *Time* and *Life*. Close to tears, she told how Bigart had shouted at her, declaring he couldn't work with someone who operated as she did. Everyone Bigart had talked to in Tokyo disliked her. But she protested that all she wanted to do was share the assignment. She began to weep. "What should I do?"

"What is more important to you, Maggie, the experience of covering the Korean War or fears of losing your job?"

Heavyhearted, she went to bed. "I felt that no matter what the cause of my colleague's hostility, it would be harder on me because I was a woman. Since I was the only woman here doing a daily newspaper job, I was bound to be the target for lots of talk, and this mix-up would supply fresh material."

She awoke before dawn, determined to go up front. She climbed into a jeep with Mydans and a young Australian reporter for Reuters. It soon began to rain. As they entered Pyongtaek, they had to drive around smouldering ROK ammunition trucks that had been mistakenly bombed and strafed by the Australians. Many dead still lay on straw pallets. The trio continued north in the drizzle until they located the command post of the 1st Battalion of the 34th Regiment. Inside a thatched hut surrounded by a sea of mud, they found the battalion commander, Colonel Harold "Red" Ayres, who had just arrived a few hours earlier.

About six miles to the north, above Osan, Task Force Smith's companies had been in place before dawn, but they had not yet completely dug in. Smith had planted one 75-mm recoilless rifle east of the highway and the other one farther east near the tracks. The 4.2-inch mortars were on the reverse slope, some four hundred yards behind the mile-wide infantry line. Two thousand yards behind them, the infantry jeeps had pulled four 105-mm howitzers into position. A fifth howitzer was brought forward to knock out any tanks coming up the road.

Despite the rain, Smith could see almost to Suwon. Just after seven A.M., he made out movement. Half an hour later he could see it was a tank column. His platoon leaders were walking up and down talking to the men in foxholes, and when the tanks were about two thousand yards from the front lines, one of the U.S. howitzers opened fire. It was exactly 8:16. The other pieces joined in, but those in front could see that the tanks kept coming closer unharmed. The recoilless rifles scored direct hits; but the tanks rumbled on firing their 85-mm cannons and machine guns. The first tanks were hit by the 2.36-inch bazookas upon reaching the U.S. infantry line. All rockets hit the rear armor of the tanks—their weakest point—but nothing stopped their relentless drive until a howitzer hit the two lead tanks with HEAT (high-explosive antitank) ammunition. The damaged tanks pulled to the side, but thirty-one others moved relentlessly through Task Force Smith. They did not stop to engage the American infantry but proceeded toward the artillery positions. At five hundred yards the tanks hid behind a little hill for protection and then, one by one, roared into the open and rolled safely on toward Osan.

While Maggie and the other correspondents were drinking coffee with Red Ayres, General Barth burst into the hut. "Enemy tanks are heading south!" he cried. "Get me some bazooka teams pronto!" For the first time Communist tanks, he explained, had met Americans—Task Force Smith. "We can depend on them to hold on, but if any tanks do get by those batteries, they'll head straight for here!"

After the tank attack on Task Force Smith, there was a disturbing silence. There were at least thirty dead, but Smith could see nothing coming down the road from Suwon. In the steady rain the men deepened their foxholes for the infantry attack that was bound to come.

About an hour later, Smith, from his observation post, spotted movement near Suwon. In another hour the head of a six-mile-long column of trucks and foot soldiers, led by three tanks, was within a thousand yards of the American line. Smith decided to throw the book at them. Mortar shells wreaked havoc among the trucks and .50-caliber machine-gun fire riddled the column. Just before noon enemy infantry began moving up the east side of the road.

Sergeant First Class Loran Chambers, a veteran of World War II, already had five Purple Hearts. When he called over the telephone for some 60-mm mortar support, the answer was: "Won't reach that far."

"How about some 81!" he yelled.

"We don't have any."

"Hell, for Christ's sake, throw in some 4.2's!"

"We're out of that too."

"How about the artillery?"

"No communications."

"How about the Air Force?"

"We don't know where they are."

"Then damn it, call the Navy!"

"They can't reach this far."

Chambers shouted an obscenity. "Send me a camera. I want to take a picture of this." A few minutes later a mortar fragment gave Chambers his sixth Purple Heart.

By two-thirty P.M. Smith's perimeter was established, but a quarter of his force was already wounded or killed, little ammo was left and there was no transportation. His task force was surrounded except for an escape corridor on the left. There was no air support, not even a liaison plane to guide them to safety because of the solid, low overcast. Nor could Smith open wire communications to the artillery, since the road was still under heavy fire.

Smith ordered C Company to fall back to the right rear with attachments, the medics, the walking wounded, and battalion headquarters; B Company was to cover the withdrawal. When Richard Dashmer's C Company got the word to withdraw, they ran down the hill like jackrabbits. "There was no longer platoon organization. Just people moving back." The gear was getting heavy and some even threw away their helmets. No one wanted to die. Will we ever get out? thought Dashmer.

Smith had planned to leapfrog the units off the ridge, but Second Lieutenant Carl Bernard never received the order. Then he learned that his platoon was the only one left on the line. He managed to collect about twenty-five stragglers—many of them wounded—and lead them to the momentary safety of the next ridge.

North Korean infantry seemed to be on all sides of Bernard when word finally came to fall back. They plowed through rice paddies to the next ridgeline. Then came a burst of fire. The .50-caliber machine gun left behind by B Company's headquarters was being turned on them.

The worst part for Smith's officers was to leave wounded and dying men calling for help. One lieutenant came upon six men lying on the ground. "What is going to happen to us, Lieutenant?" one called out. The young officer gave him a hand grenade. "That's the best I can do for you."

As the victorious North Koreans were resting after the battle, they were approached by curious villagers. Lieutenant Oak Hyung-uk had not been impressed by the Americans; many were too frightened to fight. Those who begged for mercy were not shot, but the ones who resisted were ruthlessly cut down. Oak surveyed the carnage. Dead Americans lay all over the place with mouths open. One man in his 9th Squad laughed. "The Americans are still hungry," he said, "even though they're dead! Here, have some earth to eat!" He threw a handful into each mouth to the amusement of everyone—even the villagers.

Early that afternoon Maggie Higgins and the other correspondents had been given permission by General Barth to follow a bazooka and rifle team. "Go carefully," he warned his men. "Some of those tanks may have broken through. Don't fire at them at further than 150 yards, boys."

The injunction sent a chill up the spine of Carl Mydans, a small man who always managed to get a good picture despite the danger. The correspondents, wrapped in rain-soaked blankets, followed the six-man team in four jeeps. At the crest of a hill the convoy stopped. Higgins could see GIs leaping out of the trucks and spreading out on a ridge parallel to the road. A South Korean on horseback, his helmet absurdly camouflaged with sweet potato vines, galloped towards them from the north. "Tanks! Tanks!" he shouted. "Right behind us!"

"Wait a minute," the Australian correspondent said. "Even if tanks do show, no infantry has been sighted. Tanks can't get off the road, and we can. Let's walk on."

They soon came upon a lieutenant named Charlie Payne, who told them that a tank had sighted *them* and then had turned back. "We're going to dig in here and send out patrols to hunt him down."

But a few minutes later, as the correspondents were entrenching, a Soviet tank appeared about fifteen hundred yards to the left, straddling railroad tracks. Behind was a second tank. A small U.S. ammunition convoy haphazardly rumbled up the road from the rear and two lieutenants trotted up the hill. They were obviously green and young. "Charlie," one said to Payne, "our orders are to crash through with this ammunition and to hell with sniper fire." They intended to get their valuable load up to Colonel Smith, whose tiny force was being shattered. The two lieutenants wanted a couple of volunteers.

"Things are changing a bit," said Payne, and advised waiting for further information. "Then maybe we'll make like Custer."

In the meantime Higgins noticed how the youngsters of the bazooka team were staring at the two tanks as if they were watching a newsreel. An officer prodded them to attack and slowly they left foxholes to creep through the bean field. At five hundred yards they fired a bazooka and it looked like a direct hit. But Payne said, "Damn, those kids are scared. They've got to get close to the tanks to do any damage."

There was a belch of fire from the railroad tracks. Higgins saw North Koreans leap from the tank. Machine guns chattered. Through field glasses she glimpsed a blond American head poke out of the grass, then she saw his body fall; and a few minutes later she heard someone shout, "They've got Shadrick—right in the chest." The voice was matter-of-fact. "He's dead, I guess."

Although bazookas were firing, they were having no effect, and all at once the bazooka team started back towards them.

"My God," said Mydans, who had been taking pictures of the firefight, "they look as if the ball game was over and it's time to go home."

Higgins asked a sergeant what was going on.

"They ran out of ammo," he said bitterly. And the enemy infantry outnumbered them. "Besides, these damn bazookas don't do any good against those heavy tanks. They just bounce off."

Back at battalion headquarters Higgins was talking to a medical corps sergeant when the body of Shadrick was brought in. He was laid on the bare boards of the shack. She noticed the expression of surprise on his face. His fair hair and frail build made him look even younger than his nineteen years.

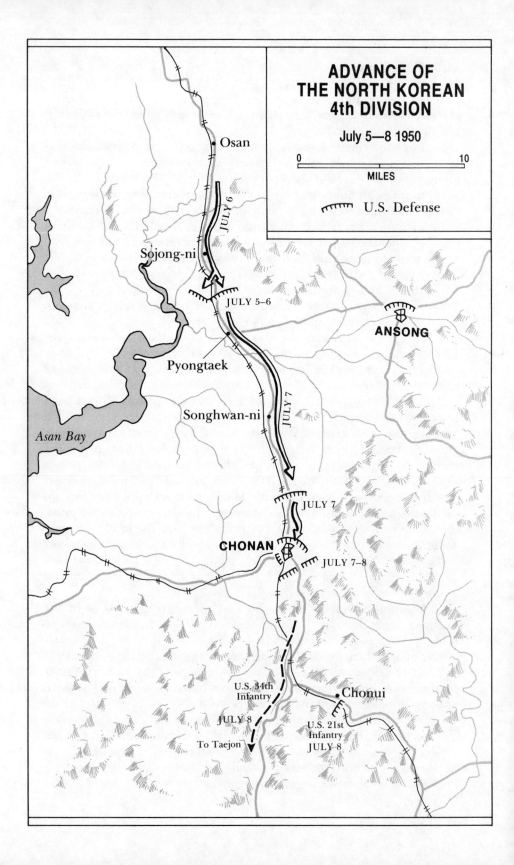

ADVANCE OF
THE NORTH KOREAN
4th DIVISION

July 5—8 1950

0   10
MILES

U.S. Defense

Osan

JULY 6

Sojong-ni

JULY 5–6

ANSONG

Pyongtaek

Songhwan-ni

JULY 7

Asan Bay

JULY 7

CHONAN

JULY 7–8

Chonui

U.S. 34th
Infantry

JULY 8

U.S. 21st
Infantry
JULY 8

To Taejon

* * *

At ten P.M. General Dean arrived at Red Ayres's command post at Pyong-taek, some fifteen miles south of Osan, to confer with General Barth. There was still no definite word of Task Force Smith, but the presence of enemy tanks nearby disturbed him. Soon after he left, four exhausted, rain-soaked survivors of the battered task force came in with a tale of utter destruction. They had been overwhelmed by tanks and hordes of infantry! Almost everyone must have been killed!

A few minutes later Lieutenant Colonel Miller Perry, Smith's artillery commander, limped into the command post. He gave a more realistic account: when Smith ordered retreat the men had removed sights and breech locks from the guns. Then Perry and Smith walked back to the outskirts of Osan where they found the artillery trucks only slightly damaged. As they rounded a bend leading into Osan they came upon three parked enemy tanks, their occupants smoking cigarettes. Smith's little convoy escaped before a shot could be fired. They then circled east and headed for Ansong. On the way they picked up at least a hundred of their own infantrymen, some without shoes, helmets or shirts. All had arrived safely in Ansong after dark. No one had chased them.

After listening to this account, the correspondents who had come to interview Ayres left the war room to sleep. The place they found was so crowded that Mydans ended up on top of a table. Just before midnight he was awakened by a chaplain. "Better get into the war room, Carl," he said. Colonel Ayres told Mydans to rouse the other correspondents. As Higgins stepped into the hushed war room, she could tell that Ayres's former confidence had been replaced by deep concern. The enemy was filtering through and the correspondents were ordered to head south. By four A.M., July 6, they reached the command post of the 34th Infantry Regiment in Songhwan. Higgins sprawled atop one of the tables and Mydans on another. Despite the mosquitoes and bugs and chill of rain, both fell asleep. It was the end of their first day of battle in Korea.

Maggie Higgins awoke at dawn. There wasn't a soldier in the place and the floor was strewn with cases of C-Rations, maps and guns. From his table Mydans was blinking with disbelief at the emptiness. The regimental commander of the 34th Infantry Regiment, Colonel Jay Lovless, came in and offered Maggie a jeep ride to his command post in Chonan, ten miles farther south. Mydans could follow in a signal corps jeep. As they set out, a heavy rain began drenching the roads. When Mydans stepped into the Chonan headquarters, a major said, "Good thing you got out of Songhwan when you did. Half an hour later tanks came in." Then Lovless turned to the major. "Keep the traffic moving through the town. This will be the front line."

By now, exhausted, bleary-eyed men were pouring into Chonan, many without rifles, field packs, helmets, or ammo belts. They were disgusted. Some cursed their government for throwing them into a hopeless cause, others blamed their officers, and some felt shame. But among them, looking just as bedraggled, were those who had fought gallantly against hopeless odds. Only those who had experienced the overwhelming terrors of the night could understand what the sight of other men running to the rear in panic could do to the staunchest heart.

Later the correspondents were briefed at 24th Division headquarters in Taejon. General Barth admitted they had given up ground needlessly. Another officer stated that there were probably 150 to 170 enemy tanks on the loose. Mydans, shaved and dusted with DDT to fight the insects, heard a major ask a captain, "Haven't you a map?"

"Hell, no," was the answer. "We've been off any map I've got for hours."

Another officer chimed in, "Don't you know we're engaged in Operation Haul Ass?"

Someone remarked that the other regiment of the division, the 21st, was digging in south of the town. "It's a kind of suicidal stand. No hills, just paddy fields."

Up front Charles and Eugene Jones, twenty-four-year-old twins, were filming the headlong retreat of GIs to the rear. When the war broke out they had quit their jobs on rival Washington newspapers to wangle jobs as NBC-TV cameramen. Marines themselves in World War II, they had as their goal to capture on film what Bill Mauldin had caught in cartoons and what Ernie Pyle had depicted in his prose: "the professional combat men with dirty faces and clean weapons."

Today the fighting had turned into a rout. Then someone saw a GI a quarter of a mile away tottering out of the ruins of a village to the accompaniment of rifle fire. He was obviously wounded, and his cries for help could be faintly heard. No one moved. Then Charlie Jones rose. "Help him! Pour it on 'em!" he yelled and dashed to the GI's aid. Gene began firing his M1 as fast as he could pull the trigger. He yelled to the others to let loose. As Charlie brought the wounded man in, Gene dropped his rifle and started filming. A rifleman nearby jumped up to help.

Maggie Higgins had been observing the scene from an adjacent hillside, and as Charlie began to dress the GI's wounds, she put a hand on the cameraman's shoulder. "Soldier," she said, "I want your name to make sure you get recognition for what you did. That was one of the bravest things I've ever seen."

Thinking she was another American civilian being evacuated as part of the great retreat, Charlie grinned up into Maggie's dancing eyes. "Hell, lady," he said. "I'm just a war correspondent."

4.

In America stories of the first few days of the fighting were being devoured. The New York *Herald Tribune* was profiting by the firsthand reports of their two star reporters. Higgins's piece, datelined "AN ADVANCE COMMAND POST IN SOUTH KOREA," was a close-up of Shadrick, the first U.S. infantryman to die in Korea, she reported incorrectly. "The medics brought the dead soldier's body in here, tenderly lifting him from the jeep. The lifeless form was shrouded in a blanket which kept the pelting rain off the blond young face. As medics brought the body in, one private said bitterly, 'What a place to die!' "

Confusion and frantic withdrawal continued. On the morning of July 8, North Korean tanks and infantry broke into Chonan. Remnants of the battered 3rd Battalion were fighting in the streets. A man of action, Colonel Robert Martin, who had replaced Colonel Lovless as commander of the 34th Regiment, grabbed a bazooka and went forward with Sergeant Jerry Christenson of the S3 (operation) section. They rushed into a small house on the east side of town just in time to see a tank coming towards them. Martin aimed the bazooka and fired. Simultaneously the tank released an 85-mm shell that cut him in two. Sergeant Christenson miraculously escaped death, but one eye popped from its socket. It took some time for Christenson to get it back in place.

More tanks rumbled into Chonan, accompanied by infantrymen; it appeared as if none of the Americans could escape. But friendly artillery laid down a white-phosphorus screen and many of the men—including Christenson—managed to rush down the road towards Taejon.

Two days earlier, on July 6, a rumor had run through MacArthur's headquarters that he planned to send the Eighth Army, whose four divisions were widely scattered all over Japan, to Korea. Its commander, Lieutenant General Walton Walker, was so disturbed by reports from Korea that, on his own initiative, he flew to Taejon on July 7. He was greeted by General Dean, whose bulldog face and aggressive stance commanded deference. Dean, who towered over the short and stocky Walker, briefed him on the tactical failures, command problems and critical shortages.

The situation was even worse than Walker had thought. It was obvious to him that neither Tokyo nor Washington was aware of what was really happening. Seeing how desperate things were, he suggested that Dean consolidate all of his briefing points in a message for MacArthur's personal attention. It was completed by nightfall.

Walker could see that Dean was overcommitted. His own staff was forced to direct the actions of his two committed regiments. Remaining

divisional units were stretched from Pusan to Taejon. And Dean's 19th
Infantry Regiment was deployed between Pohang and Taegu to protect
lines of communication. Walker told Dean his first priority should be to
consolidate his division as quickly as possible.

The next day, the 8th, Walker returned to Taejon. This time he
had good news for Dean. The whole Eighth Army was coming to Korea.
Dean was relieved. No longer would he have to wear the double hat of
division command and force command. The two generals and Walker's
only aide, Major Layton "Joe" Tyner, jeeped north to the last hill south
of Chonan. The town lay only six hundred yards before them. The scene
was chaotic. The road was jammed by refugees and soldiers. Most were
GIs, remnants of the 3rd Battalion.

They spread a map on the hood of the jeep and Tyner listened to
the two generals calmly discussing what had happened and what should
be done. Though Dean had spent a sleepless night, Tyner noticed that
he was alert and controlled. They were interrupted by an officer from
the 3rd Battalion who told of the tank attack on Chonan and how Martin
had been blown in half. Resistance had disintegrated and the troops
were bugging out.

A new decision faced Dean. The highway below Chonan divided:
the main road to Pusan followed the railroad to the southeast; the other
went straight south before angling eastward to rejoin the Seoul–Pusan
highway. Both roads had to be defended, but the more important was
the one to the southeast leading to the village of Chonui and then to an
important road junction, Chochiwon, which was halfway to the Kum
River. Once the NK forces crossed that important river, Taejon itself
would be endangered.

Realizing the exhaustion of the 34th Regiment, Dean sent them to
defend the road to the north while his second regiment, the 21st, newly
arrived and fresh, would fight a delaying battle at Chonui and Chochiwon. His third regiment, the 19th, would move into a reserve position.

Dean had already ordered the tanks, which were attached to the
19th, to come up on the line; and while Walker and he were still on the
hill, these light tanks arrived. The commander of the first platoon, a
lieutenant, came up the hill. Walker stopped him. "What are you going
to do down there?" he asked.

"I'm going to slug it out," said the lieutenant, clenching his teeth.

Walker said calmly, "Now, our idea is to stop those people. We don't
go up there and charge and slug it out. We take positions where we
have the advantage, where we can fire the first shots and still manage a
delaying action."

Dean was impressed. Right on the battlefield Walker was giving this
man "as fine a lecture on tank tactics as you could hear in any military
classroom." This was the real Walker, not the one newsmen called "Bull-

dog," but the one his friends called "Johnny." He was a disciple of General George Patton, who called him "a fighting son of a bitch." Yet he had none of Patton's flare or ego. Walker rarely swore, didn't smoke and would take only an occasional drink. Like his idol, he was religious but did not consider God his personal intelligence officer.

The two commanders then discussed problems created by having only two battalions in each infantry regiment. Since Army doctrine was based on triangular organization, changes in employment techniques were necessary. Dean explained the difficulties of trying to establish a reserve force. Walker understood, having fought much of World War II with minimum reserves. He went on to describe a technique that had worked for other units in similar situations. It involved establishing hard points in depth, and using integrated firepower to cover areas between them. "Under such conditions," he emphasized, "it is imperative that units not become decisively engaged." To prevent this, commanders at every level had to exercise extreme care when assigning missions, selecting positions, developing fire support plans, planning withdrawal routes and issuing withdrawal orders. His final challenge was to devise a way to run the battle under such complex conditions. While analyzing the problem, he remembered what Patton had said on countless occasions: "Senior leaders must focus on where rather than how to defeat any enemy." That was the key! After tailoring American and ROK forces to terrain within their assigned sectors, he would concentrate on where critical battle might take place. This would indicate which division required his personal attention at any given time. In other words, he would command by exception, and the exceptions would be based on critical combat actions.

Dean's orders were transmitted: "Hold Kum River line at all costs. Maximum—repeat maximum—delay will be effected." The 21st Regiment had to hold at Chonui or Chochiwon and could expect no help for four days. The enemy's approach to the Kum River, which ran in front of Taejon, had to be delayed, and then a final stand would be made on the south side of the Kum. The fate of Taejon depended on it.

Walker returned to Tokyo later that day to discover that he himself would not be in command until July 12. He felt ready to assume the awesome task of attempting to save South Korea and exuded the complete confidence of a man who had always succeeded.

When MacArthur learned from the reports of Walker and Dean that the situation in Korea was critical, he radioed the Joint Chiefs that there was nothing to stop the armored equipment of a well-trained enemy force of first-class quality. "This force more and more assumes the aspect of a combination of Soviet leadership and technical guidance with Chinese Communist ground elements. It can no longer be considered as an indigenous North Korean effort," he incorrectly reported. To stem this force he needed almost twice the number of men he had requested two days earlier. "The situation," he concluded, "has developed into a major operation."

On the 10th, the Security Council of the UN directed the establishment of a unified Korean Command, and MacArthur was officially named Commander in Chief of the UN Forces.

In the meantime his troops at Chochiwon were fighting so gallantly that two of the best North Korean divisions were delayed for more than two days. But the cost in casualties was dreadful. At the end of the first week of U.S. combat, two U.S. regiments had been shattered with little accomplished. Many men had panicked, leaving weapons and ammunition for the enemy. The GIs had been ill-equipped, improperly trained and, in too many cases, poorly led.

Now, except for the Kum River, there was no natural obstacle to slow the North Korean drive to the very gates of Taejon. If this key city fell, the American and ROK forces would have to fall back all the way to the next major river, the Naktong. Once behind this barrier they would be entrapped in the southern tip of the Korean peninsula.

Kim Il-sung had not succeeded in getting to Pusan in five days as scheduled, but his victories over the troops of the world's strongest nation did much to heighten the morale of his troops.

CHAPTER 6

The Fall of Taejon
(July 12–21)

1.

General Dean, determined to hold strategic Taejon as long as possible, was only too aware on July 12 that the reinforcements landing in Korea from Japan were by no means prepared for war. In the summer of 1949 General Walker had begun a training program to get Eighth Army troops into combat readiness after their long period of occupation duties. Although most of his troops had progressed through battalion training, none had advanced to regimental, division or army levels; nor had any maneuvers been carried out, since there was no space to do them in crowded Japan.

The equipment that arrived in Korea was old and worn. Some vehicles had to be towed to the LSTs (landing ships, tanks) bound for Pusan. Most radios were inoperative, and many weapons, from M-1's to mortars, were not fit for combat. The first troops arriving did not even have cleaning supplies for their weapons.

Walker knew the limitation of his troops in training, equipment, and numerical strength, but was too good a soldier to complain to those in the administration and the Pentagon who were responsible for the pitiful state of his army. His job was to hold strategic Taejon until more reinforcements arrived from Japan; and he passed on the task to Dean, who guessed the main attack would come where the Seoul–Pusan highway crossed the Kum River, twenty miles northwest of Taejon at the village of Taepyong-ni. Dean also expected a strong attack eight miles downstream at Kongju.

It was a herculean task and his understrength 24th Division was expected to carry it out. All three of his regiments—the 34th, the 21st and the 19th—were weak. The 34th had been battered and beaten the past week. Already one of its commanders had been relieved and his successor blown in two after a gallant fight. Its third commander, Colonel Robert "Pappy" Wadlington, formerly the regimental executive officer, was forty-nine years old.

The 21st Regiment under Colonel Richard Stephens had performed relatively well under difficult conditions, but was down to 1,100 men after the savage battles at Chonan and then Chochiwon. Dean ordered these worn troops to be placed in reserve near the airport, north of Taejon.

Dean's third regiment, the 19th Infantry, commanded by Colonel Guy Meloy, Jr., had a renowned history, having a century earlier won the sobriquet "The Rock of Chickamauga," for its memorable Civil War battle. But almost all of Meloy's 2,276 men were green, and there had not been enough time to organize them properly. Unfortunately, as they moved north toward the Seoul–Pusan highway bridge, they had to pass the gaunt troops of the 21st heading back toward their reserve position. The Chicks were shaken to see their condition and their own confidence faded. By July 12 they were dug in astride the bridge. That night engineers partially blew it up, planning to dynamite it again in the morning.

Eight miles downstream engineers of the 34th successfully destroyed the steel truss bridge at Kongju at four A.M. on the 13th. None too soon, for shortly after dawn infantrymen of the 4th Korean People's Division moved up machine guns on the north side of the river. Pappy Wadlington's men saw a tank approach. They huddled in their foxholes several hundred yards behind the river. Nothing happened until afternoon. Then shells began to land in the town of Kongju. The firing stopped and they wondered when the battle of the Kum would begin.

In Tokyo, General Collins had just arrived from Washington with General Vandenberg. The president had sent them to get a first-hand estimate of the situation. At nine A.M. they met with MacArthur, MacArthur's chief of staff Major General Almond, and Walker, who had flown over from Korea.

MacArthur hoped to block off support of North Korea from Manchuria or China, but this could only be achieved by medium bomber attacks. He felt sure the Soviets would not go to war but would continue to support the enemy. He urged an immediate and maximal effort to support the American and ROK forces rather than a gradual buildup. "To hell with the concept of business as usual."

Both Collins and Vandenberg agreed that the North Korean advance must be stopped. Collins said he had to integrate MacArthur's requirements with the administration's overall military program. Therefore, he needed to know when MacArthur would be able to launch his major counteroffensive. Impossible to say, replied MacArthur. He hoped to stop the advance once three American divisions were in action. His goal was to destroy the North Korean forces, not merely drive them back across the 38th parallel. And then they must "compose and unite Korea." He might even have to occupy all of Korea, and to do this he would need eight infantry divisions.

Vandenberg asked what he would do if China entered the war. Cut them off in North Korea, was the answer. What an opportunity to use the atomic bomb and to cripple their supply routes! At this point General Walker said he needed eleven infantry battalions promptly. But MacArthur had the last words: "We win here or lose everywhere; if we win here, we improve the chances of winning everywhere."

After the conference Walker and Collins flew to Korea. By late afternoon they reached the new Eighth Army headquarters in Taegu. Walker agreed with MacArthur's estimate of the combat situation and figured that, barring unforeseen developments, he could hold a sizable bridgehead in the southern tip of the peninsula.

Collins could stay only an hour, but he found the trip worthwhile. It gave him a better conception of the ruggedness of the Korean mountains and the problems facing American troops in the field.

Maggie Higgins had just received a blow that rocked her "as rudely as if it had been a bullet." She was handed orders to get out of Korea, and she jumped to the conclusion that she had been accused of writing stories giving aid and comfort to the enemy. Then she learned it was because General Walker felt Korea was no place for a lady: there were no facilities for women. MacArthur reinforced this order. Walker, he said, was in control of all war correspondents and would have "the final say on which correspondents will be allowed to stay."

Higgins was worried about her job despite reassurances by Mydans and Beech. She had heard nothing from the *Tribune* since Bigart's warning that she would be fired if she stayed in Korea. She telephoned her office in New York. "I'm going to General Walker's headquarters in Taegu," she said, "to remind him that I'm a duly accredited correspondent and to convince him that I'm here in that capacity and not as a woman."

The *Herald Tribune* printed her statement and it was carried over international wire services. Higgins also sent an appeal to MacArthur. Dean supported her, as did many officers and enlisted men. Colonel Stephens, in fact, promised to hire her for his rifle platoon if she was thrown out.

*   *   *

As soon as Generals Collins and Vandenberg left Korea, General Walker gathered a group from each section to explain policies and priorities. For most, this was their first experience on a higher-level staff in combat. He got their attention with his first words. "I want you to forget about our successes in World War Two," he said. "Remember the failures. We're like those Americans who faced the Japanese in the early days. Few of our unit commanders have combat experience. Our troops are poorly trained and in lousy shape. Equipment is in a sorry state. We lack adequate communications. The supply system is suffering from growing pains. And fire support is almost nonexistent. Many of you may think we're better than the enemy. We're not! That's being proven right now north of Taejon. But we're going to turn things around."

The enemy, he added, intended to take South Korea. "From what I've seen, he may have the capability to do it." Then his jaw tensed, and the bulldog image that had been his trademark became apparent. "I don't intend to let that happen," he continued. "Right now, we don't have the capability to stop them. But help is on the way. We have to slow them down until it arrives."

On the morning of July 14, Colonel Pappy Wadlington's 34th Regiment troops at Kongju heard more tanks on the north side of the Kum River. Then L Company lookouts reported that North Korean soldiers were crossing the river on two barges downstream. By nine-thirty some five hundred enemy had come across. L's commander, Lieutenant Archie Smith, unable to locate the machine-gun and mortar sections supporting him, ordered withdrawal and set out to find 3rd Battalion headquarters. When he reported what he had done, he was relieved of his command. By this time the entire left flank of the 34th Regiment had disappeared and the North Koreans poured into the hole. Soon enemy infantrymen, supported by accurate mortar fire, overran the regimental artillery headquarters.

Once Walker learned that the enemy was crossing the Kum, in strength, he knew the 24th Division didn't have enough firepower to stop a major attack. They needed close air support in a hurry. He notified Fifth Air Force, which began diverting aircraft from other areas.

Walker himself took to the air with his private pilot, Captain Eugene Michael Lynch, to get a bird's-eye view of the battle. En route to Taejon, Walker monitored the combat channel. The air was filled with reports of pilots finding so many targets they didn't know which to hit first. The river was "running red!" Arriving at the scene, the general was shocked. The entire 4th NK Division was attempting to cross in the 34th Infantry's sector just north of Kongju. Enemy tanks, now burning, had pulled up to the bank and delivered direct fire on the defending troops. Enemy

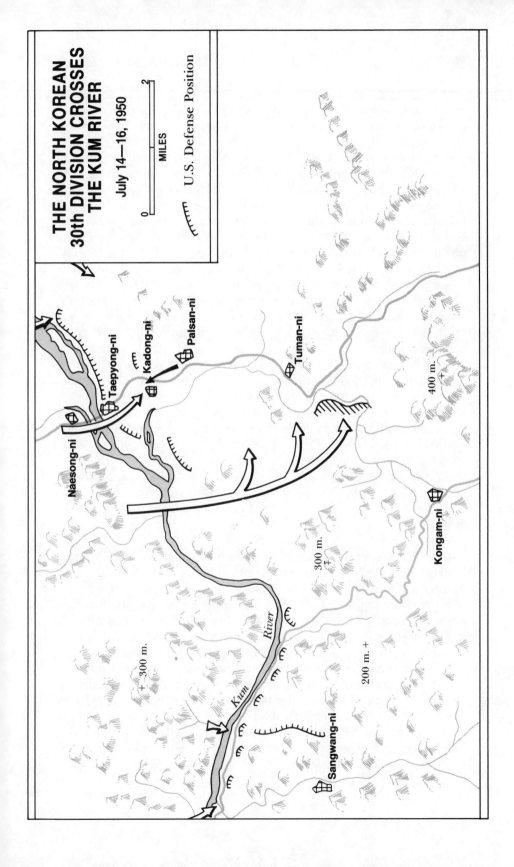

THE NORTH KOREAN
30th DIVISION CROSSES
THE KUM RIVER

July 14–16, 1950

0   2
MILES

⚬⚬⚬⚬⚬ U.S. Defense Position

Naesong-ni

Taepyong-ni

Kadong-ni

Palsan-ni

Tuman-ni

Kongam-ni

Kum River

Sangwang-ni

+ 300 m.

300 m. +

200 m. +

400 m. +

artillery was falling on the 34th's forward positions. Barges, swimming and wading riflemen and floating bodies filled the water, with more troops waiting on the shore. A second crossing site, several miles downriver, was equally active.

As Walker viewed the carnage, air controllers spotted elements of the 3rd NK Division massing across from the 19th Infantry to the east. Enemy tanks had used piles of hay and huts to hide their presence. They were spotted by a liaison pilot from the 24th Division who had noted tracks leading to the various sites but none leaving. The news was disturbing. It meant the enemy had changed his tactics and was moving at night to avoid detection. Both flanks of the 24th Division were now threatened and, if ROK units on their right were under attack as well, Dean might be cut off in Taejon. On the way back to his headquarters, Walker flew over the South Korean forces and was relieved to see them still holding positions well to the north. It was apparent that Eighth Army's timetable for organizing a final defense had to be accelerated.

Upon landing, he was met by Colonel Allan D. MacLean from his G3 section. A hard charger, MacLean wanted to see action. He didn't have long to wait. Spreading his map on the plane's wing, Walker sketched what was to become known as the Pusan Perimeter. "Mac, I want you to find the best defense positions as far forward of that line as possible." MacLean nodded. "Lynch will fly you. As a combat infantryman, he knows the terrain. Use my plane."

"When do you need this?" MacLean asked. "Now" was the reply. "How far forward of the line do you want us to go?" Walker raised his eyes from the map and looked at MacLean. "Keep flying until they shoot at you."

Pappy Wadlington didn't learn that the regimental headquarters and both fire batteries had been overrun until 3:15 P.M. He ordered an attack by his 1st Battalion, which moved out to the north more than an hour later. Nothing happened until the lead company reached the overrun artillery position. There, a few bursts of fire halted the company. Since it was dusk, the battalion commander ordered everyone to pull back.

The defense of the Kum River had begun with a disaster. In a single day the west end of the defense line had been overrun. The withdrawal of the 34th Regiment left its neighbors on the east, the 19th Regiment, with its left flank wide open. T-34 tanks and self-propelled guns, after moving across the river near the blown-up highway bridge, opened fire on the Americans. The untried Chicks of the 19th had almost thirty miles of river frontage to cover, and it was obvious that soon they would be outflanked on both sides.

* * *

General Dean sent encouraging words to both Wadlington and forty-seven-year-old Colonel Guy Meloy Jr. of the 19th, who had never commanded troops in battle. "Hold everything we have until we find out where we stand—might not be too bad—may be able to knock those people out and reconsolidate. Am on my way out there now." But even as he wrote this message, Dean must have known he could not hold Taejon. He informed Colonel Stephens that the 34th Infantry was having trouble and he must put his own regiment in a good position east of Taejon. "We must coordinate so that the 19th and 34th come out together." Colonel Stephens headed his 21st Regiment, now whittled down to 1,100 men, from the Taejon airport back north eight miles towards Okchon, a village on the main Seoul–Pusan highway. He had been ordered by Dean to occupy the hills rising on either side of Okchon to protect the rear of the scattered 34th Regiment. Stephens also sent out a company of engineers to prepare all tunnels and bridges east of Taejon for demolition.

The best Meloy could do to stop a flank attack on his left was to send out Lieutenant Colonel Thomas McGrail with one company, two light M-24 tanks and two .50-caliber-machine-gun antiaircraft vehicles—two thirds of Meloy's entire reserve force. This was Task Force McGrail and its mission was to guard the left flank.

The quiet was deceptive. Meloy knew it was only a question of time before a major attack would come. There were a few probing forays at the center of his line at the blown bridge. But these were not pressed, and shellings from tanks and artillery across the river were only sporadic.

Throughout the night came other minor attacks. Then at three A.M. a North Korean plane dropped a flare. Tank and artillery fire blasted Meloy's men. An hour later North Korean troops crossed the river in a gap between C and E companies. Lieutenant Henry McGill, commander of C Company, phoned the 1st Platoon leader, Lieutenant Thomas Maher. How was he doing? "We're doing fine," said Maher. "We eat this stuff up." Thirty seconds later a burp-gun bullet smashed into his head.

Within three hours the company was overrun, and the North Koreans rushed through the breach. It was as if a dam had burst. The entire 19th Regiment was suddenly in danger of being enveloped. Colonel Meloy hastily set up an assault with cooks, bakers, drivers, mechanics, clerks and the security platoon. It failed. While organizing a second assault, Meloy was wounded and had to turn over the regiment to Lieutenant Colonel Otho Winstead, the commander of the 1st Battalion, who ordered a withdrawal to Taejon. But after proceeding south several miles, the Americans ran into a strong enemy roadblock.

Although all frontal attacks that morning of July 14 had been stopped except at a single hill, by afternoon the entire Kum River defense system had collapsed.

2.

The ROKs responsible for holding the line east of the Seoul–Pusan highway were withdrawing south as fast as the Americans on their west, but they, too, were putting up stiff resistance. General Walker went to see Rhee to commend the ROKs. The president was charmed by his manner and his obvious determination to win. It was only a brief meeting, but when Noble called later he found both Rhees uplifted. At last they had hope. Here was a man!

Maggie Higgins was still avoiding Walker's headquarters. By now the order to send her back to Tokyo was international news. The Russian publication *New Times* depicted her in a cartoon being marched out of Korea at bayonet point. The caption read: "MACARTHUR'S FIRST VICTORY."

The next day, July 17, Walker was informed that he was to assume command of all ROK ground forces at President Rhee's request. The news was welcomed by Captain Hausman and the KMAG officers who had been working closely with General Chung Il-kwon in reorganizing the scattered ROK Army. With the heavy losses in the first days of fighting, a large-scale reequipment of the ROK Army had to be delayed because the roads and railroads were jammed with Americans; it was difficult to get even small amounts of supplies and equipment to the beleaguered ROKs on the east side of the peninsula.

Their advisory officers had recommended that the surviving ROKs be reorganized into two corps. This was already being done with the cooperation of General Chung, and now the job was to bring the five remaining ROK divisions up to strength.

Jim Hausman's first meeting with General Walker had started inauspiciously. He had come up to Hausman's desk and said rather curtly, "Are you the captain I have to see in order to move an ROK unit?"

"I hope not, sir." Hausman explained how the advisers operated, finally convincing the general that his orders would be carried out most efficiently if given through the ROK chain of command. "Tell me what you want and I will see that it is carried out. I'll have the order issued by General Chung Il-kwon. If he orders a unit to move and it doesn't, the unit commander will be shot on the spot." That order, he said, had already been signed by President Rhee and was quite effective. From that moment, relations between Hausman and Walker were good.

On the morning of July 18 Maggie Higgins walked into Walker's Taegu headquarters. She slipped by everyone because they thought she was another GI in her khakis and helmet liner, but when she asked a public relations officer for directions to the correspondents' billet, he recognized her and said, "I'm taking you to the airstrip, and right now, even if I have to call some military police. And you can write that down in your little notebook."

"Am I under arrest?"

"Don't pull that stuff. I know your publicity tricks."

Once in Tokyo, she learned that MacArthur had rescinded the order to banish her from Korea, and made plans to return to the battlefield.

When Hobert "Hap" Gay, Patton's executive officer in World War II, arrived a little later with his 1st Cavalry Division, Walker was on hand to meet him. "Just like old times" was Gay's greeting.

"Not quite, Hap," said Walker. "Things have gotten much worse since you left Japan. There won't be time to consolidate your division. In fact, you won't be able to organize by regiments. I need as much combat strength as possible behind Dean right away. Be ready to move by battalions."

Walker spent a few more minutes with his old friend. "Hap, almost all of your commanders are inexperienced. Like Patton used to say: They're vulnerable to the valor of ignorance." He went on to tell Gay the same things he had told both Dean and Kean. "We must trade time for space." He followed with a litany of basics. "Hold the high ground as long as possible. Defend in depth. Keep a reserve. Watch your flanks. Protect your artillery. Maintain communication at all costs. Don't get decisively engaged." Such actions were second nature to veterans. But inexperienced commanders always paid with blood to learn them. The 1st Cav would spill much more on the sacrificial altar of war.

As he was leaving, several correspondents cornered Walker. "Now that the Cavalry is here, are you going to attack?" asked one. Walker stared at the man, then climbed into his plane without saying a word. Lynch noted the startled look on the questioner's face. "General, you won't be very popular with those guys."

"I know it," said Walker. "But there's no way you can give an intelligent answer to a dumb question."

He headed for the Taejon airstrip to notify Dean of the Cavalry's arrival. Walker had estimated it would take two days to get Gay's first units up to Yongdong to reinforce the 24th Division. He wanted to know if Dean could hold Taejon until July 20. Together, they studied the map. Although spread thinly, Dean felt that, by fighting a delaying action to the high ground west of town, it could be done. Even so it was a desperate situation. Dean's 19th Regiment had been whipped in its first fight and was reorganizing at Yongdong, the division rear headquarters thirty miles southeast of Taejon. The 21st Regiment was in equally bad shape after its battles north of the Kum River. That left only the 34th Regiment to defend Taejon. And Dean had only two battalions of artillery left to confront a joint attack by two strong enemy divisions.

Taejon was a long, narrow city in the north-south valley below the Kum River, with a population of 130,000. It lay on the main Seoul–Pusan highway, 100 air miles south of the capital and 130 air miles northwest of Pusan, the port city at the southeasternmost point of the peninsula.

Walker ordered Lynch to fly south so they could check the road to Kunsan, which lay at the mouth of the Kum River. If the North Koreans tried to envelop Dean's division in Taejon, they would have to come this way. Lynch made a low pass over the division recon company and Walker noted that it occupied the best defensible terrain some ten kilometers south of Taejon. From there they flew over a ridge just west of the city. Here the road to Taegu passed through a tunnel. Troops were deployed along this high ground. "Fly along that ridge," the general directed. Lynch dropped down until he was at the same elevation and to the rear. This allowed Walker to get an idea of the fields of fire. All of Taejon was visible as well as routes leading to the tunnel. It was an ideal defense position with extended fields of fire. On the way back to Taegu, they passed over many 24th Division troops between the ridge and Yongdong. Walker was assured. If Dean did not become decisively engaged in Taejon, he could hold until the 20th.

By the evening of July 19, Dean had set up his defenses. Two miles northeast of the city the 1st Battalion of the 34th Infantry was dug in on a hill along the main highway a mile in front of the Taejon airstrip. Behind the 1st Battalion, and only half a mile from the city, Dean had placed the 3rd Battalion on a ridge.

To the northeast were scattered remnants of the 19th Infantry. At ten-thirty P.M., Lieutenant Robert Herbert of G Company, 2nd Battalion, whose men were exhausted from a futile attempt to break the North Korean roadblock, was ordered to move his platoon of 47 men from the company perimeter to the battalion command post as a reserve force.

Upon arrival at the CP, Herbert was informed that he was to be ready for any emergency. In the morning he was to set up a security force. It was weirdly quiet when Herbert bedded down near the CP. Uneasy, he returned to the post and, while chatting with Lieutenant Colonel McGrail, the battalion commander, he heard the sound of running feet. A soldier dashed up half crazed, babbling that E Company was completely overrun! Everyone slaughtered mercilessly!

McGrail ordered Herbert to move out and contact the enemy. No sooner had he got his platoon on the road than McGrail approached in a jeep. "Get aboard," he said. They'd make a reconnaissance. It was midnight by the time they reached the E Company area where the "butchery" had occurred. One platoon had been been pushed back, but everything was now okay, reported the company commander.

"All right, Herb," said Colonel McGrail. "Turn your platoon around and go on back to the area." While Herbert—tall, slender, fair—was preparing to do so, the man who had babbled of the massacre again appeared at top speed. "An enemy machine gun on the other side of the bridge is shooting up jeeps and slaughtering GIs!" he cried.

"Herb," said McGrail patiently, "take your platoon and see what's going on."

Herbert proceeded to the E Company area where GIs were supposed to be slaughtered. He heard nothing. What a futile night!

Three miles to the east, disquieting reports were also coming in to the CP of the 1st Battalion, 34th. The commander, Colonel Red Ayres, had himself heard the rumble of tanks and sent out a patrol to investigate. It never reported back. And just before midnight a disturbing message had come in. The enemy was on a road south of the city; a jeep patrol was stopped six miles below Taejon by a roadblock. It seemed clear that the enemy was moving around to the rear of the city. Just after three A.M., July 20, the S2 of the 1st Battalion ran into Ayres's CP, a Korean house, and exclaimed, "The enemy has penetrated the main line of resistance!"

Ayres could now hear small-arms fire. He went outside and saw flares bursting over the artillery position.

The North Korean 4th Division was coming down the main highway and was rolling up Ayres's right flank. By four A.M., small-arms fire began hitting Ayres's CP. He tried to communicate with his frontline companies. No luck. He sent a message that tanks had penetrated his lines to Colonel Charles Beauchamp, who had been flown to Korea to take over from Pappy Wadlington as commander of the 34th.

The situation was so confusing that Ayres gave orders to evacuate the CP and was gone when Beauchamp tried to communicate with him.

In Taejon, Dean was awakened at dawn by sporadic firing. He could smell the acrid after-odor of cordite from the artillery. His hope that the 34th could hold the line long enough for more help to arrive was growing weaker by the minute. His aide, Lieutenant Arthur Clarke, reported that enemy tanks had been seen in the outskirts of Taejon. As Clarke was making their bedrolls, he said, "I don't think we'll sleep here again tonight."

Just before dawn Lieutenant Herbert crossed the bridge to flush out the village. On the far side of the bridge was a smouldering jeep. The driver was burned to death, his assistant lying next to the jeep— dead. Moments after Herbert returned to his CP, a jeep roared in from

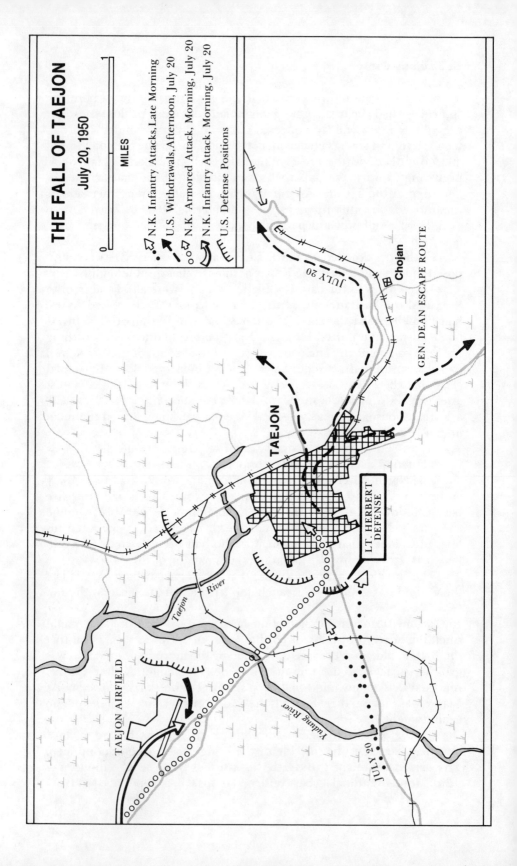

THE FALL OF TAEJON

July 20, 1950

MILES

0   1

N.K. Infantry Attacks, Late Morning
U.S. Withdrawals, Afternoon, July 20
N.K. Armored Attack, Morning, July 20
N.K. Infantry Attack, Morning, July 20
U.S. Defense Positions

Chojan

GEN. DEAN ESCAPE ROUTE

JULY 20

TAEJON

LT. HERBERT DEFENSE

Taejon River

TAEJON AIRFIELD

Yudung River

JULY 20

Taejon. The road to the city was blocked at a key road junction by three enemy tanks! Herbert could see smoke and hear explosions which seemed to be coming from the city.

McGrail ordered Herbert to open up the road with B Company of the 34th, but had no bazookas or grenades to give him. Herbert led his people up toward the junction, which was less than a mile from the center of Taejon. It was obvious that the main enemy tank attack would come down the upper road, so Herbert set up his own roadblock around a quarry near the junction.

General Dean had not left the city. He was hunting for tanks with his aide and a Korean interpreter. They came upon two T-34's which had been knocked out. Nearby was a truck mounting a recoilless rifle. Dean got the driver's attention and directed him toward a third tank, which appeared to be undamaged. The gunner set off four rounds but all missed. Frustrated, Dean commandeered two 2.36-bazooka rocket teams and began chasing on foot an enemy tank heading south. Like a bird dog, the general tracked the Soviet T-34 as it approached Herbert's roadblock. Herbert saw the tank heading towards him and was about to let loose when someone hollered, "Don't fire! It's ours!" Herbert held his fire, since he'd heard there were four friendly tanks in Taejon. The T-34 halted thirty yards away. The hatch opened and a North Korean tanker peered out at the burning vehicles and the bodies on the road. The hatch slammed down and the tank was gone before Herbert realized it was an enemy. Then through his glasses he made out a squad heading towards him from the south. He recognized General Dean following tank tracks in the dirt road.

"Sir," he said, "what the fuck is going on?"

Dean laughed. He asked why Herbert had let the enemy tank go through.

Herbert explained, then said, "The men will stay and fight, but I have to tell them what we're doing."

"We're trying to hold the ground west of town till the 1st Cav Division can get formed and attack through us."

"When, sir?"

"As soon as they can form."

"*When*, sir?" he insisted.

"As soon as they can form," repeated Dean and laughed. He added that the 1st Cavalry was assembling south of Taejon, and that nine enemy tanks had broken into the city that morning. He instructed Herbert to blast the enemy tank if it came back, then left on foot for Taejon with his squad and two bazookas.

Herbert climbed to the high ground south of the road junction, where he made out a column heading towards him from the southwest.

Was it friend or foe? There were two files seventy-five yards apart, one on the road and one in the valley. Someone shouted that the enemy tank was coming back!

The slender Herbert ran down the slope. "Get him, get him, for Christ's sake!" It was an easy shot, but the man on the bazooka was trembling. The round hit the dirt behind the tank and it lumbered on unharmed. Herbert was disgusted with himself. *He* should have been on the road with the bazooka. *He* wouldn't have missed. He rushed back to the high ground to observe the approaching column. There were too many for it to be the 2nd Battalion. It must be North Korean.

Shells from North Korean artillery began falling. Several men were killed. From his vantage point Herbert could see elements of the 34th Infantry pulling out of Taejon. He decided to hang on until dark and then withdraw, even if he got no instructions. Things looked so bad he sent a runner to find General Dean.

Back in the city the general was still looking for action. With his aide, Lieutenant Clarke, he located a team with the larger 3.5 bazooka. Accompanied by several infantrymen, they climbed to the top floor of a two-story business building. From a window Dean saw a tank below. The muzzle of the gun was only about a dozen feet away and he could have spat down its tube. He told the bazooka team exactly where to aim. A rocket hit the tank and they could hear those inside screaming. The second round from the new bazooka, recalled Clarke, "quieted most of the screaming, and the third made it quiet."

3.

At first light, that eventful day, Mike Lynch had flown Colonel MacLean to Taejon to pick up an overlay of Dean's position. Artillery was already impacting on the airstrip. Wasting little time, MacLean queried several officers in the 34th Infantry command post and was flown back to Taegu. He notified the G3 that the enemy was beginning his attack on Taejon and Dean would need all help possible.

A few hours later, an Air Force major showed up at Eighth Army's flight section. "Where's Mike Lynch? He's supposed to fly me to Taejon. The 24th needs an air liaison officer in a hurry."

"Taejon's under fire," Lynch told him. "I was up there early this morning."

"Walker's office wants you to get me there," said the major. "Besides, I've been told it's still open." They took off immediately.

Flying on the deck, they slipped into the Taegu airfield and parked near several infantrymen in a foxhole. Operating the canopy, the major prepared to step out when suddenly the soldiers began shouting. "Get the hell out of here! The gooks are in the Quonset huts across the field."

Just then a burst of machine-gun fire could be heard. Unable to taxi back to the strip, they took off across it, passing between the Quonset huts and over the heads of a surprised enemy. Once airborne, the major spotted two Yaks starting to make a run on them. Both missed. Flying south, Lynch noted that the recon company had moved. And very few infantrymen were occupying the ridge. He knew Walker considered these two positions as vital to Dean's defense of Taejon.

Upon landing, Lynch reported the changes in the 24th's situation to the G3 who notified Walker. Mike also told the general about the recon company and the lightly held ridge. Walker assumed that Dean had altered his defense plan and knew about these changes. It was a tragic assumption. Dean didn't know.

His tank hunt successfully completed just before noon, Dean was returning to the 34th Infantry CP to see Colonel Beauchamp. While lunching on cooked C-Rations, Dean expressed pleasure at destroying the tank. Not realizing what a desperate situation they were in, Dean and Beauchamp discussed future plans calmly, imagining that their combat forces were still holding off the enemy a mile or so to the west. In fact, the two battalions of the 34th were scattered in the hills, and the remnants of the 19th were doing little, except for the stubborn Lieutenant Herbert. Even so, as they finished their meal Dean instructed Beauchamp to initiate a daylight withdrawal. They would not wait until dark as planned.

At about two P.M. Beauchamp instructed his operations officer to send out messages by radio and telephone to prepare to pull out at once. But neither the 1st Battalion of the 34th nor the 2nd Battalion of the 19th could be raised. Only the 3rd Battalion of the 34th got the order.

The North Koreans were closing in on Taejon from three sides. At the roadblock Herbert's group was running out of ammunition. Then word finally came to withdraw. The men who had fought so gallantly all day piled into the remaining trucks and were soon in the center of Taejon. Herbert could see about 150 of the 19th and 34th vehicles jammed bumper to bumper. There were engineer, artillery, and infantry vehicles as well as personnel carriers and heavy weapons. Obviously everyone was worried about getting out of the city. But there was no panic.

Just before six P.M., the convoy started off, led by Colonel Pappy Wadlington in a jeep. The column rolled south through swirling clouds of smoke. Much of the city was on fire, with debris falling into streets littered with dead Koreans and Americans. In the confusion the rear half of the convoy failed to follow. It was still in place. Herbert moved to the head of the stalled line, where an artillery major was sitting dreamily in a jeep.

"Sir, we have to get moving!" said Herbert.

"Okay, okay," said the major and asked if anyone knew the way out of town.

"Get moving!" yelled Herbert angrily and the convoy started at last. Herbert assumed they'd get out of town without difficulty, so he and his runner jumped on the nearest vehicle, a 3/4-ton artillery truck. Small-arms fire came from buildings that were not burning. The Americans returned fire from their vehicles. Far ahead, Wadlington's jeep was coming under heavy fire. Everyone jumped out, but enemy fire had slackened, and Wadlington ordered the convoy to move on. He'd follow when it got under way. But his jeep could not pass the trucks. Wadlington ordered the driver to circle the block to get ahead. They got lost, ending in a dead-end street near a schoolhouse. Small-arms fire kept them from turning around. The jeep was destroyed and everyone ran.

The second part of the convoy had taken the wrong turn and, by chance, now ended up at the same dead-end schoolhouse. Like Wadlington, these men abandoned their vehicles. Lieutenant Herbert was among this second group. He walked back to find his men. No luck.

The two jeeps of General Dean's party were also lost. Dean's driver had not seen the vehicle ahead of him make a turn to the left onto the highway to Pusan. Instead, he kept going straight ahead, with the second jeep and L Company tagging behind. Lieutenant Clarke realized they had missed the turn, but before they could turn around, enemy fire broke out and they had to keep moving.

After a few miles the main convoy heading toward Pusan met heavy mortar fire. The lead vehicle, a half-track, was hit and began to burn. A second half-track pushed the wreckage off the road and continued, but its driver was almost immediately killed, and the truck set afire. Machine-gun fire raked the road. Everyone scrambled into roadside ditches. North Korean soldiers rose from rice paddies and began blasting the road with burp guns.

The Americans now rushed up to the road to drench their vehicles with gasoline and set matches to the equipment. Soon everyone began clambering up on the high ground north of the road.

Back at the dead end, Herbert heard a major order his men to head for the high ground. Some of the major's 125 men had already taken off. Others had panicked and failed to destroy the vehicles before scattering to the hills. Herbert blamed their officers, but there was nothing he could do about it. He still had an M-1 and four or five clips. He grabbed four grenades from his truck and gave two to his runner. They started up the hill. Herbert moved to the head of the column to take charge. It was now about nine P.M. and in the growing darkness Herbert could make out a column of North Koreans approaching from the northwest.

Upon reaching the top of the next ridge, a lieutenant colonel in the rear passed up word to take a break. But the resolute Herbert knew resting could be fatal and kept moving, followed by some sixty men. At the next high ground he looked back. The sound of gunfire was coming from where the other men were resting. He guessed they would soon be dead or captured. He led his exhausted men farther south, finally stealing through enemy lines to safety. And to fight another day.

After General Dean's jeep made the wrong turn, he looked at a map and decided they should take another road that would let them drive faster than the truck-jammed main route. About a mile south of Taejon they came upon walking wounded, and Dean loaded them into his two jeeps as a sniper opened fire. Dean made out a North Korean silhouetted on top of a hill. The general fired his M-1. The figure dropped. Soon the two jeeps came to a roadblock. Heavy gunfire swept the road and Dean tumbled into a ditch. He had left his M-1 behind and he had lost his pistol. Clarke was in the same ditch. With them were seventeen Americans and a terrified Korean civilian. They crawled through a bean patch and rested at the bank of a river. There were few arms and Clarke insisted that Dean take his pistol. "I can't use it anyhow." He had been hit in the shoulder.

They waded across the river and started up a steep slope, with Dean in the lead. It was pitch dark, and the main group on the road was now out of sight. At one rest-stop Dean thought he heard running water and went off to get some. "The next thing I knew I was running down a slope so steep that I could not stop." He fell and lost consciousness.

Clarke looked for him in vain. And when the general came to, he found he couldn't get up. Dazed and groggy, he looked at his watch. It was half an hour after midnight, July 21. He was alone in a dry creekbed with steep sides. All he could think of was, "My God, what's happened to those people up there? I don't know where I am."

CHAPTER 7

A Private Takes Command
(July 19–31)

1.

General Walker faced not only a breakthrough at Taejon but two other dangerous drives. On the west coast the Korean People's 6th Division had raced south undetected and seized Chonju, forty air miles southwest of Taejon. This important city had been defended only by police, and there were almost no North Korean casualties. The People's 6th was one of the two former strong Chinese divisions made up of North Korean volunteers. Combat-hardened from their battles in the People's Liberation Army against Chiang Kai-shek, these trained soldiers would be the most effective the Americans had yet faced. Now they were ordered to continue to the southwest tip of the peninsula, then swing east and launch the final attack on Pusan.

Simultaneously, the main part of Kim Il-sung's forces were moving relentlessly through the central mountains of South Korea by way of two mountain corridors east of Taejon, the area MacArthur had assigned to the ROKs. By the time Taejon came under attack, the North Korean advances down the mountainous backbone of the peninsula and along the east coast had gained alarming momentum. General Walker dispatched the newly arrived U.S. 25th Division to help the ROK Army stop one drive which had reached a point less than seventy air miles north of his headquarters in Taegu. The first American action came at Yechon, an important road hub fifty-five air miles north of Taegu. On

July 19 the North Koreans broke into the town. Walker ordered General William Kean, commander of the 25th, to retake Yechon, and he sent his 24th Regimental Combat Team to carry out the mission. This was an all-black regiment, except for some white officers, and the men were eager to disprove the common gossip that blacks were poor fighters.

Their commander, forty-nine-year-old Horton White, had never led troops in combat. On arrival in Korea he had privately admitted to First Lieutenant Charles Bussey, the black commander of the 77th Combat Engineers Company, that he was too old for action. "I didn't realize it until this morning, but soldiering is for young-uns," he told Bussey. "Mine is all behind me." But he vowed he'd do the job required.

On the morning of July 20 the 24th Regimental Combat Team moved against a village in front of Yechon. Tom Lambert of AP crouched in a soybean patch on a hillside watching the assault as two enemy companies began a flanking move under a barrage of artillery and mortar fire, a tactic the Reds had been using successfully.

To Lambert's west, small groups of Americans were legging it across the rice fields. Lambert could see a machine gunner struggling with his burden up the slopes into a grove of trees. There was silence, then the chatter of the machine gun. The correspondent's attention was drawn to the north, where black soldiers were stalking warily into clusters of houses, firing as they advanced. All of a sudden, enemy mortar rounds began falling into a mud hut the GIs had just abandoned. The GIs moved without hesitation on a forward outpost.

Part of Yechon, nestled in a cup of a mountain ridge, was burning fiercely as two Mustangs swept down to strafe. The GIs hopped nervously back and forth across the ridge to avoid the line of fire. The two flanking companies had reached the outskirts, and the GIs again came under heavy mortar fire. The American commander withdrew his troops into a perimeter defense and called for artillery. All through the night harassing fire continued to keep the Reds from infiltrating the American lines.

After midnight a combat battalion team of the 24th RCT moved into position while their officers learned the plan of attack. L Company would lead. After dawn of the 21st its commander, Captain Bradley Biggs, a black paratrooper, deployed his men by the book. They met heavy machine-gun and mortar fire but pressed forward, methodically wiping out North Korean positions.

Lieutenant Bussey was approaching Yechon in a jeep with the first mail to his engineers when, at about one P.M., he heard the sound of battle. Encountering a column of trucks, he asked an infantryman where his engineers were. They were spearheading the attack. Bussey could see huts burning. He climbed a hill and looked down at Yechon. There, in a gulch between the town and a mountain, were about twenty-five

white-clad men. Then more and more figures ran out, at least two
hundred, attacking like soldiers. If they got to the column of trucks and
set them afire, his whole battalion would be trapped in Yechon. Bussey
ran down the hill and commandeered soldiers, two machine guns and
cases of ammunition. He emplaced the guns just as the white figures
approached and put a burst over their heads. If they were civilians they'd
run. They didn't, and he ordered both machine guns to fire for effect.
Enemy mortar rounds began landing. A fragment hit Bussey. One of
the gunners was killed and the other gun overheated and wouldn't fire.
Bussey took over the good gun and raked the approaching North Koreans. Scores dropped and he knew it was a slaughter. A body count
after the action indicated 250 enemy dead.

Tom Lambert's dispatch on the previous day's fighting was already
proclaiming throughout America that the blacks had scored "the first
sizable American ground victory in the Korean War." Bussey received
a Silver Star and a Purple Heart from General Kean, who declared it
was only a down payment on a "bigger medal."

On July 23 the exhausted remnants of Dean's division were still falling
back helter-skelter to the south, southwest and southeast. Charles and
Eugene Jones, the twin NBC-TV cameramen, were filming dazed GIs
drifting through Yongdong along the Seoul–Pusan highway. Scared
men began yelling, "The gooks are coming! Get the hell out!"

The brothers could see drab-brown figures—the North Koreans—
crawling over the northwestern horizon. They took pictures of GIs sitting
or lying on the main street, exhausted and disconsolate. "How far away
are the lines?"

"This *is* the line, buster," said a man caked with sediment. "There
ain't nothing out there but gooks. We're the last of the last."

Someone shouted commandingly and the man picked up his rifle
to merge into the moving column. All was quiet except for the rattle of
equipment. Sullen, perplexed faces stared vacantly at the cameramen.
They looked away. It was painful to see one's countrymen in defeat.

They joined the column passing a battered brick building, its roof
partially ripped off. Inside, a battalion was packing up. Shells screeched
overhead and everyone dove onto the dusty road, then rose slowly,
sheepishly. The stench of death was heavy. A rabbit hopped across hot
ashes, chased by a dog crazed by concussion. They heard a tiny squeak.
End of the rabbit. It was unbearably hot. Artillery bursts flashed overhead exploding in the rear. The army of the United States was pulling out.

They passed a stable. Ammo lay stacked neatly amid manure.
Nearby was a wrecked 3/4-ton truck on fire. The rear half was blown
off and in the scattered metal the Jones brothers could see what was left

of two men. The blackened torso of a GI sat upright, bony hands on the steering wheel as if he were still driving.

They hailed a passing jeep and scrambled aboard, then asked, "How far you going?"

"All the way!"

That same day General Dean's aide, Lieutenant Clarke, returned safely to Taegu. He told Major Joe Tyner, Walker's aide, about the gallant fight Dean had put up at Taejon and how he had been lost while getting water. Dean was dead or a prisoner of war.

Maggie Higgins had also returned to Taegu. She found General Walker correct and frank. Although he still felt the front was no place for a woman, he did not object to General MacArthur's action, and assured her that from now on she would get absolutely equal treatment. He didn't tell her that the order to send her out of Korea had been initiated by a public relations officer and he had merely okayed it. "If something had happened to an American woman," he now told her, "the American public might never have forgiven me. So please be careful and don't get yourself killed or captured."

General Walker had ordered the 1st Cavalry Division to stop the victorious enemy surging out of Taejon. "Protect Yongdong," he told Major General Hobart "Hap" Gay, the division commander. "Remember, there are no friendly troops behind you. You just keep your own back door open. You can live without food but you cannot last long without ammunition, and unless the Yongdong–Taegu road is kept open, you will soon be out of ammunition."

Gay had been Patton's efficient executive officer during the war in Europe. Now, for the first time, he would have to lead men in combat. His attempts to slow up the North Korean advance north and northwest of Yongdong failed, and by the morning of July 25 three of his battalions had been wiped out or scattered. To make matters worse, massive numbers of refugees (including North Korean agents) were crowding into Yongdong, impeding the movement of his own troops. Gay was desperate. He had to follow Walker's definite orders to keep open the main highway to Taegu, and the only solution was to pull back immediately.

This distressing news was followed by a report that the North Koreans, after being whipped by the American blacks at Yechon, were again threatening Taegu from the northeast. What concerned Walker more, however, was an aerial reconnaissance report indicating that the enemy had apparently begun a drive on the west coast from the estuary of the Kum River. He guessed this force would swing east behind the western flank of Eighth Army. Although his intelligence officers still had no idea that the 6th Korean People's Division was already nearing the southwestern tip of the peninsula and was about to swing east to assault Pusan, Walker concluded that a crisis could be developing in the west far behind the lines. To counter this danger, on July 24, he summoned General Church, who had replaced the still-missing Dean as commander of the 24th Division. Walker told Church he would have to move this unit to the threatened sector in the southwest. "I'm sorry to have to do this, but the whole left flank is open and reports indicate the Koreans are moving in." Church was to cover a vast area of wild mountains ending at Chinju, fifty-five air miles west of Pusan.

Realizing that the two remaining regiments of the 24th Division were too weak to halt this thrust, Walker sent two battalions of the 29th Infantry Regiment to help Church's exhausted troops. The reinforcements were raw recruits who had arrived only yesterday from Okinawa, where they had been briefly trained. Without time to zero in and test-fire their weapons, they were expected to stop the onrushing enemy. On the night of the 25th their commander, Lieutenant Colonel Harold Mott, was ordered to occupy Hadong with one of his two battalions. This town was an important road junction twenty air miles west of Chinju near the tip of the peninsula. They were supposed to stand off some 500 enemy reportedly coming toward Hadong from the west.

Captain Hausman sent General Fat Chae, the former ROK chief of staff, to this area to determine how critical the situation was. Chae offered to accompany Mott's troops, since he was familiar with the terrain and could serve not only as guide but interpreter. Half an hour after midnight, Chae led Mott's motorized column through the rugged hills. They had to detour because of an impassable ford and it took all night.

At daylight an approaching truck stopped. Inside were about twenty badly wounded South Koreans—the only survivors of the local Hadong militia. Since there was no radio communication with 19th Infantry, the executive officer jeeped back to Chinju for instructions. The battalion was ordered to continue and to seize Hadong. By dusk Mott had brought his men to a small village three miles from Hadong. Tomorrow morning, July 26, they would attack.

Fifteen air miles southwest of Hadong, General Pang Ho-san, commander of the 6th Korean People's Division, was issuing final orders for the attack toward Pusan. Although this NK unit was poorly prepared for such an ambitious operation and their rations had already been cut in half, Pang called upon his troops that evening to win the victory. "Comrades, the enemy is demoralized!" he said. "The task given us is the liberation of Chinju and Masan and the annihilation of the remnants of the enemy." The liberation of these two towns, he promised, "means the final battle to cut off the windpipe of the enemy!"

The response was generally enthusiastic, but Major Park Ki-cheol, an artillery commander, was not impressed. He could not fathom the stupidity of the North Korean high command for allowing the division to take so much time getting in position for the attack on Pusan. Instead of wasting days preparing to seize an unimportant port city, they should have already taken Pusan by surprise.

Park had been unhappy with commands from above ever since the transfer of his division from China to Korea. For one thing, he preferred the Chinese method of having no rank. A man was only known by his position as infantryman or commander of a battalion. All troops wore the same simple uniform with no insignia. All were comrades. Now he sported the rank of major and was distrusted by everyone beneath him while he avoided everyone above him.

For the past year his brother, an intellectual, had tried to convince him that the Kim Il-sung regime was corrupt and inept. Even before the attack on June 25 Park had had doubts about Kim's brand of Communism, and now, after so many frustrations, he concluded that his brother was right. There was only one thing to do: go over to the ROK side and democracy. He felt sure the Americans would eventually see that the country became a true democracy despite President Rhee's autocratic ways. He felt deep shame for abandoning his comrades, but it was time to cross over.

Just before dark that night he informed his superiors that he was going to reconnoiter. He came to a farmhouse. Inside he found Korean clothes, including a *gat*, the horse-tail headgear of a Korean gentleman. He put this disguise over his uniform and kept walking east. After dawn he proceeded cautiously until he came to the U.S. lines. He held up his hands. A GI guard didn't bother disarming him; he just took his wristwatch and money, some 800,000 *won*. Another American came up and slapped his face. Major Park was incensed. Was this democracy? The propaganda *was* correct. The Americans and South Koreans were interested only in money! A bolt of regret swept through him. But what could he do now?

2.

Earlier that morning of July 26, Mott's 3rd Battalion started off on the three-mile trip to Hadong over rugged hills for their first taste of battle. Captain George Sharra's L Company led the way with a platoon of the heavy weapons company, followed by Mott's command group and K, M and I companies. Sharra was an old hand, having seen action in Africa, Sicily, France and Germany. Less than an hour later, when they were about half a mile from the top of the Hadong pass, he glimpsed a dozen or so camouflaged NK soldiers. The heavy weapons company fired their recoilless rifles. As the rounds whizzed over their heads, the North Koreans ran. Sharra ordered L Company to go to the top of the pass and secure it. There they dug in and waited for a scheduled 9:45 A.M. air strike on Hadong, a mile and a half away.

Colonel Mott, his staff, and General Fat Chae and his aide, Colonel Lee Sang-gook, hurried to the pass, where Sharra pointed to a group of men moving up higher ground in the north.

"Yes," said Mott, "I have K Company up there."

Another column of soldiers appeared at a curve on the south side of the road to Hadong. Mott pointed it out to the executive officer, who was standing next to Chae. They tried to figure out who they were. Some were wearing U.S. fatigues, but others were in the mustard brown uniform of the enemy.

Private Charles Dawson of the heavy weapons company saw these officers who seemed to be enjoying the beautiful scenery. Then he heard General Chae shouting toward figures at the road curve. Apparently he was demanding that they identify themselves. They reacted by scrambling into ditches. L Company's machine guns opened fire. The North Koreans replied. The liaison jeep near Dawson was hit and parts flew everywhere. Boy! he thought. This is just like the movies! He saw Fat Chae collapse, blood spurting above his right ear.

After dragging the huge general to a vehicle, Colonel Lee cradled Chae in his arms. "Tell Minister Shin, I'm sorry," uttered Chae and slumped. Lee was sure he had died as he wished: honorably in battle.

Mott and three other staff officers were also hit. Although creased across the back, the colonel scrambled below the pass and was helping unload ammunition when a box fell and broke his foot. A GI dug him a foxhole. In the meantime, with no one in command, there was confusion all over the hill.

By now I Company, the reserve, had arrived. As Private Baldwin Frank Myers's squad rounded the curve at the crest of the hill, he could see an open rice paddy and a horseshoe of hills in front. The point of his own column was firing. An American jeep racing towards Myers was raked with enemy machine-gun fire. It shot off the road, rolled several times. Everyone inside was dead.

Moments after swinging around the road curve, Myers's group was hit by mortars. Two men were wounded. Myers helped drag to safety one whose guts were blown open, then made a shallow hole on the crest and, through the scope of his sniper rifle, peered across the rice paddy at the battle some five hundred yards away. It was obvious the battalion had taken heavy casualties and some of the men were running without weapons, half-clothed, across the paddy. Myers wanted to fire but was afraid of hitting his own people. K and L companies were trapped, and there seemed little hope that any could escape.

Late that morning Lieutenant Makarounis told I Company to advance and rescue the trapped two companies. "It's suicide to cross the paddy!" Myers replied. They should hold the hills and give covering fire for K and L so they could withdraw at dusk.

Makarounis ordered Myers to go and threatened him with court-martial if he didn't obey. "I will tolerate no cowards in my outfit!"

This angered Myers; he was no coward. He zigzagged his way across the paddy at top speed. There was sporadic fire, but he was not hit. By the time he reached the far side, the rest of his company was 250 yards behind.

He found the trapped companies beneath the horseshoe of hills. Everywhere there lay wounded and dying. No one seemed to be in charge. Seeing a group unloading ammo from a munitions truck, Myers decided to get some grenades, then scrambled a hundred yards up a ravine to be near the crest. He rested where he had a panoramic view of the battle. Suddenly came a series of whistles, and a cluster of mortar rounds landed in the ravine where the munitions were being unloaded. The soldiers there must have caught hell. The volume of fire caused a steady roar. There seemed no way out.

In the paddy ditch below, he heard Makarounis shouting, "Keep moving!" But most of those who had made it that far kept crouching in the ditch.

Shortly afterwards word was passed from Makarounis that they were to "make an orderly withdrawal." How? thought Myers, but then realized someone was going to have to do something or they'd all be killed or captured. "I could only see certain death in any direction. The choices were retreat and die in the rice paddy as the others would, surrender and be executed, or go forward and try to get them off the hill. I accepted certain death. I was calm with a gnawing anger while seeing the helpless slaughter of my company below. In an instant, I visualized charging up the hill into the face of the enemy, throwing hand grenades and firing in their faces, charging into them, frightening them, and bashing their heads with my rifle. I worked myself into a rage that overcame any fear or trepidation I may have had. All I could think of was charging up the hill and killing the enemy. I was not afraid. I felt protected."

"Come on!" he yelled. "Let's go get those bastards!" Swearing in rage, he dashed up the hill. Nearing a clump of brush, he heard Jim Yeager yell, "Get down!" Shots whistled past him. The roar of fire became deafening but it was directed over his head into the rice paddy below. As he got closer, he saw the brush was the enemy in camouflage. Three jumped up. He emptied eight shots at them and hit the ground after finishing the clip, and saw more "brush" to his right with rifles poking out, firing.

Myers sprinted in a crouch to safety under the crest of the ridge, and threw two grenades. He flopped to the ground as they exploded, then crawled over the crest towards the enemy, not knowing what to expect. He saw half a dozen smoking bodies and NK survivors running down the hill with bloody clothes, dangling arms. A North Korean officer whipped the poor devils with a stick, but they kept retreating. Myers was furious. He aimed at the despicable officer's stomach and fired. The man's left arm jerked and he spun around. Myers fired again, and the North Korean dropped as if punched in the stomach with a pole. Then he noticed three enemy columns heading toward the position I Company had held before advancing across the paddy. If the North Koreans secured that position, Myers knew his comrades would be caught in a fatal crossfire. It seemed hopeless for I Company. They were outnumbered ten or fifteen to one and were surrounded except for an opening to the south across another rice paddy.

He had to get back and warn them of the encirclement. He continued firing as fast as he could reload until his sore shoulder could hardly stand the pain. The weapon was so hot the wood was smoking. He feared his next shell would explode from the heat. Bullets were splattering all around him and he finally decided to get the hell out of there. Enemy were all around and closing in, shooting everything—even their own dead. He could hear the NK jabbering and yelling. He had one grenade left; he would take his own life rather than be captured. The butt plate of his rifle had been shot off and the rifle was no longer of much use. He said a prayer that he would make it back to his own lines.

He ran down the hill as fast as possible past wounded and dead. At the paddy he came upon GIs crouched behind a bank. Only four were shooting at the enemy on the hill. Lieutenant Makarounis, who had ordered them all to cross the paddy, was now doing his best to move his men east. Myers yelled at him not to go in that direction. "What shall we do?" asked Myers.

"What *can* we do?" said Makarounis. "Every man for himself!"

Myers was furious. "Why can't you tell us how to get out? You're the one who got us in this position!"

Tears came to the lieutenant's eyes and Myers suddenly felt sorry for him. Makarounis was an MP, not a combat officer. At the same time, he *was* responsible for the stupid excursion across the paddy. Myers had lost respect for his leaders. Two had already bugged out. At least this officer was there to share the hell he had sent them into. As Myers started toward four men who were still firing, he abruptly stopped, feeling something like a huge hand press his right shoulder. It forced him down. Then he heard the ominous sound of incoming mortars. Rounds landed in the paddy fifteen yards away, blowing off his helmet and showering him with mud and warm water. But he was unharmed, thanks to the huge mysterious hand. He noticed that Makarounis, despite Myers's warning, was leading his men east. There were bloodstains on the lieutenant's back. Flanking fire from the east suddenly opened up. The 150 or more men following Makarounis down the ditch were rapidly dropping. Myers, feeling a near miss on the right and a slight tug at his fatigues, looked down at the crease of a bullet across his jacket.

The survivors following Makarounis were already two hundred yards to the rear, but there were still two or three hundred men lying cowering in the ditch. Some were crying, some whimpering. Myers yelled at them to get up and use their damned weapons or they'd all die there. His words had no effect.

Myers found a BAR (Browning automatic rifle) and started firing. The weapon blew up, the powder flash searing his already burned face. His ears rang. A machine-gun burst caught the man next to him. Grabbing Myers's wrist, he said, "Mama," and died. Myers had to pry his wrist free. Enemy fire continued. Myers had used up all the weapons he could find.

"I think I may have a way out," he told the men near him. "If I make it, you guys follow and bring your weapons." He started down the ditch with one grenade, a bayonet and his canteen. At the far bank he floated down the stream, going with the current as if he were dead. Finally he came up for air and slowly rolled his face toward the hill. He could see the enemy had stopped firing and were standing along the ridge. He was in plain sight and thought bullets were going to rip through him at any second. But the battle was over. There were only a few sporadic shots. He waded out of the river. As he proceeded up the hill a rifle cracked. He thought it was one of his men and approached until he noticed a pair of shoes sticking out from the brush. A North Korean emerged swinging a long-barreled rifle at Myers. He felt helpless. He was standing dripping wet with only a grenade in his hand. If he pulled the pin, he himself would probably be killed. He threw the grenade as if it were a rock. It struck the North Korean in the stomach. Myers leaped forward and, grabbing the barrel of the Korean's rifle, jerked it from him. He was as scared as Myers. In a frenzy of hate Myers beat him with the rifle, cracking the stock. He tossed it back to someone without a weapon. "Cover me. More enemy up here."

While the battle near Hadong was raging, General MacArthur landed at Taegu. During a closed conference with Walker he emphasized the need for the Eighth Army to stand its ground. He declared that there would be no evacuation—no Korean Dunkirk. Walker, too, was determined that there should be no more withdrawals.

Early that evening, while there was still light, the survivors at Hadong were trying to work their way east. They had left behind more than three hundred dead comrades, most killed in or near the rice paddy.

Some, like Lieutenant Makarounis, sticking with his men to the end, had already been captured. But the resourceful Myers was still free. He had led a group towards friendly lines. Upon reaching a village late that night, they split up to find places to sleep.

At four-thirty A.M., July 27, Myers was awakened by one of his men. The enemy was approaching! They hurriedly split into two groups. Myers and five others went up a hill to pick off the approaching enemy. The others moved up the road with their wounded as quickly as possible.

Myers and his people waited on the crest of a ridge for hours. At about nine A.M. a convoy of three-wheeled camouflaged motorcycles, followed by trucks hauling howitzers and several jeeps, pulled into the village. These were North Koreans with captured U.S. equipment. As men hopped out of the trucks and rushed into the river for water, Myers thought, "Now's the time for us to get some revenge." He felt calm and in control. He directed fire at those in the water and then at the fuel tanks of the trucks. Vehicles burst into flame as the enemy scrambled for cover.

Myers headed southeast as fast as a badly sprained ankle would allow and finally came to Americans setting up a roadblock. "Seeing a friendly face was like seeing God." When they finally got back to head-quarters in Chinju, dead tired, he swallowed a shot of brandy, collapsed in a bunk and, after living a lifetime in two days, passed out.

At about four A.M., July 28, he was awakened and told that the enemy was breaking through American lines only about five miles to the northwest. Armed with a new sniper rifle, he jumped into one of the trucks bound for the front lines. There he and 125 others marched up a hill to the crest of a ridge. A sergeant was in charge, but there were no officers. Who, Myers wondered, would lead them into battle this time? They spent all of the next morning digging in on the ridge and preparing positions. In the afternoon Myers darkened his powder-burned face with mud and stuck on a few scraps of brush for camouflage. Then he moved a half mile forward to the finger of the hill so he could see what was taking place. Below, trucks were unloading North Korean troops. There were thousands of them! Less than half a mile away! He was tempted to use his sniper rifle but decided to hold off. Then a runner came up and told him to get back to the ridge. But Myers said he was doing something important. He told the runner to take a message back to battalion. A substantial enemy contingent was out front and they should call in an air strike and artillery as soon as possible. Once the runner left, Myers returned to his observation position.

More than an hour passed and then came a roar from the south. At least a dozen Navy Corsairs and one Mustang moved in, causing the enemy troops to scatter in all directions. One group ran into a building. A Corsair swooped down and Myers saw something tumble out. Then the building seemed to explode. Three soldiers ran through a back door and plunged into a rice paddy. Myers brought down two North Koreans with the first clip but it took nearly the entire second clip to deck the third man. He continued firing until his arm, still sore from yesterday, ached.

All at once the P-51 glided down at him! He waved with his free arm, motioning the pilot where the enemy was. At the last moment the Mustang slid off to the right. The pilot waggled his wings and waved at Myers.

He fired another clip for good luck before returning to tell his comrades what they could expect that evening. It began to rain a little at midnight. All was quiet, but he knew the enemy would be back. Near the bottom of the hill a friendly booby trap went off. The enemy was directly below and coming up the hill. Two men ran past Myers. Not sure whether they were friend or foe, he yelled at them, "Get down!" A silhouette suddenly popped up on the hill to the left and fired twenty rounds at the two running figures. The shots appeared to be coming from the rear. How could the enemy have got that far?

He took aim at the silhouetted figure. It might be the enemy, but he didn't want to take a chance. Myers crept close. "Hey, you GI?" No answer but Myers could see the man tense up and raise his weapon. He thought feverishly. Who the hell could it be? The sergeant in charge of the position? "Sarge, is that you?" he yelled. The figure relaxed. It *was* the sergeant. Myers jumped forward. "Halt!" said the sergeant. "Password!"

"You didn't tell anybody the password," yelled Myers. He yanked the carbine from the sergeant's hand. "Get off the hill or I'll kill you. You just shot two of our men!"

A captain and an MP appeared. "What happened?"

"This crazy son of a bitch just shot two of our men and I told him to get off the hill or I'd kill him." He was surprised to see a captain this far front.

"Who's in charge?" asked the captain.

"The sergeant."

The captain asked Myers how long he'd been in the army, and what experience he'd had. Myers told him he'd only been in the service a short time but he'd been in Leadership School.

"Were you the one who sent in reports on enemy troops?"

When Myers said, "Yes," the captain asked what he'd do if he were in charge of the unit. "I'd hold the position until just before dawn and make the enemy think we were here to stay and would give them hell at first light." Then he'd move off the hill while it was still dark and get across the rice paddy. He remembered what had happened at Hadong. "If we don't do this, we won't have a chance."

"Your plan sounds fine," said the captain and put him in charge of the 125 men. Figuring he'd just been given a temporary battlefield commission, Myers passed the word to hold until he gave the word for an orderly withdrawal just before daylight. Ten minutes later the enemy attacked. Flares went off and he could see a vast sea of North Koreans coming up the hill. At two hundred yards Myers gave the command to fire. They had no machine guns and only a few grenades and it looked as if they'd be overrun and annihilated. Then friendly artillery fired again and the North Koreans ran into booby traps. The hill on the right also joined in the attack, and between grenade explosions Myers could see the enemy veering toward the right. The attack was furious, but just when it looked as if Myers's people would be overrun, the North Koreans abruptly backed down the hill. For two hours there was quiet; then at about four A.M., July 29, Myers again heard horns, bugles and other noises mixed with a babble of voices. It was just getting light, and Myers passed the word to fire with everything and then pull back.

Just as Myers's men opened up on the North Koreans at the bottom of the hill, so did friendly artillery. Many North Koreans were felled, but others came on relentlessly, and when they were within a hundred yards Myers passed the word to withdraw. It would only be a question of minutes before the enemy reached the crest. Myers started down the other side of the hill. Everyone was running, some already trying to cross the river. One man, swept away by the current, shouted for help. Myers yanked him to safety. The North Koreans began firing from the crest with burp guns. Bullets struck all around, but no one was hit.

As they headed for the battalion command post Myers looked back to see North Koreans swarming over the hills like ants. Then Mustangs, flying three abreast, swooped by, launching rockets over Myers's head into the enemy concentration on the hill. Perfect timing! The Mustangs began strafing, and to make things even more miserable for the enemy, 82-mm mortars broke loose with white phosphorous and high explosives. The whole hill erupted with flashes and explosions. He could see bodies cartwheeling in the air like debris. A good day for *us* at last! thought Myers.

At Eighth Army headquarters in Taegu, Walker was mulling over the apparently desperate situation. In the east the ROKs and his 25th Division were gradually falling back. On the Seoul–Pusan highway the 1st Cav had not succeeded in holding the enemy. And in the west a ghost enemy division had suddenly wiped out a new battalion and was driving towards Pusan.

Walker had spent most of the past few days not only visiting units but also being flown over the entire battlefield by his private pilot, Captain Mike Lynch, in an observation plane. He rarely talked to Lynch but did remark that he was pleased with the recent fight the 27th Infantry Wolfhounds had put up in the east. Their colorful commander, Colonel John "Mike" Michaelis, a veteran of the war in Europe, had decisively stopped a heavy enemy attack, destroying six T-34 tanks. He had then withdrawn intact, ready for the next assault. Walker planned to use the Wolfhounds as a fire brigade in case of emergency.

The general did not reveal that, unlike many of his own staff, he was confident he could hold off the powerful NK division in the west that was being slowed down by Private Myers and others like him. Walker remembered how the GIs had withdrawn in confusion in the Battle of the Bulge, only to come back a few weeks later to crush the Germans. Americans, armed properly and well led, would do the same in Korea.

On the afternoon of July 29 he drove with his aide, Major Tyner, to the 1st Cavalry Division command post in a schoolhouse midway between Taegu and Taejon. After Walker questioned Hap Gay's order to withdraw, Gay admitted it might not have been a sound move, but he feared his communications would be cut. Walker tersely replied that there would be no more such withdrawals.

Walker also jeeped east to confer with General Kean, commander of the 25th Division. Then he spoke to Kean's staff. "We are fighting a battle against time. There will be no more retreating, withdrawal or readjustment of the lines or any other term you may choose. There is no line behind us to which we can retreat. Each unit must counterattack to keep the enemy in a state of confusion and off-balance." Tyner was impressed by Walker's calm authority. "There will be no Dunkirk, there will be no Bataan. A retreat to Pusan would be one of the greatest butcheries in history. We must fight until the end. Capture by these people is worse than death. We will fight as a team. If some of us must die, we will die fighting together. Any man who gives ground may be personally responsible for the death of thousands of his comrades." He still had not raised his voice, but his concluding words were etched in his listeners' minds: "I want you to put this out to all your men. I want everybody to understand that we are going to hold this line. We are going to win."

Walker did not reveal that his plan was to form a horseshoe defense in front of Pusan with Taegu as the apex. He intended to pull the South Korean and American troops back to this beachhead, which would soon be strongly supported in the west by the Marines. The movement would not be like the frantic withdrawals of the past, but an orderly pullback.

The word soon spread to the troops. Some commanders thought the order impossible to execute, and some thought the men would take it to mean, "Stay and die where you are." But many of the troops up front were greatly relieved by Walker's order. The day of withdrawals —and this meant bugouts—was over. They all had to stick together.

*   *   *

That night President Rhee ordered his wife to leave at once for MacArthur's headquarters in Tokyo. She refused. "Mommy," said the distressed Rhee, "if the enemy breaks through the Taegu defense line and comes closer to us, I will have to first shoot you and then go to the battlefront." She pleaded. She must stay until the end. She would not be a burden. He held her hands. "I will never form another government in exile," he said emotionally. "Let's have our finale here with our boys."

At the western front, Private Myers, after another night of battle, was given a rest. As he was limping up to his position carrying a heavy BAR, a jeep slowly passed with a chaplain who asked, "Where are you going?" He said he was heading up the river to stop any enemy advance. The chaplain looked at his eyes. "You're fatigued and should get back to the dispensary." Myers climbed wearily into the jeep and was taken to a small concrete farmhouse where wounded were being treated. He leaned his weapon against the wall and flopped down. Hours later he woke up, aware that he was in great danger. He could hear explosions, gunfire and the richochet of bullets. He couldn't find his BAR but came upon a carbine. He could hear screams and explosions in the courtyard. Bullets crashed through the window, ricocheting around the room. People were running past the doorway and he heard American voices saying, "Come this way!" Others in white clothes ran past. He stumbled to the door and began firing at them. To the right about forty were swarming over the hill. He pushed forward the selector spring on the carbine to automatic and began firing at close range. The thirty-round clip was empty and he had difficulty inserting a new clip. Grenades were falling nearby. He ran toward the road, stumbled headlong into a ditch, and lay there a few minutes to determine what was going on. He guessed the GIs had evacuated. He could hear their voices a quarter of a mile down the road. He could also hear the jabbering of Koreans. Once firing ceased he crouched and dashed down the road toward the American voices, despite his sore ankle.

Somehow he made it to safety. Exhausted, he was taken to the Chinju dispensary. His ankle was greatly swollen, but he had no sooner lain down than someone ran in yelling, "Gooks are surrounding the place!" Myers sprang up, grabbed a rifle and limped into the street. He was so surprised to see half a dozen North Koreans that he lost his balance and fell. One Korean slashed at him with a bayonet but it only scraped the side of his leg. He fired from a sitting position, forcing the NKs to take cover, then hobbled to the train station where wounded were being loaded. No sooner had Myers piled into the train than he saw enemy troops running towards him. He and other wounded began firing out the windows. Myers figured he alone must have hit seven enemy before the train finally started.

The next thing he remembered was an ambush, and he again began shooting out of the train window. He passed out, and when he came to, he was on a stretcher and a nurse was trying to take the rifle out of his hand while he mumbled something about getting back to his unit. Next he heard a loud, strange sound and jerked upright. He was in a clean white room between fresh clean sheets. The sun was bright. Through a window he saw a beautiful green hill. Then he saw a pretty lady in a white dress.

"Where are Mom and Dad?" he asked. "Where am I? In heaven?" Once he realized he was alive, Myers wondered if he was still an officer after his temporary battlefield commission. But, of course, he was still a buck private and nobody was writing up any decoration for bravery.

Nevertheless, it was men like Myers that Walker was depending on. The general remembered that in the Battle of the Bulge the lines also had often been nonexistent or fluid. As in Korea, there had been a series of isolated actions with one or two men fighting lonely battles that determined great issues. In this kind of fight Walker knew, through experience, that the American soldier excelled. His love of luxury made him a poor soldier in the first moments of battle. But in the Bulge the GI soon learned that there was only one way to survive: he had to fight. And he had fought, not for political or ideological reasons, but for his life.

Back home General Walker had suddenly become a national figure; his bulldog face was on the cover of the current issue of *Time*. The accurate description of his World War II feats as one of Patton's favorite generals gave the readers confidence in his ability to settle the mess in Korea. "There is no question whatever about the outcome of this struggle," he had told correspondents after the Taejon disaster. "We shall win."

At last an old pro had taken command, and readers felt their sons were safe in his hands.

CHAPTER 8

"General, This Is Complete Chaos and Desolation!"
(July 11–August 13)

1.

While General Walker was pulling his troops into the horseshoe defense of Pusan and numerous vessels from the United States, Okinawa and Japan were bringing in men, arms and equipment hastily assembled by the still-stunned Pentagon, the North Koreans were spreading through occupied territory, attempting to free the south from what they called the slavery of Rhee and the imperialistic Americans.

In this civil war they were winning many adherents to their cause through persuasive pamphlets that declared the U.S. forces were fighting in Korea not for democracy but on behalf of their own imperialistic aims in the Far East. The Americans cared nothing for the Korean people, whom they despised as inferiors; they were using Rhee only as their puppet. "Now they attack our land with their own armed forces and kill Korean sons and daughters by bombing and shootings."

North Korean pamphlets also pointed out that the U.S. forces were sacrificing ROK soldiers rather than waging the decisive battles themselves. They claimed that American "liberation" meant destruction. Some called for cooperation with the Korean People's Army, which wanted only to unify the land into one free country. Who had set Korea free from the oppressive Japanese? Not the United States, which was already an ally of the hated Japanese. The glorious Soviet army had swept down to bring freedom!

The pamphlets also extolled the humanity of the Korean People's Army, expressing pity for those forced to fight in the ROK forces. They would be forgiven. Have no fear! "Quite contrary to the propaganda of Syngman Rhee, the People's Army is a kind, modest, and merciful lot of young people."

Loudspeakers in every liberated town were installed, and posters and placards were mounted everywhere. School texts had been long prepared, and these had a great effect on Korean parents, to whom education was a religion. The most effective propaganda messages were taken from Communist newspapers and magazines in North Korea, China and the Soviet Union.

Such propaganda was followed by action. Kim Il-sung's invasion had been designed not only to bring the South under control by force but also to reform the existing social system. The first priority was land reform. Tenant farming had already been abolished in the North, and working farmers had become owners of the land. Now they were freeing South Korean farmers from paying high rents, and living standards would be raised. Already thousands of farm village committees had been organized to implement radical land reform. Farmers were grateful for the abolition of taxes on summer crops for all of 1950.

But other measures were not popular. At first, arrest and liquidation of key South Koreans was tolerated by those who disliked the Rhee regime, but the excesses soon became abhorrent. Conscription of young South Koreans for the North Korean "volunteer force" did not start in earnest until the morning of July 3, when some sixteen-thousand students from eighty-five schools in Seoul were assembled in Seoul Stadium and Kumwa Primary School. Three days later, recruiting of so-called volunteer forces was drastically enforced.

An Hong-kyoun, a senior at high school, had been shocked to see tanks and North Korean soldiers stream into Seoul. He came from a traditional Confucian family and was opposed to any totalitarian government. He thought Rhee, who had fought forty years for Korean independence, was a great leader, and he was confident that America was going to lead his country to democracy. At first he had not been frightened by the invaders. The soldiers were polite and good-natured. Youngsters like An were invited to theaters to see Soviet movies, a treat, since they were artistic and entertaining films. But soon the young men found the theater doors locked, and except for a few, all were forced into trucks and hauled away. An's family dug a small hole under the floor, where he would hide throughout the day in the dark, sweltering place alive with roaches. At night he crept out to sleep. He became weak from malnutrition.

Some who fled Seoul during the battle returned to find their homes occupied or ravaged by the invaders. But when young Lee Yun-sook and her family returned, their home was intact. Nor was life bad. The North Korean soldiers were disciplined and minded their own business. She heard that many neighbors had been imprisoned, but the new officials announced that only bad people had been put in jail—and none of these had been murdered. *That* was only Rhee propaganda. The new government seemed to serve everyone's best interest, for some of the officials in the Rhee regime *had been* corrupt.

She was free to barter for food with her mother's clothes, since she could bargain best in her family. And because she had gone to high school, she was given a job in a political office answering phone calls and clerking. Then she heard there was work at a bread factory. It was a lovely job! She could eat all the bread she wanted, and was allowed to bring home three loaves a day.

Others were not so lucky. Thousands of Seoul citizens had already been "migrated" to the North. Those selected were given tempting inducements "You, the beloved populace of the city!" announced one pamphlet, "If you migrate to the northern half of the People's Republic there is waiting for you ample food, housing, furnishings, and places of occupation."

On July 11 the Apostolic Delegate, Bishop Byrne, and his secretary were arrested in Seoul and taken to a commercial building which had been transformed into a jail. They were herded into a dark corner of a basement room. Here they found other missionaries, including Father Paul Villemot, an eighty-two-year-old French priest. Later came Mother Béatrix, the elderly superior of the Sisters of St. Paul Chartres, five Carmelite sisters, two Belgians and three more Frenchmen, one of whom was blind, as well as Father Philip Crosbie, an Australian who had been a prisoner of the Japanese during World War II.

The room, about twenty feet square, was crammed with more than three hundred people. Just inside the door sat a guard who kept shouting at terrified Korean civilians squatting before him. This, Father Crosbie soon learned, was Communist indoctrination. Night and day he was forced to witness the badgering, which always ended with the shout: "Confess! Confess!"

After the religious prisoners were cross-examined, they were brought before a People's Court. Here, hour after hour, they were tried before five hundred Seoul civilians sympathetic to Kim Il-sung. When the aged Father Villemot, weak and suffering, asked for a cup of water, the mob cried: "Why befriend this foreign devil?" And when the court asked Bishop Byrne why he had come to Korea and he replied it was to teach religion, the crowd yelled, "Kill the American!"

The judge said, "Either Bishop Byrne will broadcast by radio a

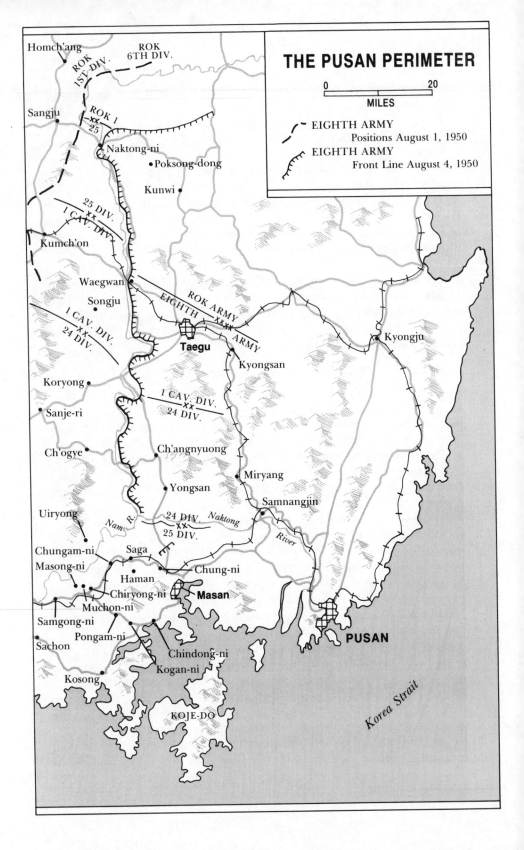

THE PUSAN PERIMETER

0   20
MILES

-- EIGHTH ARMY
    Positions August 1, 1950

EIGHTH ARMY
    Front Line August 4, 1950

Homch'ang

ROK
6TH DIV.

ROK
1ST DIV.

Sangju

ROK 1
XX
25

Naktong-ni

Poksong-dong

Kunwi

25 DIV.
XX
1 CAV. DIV.

Kumch'on

Waegwan

Songju

EIGHTH

ROK ARMY
XXX

1 CAV. DIV.
XX
24 DIV.

Taegu

Kyongsan

Koryong

Sanje-ri

1 CAV. DIV.
XX
24 DIV.

Ch'ogye

Ch'angnyuong

Yongsan

Miryang

Samnangjin

Uiryong

Nam R.

24 DIV.
XX
25 DIV.

Naktong

River

Chungam-ni

Saga

Masong-ni

Haman

Chung-ni

Chiryong-ni

Masan

Muchon-ni

Samgong-ni

Pongam-ni

Sachon

Chindong-ni

Kogan-ni

Kosong

KOJE-DO

PUSAN

Kyongju

EIGHTH ARMY

Korea Strait

denunciation of the United States, the United Nations, and the Vatican, or he must die."

"There remains only one course for me," said the bishop calmly. "That I die." His courage must have impressed the judge, who did not enforce the sentence.

After the trial the missionaries were taken by freight train to Pyong-yang. During the trip Byrne was wretchedly ill, and Father Crosbie recalled the kindness shown to the bishop by three laywomen. To Crosbie it was a touching version of United Nations—an American bishop being nursed by a German, a Turk and a Polish-Korean, while representatives of France, Belgium, Ireland, America and Australia looked on.

They arrived in Pyongyang on Friday, July 21, and were lined up —foreigners first—then marched through the streets to the courthouse. Crosbie wondered what thoughts were in the minds of those watching such a strange parade. Did they feel shame or pride at the sight of these prisoners, eight foreign women, and eight foreign men, two very old, and the others chronically ill?

2.

Far to the south, a British correspondent from the London *Daily Worker* had just been escorted into Taejon by the North Koreans. Alan Win-nington, an intellectual adherent of the Communist party, was appalled at what he saw after crossing the Yalu River. He passed through hordes of refugees fleeing the American bombings. He had seen a Mustang rake the people with its guns. "It left screams, moans, babies' cries, calls for help, blood, bereavement and life disfigurement."

What Winnington had witnessed and heard during his trip to Taejon convinced him that the South Koreans, egged on by the Americans, had started the war. It was just another step of the imperialists to enslave the world. He was now learning of the "very big slaughter" of thousands of political prisoners near Taejon, where villagers had been forced, so he was told, to dig great pits and shovel earth on dead and dying victims. Winnington was shown the valley where a thin crust of rain-washed soil covered rotting corpses. "Through the fissures could be seen among the stinking masses of flesh and bone, hands, legs, grinning skulls stripped to the bone, heads burst open by bullets, wrists tied together." He was told there were at least seven thousand corpses. As they were leaving, one of his escorts sank up to his thigh in the mess below. Winnington pulled him out. For days Winnington could taste and smell and see the waxy flesh and limbs thrusting up through the light soil covering.

Many regarded his story in the *Daily Worker* a manufactured report by a leftist correspondent. But Major Peach, the Australian member of the United Nations observer mission, had earlier reported similar atrocities he had witnessed in the first days of the war.

There were atrocities on both sides, and Kim Il-sung became so concerned by those committed on American and ROK prisoners that he issued this order: "Some of us are still slaughtering enemy troops that come to surrender. Therefore, the responsibility of teaching the soldiers to take prisoners of war and to treat them kindly rests on the political section of each unit." No similar order was issued by President Rhee.

3.

Walker's need to move his 25th Division from the central to the southern front and deploy what troops he could to stop the dangerous drive of the People's 6th Division in the west forced him to withdraw the entire Eighth Army across the Naktong River.

The withdrawal began on August 2 and brought with it frantic refugees, who crowded the highways. Already a half million homeless had crossed into UN-held territory. Their entry was intensifying the panic of the citizens of Taegu. Ambassador Muccio did his best to allay fears, expressing buoyant optimism, shared by his staff, none doubting, no matter how desperate the loss, that UN forces would win. Their confidence did much to allay fears of correspondents, local government officials, and civilians. Walker never wavered in his assurances but did confide to Muccio and Noble that some of his own staff were in despair.

Walker spent little time at his headquarters. Every day he reconnoitered enemy positions at dangerously low altitudes with his private pilot, Captain Mike Lynch, or Major General Earle Partridge, commander of the Fifth Air Force. Afterwards he would ride off in his jeep cavalcade, often erroneously described as a traveling circus with sirens and flashing red lights. In fact, there were only two jeeps, each with a mounted machine gun. Walker, in the first, was driven by Master Sergeant George Belton, who had served with him in Europe. The general's aide, Major Tyner, in the second jeep was thankful not to be riding with the general, since Belton was noted for daring. It was a miracle Walker hadn't been killed in Europe, but like Patton, he always put speed above personal safety; the delay of a minute might cause the loss of a battle.

Both jeeps had been modified, with armor plates welded on the bottom in case they ran over a mine. There was a wire cutter on the hood to sever anything strung across the road.

In addition to his air and field trips, Walker attended Eighth Army briefings almost every morning, as well as meeting often with Muccio. He also made himself available to General Chung Il-kwon and the ROK defense and home ministers, all of whom were invited to special briefings.

By August 2 Walker's troops were enclosed in a roughly rectangular area some seventy air miles from north to south and sixty air miles from east to west. In an area half the size of Maryland, he was to wage his battle to preserve a bridgehead in this Pusan Perimeter.

Those in Walker's small command group had come to know two Walkers. One was the aggressive leader who was merciless when senior commanders made casualty-causing mistakes. The other was a reflective scholar who, after each battle, sought firsthand knowledge of both friendly and enemy actions. Once in the privacy of his jeep or plane, he would critique those actions aloud, citing mistakes made and corrections needed. His aide, Joe Tyner, and his personal pilot, Mike Lynch, were convinced he was really rehearsing. For they noted that his observations became subjects for discussion at his next stop.

They became aware of the great influence of General George S. Patton on Walker. Although he seldom mentioned his old boss in the presence of others, he quoted him often during those critiques. He kept a copy of Patton's *War As I Knew It*, in his quarters. Everpresent on his desk was a summary of "combat lessons learned" as compiled by Third Army during numerous battles in Europe.

The three officers most closely associated with him—MacLean, Tyner and Lynch—became convinced that Walker was fighting the NKPA much as Patton would have. His "armor state of mind" allowed him to assess and respond to the rapidly changing situations more swiftly than the enemy. And his broad experience in mobile operations provided a reservoir of options to draw upon when either surprised by enemy actions or disillusioned by friendly performance.

Walker never forgot Patton's repeated advice that "senior leaders must focus on where rather than how to defeat an enemy." But because of the rapidly deteriorating situation in Korea, Walker had to concern himself with both problems simultaneously.

To do so, he applied two techniques. In determining where critical battles might take place, he used what are known in military parlance as essential elements of information, or EEIs. These are intelligence items a commander deems significant in order to assess an opponent's capabilities. Walker concentrated on enemy movements.

The second technique involved what could be called critical combat indicators, or CCIs. These are the operational items a commander relies upon to determine how and when an enemy will act. Here his focus was on logistics, strength, weaponry and methods of operation.

By the time Eighth Army withdrew to the Pusan Perimeter, Walker had learned much about the enemy. Within days of taking command, he had become convinced that Pusan was Kim Il-sung's final objective. Therefore Walker's first EEI concerned enemy movements in that direction. While concentrating on actions along the Taejon–Taegu corridor, he used the remainder of his small aviation section to monitor movements to the south. His own pilots, flying G2 and G3 staff officers, were the first to detect an enveloping force consisting of the 4th and 6th NKPA divisions. They, too, had been given orders by Walker to "fly until you get shot at."

Within days of this discovery, he faced a serious crisis. Remnants of the 24th Division were all that stood between this new NK force and Pusan. When his pilots confirmed that there were elements of at least two enemy divisions, he decided to move the 25th Division, currently northwest of Taegu, to reinforce the 24th. Having cleared his interior lines of excess traffic, despite Almond's opposition, he was able to move the entire division a distance of 100 miles in less than 24 hours. Dario Politella, who served as Eighth Army's aviation historian, noted that ". . . experts who have since evaluated military tactics during the Pusan Perimeter operations feel that this one shifting of troops during the critical period had been responsible for the successful defense of Korea." Walker's vision and daring had made it possible.

Of equal importance was his selection of CCIs. In reviewing combat actions, he noted a number of key trends. First, enemy forces could only sustain offensive operations for a period of three days. Then they had to break off the attack until resupplied. Second, once casualties were inflicted among first-line units, they had to rely on poorly trained replacements to continue. Third, although the Russian T-34 tank had dominated battles during the first weeks, it was no match for the American Sherman E-8, the Pershing M-26 or the new Patton. Furthermore, successes achieved by the new 3.5-inch rocket launcher had instilled a new confidence in infantrymen when facing NK armor.

His most important finding concerned combat methods. The North Koreans had proven to be masters of the double envelopment. And they applied this scheme at all levels, from company to field army. But Walker noted a fatal flaw. Whenever UN forces disrupted an attack, a lull always followed as the enemy sought to regroup. He decided to exploit this weakness by applying a tactic the Germans had used against him in Europe. They would delude by appearing to be present in strength at a given point. When U.S. forces deployed for an attack, the Germans would distract them by appearing to provide a safe flanking route. But when the Americans sought to execute such a movement, they would attack by fire to inflict maximum damage. Once done, they would disengage.

Walker tried to teach this tactic to his subordinate commanders. But, once more, lack of experience was his greatest enemy. Only Colonel Mike Michaelis had sufficient combat acumen to grasp the concept. He developed an "inverted snake procedure" following Walker's advice. Time and again he was able to delude, distract and inflict maximum damage on the enveloping NKPA forces before disengaging. His success earned Michaelis and his Wolfhounds a prominent role in battles where the need for ingenuity was critical.

Walker's greatest challenge was to devise a scheme for defense of the perimeter. Again, Patton's sage advice played a role. He remembered a letter of instructions Third Army had issued to general officers in September, 1944, when lack of supplies forced them to halt. It was one of the few times in Patton's career when he was forced to assume the defensive.

Walker had to modify the letter to fit his own situation. It had been written to cover a temporary defense pending renewal of the offensive. He was a long way from achieving that status. Patton had not wanted the enemy to recognize his scheme as being defensive in nature. But Walker had no choice. Third Army had been made up of veterans who could respond to combat challenges with minimum warning. Eighth Army was still an inexperienced force paying heavily for its mistakes. Patton had inflicted such damage that enemy commanders were reluctant to challenge him while NKPA successes against UN forces had whetted their appetite for ultimate victory. Lastly, Patton and his commanders had come to know the enemy they were facing and how to deal with them. Walker and his subordinates were still learning.

Applying Patton's ideas, he developed his plan. He would begin by establishing "a thin outpost zone backed at suitable places by powerful mobile reserves . . . with all possible avenues of tank attacks registered in by all [artillery] batteries . . ." Defense within units of battalion-size and smaller would consist of "mutually supporting small groups arranged in depth and completely wired in . . . with mines in place." To prevent envelopments or ambushes, he directed that units would "use roads to march on and fields to fight on." Confident that these criteria were sound, Walker set out to build his perimeter defense.

4.

When Maggie Higgins learned that the "fire brigade" of Colonel Mike Michaelis was in action at Chindong-ni, a small town on the southern coast, thirty-three air miles from Pusan, she drove a borrowed jeep over the mountains to where she found Michaelis in a battered schoolhouse.

The next morning, while she was finishing breakfast, a fusillade of small-arms fire hit the schoolhouse and cracked the windows. A grenade exploded on the wooden grill where she had slept. Everyone started to run, but bullets from two directions made them hit the floor. Higgins wondered what had happened. They were miles behind the front lines. How could the Reds have come so close? What had happened to the perimeter defense?

The battle raged. Someone brought three wounded prisoners into the room. They crawled on their stomachs making moans like injured puppies as bullets cut through the paper-thin walls, ripping up the floor-boards. Higgins mumbled to Harold Martin of *The Saturday Evening Post* that it looked as if they would have an intimate account of the battle for the public.

As she started toward a window, she saw that the three prisoners were lying dead in their own blood. She leaped out the window; officers and noncoms were trying to dodge the incoming fire and locate their men. Michaelis, his executive officer, and company commanders were beating GIs out from under jeeps and trucks, forcing them to get the hell to their units. An officer shot and wounded a GI machine gunner who had gone beserk and was firing at his own vehicles and men.

An emergency command post was set up between a stone wall and the radio truck, and Higgins heard a reconnaissance lieutenant report that a new group of enemy forces was massing in a gulch to the north and that several hundred North Koreans had just landed on the coast a thousand yards beyond.

She tried to say something to Martin, who was writing in his note-book. But her teeth were chattering uncontrollably; only a disgraceful squeak came out. For the first time in the war, she experienced the cold, awful certainty that there was no escape. "As with most people who suddenly accept death as inevitable and imminent, I was simply filled with surprise that this was finally going to happen to me." She felt comparatively easy and her teeth stopped chattering. And when Michaelis asked, "How you doin', kid?" she was able to say, "Just fine, sir."

Ignoring bullets, he jumped up and yelled, "Cease firing! Let's get organized and find out what we're shooting at!"

Gradually, order was restored. A recon officer reported the "enemy" landing on the coast was an ROK unit coming to help. On the crest of the hill two enemy machine guns were eliminated by A Company, led by its commander, Captain Logan Weston. He limped down to get a wounded thigh treated in the schoolhouse, where Higgins was helping a doctor administer plasma. He went back up the hill and half an hour later came down again with two more bullets in his shoulder and chest. As he sat smoking a cigarette, he said calmly, "I guess I'd better get a shot of morphine now. Those last two are beginning to hurt."

After the battle, Higgins prepared to leave, taking a carbine in her jeep. She asked Michaelis if he had any message for General Kean. "Tell him that we will damn well hold."

5.

On August 3 Truman and the National Security Council discussed the hasty trip MacArthur had made three days earlier to explain as tactfully as possible to Chiang Kai-shek that any Nationalist raid on mainland China would be intercepted by the U.S. Seventh Fleet. MacArthur's brief statement to the press caused little stir, but a communiqué by Chiang was a bombshell. He stated that the talks had covered not only the joint defense of Formosa but "Sino-American military cooperation." Victory over Mao's mainland armies, he concluded, was now "assured."

Chiang's statement infuriated both Truman and the Pentagon. They wanted no trouble with Mao that might result in his entry into the Korean war. Acheson agreed and, irked that MacArthur had kissed Madame Chiang's hand, shot off a testy message to the American ambassador in Tokyo, demanding a full report on the talks.

MacArthur affected surprise at the sensation he had caused. The mission to Formosa, he said, had not been *his* idea. Furthermore, his own statement had been discreet. But after Acheson's insistence he be reprimanded, Truman informed the general that he was sending Averell Harriman to Tokyo to discuss the Far Eastern political situation. "As a soldier," MacArthur told the urbane Harriman, "I will obey any orders that I receive from the president. I have discussed only military matters with the generalissimo."

Truman was generally reassured by Harriman's report. He sincerely shared MacArthur's conviction that they should fight Communism everywhere, except for Formosa. And so the president told a press conference that he and MacArthur saw "eye-to-eye on Formosa." He assumed that this "would be the last of it."

6.

On August 2 the *Clymer*, the lead ship of the convoy carrying U.S. Marines to Korea, steamed into Pusan Harbor. Its troops, the first contingent of the 1st Provisional Marine Brigade, crowded the rail to hear a tinny rendition of "The Marine Corps Hymn" by an enthusiastic Korean band.

On the pier, Brigadier General Edward Craig, commander of the brigade which, with its air components, would consist of 6,534 officers and enlisted men, was dismayed to see Marines hanging over the rails and waving as if they were landing in San Diego. He shouted up to an officer, "Did you get my orders?" He had sent a radiogram saying the men should be ready for combat on landing.

"No, sir."

There was bedlam on the Pusan waterfront as ship after ship arrived and thousands of Marines poured onto the docks. At last the *Henrico*, dogged by mechanical failure, arrived carrying the 1st Battalion of the Fifth Marines. Those aboard were disappointed. The hills were beautiful, but only a few buildings in the city reached above the treetops. Private

First Class H. R. Luster, a lanky Arkansan, thought everything looked makeshift and temporary.

"Hey, Ellis," he called to his corporal. "Is this really Korea?" He had the feeling they were not near any war front. "I don't hear any guns."

"Well, we'll soon find out," said Dale Ellis. "Come on, let's go get chow."

For some reason they stayed aboard the ship that night. It was still dark when they were awakened and ordered ashore. The docks lit up as they shuffled down the gangplank and picked up live ammunition, the first Luster had seen since he'd left the rifle range near La Jolla. They were trucked down a brick street that reminded him of Honolulu. After crossing a river about one third the size of the Arkansas, they jumped out of trucks and were ordered to place packs in one great pile. Luster didn't want to leave his Bible, but he realized he hadn't come to Korea to read.

He joined the others marching along a gravel road, weighed down by his thirteen pounds of ammo and twenty-one-pound BAR, in addition to his regular equipment. The Marines trudged past a dead, bloated cow and started through a rice paddy toward a distant hill. The sarge told them this was their spot for the night. They covered their clothes with mosquito repellent. The bugs loved it.

Suddenly a red flare went up. Then came a green one. The enemy! "Ellis," Luster asked his corporal, "can I fire my BAR?"

"Not yet."

Also newly arrived in Pusan were GIs of the 5th Regimental Combat Team, which was attached to General Kean's 25th Division. Because of the dangerous drive of the 6th Korean People's Division, Walker was forced to send both the 5th RCT and the Marines to strengthen the southwestern end of the Pusan Perimeter. These two units comprised six battalions with supporting tanks and artillery and, once in place, would change the weakest flank to the strongest. Here, Walker decided, was the place for the first American counterattack. Task Force Kean, commanded by General Kean, would launch it. Together with the Marines, he would have 20,000 men.

While these plans were being prepared on August 5, a company of the 25th Division took a hill about ten miles north of the schoolhouse where Maggie Higgins had recently faced death. There had been little opposition, but at dark the company was hit by a counterattack. That night Second Lieutenant Chester Lenon of the all-black 77th Combat Engineers was awakened and told by a white captain that the company, which supposedly had scored a victory, was being slaughtered. Lenon, the thirty-one-year-old son of a Louisiana Baptist minister, had fought in Europe as a sergeant and later was commissioned in the Corps of Engineers.

"I've got to mount a counterattack," said the captain, "but I don't have any officers to send up there. It's between you and me."

Lenon volunteered. He gathered about 125 men, including drivers, cooks and clerks, and briefed them thoroughly. This was their baptism of fire, he said, and he made sure they knew how to use rifle grenades. "I have faith in you," he said. "I know you can do it. God bless all of you." Half an hour after midnight they marched toward the dark hill. Lenon had no maps. They felt their way up the hill crawling through underbrush and ravines. Just before dawn they heard occasional firing. At first light, bullets screeched all around them. They had been discovered. Lenon ordered everyone to lie low, then crept forward with a sergeant toward a machine-gun nest, and both flung grenades. Lenon was shot in his left thigh. "Oh, I got it," he said, and passed out.

When he came to it was early afternoon. He couldn't hear anything. He felt numb, but when he tried to move it was painful. He waited. Still no noise. "Is anyone else here?" he said. He raised five voices. All were wounded. They managed to find each other. Lenon remembered seeing a small stream on the way up the hill. "Let's see if we can crawl back down there and get us a drink of water." First they took an inventory. No one had any food. Among them there was only half a pack of cigarettes. By dark they had still not reached the stream. A big man said, "Lieutenant, I just can't go."

"We'll all stay here until you feel better," said Lenon. He was proud of his men. Nobody panicked, no one complained. The big man, a Pfc., said, "I can't move at all. I'm just in too much pain."

Lenon put the Pfc.'s head in his own lap, nursing him. The Pfc. said, "I'll see you, Lieutenant," and died.

"Okay," said one of the men. "There are five of us now."

It was so hot they had to creep under bushes for cover. There was no sound except for several passing planes. They waved but no one noticed them. Lenon began to hallucinate. His wife appeared and he said, "Babe, I'm hungry." She said, "Don't worry about it," and opened a box with the most beautiful steak he'd ever seen.

They continued painfully for hours until finally, parched for a drink, they reached the stream. It was only about six inches wide, and they built a dam to collect water.

On the day Lenon was wounded, August 6, the Marine brigade was attached to General Kean's division and ordered forward to Chindong-ni where Maggie Higgins had faced death in combat. Leading the way was the 3rd Battalion, Fifth Marines, commanded by Lieutenant Colonel Robert Taplett, a thirty-two-year-old from South Dakota. The tall, lean Taplett reminded the battalion surgeon, Navy Lieutenant (j.g.) Robert Harvey, of a racehorse. "What an enlistment poster he'd have made! He spoke in a staccato way with no warmth and seemed hard as nails." Taplett was told there was some trouble at Chindong-ni and he was to relieve the 27th Infantry Regiment.

Taplett arrived at Michaelis's CP about noon. The troops there didn't know where the colonel was. Taplett asked what the dispositions were. Learning he was to cover ground now held by three battalions, he drove forward a mile and a half to find a good place for his command post.

He found an Army CP on the road.

"This is a great spot," the Army commander remarked. "Right on the road."

"You've got to be crazy, mister," said the outspoken Taplett. "In the Marine Corps we stay the hell off roads." He pointed to a slope. "I'm going way up on the top of the reverse slope of that ridgeline. That's where my battalion CP is going to be."

"*You've* got to be crazy," said the GI commander. "That's not the way we do it."

Taplett was no diplomat. "I don't give a damn how you guys do it," he said. "I don't think you've been very successful so far anyway."

As soon as Taplett's CP was set up, he got a message from General Craig; he was being detached from the brigade and would be under the operational control of Michaelis. He was in the Army now. Late that afternoon he reported his location and defensive positions to Michaelis, and then ordered mortars and artillery to lay registration fires just to the north.

Task Force Kean's counterattack jumped off the next morning, August 7; its main purpose was to recapture Chinju, about twenty air miles west of Taplett's CP. The Army 5th Regimental Combat Team was to start from Chindong-ni and head west; the Marines would follow, then branch out along the coast road; while the Army's 35th Regiment, starting thirteen air miles north of Chindong-ni, would meet the 5th RCT at a village named Muchon-ni, halfway to the goal.

The attack had gone well in the north, with the 35th shattering a key North Korean position and then racing towards Muchon-ni. But when the 5th RCT got bogged down at Hill 342 before it could start, General Kean telephoned General Craig, directing him to assume control of all troops in the Chindong-ni area until further orders. It was welcome news to all Marines. Craig jeeped to see what was going on with the 5th RCT. He found the key road junction at Tosan, three miles south of Hill 342, jammed with GIs and equipment. On the high ground, infantrymen were trying to wipe out snipers and infiltrators. No question about it: the 5th RCT was stalled, the GIs done in by the 110-degree heat.

*   *   *

Lieutenant Lenon and his four wounded comrades were still lying near the little brook with no food. During daylight the five men would come out of the brush to wave at passing planes, to no avail. "Lieutenant," said a private named Sanders, "all we're going to do is lay out here and die." He was hit only in one ankle and offered to go down the hill to find help.

"You couldn't crawl two blocks," said Lenon. "I'm wasting you if I let you go."

But the others persisted until Lenon agreed to let Sanders take off.

Far to the north, General William Dean was still wandering behind enemy lines—exhausted and half-starved—escaping capture by his ingenuity.

7.

On the morning of August 10 the 2nd Battalion of the 5th Marines pressed forward from the tangled Tosan junction, where their progress had been stalled for two days. They headed southwest to Paedun-ni, more than an air mile away. General Craig was not happy with the pace and ordered them to continue the march on Kosong, the next target, with "all speed." This was another seven air miles south. About a third of the way there they would have to get through Taedabok Pass, a defile a thousand yards long, where they could run into real trouble.

By midafternoon, the first reconnaissance jeep entered the pass. Suddenly machine-gun fire and automatic weapons raked Dog Company. An antitank round hit one of the jeeps as the Marines took cover in the ditches. At four-thirty P.M., two Marine tanks arrived and drove the enemy into hiding.

Just then, Taplett's 3rd Battalion came up in trucks. The regimental commander, Colonel Raymond Murray, ordered Taplett to get ready to pass through the 2nd Battalion. The two men climbed a rise where they could peer down on Kosong, five miles away. Murray ordered Taplett to continue the attack immediately.

As Taplett's men started down the road, an F-51 streaked out of the sky and began to strafe them. Shells hit the hard road and exploded on contact. Someone yelled, "Get out the air panels!" But the attack by the U.S. Air Force was over. One Marine had jumped into a bush for safety and landed on top of a North Korean, who leaped out firing his submachine gun. After six rounds he dropped the weapon and tried to run away, but a dozen slugs hit him in the back.

After a talk with Taplett, Murray went down to see Lieutenant Colonel Harold Roise, commander of the 2nd Battalion. Neither Roise nor anyone else knew exactly where the enemy positions were, and Roise's S3 offered to lead a patrol to find out. Major Morgan McNeely headed down the hill in a jeep with a radio operator and a three-man fire team. All were killed.

That night Taplett got orders to continue the attack at eight the following morning, August 11. He in turn ordered G Company to lead. At first light they were hit by a brief assault. Although the attackers were wiped out, First Lieutenant Robert Bohn was hit in the neck and shoulder by grenade fragments. The wounds weren't serious enough for evacuation and Bohn told a corpsman to dress him up, but G Company was almost half an hour late reaching the line of departure.

Colonel Murray was furious. "When I say 0800, I don't mean 0801!"

They did kick off at eight-thirty, and despite his wounds, Bohn was eager to fight. The main body started down a single-lane gravel road and headed for Kosong. The sun was already scorching. Bohn sent out flank patrols and guards to the high ground. He told them to run, and kept relieving them so the fast pace could continue. He knew that only speed could prevent an ambush.

Bohn stayed with the first platoon and could see the men ahead checking under culverts for mines. At a blown-up bridge over a dry river, someone saw movement underneath the wreckage. After a BAR-man sprayed the area, he saw he'd hit a Korean woman and several children. The Marine dropped his weapon in horror and began sobbing. "Hey," said Bohn, "what if that wasn't a South Korean woman down there?"

Guessing that the woman thought the Americans had done this on purpose, Bohn asked a South Korean interpreter to tell her it was a terrible accident. At first she refused treatment by a corpsman, but finally, and reluctantly, she accepted help.

Bohn continued the fast pace despite increasing heat. Everything was working. This smooth, rapid movement was about the most satisfying thing he'd ever done in combat.

Taplett ordered Captain Joe Fegan's H Company to make a turn to the right and sweep into Kosong. Bohn would drop in behind. Taplett then sent up two tanks to reinforce Fegan while he himself went up front with his forward air controller, First Lieutenant Daniel Greene, in the radio jeep. They came to the blown-up bridge.

"Well, what do we do now?" asked Greene.

"It's simple. Put on a backpack and go up to the point."

"Colonel, you're going to get me killed."

"No, Danny," said Taplett, who couldn't imagine himself getting killed, "'cause I'm going to be right with you and make sure you get there."

Greene followed Taplett and the radio operator to the outskirts of

Kosong, where they found a large schoolhouse and set up a CP. A little later a jeep towing an ambulance came roaring from behind. It careened past them and turned right towards Sachon. In seconds came three quick explosions. One round went through the jeep, killing two sergeants. Another round smashed the ambulance, killing the driver and corpsman.

If Fegan had gone first with four tanks loaded with his entire company, it would have been a catastrophe. Taplett sent forward a fire-team patrol to find the exact position of the antitank guns. There were two, and Fegan's tanks efficiently knocked them out, then discovered a third antitank gun, which had run out of ammo. This too was wiped out and the attack began with the tanks leading. Taplett was right behind H Company with his forward CP. He didn't even send patrols on the side. Bohn brought up the rear. They made good progress but Lieutenant Greene was nervous.

"You know, Colonel," said Greene, "I can't think why the forward air controller should be up with the point. All that's ahead of me is a fire-team."

"Well, Danny, that's the way it is. We'll soon know if there's any opposition. If they start shooting, then we'll take some cover."

Whenever there was opposition Greene would call in air coverage and then Taplett would rake the hillside with all his weapons for about five minutes. On each occasion the column stopped only briefly. It was working so beautifully that even Taplett was amazed. "Danny, too bad you weren't with us at Camp Pendleton. Everything is going just the same way."

Once, when the column stopped, Private First Class Fred F. Davidson, a tall, lanky, blue-eyed Oklahoman who believed in America and the U.S. Marines, suddenly had to defecate. He went to an almost dry creek on the left side, thinking how strange it was that humans always wanted to do this out of sight of other humans. He slid down the five-foot embankment on his rear. As he got to his feet he saw a North Korean peering through the bushes at the Marines on the road. He was about fifty feet away from Davidson and apparently hadn't heard him slide down the embankment. The man's back was toward Davidson, who quickly raised his carbine, sure it was set on automatic fire. Davidson pulled the trigger. Nothing! The damned safety was on. Without taking the carbine from his shoulder, he searched for the safety catch with his fingers. He found it and pushed. But instead of a burst of fire, the loaded thirty-round magazine dropped from the carbine to the ground. He'd pushed the wrong catch. The startled North Korean soldier turned around to face Davidson for the first time. Davidson retrieved the magazine with the enemy staring at him in wonder. Davidson pulled back the bolt, rammed a round in the chamber and pulled the trigger. This time it *was* on full automatic. The bullets ripped across the North Korean's body from his crotch to his chest and he dropped on his back.

Davidson jumped across the brook bed. The man's eyes were open but he was dead. He kicked the burp gun away just in case the North Korean was playing possum and went through his pockets. All he had was a pack of Korean cigarettes.

By now the place was full of curious Marines trying to see what the shooting was all about. They crowded around the body to get a good look at a dead enemy. Then they heard the column start moving and hurried back to the road. Davidson forgot he had to defecate. He was thinking this was his first true kill. Every other time he'd fired he never knew his bullet had actually killed a man. There was no doubt this time. It was all *his*.

Just before Taplett was preparing to enter Kosong, a division of VMF-323 Corsairs had swept down to strafe more than one hundred enemy vehicles trying to escape the 3rd Battalion. The North Korean column telescoped to a grinding halt with trucks and transports crashing into each other and bouncing into ditches while troops scattered into the hills. The pilots began rocketing individual targets. Despite intense automatic and small-arms fire from the enemy, the Marine pilots persisted and set afire at least forty vehicles before being relieved by another flight of Corsairs and U.S. Air Force planes.

When Taplett's battalion finally reached the debacle they were amazed to find in the wreckage some captured American jeeps, Russian jeeps and trucks, as well as duffle bags containing Russian officers' uniforms. Then the order came from General Craig to stop the attack. The 1st Battalion would pass through the 3rd Battalion in the morning. Taplett and his communications officer, First Lieutenant Hercules "Herb" Kelly, walked back to find a suitable CP and fifty yards off the road came to a streambed where Taplett saw a dead North Korean. At first he was going to use the body as a bridge but then thought that wouldn't be a nice thing to do. He'd jumped across and taken several paces when he heard a shot. He turned to see Kelly with a smoking .45. "What the hell are you firing for?"

"Colonel, I just saved your life. That gook in the ditch wasn't dead. If I hadn't been right behind you, he'd have cut you in half with that burp gun."

Taplett started to shake. "Well, maybe we'll just set up alongside the road tonight." It had been a long day, and it could have been his last. "Deploy the two companies ahead on the right and left of the road. And for once, I'm going to violate my principles and just take that clump of trees over there for a CP." He looked around. "I don't think they have any artillery; otherwise I'd climb that slope and set up there."

8.

August 11 had been a long day for the entire 5th RCT in its attempt to link up with the 35th Infantry Regiment. Things had gone wrong with the GIs from the beginning. General Walker was displeased with the performance of this unit. While the Marines were roaring through Kosong and proceeding to their next goal, the 5th RCT was still stalled a few miles northeast of the Tosan junction. Although Walker kept pressing General Kean for results, little was being accomplished, and the road back to Chindong-ni, the main supply route, was still under sniper fire. It took three tanks and an assault gun to escort supply columns to the forward positions.

At midnight, the all-black 555th (Triple Nickel) Field Artillery Battalion was emplaced near Pongam-ni, five miles from Tosan. Nearby was the 90th Field Artillery Battalion. Soon after daybreak of August 12 both artillery units were heavily attacked from three sides. The howitzers of the 555th were ineffectual against enemy armor, and the 90th couldn't depress its howitzers enough to engage the T-34's and self-propelled guns. Enemy infantry then closed in on the Triple Nickel emplacements, overrunning their positions by midmorning. The 90th, also savaged, lost all six of their 105-mm howitzers.

At six-thirty that morning the 1st Battalion, 5th Marines, passed through Taplett's lines with the mission of seizing Sachon, moving at a brisk pace. Everyone was eager to get there. But the advance was stopped. With the 555th and 90th Field Artillery overrun and enemy forces ravaging the area, General Kean was forced to call for help from the Marines. At noon a brigade helicopter landed fifty yards away. General Craig got out and headed up the road to confer with Taplett and his staff. Craig reported that the 5th RCT had bogged down and the Triple Nickel Field Artillery had been overrun.

"You're to go back at once," Craig told Taplett, "and contact General Kean of the 25th Division." Taplett would meet Kean a few miles forward of the 25th Division CP at Chindong-ni. "I'll arrange to have your battalion trucked back. You're to find out what the hell the situation is."

By one-thirty P.M. Taplett and Lieutenant Colonel Joseph Stewart, Craig's operations officer, were flying over the area northeast of Chindong-ni. Below they could see artillery pieces, their barrels in disarray. Bodies were lying in a long streambed. Jeeps were on fire. Nearby was a bridge. It was here that Craig had said a 25th Division liaison officer would meet him. He would come in a jeep with a red air panel on the hood. Taplett pointed to the streambed. Nearby was a table covered with a white sheet. "Somebody's alive down there," he told the pilot. On the ground a jeep approached, but it had no red panel.

The helicopter landed. Taplett and Stewart got out and approached the jeep. "Who the hell are you?" Taplett asked the driver.

"I'm Lieutenant Tolman." He was from the 25th Division and commanded an armored recon company with several personnel carriers and troops. He told how the Triple Nickel had been slaughtered. "I've been trying to go up there and rescue some of the people, but every time I do we get shot at."

They walked up to the table Taplett had seen from the air. An artillery lieutenant colonel was sitting there with several officers. They were getting ready for lunch.

Taplett was stunned. The damned table was set with glasses and silverware. Everyone seemed in complete shock. They'd been overrun and lost all their batteries except one. They had no idea where the 5th RCT was.

"For Christ's sake!" exclaimed Taplett. "Where's the 25th Division CP?"

No one knew.

Tolman offered to help Taplett and Stewart find General Kean, and the three drove back in a personnel carrier to Chindong-ni. On the road were many long strands of wire. Since Tolman had a phone set-up, Taplett suggested they tap into the lines. "Let's see if we can find a live one so we can talk to somebody."

They tapped about forty lines but couldn't raise anyone and returned to the streambed, where the helicopter was still sitting, its props turning. The pilot said a message had come from General Craig. Tap's battalion was en route in trucks to the streambed near the 555th wreckage.

"There are two roads," said Taplett. One went through Kosong and the other was a shortcut into the mountains. "That's where the artillery commander told us all the gooks were." He had to make sure that Major John Canney, his exec, was taking the correct road. He boarded the helicopter and told his pilot to look for the leading elements of the battalion.

They flew up along a ridge. It was empty. As they started toward the other road Taplett spotted his 3rd Battalion. Canney was sitting in Taplett's radio jeep smoking a big black cigar. They waved at each other and Taplett kept yelling, "Go back! Over the other road!"

Canney waved back, yelling, "Yeah, yeah!"

"They're too far committed down this road," Taplett told the pilot. "Let's just fly up ahead of them and see if we can see any likely resistance." There was none, and Taplett started leading his battalion from the air.

He still had no instructions on what the hell to do, and finally raised Craig. "General," he said, "I haven't been able to find the 25th Division CP, nor the officer I was supposed to meet at the bridge to give me orders. This is complete chaos and desolation! Nobody knows anything." He admitted that he didn't even know where the enemy was—probably on the high ground above the remnants of the Triple Nickel Field Artillery.

Craig himself had just been ordered by General Kean to commence a tactical withdrawal from Sachon. The preparations lowered the spirits of the Marines, who believed they had smashed the enemy in the Sachon area. Instead, they were giving back all the territory they had won at such cost. Exhausted and hungry, all they were looking forward to was a hot meal. They hadn't even had coffee or soup, and now they had to watch all the food and PX supplies being burned so the enemy couldn't get them. What the hell kind of a war was this?

Taplett's battalion arrived at the streambed near dusk and again he radioed General Craig for instructions.

"Do what you think is necessary," he said.

Taplett ordered an attack on the high ground north of the streambed. G and H companies started up the precipitous slope, and by nine P.M. both Bohn and Fegan reported that their positions were secured against little opposition. Taplett ordered them to set up a defensive perimeter.

During the night, Brigadier General George Barth, commander of the 25th Division artillery, finally arrived at the streambed. He asked Taplett when his battalion would be ready to attack. "I have two companies at the first objective," he said. Barth congratulated him on his promptness, approving Taplett's plan to seize the rest of the dominating high ground in the morning. The general ordered several light tanks and three armored personnel carriers to support the Marine attack.

Early the next morning, on Sunday, August 13, a Catholic chaplain, Father Bernard Hickey, held services. Then Taplett's attack started. All at once enemy machine-gun bullets zinged overhead. Marines jumped to the right to avoid the fusillade, but there were no North Koreans in sight. By ten A.M. G and H companies were in possession of the two commanding ridges. And no one had been hit. Nor had they hit anyone.

Back at his CP, Taplett learned that the GI troops supposed to relieve the 3rd Battalion had not arrived. He told Canney to find them. The exec tried, but in vain.

"They've got to be someplace," said Taplett. "Every time I call brigade they say the army outfit is nearing our position."

Finally, at about two P.M., Canney did run across the army outfit that was supposed to relieve them. He told an Army colonel where the 3rd Battalion was located. "You're to relieve us of our positions."

"Like hell I am," was the answer. "I'm going to set up here." The spot was a mile and a half to the rear of Taplett, and the irate Marine colonel called Craig. "General," he said, "this Army outfit doesn't want to relieve us. What do I do now?"

"Pull out," said Craig.

Taplett, disgusted, ordered his exhausted 3rd Battalion to board trucks and head for a rest area near Miryang.

9.

Early that same Sunday morning—only a few miles to the rear of the Triple Nickel wreckage—Lieutenant Lenon and his men were still lying near the little stream. He had kept up the spirits of his four men despite terrible pain, exhaustion and no food. He had lost considerable weight in the eight days since being wounded and was as gaunt as a skeleton. In his semidaze he heard someone calling out, "Hooo!" but was afraid to answer. It could be a North Korean. The cries came closer, and finally he knew it was an American voice. His answering shout was faint and cracked. Help had finally arrived. It was Lieutenant Bussey with a rescue party. Bussey, who had fought so effectively at the victory in Yechon, learned from Sanders who had crawled out to get help, that four comrades were still alive. Sanders had been captured and brutally beaten by North Koreans before being left for dead in the ditch where Bussey found him.

The four emaciated men were carried as gently as possible down the rugged hill. It was a slow, painful trip. The bearers had to relieve each other every few minutes because of the steep terrain. But Bussey, a born leader, knew how to get the most out of his men, and after five grueling hours the wounded arrived at an aid station. Bussey had carried Lenon the entire way himself.

Lenon was conscious on the trip back. He didn't know how seriously he was wounded, only that he hurt. A sergeant with a clipboard asked him his name, rank and serial number. "Sergeant," said Lenon, "I have barely enough strength to tell you I am hungry. I'm answering no more questions until you give me something to eat." He was fed a thimbleful of some watered-down soup, but they refused to give him anything else.

He asked, "How long will it be before we can get back there with the rest of the fellows?" He was told he would never walk again. But Lenon, a religious man, wouldn't believe this, even though he couldn't feel his bad leg and now weighed only a little over a hundred pounds. He had arrived in Korea weighing 220.

The rescue of Lenon and his comrades was one of the few positive events that day in the area of Task Force Kean. The first American counteroffensive collapsed, and by nightfall Task Force Kean was at almost the same position in which it had started. Although Murray's 5th Marine Infantry had wreaked havoc on the 6th Korean People's Division with the cooperation of air and artillery, it had been forced to give up all the territory it had won.

The Americans had far outnumbered the North Koreans; their artillery was far superior and their air power was overwhelming. Yet they lost. The North Koreans' victory came not only from the poor performance of the 25th Division but also from the dogged, courageous actions of Kim Il-sung's soldiers, who did not panic when outflanked and fought tenaciously in unconnected groups. Although the Americans were mobile and could control the roads, it was the North Koreans who dominated the mountains. They could climb all day in the terrible heat, whereas the bigger and stronger Americans collapsed.

The North Koreans refused to fight a Western-style war, with units neatly connected. The Americans rarely knew where their enemy was. It was a new kind of war, with regular People's Army troops often fighting like guerrillas, changing into the white dress of farmers and striking from behind. America, the mightiest nation in the world, was learning that power and technology were not enough in Korea. Could they profit by the bitter lessons of the past week?

PART III

THE PUSAN PERIMETER

CHAPTER 9

The Battle of the Naktong River
(August 14–23)

1.

As the North Koreans closed on the Pusan Perimeter, Monday, August 14, the main target—Taegu—became a city of terror. General Walker was faced not only with the collapse of Task Force Kean in the west but also with two enemy crossings of the Naktong River, one fifteen air miles northwest of Taegu and the other at Yongpo, fifteen miles to the southeast. The river, flowing from north to south, was vital to the defense of Taegu. More than a week earlier, two North Korean divisions had crossed the Naktong, and forward elements were less than twenty miles due north of the city.

Another disaster was brewing thirty air miles to the south, near Yongsan. The 4th People's Division had crossed the Naktong eight days ago and now had breached the perimeter with a large bulge which threatened to reach Miryang and cut the main supply highway from Taegu to Pusan. Despite despair among some of his staff officers, Walker remained cool and was preventing disintegration of the perimeter by prompt shifting of special troops to the most endangered positions.

The growing noise of enemy artillery unnerved the people of Taegu, since it indicated that Kim Il-sung's troops would soon cross the Naktong River in force and seize the city. At Rhee's residence Ambassador Muccio, concerned for the safety of the president, was suggesting the government

149

move south to the island of Cheju, safe even if the entire peninsula fell into North Korean hands. Rhee could form an exile government there.

Rhee angrily drew his pistol and advanced on Muccio, who paled. Madame Rhee was also shocked. "I am going to use this gun to shoot my wife when the enemy appears. Then I'll use the last bullet on myself." Rhee was trembling with indignation. "We have no intention of moving our government outside of the land."

Muccio, though a courageous man, said not a word but hastily departed.

In New York City, Edward R. Murrow was recording a broadcast for the 7:45 P.M. news, a startling condemnation of the conduct of the war in Korea. Murrow had witnessed the disorderly retreat to Taegu as well as the desperate fight around the Pusan Perimeter. He was shocked by the humiliating defeats. There had been nothing like this in the European war.

"This is a most difficult broadcast to do," he began. "But the question now arises whether serious mistakes have been made." He blamed MacArthur for the disastrous counteroffensive of Task Force Kean. It had vitiated vital defenses and cost innumerable lives, all for nothing. "This was not a decision that was forced on us by the enemy. Our high command took it because, in the words of one officer who was in a position to know, 'We decided we needed a victory.' "

The transcript of this proposed evening broadcast was rushed to Ed Chester, the director of news for CBS. Within minutes it was on its way to a top-level conference that included the CBS president and the chairman of the board. Chester returned with their decision. "It's killed," he said.

There were some protests. But the answer came: "The kill order stands."

Murrow did not resign or go public. But hundreds of correspondents at the Overseas Press Club cabled their protest to MacArthur, and *Newsweek* broke the story. "Murrow's stormy objections brought the censorship problem to a head in the network's newsroom and for other Americans trying to report the war in Korea." Under a picture of the grim Murrow was this caption: "Murrow: Censorship started at home."

While Murrow was being muzzled, General Walker was preparing a decisive attack to eliminate the dangerous enemy bulge across the Naktong, thirty air miles south of Taegu. It was scheduled to begin on August 17, this time to be carried out by the 5th Marines and their deadly Corsairs, along with three GI regiments.

At the same time Walker was deeply concerned about the attacks on Taegu by five enemy divisions from the north and northeast. For the

moment, General Gay's 1st Cavalry Division was holding off those coming from the north, and two ROK divisions were standing off with those
from the northeast. Taegu was the keystone of the Pusan Perimeter and
no one was more conscious of this than Kim Il-sung. He issued an
exhortation to the troops calling for its capture on August 15, the fifth
anniversary of the liberation of Korea from the Japanese in 1945. "Our
victory lies before your eyes." He asked all fighting men to pledge their
lives in the struggle that lay before them.

The day before this anniversary, the 10th People's Division had
already crossed the Naktong River and established a bridgehead, despite
U.S. air strikes and heavy fire from General Gay's artillery. Although
Gay's troops rallied to wipe out the bridgehead by dusk, the action caused
crippling American losses.

Panic reached the government offices in Taegu, where crowds of
politicians and those civilians seeking the favor of Rhee were trying to
find out when the president was going to flee to Pusan. They wanted to
stick with him.

General Walker had already advised Ambassador Muccio to leave
and to persuade Rhee to do the same. But Muccio, threatened the day
before by Rhee's pistol, pointed out that August 15 was the anniversary
of the surrender of the Japanese, a symbol of liberation; the Republic
of Korea had also been founded on the day in 1948. If the government
left Taegu now, morale would collapse. While admitting the wisdom of
this argument, Walker insisted that, if the situation became genuinely
desperate, they would all have to leave.

And so the day of liberation was celebrated formally in besieged
Taegu by Rhee, his Cabinet, the National Assembly, and the heads of
the foreign diplomatic missions. There was a common show of defiance
as well as full confidence that the enemy would be defeated.

While all this was going on, elements of two NK divisions were being
held off, only ten miles north of the city, by the ROK 1st Division led
by Brigadier General Whitey Paik. His right flank was connected with
Gay's cavalry division, but the enemy was trying to drive a wedge between
them. By nightfall an attack on Gay's left flank at Hill 303, together with
pressure on Paik, made it evident to Walker that Rhee must leave Taegu.

About 750 Korean police officers were lined up on the outskirts of
the city to handle the restless crowds. Taegu's normal population of
three hundred thousand had swollen to seven hundred thousand. On
the morning of the 16th, Walker again spoke to Muccio. MacArthur, he
said, was concerned that a sudden enemy breakthrough might result in
the death or capture of the president.

Muccio, accompanied by Noble, who was still armed like a commando, called on Rhee. The president had often told Noble that he
would never retreat again and, if necessary, would fight in the streets

with a hundred loyal men. Until now Muccio had always given the president the bright side of the picture, and Noble backed him up. But today the ambassador solemnly revealed that the troops defending Taegu could collapse at any moment. Both General Walker and General MacArthur urged the president to go south immediately.

Rhee characteristically snapped back that he would never leave Taegu. If others in the government wanted to go, let them. He was staying. He again mentioned that he had a hundred loyal men. All they needed was rifles. Muccio argued that Rhee could not act like a common soldier. The stability of the government depended on him.

"I'll resign then!" retorted Rhee. "Let someone else be president." He raved on and on but finally agreed to fly out the following morning.

2.

Misled by American intelligence reports, *The New York Times* wrote that American and South Korean troops were "still outnumbered at least four to one." The fact was that Kim had only 70,000 while the American-ROK strength was 92,000. Most young American soldiers arriving in Korea were led to believe that the Koreans were an inferior, ignorant, thieving bunch of people—"gooks." Few knew anything at all about Korean history or culture, and almost all were totally perplexed when a Korean would say, "Me no gook. *You* gook." In Korean the word *Miguk* meant "American."

To Captain Jim Hausman, who had worked for years with the ROKs, the stiff resistance they were now putting up came as no surprise, and he had faith that men like Generals Chung Il-kwon and Whitey Paik would perform brilliantly. He was so confident the latter would hold his lines that he never went to oversee him. "You don't need me," he told Paik.

By August 17, the critical point north of Taegu was on Paik's right, at Hill 303. This was an elongated oval mass more than two miles long and a thousand feet high. Whoever held it controlled the Seoul–Pusan railroad and the main highway crossing of the Naktong.

An enemy battalion had crossed the river, surrounded one of Gay's companies and seized the hill. Before dawn of the 17th, two of Gay's battalions, supported by a tank battalion, counterattacked. After heavy artillery preparation and an air strike, the Cavalry infantry stormed up the hill against no opposition. The Koreans, after suffering heavy casualties from artillery and air, had withdrawn. But they left behind the corpses of twenty-six captured Americans. After being stripped of equipment and shoes and made to haul water and ammo up the hill, they had been herded into a gully, hands tied behind their backs. Then four Koreans appeared and spat fire from their burp guns onto the helpless prisoners. Private Roy Manring, a nineteen-year-old from Chicago, managed to burrow under his comrades' bodies and, though wounded in both legs and an arm, crawled to safety to tell his story to shocked troopers.

3.

While the battle for Hill 303 was coming to a conclusion, the 5th Marines were resting near Miryang. They would be there only briefly, for they had been selected to spearhead Walker's attempt to wipe out the enemy bulge south of Taegu. At a staff meeting Craig outlined Walker's plan of the attack, which was to start on the morning of August 17 with an assault on the enemy bridgehead across the Naktong River. Two GI regiments would converge on the bulge from the northeast while the 9th RCT and the Marine Brigade struck frontally, the GIs on the north and the Marines on the south. The latter would hit Obong-ni Ridge, which lay ten air miles west of Miryang. The ridge stretched out like a huge prehistoric reptile, its blunt head extending to the southeast more than a mile before becoming a complex of swamps and irregular hill masses. The reptile's high, narrow spine was a series of peaks ranging in elevation from three hundred to five hundred feet.

The Marines would deliver the first punch of the drive, with the 2nd Battalion seizing the first objective. Then it would be the 1st Battalion's turn, and finally, that of Taplett's 3rd Battalion. At eight A.M. on the 17th the two rifle companies of the 2nd Battalion jumped off abreast to be greeted with a hail of lead. Despite supporting artillery fire, progress was slow and deadly.

By noon the entire 2nd Battalion was wobbling after four hours of fighting and 143 casualties, most of them in the two rifle companies. Then 1st Battalion, under Lieutenant Colonel George Newton, passed through the mauled 2nd to assault Obong-ni Ridge with two companies, Able and Baker. They too ran into a buzz saw, and the commander of Baker Company, Captain John Tobin, was wounded. His executive officer, Captain Francis "Ike" Fenton, took over. Eager to get to Korea, he had been willing to become company exec, even though it was below his rank. His father had been in the Marine Corps for thirty-four years. His younger brother, a Marine private, had been killed in Okinawa; and his wife's father was a Marine colonel. Now, at last, he was in command of a company!

The fighting continued until seven P.M. Then came a prolonged lull, and Fenton was able to tie in with Able Company and prepare for a night defense. While his men were still digging in an hour later, someone spotted two T-34 tanks on the road below. Fenton immediately gave the "flash," reporting enemy tanks in the area. Soon P-51's were scream-

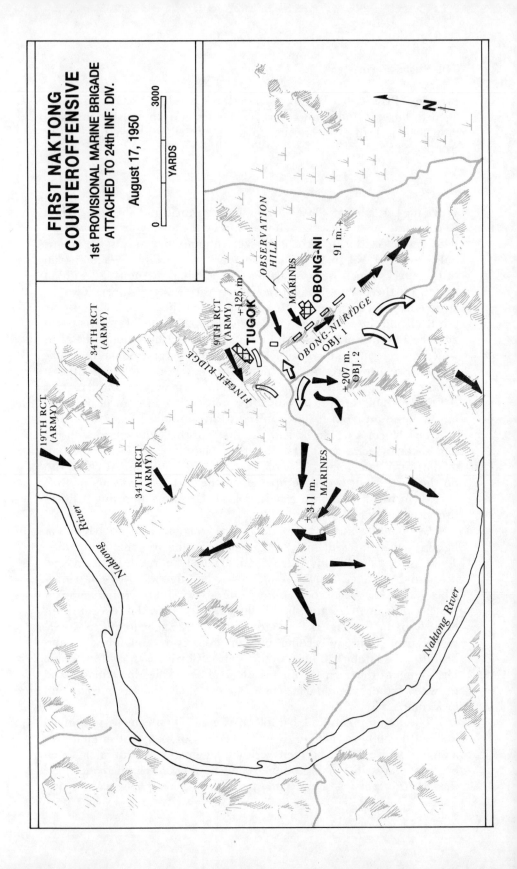

FIRST NAKTONG
COUNTEROFFENSIVE

1st PROVISIONAL MARINE BRIGADE
ATTACHED TO 24th INF. DIV.

August 17, 1950

YARDS

0   3000

N

34TH RCT
(ARMY)

19TH RCT
(ARMY)

34TH RCT
(ARMY)

Naktong River

9TH RCT
(ARMY)

+125 m.

TUGOK

FINGER RIDGE

OBSERVATION
HILL

MARINES

OBONG-NI

91 m. +

OBONG-NI RIDGE
OBJ. 1

+207 m.
OBJ. 2

+311 m.

MARINES

Naktong River

ing down, but their fire was ineffective and the tanks kept rumbling down the road.

While talking on the phone to Colonel Newton, the battalion commander, Fenton noticed a third tank following the two leaders, which were now only a little more than half a mile away. "Let the tanks pass through," said Newton. "We'll take care of them with antitank weapons."

Fenton watched, fascinated. It was like sitting on the fifty-yard line at the Rose Bowl, a good seat for the show that was about to take place. The three tanks were coming along with complete disregard for tactics—as if they owned the world. They should have maneuvered, since there was firm ground on both sides of the road. But they kept heading for the battalion CP. The P-51's continued making their runs on the tanks but they were shooting into Company B's area and Fenton's forward air control called them off.

As the first black tank rounded the corner and neared the battalion CP, 3.5-inch bazookas and recoilless rifles opened up from the high ground on both sides of the road. The first tank was hit in the right track by a bazooka. It kept shooting wildly until recoilless rounds blasted its left track and front armor. Fenton watched it burst into flames as it wobbled around the curve to be battered by a Marine tank's 90-mm gun. It exploded. A man scrambled out of the burning tank but was cut down by rifle fire.

The second T-34 was blazing away with all guns. Hit by a bazooka, it went out of control at the curve of the road, its right track damaged. Another rocket hit its gas tank. Then the recoilless rifles and blasts from two Marine tanks ripped into the crippled vehicle. Somehow its crazy firing continued until seven more rounds ripped through its turret and the hull exploded.

The third tank stopped behind its two blazing comrades. There was a thundering salvo from recoilless rifles, bazookas and the two Marine tanks. It shuddered, then erupted. The entire action took five minutes and put an end to the myth of the indomitable T-34. It had been a great show for Fenton, but he was worried about another night counterattack and cautioned his men to set up a listening watch, with twenty-five percent of the company awake at all times. Baker Company settled down to sweat out the night. Luckily everyone was ready at two-thirty A.M., August 18, when a flare went off and the NKs smashed with great force at the crucial point, where Fenton's company was tied in with A Company.

Fenton's left front held firm against a two-platoon assault, but some North Koreans slipped by Marine foxholes to charge into Fenton's CP. A desperate hand-to-hand fight ensued. Rocket gunners, mortarmen and clerks all fought as infantrymen. In the midst of this melee, Colonel

Newton called and asked how things were going. Fenton said he really couldn't tell. "We have gooks all around us."

"You must hold," said the battalion commander. A Company on the left had had three breakthroughs.

"Don't worry, Colonel," said Fenton. "The only Marines that'll be leaving this ridge tonight will be dead Marines!" He realized he sounded like John Wayne and wasn't too damned sure that Baker *could* hold.

In the pitch darkness, Fenton's noncoms re-formed scattered members of the company and led them in a counterattack. Fenton then tightened his left flank by pulling it over to his 3rd Platoon's reverse-slope position. He had successfully closed out the enemy from his perimeter. But the cost had been high. Baker had gone into combat that afternoon with 190 men and 5 officers. At daylight, Fenton seemed to be the last officer left in the company, and there were only about 88 men out on the line. Morale was high; they had done well in holding their line through the long night. Now they could see groups of NKs on the high ground along the ridgeline on their left flank, and A Company's right flank was down below the red slash of Obong-ni Ridge.

In the assault Second Lieutenant Schryver was badly wounded in the head by a grenade. He had been evacuated to the battalion aid station and Fenton was startled to see Schryver walking up the ridge, his head encased in bandages like a mummy. Fenton was speechless and finally said, "Nick, what are you doing here? I thought you were dead!"

"Well," he explained, "when I was in the aid station I got thinking that very seldom does a second lieutenant ever get a chance to command a company, and I thought your luck must be running short. You know, Skipper, you haven't been hit yet, and you're way overdue. So I figured I'd get back up here so I'd get this company if you did get hit."

Taplett was scheduled to pass through Fenton later that morning, and he and two of his infantry company commanders, Bohn and Fegan, climbed to where they could reconnoiter Hill 207, objective two. Taplett set up his observation post on the northern section of Obong-ni Ridge, while G and H companies proceeded to the base of the ridge. About nine A.M. Taplett called down heavy artillery, as well as air and mortar preparations, on this objective. An hour later Bohn attacked up the eastern spur of the ridge while Fegan started up the western spur.

At first both made slow progress. They could see North Koreans at what appeared to be a regiment CP, although the enemy usually stayed hidden during the day. Marine Air Group 33 blasted the area, shattering communications equipment and weapons of the 18th KPA Regiment. At the same time that Bohn was calling in air support, he was advancing quickly up his slope.

The greatest difficulty to Private First Class Fred Davidson—the youngster who believed in America and the Marines—was the steep climb. It was a damned good thing, he thought, that the gooks weren't putting up much of a fight. At about noon, sooner than expected, he reached the top of Hill 207. He counted eight dead enemy.

Fegan's men had been advancing more slowly against heavy opposition, but finally they were nearing the top of their spur. The North Koreans were fleeing south along the ridge.

The double attack and the tremendous air and artillery fire had ousted the North Koreans. What had begun as a retreat of small forces had become a major rout of the entire 4th NK Division.

Taplett, watching from his OP, could see masses of enemy coming down the slopes and running towards the Naktong River over flat ground. He called in artillery, and their shells caused havoc. Air observers kept reporting to Taplett that there were all kinds of bodies floating in the Naktong.

Nearby, across the valley, Lieutenant Bohn had been "sniping" with a light machine gun. Davidson borrowed an M-1 and joined in the hunt. Through binoculars Bohn was watching the flight of the North Koreans shattered by small-arms, machine-gun, and artillery fire. "Look, Gunny," Davidson heard him exclaim to a sergeant, "they're killing them in the river by the dozens!"

At two-thirty P.M. Taplett ordered both of his companies to come down Hill 207. At the bottom they were led by a platoon of tanks to the base of Hill 311, objective three. Marine planes had already scorched the high ground with napalm while artillery, mortars and recoilless rifles blasted the slopes.

Davidson walked to a spur of Hill 311. To the left was a cane field. He put his carbine on full automatic and sprayed the field with thirty rounds. He didn't know if he hit anything, but started climbing. After a while he passed a North Korean who had been wounded in the legs by the machine-gun "sniping" from Hill 207. Guarded by a Marine, he was smoking an American cigarette and grinning like a monkey.

"Are you in much pain?" Davidson asked.

The enemy soldier nodded. Davidson explained that a corpsman would soon take care of his wounds—and continued up the hill.

The battle of the Naktong was over except for the mopping up.

4.

Fifteen air miles northeast of the center of Taegu, another ferocious battle was being waged, this one in the rugged, barren hills on both sides of a long valley that had once been fertile and peaceful. The area was that defended by Brigadier General Whitey Paik's 1st ROK Division, but such a host of enemy had converged on this approach to Taegu that General Walker had been forced to send his fire brigade to Paik's aid.

While the Marines were seizing Obong-ni Ridge on August 18, Mike Michaelis, now promoted to brigadier general, was ordered to attack north on the road leading to Taejon with the 27th Infantry Regiment of the 25th Division. At the same time, Paik was ordered to attack with two regiments on either side of the almost straight, poplar-lined highway.

Michaelis's trucks rolled northward until they could see NKs and ROKs fighting on the high hills overlooking the road. His infantry dismounted, then deployed with one battalion on each side. Tanks led the way and at about one P.M. opened fire on the mountain escarpments. The rumble of their cannonade made an unearthly echo through the narrow valley. An enemy outpost withdrew, and for an hour the American infantry advanced with almost no opposition. Then Michaelis got word that Paik's two regiments on the high ground flanking the valley had not been able to advance. Michaelis was ordered to stop and form a perimeter defense. A platoon of tanks took positions at the front, with two on the road and four behind in reserve. The artillery set up their guns, and six bazooka teams set up in front of the infantry. Shortly after dark, NK mortars and artillery unleashed heavy preparation fire. Two T-34's and a self-propelled gun moved to within two miles of the American lines. There was a fierce encounter and both T-34's were destroyed. Three more NK tanks came down the road, then suddenly switched on their running lights and scurried back north. Soon after midnight all was quiet. A second, weaker attack was dispersed by artillery and mortar fire.

This was only a taste of things to come for Paik, who had already narrowly escaped capture twice during the past week. Now he and Michaelis faced two strong North Korean divisions, the 1st and the 13th, whose tank regiments had been recently supplied with twenty-one new T-34's.

During the day a public relations officer in Taegu told Bert Hardy, a newly arrived British correspondent, that the other correspondents had cleared out, since it appeared obvious that Taegu was falling. A short, stocky man entered. It was General Walker. Annoyed at the depressing picture the public relations man was giving, he exclaimed gruffly, "Lot of damn nonsense! They'll never take the town. My advice to you is to stay put!"

The past week had been a hectic one for Walker. He was spending most of his days flying low over enemy lines with Mike Lynch or jeeping up front with Joe Tyner. Walker was in his element, sending his fire brigade wherever it was needed most, and quietly relieving officers who were too old or inexperienced to handle battlefield crises. His appearance up front was reassuring to those men whose officers had misled them. He often stopped to give short pep talks to enlisted men. They were up against a tough enemy, he would say, and things were rough, but there would be no bugout back to Pusan. The perimeter was going to hold, and reinforcements were arriving every day.

His appearances on the streets of Taegu were equally reassuring to the civilians. That day shells had landed near the railroad station, and his presence helped turn panic flight into a more orderly withdrawal towards Pusan. Sunday, August 20, was relatively quiet, with U.S. planes strafing North Korean positions so close that expended cartridges fell onto friendly foxholes.

Walker went up northeast to observe how Paik and Michaelis were doing, and returned to the city to tell correspondents that Taegu "certainly is saved." On Monday morning Michaelis's men saw white flags out front. Natives reported that some North Korean troops wanted to surrender. An American patrol received scattered rifle and artillery fire. They found five disabled T-34 tanks.

Late that evening artillery raked the 27th Infantry positions until midnight. Then the People's 13th Division struck at Paik's troops on the high ground and the Americans in the valley. Tanks and self-propelled guns hit the 27th as enemy infantry came forward on both sides of the road. Other infantry attacked on the high ridges.

Pershing tanks held their fire until the T-34's came close, then blasted the lead enemy tank, while a bazooka team knocked out a self-propelled gun. The T-34 in between was trapped and disabled by bazooka rounds. In a battle lasting five hours, the Americans destroyed seven more tanks and three more self-propelled guns, along with trucks and personnel carriers. It was a slaughter, and enemy prisoners revealed that only a quarter of their number survived. To those who heard the shells from enemy tanks and saw the balls of fire hurtling down the road through the night, it was like a bowling alley in hell.

During all this, Paik's men fought valiantly to hold the high ground and prevent the enemy from enveloping the Americans on the road. During first daylight of the 22nd, exhausted groups of his division came down to the valley to bathe in a stream and find food, but they always climbed back to their positions covered by American artillery.

At one point, however, a battalion commander called Paik at his CP and said, "General, I must retreat."

"Retreat? What do you mean?"

"I must withdraw." His left flank was already falling back. "I can't hold."

"You're going to stay there, Colonel, until I come up and investigate." After a short jeep ride, Paik started climbing to the battalion position. Men were fleeing in disorder. Paik managed to gather a large group. "Gentlemen," he said, "I am going to lead you and we are going to attack. If I retreat, you must shoot me." He gave the order to charge and, armed with a pistol, led the way back to the original position. Heavy fire broke out, but Paik continued as if impervious to bullets, followed by the battalion. The enemy started to fall back, and after half an hour his men begged him to stop. He was a division commander and didn't belong up front.

He watched as they retook the hill, then returned to his CP. Michaelis had learned of the retreat and sent an urgent message to Walker, claiming that ROK troops on his left had fallen back and "are not fighting." Paik bitterly protested, and investigation proved that his people were back in place. When Michaelis learned what Paik had done, he apologized and praised him for his heroic performance. From then on they were close friends.

Another North Korean attack that night was easily repulsed, and by early afternoon of August 23 Brigadier General Michaelis reported to Walker that the People's 13th Division, after blowing up and mining the road out front, was pulling back. Walker ordered his fire brigade to return to the 25th Division near Masan; the Battle of the Bowling Alley was over and Taegu was saved.

CHAPTER 10

"This Is an Impossible Situation"
(August 31–September 7)

1.

The first major American–South Korean victory had not only saved Taegu but came at a critical moment, too. Kim Il-sung had just finished assembling 98,000 new troops for a final grand offensive designed to sweep into the Pusan Perimeter on a broad front and drive Walker into the sea.

Some of Kim's officers warned him that he was overestimating the strength of his own troops, which had raced all the way to the Naktong River, and underestimating the staying power of Walker's Eighth Army. The sensational advance south had come at great cost of NK manpower and matériel. UN air attacks had disrupted rail and road communications and had also destroyed vast amounts of ammunition and gasoline bound for the southern front. The People's troops, newly arrived at the Naktong River in preparation for the grand attack, were already suffering from lack of food. Almost a third of them, moreover, were raw recruits, with little training, who had been rushed south so fast that many did not have weapons.

But Kim angrily rejected such advice. Expecting the Bowling Alley to collapse, he figured his troops would easily sweep across the Naktong River. But the Pusan Perimeter, although pierced in several places, was still held, if precariously, by 120,000 Americans and ROKs.

The North Korean commanders were aware of their troops' loss of

161

stamina and, on the eve of the great assault, issued encouraging instructions in hopes of raising morale. Kim's attack, however, did not start soon after sunset on August 31 as scheduled. It did not get under way until midnight near Haman, where Lieutenant Lenon had been wounded. Before daylight of September 1, two battalions of Lenon's regiment had been driven back to high ground east of Haman; and most of two regiments of the People's 6th Division poured through a three-mile-wide gap near the southern end of the Pusan Perimeter. About eight air miles north, the right side of the 25th U.S. Division was also hit hard and, although the 35th Infantry Regiment held its original positions, there were almost 3,000 North Koreans behind its lines by morning. Another eight miles to the north, the 9th Infantry Regiment of the 2nd Division was severely attacked near the NK bulge across the Naktong River, where heavy fighting had taken place two weeks earlier. The Americans had been planning their own offensive and were caught flatfooted. Before dawn North Koreans had split the 2nd Division in two and again owned Obong-ni Ridge, which had been won at terrible cost by the Marines. The 2nd Division commander, Major General Lawrence Keiser, telephoned Eighth Army headquarters at 8:10 A.M. to report the situation; a hole, six miles wide and eight miles deep, had been punched into his line.

At nine o'clock General Walker requested the Air Force to make a maximum effort along the Naktong River in order to isolate the battlefield and prevent enemy reinforcements and supplies from getting through to the advance units. Walker was also faced with the crisis of his 25th Division. To which place should he send his perimeter reserves? These consisted of three understrength infantry regiments as well as two battalions of the newly arrived British 27th Infantry Brigade, which was not ready to fight. Although he now had the 2nd Division, these were troops commanded by a man about whom Walker knew little.

From the very beginning Walker's assessment of NKPA intentions had clashed with those of MacArthur, whose contact with Eighth Army, except for infrequent visits, had been through his staff. This was a new experience for Walker. While commanding George Patton's Ghost Corps, Walker had earned a reputation as being one of America's finest tactical commanders. He was used to talking personally to Patton, Bradley, and, on occasion, Eisenhower during critical phases of World War II. Walker had another problem. As one of Eisenhower's close friends, he was privy to MacArthur's failures as a tactician in the past. From his arrival in Korea Walker never doubted his own fate or how he might be treated by history. But he was too much of a soldier to let it bother him.

Familiar with NKPA tactics, he anticipated a classic double envelopment. Three actions would be involved. He could expect a limited attack to fix the 1st Cavalry and 1st ROK divisions in positions northwest of Taegu. At the same time, he would face major thrusts along the Masan–Pusan corridor in the southwest and down the main east coast road out of Pohang. He had to be ready.

Of the two envelopments, the Masan attack was more dangerous. It was closest to Pusan. Terrain was adequate to support major forces. And, if the enemy gained control of a critical pass south of Miryang, he could no longer mount an effective defense between there and Pusan.

Once enemy intentions had been identified, Walker realized the need to change current dispositions. He withdrew the Wolfhounds and 23d Regiment from the Bowling Alley, returning them to their parent divisions. He requested retention of the Fifth Marines until after the expected assaults. And he reordered staff priorities to ensure rapid response once the battle was joined.

To provide depth in the Masan area, he deployed the Marines behind both the 25th Division in the southernmost sector and the 2nd Division to their north. To cope with northern and eastern threats, he positioned the 19th and 21st regiments of the 24th Division along the axis between Taegu and Pohang. From there, they could either reinforce the 1st Cavalry to protect Taegu, or support ROK units holding down the perimeter's east flank. Finally, all available ammunition was stockpiled at gun sites to ensure sustained support once the action began.

In studying needs, Walker concluded that ammunition on hand was marginal. He asked GHQ to release stocks held to support the coming amphibious landing at Inchon. To him, his own upcoming battle would really decide the Korean issue. His request was denied. Thus, a battle yet to be fought was given priority over a battle that could be lost. To Walker, this was one more example of his stepchild status from the war's onset.

Eighth Army had one major weakness, the newly arrived 2nd Infantry Division. Neither the division commander, Major General Lawrence Keiser, nor the three regimental commanders had ever led troops in battle. The division itself, hurriedly put together, was short of battle-experienced officers and NCOs. Walker could not afford failure on a division scale.

For these reasons, he assigned the 2nd to what he considered his least-threatened sector, the Naktong Bulge. Recent destruction of the NKPA 4th Division in that area, and an assumption that the enemy would commit all forces to support the Masan attack, led Walker to conclude that the 2nd could handle this assignment.

Shortly after midnight on September 1, reports began showing enemy activity along the entire perimeter. The expected offensive was under way. But this time Walker was ready. All his troops had to do was hold the line and inflict maximum damage. If this plan was successful, the enemy would be defeated with minimum loss to his own forces.

By dawn, the 6th and 7th NKPA divisions, reinforced with tanks, were advancing out of Chinju toward Masan in the southwest. North and west of Taegu, elements of the 1st, 3rd and 13th divisions were pressuring the 1st Cavalry and 1st ROK divisions. In the Taebaek Mountains and along the east coast, units of the 5th, 8th, 12th and 15th divisions were moving against the four ROK divisions. Only the under-strength 2nd, the green 9th and the remnants of the 10th Division were unaccounted for. Walker had been right about his plan. He was confident of success.

First indication of trouble came from the 25th Division. There had been a penetration of the 24th Infantry's position. General Kean wanted to commit the 27th Wolfhounds, currently under Eighth Army control, to restore the line. Walker released a battalion for this purpose. Several minutes later, a new request was received for additional forces. A second battalion of the 27th was released.

Before leaving his headquarters, Walker received a call from Major General Lawrence Keiser that his forward units were under attack. This was puzzling. They were occupying what had been assumed to be the least-threatened sector. Furthermore, he had approved a request for the 2nd to conduct a reconnaissance in force to the Naktong the day before. If done properly, it should have preempted surprise. Deciding the report was probably an exaggeration by shaky leaders in their first battle, he asked his Fifth Air Force counterpart, Major General Earle Partridge, to make a maximum effort in their sector along the Naktong River. He wanted to isolate the battlefield and prevent reinforcements and supplies from getting through to any units that might have made a crossing.

In the few minutes it took to travel to the small airstrip where Mike Lynch was waiting, the situation had escalated. It now appeared the enemy's penetration was endangering the 25th's right flank. Walker had planned to visit all the divisions, taking his G3 and Joe Tyner with him. His four-seated L-17 was in readiness. But reports from the 25th and 2nd changed his mind. He shifted to his two-place L-5. This would allow him to conduct low-level observation in the critical area and land if emergencies arose.

He informed Joe Tyner of his intention to assess the 2nd's situation firsthand and climbed into the aircraft. Mike asked where the general wanted to go first. "I don't know where we should begin," he said. "But there's one area where we cannot let them through, and that's the Naktong Bulge." They flew level down the river. Earlier they had discovered two sandbag bridges constructed several feet underwater by the enemy, and had called for bombs. But today the bridges were still intact.

Walker concluded that elements of the North Koreans' 2nd, 7th and 10th divisions had come secretly across the river during the night and were headed for Yongson and then Miryang, the main road and rail corridor from Taegu south to Pusan. Ignoring ground fire, Walker instructed Lynch to get lower. They swept down and discovered the North Koreans had struck between Keiser's 9th and 35th regiments. There was already a great gap in between! The 9th must have panicked and were trying to get south.

They could see the junction of the Nam and Naktong rivers. Here, where the Naktong turned east, there was almost a direct open alley to Pusan, and if the enemy got through, there would be chaos. If the enemy had gotten tanks across, there would be no stopping them.

"Mike," yelled Walker, "could we make it through if we try to go down the river? We've got to see how many are coming across and if they have armor." They had to shout since they couldn't use the intercom system. They decided to skim a few feet above the water. Mike was to look at the right bank while the general checked the left. If tank tracks were spotted, Walker knew he was in real trouble.

Lynch began to fly down the river with the throttle against the stops. At times the wheels touched the water. Catching the enemy by surprise, they passed the underwater bridges in full sight of guards posted on either bank. By the time NKs raised their rifles to fire, the plane had passed beyond range. Walker was relieved. There were no signs of tank tracks.

Returning to the area where American troops had been seen, they could see GIs pouring back through streambeds and trails. "God," shouted Walker. "They're not even massing where they should! We've got to stop them!" But there was no place to land. "I've got to talk to them!" insisted the general.

"Okay," yelled back Lynch, "I'll get up high enough and then kill the motor and hope it'll start again. We'll come right down over their heads and you can yell at 'em."

Lynch climbed up to two hundred feet, cut the throttle and lowered the flaps. The back door was dropped and Walker leaned out and shouted, "Get back there, you yellow sons of bitches! Get back there and fight!" He turned to Lynch. "Have you got three stars on the plane?"

"No, but I've got one of your star flags." Lynch stuck the flag out as they clipped the tops of trees in a creekbed. He now had the motor idling as Walker kept yelling, and put on power just before it stalled. The men were running, many without helmets and weapons. Lynch could hear someone shriek, "They're going to kill us!"

After twenty minutes the plane was drawing enemy fire. "Jesus Christ," said Lynch, "we can't do this anymore!" Besides, the shouting of Walker had no effect. The men were petrified.

As they flew down the road, they could see that the pass was a nightmare. Trucks were trying to come up to the front, while other vehicles were relentlessly heading for the rear. They lowered and circled the pass so they could see what was happening with the 35th Regiment.

Suddenly a line started forming on a hill and vehicles heading forward with ammo began to move. Without getting permission from Walker, Lynch lowered to fifty feet. Walker was amazed at what was going on. "It looks like this situation is being stabilized! Let's go find Dutch Keiser's headquarters."

They flew to 2nd Division headquarters and landed on a road. Both walked into Keiser's tent. "Dutch," said Walker, "where's your division?" Keiser replied that he'd sent an officer to the 9th Regiment to find out what was going on.

"Where are your reserves? What are you doing about positioning your reserves? You can't lose Yongsan. If we lose that, we'll lose Miryang and then Pusan. Now we're in the heart of this whole thing, and you don't know what the hell's going on!" Determinedly Walker added, "I'm not going to lose this battle!"

He walked over to Keiser's situation map. One look told him all he needed to know. In conducting the reconnaissance in force, no effort had been made to provide security between forward elements and the main defense line. The enemy had exploited this tactical mistake.

The officer who had been sent to the 9th Regiment arrived, map under arm, out of breath. "I'm sorry, sir," he told Keiser. "I was delayed. In fact, I almost didn't get back here." Why not? "Because there's a tall, red-faced colonel up there at the pass who said, 'No son of a bitch who is able to fight is going to go past this line!' "

"What did you tell him?"

"Boy, I really had to talk my way out of there. Who the hell was it?"

"That's my G3, Colonel Allan MacLean," said Walker, who realized why the line had miraculously stabilized on the road to Pusan. One good man could do wonders.

When they finished, Keiser started to escort Walker back to the plane. "You get busy now," said Walker. "I don't need anyone to walk me back."

Once in the plane, Lynch and Walker studied the map. Where the hell do we go next? thought Lynch, then said aloud, "This is the Battle of the Bulge revisited. Nobody knows what's going on, rumors are rampant. Guys are panicking for no reason and people are saying the enemy is all over."

Walker said nothing but suddenly rested his hand on the map. Tears rolled down his cheeks. "Here I'm losing the whole army and I can't do anything about it."

Lynch felt bitter. He hated everyone above Walker and everyone below. But that's what you get, he thought, when you take a bunch of administrative guys and give them a command in peacetime so they can get promoted.

Walker said little on the trip back but did admit that they no longer owned the Naktong. He had to find out what enemy matériel was coming across the river. Any heavy stuff? Was he going to have to fight heavy artillery or would there be tanks? All the way back to headquarters Walker wondered if his 2nd Division would hold.

The next day three People's divisions attacked the 1st Cavalry Division, pushing Gay's troops all the way back to the Bowling Alley. Things were so serious at Yongsan that Walker again had to call upon the Marines. With MacArthur's approval, the 5th Marines were ordered to join the 2nd Division in a coordinated counterattack. Upon hearing they were going back into the Naktong Bulge, the 5th Marines were shocked and disgusted. Word filtered down that the enemy had already recrossed the Naktong and were at Yongsan.

"We were beginning to feel like the queen on a chess board going around checking everything," recalled Captain Fenton. Soon after midnight of September 2, his Baker Company moved out.

Just before nine A.M., the 1st Battalion jumped off with Fenton's company on the right. They crossed a rice paddy, wading through deep muck, and met many GI stragglers without weapons, who had been cut off in enemy territory for several days. Most were wounded and all were exhausted. The Marines started up the hill and by late afternoon had seized Hill 117.

2.

That afternoon, on the ridge line leading to Obong-ni River Taplett's 3rd Battalion came across a GI bivouac area. It must have been a command post. Dead bodies littered the ground. Some men were still in sleeping bags or on cots. Laundry hung on a line. Servings of chow were on the tables; they must have been about to eat. Taplett guessed the North Koreans had ransacked the place. The 3rd Battalion moved on, passing through the 2nd Battalion, which had endured many casualties from heat prostration. There was supposed to be a GI unit from the 2nd Division on the right, but Taplett could see no one around. As it grew dark, rain pelted down and the men were told to dig in for the night.

Just before dawn on September 4, Colonel Murray ordered Taplett to contact the Army's 5th Regimental Combat Team, supposedly attacking on the right. Taplett radioed back, "There isn't anybody out there except North Koreans." He sent his executive to locate the 5th

RCT and found that these GIs hadn't even come up to the line of departure far to the rear. A few hours later First Lieutenant Bohn of G Company reported, "There's all kinds of North Koreans coming down the stream bed." Taplett moved his headquarters and service company, which had extra machine guns, to the high ground commanding the streambed. Rarely had this company had such an opportunity. From above, Taplett watched the action. The H and S company began mowing down the enemy with machine guns and mortars. Despite the slaughter, the North Koreans kept coming. Taplett could hear his H and S people yelling and screaming exultantly. "I got one!" "I got one!" "I got *two!*"

At about eight A.M., Murray ordered Taplett to sideslip to the left of the 1st Battalion and attack Obong-ni Ridge with the two battalions abreast. In the process, Taplett's men would have to slog across a wide and muddy rice paddy. No sooner had his troops taken the low hill mass at the base of Obong-ni Ridge than a call came from Murray, "Halt the attack!"

"Gee, thanks," replied Taplett.

"We're going to change the disposition." The Army was supposed to attack on the other side of the ridge but had bogged down. "We're going to consolidate, and I want you to move your two rifle companies. Sideslip them to the right and tie in with the 1/5, part way up the ridge."

But Taplett's forward command group was under heavy enemy fire, and it was late afternoon when he finally crawled out of the paddy— only to be told to report at once to Murray. By the time he reached Murray's CP, the soaked, foul-smelling Taplett was in a rebellious mood. "We can't seem to make any sense out of what George Newton's trying to report to us," said Murray. Newton was commander of the 1st Battalion. "I think he's lost control of his unit. Would you go up the road and see what's going on in the 1/5?"

Taplett said to himself, "For Christ's sake, he's got an S3 and he's got his staff and he's got his exec. Why don't they go up or why doesn't he go himself?" Taplett had a tough enough job ahead trying to maneuver his own battalion.

"What's my authority with George?" he grumbled.

"You find out what's going on," Murray repeated. "And if necessary, straighten out the mess."

Taplett said nothing. Since it was dark, he climbed into the jeep and took the backpack radio operator and two riflemen up the road. As the jeep came around a bend, Taplett saw Newton, Ike Fenton and a bunch of 1/5 CP people standing off to one side of the road.

"Any problems?" he asked Newton.

"No. Other than we're catching hell. Every time I tell Murray we're not going to be able to take this ridgeline tonight because there's just too much opposition, he just tells us to take it."

Taplett turned to Fenton, a close friend. "Ike, everything all right?"

"Yeah." Rain was pelting down. "Regiment won't listen to what we're saying to them—that this is an impossible situation."

Taplett understood, since his people were in trouble too, and they were only on the reverse slope. He'd just heard that troops near the top were getting grenades thrown at them from the other side. He called Murray on the radio. "Everything is under control up here," he said. "George is fine. They're just catching a lot of hell is all. Even my two companies are pinned down. We can't move, especially during the night."

Murray, reassured, said, "Well, we'll halt where we are."

3.

That night, General Walker was forced to issue an order which he knew would endanger the perimeter. He released all his Marines effective the next day. The command had come from MacArthur, who was planning to use the Marines to make a top-secret amphibious landing at the port of Inchon near Seoul. Walker had protested but bowed to the inevitable, even though the situation was critical in the Naktong Bulge and the defensive lines north and east of Taegu were being battered.

By the morning of September 5 the battlefield near Taegu was a quagmire. The Jones twins jeeped forward in the pouring rain, determined to film the action despite the weather. They stopped at a regimental CP and saw its commander silently standing near a radio. Over the static and beating of rain they could hear dim, broken voices from up front: "Baker to Rosemary . . . they are at the stone wall; give us fire support."

"Fox Able to Fox . . . we hear tank motors . . . send . . ." Then came a metallic voice, calm as a church deacon: "Yes . . . yes . . . Their people are all around on the ridges . . . yes . . . in back of us now . . . we got wounded all over up here . . . await your words . . . yes . . . yes . . ."

The twins had heard enough and left the silent group huddled around the radio. Their jeep sloshed through the mud until they came to a roadblock. A six-by truck lay in the ditch, chow cans spilling out, the hot food containers steaming in the rain. There were no people, but the echo of gunfire cracked back and forth as the two cameramen kept moving forward. Something went "*umph-thut*," and they saw a blister raised on the jeep's hood from a stray bullet. They jumped, sprawling into the ditch. There, hunched in the rain, were two GIs peering at a mist-covered hill. One fired. The other leaned over the stock of his BAR watching tensely. The high ripping sound of enemy guns was joined by the heavy bark of friendly weapons. The twins found themselves in a dim, unearthly, mist-shrouded place. They saw an animal slithering towards the wrecked food truck, a GI. He sank to his knees and began cramming food into his mouth, glancing furtively from side to side like a trapped creature. Above the rain, they could hear him chant, "Mother-fuggin' bastards . . . starve me . . . hell."

Ignoring the rain, they kept filming the scene. On the ridge in front they heard an eerie wail, then three figures appeared, mumbling to each other, twisting their heads back and forth. Their eyeballs gleamed whitely. Glancing briefly at the twins, they trotted down the road. Other riflemen scurried from the undergrowth, bent double, straining, push-ing. The crack of rifles closed in from both sides. Two men crashed out of the bushes carrying a wounded comrade with an old-young face. He clawed to hold the skin of his cheek in place, scarlet blood seeping through his fingers. He sang, "Chow . . . uhu . . . chow," a gurgling croon. The trio stumbled down the road, their feet making sucking noises in the mud.

Behind came a man, sodden blanket over his shoulders, mumbling vaguely, "Told 'em . . . knew gooks . . . hit the stone wall. Hear they're gonna try an end run . . . Christ, better try somethin'. . . . Inchon . . . yeah . . . said they call the place Inchon."

By some magic, enlisted men always seem to find out the most carefully protected secrets. Or perhaps there could be no secret in a civilian army, even that of MacArthur's top-secret amphibious landing, whose success depended on stealth.

Walker was saying little to Lynch, his pilot, or Tyner, his aide, but both knew what was bothering him. With the Marines leaving the front lines at midnight they were going to be totally on their own. They couldn't seem to get the 2nd Division going in the south, and things were looking bad in the north. There would be no more naval support for the perim-eter, since the aircraft carriers would soon be heading north for the surprise landing at Inchon. That morning Walker had to make a deci-sion. Was it time to move back to the Davidson Line?

About four weeks earlier, Walker had verbally instructed Brigadier General Garrison H. Davidson to lay out a secondary line of defense, designated by MacArthur himself, in case Eighth Army couldn't stop the enemy at the Naktong River. It began on the east coast just above Pusan, and extended generally west along the high ground to a point northeast of Miryang before curving down to the high ground northeast of Masan.

"Would you take me over the Davidson Line so I can get a good look?" Walker asked Lynch. His pilot had already flown over it many times; and despite the beating rain, they swept as low as ten feet off the ground so the general could see the barbed wire and prepared positions. Starting from the east coast, they skimmed the ROK lines protecting

Taegu, purposely circling so the men could see the three stars on the plane. Those below waved enthusiastically. Lynch then headed to the area just north of Taegu, where he descended so the 1st Cavalry Division could identify the general's plane. Again the troops waved. They continued west to the 2nd Division area and finally surveyed the lines of the 25th Division. Again and again, Walker waved and those on the ground gave him the high sign.

When they finally landed, Lynch said, "You know, General, those men look like they're ready to fight. I'm tired of hearing all this about 'whipped guys.' They've all taken the worst the enemy could give them, and as far as I'm concerned, they look like they're ready to charge."

The previous night Walker had been convinced he should pull back. Now he said, "I believe the same thing, Mike. It's a big relief to see what we saw." Back at Eighth Army HQ, Walker gave a curt order to his staff: "We're holding."

Despite the rain, the ROKs and Americans held firm all along the front, and in the south, those Marines not being readied for the Inchon landing were counterattacking. At 8:20 A.M., September 6, the 1st Battalion jumped off. They were scheduled to seize two hills and then take the final objective, Obong-ni Ridge, which blocked the route to the Naktong River. Captain Fenton's Baker Company was still waiting for the order to take off. Just as hot coffee arrived, the word came and the men had to leave before the coffee could be distributed. Despite scattered mortar and sniper fire and an occasional machine-gun burst, the company kept advancing and covered the three thousand yards to a ridgeline parallel to Obong-ni Ridge. A few minutes later, A Company joined them. Orders came to hold until adjacent units arrived.

Captain Fenton guessed the enemy was withdrawing all the way to Obong-ni Ridge to set up their main line of resistance. He felt sure they expected him to come over the little ridge and get down into the mucky paddy that had already caused so many casualties. Then they would open up and hit him hard.

While he was preparing a hasty defense, heavy mortar rounds and antitank high-velocity fire came in from the ridge. The rain was so dense that Fenton was unable to call in close air support. The soaking had already knocked out all five of his 536-type radios; and now his battalion tactical radio went dead. A runner arrived; GI elements were coming up abreast of his right flank.

Then the NKs attacked, supported by three tanks. One was camouflaged to look like a half-track. Fenton estimated 350 infantrymen were coming at him. He sent a runner to the army coming up to ask if they had any artillery support, and if they did, to call it down on the enemy in front of Baker Company. Two other runners went back to battalion to notify Colonel Newton what was going on. A fourth man was sent to warn their tanks down on the road to be cautious. T-34's were coming around the bend just as they had in the first Obong-ni battle. But this time the NK tanks caught the lead Marine tank with its guns trained in the wrong direction, and a T-34 scored a direct hit on its turret. The second Marine tank made the same mistake the enemy had made in the previous encounter—it tried to go around the lead tank. It too was knocked out.

Up on his ridge, Fenton at last got lucky. Artillery support came in from the army, enabling him to move his bazooka teams into position. They rained rockets on the three enemy tanks, threatening to cut them off. The first two T-34's were hit and the turrets jammed so they could not fire at Fenton. Two more rockets hit each of the wounded tanks and set them afire.

While this was going on, enemy infantry again attacked through the heavy rain. Because the ridge Fenton was defending was oval-shaped, visibility was poor and it was practically impossible to see the NKs as they approached the base of Fenton's position. He kept getting reports from up and down the line that they were being hit by groups of forty to a hundred. Things became so critical that he had to send every man he had to the lines—rocketmen, corpsmen, and mortarmen were rushed up front. And ammo was getting low. Things looked grim until a platoon from A Company suddenly appeared with five boxes of grenades. The North Koreans were now so close that Fenton's men tossed them to the men on the line, who immediately pulled the pins and threw them at the enemy.

Fenton had managed to get one of his radios back into working condition. He gave it to the forward observer, who called for immediate 80-mm fire-for-effect, since the enemy was less than a hundred yards away. The 80's laid down a deadly blanket, and when the forty-minute counterattack finally broke up, there were only eighteen rounds left.

Meanwhile, Taplett had been told by Colonel Murray that a GI unit was to relieve him at nine P.M. It was already almost eleven. "We're all here, all by ourselves," he told his exec, Major Canney. "Where in hell's the army unit? John, go back down the road and see if you can find it."

Canney returned with news that there was no sign of them. Taplett radioed Murray. "Say, what the hell do you want me to do?" he complained. The army was already two hours late.

The patient Murray told him to be patient.

Word came from Bohn that his company was receiving sporadic fire, and his men were uneasy as hell. Taplett ordered both G and H companies to pull back because they were about to be relieved. Then a man from CP security reported that he'd heard some rustling. "We challenged them and they said, 'We're army! We're army!' " Soon Taplett was talking to a GI first lieutenant who had part of a rifle company. "Where's the battalion?" asked Taplett.

"I don't know, but we have orders to come up here and relieve some Marines." He was the company executive officer and had about 45 men. They had rifles, carbines, grenades and two 60-mm mortars.

"Where's your company commander?" asked Taplett.

"Well, we had a firefight up at Taegu a day or two ago. Things got rough and the ammo was low and the captain said to me, 'Take charge of the company. I'm going back to get ammunition.' And I haven't seen hide nor hair of him since." When the lieutenant found out he was to relieve two companies he was shocked. "Can you loan me a radio?"

Taplett said he'd loan him two radios, three mortar tubes and ammo, as well as some rockets and machine guns. "What do you plan to do?"

"I think I'll just take over the position your CP people have."

"I'm supposed to be relieved by a battalion," said Taplett. He called Murray. "Ray, what do I do? It's getting awful late." The 1/5 had already passed down the road and Tap's battalion had covered their withdrawal. "It will soon be morning and there's only this poor first lieutenant up here with about 50 army troops and very ill-equipped."

"Turn over the responsibility to them," said Murray. He promised to send a message to Eighth Army that the Marines were turning over this entire sector to the GIs. "Now start forming a file," concluded Murray. "And march back down that road."

As Taplett was preparing to leave, the Army lieutenant said, "As soon as you leave, we're not going to stay here very long. We're going to be leaving right behind you."

And they did.

It was dark when someone came walking up the ridge yelling, "B Company!" Fenton's people were veterans, and not a man replied. It could be an enemy trick. Finally an Army lieutenant appeared and asked if this was B Company.

"Yes," said Fenton.

"Why didn't you answer me?"

In a few well-chosen words Fenton told him why.

When the embarrassed lieutenant asked where his outfit should be placed, Fenton, assuming he had a company, suggested he put two platoons on the line. The lieutenant confessed he had only 40 men.

It was the same old story. The Army was going to relieve with a mere platoon! And when the NKs started to feel out the line, the Army outfit would probably pull out. Baker Company of the regiment's rearguard started moving back by foot to Yongsan, where they would entruck for Pusan. The Marines' battle was over.

Back at Observation Hill, Bob Bohn's company was told at about midnight that they were to keep together in the dark and walk to the bottom of the hill, then out to the road. There they would join the rest of the battalion.

Taplett's men had been sloshing through rice paddies and climbing the damned hills and now they had to march through the rain. Everybody was cold and ornery from fatigue. After about five or six miles they finally reached trucks. While they were milling around, B Company arrived and Fenton came up to Taplett. "Hey, Tap," he said, "would you like a bottle of brandy?"

"Ike, where in hell did you get the brandy?"

"I got it from Dr. Harvey," he said and pulled out of his combat jacket half a dozen miniature bottles. He gave Taplett two.

They drove all night, arriving in Pusan soon after dawn. By now a rumor had spread among the men that they were going by ship to Japan. Cheers! Then came a more accurate rumor. They were to line up with the 1st Marine Division for an amphibious landing at a port near Seoul—Inchon.

Murray told Taplett that his battalion would be the first to land. They would seize a little island connected by a causeway to Inchon, while the rest of the 5th Marines would later hit the seawall with other troops of the 1st Marine Division. Taplett was ordered to prepare his operation plan but tell his men nothing. Taplett followed orders, then he had a long sleep.

The next day, September 7, survivors of the People's 7th Division were escaping over the Nam River near its junction with the Naktong, while the Americans were burying more than two thousand North Korean dead discovered behind their lines. Walker's casualties had been heavy, but those inflicted on the enemy were far more serious. The outnumbered, outgunned enemy had fought fiercely but to no avail. The Pusan Perimeter was intact. The crisis was over.

CHAPTER 11

Inchon
(August 21–September 15)

1.

From the outset, the Navy, the Marines and the Joint Chiefs opposed MacArthur's top-secret amphibious assault on Inchon. It was a quixotic project, doomed to disaster. The channel to Inchon's harbor was narrow, treacherous, and easy to mine. Most of the time it was a vast, mucky mud flat. MacArthur stubbornly maintained that such problems would make attack a bigger surprise to the enemy.

He selected his iron-gray-haired chief of staff, Ned Almond, to command the operation. Almond had served thirty years as an infantry officer. Despite his fifty-eight years, he was bursting with energy. A combat major in the first world war and a division commander in the second, he expected everyone to be as devoted to duty and hard work as he was. Lightning flashed from his blue eyes whenever he met with hesitation or incompetence. Although of medium height, he seemed far bigger when angry—which was much of the time. Implicitly trusted by MacArthur, he, in turn, revered his chief and applied all his boundless vigor to the great assault.

Although the Joint Chiefs of Staff still maintained that the invasion was too chancy, they reluctantly went along with the idea. On August 21, Army Chief of Staff J. Lawton Collins and Admiral Forrest Sherman, chief of naval operations, were selected to review the operation person-

ally with MacArthur. Plans were set for a full briefing and discussion in
Tokyo on August 23.

On the previous afternoon, Major General Oliver P. Smith, commander of the Marine division that would land at Inchon, met Ned
Almond. The white-haired Smith, a quiet, reserved man, was the antithesis of the buoyant, restless Almond. It was apparent that these two
would not always see eye to eye; and Almond, who had just been made
commander of a brand-new corps, the X Corps, would be in charge of
the two assault divisions at Inchon. Almond had first protested, since it
would mean he would have to wear two hats. But MacArthur assured
him that he would temporarily remain his chief of staff "in absentia."
The war would end soon after Inchon, and Almond would be back in
his real berth in Tokyo.

Smith politely questioned landing at Inchon, but Almond swept
aside all objections. There were no organized North Korean forces in
the area, and the landing would be purely mechanical. Then Smith was
brought in to meet MacArthur, who greeted the Marine warmly. As he
reflectively puffed on his pipe, MacArthur spoke eloquently of his concept of the landing. It was more than a "concept" in the military sense;
it was a vision of victory that could end the war in a single bold stroke.
To Smith he seemed to have a supreme and almost mystical faith that
he would succeed. Yes, the war could be concluded in a month, and it
was Smith's Marines that would do it. They would make September 15,
1950, a glorious date in American history.

Walker looked forward to General Collins's arrival on August 22. Without delay they made a flying visit to the American divisions. Lynch
remembered details for several significant reasons. It was the first time
he had been warned not to mention what was discussed in the plane.
He was also privy to a tactical analysis by two of the Army's most experienced combat leaders. After take-off, they began discussing the
forthcoming amphibious operation. Neither favored a landing at Inchon. Collins said that most JCS members were opposed as well. But
GHQ had waged such an emotional campaign that it was impossible to
discuss the operation on its military merits. Obsessed with Inchon since
the 29th of June, MacArthur had too much personal prestige invested
to allow himself to be proven wrong.

Collins disliked the way GHQ had misrepresented the key issue. No
one opposed an amphibious operation. Militarily, it was a logical action
to take. Furthermore, U.S. naval and air superiority were such that a
successful landing could be made anywhere on the Korean coast. Only
the landing site was in question. That fact was being obscured. At the
same time MacArthur had built his case in such a way that opposing

Inchon was tantamount to opposing *any* amphibious operation. Thus, to the uninitiated, this routine action would be seen as a stroke of genius.

Beyond the site itself, there were deep differences about the purpose and objectives of the envelopment. Walker remembered Patton's views: "Most American officers don't know a damned thing about envelopments. They call any move in the enemy rear, for whatever reason, an envelopment. Too often, they make the mistake of becoming so engrossed in their own plans that they forget about the enemy." Patton felt that "best results are attained when the envelopment arrives in or just back of the enemy's artillery positions. Here you disrupt his supply and signal communications and his guns, and are close enough to the troops advancing along the axis to be sure of making contact in a reasonable time." He cautioned that, for envelopments to succeed, "they should not go too deep or be too large."

This led to discussion by Collins and Walker of the Falaise Gap fiasco during World War II, in which both men had been involved. That operation had failed because enveloping forces couldn't close the gap quickly enough to gain desired results. Now they both felt that Inchon could result in the same failure. It was too far from the link-up forces to have an immediate effect. Ability to mass forces was at the mercy of tides and weather. Troops would have to attack a built-up area almost immediately. Momentum could not be maintained after landing, thus giving the enemy time to plan ways to oppose or escape. And, beyond the political act of seizing Seoul, there was no assurance that the primary military objective of destroying NKPA forces in the south could be achieved.

When the Army chief of staff said that he favored Kunsan as the landing site, Walker was ready. He and General Partridge had recently flown over the Kunsan-Taegu area at low levels. Unfolding a map, Walker presented an alternative to Inchon that could change the war's outcome. The combat situation since MacArthur first selected Inchon, he explained, had altered drastically. Recent radio intercepts indicated Kim Il-sung planned to commit everything to capture Pusan before the UN could introduce forces to stop him. The southernmost attack would be given priority. This meant the bulk of KNPA combat units would be south of the Taejon–Taegu axis on the proposed landing date. While much of the NK tactical and logistical reinforcement could bypass Seoul when traveling south or north, it *had* to pass through Taejon to influence the battle. Therefore Taejon, not Seoul, was the key to a successful development.

Walker's map showed two enveloping arrows. One began at Kunsan; the other, at the northwest pivot point of the perimeter. Both met at Taejon. A series of "button-hooks" were drawn along the northern line of contact. These indicated infantry attacks by the ROKs to penetrate and entrap enemy units in the more mountainous terrain. The cities of Sangju, Andong and Yongdok were shown as key objectives.

Walker felt that elements of the landing force could reach Taejon no later than the second day. If his own perimeter units were reinforced with river-crossing equipment, armor and adequate fire support, they could link up by the third day. This closure speed would deny the enemy time to react. After the trap was closed, he would rely on firepower to destroy remaining elements, thus minimizing his own casualties.

Once NKPA forces had been eliminated, U.S. and ROK troops could secure the best defensible line in vicinity of the 38th parallel. Because of the terrain, this would involve occupying positions north of the boundary. At that point, ROK units could take over while the Americans withdrew. Surplus weapons and equipment would be used to increase the size of Rhee's military forces. This would give him the capability to handle future threats while the UN resolved political issues.

As to NKPA units on the northeastern front, Walker said that the best way to keep them from escaping was to "hold them by the nose with fire and kick them in the pants with movement." This had been Patton's policy for overwhelming a defending enemy.

Collins seemed to agree with Walker's plan. Lynch had flown over the terrain in question and he was convinced the plan would work. Naively, he assumed that since Collins favored Kunsan on a military basis, *and was MacArthur's nominal superior*, he would override GHQ's political arguments and change the landing site. That was how things worked at the fighting level.

But the crucial conference that took place on the sixth floor of the Dai Ichi Building the next afternoon at 5:30 was dominated by personalities and politics. It was well staged by MacArthur, for he knew he had to convince Collins and Sherman or else the JCS would not give final approval to the operation. Present also were Vice Admiral C. Turner Joy, commander of the naval forces in the Far East, Vice Admiral Arthur Struble, Seventh Fleet commander, and Rear Admiral James Doyle who would lead the amphibious force.

Eight of Doyle's amphibious specialists spoke of the natural aspects. They gave little hope that the attack would be a surprise, since there were only a few days each autumn when the tides could float the landing craft and supply ships over the mud flats of Inchon harbor. They also pointed out that Wolmi-do (the *do* meant *island*), which lay just off Inchon, would have to be neutralized before landings could be made, otherwise, Wolmi's big guns would wipe out the landing craft. Moreover, the channels to the harbor would probably be sown with moored and magnetic mines. Finally, September 15 would be at the height of the typhoon season. Doyle concluded by stating that he could not recommend the operation.

For an hour and a half MacArthur listened gravely. Then for forty-five minutes he spoke brilliantly. His eloquence, even while using a conversational tone, impressed everyone. "The bulk of the Reds," he said, "are committed around Walker's defense perimeter. The enemy, I am convinced, has failed to prepare Inchon properly for defense. The very arguments you have made as to the impracticabilities will tend to ensure for me the element of surprise. For the enemy will reason that no one would be so brash as to make such an attempt. Surprise is the most vital element for success in war." In 1759, he said, General Wolfe had won a stunning victory over Montcalm in Quebec. "Like Montcalm, the North Koreans would regard an Inchon landing as impossible. Like Wolfe, I could take them by surprise."

He admitted that the Navy's objections were substantial. "But they are not insuperable. My confidence in the Navy is complete, and in fact, I seem to have more confidence in the Navy than the Navy has in itself."

By seizing Seoul, he said, he could effectively freeze the enemy's supply system. "This in turn will paralyze the fighting power of the troops that now face Walker." The only alternative to such a stroke would be a continuation of the savage sacrifice American troops were making in the Pusan area. "Are you content to let our troops stay in that bloody perimeter like beef cattle in a slaughterhouse? Who will take the responsibility for such a tragedy? Certainly, I will not."

The prestige of the Western world hung in the balance. "Millions are watching the outcome. I realize that Inchon is a 5,000-to-1 gamble, but I am used to taking such odds." But Inchon would *not* fail. It would succeed and it would save 100,000 lives. "We shall land at Inchon," he concluded, "and I shall crush them!"

The listeners, spellbound, sat silently. Finally Sherman, who had been most critical, rose. "Thank you. A great voice in a great cause." As the Marine and Navy officials filed out to the noisy street, most of them felt that the last word had been spoken.

Later Mike Lynch asked General Walker why Inchon had been selected over Kunsan. Walker's reply was short. "MacArthur has everyone thinking of Korea as an island and Seoul the final objective. Once it's taken, the war would be over."

The next day, August 25, General William Dean was still hiding in the hills south of Taejon. For thirty-six days he had been wandering over an area controlled by the People's 6th Division, narrowly escaping capture several times. He had managed to get some food from farmers but lived mostly on berries, kaffir stalks and grass. He still had twelve rounds of ammunition and was determined to knock off eleven Communists, then use the last one for himself. Because of his rank, he knew he couldn't surrender. The Communists would be sure to capitalize on the surrender of a general. His pockets were full of peaches he'd found in an orchard and his spirits were rising. While resting under a chestnut tree he could hear the rumble of artillery in the east. He hadn't heard such noise since leaving Taejon. It was like hearing from an old friend. "I'm on my way back," he thought. "I'm going to make it."

That afternoon he came upon an old man and several boys. He had found that if he asked for food, people would help him. The old man smiled and gestured towards a village. "Well, damn it," Dean thought, "things are going my way now." He would be well fed and could then head east towards the American lines. "Everything favors me, so I'll just continue to ride my luck."

He was given rice, with garlic beads as a side dish. It was delicious and he asked for more to wrap in his handkerchief. Later that afternoon he met another friendly Korean named Han. Han could speak no English, but he understood Dean's offer of a million *won* to guide him to Taegu. They waded across a stream, only to be faced on the other bank by a dozen villagers armed with clubs and spears. One motioned Dean to go back across the river. But Dean pointed his pistol at the group. He and Han were allowed to pass through. After walking about eight miles, Han turned into a house for more food. Dean took one small glass of *sake* and ate garlic beads. The people of the house offered more *sake* and Han urged him to accept. He thought, "Are these people trying to get me drunk?" But he took another glass. Finally the two started down the moonlit road. When he and Han sat down on the road to rest, fifteen or so men appeared. Someone fired a rifle and as Dean reached for his pistol, Han grabbed his wrist. As they wrestled, Dean kept kicking out and shouting, "Shoot! Shoot, you sons of bitches! Shoot!" What an ignominious way to have your lights put out, he thought.

They bound his hands behind him and he was marched to the police station. Han was standing next to the door looking pleased with himself. While the general was being searched, he noticed a Korean calendar hanging on the wall. It was the 25th of August, his wedding anniversary.

2.

On the way back to Washington, General Collins reviewed what he would tell his colleagues and Truman. The visit *had* served a useful purpose; it had crystallized MacArthur's determination to proceed with Inchon. He would impress upon the president the utter confidence of MacArthur, while stressing the warnings of Sherman and the Marines.

Collins's report did nothing to abate Truman's growing anger with

MacArthur. The president was still seething over the general's recent praise of Chiang Kai-shek's determination to "resist Communist domination." In addition, in a message sent to the Veterans of Foreign Wars to be read at the organization's annual encampment in Chicago, the five-star general referred to Formosa as "an unsinkable aircraft carrier and submarine tender," and criticized those who opposed aggressive American aid to Chiang. Outraged, Truman seriously considered dismissing MacArthur for such "insubordination." He not only controlled himself, he also allowed the plans for Inchon to proceed. While almost 70,000 troops were being assembled for the assault, the Joint Chiefs had strong reservations. On August 28, with the Pentagon still buzzing about the VFW squabble, the Joint Chiefs finally sent MacArthur approval for the operation, yet still did not fix a definite location for the landing site. It was a masterpiece of Washington ambivalence. The troops were to land "either at Inchon in the event the enemy defenses in vicinity of Inchon prove ineffective or at a favorable beach south of Inchon if one can be located." MacArthur didn't even respond, and on August 30 issued his own operations order for Inchon. He took care not to send a copy to Washington immediately.

Even as MacArthur proceeded with his plans, the Joint Chiefs sent him a final warning of the disastrous consequences if the landing failed—or even if the landing did not lead to a quick victory. "While we concur in launching a counteroffensive in Korea as early as possible, we have noted with considerable concern the recent trend of events there."

MacArthur was chilled to the marrow to read such words, since they implied that the whole plan should be abandoned. But he promptly replied that it was the only way to wrest the initiative from the enemy. "To do otherwise is to commit us to a war of indefinite duration."

The Joint Chiefs replied dutifully that they endorsed the plan and had informed the president of their decision. Even so, MacArthur feared a last-minute cancellation and did not send the Joint Chiefs the operations order for Inchon with all details until September 10.

"Don't get there too soon," he told the courier, Lieutenant Colonel Lynn Smith, jesting in earnest. "If they say it is too big a gamble, tell them I said this is throwing a nickel in the pot after it has been opened for a dollar. The big gamble was Washington's decision to put American troops on the Asian mainland."

While Colonel Smith was leaving Tokyo for Washington, the 5th Marines were in Pusan preparing for they knew not what or where. Taplett had still told no one that their battalion would make the initial landing at Wolmi, the small island honeycombed with hidden emplacements for enough guns to endanger the entire landing. While Taplett was getting his men into top physical shape, on that September 10, twenty-eight Marine planes began softening up Wolmi with napalm. The first attack scorched the eastern side of the island, and the second flight had to orbit until the smoke cleared. They were met by antiaircraft fire from the island and the mainland. Several hours later the third strike left the hump-backed island in flames.

By the next day, ships carrying vital equipment for the expansion of Inchon's port facilities, tanks, supplies, and landing craft were slowly heading toward Inchon. Again Wolmi and the Inchon area were worked over by Marine planes.

3.

For the past twelve days MacArthur had been receiving secret information from an intelligence team hiding on a small island only a few miles from Inchon. In charge was a thirty-nine-year old Navy lieutenant, Eugene Franklin Clark. Formerly a skipper of an LST working the China coast and, having been chief interpreter-translator for the War Crimes Trials on Guam, he was fluent in Japanese. At the end of the trials in 1949 he was transferred to G2 of MacArthur's staff in Tokyo, his wife, Enid, and two children, accompanying him. Clark's potential was recognized by Captain "Eddie" Pierce, USN, then with G2, and also a Japanese linguist. He had read Clark's contribution to a terrain study of Inchon and its environs and, in the light of his recent background, asked if he would be interested in leading an intelligence team to that area, adding, "We need additional information from up there."

Clark promptly accepted. In addition to gathering information he would also be in charge of a group of Korean agents who would be sent daily as far as Seoul to determine if any preparations were being made to repel the landing. Clark met with Hans Tofte, in charge of special operations for CIA, and asked for what help he could give in securing qualified agents. Clark also sought assistance from counterintelligence (CIC), and was able to obtain the services of an energetic bilingual Korean Navy lieutenant, Youn Joung, as well as a middle-aged ROK colonel, Ke In-ju, Rhee's former head counterintelligence officer, who had been fired when he failed to predict the North Korean attack. Fearing for his life, Ke had turned himself in to the U.S. Army for protection.

On August 28, Tofte set up a CIA flight for Clark and his two aides to Sasebo, the U.S. naval base in southern Japan. Here, in a safe house, he met his three-man communications team. The team was led by a major in his late thirties, a first lieutenant, and a corporal. Clark also helped select ten Korean civilian agents known as "line-crossers." All of these agents were young except for one, a very old and wizened man. After discussing the operation with several CIA men as to procedure, he requisitioned burp guns, three .50-caliber machine guns, a number of semiautomatic rifles and necessary ammunition. These would be used by eager civilian Koreans on Yonghung-do, too young for the ROK draft, to defend their camp. He also acquired plenty of rice, dried fish, sugar, and other edibles that would not need refrigeration. Youn advised him to take extra sacks of sugar for trading purposes and whiskey to loosen tongues.

Following a briefing by Clark of Vice Admiral Andrewes, RN, who was in charge of the blockade of the east coast of Korea, everything was loaded aboard the British destroyer HMS *Charity*, then moored in Sasebo. On the last day of August they were under way for Inchon. The destroyer took them to the entrance of Flying Fish Channel, where everything was transferred to the Korean frigate *PC-703*. The PC delivered them to their destination, Yonghung-do, ten miles south of Inchon. Although it was midmorning, Clark did not feel threatened. He had been told that all the little islands they had passed were occupied by civilians only. Transfer to the beach was completed without incident by means of a small powercraft, a one-lunger, operated by an old Korean civilian.

Yonghung-do was about four miles long and four miles wide and Clark and his men could see to the northeast all the way to Inchon. Also in sight, four miles to the north, was the little lighthouse island of Palmi-do, jutting up where East and Flying Fish channels joined. The weather was fine, and by the end of the day Clark had set up camp and stationed his locally recruited defense force. An island about twice the size of Yonghung-do, Taebu-do, lay several hundred yards to the east. Clark faced his defense in this direction and, several days later, discovered to his amazement North Korean soldiers wandering on the Taebu beach, apparently paying no attention to the presence of the spies. In the first few days he and Youn visited other nearby islands in their little motorboat and bartered sugar for sampans and local information from friendly fishermen. During the night Clark sent his Korean line-crossers to Inchon by sampan. On various occasions they sneaked over to Wolmi-do to check on gun emplacements while the line-crossers went as far as Seoul to detect any North Korean troop movement which would indicate a breach of D-Day landing security. His best agent, though partial to a little nip of whiskey, turned out to be the old man, who always brought back valuable information from as far as distant Seoul.

Clark personally had to get the vital information about tides and the seawall that protected the Inchon waterfront. The tidal range varied from an average of twenty-nine feet to a high tide of thirty-six feet and a low low tide of six feet with these latter extremes occurring during a six-hour period on D-Day, September 15, and with a five-knot current.

A depth of twenty-five feet was needed to navigate the channel and harbor, and the LSTs required twenty-nine feet. Only during a few days in the middle of September and again in October did the tide provide such depths. MacArthur rejected October so September 15 had been chosen. But the U.S. Navy's tide tables differed from those of the Japanese. It was Clark's job to get exact figures and also test the muddy bottom during low tides, as well as check the height of the seawall.

On the sixth night, during low tide, Clark and Youn sculled a sampan to the seawall, which ran for hundreds of yards. They took off their clothes to test the mud and sank up to their knees in greasy muck. It was a great effort to walk, and a man in combat gear would probably sink up to his waist. Then they slithered back into the sampan and went up to the seawall. It was about ten feet high. They waited until the tide came in and took visual measurements as the tide ebbed. The measuring technique was, Clark realized, by guess and by God. You couldn't obtain accuracy in the dark and the threat posed by occasional patrols.

Since there were several contours on the lengthy seawall, they came back the next two nights to repeat the same rigorous routine. Clark reported in a "one-time pad" code (destroyed after one use) that the Japanese tidal figures were more accurate, and that the mud would be almost impossible to wade through.

Two days later, during low tide, about sixty NK soldiers started wading across from the island of Taebu. Clark's ten-man defense force opened fire and finally drove them back. Fearing a stronger attack, Clark called in an air strike, and soon British planes bombed the enemy beach for fifteen minutes and departed. The North Koreans did not attempt another raid, and Clark assumed they probably had most of their troops in the South and didn't take his group seriously.

During the next five days Clark's South Korean agents continued to reconnoiter the mainland. Clark already knew that Wolmi-do had more gun emplacements than first believed. Those had to be taken out. On daily sampan patrols, his line-crossers were finding mines in the channel, which had to be very gingerly towed clear of navigable waters. One of these in the narrow channel could create havoc with the invasion column should it hit a lead vessel.

On September 12 his main concern was the weather. It had worsened throughout the day and by nightfall heavy winds from the edge of typhoon Kezia were sweeping the channel. He feared for his people in sampans trying to return to base. Clark was apprehensive that he might have to scrub the operation after all they had accomplished, but fortunately Kezia weakened and finally dissipated altogether.

4.

Despite the weather, MacArthur was going ahead as planned. That afternoon he and six of his staff took off from Haneda in his new plane, the *SCAP*. Their departure was secret. In fact, no written orders were issued. Because of the storm, however, they landed at an airfield in

Kyushu instead of at Fukuoka; from the Kyushu mainland they proceeded to Sasebo in a new car that bore only four stars. The driver apologized but the general was amused.

At Sasebo they were not able to board MacArthur's flagship, the *Mount McKinley*. She had been delayed by the typhoon and had to be warped into the dock. It was almost midnight when the MacArthur party boarded. The ship's captain was as nervous as a cat. "General," he said, "we're going to have to cast off very quickly. There's a storm coming up and I've got to clear the breakwater within fifteen minutes or the wind and the tide will be against me."

MacArthur thanked him and calmly walked back to the car, shook hands with the driver, exchanged pleasantries, then majestically walked up the gangway.

The next day, September 13, six U.S. destroyers moved to within eight hundred yards of Wolmi-do and fired at the island to augment the earlier softening-up by Navy planes. At the same time, two U.S. and two British cruisers began pouring in salvos, while planes made bombing runs. After half an hour of punishment, the North Koreans on Wolmi finally retaliated with their undamaged guns. Three of the destroyers were hit and slightly damaged, but it cost the North Koreans dearly because their return fire revealed their still-intact positions. The cruisers and destroyers replied with deadly accuracy.

At dusk Clark was shocked to see a large hull with no superstructure floating towards Flying Fish Channel. It was at least seventy feet long and twenty feet wide, moving at five or six knots because of the ebb tide. He feared it was loaded with explosives designed to blow up one of MacArthur's assault ships. Clark and several others boarded from their motorboat and discovered it was just an empty hull, apparently broken loose by accident. They grounded it on another island so it wouldn't be a hazard when the assault fleet came down the channel in the dark.

At Eighth Army headquarters, General Walker had just learned that an ROK division had scored a substantial victory over the NK 15th Division at Yongchon. It was particularly important, since the defeated division was commanded by Major General Pak Sung-chol, until recently the vice-president of North Korea. Walker hurried to the headquarters of General Chung Il-kwon and told the ROK chief of staff he wanted to speak to all his staff officers. About forty men listened to Walker praise the ROKs for their victory. In his enthusiasm he mentioned that General MacArthur was about to surprise the North Koreans at Inchon. He hastily added that this was top secret and must be revealed to no one.

When AP correspondent Shin Hua-bong heard the cheering inside the building, he stopped Major Kim Kun-bae as the latter was coming out. They were drinking buddies, and Shin guided him to a bar. After feeding the major drinks, Shin said that he understood General Walker told the staff officers something fantastic. The major was reluctant to say anything until Shin said there must be an amphibious landing at Kunsan, a port far south of Inchon. "Not Kunsan!" exclaimed the intoxicated staff officer. "It's Inchon!" Realizing what he had said, the officer immediately denied his own statement. The reporter told him not to worry, since all this would be public knowledge in three days. "Stupid!" exclaimed the tipsy Major Kim. "It's going to be the day after tomorrow." Shin sent his story to Tokyo.

At sundown MacArthur's ship, the *Mount McKinley*, was steaming north for Inchon.

Taplett's battalion was also on its way up the coast in a high-speed transport.

5.

D-day minus one, September 14. U.S. destroyers returned to Wolmi-do in the morning and fired more than 1,700 five-inch shells, receiving back only a few scattered shots. Apparently the big guns were silenced. Lieutenant Clark woke in relief. The typhoon had come and gone, and there were only a few more hours to wait.

Later that afternoon there was activity on the beach of the neighboring island of Taebu. It looked as if the North Korean soldiers were preparing to cross over in force, so Clark ordered everyone to make for Palmi, the little lighthouse island. They abandoned everything of size, including their machine guns and the little engine that ran the communications generator.

Clark had already signaled Tokyo that he would do his best to light the ancient, French-made oil lamp of the Palmi lighthouse to guide the American ships down Flying Fish Channel. Before turning in to sleep, Clark wrote on the lighthouse door "KILROY WAS HERE." He could imagine the look of surprise on the faces of the Marines when they tried to figure out who in hell got there before them.

Earlier in the day General Walker had phoned Chung Il-kwon that he had just received a call from GHQ in Tokyo. They wanted to know who had leaked the story of the Inchon invasion. Chung brought a letter of resignation to Rhee. The president only said casually, "Don't give it a thought." Rhee laughed. "Kim Il-sung will think it is another Rhee trick."

Early that evening MacArthur and his staff went to bed on the *Mount McKinley*. Courtney Whitney, one of MacArthur's closest friends, felt he had been sleeping only a few minutes when a Marine sentry informed him that the general would like to see him in his cabin. Whitney threw on his bathrobe and found MacArthur also in his robe. "Sit down, Court," he said. His brow was wrinkled in meditation as he paced the room. Both men were thinking that soon they would be threading through the shifting bars of Flying Fish Channel. MacArthur had made many landings before, but this was the most intricate amphibious operation he had ever attempted. Here thousands of men would act boldly, but he alone would be responsible for failure. "The dreadful results would rest on judgement day against my soul."

Whitney knew the general needed someone to listen to him express his thoughts. As MacArthur continued pacing, he carried on a monologue about all the hazards so graphically outlined by the chief of staff and others who had tried to talk him out of such a dangerous, chancy operation. As he continued his remarkable soliloquy, it seemed to Whitney that the general was feeling the physical pain of the memory of so many battlefields. Fortunately for MacArthur's frame of mind, he had not yet heard that an AP correspondent had leaked the story.

He harped on the element of surprise. It had saved the lives of thousands of his men in World War II and would now protect most of those steaming toward Flying Fish Channel in their blackened ships. But if the North Koreans were waiting for him, the day September 15, 1950, could go down in history as one of the greatest American military disasters.

At last he stopped his pacing and said, as if speaking to himself, "No, the decision was a sound one; the risks and hazards must be accepted." The worried creases disappeared. "Thanks, Court," he said. "Now, let's get some sleep."

As Whitney closed the cabin door, he heard five bells. It was two-thirty A.M. September 15. At the other end of Flying Fish Channel, Lieutenant Clark had just lit the old lamp that would guide the invaders. He also set up a small shoals light on top of a large rock.

Whitney decided to take a turn around the deck. Crew members were alert but silent. Whitney stood at the bow listening to the rush of the sea when he noticed a flash of light, winking on and off. He was elated. They *were* taking the enemy by surprise! The North Koreans had not even turned off the navigation light. Clark's message to Tokyo that he would do his best to turn on the light had not reached the *Mount McKinley*.

In Washington, MacArthur's envoy, Lieutenant Colonel Lynn Smith, was just handing over the operation orders for Inchon to the Joint Chiefs—too late for canceling the landing.

There would have been panic aboard MacArthur's ship if they had known Kim Il-sung was aware they were coming, having been warned by Mao. In late August, after studying disturbing intelligence reports, Mao had made an intense study of the unusual movements and preparation for some sort of Marine offense in the Pusan Perimeter. After mulling over the situation with his young assistants and reexamining MacArthur's past victories, Mao and Cho En-lai concluded that it would be an amphibious landing, since this was the famous general's specialty. Logic dictated it would come on the west coast at one of five possible ports. Inchon, it was deduced, had to be the target, since it was closest to Seoul, the heart of Korea. And because of the exceptional tides and the weather, the most likely date for the assault would be September 15.

This prediction was passed on to Kim Il-sung, and several days later North Korean intelligence agreed with Mao. Any doubt had ended after the September 10th napalm attack on Wolmi-do by Marine planes.

Aware that MacArthur was about to land, Kim Il-sung composed a fervent message to his troops: "Protect and defend all liberated areas! Defend with your blood and life every mountain and every river!"

PART IV

THE ROAD BACK

CHAPTER 12

"It's a Piece of Cake!"
(September 15–19)

1.

At three A.M. the *Diachenko*, a high-speed transport, stopped its engines. The compartment lights came on and reveille was played over the ship's PA system. Most of Taplett's 3rd Battalion were already wide awake. As soon as chow was sounded, Private First Class Fred Davidson headed for the galley. He had heard that Marines always had a big breakfast of eggs, steak, bacon, and hot muffins before a landing. But George Company got only powdered scrambled eggs, toast without butter and some canned apricots.

As Colonel Taplett was approaching Wolmi in the *Fort Marion*, he noticed that the land ahead was completely dark. Off towards Inchon there wasn't a single charcoal fire, and he could see Cemetery Hill against the sky. Would they get there alive?

"This is weird," he softly told Canney, his exec. "Here we are right in the middle. And the worst part—it's such a high-risk operation." A few hours earlier the landing force commander had shown him a dispatch from Admiral Doyle and MacArthur stating that Taplett was to continue the operation until he had sustained eighty-seven percent casualties. Eighty-seven percent was suicide!

He summoned the battalion surgeon, Lieutenant (j.g.) Robert Harvey. "Be very quiet," whispered Taplett. "Don't say a word. Come with me." He took Harvey topside. "You're going to see the island we're to strike in the morning."

Harvey could make out the black silhouette of Wolmi. There was a tiny lighthouse island adjacent to it, Sowolmi. "My God, he said, "we're sitting between two islands. Is there anyone on this other island?"

"I hope not."

When Dr. Harvey had first seen Taplett in the Pusan Perimeter, he thought he was arrogant. But once they were in battle, it was obvious that Taplett's goal was to seize real estate with the least possible loss of lives.

On Wolmi the 300 or so survivors of the brutal bombings, napalm and shellings were still strong enough to put up a stiff fight. The seven-hundred-yard causeway leading to the city of Inchon was practically undamaged. A massive force lay quietly in Flying Fish Channel and a battalion of battle-hardened Marines was preparing to attack them. At first light, lookouts on Wolmi shouted that many ships were standing in the channel!

At 5:45 shells from six- and eight-inch guns began landing in Inchon from four British and American cruisers. Then six U.S. destroyers moved in on Wolmi and began pulverizing the little island with their five-inch guns. As Wolmi lay silent in a pall of smoke, Marine Corsairs flashed through the overcast to unleash rockets and bombs.

At six A.M. Taplett's men started boarding in LCVPs (landing craft, vehicles, personnel). Davidson buckled on his helmet's chin strap and started climbing down the boarding net. Thirty-three minutes later Davidson's platoon of Lieutenant Bob Bohn's G Company and three platoons of H Company stormed Green Beach at the northwest end of the island. Three minutes later the remainder of both assault companies hit the beach.

It seemed deathly quiet to Davidson. Then he was startled by the roar overhead as Corsairs abruptly swooped down. Empty machine-gun shells fell on the LCVP. Talk about *close* support! He hit the sand and turned to the right. He could hardly see because of the smoke. They came to a cave and threw grenades inside, hollering, "Fire in the hole!" They waited for those who survived to stumble out, then started up the slope of Radio Hill.

Taplett came in the third wave. His main worry had been Green Beach, a narrow strip with a steep hill behind it. He feared they'd catch a lot of enfilade fire from the slopes as they landed. But things were going well and an officer shouted to Davidson and several others to go east while the rest of Bohn's company continued straight up.

Davidson's little group came upon a trench cut across the side of the hill where they set up a light machine gun. They could look down on Inchon and see the Corsairs raising hell with strafing runs. They

Photographer David Douglas Duncan captures the exhaustion of combat during the battle of Obong-ni Ridge in the face of a Marine captain. "Ike Fenton's eyes," commented Duncan, "were those of an apostle being crucified upon his own anguish and faith."

Pfc. Fred Davidson, another survivor of Obong-ni Ridge
Fred Davidson

Navy Lieutenant j.g. Eugene Clark (*far right*) and Korean agents hide for two weeks on a small island near Inchon to spy on the enemy. *Eugene Clark*

General Douglas MacArthur aboard the U.S.S. *Mount McKinley* watches Lieutenant Colonel Robert Taplett's battalion seize Wolmi Island in Inchon Harbor. *National Archives*

Father Philip Crosbie, an Australian priest, one of the survivors of the Death March endured by civilian prisoners of war
Father Crosbie

MacArthur's troops storm north and seize Pyongyang. They take over Kim Il-sung's office in the Capitol Building. *National Archives*

TOP: MacArthur and General Walton Walker, commander of the Eighth Army, savor the victory. *National Archives*

CENTER: MacArthur unexpectedly orders his pilot to fly all the way to the Yalu River. Here he gazes across at Manchuria on November 24, 1950. *National Archives*

BOTTOM: NBC News correspondent Eugene Jones, wounded at Inchon, insists on dropping with paratroopers north of Pyongyang. *Eugene Jones*

Mao's troops had already crossed into North Korea in great numbers. Secreted in a small house near the Forbidden City, he directs the battle from afar. *People's Military Museum, Beijing*

Lost North Korean baby at Taedong River, December 4, 1950, after Chinese sweep all the way back to Pyongyang, forcing large numbers of civilians to flee south. *National Archives*

Chinese mortar attack *People's Military Museum*

Kim Il-sung. A charismatic
leader despite Western
ridicule. *People's Military
Museum*

could also see How Company approaching at the back side of their island. Davidson's group gave covering fire before being ordered to rejoin the rest of the company on top of Radio Hill.

Lieutenant Bohn had already run up the American flag by the time Taplett arrived at seven-thirty. Taplett had never been so winded in his life. He and his staff had taken a short climb through torn-up ground. How Company reported the road was heavily mined, but they were filtering through the wreckage of the industrial area. The battalion reserve, I Company, was mopping up with tanks; by eight A.M. Taplett was able to report that the island was secured. And not one of his men had died.

Davidson had nothing to do now but sit on top of Radio Hill and watch the assault platoon, led by Second Lieutenant John Counselman, move across the causeway with a few tanks to Sowolmi Island and quickly kill or capture those in the lighthouse garrison. In an hour and a half the 3rd Battalion had taken MacArthur's first objective at the cost of only seventeen wounded.

Taplett had told Dr. Harvey that he could not evacuate any wounded from the island because the tide would not last long enough. Harvey treated them on the beach and then placed them on amtracs (landing craft) that had become mired in the mud flats.

Captured soldiers and civilians from the little village on the island were being herded behind barbed wire near the beach. All of them were stripped, since they might have hidden weapons. But Taplett objected when he saw a naked elderly man. "That guy is a civilian not a combat man."

"Yeah," said a Marine guard, "but he's hung like a stud horse, and we like to look at it."

Taplett was not amused. "Get some clothes on him," he ordered.

MacArthur, aboard the *Mount McKinley*, had been awakened by the bombardment. After a quick breakfast he scanned the shorelines of Inchon and Wolmi-do through field glasses. Immense explosions were erupting all along Inchon's shores. Endless circles of landing craft churned around, and the first assault waves started toward Wolmi. If they were thrown back by superior forces, it would mean Inchon itself was protected by an enemy in force. He watched anxiously as Taplett's men hit Green Beach and fanned out. But smoke obscured their progress.

About an hour later Carter Printup, the captain of the *Mount McKinley*, was informed by a lookout that a strange, small craft was approaching. Through binoculars he saw a motor-driven sampan. The occupants looked like Koreans. But one was tall and waving what looked like a naval officer's cap. It could be an enemy suicide mission and Printup shouted, "Stand off! Stand off, there!"

An LCVP was lowered and sent out to the sampan. When the ensign

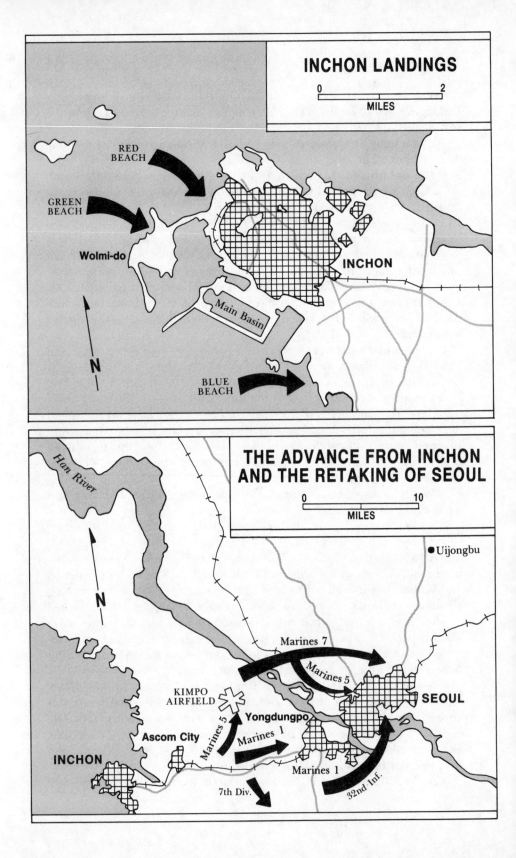

commanding the vessel saw that the tall man in green fatigues and Navy hat was a Caucasian, he pointed a machine gun and shouted, "Who the hell are you?"

"I'm Lieutenant Eugene Clark of the United States Navy. And put down that gun before you hurt somebody."

From the top deck Admiral Joy's intelligence officer recognized Clark. He was welcomed aboard and commended for lighting the path to Inchon.

At eight A.M. an orderly climbed to the bridge where MacArthur was watching Wolmi with concern and handed a message to Admiral Doyle, the amphibious commander. Admiral Struble reported from the *Rochester* that the landing party was ashore and had advanced inland.

MacArthur clapped his hands, laughed. "Good, now let's go down and have a cup of coffee!" He told Doyle to send a message to the fleet: "The Navy and the Marines have never shone more brightly than this morning."

During breakfast Admiral Struble arrived. He said he was going to take a look at Wolmi. "If you want to go in, General," he told MacArthur, "I'll take you."

"Yes, by all means." MacArthur went below to get a warmer jacket and sent word that some of the correspondents could go with him. Struble agreed to take them. He had already invited Generals Almond and Shepherd to come along. By the time MacArthur returned, more than thirty people were waiting to be taken to Wolmi. It took two barges to transport the party. As they approached Wolmi, the general looked toward Green Beach. The crackle of small-arms fire on the other side of the hill must have inspired MacArthur. "Let's go around and take a look at Red Beach." This was on the mainland just north of the causeway from Wolmi-do and would be one of the two principal landing areas to be hit late in the afternoon.

It was a hazardous proposal, but Admirals Struble and Doyle directed their barges to the northern tip of the island, where they could see Red Beach. Fortunately there was no fire from the mainland, and the barges returned safely to the *Mount McKinley*.

As early afternoon wore on, Taplett was intently surveying Inchon from his observation post. The 5th Marines would land at Red Beach just left of the causeway, while the 1st Marines, which had yet to see action in Korea, would hit Blue Beach some two and a half miles to the southeast. But a strange silence hung over both objectives. Where were the North Koreans? There was almost no evidence of any defenses. He radioed his regimental commander. "Colonel Murray," he said, "I'd like permission to cross the causeway. I don't think it's very heavily defended. Can I send a patrol in?"

"No. Just stick to plans."

"It's a piece of cake!" Taplett insisted. His tanks and engineers had now landed. "Hell, we could take a tank force"—a company reinforced with tanks—"right across the causeway!" They could clear out Red Beach so the rest of the 5th Marines could land there without opposition. But Murray refused to budge. Taplett would have to be a spectator.

At two-thirty P.M. the four cruisers and six destroyers began the final bombardment of Inchon. Shells poured into the seaport, smashing every landmark of tactical importance. Fires blazed across the entire waterfront. Taplett had instructed Dr. Harvey to join him at the observation post. "I want you to see something you'll never see again," he said, and told Harvey to climb a tree.

By now the naval and air bombardment had covered Inchon with smoke. Clouds blew in from the sea and a slight drizzle began. Taplett hoped the amtracs would get off on time, since the sun would set an hour and thirteen minutes after the scheduled takeoff. The landing force would need every minute to secure the beaches before dark.

At 4:45 the naval and air bombardment stopped and three rocket ships moved in, showering Red and Blue beaches. At exactly 5:22 P.M., Marines from both regiments began scrambling from transports into amtracs. Taplett and Harvey watched eight LCVPs carrying two platoons of the 5th Marines toward Red Beach. They were to climb Cemetery Hill.

Dr. Harvey was enthralled. From his tree he could see what looked like every ship in the world standing off Inchon, as hundreds of landing craft headed for the seawall. Above were clouds of planes.

Taplett's mortars and heavy machine guns were providing cover for the 5th Marines. It was almost impossible to see what was happening at the seawall because of the smoke and explosions. Everyone on the hill around Harvey who had an M-1 was using it.

On their right the 1st Marines were approaching Blue Beach. Eugene Jones, the NBC-TV cameraman, was filming them as his amtrac neared a narrow strip of industrial waterfront. Only one of the twins was allowed to land, and Gene had won the toss. It was like the day five years ago when he was heading for beaches held by the Japanese. Today he heard a corporal grumbling: "You goddamn people! Won't you never learn to tape your grenades . . . you're gonna kill yourselves that way someday!"

At last the motors slowed and idled, and the column swung abreast. Then, at a signal, all motors ripped up in a crescendo. They had reached their line of departure, and headed forward into haze and smoke. The amtracs on both sides of Gene were invisible. It seemed as if they were rushing and rocking on a railroad track of motion.

"First wave," someone shouted. "Just ahead . . . mixup . . ."

All around Gene men got down to one knee. Eyes intent. No emotion. No feeling. "Pick up your brass, and move out, mister," said someone coolly. Gene looked over the edge. Amtracs, visible now, were moving in front and to the side like waterbugs. They circled, floundered, rose and fell, and bounced off the seawall. Men crouched behind the shields, firing. Two men started up. The first lifted his foot until a bullet smashed into him. He jerked, sagged, and rolled over the wall. The second man slid back on the amtrac's treads—shot. Jones ducked back onto the steel bottom. All around him were the crackling of rifles, the rattling of machine guns.

"Make for the hole in the wall!" someone shouted and pointed to a gaping shell hole. The amtrac plunged forward, bounced off another amtrac and all at once the huge wall loomed. The man nearest the bow jumped ashore, flung a grenade and dropped flat as it exploded. Up he popped, low and weaving, disappearing in the smoke and dust. The rifleman, thought Jones, was a man to know. Everyone followed him. Jones plopped into a dugout with the others. They could hear their amtrac backing down and someone yelling, "Down to the boat basin . . . can get over there . . . back with you in a minute." Then silence. As they lay in the dugout, mortar rounds rained down and shrapnel thudded around them.

Jones could hear someone down the wall saying in a flat, dry voice, "Yellow jacket to Fox five . . . 3rd Battalion over the wall . . . receiving mortar and small arms . . . moving inland . . . authority Big Jack." Then their amtrac was back. A Marine wearing a baseball cap holding a .45 in one hand, trotted forward shooting and waving imperiously, signaling directions. Jones watched him disappear down the seawall, the amtrac jerking, lumbering behind, the .50-caliber machine gun spitting fire over the guide's head like some great dog protecting a puppy.

"Move out!" someone yelled. "Man says to move out!" Thirty minutes had passed since they had come over the wall. It was getting dark fast. Behind Jones the blood-red ball of the sun rested flatly on the sea.

Everyone sprinted in a crouch, then dropped to one knee, then ran again, falling in holes or among the rails. Ahead Jones could see dimly, in the flames of Inchon, the blurred shadows of other Marines. All were moving forward in the twilight. A mortar burst nearby and shrapnel tore into Jones's stomach. Although seriously wounded, he crawled five hundred yards down the waterfront, refusing medical attention until he found a Marine who promised to take the precious film to his brother.

As the landing craft of the third wave carrying Able Company 5th Marines approached the seawall, Private First Class Ray Walker could make out through the smoke those in the preceding waves climbing the two ladders in the front of their LCVPs in order to get over the seawall. It was just like the movies. Funny thing though, while watching war movies he was always chewing his nails. Now he was calm. In fact, he felt good. "Cox'n," someone shouted, "hold the fucking boat still!" Then over the seawall they all scrambled. Walker hugged the dirt with everyone else until a sergeant shouted, "Come on, move out, Marines! You can't live forever!" No one moved. Walker sure as hell was not going anywhere until he was told by someone he knew.

A grenade dropped into their midst. Some brave soul threw it back. Walker tossed a few grenades out front. Poof! Thank God *they* didn't come back. A sergeant ran up to an enemy bunker and thrust his arm through the slit, holding the grenade until it went off. Christ, what balls! Then Walker learned that the gutsy sergeant's squad had just been chewed up by that bunker. Finally they were up and over the trenches led by someone or other up Cemetery Hill.

Maggie Higgins had gone in with the fifth wave. As they neared the seawall, an amber starshell burst over Red Beach. It meant the first objective of the 5th Marines, Cemetery Hill, had been taken. But before she could relax, brightly colored tracer bullets ripped across the bow of their landing craft. Everyone hunched deep.

Higgins peered at the men. Their faces were contorted with fear. The boat smashed into the seawall as bullets whined above.

"Come on, you big, brave Marines!" yelled Lieutenant R. J. Shening. He gave them hard shoves and the men scampered out of the bow. A burst of fire inspired her to get out of the boat fast. She dropped over the side into three feet of water, then reached back for her typewriter.

She vaulted the trenches on the other side of the seawall and ran to a mound for protection from bullets. In the half dark, Marines were zigzagging toward a cliff. By about seven P.M. Red Beach was secure and there was only intermittent small-arms fire. She decided to go aboard an LST and write her story.

The day had been a roaring success, and only 20 Marines had been killed and 179 wounded, including the cameraman, Gene Jones.

2.

Kim Il-sung had been warned by Mao that MacArthur would probably land at Inchon on September 15. Why wasn't a stronger force dug in along the beaches? Why hadn't artillery blasted the American fleet? Like the hero of a Greek tragedy, Kim had been brought down by hubris. Ignoring advice from subordinates, he had insisted on launching, on September 1, his all-out assault on the Pusan Perimeter, expecting to destroy Walker's Eighth Army, end the war, and receive worldwide acclaim as a military leader.

He had thrown everything available into this ambitious operation, but the troops who were to carry it out were already exhausted and running out of ammunition. Their tanks and vehicles had little gasoline. Moreover, UN air attacks had so badly damaged road and rail communications to the south that few reinforcements and supplies reached the frontline troops.

Kim's staff, shaken by the severe losses suffered in reaching the Naktong River, had warned him that the People's Army was in no condition to launch such an attack. They advised retreat in good order to mountainous terrain favorable to their troops. Here they could get food from friendly South Koreans and set traps and ambushes for the attacking Americans. When Kim angrily rejected this plan, Major Ju Yeong-bok, the translator from Russian to Korean of the invasion plans, feared the war was lost. Then word reached the North Korean engineering HQ in Seoul: "MacArthur has landed in force at Inchon!" Major Ju ordered his men to burn all papers and prepare for battle. As engineers they would be responsible for river crossings and putting up road blocks. "For the first time," he told them, "we will be under enemy fire."

Ju and two other subordinate officers were summoned by their chief, Colonel Park. "From a strategic viewpoint," he said, "we will have to hold our position until the main force fighting on the Naktong River has pulled back to the Han."

When Ju's fiancée had been killed in a recent bombing raid at Pyongyang, he had blamed Kim Il-sung and Stalin, not the Americans. Now, the debacle at Inchon brought Ju's latent hatred of Kim and communism to the surface. Why, he asked, had their leader done nothing after the prelanding enemy bombings of Wolmi-do? What was Kim doing when hundreds of enemy warships and convoy of transports were gathering off Inchon? And why had he sent the newly arrived 18th Division south toward the Naktong? It should have gone immediately to Inchon! And what was General Shtykov thinking about in this crisis? Ju knew that the Soviet ambassador was really the brains behind Kim. There were from 15,000 to 20,000 People's Army troops in the Inchon-Seoul area, but most of them were recruits with little training, and some had no weapons. Moreover, there was no air cover and few tanks. In spite of all this, their last order from Kim was to defend Seoul—to defend their capital to the last man. And where was Kim now? Hiding in his air-raid shelter in Pyongyang!

Ju soon learned that Kim had already taken makeshift measures after consulting with General Shtykov and other Soviet officials: the 105th Tank Division and the 87th Infantry Regiment of the 9th Division were instructed to leave the Naktong River area and head immediately for Seoul. Desperate orders had already been sent to all People's Army units: "Defend with your blood and life every mountain and every river! Defend to the death our capital, Seoul!" Yet the 105th Tank Division was down to fifty dilapidated tanks, and their movement was restricted by U.S. Air Force surveillance. The infantry units by now had lost almost all of their heavy equipment and were low on ammunition and food.

Later that afternoon, Colonel Park summoned Ju and the other two senior officers. "Your mission," he said "is to assure engineering security to the end." One man was to be responsible for the Seoul–Inchon highway; a second for the Suwon–Inchon road; and Ju was to take the Seoul–Kimpo road. All three groups were to set up obstacles, destroy bridges and railroad tracks. He told them to assemble their men and prepare to load trucks with mines and explosives at dusk. Ju followed instructions energetically. Despite his disillusionment, he still welcomed the chance to fight for his country.

Ju gave orders to his men to meet at the munitions depot in an hour, when they would start for Kimpo. Meantime, he had business to attend to. His uncle lived nearby and it was his family duty to say farewell, even though it would be difficult to face this relative, who was bitter about the Communist party and hated the People's Army.

But his uncle was in a state of excitement because of the latest news broadcast from Tokyo. "American entry into Seoul is near!" he exclaimed. "Ah, true liberation!" His worn face brightened.

Then his uncle began attacking the South Korean government. In June they had deceived the citizens of Seoul with false broadcasts and escaped like rats to Pusan. "We citizens hated and resented the Rhee government and so recognized your People's Army and welcomed them. But the hardships under the Red occupation are beyond description."

Ju tried to express his sorrow, but his uncle overrode him. "We citizens forgave the government that fled and have been waiting for the national army to return. They have just landed with the U.S. Army at Inchon! The entire people of South Korea are rejoicing!"

His uncle grasped Ju's hand with his own weak one. "The next time we meet, our country will be unified. President Rhee has announced cancellation of the 38th parallel on the radio today."

When Ju asked that his greetings be sent to his mother and her sister, he learned that his aunt had been arrested and badly beaten many times by Kim's police because she had been vice-chairman of a woman's anti-Communist group. "Her four children are on the verge of starvation."

Cursing the Reds, Ju went out to his jeep to head for the depot. The Capitol Building looked like a skeleton in the dark. Soldiers were rushing around as trucks dashed recklessly through the streets blasting their horns. Nearby, gunfire crackled. As the jeep headed down a narrow street, Ju and his driver came upon a mass of civilian prisoners, about three thousand, escorted by guards with automatic rifles. Ju could see that the prisoners, bound together by heavy chains on their ankles, were panting from the burdens on their backs. Home Ministry guards shouted for more speed and the prisoners quickened their steps, their chains clanking, *zah zack zack, zah zack zack,* as they scraped the road.

Then came a column of women painfully dragging their bare feet, hair disheveled. Ju imagined they were mourning the loss of husbands and children. He felt a surge of rage. Who had ordered this?

At the munitions depot, Ju found that the trucks were loaded and his troops assembled. From the nearby ferry they were transported to the southern bank of the Han. It was so dark they couldn't see the streets of the suburbs of Yongdungpo. After a few miles they came to burning buildings, but curiously the streets of the city were empty. From the south and east came the sound of gunfire. On the balcony of one large building were portraits of Stalin and Kim Il-sung ablaze from flames below.

The little column kept moving slowly toward Kimpo Airfield.

3.

At daybreak, September 16, the 5th Marines left Cemetery Hill and started for Seoul. They passed through the southern section of Inchon, leaving the mopping up to the South Korean Marine Corps. Inchon's streets were silent. Terrified civilians watched from their windows and alleyways, relieved to see no enemy. By dark the Marines were six miles inland. On their right, the 1st Marines, commanded by Colonel Lewis "Chesty" Puller, were also progressing, doing more hiking than fighting. Where were the North Koreans?

Aboard the *Mount McKinley,* the commander of the 1st Marine Division was getting ready to go ashore to his command post. "Good luck, General Smith," said MacArthur. "Take Kimpo Airfield as soon as you can."

Just before dawn of the 17th an advance platoon of Dog Company of the 5th Marines spotted six T-34's and infantrymen approaching. In minutes a bazooka team knocked out one tank, and the other five were quickly set afire by M-26's and recoilless rifles. Puller's 1st Marines on the right of the road joined in the attack and helped wipe out 200 infantrymen.

MacArthur was not far behind. He had landed that morning accompanied by a large group of generals, staff officers, and correspondents. As he approached the battlefield, the stench of high explosives still polluted the morning air. The cavalcade stopped so MacArthur could inspect a dead North Korean. Keyes Beech watched him poke the body with his toe and say, "That's the way I like to see them!" He was in a happy mood. "A good sight for my old eyes!" He turned to a doctor. "There's one patient you'll never have to work on, doc!"

The column continued down the road and came upon the wrecks of several Soviet tanks. MacArthur leaped out of his jeep to admire the blazing heaps of twisted metal. "Considering that they're Russian," he said, "these tanks are in the condition I desire them to be."

It had been another day of triumph for MacArthur, and his appearance at the front impressed not only the Marines but civilians. As his gig headed back for the *Mount McKinley*, he turned to Admiral Struble and Lieutenant General Lemuel Shepherd, Jr., commander of Fleet Marine Pacific. "Well done," he said solemnly.

The 5th Marines had advanced through desultory sniper fire and were within a thousand yards of Kimpo Airfield. Advance units came under moderate small-arms fire, but a rifle platoon knocked out one automatic weapon and Marine tanks smashed the remaining enemy resistance. By six P.M. the 5th Marines had reached the southern tip of Kimpo's main runway.

4.

It had been a hectic day for Major Ju and his engineers. After many delays, they had approached Kimpo Airfield at dawn. But he could see no activity nor any sign of retreating troops. Where was the People's Army?

Ju was at a loss. Should he advance or withdraw? This was his first experience in battle, and there was no one to advise him. Sitting at the foot of a large tree, he wrote a report to Colonel Park.

After dark a runner brought a reply from the colonel. The main U.S. force, he said, was approaching and would come across where the defense was weak and then advance toward Seoul from the northwest. The high command had ordered advance general headquarters to withdraw from Seoul. Therefore, there was no need to lay mines. "Stop work immediately and return to field headquarters."

Ju felt as if he had been struck by lightning. Summoning the company commander and platoon leaders, he told them to collect the mines and retreat. The ambition of Kim Il-sung had been crushed. This war had been approved by Stalin; but now the Russians weren't lifting a finger for fear of international repercussions.

Ju was at a turning point of his life and he had to act. Such a chance would never come again. He decided to seek freedom, even though it might seem an act of betrayal. He was determined to fight Communism and asked to be taken to an ROK Army unit, but no one knew where one was. Suddenly Ju felt worn out. He was taken to a nearby house where he fell asleep on the floor.

He was awakened by someone yelling, "American soldiers coming." Three men wearing dark green uniforms shouted in English while pointing their rifles. A young villager called out, "Hey, elder brother, the Americans are telling you, 'Hands up!' They'll shoot you if you don't do as you're told."

Ju was indignant. "I'm not a prisoner!" he exclaimed. But he slowly raised his hands with mixed feelings of regret, shame and desperation. His existence as a man of freedom was finished.

He was put in a jeep, which headed toward the airfield, seized while he had slept. He was astounded by the piles of oil drums and boxes of ammunition along the road. Occasionally a driver would shout curses at Ju and, for some reason, stick up a middle finger threateningly.

At the landing strip Ju was turned over to two Marines, who yelled, "Get moving!" One smacked him in the rear with the butt of his rifle. Then he heard an American officer talking on the phone in Korean. It was as if he had met Buddha in Hell. Now he could explain why he shouldn't be treated as a prisoner. But the officer glared at him. "Just answer my questions. Where should we bomb?"

Ju was thunderstruck. "Bombing should be limited to military targets," he said critically, and described several indiscriminate bombings that he had witnessed.

The American became so angry his white face turned red. "Because of shameless criminals like you we *have* to bomb indiscriminately!"

Ju was taken to a press tent, where two American correspondents queried him in poor Korean. When asked, "In which battle were you captured?" he replied, "I didn't fight. I wasn't captured. I walked in on my own two legs."

"Goddamn it," said one reporter. "You're captured now!"

At last Ju was brought to a small, barbed-wire enclosure. Fatigued, he threw himself on the grass, thinking of his humiliation. He wanted to die.

CHAPTER 13

Crossing Two Rivers
(September 16–22)

1.

In the south General Walker was planning his breakout from the Pusan Perimeter. But he did not have sufficient strength to concentrate an effective force; the enemy still held the initiative. The 24th was his only division not pinned down, and he planned to move it piecemeal from the east. If only he could have kept the 5th Marines, he would already be across the Naktong River with tank task forces racing towards Seoul.

Figuring that the enemy troops would be demoralized upon learning of the Inchon landing, Walker calculated that he would finally be ready to move by September 16, and got permission from MacArthur to cross the Naktong on that day. But the weather was so bad on the 16th that the saturation bombing planned for the area was canceled.

To the left of Hap Gay's 1st Cavalry Division, the 2nd Division under Lawrence Keiser smashed into the western flank, capturing Hill 208, which overlooked the Naktong. Two days later, September 18, two companies of the 2nd Division crossed the wide Naktong against a twelve-foot-deep current.

North of Taegu, the 8th Cavalry Regiment of the 1st Cavalry Division had been held to a standstill by the battered People's 13th Division. Walker, unhappy, told Gay in no uncertain terms that he was not pushing his men hard enough and that his failure to emulate those in the south was endangering the entire operation. Fortunately the ROK 1st Division to Gay's right had an aggressive commander. General Whitey Paik was charging forward, inflicting heavy casualties on the 13th People's Division. Even so Walker felt his efforts to break out of the perimeter were not going well and when, two days later, Eighth Army received the first briefing of Inchon, he realized the reason why. Whereas Inchon units had met scattered resistance, perimeter troops were encountering fanatical forces in prepared positions on dominant terrain. Every attack was fiercely resisted. To Walker, this indicated two things. Enemy commanders were still under orders to protect their gains. Failing that, they would try to inflict maximum casualties before being forced to withdraw.

Beyond discussing technical problems during the landing, there was scant coverage of the combat situation in the Inchon briefing. Things were quiet until the briefer mentioned the massive firepower used to support the landing. These figures brought gasps from the ammo-starved audience. Walker was heard to say: "They expended more ammunition to kill a handful of green troops at Wolmi-do and Inchon than I've been given to defeat ninety per cent of the North Korean Army."

Although the casualties of General Almond's X Corps had so far been light, Walker was convinced they would increase as his troops approached the more densely populated areas of Yongdungpo and Seoul. Furthermore, if forces were directed to assault rather than to encircle and isolate these complexes, their progress would be slowed. This would give the enemy time to react and reinforce. European commanders had learned this lesson during their sweep across France. Whenever possible, they avoided cities. To Patton, street fighting was but "a variation of pillbox fighting." To an infantry soldier, that was the worst kind.

Discussions about military matters had already convinced Walker that Almond's knowledge of combat fundamentals and principles was limited. Even worse, his impetuous nature led him to underestimate the enemy while overestimating his own competence.

Again, Walker remembered Patton's words. In differentiating between haste and speed in military operations, he warned that "there is a great difference between these words. Haste exists when troops are committed without proper reconnaissance, without the arrangement for proper supporting fire, and before every available man has been brought up. The result of such an attack will be to get the troops into action early, but to complete the action slowly."

In discussing speed, Patton emphasized that such attacks should be launched "with a predetermined plan so that time under fire will be reduced to the minimum." Walker considered Almond too compulsive to follow Patton's advice. If he encountered problems in his effort to take Seoul, he would probably ignore existing plans and start improvising. Were he to do so, there would be no "anvil" against which "hammer" forces from the Pusan Perimeter could strike. The bulk of enemy forces would simply bypass Seoul and escape to the north.

Following the briefing, Walker made his customary flight along the front with Lynch. The general appeared to be deep in thought. Shortly after noon, he had Tyner alert the airstrip to again ready his plane. This came as a surprise since MacLean had been directed to make a detailed reconnaissance of the Bowling Alley. He and Lynch were preparing to take off when Tyner called.

Normally, Walker would climb into the cockpit as soon as he arrived. But this time he paused at the wing. He was carrying the same map shown to Collins during his visit. Beyond ear-shot of others, he made a startling request. "I want to fly along this line." It was the one in his Kunsan plan.

"How far, General?" asked Lynch.

"To Taejon," he replied. "I want to see what shape the roads are in." He had made this same flight with General Partridge a month before. But that was in an Air Force T-6. Its low wing had prevented him from studying the roads.

"We can take the L-5," said Lynch. "But it won't be as safe." His other plane, the L-17, was almost 50 knots faster. However, like the T-6, it, too, had a low-wing configuration.

"Which one gives us a better chance of landing if we get hit?" the general asked.

"The L-5. I can put it down anywhere." Surprisingly, taking the flight in the first place was never discussed.

Walker asked his driver, Sergeant George Belton, to put his ever-present shotgun in the plane. Lynch tucked his own carbine under the front seat. He also put four grenades in the map pocket. Climbing into the cockpit, he glanced toward the rear. Staring back at him were two twelve-gauge barrels. Belton had propped the shotgun against the front seat. "General," said Lynch, "will you turn that gun around? I sure as hell don't want to be shot down by us." Walker laughed.

Once airborne, they headed toward the Bowling Alley. After climbing above small-arms range, they flew north to the town of Naktong, studying the river below. From there they turned west toward Sangju. At that point, Walker asked Lynch to drop down to get a better look at the road. They continued west to Poun at a low altitude, then began climbing as they approached Chonan. Finally, they turned south toward the battered city of Taejon.

There was no traffic along the route to Chonan. But it was evident that armored vehicles had used the road running north from Taejon. This meant the enemy was moving tanks at night. Their direction could not be determined.

They passed over Taejon at eight thousand feet. Walker had a good view of the road toward Kunsan. It was completely void of activity as far as he could see. They'd have had Taejon by now if only MacArthur had followed Walker's plan to land at Kunsan. "And," he muttered, "we could have trapped those forces facing us in the perimeter. All I needed was a small part of what they gave Almond."

Having just flown the route Walker planned, Lynch was sure he was right. "How do you want to go back, General?"

Walker thought for a minute. "I don't think it would be safe to fly directly to Taegu. They're strongest along that route. They know we're back here and might fire everything to knock us down." He decided. "Let's fly toward Chinju. We might be lucky enough to spot something in front of Kean." They didn't see a man or vehicle on the road leading back to the perimeter.

After having spent more than two hours behind enemy lines, they finally landed at Eighth Army's small airstrip. Tyner was waiting. "Did you have a nice flight?"

"I enjoyed it," was all Walker said. Later Tyner asked Lynch where they had been so he could enter it in the general's personal log. Mike tried to be as casual as Walker. "We visited Taejon." Joe stared in disbelief. This trip of seventy-five miles behind the enemy lines was the deepest of any flight in the Korean War by Army aircraft.

2.

On the 18th, soon after Major Ju was incarcerated at Kimpo Airfield, General Almond, commander of all ground forces in the operation, arrived at the headquarters of Colonel Ray Murray in the basement of the airfield operations building. Almond informed the 5th Marines commander that he intended taking Seoul in a pincers movement. On the right the 1st Marines, heading for Yongdungpo under Colonel Puller, had so far met little opposition from the disorganized North Korean troops. Once Yongdungpo was seized, Colonel Puller would cross the Han River and assault the capital on the right flank. Murray's 5th Marines would cross the Han at Kimpo and head along the north bank of the river so they could hit Seoul simultaneously.

Late on the afternoon of the following day, Ray Murray held a staff meeting in the operations building also attended by correspondents. In the light of Coleman lanterns, he said they would cross the Han early the next morning. Taplett had serious doubts about the plans. The crossing point was a ferry route, and he felt sure it would be heavily defended.

Taplett left, convinced that it had been a show for the press. A lot of bravado and big statements. We'll be across the Han, and soon we'll be in Seoul, and all that baloney. Murray had already ordered Captain Kenneth Houghton to swim across the river with his recon company at dark and seize a bridgehead formed by three hills. Then at four A.M. Taplett's 3/5 was to go over, followed by Roise's 2/5 with the 1/5 remaining in reserve. Tanks and vehicles would be ferried across on fifty-ton floating-bridge sections.

Taplett had reservations about the feasibility of recon's Han River crossing and their ability to seize and hold the three objectives on the north bank as ordered. His battalion was supposed to come over in an administrative crossing—that is, without any preparation for an assault crossing. The 3/5 would simply pass through the recon company and continue the attack toward Seoul. "I have misgivings," he said to his exec, John Canney, and his S3, Major Lawrence Smith. "I just don't think it's going to happen that easily."

At eight P.M., Captain Houghton, Second Lieutenant Dana Cashion, ten enlisted men and two Navy reserve officers, Horace Underwood and Ensign Judah Siegal, the latter a Navy information officer armed with a tape recorder, arrived at the riverbank. It was a small advance party. After checking the current and stripping to their skivvies, they slowly waded into the warming water. They silently swam breast-stroke across the Han in about thirty-five minutes. After getting a report from civilians that there were no North Koreans in the area, Houghton decided it was time to bring across the rest of the recon company in amtracs. He radioed back, "The Marines have landed and the situation is well in hand!" Ensign Siegal, who was giving a running account of the action on his tape recorder, was thrilled. This was history in the making! And he was putting it on tape.

The nine amtracs clanked down to the embarkation point and revved their motors. The din was deafening as they plunged into the river one by one. Suddenly shells started to explode among the amtracs. Four foundered in the mud, their treads spinning helplessly. Mortar rounds were dropping around them, and Houghton decided to swim out and guide their occupants to the beach. One round burst near the swimming Houghton. The explosion sprained his back and gave him double vision. One of Houghton's party, a corporal, dragged him to a mired amtrac. No one was aboard. All had swum back to the south bank.

By now the mobile amtracs were also heading back, although no one knew who had given the orders. The other men in Houghton's party soon left the beach and swam the four hundred yards to the safe side of the Han. Sergeant de Fazio and eight men swam back and finally located Houghton, still dazed, on the grounded amtrac. The conflicting accounts to Colonel Murray, particularly Ensign Siegal's excited report of his first combat action, made it almost impossible to discover what had really happened. Taplett's hunch had been right. The prospect of an easy advance was baloney.

Taplett was supposed to cross at four A.M., and while Houghton's team was landing at their beach, he had instructed Item Company to lead, followed by How Company, sandwiched by the H and S and weapons companies. As Taplett was dispatching these units from their positions, he heard Houghton announce, "The Marines have landed and the situation is well in hand!"

"I've still got the horrible feeling," Taplett said, "that things aren't going right."

When he heard that Houghton was withdrawing, Taplett told his staff to head for the embarkation site to load up for the crossing, then took off in a jeep with his radio operator to see Colonel Murray. He was told that Murray was asleep. "We're going to have to change the orders," Major Charlie Brush, the operations officer, told Taplett. "You're to make the assault crossing, but we don't think there's enough room on the beach to land tractors [amtracs] abreast. Therefore you're going to take this battalion across in single file."

"Get the regimental commander up," said Taplett. "I think it's suicide to go across single file. They'll just pick off one tractor after another."

"Those are my orders, and those're the orders of the regimental commander."

Taplett knew only one way to talk—straight out. "Well, you tell him I disagree with him," he said and left to order his company commanders to reload all the tractors and get the fire team's platoons organized so they would have cohesive assault by fire teams and combat teams in each tractor instead of being loaded up with a lot of administrative supplies.

Then he and his radioman, Private First Class Green, jeeped back to the Regimental CP to face Colonel Murray. Only Brush was in the office. Taplett demanded to see the colonel. Brush said he was still asleep and could not be disturbed. Never had Green seen Taplett so furious —and he too was incensed that they weren't able to see the man who was supposed to lead the attack in a few hours.

"Charlie," said the fuming Taplett, "I'm going to go across in waves of tractors and land my companies in columns. But I'm going to land in waves of tractors—four or five in each wave."

Taplett left without getting approval from Murray. He and the commander of the amtrac company started off in the jeep for the tractor site. Upon arrival Taplett received a radio message from Murray. Taplett, prepared for court-martial, was stunned when his superior said as calmly as if nothing had happened, "Can you make an assault crossing at four o'clock?"

"No way. I'll try to make it by five or five-thirty at the most." Then he said, "Ray, give me some artillery support and get me some air on station so we can use it 'on call.' "

3.

That day Walker was making some progress against a far more numerous foe. In the Naktong Bulge area the U.S. 2nd Division was still pushing forward. A battalion of the 38th Infantry crossed the Naktong River with tanks, artillery and mortars. And to the right of Gay, Whitey Paik's ROK 1st Division, having found a gap in the NK 1st Division in the high mountains, had plowed through to the key highway northeast of Tabu-dong. Paik's position thirteen miles past the most advanced units of Gay's division forced the NK People's 1st Division to withdraw two regiments from its strong mountain fortifications. Now Paik was in the rear of two enemy divisions, the 1st and the 13th.

Despite this progress, MacArthur expressed concern that night about General Walker at a meeting aboard the *Mount McKinley*. Was Walker aggressive enough to break out of the Pusan Perimeter in time to link up with X Corps in the Seoul area? Should he be replaced?

Learning about this, the indignant Walker phoned Major General Doyle Hickey, temporarily taking over Almond's desk duties in Tokyo, to say he was "ready to break loose" but was having difficulty getting his armor across the Naktong because of bridging problems. Almond's X Corps, he complained, was being given greater logistic support than Eighth Army. "We have been bastard children lately, and as far as our engineering equipment is concerned we are in pretty bad shape." He added, "I don't want you to think that I am dragging my heels, but I have a river across my whole front."

At five-thirty on the morning of the 20th, the 24th Division began crossing the Naktong near Taegu in the murky fog. This success on Gay's left, combined with Paik's breakthrough on his right, was followed by another victory of sorts. Just before dawn of September 21, the chief of staff of the 13th People's Division, Senior Colonel Lee Hak-ku, had awakened two sleeping 8th Cavalry men to surrender. He readily gave full information on the state of his division which was down to 500 men and no longer battle effective. They held no line. The regiments had lost communication with their division and men were fleeing for their lives. He said that about seventy-five percent of the troops were South Korean conscripts. Rations were down to a half, there were no tanks, and only a few self-propelled guns and mortars. Of their three hundred trucks, only thirty could run.

Although Lee talked at length, he did not give the full story of why he had come over to the United Nations. During World War II he had been a grade-school teacher and afterwards became a Communist. In 1946 he joined the North Korean Army and after four years was a four-star colonel, a rank equivalent to an American brigadier general. His relationship with the commander of the 13th Division, Major General Choi Yong-jin, worsened as the division advanced to the Bowling Alley. Because of Choi's reckless tactics, the division suffered heavy casualties and by August was down to 3,000 men. Despite their low strength, Choi insisted on headlong attacks. Lee protested as the casualties increased, but Choi drove his men relentlessly. On the night of September 20 he ordered Lee to prepare a final all-out attack. Lee was appalled. "While we are alive, we can attack!" cried Choi.

Lee protested that the men were exhausted and starving. They had almost no ammunition. "This is not my order," said Choi. "It is the supreme commander's." He ordered Lee to collect all the hungry and wounded men "as one human bullet" and attack the Americans.

"But Comrade Choi, we have already lost the war!" News of MacArthur's landing at Inchon had finally reached the troops and morale was low. Colonel Lee begged Choi not to throw away the lives of his men.

"If you do not obey me," shouted Choi, "you are a traitor of the party."

"*You* are the traitor of the people!"

Choi called him an American spy, and drew his side arm. But Lee was faster and shot the general in the arm. He ordered a retreat of all the survivors, then at dark went forward looking for a South Korean unit. He finally found two sleeping Americans and surrendered.

4.

By dawn of September 20, the 5th Marines had recovered from the foul-up of the 19th. Murray had not only gone along with Taplett's request for an assault landing but had postponed the four-thirty A.M. crossing until everything was properly prepared.

At six-thirty Taplett's 3rd Battalion started across in amtracs. Item Company led, with G and H companies to follow. Taplett's plan was to secure the landing site and immediately turn right up the massive high ground which controlled the landing area.

From the south bank MacArthur, Almond and a score of generals and admirals watched Taplett's battalion successfully cross the river against heavy firing from the enemy.

One tractor was hit by machine-gun fire as its gate dropped and the men piled out. Despite casualties, the 3rd Platoon started up the slope to the high ground with no hesitation while the 2nd Platoon attacked on the left. The going was rough, with the mortar section cut down by enemy machine guns. The 2nd Platoon's commander was among the wounded, and the platoon fell back to deploy. Reinforced by engineers, they rushed over the first spur with the help of the other two platoons. The Item Company commander radioed to Taplett, "I'm over the first one!" With this news that no more rifle and machine-gun fire was directed on the landing site, Lieutenant Bohn started across the river with his infantry company. It landed without casualties and headed east toward its objective.

When Bohn reported, "There's no resistance whatsoever," Taplett sent H Company across. They, too, arrived safely and met no resistance. It was 9:40 A.M. and twenty minutes later a wave of amtracs brought the 2nd Battalion to the north side of the Han.

MacArthur was delighted.

Before Taplett had gained his three objectives on the north bank, Almond was already racing to Colonel Puller's command post on a hill overlooking his objective, Yongdungpo. Puller, having methodically deployed his regiment around the city, was standing next to a jeep, puffing his pipe and studying maps, when Almond arrived.

Glaring at Yongdungpo, Chesty pointed at it. "There's only one way to flush 'em out, General Almond," he said. "This town ought to be burned."

"Then why don't you go ahead and do it?"

He needed permission and had been trying to reach Major General Oliver P. Smith, commander of the Marine division.

"I'll give you permission," said Almond, exhilarated by the sound and smell of battle. He had commanded a division in Italy, and although he enjoyed being MacArthur's chief of staff, he yearned for combat. As commander of X Corps, he was in charge of the entire Inchon-Seoul operation, but he would have preferred being out front where he could personally supervise regimental and battalion commanders. "You go ahead and do what you think is best. Just take that town."

By the end of that memorable day, Yongdungpo was in flames from Puller's howitzers, 105-mm guns, and incendiary shells from 4.2 mortars. Adding to the holocaust were strikes by Corsairs with rockets and napalm. All through the night the town burned, and at six-thirty the next morning, September 21, Puller launched a major attack. The fighting was fierce, and the North Koreans fell back slowly.

The next day Puller's men broke through enemy defenses with the help of the 32nd Infantry Regiment of the 7th Division. These GIs had entered the battle only two days earlier and were already making sizable gains on the right flank. The enemy was retreating on all sides, and the 1st Marines had occupied Yongdungpo by midafternoon. They found the streets littered with dead as well as abandoned heavy equipment and supplies.

Across the river the 5th Marines were also progressing. Taplett had taken three little hills, and the 1st Battalion had advanced three thousand yards against light-to-moderate enemy resistance. Murray was pleased. His regiment was now less than a mile west of the Capitol Building in Seoul, but the real battle was yet to come.

At Kimpo Airfield Major Ju and other prisoners were being loaded into five open trucks, their destination a large POW camp near Inchon. As they went through the first village, people cheered the U.S. Army shouting, "Long live President Truman! Long live President Syngman Rhee!" But upon espying the prisoners they yelled, "Kill them! Down with Kim Il-Sung! Down with Stalin!"

Someone noticed Ju's uniform. Boys threw stones at him while their elders called for his death.

Late that afternoon the convoy reached a temporary POW camp on the outskirts of Inchon. Ju was led down a dark corridor to a cell. As he entered, five men stood up, saluted. They had been captured on Wolmi and only forty-five of their battalion survived. "On our march here we had to walk stark naked with our hands on our heads," one said. "People threw stones at us and beat us with sticks."

"That is because we were forced to fight in this unjust war," said Ju.

"We all want to join you," replied their spokesman. "We'll fight with you against the Communists."

Ju felt renewed spirit.

CHAPTER 14

The Fall of Seoul
(September 23–29)

1.

On the north side of the Han River, Baker Company of the 5th Marines was hanging on to rugged Hill 106 despite heavy enemy fire. It was noon, September 23. The company commander, Captain Ike Fenton, was teed off. "Dave . . . *please*, you goddamned idiot!" he exclaimed to *Life* photographer David Douglas Duncan. "I can't get you out of here if you're hit. Keep your tail down."

"Mid-autumn sunlight had filled our world," recalled Duncan. "It still did. For all but one of us, that is. For him, the Marine beside me who had been opening his K-Ration almost with anticipation—the sunshine made everything look better than it was that day—for him, night was already near. A North Korean sniper's bullet had just thudded into his chest, crumbling him sideways into our hilltop trench. The boldface label on the waxed, half-open carton seemed ironic: RATION, INDIVIDUAL, COMBAT."

Fenton ordered four riflemen to carry the wounded man back to where the helicopters could land. "The dead are dead," he said. "It's the wounded that wreck us." Ike's eyes were angry, bloodshot. "Okay," he said to Duncan, "get your pictures. But for Christ's sake, don't get wounded!" He tore open his K-Ration.

"How about killed?" asked Duncan.

Ike Fenton almost smiled. They were old friends.

214

At dusk the photographer found Leonard Hayworth. "He was my reason for rejoining Ike Fenton's assault company after the Inchon landing for the attack upon Seoul. Corporal Leonard Hayworth stood six feet three and resembled actor Errol Flynn playing a Marine corporal in Korea. Except Leonard Hayworth was small-town, shy and gentle, and a master machine gunner. I had photographed him in tears late one rain-and-bullet-swept afternoon two weeks earlier on the Naktong River Perimeter when he had crawled back from his empty gun to plead for more ammunition from his captain, Ike Fenton—his captain who had neither ammo nor replacements for the wounded nor the dead nor aerial support nor radio contact with the rear. And the gooks were attacking. Leonard Hayworth wept his frustration. Ike Fenton's eyes were those of an apostle being crucified upon his own anguish and faith."

The next morning at dawn a North Korean machine gunner shot Hayworth between the eyes. A little later Duncan scratched a chest muscle that suddenly tingled. Fenton laughed, held out his fist. A scrap of metal dropped into Duncan's hand. An enemy bullet, at the absolute end of its flight, had just struck Duncan over the heart and fallen to the dirt below. Later in the day he wondered a little about luck and fate. "And I pondered a bit over my profession. It had started simply as fun."

Late the next afternoon, September 23, General Almond was telling General Smith at X Corps headquarters that he wanted the 1st Marines to attack Seoul from the southeast while the 5th Marines continued their assault from the northwest. He would give the Marines twenty-four hours longer "to make headway," and asked Smith to "guarantee that the 1st Marine Division would capture the city by 25 September."

The courtly Smith may have looked unaggressive to Almond. It was well-known that he was a Christian Scientist and his side-arm holster was always empty. He also spoke quietly and controlled his temper. But he was extremely stubborn about anything that involved the safety of his troops. "I can't guarantee you anything," he said coldly. "I leave that up to the enemy." He added that his troops would do the best they could and go as fast as possible.

Smith did point out that the 5th Marines had run into much stiffer resistance than anyone had anticipated, indicating that the North Koreans were going to put up a desperate battle for Seoul.

The tension between the two men increased. Smith knew about Almond's many trips to Marine command posts during the past two days and could not refrain from remarking that he preferred handling his own regiments.

"I'm not handling your regiments!" retorted Almond sharply. "I'm just seeing how they do after *you* handle them." He added that he was going to visit the Marine regiments the next day; if they had made no advances, he would narrow the Marine sector so that the seizure of South Mountain, the most dominant feature of Seoul, could be assigned to the U.S. Army—General Barr's 7th Division. He would announce his decision at another meeting the following day in Yongdungpo; General Barr would be there.

During the night Puller finished preparations for crossing the Han at dawn the next day, September 24. But mine-clearing operations at the crossing site caused a delay, and the reconnaissance and assault elements of the 2nd Battalion did not embark until eight A.M. With no tank support for the enemy and only scattered fire, the entire 2nd Battalion was safely across by 9:45.

Instead of observing this maneuver, Almond went to Barr's 7th Division command post and instructed him to prepare for his crossing the next day. He was to attack Seoul on Puller's right flank. Almond then visited both Puller and Murray, informing them in person what he wanted done. He rushed back to his own CP, had lunch, and hurried back with two staff officers to Yongdungpo in time for a two P.M. commanders' conference. Smith and Barr were already there with the 32nd Infantry Regiment commander, Colonel Charles Beauchamp, who had been reassigned to his old regiment from the 34th. A group of correspondents crowded around the conferees. Almond announced that he had decided to narrow the Marine sector and let the 32nd Regiment cross the Han the following morning.

The antagonism between Smith and Almond was obvious even though both tried to remain calm. "Where are your amtracs?" Almond asked Smith.

"They're up near Kimpo."

Almond said he needed them to make a crossing for the 32nd. Smith bridled. Puller's regiment had to have them to complete his crossing. "They've been assigned to the 1st Marine Division," he added.

Almond retorted that this didn't concern him in the least. "How long will it be before I can get them?"

The Marine major in charge of amtracs said they could be available before dark. But Colonel Beauchamp protested that his men had never used amtracs. "They wouldn't know how to run them."

"No sweat," said the Marine major. "You put sixteen men in each one, and we'll get them across."

It seemed that the short meeting was over without much rancor until Almond remarked he had seen both Murray and Puller earlier in the day, explained the plan and told each exactly what he had to do. To Smith it was a slap in the face. Only yesterday he had protested that Almond was trying to run Marine regiments. "Smith just hit the ceiling," recalled Barr.

This sudden display upset Almond, who noticed that the other officers were startled and the correspondents were drinking it all in. He attempted to soothe Smith by saying they could discuss the matter privately after the conference. Once alone, Smith repeated his request that Almond not give direct orders to his regimental commanders. For once the X Corps commander was on the defensive. There must be some misunderstanding, he said. He had never given any orders to Murray or Puller.

Smith icily replied that Puller and Murray thought they had been given orders. Almond hastily replied that he would certainly correct that impression, and as Smith wrote in his log, "There the matter rested."

While Puller's men were establishing a strong bridgehead in Seoul, Murray's 5th Marines were meeting fierce opposition in the rugged hills to the left. The actions of men in Taplett's battalion were typical of the scores of small-unit firefights and hundreds of individual battles being waged northwest of Seoul. For Private First Class Preston Parks, Jr., of G Company—gunner in a fire team—tribulations lasted all day. He was an enormous man, whose size could be a disadvantage, since he presented such a huge target. But today it turned out to be an asset. Parks was big enough to play professional football. He was also a rugged individualist. He had been lying peacefully in a gully when his sergeant disturbed his serenity. "I want you to go up that hill and look down in the valley and see what's there."

"If you want to know what's over that ridge, you go and look. I'm not sticking my head out."

Lamb, Parks's assistant gunner, said, "I'll go!" and started off. Seconds later there were two bangs. Lamb went down. "I'm hit!"

"Well, damn it, crawl on back down here."

He did, and Parks pulled him into the gully. "Get me a corpsman!" he shouted. A few minutes later one appeared and began complaining. "I'm not supposed to be up here," he said. "I belong in a field hospital."

"I didn't give you the assignment," growled Parks. "Now get your ass up here and help me with this man."

Moments after the corpsman left, a round hit between Parks and his fire-team leader, Pop Miller. Ears ringing, Parks dove to the right. Miller, a veteran of World War II, jumped to his feet and started up the hill. There was another bang and Miller fell.

Parks, grabbing his collar, pulled Miller down and again hollered for a corpsman. After a battle-dressing had been applied to Miller's elbow, Parks told his two wounded buddies he'd bring them them to the aid station. With his BAR strapped around his shoulder, Parks carried them like babies, Lamb on the right, Miller on the left, their arms around his neck. He started up the hill. Near the top Pop whispered, "Goddamn it, look at that!"

Forty yards ahead they saw two North Koreans behind a machine gun, gazing down into the valley. Parks cautiously laid down the two wounded men and gave them rifles. When he said, "Three," they all fired.

"Did we get them?" asked Pop.

There was the machine gun but no enemy. Parks crept up to the gun. It was a Nambo with two magazines. No sense leaving a good souvenir. He picked it up. Now he had a BAR, a machine gun and two wounded men. He got them all down the other side of the hill to the aid station.

No sooner had he returned to his position than a lieutenant appeared. "Saddle up," he said. "We're taking that hill across the valley."

Parks shook the man next to him. "Jones," he said, "we're moving out." Jones didn't want to move out and said, "Goddamn it, I'm not going this time. I'm sick and tired of hearing, 'Saddle up, we're moving out.' I'm staying right here." Parks finally persuaded Jones to follow the others, who were jogging in a crouch. Then came withering machine-gun and rifle fire. Everybody dropped. The forward observer raised himself up to look through his glasses and four rounds came in near his chin. "The hell with this shit," he said, and fell back.

Irked, Jones said, "They can't hit me," and stood up. As he peered out front, he suddenly turned. "Parks, I'm hit." Parks opened Jones's field jacket and saw Jones had been shot above the left pocket. A small trickle of blood oozed out. Parks talked to him as he breathed heavily. Then there came a heavy, deep snoring, like a death rattle. Parks screamed, "Corpsman!"

At last one came, but said there was nothing he could do for Jones. "He's dead."

"Like hell," said Parks. "He's still breathing. By God, you do something for him or *you're* going to be dead."

The corpsman gave Jones a shot of morphine and then addressed Parks. "I'm sorry. He was dead when I got here," he said and left.

Parks had run out of cigarettes and reached into Jones's left-hand pocket for a package of Camels. The first three were bloody and Parks tossed them aside. He found a dry one and lit it. A youngster nearby said, "Goddamn it! Are you going to smoke his cigarettes? He's dead!"

"I want to tell you something, sonny. Jones and I were friends, and if he was alive and I asked him, he'd give me the cigarettes."

"That's not the point. You're smoking a dead man's cigarette."

Enemy firing was still heavy. Parks laid Jones down and put his weapon beside him. A few minutes later their lieutenant leaned over the body. "Jones," he said, "you're going to be okay. We have a helicopter coming to get you."

Parks puffed on his cigarette. "He'll never believe that. Can't you tell a dead man when you're talking to one?"

"If that man is dead, goddamn it, cover him up with a poncho!" The lieutenant stalked angrily down the hill. Parks sat silently as two men covered Jones with a poncho. There was nothing to do but wait for artillery or mortar fire.

They sat there till dusk without any artillery. Then came the shout, "Fix bayonets, we're going to take that hill!" As Parks prepared his fire team, Marines started shouting and shooting all along the line. Parks's team rushed forward and, after a firefight, took about seven prisoners. Parks sent a new replacement to find out what the CP wanted to do with them. One captured NK kept saying, "Give me a cigarette, Joe. Give me a cigarette, Joe." Nobody paid any attention to him.

It was the end of a typical day in Taplett's battalion.

The battle for Seoul entered its final stage at dawn of September 25, when Chesty Puller's 1st Marines crossed the Han and entered the city. By midafternoon they had seized a hill in the southwest section of the city not far from the industrial area.

The next morning General Smith's division was at last in position, for the first time since the landing, to attack with all three regiments abreast. On the left flank the 7th Marines had entered the battle. In the center were Murray's 5th Marines, and on the right flank, within the city itself, were Puller's 1st Marines.

2.

That evening in Peking, Indian ambassador Kavalam Panikkar dined with General Nieh Yen-jung, the aging Army chief of staff who was also the military governor of Peking. With his round face and shaved head he reminded Panikkar of a Prussian officer. But he was always pleasant, friendly and frank. After dinner they talked about the war in Korea. In a quiet manner Nieh revealed that the Chinese did not intend to sit back with folded hands and let the Americans come up to their Manchurian border. Panikkar, taken aback by the news, was impressed by the general's quiet and pleasant tone.

"We know what we are in for," continued Nieh. "But at all costs American aggression has to be stopped. The Americans can bomb us, they can destroy our industries, but they cannot defeat us on land."

Panikkar warned that such destruction would put China back half a century. Even the interior could be bombed.

"We have calculated all that. They may even drop atom bombs on us. What then? They may kill a few million people. Without sacrifice a nation's independence cannot be upheld." He calculated the effectiveness of atom bombs, then said, "After all, China lives on the farms. What can atom bombs do there? Yes, our economic development will be put back. We may have to wait for it."

3.

In the hills northeast of Seoul Taplett's people were running into heavy opposition—as usual. How Company was moving slowly down a huge spur on the left flank after taking heavy casualties. Late in the afternoon, just as Item Company was passing through to continue the attack, a force of 200 North Koreans hit hard. The fight raged until dark, and the enemy, badly mangled, finally withdrew. Taplett's battalion was almost in position to pass the 2nd Battalion and continue down the pesky spur to the outskirts of Seoul.

At 8:08 P.M. General Almond sent a message to Smith's 1st Marine Division: "You will push attack now to the limit of your objectives in order to insure maximum destruction of enemy forces." When Colonel Alpha Bowser, the operations officer, read the message, he was worried. How could the division attack when Taplett was still under attack himself? He telephoned X Corps, but there was no mistake and Bowser reluctantly took the order to General Smith, who strenuously objected to Almond's chief of staff. Smith was told that Almond had issued the message himself.

The Marine general ordered both Puller and Murray to coordinate their attacks but to keep to avenues of advance that could be identified in the dark. Distressed, Murray consulted Lieutenant Colonel Joseph Stewart, a veteran operations officer, who said, "I'm afraid we'll have to delay pursuit of the fleeing enemy until we see if Tap can beat off this counterattack." And when Taplett, who had been taking casualties all day, heard the order, he told Murray, "I can't pursue anything!"

Even so, the order had to be obeyed, and both Puller and Murray planned to launch attacks at 1:45 A.M. While these were being organized, Almond, glowing with confidence, told correspondents that the North Koreans were fleeing to the north and his troops were already making significant progress in Seoul.

At about midnight Lieutenant Colonel Thomas Ridge, commander of Puller's 3rd Battalion, was ordered to prepare a night attack. He protested as forcefully as he could. When this failed, he passed on the order to Major Edwin Simmons, Weapons Company commander, who also protested.

"What are our objectives?" he asked.

"No objectives. Just go straight ahead. We'll lay down very heavy fires."

Simmons had already sent out a patrol to make contact with Taplett's battalion on the left. "Well," he protested, "the fire will land straight on top of Corporal Collins and his patrol!"

"That's the fortunes of war," said Ridge.

At 1:15 A.M., NK infantry, tanks and propelled guns were reported approaching the Ma-Po Boulevard roadblock that Simmons had helped set up early in the evening.

Simmons and his radio operator were standing outside his CP, a house atop a hill overlooking Ma-Po Boulevard where it crossed a bridge spanning a stream. On the other side was a walled building heavily defended by the enemy. Simmons was about to give orders for the artillery preparation when he heard enemy tanks rumbling down the boulevard toward him from the center of Seoul. He flashed a warning to all units just as the lead tank fired its first round. Simmons shouted for his radio operator, Vargas, to follow him and darted for the cellar steps leading to the CP. But Vargas was dead. A shell had gone through his stomach. Simmons got the radio belonging to a mortar observer, switched frequencies, and called battalion: "Enemy tanks are coming down the boulevard! They're about to hit us!"

"Thank God!" said Ridge.

"What did you say?" said Simmons.

Two T-34's and a crowd of enemy infantry approached the bridge. They were met by close-range Marine fire. One tank was stopped, the other spun on its tracks and hid behind a corner.

Simmons ordered the artillery behind him to shorten range to the minimum that would clear the mass of high ground he occupied. The 81-mm mortars should also continue firing at closest range.

Simmons began using heavy machine guns against the tanks and, though the guns could not penetrate the armor, the steady firing kept them buttoned up. He figured this was an attack of battalion size, and by four A.M. the foxholes of the machine gunners were almost knee deep in cartridge cases. G Company's first sergeant, Rocco Zullo, kept the men in position; and his runner, Cecil Sanders, the best machine gunner he had, was going from foxhole to foxhole, laying each gun properly and checking to see the lay was not changed.

During the long fight, Simmons stayed on the cellar steps so he could keep in touch with everyone. Fortunately, the enemy was firing at his hill a bit too high. But he was sure that with first light, at about five-thirty, the enemy would correct that error.

He knew he had to prepare for a tank attack and called down to the roadblock, "Send up a recoilless rifle!" The rifle was an especially accurate weapon, and its best position at dawn would be on top of the hill. Simmons positioned the gun with its crew in front of his cellar steps. He told them the approximate location of the tanks. One T-34 in particular, he explained, was causing trouble.

Simmons told the gunner, "I want you to look through that sight, and as soon as there is enough light for you to see that tank, you let me know. You'll only get one chance. If you don't hit him the first time, he's going to see us." As the time approached, Simmons crouched behind the gunner. "I can see it!" said the gunner.

"Fire!" said Simmons.

The round hit the tank, but before they could congratulate each other, the back-blast of the recoilless rifle smashed into the house and they were covered with mud and wattle. Simmons, a model of neatness, was a mess. He picked himself up and looked down. All was quiet. There was one dead tank on the bridge. Several others were smoking. He went down to the roadblock to check on his men. They and G Company were in good spirits but were exhausted after fighting all night. Miraculously, Corporal Collins and his patrol came in unscathed. They had taken cover in a culvert and the North Korean attack had rolled over the top of them.

A little later Puller came up to Ridge's CP. The expenditure of shells the night before had been tremendous. He glowered at Ridge. "You had better show me some results of the alleged battle you had last night." The report of damage done by Simmons and the artillery was just coming in: seven tanks, two self-propelled guns and eight 45-mm antitank guns. Eighty-three shell-shocked prisoners had been collected and more than four hundred dead had been found. Two companies of determined Marines, led by a determined major, without a tank but with the help of formidable artillery and mortar fire, had destroyed a battalion reinforced with Russian tanks and self-propelled guns.

Fuller's men continued the drive up Ma-Po Boulevard. Charles Jones was near the point, filming the advance. He was alone, since his twin was still recovering from his wound at Inchon. At first there was little resistance; then rifle fire crackled from a building on a rise to the right. The Marines scattered, their heavy packs twisting and jumping up and down as slugs whined off the cement. Charlie followed a group into an alley and made out tiny figures running down a side street only a block away. Riflemen were jumping in all directions, yelling and bringing up their weapons. Jones filmed the first prisoner who crawled out with hands upraised, bleeding from concussion. Soon the sidewalks were massed with the 2nd Battalion, 1st Marines, moving forward. Assault companies took off at a dead run, the men spaced at twenty-foot intervals, bobbing and weaving. They approached barricades of earth-filled rice bags, shoulder high, stretching across the boulevard. Jones swung his camera onto a bazooka team running forward to blast a hole in the barricade for those behind, then set off another rocket, which hit a heavy power cable dangling thirty feet ahead and exploded, spraying shrapnel onto the street. One Marine lying in the debris stared sullenly at the bazooka man. "Christ sake . . . dumb bastard . . . could get killed around here."

Reginald Thompson of the London *Daily Telegraph* was shocked at the destruction. "Few people," he reported, "can have suffered so terrible a liberation. Great palls of smoke lie over us as massive buildings collapse in showers of sparks, puffing masses of smoke and rubble upon us in terrific heat."

Early that morning Taplett launched an attack to clear the last resistance of the nettlesome hill complex protecting the northwestern section of Seoul. In the lead was George Company. Its commander, Bob Bohn, had been seriously wounded after crossing the Han. His replacement, First Lieutenant Charles Mize, a soft-spoken southerner, led by example, not shouting. His men already trusted him. As George battered through a maze of trenches held by stubborn North Koreans, a bullet went through Mize's leg. A corpsman bandaged him, but he refused to be evacuated.

His company finally started down the spur and reached the outskirts of the city. At one crossing, Private First Class Fred Davidson thought he saw a head and rifle barrel at the window of a small, one-story building. He crept to the doorway, carbine at the ready, wishing he had a grenade. Taking a deep breath, he jumped through the opening and saw a North Korean as he landed. He pulled the trigger but only one shot fired. The damned carbine had jammed. But the single bullet had dropped his man, who was on the floor screaming and crying. The bullet had somehow gone through his buttocks to take three fingers off his right hand.

Davidson tried to clear the jam while cautiously approaching the enemy. The North Korean was a kid—about his own age. Davidson kicked his rifle away and peered into the next room. Empty. He cleared the jam and aimed the carbine at the youngster's head. Just then two Marines burst in to help. Soon the room was crowded with Marines who had come to see what all the excitement was about. A Navy corpsman began working on the Korean's wounds, and Davidson drifted outside. All he could think of was what that one bullet had done. Amazing!

A few hours later MacArthur released United Nations Communiqué 9: "Seoul, the capital of the Republic of Korea, is again in friendly hands. United Nations Forces, including the 17th Regiment of the ROK Army and elements of the U.S. 7th and 1st Marine Divisions, have completed the envelopment of the city."

Radio Pyongyang's report—that the People's Forces in Seoul were still desperately resisting and would "fight to the last man"—was more accurate. The battle for Seoul was far from over.

4.

General Walker was in his element. His troops, led by armored spearheads, had smashed through the enemy cordon in the south. On all sides Kim Il-sung's troops were retreating north in disorder, with some units disintegrating. In the past four days his 1st Cavalry Division had broken loose for a tremendous gain. The 24th Division to Gay's right was also making progress. Walker had been constantly on the move—on the ground with his aide, Tyner, or in the air with Mike Lynch.

Eighth Army headquarters was already back in Taegu, and Major Tyner noticed that every night before retiring the general would study his precious copy of Patton's treatise on armed warfare. Satisfaction with his troops' success was augmented by the Silver Star his son—Lieutenant Sam Walker, a company commander in the 24th Division—had been awarded for heroic action in the seizure of Songju.

On the morning of September 26, Walker had high hopes for Task Force Lynch—a battalion from the 7th Cavalry Regiment reinforced by an engineer company, seven tanks from another battalion, an artillery battalion, a heavy mortar company and a tactical air party. Since leaving Tabudong near the Bowling Alley, this powerful mobile force had ripped north all the way to Poun, 106 miles from Osan, recently taken by Barr's 7th Division on the right flank of Almond's X Corps.

The deeds of Task Force Lynch reminded Walker of his idol's dash across France after D-Day. General Patton would have loved these young tankers who were refuting the theory that Korea was not tank country. The first elements of Task Force Lynch, led by First Lieutenant Robert Baker's platoon of tanks, left Poun at eleven-thirty A.M. Mile after mile they met only cheering villagers.

Walker was following their rapid progress in a plane piloted by General Partridge. They flew over Task Force Lynch and at midafternoon landed unannounced at Suwon Airfield, held by troops of the 7th Division. For an hour Walker conferred with the commander of the GIs, informing him that Task Force Lynch was on its way to Osan for a linkup with X Corps and would arrive within thirty-six hours. But Lieutenant Baker was far ahead of schedule and by six P.M. had advanced fiftyfour road miles. He soon reached the main Seoul–Pusan highway, the scene of bloody fighting in July, where General Dean's troops had been savaged.

Upon reaching Chonan, Baker didn't know which way to turn at an intersection. Sticking his head out of the turret, he called to a North Korean soldier on guard, "Osan?"

The soldier nodded in affirmation and then was terrified to see that Baker was an American. Other enemy soldiers gaped in wonder as the Americans drove through town. A few miles north they ran into more enemy troops, fired on them, and continued. Baker was now out of touch with the rest of Task Force Lynch, several miles in the rear.

Baker's tanks continued, receiving enemy fire three miles short of Osan, not slowing when the fire increased. An antitank shell sheared off the machine-gun mount of the third U.S. tank, killing one man. Nearing the 7th Division lines, they were met with small-arms and recoilless-rifle fire. Tankers of the 7th Division prepared to repel a tank attack. But when Baker's lead tank increased speed and turned on lights, the 7th Division tankers hesitated momentarily. Just as they were about to fire, a white-phosphorus grenade lit up the American star on Baker's tank. Another American-versus-American battle was narrowly avoided. And Baker's tanks were safe after traveling 106 miles in one day. It was 10:26 P.M.

5.

Dawn of September 27 revealed a smoking, dying Seoul. Puller's men were already moving into the business section. Puller had ordered his company commanders to keep the men moving because the buildings and rooftops were full of Reds. They were to circle to the side streets if held up by barricades and let the ROK Marines mop up behind them.

Taplett's battalion had started the day expecting heavy resistance but had met only a few shots from snipers. Making their way down the hill through the smoke and haze drifting up from Seoul, they reached the western streets of the city by midmorning. The way was guarded by barricades at every intersection. Private First Class Davidson ran up the flight of steps leading to a theater to look ahead and see what lay in store for them. On the boulevard, streetcars were used as part of the next barricade. Supported by a Pershing tank, George Company got through this obstacle with supporting fire from the machine guns of Weapons Company. As they headed for the next barricade, Davidson saw Big Jack Westerman, his platoon leader. As usual, the lieutenant was leading his men down the street as if he were bulletproof. Big Jack stepped out from a building and was suddenly slammed backwards, brought down by a sniper. He turned onto his stomach as the man next to him leaped protectively on top of him and fired. The sniper continued to shoot, his bullets spattering all around Big Jack and his guardian. Davidson spotted the sniper's hole and raised his carbine. As he pulled the trigger, he saw a bullet strike Big Jack in the right shoulder. It was incredible, but he actually saw the bullet hit. This inspired Big Jack to scramble on all fours for cover behind the building.

After a Pershing tank had come up and blasted large holes in the sandbags on the barricade with its 90-mm cannon, a rifle squad from Westerman's platoon rushed forward, catching the defenders before they could reman.

Davidson and the others took cover while a demolition team set explosives in and around the obstruction and blew it apart. Davidson went up to Westerman, who was being bandaged by a corpsman. He'd been hit twice in almost the same place. Davidson was about to say, "You've got the million-dollar-wound, Big Jack!" but realized in time that Westerman might lose his right arm. "Take it easy, skipper," he said.

At noon two Red flags were still flying on both sides of the great dome of the Capitol Building. Taplett ordered G and I companies to continue the attack, and advance units cautiously approached the Capitol grounds. One tank backed up, then charged forward, smashing through the huge gate. Infantrymen followed. There was a little firing but not a living soul in sight, only bodies.

By now hundreds of Marines were in the grounds. A youngster named Keyton shinnied up the flagpole, tore down a beautiful silk-and-nylon North Korean flag and replaced it with the Stars and Stripes. While some Marines watched, others like Davidson were answering scattered small-arms fire. Those around the flagpole broke into cheers when the American flag finally waved in the breeze. Meantime, Marines were charging into the main building, clearing out North Koreans, room by room, floor by floor.

Davidson saw one Marine strutting from the building with a Tiger skin, tail and all, draped around him. Another was wearing an antique warrior's helmet, and others were decorating each other with fancy medals that turned out to be national treasures.

Taplett was catching hell because of G Company's audacity in running up the American flag. X Corps sent a UN flag to replace it. Fortunately there were two flag poles, and the UN flag was placed on the second staff. Taplett saved one of the North Korean flags for the battalion and gave the other to General Smith, an act which did not endear Taplett to X Corps.

While Taplett's men were raising the American flag, Puller's 2nd Battalion was raising one above the Russian consulate. And eight minutes later another went up over the U.S. consulate nearby.

The city flamed, rocked and shook. It was four-thirty P.M., and except for the mopping up, the Battle of Seoul was over.

Taplett was in a helicopter bound for Almond's headquarters across the Han. Here he was briefed on the ceremony that MacArthur had planned for returning the Korean government to the city of Seoul. Taplett was to ensure the complete security of the area around the Capitol Building where the event would take place.

He returned by helicopter, landing between the huge shattered gate and the domed building. It was getting dark and he decided to spend the night there. By now the place was swarming with his men searching for souvenirs. He chased everyone out of the museum with orders to return all artifacts. In the morning Taplett's troops began setting up security for MacArthur's arrival the next day. The 1st and 7th Marines and the GIs of the 7th Division were still busy seizing the heights on both sides of Seoul and mopping up the streets, while Rhee's police were scouring the city for civilians who had supported Kim Il-sung. The Marines and GIs were appalled at the slaughter performed by these police. Hundreds had been slain on the spot and thousands imprisoned.

While MacArthur was preparing for the historic ceremony, he was astounded to get a message from the Joint Chiefs admonishing him for his plan to restore the Rhee government. Such an act "must have the approval of higher authority."

The general promptly replied. "Your message is not understood. I have no plan whatsoever except scrupulously to implement the directive I have received." The UN Security Council, he said, had called upon all its members to assist the Republic of Korea, to repel the armed attacks, and to restore security in the area.

"The existing government of the Republic has never ceased to function," he added. It was the only Korean government whose legality had been recognized by the UN. What he planned to do in Seoul was merely return Seoul to this government. "Such action is not only very much desired by the American ambassador and all others concerned, but appears to be implicit in my directives."

His response ended attempts in Washington to undercut Rhee by those who felt he was too headstrong and dictatorial. In Taegu, Muccio and his staff enthusiastically backed MacArthur. Early that evening two C-54's arrived to carry Rhee, Muccio and their staffs to the ceremony.

At dawn of September 29, Marine guards were unobtrusively placed along the route from Kimpo Airfield to the domed Capitol Building, also known as Government Palace. While Taplett was setting up security around the area, a vehicle burst through the gates, horn blowing. Taplett stared at a bunch of characters in Army fatigues and battle gear leaping out as if about to launch an attack. They said they were intelligence officers and wanted a place to change clothes. Taplett invited them into the building. Soon they emerged in dress uniform to announce they were the honor guard.

Sergeant Ted Sell and Private First Class Sam Jaffe of the 1st Marines were ordered to jeep down to Ascom City Airfield and greet MacArthur. "Don't let him get killed in our sector," their commander said. The two arrived at the airfield an hour before MacArthur's estimated arrival. They were still in dirty dungarees, and the Air Force cooks refused to serve them because they didn't have mess kits. Sell reached for a pancake and told the mess man to put bacon on it. So did Jaffe. Then they went outside to wait for the great man, wiping their greasy hands on their fatigues.

At 10 A.M., the *SCAP* touched down. The general and his wife stepped onto the asphalt taxiway. He was wearing a beautifully ironed field uniform without a necktie. The MacArthurs were led to the first of five Chevrolet staff cars. Behind followed five spotless jeeps for the press and less important guests. Soon they came to the Han and approached a pontoon bridge, which Lieutenant Colonel Edward Rowny's engineers were still repairing. The bridge had been finished the night before, but a squall had knocked it apart, and the bent sections had to be taken to forges set up in Inchon for straightening. The colonel was still making last-minute repairs as the procession started across. Rowny, who had written his wife that he really wished MacArthur could walk on water, watched anxiously as the general's car reached the other side safely. MacArthur had refused to take a helicopter to the Capitol Building, insisting that a parade would impress the people of Seoul.

The streets were lined with civilians who had been routed out to cheer the general. But the procession was going so fast that many didn't know what was going on. Then Jaffe, who with Sell was directly behind MacArthur, mounted a small American flag on the windshield, and this sight brought cheers.

As they passed through the big gate to the Capitol Building, Sell told the driver to park. He and Jaffe leaped out to follow MacArthur. Emotionally stirred, the general was pinning Silver Stars on both Almond and Walker. The two filthy Marine enlisted men were shooed away. But Sell remembered his orders to stick closely to the general no matter what. Learning where MacArthur's speech would be given, he and Jaffe, despite glares from high-ranking officers, forced their way inside to a balcony overlooking the spot.

Rhee's plane landed at eleven, and the presidential procession headed for the Han. As Noble crossed the river, he remembered their hectic departure three months earlier. As they entered Seoul, people along the road cheered. Many were weeping with joy.

Noble was appalled at the sight of the ruined city. It was worse than Tokyo after the war. The first streets were battle torn, but as they came to the center of town it was obvious that many of the buildings had been burned by the retreating North Koreans. Most of the windows in the

Capitol Building were smashed; its great copper dome was twisted and blackened.

Chesty Puller's jeep arrived at the gate a few minutes later. Damned if he'd dress up for the occasion, he wore his rumpled, dirty utilities. He hadn't shaved since the landing and looked like what he was. An Army MP, a natty major, stopped his jeep. Only staff cars were allowed in the compound.

Puller removed his pipe. "This is our real estate, Major. My boys took this damned place."

"Orders, Colonel. I'm sorry. I can't let you pass."

Puller grabbed the windshield and stood up. "I don't give a damn what your orders are, old man. My orders are to go in there, and I'm going. Now get out of the way."

"Not today, Colonel."

"Listen, Major, if you wanted to throw your weight around, you should have been here when you could get your nose bloody, while the 1st Marines were coming through the streets."

"My orders, sir. You cannot enter here."

Puller turned to the driver. "Run over him, Jones!"

Jones gunned the motor, flinging Puller back into the seat. The MP major leaped aside shouting, "I'll see you when you get out of there!"

The main room of the building, the vaulted National Assembly chamber, was thronged with numerous U.S. Army and Navy officers; United Nations officials; diplomats, such as Ambassador Muccio; President and Mrs. Rhee; and many South Korean officials and officers, as well as several British officers wearing whites.

The room was topped by large skylights. In the balconies curving above the platform, MacArthur's honor guard, in shining helmets, stood as still as statues, irking the few Marines present. "You'd think," remarked Craig to Puller, "that they'd have the decency to give some of the honor to men who captured the place."

As the clock struck twelve, MacArthur and Rhee strode into the room, arm in arm. All stood silent and respectful, except for photographers leaping about to snap pictures. Sergeant Sell's presence in a balcony with Private First Class Jaffe still caused dark looks. Sell counted three full rows of Army generals in starched khaki. He hadn't known there were so many. There were also several rows of State Department people and other dignitaries, but only four Marine officers—Colonels Puller and Murray and Generals Smith and Craig.

The place still smelled of smoke, and Sell could hear the sound of distant small-arms fire. Occasionally an artillery boom shook the building. MacArthur strode to the lectern. Behind him the president sat with Mrs. Rhee and a junior army officer few people recognized, James Hausman.

"By the grace of a merciful Providence," began the general, "our forces, fighting under the standard of that greatest hope and inspiration of mankind, the United Nations, have liberated this ancient capital city of Korea. It has been freed from the despotism of Communist rule and its citizens once more have the opportunity for that immutable concept of life which holds invincibly to the primacy of individual liberty and personal dignity. . . ."

Glass, loosened by the artillery, suddenly began to rain from the molded skylights high above. It was like the hand of God, recalled one Marine. Officers hastily donned helmets, but the bare-headed Mac-Arthur never flinched and kept talking unhurriedly as if nothing had happened. "On behalf of the United Nations Command I am happy to restore to you, Mr. President, the seat of your government, that from it you may better fulfill your constitutional responsibilities."

He paused and then asked the audience to rise and join him in reciting the Lord's Prayer. Helmets came off as everyone rose.

"Our Father, who art in Heaven, hallowed be Thy name . . ." Tears were flowing down MacArthur's cheeks, but his voice was strong and steady. After the prayer, MacArthur turned to the aged Rhee and said with emotion, "Mr. President, my officers and I will now resume our military duties and leave you and your government to the discharge of civil responsibilities." Rhee rose and clasped MacArthur's hand. "We admire you!" he exclaimed as tears coursed down his furrowed cheeks. "We love you as the savior of our race! How can I ever explain to you my own undying gratitude and that of the Korean people?"

Puller had been observing Rhee with admiration during the ceremony. "He had fought the Japanese for thirty or forty years, trying to save his country. His fingers had been ruined, all broken and gnarled where the Japs had tortured him. And he'd fought the Reds just as hard. Now people in Washington were trying to dump him." As Puller left the building he looked around for the Army major who had threatened him. It was fortunate he didn't find him, for Chesty was fuming. "They never said a damned word about the Marine Corps!" he muttered. "Can you imagine that? Who the hell do they think carried this whole fight?"

Maggie Higgins watched as other correspondents and dignitaries surged around MacArthur. She was still in bedraggled battle dress and tried to avoid him, but he caught sight of her and called out, "Hello there, tall, blond and ugly! Come up and see me sometime!"

He was soon aboard the plane bound for Tokyo. As he strode the aisle with long, deliberate steps, pipe clenched in his teeth, he was making plans to finish the job in Korea.

The war had suddenly turned around. After suffering the humiliation of being driven almost to the bottom of the Korean Peninsula, he had stunned the world by charging all the way back to Seoul. Complete victory lay just ahead.

PART V

THE CHINESE PUZZLE

CHAPTER 15

Across the 38th Parallel
(September 29–October 15)

1.

Two days before the gala occasion in Seoul, the Joint Chiefs informed MacArthur that his military objective was the destruction of the North Korean armed forces, but under no circumstances were his forces to cross Manchurian or Soviet borders. MacArthur replied that the Eighth Army would attack across the 38th parallel with the objective of seizing Pyongyang. X Corps would make an amphibious landing on the east coast at Wonsan and then drive across the peninsula to help Walker take the capital.

But MacArthur's vision took him far beyond Pyongyang. He wanted *all* of Korea. MacArthur, at the peak of his military fame, held the upper hand in Korea a few hours after he strode triumphantly out of the Capitol Building in Seoul on that afternoon of September 29. But it was President Rhee who took the first military initiative, and he did so without consulting the general. Rhee summoned Chief of Staff Chung Il-kwon and asked if there were any markings along the 38th parallel. Chung's answer was negative. All stones and signs had been removed. "Do you think they should be disregarded?" asked the president.

"The parallel," said Chung, "is only a line drawn on a map. There is no such thing."

This was what Rhee wanted to hear. To him the 38th parallel was a symbol perpetrated by foreigners. *All* Korea should belong to the

Republic of Korea. "Why don't you let those two regiments you have up there through it?" Chung protested that the operational authority to do so was in the hands of General MacArthur as commander of the UN forces. "Well, are you the chief of staff of the United Nations or the chief of staff of the Korean Army?" The latter, Chung replied. "In that case," said Rhee, "don't you think you should obey the order of the president of Korea? I gave General MacArthur authority over the ROK Army temporarily. If I want to take it back, I can take it back today."

"Yes, sir. Mr. President, if you give me the order, I will immediately execute it."

Rhee scribbled on a piece of paper. "This is my order." It directed Chung to march his forces north immediately and was signed by the president.

Chung was soon flying in a light plane towards his advance regiments. The next morning, September 30, he was in a jeep chasing up the east coast highway after his 3rd Division. At eleven A.M. he met a regimental commander who told him the men were excited; they all wanted to be first into North Korea. "I can't hold them any longer!" he exclaimed, adding that one battalion was already nearing the 38th parallel. Where precisely was the battalion commander? asked Chung. The embarrassed answer was that *he* was leading his men. "He is already in a town six miles on the other side of the parallel."

"Can you communicate with him?" asked Chung.

The regimental commander reached him by radio.

"Are you aware that you are disobeying army rules?" said Chung.

"Yes, sir," said the battalion commander. "However . . ." he hesitated, "isn't the 38th parallel no longer valid?"

"I understand how you feel, but you have violated military law. Are you prepared for a court-martial?" He was. "What kind of terrain is up there?"

"One company is in back of a mountain."

"Can you see any North Korean troops?"

"Many, sir! They're busy escaping and are burning rice warehouses. Please give us the order to go ahead. We must not lose this great opportunity!"

"Do you think one company is enough?"

"One platoon would be enough right now."

At that moment there was no United Nations, no General Walker, no President Rhee. Just one courageous battalion commander. "Advance to the north," Chung told him.

MacArthur made no public announcement that the parallel had been crossed, but it was clear he assumed he had authority to do so from the message he sent the secretary of defense: "Unless and until the enemy capitulates, I regard all of Korea open for our military operations." The following day, October 1, he called upon the commander in chief of the North Korean forces to surrender.

It was no coincidence that Premier Chou En-lai, in a speech that same day—the first anniversary of the Chinese Communist state—warned the West that the Chinese people "will not tolerate foreign aggression and will not stand aside should the imperialists wantonly invade the territory of their neighbor." This clear threat to intervene in the Korean War if UN troops crossed the 38th parallel was ignored in Washington. The Joint Chiefs cabled MacArthur: "We desire that you proceed with your operations without any further explanation or announcement and let action determine the matter."

The Joint Chiefs had already told MacArthur that Truman wanted to downplay the crossing of the parallel and that any announcement might "precipitate embarrassment in the UN." On both sides of the world there were already repercussions. The Soviet delegate in the UN proposed a plan on October 2 calling for a cease-fire in Korea and the withdrawal of all foreign troops. Near midnight in Peking, Indian ambassador Kavalam Panikkar was awakened to learn that Chen Chia-kang, the director of Asian affairs of the Chinese Foreign Ministry, was waiting for him in his drawing room. Apologetically, Chen asked Panikkar to see the prime minister at his residence immediately.

As Panikkar left his house half an hour later, the streets of Peking were almost deserted. Guessing that the sudden call was connected with Korea, he was bursting with impatience to know what had happened. Did Chou En-lai have fresh proposals to communicate to Nehru? Had the Chinese entered the war? He found Chou as courteous and charming as ever. After the usual tea, Chou thanked Pandit Nehru for his contributions to peace, then said that, if the Americans crossed the 38th parallel, China would be forced to intervene.

Did he have news that the Americans had already crossed the border? asked Panikkar. Yes, answered Chou, but he didn't know where.

At one-thirty A.M., October 3, Panikkar telegraphed the gist of their conversation to New Delhi. Although MacArthur would not announce that the ROK 3rd Division had crossed the parallel until later in the day, Panikkar guessed it had been done; and he was sure the Chinese troops concentrated in Manchuria had also moved across the Yalu. In the morning he shared this information with the British minister.

When the news was passed on to Acheson, the secretary of state did not take it seriously, because he distrusted Panikkar. "He was not a good reporter." Nor had Acheson taken seriously Chou's recent speech declaring that China would not stand aside if North Korea was invaded.

Panikkar, nevertheless, *was* an accurate reporter. Chou En-lai's warning had not been mere rhetoric, and Chairman Mao had decided that very day to send troops to Korea to fight the Americans and South Koreans. Eighty percent of Chinese heavy industry lay in Manchuria; it *had* to be held. The Chinese troops, called the Volunteers Army, were to be led by their top field officer, Lin Piao, commander in chief of the Fourth Field Army. A wily man, Lin claimed to be sick, but many believed he had no relish for fighting the Americans.

Near noon on October 4 a plane arrived at the First Field Army headquarters in the northwest with orders for its commander, Peng Teh-huai, to leave immediately for a special conference of the Communist Party of China (CPC) Central Committee in Peking. Born a peasant, Peng had attended a military academy and become a regimental commander of warlord troops. Then he had joined Mao.

It was after four in the afternoon when Peng arrived in the capital. The conference had been in session at Yi Nien Hall for some time, and a comrade informed Peng that Chairman Mao had started by asking the Central Committee to spell out the disadvantages of sending troops to aid their North Korean brothers. After listening to a frank recital of the drawbacks, the chairman had said, "Everything you say is true, but when a neighbor is in mortal danger, it is hard just to stand by and watch, no matter how logical such a course may be."

Although Mao was supported by Chou En-lai, Peng felt that most of those present were against going to war. Convinced that Mao was right, Peng did not speak up because of a feeling of inferiority. During the war with Japan, Peng had organized a massive offensive of a hundred regiments which had stunned the enemy. But envious colleagues later criticized this campaign as unnecessary and costly. In Chinese political and military life, such controversial matters as "The Battle of a Hundred Regiments" were never forgotten.

The meeting adjourned and Peng was taken to dinner at a restaurant by comrades on the administrative staff of the Central Committee. Peng still kept his opinion to himself, but that night he could not sleep. "I thought the spring bed might be too luxurious for me, so I tried sleeping on the rug." But he couldn't get the meeting out of his mind. The United States had invaded North Korea and was threatening northeastern China, only a river away. America also controlled Taiwan and was threatening Shanghai and China's eastern seaboard. "If the United States wanted to invade China, I thought, they would always find some excuse. Sooner or later the tiger devours the man; the timing only depends on the tiger's hunger."

Peng concluded that they must resist and defend every inch of ground. If they didn't fight American imperialism to the death, they would never be able to build socialism in China. "And if the United States should wage war on us, an early end would favor the Americans.

But a protracted war would favor us. So too would a conventional war favor the Americans. We could only gain the upper hand by using the same tactics we used against Japan. Now we are much stronger, our government controls all of China and we are getting some aid from Russia. Sending troops to Korea would also help the future construction of the fatherland."

Peng kept hearing the fervent words Mao had spoken at the meeting: "When a neighbor is in mortal danger, it is hard just to stand by and watch." The cautious words of the others were those of nationalists and not internationalists. "I came to the conclusion that sending aid and troops to North Korea was the correct, necessary, and farsighted course of action, and that the situation was so serious we could not hesitate any longer. I became completely convinced that Chairman Mao was right."

The next afternoon the Central Committee reconvened in Yi Nien Hall. After several comrades expressed their contrary views, Peng finally spoke, and did so emphatically. "It *is* necessary to send troops to aid North Korea. If the fatherland suffers great destruction, it only means that our victory will be delayed by several years, as it was in the war of liberation. If the United States has troops stationed in Taiwan and on the banks of the Yalu River, it can always find some excuse to start an invasion."

Chairman Mao promptly declared that Peng would be commander of the Volunteers. Peng accepted without reservation. Afterwards a comrade congratulated him: "You never seem to age!"

And so China reluctantly entered the Korean conflict, not to further world communism but to protect itself from invasion by a powerful enemy threatening to use atomic bombs. The irony was that the United States had already won the Korean War. Kim Il-sung's armies were soundly defeated and were no longer a threat to South Korea. But MacArthur's dream of taking *all* of Korea and perhaps pushing even farther north had forced Mao into a war he had tried for months to avoid.

Because the Americans had refused to take Chou En-lai's warnings seriously, their troops were unknowingly facing disaster. Who was to blame? Not only MacArthur, the dreamer, but the Joint Chiefs and the Truman administration. The JCS and the administration could have restrained MacArthur but bowed pusillanimously to the man who was still riding high in public opinion polls all over the Western world for his astounding victory at Inchon—which, in truth, had been handed to him by Kim Il-sung and could be termed a Pyrrhic victory. Now America and her allies were entering the Second Korean War, a war against a more powerful adversary, Red China.

Mao's decision to intervene had not been influenced by the Soviet

Union. Although Stalin had been blindly optimistic in the first days of the conflict, the retaking of Seoul had convinced him the war was lost. He had cabled Peking: "Comrade Kim Il-sung will be forced to come to northeast China to form an exile government." But when Stalin learned of China's decision to send troops, it was reported that he shed tears and praised the Chinese. To Harrison Salisbury of *The New York Times*, however, these were crocodile tears. He believed Stalin had caught Mao in a nutcracker.

2.

At a meeting of the UN at Lake Success, there was so much controversy over the ROK crossing of the 38th parallel that the U.S. delegation brought the Korean question before the General Assembly, where American influence greatly outweighed that of the Soviet Union. This maneuver served its purpose. The General Assembly passed a resolution giving implicit assent to MacArthur's conquest and occupation of North Korea. As far as the Joint Chiefs were concerned, this resolution supported operations north of the 38th parallel. They sent a copy of the declaration to MacArthur, who regarded it as permission to destroy the North Korean Army, since Kim Il-sung had ignored his recent call to surrender.

Walker's ROK I Corps, comprised of the 3rd and Capital divisions, was pushing up the east coast by land. Despite heavy casualties, it was finally approaching the port of Wonsan, 110 air miles north of the 38th parallel. This was the goal of Almond's X Corps in an amphibious operation which was not even ready to set sail. Walker was champing at the bit. Although continuing to be plagued by supply shortages, he was ready to start his main drive to Pyongyang on the west coast. The ROK I Corps and the American IX Corps (2nd and 25th divisions plus the Puerto Rican 65th Regiment) would attack then in the center, with the ROK corps in the east. Walker thought MacArthur's order to send X Corps to Wonsan by ship was illogical and risky; it would take too much time and complicate supply lines. Walker's ROK I Corps could get to Wonsan overland in a few days.

The Joint Chiefs also were dubious of the amphibious maneuver but felt they could not question the judgment of the man whose Inchon operation had won acclaim from all Americans, including his political enemies.

On October 6, Walker's ROK 6th Division also crossed the parallel, followed the next day by the ROK 7th Division. Walker called General Hickey in Tokyo and wanted to know when he would get MacArthur's order to kick off on the main attack to Pyongyang. Hickey, still acting chief of staff, replied, "Your A-Day will be at such time as you see it ready."

Two days later Walker informed MacArthur that he had ordered his commanders to strike out for Pyongyang. The 1st Cavalry Division was already across the parallel north of Kaesong, the city taken by North Koreans on the morning of June 25. Gay's troops were joined by the British 27th Brigade, Whitey Paik's ROK 1st Division, and the U.S. 24th Division. Walker was confident. Again he and Lynch had flown far ahead of current dispositions and had assessed the threat. To others his advances may have appeared rash. But by his combat instincts and personal reconnaissance, he had left little to fate. The attack would be conducted in a professional manner.

Buoyed by this sudden action and the UN resolution, MacArthur sent Kim Il-sung another radio call to surrender. Predictably, Kim Il-sung, even though aware that MacArthur's troops were already swarming into North Korea, rejected this demand. On that same day, the Joint Chiefs, fearing MacArthur might act rashly, ordered him to "obtain authorization from Washington prior to taking any military action against objectives in Chinese territory." The message did not deter MacArthur. Nothing succeeded like success. On October 10 troops of Walker's two ROK divisions on the east coast entered Wonsan, and fierce fighting on the streets lasted throughout the night. By dawn the city was secured. Walker was triumphant. Wonsan was his while Almond's X Corps was still at sea. Walker was confident that such good news would cause MacArthur to put him in command of X Corps.

The innocent belief that his commander was going to do the proper thing soon collapsed. MacArthur had no intention of placing Almond under Walker. "Wonsan port facilities will be secured and utilized for operations of X Corps," he radioed Walker. Then he lowered the boom. Once Almond's troops landed in Wonsan, Walker would lose command of all the ROK forces in the area. "I now plan to place X Corps in operational control of I ROK Corps." This meant a divided command in North Korea, with Walker controlling the west and Almond in complete charge of the east. Almond would also have the veteran troops that Walker had counted on so heavily in the Pusan Perimeter—the Marines. To make matters worse, MacArthur had already shifted to Walker complete responsibility for coordinating the logistic support of all UN forces in Korea. The reason was not clear to Walker. He had been given the mission of coordinating support of *all* forces in Korea, yet he was allowed to control only the west. It didn't make sense.

3.

The day before MacArthur's second ultimatum to Kim Il-sung, the Chinese ambassador to North Korea had informed Kim that the CPC Central Committee had decided to send the Chinese Volunteers Army to fight in Korea. Meanwhile, Chou En-lai had just arrived in Moscow to discuss with Stalin China's entry into the Korean War and what war matériel the Soviets would provide.

A representative of Kim Il-sung was also in Moscow urgently requesting more aid from Stalin. But Stalin's bland reply was disappointing: "I wish the Korean people, heroically defending the independence of their country, a successful conclusion to their struggle of many years' duration for a united, independent, and democratic Korea." There was not one word about equipment or Russian troops. It was evident that Stalin regarded the North Korean cause as hopeless after Inchon and was passing the torch to Mao. On October 10, the Chinese Foreign Ministry alerted the nation for mobilization: "The American war of invasion in Korea has been a serious menace to the security of China from its very start."

The recapture of Seoul and the American–South Korean drive north forced Kim Il-sung to realize his precarious situation. He set up a new capital at the mouth of the Yalu River. He also issued an order to all his troops explaining why they had been defeated: "Some of our officers have been cast into utter confusion by the new situation and have thrown away their weapons and left their positions without orders." They were not to retreat one more step: "Now we have no space in which to fall back." He warned that all agitators and deserters would be executed on the spot. To carry out this order there would be a "Supervising Army," composed of men who had distinguished themselves in battle.

4.

When Truman learned that two U.S. fighter planes had attacked a Soviet airfield sixty-two miles above the North Korean border near Vladivostok on October 8, he was so deeply concerned that he decided he must have a private talk with MacArthur. And so, two days later, Truman's press secretary handed reporters a statement announcing that the president was meeting with MacArthur the next weekend somewhere in the Pacific. The site, Wake Island, was not mentioned. He would be accompanied by a distinguished group, including Averell Harriman, Dean Rusk, Chairman of the Joint Chiefs General Omar Bradley, and Secretary of the Army Frank Pace.

This announcement brought Truman back to the front pages that had been dominated by MacArthur's great victories. The statement emphasized that the meeting was not due to any "sudden emergency"; and although a White House spokesman declared their meeting was not political, it was widely assumed that the trip was designed to help the Democrats in the coming election.

On October 11 the president boarded the DC-6 *Independence* and, after two stops, flew to Hickam Air Force Base in Hawaii, landing on the 14th at eight A.M. After a tour and dinner, he bedded down in the *Independence* which took off at twelve minutes after midnight. In five hours his entourage crossed the international date line, and it suddenly became Sunday the 15th.

MacArthur was already in Wake, having arrived with a small party including Ambassador Muccio. The general was not in a happy mood. On the trip from Japan he had clearly expressed to Muccio his disgust with "being summoned for political reasons." He was "mad as hell." His watch was still on Tokyo time, three hours earlier than that of Wake, and he didn't get to bed until two A.M. Yet he seemed completely rested when Whitney woke him an hour and a half later to give him time to bathe, dress, and have breakfast before the president's scheduled arrival at six.

Half an hour later the *Independence* appeared. As it came to a stop, MacArthur strode to the foot of the launching ramp, greeting Truman with apparent warmth and friendliness. Instead of saluting his Commander in Chief, he seized Truman's right arm while pumping his hand, and said, "Mr. President!"

Truman smiled. "How are you, General? I'm glad you are here. I've been a long time meeting you, General."

"I hope it won't be so long next time, Mr. President."

As the two shook hands, photographers and correspondents swarmed around. For almost forty-five minutes president and general talked privately. MacArthur expressed his regret that any misunderstanding had arisen because of his message to the VFW on the strategic importance of Formosa. But Truman brushed this matter aside. "Oh, think nothing more about that." He was finding MacArthur a stimulating and fascinating person.

The formal meeting in the one-story concrete-and-frame building at the southeast tip of the island was under way by 7:45 A.M. Truman removed his jacket and MacArthur pulled out his briar pipe. "Do you mind if I smoke, Mr. President?"

"No," said Truman wryly, "I suppose I've had more smoke blown in my face than any other man alive." Those in the room laughed. This air of informality prevailed throughout the meeting.

After discussing the rehabilitation and unity of the two Koreas, Truman asked the question that everyone was waiting for: "What are the chances for Chinese or Soviet intervention?"

"Very little," said MacArthur. "Had they interfered in the first or second month, it would have been decisive. We are no longer fearful of their intervention. We no longer stand hat in hand. The Chinese have 300,000 men in Manchuria." Of these probably not more than 100,000 to 125,000 were distributed along the Yalu River, and only 50,000 or

60,000 could have gotten across it. "They have no air force. Now that we have bases for our Air Force in Korea, if the Chinese tried to get down to Pyongyang, there would be the greatest slaughter."

He did not underestimate Russian air power, but the Soviets had no ground troops available for North Korea. "The only other combination would be Russian air support of Chinese ground troops." And ground support was very difficult. "I believe it just wouldn't work out with Chinese Communist ground and Russian air. We are the best."

Both men quickly approved a communiqué, which, in 748 words, praised the conference, claiming that, "The very complete unanimity of view which prevailed enabled us to finish our discussions rapidly."

"I've never had a more satisfactory conference since I've been President," Truman told reporters; but MacArthur, reluctant to talk, walked away.

On the way to the airstrip MacArthur asked Truman if he was going to run for reelection. He countered by asking if the general had any political ambitions. "None whatsoever," was the reply. "If you have any general running against you, his name will be Eisenhower, not MacArthur."

Truman chuckled. "Eisenhower doesn't know the first thing about politics. Why, if he should become President, his administration would make Grant's look like a model of perfection."

As the president mounted the ramp to the *Independence*, the general gave a friendly wave. At 11:35 A.M. the plane started down the runway with MacArthur still waving.

What had been gained at Wake was a friendly connection between the administration and a general at the height of his popularity. There had been no serious discussion of the likelihood of Chinese intervention in Korea. Whether planned or not, the publicity received by the president, generated by a military hero's reflected glory, appeared substantial, yet it would have no effect on the election several weeks later.

CHAPTER 16

"Many, Many Chinese Are Coming!"
(October 14–26)

1.

Four days after the Wake Conference troops of the 40th Chinese Army crossed the Yalu River at Andong in the twilight over two bridges built long ago by the Japanese. Soon troops of the 39th and 42nd armies were marching into North Korea at seven additional points along the river. In all there were now in South Korea four armies, three artillery divisions and one antiaircraft regiment. But Commander in Chief Peng and Chairman Mao still had no definite plan for the opening campaign. These troops were only getting into position for the initial assault.

The crossings were undetected by American fliers, and MacArthur remained convinced, as did the CIA, that there was no real threat of Chinese intervention. Just before leaving Wake, the general, still glowing with good humor, called out to the correspondents, "Come on up to Pyongyang. It won't be long now!"

Well on their way to the North Korean capital despite difficulty getting supplies, Walker's troops had broken through the principal prepared enemy positions between the 38th parallel and Pyongyang. NK troops were pulling back in confusion, and MacArthur's remark that his men would soon be in Pyongyang was not a fanciful boast.

The dirt roads had been turned into mud by torrential rains, and it was a race between Gay's 1st Cavalry Division on the left and Whitey

243

Paik's ROK 1st Division on the right to see who would be first to reach the capital.

The Jones twins, the NBC-TV cameramen, had been on the road sixteen hours; finally, at dusk on October 16, they caught up with the regimental armored unit selected to lead the assault on Pyongyang, fifty-seven miles away. Recovered from his wound at Inchon, Eugene was eager to film more action.

At dawn, garbage pails filled with hot coffee steamed outside the schoolhouse CP. Inside, a colonel was addressing his staff, fur parka carelessly draped around his shoulders. He was like a father lecturing sons. They were to seize a place up the road called Sariwon. It was a vital industrial area turning out most of the North Korean Army's equipment. It was also the open door to Pyongyang, thirty-five miles farther to the north. From prisoners they had learned that the last big stand would be made here.

Infantry clustered atop tanks as the column approached their first objective, a village called Mulgaeri. It was filled with burning mud huts and sharpshooters. Riflemen slipped off tanks to flush out the snipers on both sides of the road. The Jones twins followed, filming troopers deployed on either side of the ridgeline bordering the road. Tanks began firing down the defile, throwing white phosphorus into the town. Buildings flared up, yet no figures came out. Mortar fire was coming in, but so far there were no casualties. When the order came to advance, the troops fanned into the edge of town in columns, with tanks lumbering between, their machine guns spraying the side streets. Infantrymen were firing at anything moving inside the buildings.

The twins followed the first platoon across a cement bridge at the far edge of the town. Slugs whined off the heavy pillars as riflemen sprinted to get past the suburbs into the open country around the town. To stand still invited death. At last they were in the outskirts and then in the safe flatlands. The town was in flames, still rocking with gunfire as supporting tanks and infantry reduced the place to rubble.

The advance was fast; all the villages and towns the troops passed had been blasted by friendly air working ahead of them. The smell of burned thatch and charred dead was nauseating. All day long the attackers roared ahead. At the outskirts of Younghyeni, the second objective, the twins found Brigadier General Frank Allen, Jr., Gay's assistant division commander, chatting with the colonel who'd led the tank attack on Mulgaeri. They reminded the twins of two elderly professors planning an academic course. Then the general slapped the colonel on the shoulders and vaulted into his jeep while the colonel climbed back to his turret. Raising an arm, the colonel pointed down the road. The column moved forward and late that afternoon reached the hills just south of Sariwon. Suddenly they were hit by enemy fire from an orchard, and everything came to a halt.

General Allen reappeared. He jumped out of his jeep, stamping up and down the road angrily and waving his map and shouting, "God-damnit, they're in that orchard. Rake 'em, damnit! Blast them the hell out of there!"

A British patrol went forward, the twins following with their TV camera. As they neared the lead tank, a volley came from the orchard. Two men went down and the tank officer was wounded in the face. The assault company started forward with the twins behind the lead platoon. Midway to the tank they hit the ditch, rolling into its safety as fire sprayed from the apple trees.

The twins looked at the faces around them—troopers of the British brigade fresh from the jungles of Malaya and from Hong Kong. The Joneses couldn't understand their jargon. A fierce, proud lot, disdaining helmets, these men reminded the twins of Marines. Professional killers, the cream of service shock troops, they showed little emotion, exchanging small jokes in their weird tongue. They were proud of their long, wide bayonets and caressed the barrels of their weapons. A hairy corporal made a joke about the "two bloomin' camera fellers," and others ribbed the Joneses. But it was obvious they liked the idea of having such civilians attack with them. The twins felt flattered.

The lead tank crawled forward to give the platoon flank-fire support. The word passed to assault the orchard in seven minutes. Suddenly the orders came, and the British troops gave a high yell and dashed across the road and up a hill. The twins found themselves running with everyone else. At last they too were in the orchard, filming the British, who were weaving through trees covered with freshly ripened fruit. Above, bright little apples bobbed freely in the wind. Enemy dead littered the place, some almost ripped apart by tank fire. Two wounded North Koreans gurgled and twitched. A Tommy shot them.

Another Tommy jerked the rifle from beneath one of the dead and hefted it over his head with a yell. Soon, at the far end of the orchard, the attackers found themselves barred by a hedge. Brambles tore at their clothing, and the assault stopped.

An enemy machine gun from the ridgetop was raking the hedge. Leaves from the apple trees drifted down. A light mortar team joined them, and as the tiny shells whistled up to the ridgetop, the Tommies moved out in groups of three and four.

The twins crawled out past the line of troopers. A young, blond officer stood up slowly and began yelling at his men, calling them foul names. Like the hero of a movie, he ordered them to move forward, seize the ground, and hold it. The men rose and leaned forward as if against a strong wind. Bayonets lanced out in chopping motions, and the twins raised their camera to catch the snarling expressions of the charging Tommies.

A hedge fence atop the ridge was the final objective. When it loomed up, men flopped down, using it as protection. It felt wonderful to hit the soft, wet earth. The contour of the plowed field seemed to fit the curves of their bodies. Everyone was thirsty and canteens came out. The battle was over.

That day, October 17, MacArthur issued Operation Order 4 establishing a boundary between Walker and Almond along the watershed of the Taebaek Mountains from the 38th parallel to the Yalu. Walker was ordered to advance north on the west flank while Almond was to advance north on the east, fifty and a hundred miles above the old lines.

Morale in Gay's division was high, since it was rumored that Pyongyang was the final objective of the war. They'd all be having Thanksgiving dinner in Tokyo. Given the green light, Gay ordered his 7th Cavalry Regiment to resume its advance at dawn. The leading battalion rushed forward against light resistance until it was halfway to Pyongyang. The next morning two other cavalry battalions started to flank the enemy and found its positions abandoned.

On the right flank, Whitey Paik's ROK 1st Division was only eight miles from Pyongyang. He was delighted by the support he was getting from the rockets of the F-80 jets. "Now at least we have some tanks too," he told a *Time* correspondent, "and it is wonderful! My tactic is 'no stop.' Now we can be like General Patton." Praised for his driving spirit, he explained that this was partly because he was a native of Pyongyang. He was worried about his sister and her six children who had been left in the capital. "Pyongyang is a beautiful town, but the Communists will fight to the death for it and we will burn all of it if necessary. Under the Communists nobody can talk, nobody can take trips, nobody can do anything. I would gladly die for freedom from the Communists."

On the afternoon of October 18, Paik explained to his staff how they would break through the last enemy line of defense, which lay six miles in front of Pyongyang. The 12th Regiment would lead the main attack that night on the Taedong River Bridge—the southern gateway to the city—with a U.S. tank battalion providing supporting fire. His other regiment, the 11th, would secure the Pyongyang Airfield.

Throughout the night, Paik's two regiments fought bitterly but in vain to break through a strong line of pillboxes beyond which lay favorable terrain for tanks and artillery. Finally, just before dawn of the 19th, the North Koreans began retreating. Paik pushed the attack with a solid line of four artillery battalions and two regiments reinforced by

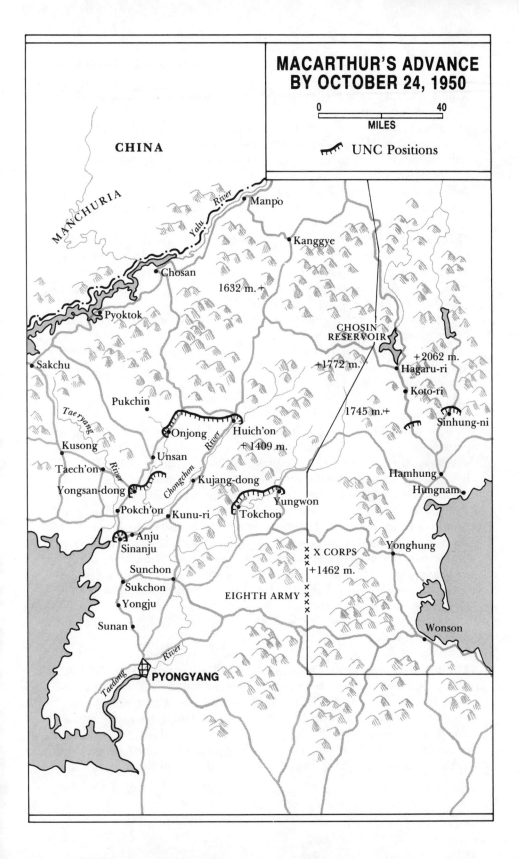

MACARTHUR'S ADVANCE BY OCTOBER 24, 1950

0   40

MILES

UNC Positions

CHINA

MANCHURIA

Yalu River

• Manp'o

• Kanggye

• Chosan

1632 m. +

• Pyoktok

CHOSIN RESERVOIR

+1772 m.

+2062 m.
Hagaru-ri

• Sakchu

• Koto-ri

Pukchin

Taeryang

+1745 m.

Sinhung-ni

Kusong

Onjong   Huich'on

+1409 m.

Chongchon River

• Unsan

Taech'on

River

• Kujang-dong

Yongsan-dong

Hamhung •

Hungnam •

• Pokch'on   Kunu-ri

Yungwon

• Tokchon

Anju
Sinanju

X CORPS

Yonghung •

Sunchon

+1462 m.

Sukchon

EIGHTH ARMY

Yongju

Sunan •

Wonson •

River

PYONGYANG

Taedong

American tanks, which overran the entrenchments, crushing machine guns and enemy troops.

When Paik learned that the Taedong River Bridge had been blown up, he ordered his 11th Regiment to cross the river at shallows several miles upstream, where he had swum as a boy. The 11th had no trouble and soon was turning west towards the city. Just before eleven A.M. the 2nd Battalion reached the northern end of the blown bridge.

Across the river, Gay's tanks were approaching the southern bank, only to find that the highway bridge had been blown. Undeterred, the 3rd Battalion, 5th Cavalry, managed to get across the river by noon.

As they landed, Paik saw a GI from the U.S. tank battalion attached to him putting up a sign on the bridge which read, "WELCOME 1ST CAVALRY DIVISION FROM 1ST ROK DIVISION."

"It's not good to brag," scolded Paik.

"I'm on your team," said the GI, "and I'm proud of it. *Our* team won the race to Pyongyang."

Paik had left Pyongyang as a refugee five years earlier, carrying all his possessions in a bundle on his back. Now he was returning to his home town as commander of conquering troops. It was probably the greatest moment of his life. He had savored every day, every single hour of their advance on Pyongyang.

Throughout the city, bells in Christian churches were ringing as people thronged to welcome American and ROK troops. Despite the wreckage, the capital was still impressive. Private Julian Tunstall of the British Middlesex Regiment was shocked to see the Americans take over the few remaining buildings and houses, ejecting civilians and seizing their property. GI troops were smashing things they didn't want. They blasted open safes, grabbed pictures, chairs, clocks and embroidery, loading up trucks and trailers with assorted booty. Americans in jeeps stopped to round up male civilians on the excuse that they were soldiers or Communists or thieves. The victims were stripped of watches and other valuables. Most officers, Tunstall noticed, managed to close their eyes to the looting by their men.

2.

The following morning, October 20, Kim Il-sung and Peng Teh-huai met at the new North Korean capital near the mouth of the Yalu River. Peng revealed that the CPC Central Committee and Chairman Mao had decided to send thirty-nine divisions to Korea. The first contingent had consisted of about 260,000 troops. The second and third groups of the remaining twenty-four divisions were being formed. The Chinese Volunteers Army, said Peng, would first concentrate on defense, and not attack unless the enemy launched an offensive. Peng noted that it had been difficult for the Central Committee and Chairman Mao to make this decision because China was faced with its own enormous difficulties. The goal of the Chinese in Korea, he said, was to assist North Korea in the reasonable settlement of its problem by wiping out the U.S. troops. At the same time, they had to be prepared in case the United States declared war on China and bombed Manchuria as well as the Chinese coastal area.

There were three possibilities, said Peng. First, they could annihilate their enemies and secure a peaceful settlement for Korea; second, they could stand firm but be locked in a stalemate; third, they could be unable to stand firm and be forced to return home. The Volunteers, he concluded, would strive for the first possibility.

Kim Il-sung thanked Mao and the CPC Central Committee and briefed Peng on the current situation. He had little more than three intact divisions: two infantry and one tank, plus a workers' regiment and a tank regiment. All the troops hit by Walker in the south were now withdrawing or hiding in the mountains to fight as guerrillas.

The results of this meeting were radioed to Mao, who the next day ordered Peng to abandon the original plan. Peng should *not* prepare for defense but seize the right moment for assaulting the enemy in force, using mobile tactics. On the evening of the 21st, following Mao's instructions, Peng ordered the concentration of three armies (the equivalent of three U.S. corps) on the western front. They were to destroy the ROK 6th, 7th and 8th divisions.

3.

The day after Pyongyang was seized, MacArthur launched an airborne assault on two objectives thirty air miles north of the capital. From his plane MacArthur watched the air drops with great satisfaction. Then, upon landing at Pyongyang, he told reporters the maneuver had apparently taken the enemy by complete surprise, and he estimated that 30,000 NK troops—probably half of those remaining in North Korea —had been cut off. "This closes the trap on the enemy." After conferring with General Walker, he returned to Tokyo convinced that his military mission in Korea was accomplished. The next day he predicted that "the war is very definitely coming to an end shortly." There was only one detail left for MacArthur: he once more called upon Kim Il-sung to surrender. The answer, of course, was negative.

The twin airdrop at Sukchon and nearby Sunchon had been a magnificent exhibition. Although it was probably the best combat jump the Army had ever staged, little had been accomplished. By now the main body of the retreating North Koreans was already safe across the Chongchon, the river running parallel to the Yalu, less than sixty air miles to the north.

MacArthur was convinced that President Truman would take immediate diplomatic action to exploit his victory, and was astounded to get a message from the State Department asking him to issue a statement saying that he did not propose "to interfere with the operations of the Suiho Hydrolectric Power Plant near Sinuiju in North Korea." This plant on the Yalu supplied power not only to North Korea but to plants in Manchuria and Siberia. MacArthur regarded this as a prime military target and replied, through the Joint Chiefs, that he did not believe such a statement was advisable. Washington did not press the issue, but MacArthur wondered what authority would be taken away from him next.

On October 24, the Eighth Army crossed the strategic Chongchon River; and one division, the ROK 6th, raced all the way north to a village only fifty-five air miles from the Yalu River. That same day MacArthur ordered both Walker and Almond to drive north with all possible speed. Restrictions previously limiting use of American troops in North Korea were now lifted with Walker and Almond "authorized to use any and all ground forces" necessary to secure all of North Korea. This order decidedly enlarged the U.S. role. Within hours a fired-up regiment of the ROK 6th Division was within ten miles of the Yalu.

When the Joint Chiefs asked for an explanation of this drastic action, which had not even been submitted to Washington for approval, MacArthur replied that his decision was a matter of military necessity forced upon him because the South Koreans lacked sufficient force and experienced leadership to seize the Yalu River border. He reminded the Joint Chiefs that General Marshall had recently told him to feel unhampered tactically, and concluded by hinting at possible dire consequences if any other course of action was taken.

Acheson was furious. What an extraordinary reply! MacArthur had violated a direct order of the president of the United States, commander in chief of all the military. Acheson was reminded of the Civil War when Lincoln, in despair, had given General Grant complete operational control with no more directions from Washington. This decision had led the U.S. military establishment of the future to believe that the theater commander was always to be in complete command.

Despite Acheson's protests, the Joint Chiefs bowed to MacArthur and the dash to the Yalu continued apace. Now MacArthur, like Grant, had total control. Walker himself was concerned by his own rapid progress, since there was a huge gap between his troops and X Corps. Many thousands of North Koreans were still escaping to the north through this opening. Almond's main force, the Marines, had not yet landed on the east coast. For a week their ships had been steaming slowly back and forth just outside the Wonsan Channel while minesweepers cleared the harbor. The restless Marines called it "Operation Yo-Yo." Finally, on October 25, the twenty-one transports and fifteen LSTs dropped anchor. GIs greeted the Marines with raucous catcalls. Even Bob Hope and his USO show had beaten them to Wonsan. "This is the first time I've ever been on shore waiting for the Marines," Hope quipped.

4.

While the three ROK divisions were advancing north, Peng's three armies were coming south on foot, moving slowly at night, impeded by road jams and obstructions. On October 25, the day after Walker crossed the Chongchon River, only two divisions of Peng's Fortieth Army had reached the point, fifteen miles northwest of that river, which Mao had selected as the first battleground. The vanguard divisions of the other two armies were still twelve to thirty miles from their designated positions. This situation forced Mao to change his plans. He ordered Peng to attack the three ROK divisions to the east of the Americans and British. After their annihilation, Peng should attack the Americans and British. Using the new mobile system, the Volunteers were to lure enemy troops into mountain areas, then encircle them and wipe them out.

Mao ordered Peng to win a decisive victory in this first campaign while maintaining high morale in the face of enemy bombing and strafing. His mission was to inflict heavy casualties on the enemy before more UN reinforcements could be brought to Korea. "The People's Volunteers," he concluded, "must fight hard for victory but on a safe and reliable basis.

"Annihilate several regiments at first," Mao ordered Peng, "then destroy more enemies gradually. This will raise our troops' morale and put us firmly on our feet." Following these orders, Peng issued the command to use overwhelming force. A division, for example, would concentrate on a single enemy regiment. In that way, they could not only stop the enemy advance but annihilate one or even two divisions.

5.

On the day Almond's X Corps began landing at Wonsan, General Walker told correspondents, "Everything is going just fine." His optimism was not shared by General Whitey Paik, whose ROK 1st Division was approaching the village of Unsan, some fifteen air miles northwest of the Chongchon River. Paik was uneasy over the rapid advance to the Yalu. His supply lines had already been stretched to the limit. Supplies had to come by truck all the way from Inchon and Pusan, since the railroads were out of service. What concerned him even more was the wide dispersal of the Eighth Army.

Korea was only 120 miles wide from Pyongyang to Wonsan, but as the Eighth Army moved north to the Yalu, the peninsula spread out like a fan to 400 miles. As each regiment headed north, gaps of 20 to 30 miles opened up between units. To make matters worse, communications between Almond and Walker were poor.

Once Paik entered Unsan at about eleven A.M., his fears became a reality. Enemy mortar fire suddenly exploded near a bridge as American tanks approached. They took a prisoner who admitted he was in a Chinese division and revealed that vast numbers of other Chinese Volunteers had also crossed the Yalu River and were heading south. Paik immediately reported to I Corps that "many, many Chinese are coming!" But no one would believe him. The prisoner must be a Korean who had just returned from China. Paik insisted on speaking to the corps commander, General Frank "Shrimp" Milburn. "I'll do the interpreting," said Paik, who spoke Chinese. "Come over and interrogate him yourself."

Milburn was soon in Unsan listening to the Chinese soldier. He asserted that tens of thousands of Chinese troops were already in the nearby mountains. Milburn was convinced this meant the Chinese had intervened in force. Walker, when told, agreed. His right flank, held by the ROK II Corps, was in danger of collapse. Its 6th Division had already been savaged; by the morning of October 25 not a single company of the 6th Division's 2nd Regiment was intact. The men had broken and were scattered in the hills. The 7th Regiment, 6th Division, unaware of the plight of their comrades, was far to the north. It had been ordered to race to the Yalu and was expected to reach its goal in the morning. It would be far out on a limb.

MacArthur, however, still refused to take the Chinese seriously, even though his intelligence chief had just received confirmation of a tremendous force already across the Yalu. The report had come from the intrepid Navy lieutenant, Eugene Clark, who had had the dangerous mission of spying on the North Korean defenses at Inchon just before the landing. Early in October Clark had been sent north on a triple mission. First he was to provide areas where Air Force pilots could "ditch" their damaged planes, other than in enemy territory or freezing water. To accomplish this he was to secure all of the offshore islands from Inchon to the Yalu River that were suitable for this purpose and, in the course of this activity, obtain, for study of its characteristics, a North Korean radar (or parts of it) that had been located on the mainland near the mouth of the Yalu. Second, he was to find out and pinpoint the site from which, and learn just how, the enemy was transporting or floating mines south into Inchon Harbor and shipping lanes along the east coast.

Third, and most important, he was to determine if there actually was a substantial Chinese buildup along the Yalu or crossing into North Korea.

Clark had recruited South Korean agents and guerrillas to perform these tasks. With an adequate assortment and amount of arms and food, the agents and 150 guerrillas were loaded into four civilian power craft, while Clark and his staff boarded an ROK patrol craft. All got under way on 15 October.

They found the first island along the coast, Taechong, free of enemy troops, but with several farming and fishing families. They continued north, finding several unoccupied islands suitable for planes to "ditch" in an emergency.

By now Clark's force was far up the west coast, about ten miles from the mouth of the Yalu. He had lost two boats in a storm and was down to about 75 men. He set up a reconnaissance camp on a peninsula nearby and in the vicinity of the city of Sinuiju. This seemed the best location for quick runs in and out of the target areas. It was intolerably cold and Clark had furnished his men with padded Chinese-type clothing both for warmth and for disguise. The agents were dispatched to locate the enemy radar. It was not found but several returned to report a massive buildup of Chinese troops in the Sinuiju area and farther to the north in Manchuria. They had talked to natives who said the Chinese boasted they were coming into Korea with 300,000 troops.

Clark was astonished but reported this by radio. He would need several separate sources before the buildup could be taken seriously. Two days later other agents also learned there were 300,000 Chinese swarming into Korea. The area along the river was literally alive with the movement of troops and equipment. Clark reported again—the figure remaining steady. And the following day the evidence was so overwhelming that he was constrained to radio: "Am confident of these figures and Chinese troop movement."

Walker had already reported Eighth Army's logistical weakness to MacArthur. Walker was only too sure that the all-out drive to the north was a calculated risk. There was no possibility of accumulating supplies to meet heavy opposition, and Walker had taken Whitey Paik's report seriously.

But his concern was still not reflected in either Tokyo or Washington. Truman had been assured by the CIA that a study of all known factors led to the conclusion that full-scale Chinese intervention was unlikely in 1950 unless the Soviets decided to start a global war. All Chinese aid, the CIA analysts had concluded, would probably be confined to cover assistance.

Even the defeat of the ROK 6th Division had not alarmed Tokyo. MacArthur's stature was now so great that the Joint Chiefs felt incapable of defying him. They were also convinced that the tactical plans of a theater commander were his prerogative. They not only did not question his decision to drive to the Yalu, they approved it. Even Army Chief of Staff Collins agreed. To him it was "a wholly reasonable proposition," and MacArthur's new plan was consistent with the overall goal to end the war quickly and unify Korea. Truman also made no protest, for he knew what such a military victory might mean for the Democrats in the forthcoming November biennial election. Ignored during these deliberations were concerns of the senior tactical commander, General Walker, who would be forced to fight against overwhelming odds if the entire chain of command above him was wrong.

And so the race for the Yalu resumed despite the warnings of Lieutenant Clark and General Paik.

The Jones twins were with the advance troops, in hills across the Chongchon River. By now Charlie had rescued a number of wounded American infantrymen and become a legend. He and Gene lay in a ditch with riflemen. Rumor had it that a new kind of fighting man was out front: one with slanted eyes who wore a padded cotton uniform.

The TV cameramen saw a jeep coming down the dusty road. When it stopped, the driver, a KMAG first lieutenant, walked towards them while three Koreans remained in the jeep, staring impassively. The lieutenant, a big, gray-haired, dusty man who hadn't shaved or slept for a long time, stared down into the trench and asked in a drawl, "Which way is forward?"

A rifleman pointed to a crossroad in the distance. The lieutenant returned to his jeep and climbed in, a long leg draped over the side. "Which way did you say was the right one?" he again asked politely.

"Don't rightly know, Lieutenant," said a somber infantryman. "But all them roads end the same. Where you going?"

The KMAG officer grinned. "Goin' no'th to dip ouah swords in the waters of the Yalu." His three Korean companions remained silent as the jeep rattled off.

There was a clicking of bolts. A long silence. "Jesus, what a craphole this is!" said someone from the depths of the ditch bottom. Ahead the twins could hear the voices of unseen people yelling. They anxiously peered further north past the ridge, toward the unknown.

CHAPTER 17

The Death March
(Late October–November 8)

1.

By autumn most of the UN prisoners of war were in camps near the Yalu River. General Dean was housed in the city of Manpo, 125 air miles east of the mouth of the great river. Dean had been thinking of escape because of the retreat of the North Koreans and the appearance of many UN planes. But he was still so exhausted he couldn't walk a hundred yards without having to rest. In late October he was taken across the Yalu to the north side. He noticed immediate differences. There were vendors with cartloads of meat and other food. He asked the captain in charge if this was his first trip to Manchuria. "This isn't Manchuria," he was told. It was a Chinese section of Korea.

"Then what was that river we crossed?" asked Dean, and got no answer, since his transportation into a neutral country would violate the Geneva Convention. Several days later Dean was brought back to Manpo alone; he figured they could not afford to have him killed, since he could be used as a bargaining point in any peace negotiation.

He was correct. Many other prisoners located in camps along the Yalu were being shifted back and forth from east to west to prevent their being retaken by one of the UN spearheads heading for the Yalu. Although Dean was the most prestigious captive, eighty-seven noncombatants of various nationalities were also of great importance. These included an Englishman, Herbert A. Lord, lieutenant commissioner of the Salvation Army, and three men from the British legation in Seoul: Captain Vyvyan Holt, Minister George Blake, and Vice-Consul Norman Owen. In addition, there were the many Roman Catholic sisters and priests headed by Bishop Byrne, and six men and women from the Methodist Mission in Kaesong, including the Reverend Larry Zellers, who had been captured near the 38th parallel. Father Philip Crosbie, the Australian priest, also picked up near the border, had been keeping notes ever since his capture.

This group had been unexpectedly ordered to prepare for departure from their Pyongyang jail early in September and had left on a train for Manpo ten days before the Inchon landing. Through September and early October the days had been unusually sunny and occasionally warm enough for swimming. They were taken to the Yalu by a guard so that they could launder clothes, bathe, and bask in the sunshine. But such pleasures ended by mid-October, and a week later extreme hardship began. They were forced to march twelve miles behind a large group of UN prisoners of war from Manpo to a broken-down mining town. During the next few days they could occasionally hear bombing in the distance. It sounded like artillery; UN troops must be coming. Every so often, small disorderly bands of North Korean troops passed by, often without arms. On October 26 they were ordered to move again. They lightened their baggage and improvised a stretcher for an ailing nun, Mother Thérèse. Another nun, Sister Mary Clare, still lame from a fall, and eighty-two-year-old Father Villemot could walk only with help. As they set out at dark it began to drizzle. It would be impossible for those carrying Mother Thérèse to negotiate the winding, slippery mountain paths, so the guards brought everyone back to camp.

For three days they trudged through rain in the bitter cold. On the last day of October they were lined up and ordered by a North Korean major to empty their pockets and surrender all penknives. The old people had to give up their walking sticks. "I am to be obeyed," said the major. "You are now under strict military discipline. We are going to march to Chunggang-jin." This was more than a hundred miles distant. He coldly surveyed the miserable group in its tattered clothing. "No one is to fall out of line without my permission. If anyone does, I will deal severely with him."

Monsignor Quinlan, superior of the Columban Fathers in Chunchon, was nominated as group leader and approved by the major. Who would lead the women? he asked. Nell Dyer, of the Methodist Mission, a tall, resourceful native of Arkansas, was chosen.

Father Crosbie was gravely concerned. Was the major a fool or a knave to expect this group to march in military column? There were mothers with babes in arms, a blind nun, the tottering Father Villemot, and frail Mother Béatrix, as well as consumptive Mother Thérèse.

Commissioner Lord stepped forward to voice his concerns. "They will die if they have to march!"

"Then let them march till they die. That is a military order!"

The prisoners were too stunned to talk to each other, but Crosbie was certain there were few who didn't breathe a prayer to their creator.

The march began with Father Villemot helped by Father Quinlan and another young priest. Bernadette, the sturdiest of the Carmelites, led blind Sister Marie-Madeleine. As they moved eastward, Zellers could see a large group of American military prisoners lining up in preparation for the march. While the POWs milled around, the major halted the civilians and took advantage of the wait to deliver a propaganda speech: "Suppose you were an engineer on a train and the locomotive broke down. What would you do? Would you kneel down and pray that it would run? Or would you get an expert who knew about such things to repair it? In this country we know what we would do. We don't need you religious people anymore. You are parasites. There are things in this world that need repairing. We know what to do about that."

At last the POWs were ready. First came oxcarts piled high with their supplies—bags of grain, dried fish, and cigarettes. They were followed by a long line of some 700 soldiers, led by their senior officer, Major John Dunn. As they passed, Crosbie was shocked to see that a number had bleeding feet.

The civilians fell in behind the POWs. Although no one was barefoot, a number were poorly shod. Many of the civilians needed help to keep going. Zellers and Nell Dyer took turns assisting Sister Mary Clare. Mother Eugénie supported Mother Béatrix.

As they approached a city, they realized it was Manpo—they were back where they had started. The POWs moved into a field, and the civilians followed. They squatted on the ground for several hours wondering what was wrong. The major had told them they were to walk sixteen miles that first day, and they would pay dearly for the long wait.

At last the guards roused them as if they had been responsible for the delay. "*Bali! Bali!*" (Hurry!) they shouted as they ran up and down the line like sheepdogs. The grueling pace was hard on everyone. Ahead Crosbie could see emaciated young soldiers who had fallen out. Hounded by guards, they were stumbling back in place.

It was dark by the time they straggled into Manpo and headed east. In the gloom, riflemen and machine-gun crews passed them at a bobbing, constant pace. Behind were men carrying heavy burdens at the end of poles that swayed as they moved at a steady trot. These were the tireless Chinese Volunteers.

The POWs and civilians plodded on but were halted after having traveled only about six miles. Sleep, said the guards. They huddled together for warmth in groups of three and four. But there was little rest or sleep.

At dawn, November 1, they were awakened and served boiled corn. After they had walked about two or three miles, there was a sudden stop. At the head of the column Commissioner Lord was interpreting a conversation between the major and some POWs. Crosbie saw them move over to the top of a small knoll, still talking. "I order you not to allow anyone to drop out," said the major. "If you do, I will punish you with the extreme penalty of military discipline. Even the dead must be carried."

The march resumed, but in a few hours POWs began to falter. The major again stopped the column and summoned the platoon leaders. Through Lord he said, "You have disobeyed my orders. I have authority to punish you. I will now shoot you all."

Lord pleaded for the lives of the young soldiers as the major placed his pistol at the head of the Salvation Army commissioner, who kept talking, unmindful of his peril. The major asked whose platoon had the greatest number of dropouts.

There was a pause. Then Lieutenant Cordus Thornton walked up the knoll.

"Why did you let those five men drop out?" the major asked Thornton.

"Because they were dying, sir."

"Why didn't you obey my orders?"

The young lieutenant replied that would have meant condemning the carriers of the dead to die themselves from exhaustion.

The major, glaring, stood as if in doubt, then called to a band of passing NK soldiers. "What should be done to a man who disobeys the People's Army?"

"Shoot him!" they shouted.

"There," said the major, "you've had your trial."

"In Texas, sir," replied Thornton, "we would call that a lynching."

The major handed a guard a small towel to blindfold Thornton. Another towel was used to tie Thornton's hands behind his back.

Wilber Ray Estabrook, a private first class captured near Taejon, and Jack Browning, of the shattered 34th Infantry, watched in horror as the major stripped off his overcoat and pointed to the insignia of his rank. "I have the authority to do this." As the major cocked his pistol and stepped behind the lieutenant, parents tried to shield their children's eyes.

The major flipped up the back of Thornton's fur cap, then pulled the trigger. Thornton collapsed to the ground.

A sixteen-year-old girl screamed. "Stop!" shouted the major, "or I'll kill you too!" He surveyed the shocked crowd. "Now," he said in dead calm, "you see what can happen to you." It was the first death eight-year-old Shaucat Salahutdin, son of a Tatar businessman, had ever seen. His legs wobbled and he had to pull down his pants to defecate. He had seen the brains actually blown out of a man!

Crosbie prayed. They were in the hands of a lunatic. Sergeant Henry Leerkamp stepped calmly from the ranks. "This will help us to work better together in peace and harmony," he said and began to dig a grave with a stick at the foot of the knoll. The ground was hard and Leerkamp called to the men staring down, petrified. "Won't some of you help me?"

His words broke the spell of horror and several soldiers carried the body down while others helped Leerkamp dig with sticks and fingers. Thornton was laid in the shallow grave and covered with dirt and stones.

The march resumed. From then on the major had a new name: the Tiger. And both the POWs and the civilians had a martyr, Lieutenant Thornton. It was obvious to Crosbie that the POWs were in worse shape than the civilians. Stronger comrades helped the weak and carried those unable to walk.

The Tiger set such a grueling pace that Crosbie wondered what would happen when it became physically impossible to obey his orders. Would there be mass murders?

At the first rest-stop, the ranking guard approached the civilians. Kneeling, he said in a quiet voice, "We do not like to see what happened this morning. Our commander is a determined man. He will do whatever is necessary to complete this march. Please do as he says."

Within an hour Mother Thérèse was no longer able to keep moving, even with help, and dropped to the ground. Crosbie called to Zellers, "Larry, we just can't leave Mother Thérèse behind to die." Two others helped Zellers and Crosbie hastily construct a makeshift litter, and the four of them carried her to the next rest-stop. As they sat by the side of the road, all were so exhausted that it was agreed they simply could not proceed. Mother Thérèse would have to walk. But when the signal came to resume the march, the four picked up the litter and plodded down the road. After a quarter of a mile one priest exclaimed, "We agreed, didn't we, that we couldn't continue? What are we going to do?"

They stopped and gently lowered the litter. Mother Thérèse struggled to her feet and, with the help of another nun, somehow managed to keep pace with the march.

Zellers was amazed. "Bing," he remarked to Crosbie, who had been given this nickname by the Americans, "how does she do it?"

"It isn't physical strength anymore. Mother Thérèse ran out of that a long time ago. When you are as weak as she is, you just put one foot in front of the other and leave the rest to faith."

What a privilege, Zellers thought, to be with such people. He'd first met Bing on the train heading for Manpo. It was cold lying on the decking next to an open window, and Crosbie had taken off his zippered jacket. "Here, put it on." Zellers protested. "Wear it for a while. We'll share it," Crosbie insisted. All his life Zellers had heard of the hypothetical person who would take the shirt off his back to help someone in greater need. Now he had actually found such a man.

That afternoon they followed the course of a river that wound between sunlit hills. At dusk Father Villemot collapsed and POWs helped carry him in a blanket. At last they halted in a field beside a farmhouse. They had covered twenty miles. The POWs stayed in the open field, but the civilians were conducted to the farmhouse, where the Tiger told them that those who had fallen out were being cared for in the People's Hospital. Then, taking Lord aside, he forced him to sign a paper certifying that those who dropped off, including Thornton, had died of heart failure.

Diplomats were assigned to one room and families to another. The rest slept on straw in the farmyard, huddled together in the cold. Few were able to sleep. Larry Zellers and Louis Dans, the assistant manager of the Traders' Exchange in Seoul, spent the night visiting with POWs.

Some prisoners tried to draw near to fires built by the guards but were driven back. By dawn a dozen POWs had frozen. Eight others could not walk. The Tiger ordered them left behind. Lord heard the Tiger tell local people to bury the dead. The number he gave included those unable to walk.

On November 2, the march covered another twenty miles, with only a few rest-stops. Mother Thérèse started out, supported by a priest, Father Canavan, and Crosbie, but then became faint and had to be carried in a blanket. Yet after two hours, she insisted on walking again. Bishop Byrne and Dr. Kristian Jensen, the Methodist missionary, had been helping each other, but were finding it difficult to keep going. So were seventy-six-year-old Madame Martel, of France, and the elderly Russians: Madame Funderat and Ivan Tihinoff. But the march was not slowed or held up when these people fell behind. They were forced to catch up no matter how agonizing their ordeal.

They halted at school grounds for the night. After a meal was served to POWs and civilians, the civilians were taken inside. Again, one room was set aside for diplomats and another for women and children. The others were put in the corner of a large schoolroom filled with POWs. The place was jammed, but hundreds of freezing soldiers were still outside. Their pleas inspired those inside to jam together even closer. The room soon became a bedlam as men moaned in pain from their cramped, twisted limbs.

Twice a guard demanded quiet. The third time he shouted, "This is my last warning. If I have to return, I will open the door and fire into the room!" He left, slamming the door.

A quiet voice from the dark said, "Men, you heard what the guard said." It was Major John J. Dunn, the senior ranking American officer. "I order you to be quiet for your own sake. I don't know where the officers and noncoms are in this room," he added. "You must be scattered all over. From now on, when anyone screams, he is to be thrown outside."

There was no noise for half an hour, then someone cried out. The offender was passed overhead to the door and heaved through it. There was again quiet, but then another men screamed. This one fought back until someone struck him hard and yelled, "Now throw him out!"

There was dead silence until a loud, clear voice rang out, "An officer hit that man!" The officer gave his name, rank and serial number. "If anyone wants to make anything of it before some board of investigation after the war, then speak up!"

There was dead quiet, and for the rest of the night no one made a sound.

Soon after dawn the door was flung open to reveal the smiling face of the Tiger. "Everyone stand up!" he ordered. Only about six men were able to do so. Those next to the door fell forward and crawled outside. The next row followed.

After breakfast the Tiger stepped up on a box. The People's Government, he announced, was concerned for their health and ultimate release. Therefore, they should appreciate everything being done for their welfare and cooperate. There need be no anxiety about those who had fallen on the way! But finally the Tiger brought cheers: there would be transport for all women who found difficulty in walking.

When it was time to leave, the guards would not let Crosbie and others who had helped the women remain behind. Only Commissioner Lord could stay. He was needed to interpret. As soon as the men were out of sight, Nell Dyer was told there would be no transport after all; everyone must walk, including the three elderly woman—Mother Béatrix, Mother Thérèse and Madame Martel.

Nell Dyer did her best to keep the women together, but the three weakest soon fell behind. Lord stayed with them. The women ahead were also having difficulty. Nell begged their guard for a rest, and he finally consented. But as soon as they stretched out on the roadside, the guards began kicking Nell in the legs. The women dragged themselves up and continued. After a while the guard, who could understand English, did let them rest, but they were not to lie on the road.

"Why do you treat us like this?" asked the intrepid Nell. "We are elderly people and isn't it a Korean tradition to have respect for age?"

"That is true," said the guard, "but now that we are in the People's Army, we are not free in these matters anymore."

Far in the rear Mother Béatrix and Mother Eugénie were alone. Mother Béatrix sank down and could not rise. Guards tried to rouse her in vain. Mother Eugénie too was at the end of her strength. She pleaded with the guards that the woman they were mistreating was seventy-six years old and had spent fifty years caring for the poor and orphans of Korea. The guards ordered her to go ahead, but she clung to her companion. "Go, my sister, go," said Mother Béatrix. The guards pushed Mother Eugénie down the road. She heard a shot and turned. Mother Béatrix's body was being shoved down a steep slope! The tiny form rolled over and over, finally landing with a thud at the bottom of the ravine.

The last two stragglers finally appeared. Commissioner Lord was towing the Russian widow, Madame Funderat, with a rope. After a meal, they resumed the march, but the guards insisted Lord leave Madame Funderat behind. She never overtook them. By now the priest who helped Monsignor Quinlan support Father Villemot had hurt his knee. Crosbie took his place, but the aged Villemot was exhausted.

"Leave me here," he said. "These people will surely let me die in their yard and then bury me."

The guard told Quinlan and Crosbie, "You can't leave him here. He'll have to go on."

The two priests continued supporting Villemot for another mile. At a bend they espied in the distance a stalled oxcart and hurried forward, praying the cart would not move away. They reached it at last to find the French diplomatic group and the Tiger. He had stopped a passing supply cart to give Madame Martel a ride. To Crosbie's surprise he agreed to let Father Villemot join her. As the afternoon progressed, the Tiger also found transport for a family in distress.

That night the POWs bunked in a school while the civilians stayed in a church. There was no window and a sympathetic guard lit a fire which, Korean style, heated the floor. It grew so warm that lice, dormant in the cold, began to run amok.

At dawn the guards came to end the uneasy rest of the civilians. Zellers looked out the door of the schoolhouse at gently falling snow. He surveyed the ribbon of slippery road they were to travel. It stretched into layer after layer of mountains. They had to get over the summit before the snow blocked it. "I'm afraid some of us aren't going to make it," observed Zellers.

"Larry, me boy, you're right," said Monsignor Quinlan. "But the Good Lord will give them a better welcome in heaven than the Communists have ever given them in this unhappy land." He had known this part of the country before it became Communist.

Because of the snow, they started off without breakfast, even though only a meager dinner had been served the night before. Again Father Villemot and Madame Martel were allowed to ride in the cart, and the others did their best on the road that snaked its way up the mountain in a series of wide loops. Larry Zellers, always dependable, was helping Sister Mary Clare. Behind them were the blind Sister Marie-Madeleine and Sister Bernadette, who was escorting her through the carpet of snow. Next to them Father Crosbie was guiding Mother Thérèse.

As the climbing became difficult and dangerous, Crosbie heard shots ahead. He figured the guards were amusing themselves as usual with some practice rounds. At the mouth of a ravine they encountered an NK officer and several guards returning down the road. They were laughing, and neither Zellers nor Crosbie thought anything of the incident. A few minutes later they found two exhausted POWs sitting by the roadside with guards standing behind them.

The civilian group moved around another bend and heard two more shots. Crosbie's head reeled and his knees went limp as the shocking truth hit him. POWs were being murdered!

They came upon a POW sitting helplessly in the middle of the road, unable to go another step. A guard stood nearby, waiting for the civilians to pass. About a minute later Zellers heard the crack of a rifle. He turned and saw the guard rolling the body toward the edge of the road. At first, the thought that the murdered POWs would soon be in the presence of God almost succeeded in converting this barbaric scene into one of tranquillity for Zellers. Then he was brought back to reality. They approached more young soldiers unable to move. Zellers could tell by looking into their eyes that they knew what was coming.

Father Crosbie was overwhelmed with a feeling of helplessness as he saw more and more POWs sitting or lying exhausted, with guards waiting ominously until the civilians passed. If there had been any hint of humanity the day before, it came to an end that horrifying day, November 4.

The slaughter continued. Each time they approached exhausted POWs—now feeble, tottering skeletons—Crosbie passed as closely as he dared in order to speak a few words about God's love and mercy in this dark hour. His forgiveness . . . His reward was waiting for them. Some nodded as if they understood. Up ahead he could hear a youthful voice singing, "God Bless America."

Zellers came upon four emaciated GIs struggling to carry a comrade, unable to keep up the pace. A guard ordered them to lower the man and rejoin their group. As they regretfully obeyed, an American officer appeared. Major Newton Lantron simply threw the inert man over his shoulder and strode swiftly ahead. How long would his strength last? wondered Zellers. Like Crosbie, he was overwhelmed by his own helplessness. He saw a barefoot POW trying to help a buddy who had fallen behind. But the weaker one fell to the ground. The guard shoved the stronger man away, motioning him to go on alone. The barefoot soldier started up the road, but after a few paces returned to his fallen comrade, removed his shoes and then, prize in hand, hustled forward to join his group. Neither the man on the ground nor the guard objected.

During that ghastly morning, twenty-one POWs had been murdered, and Crosbie and Zellers now realized what had happened to Mother Béatrix and the eighteen soldiers who had fallen out the day before.

For some reason, the deadly march that morning was followed by almost humane treatment. Pleas by Monsignor Quinlan and Commissioner Lord resulted in a truck and a bus being provided to carry all the women, children, old men and five sick POWs. In addition, they were allowed to rest the next morning. The following afternoon the civilians started off with the main body of POWs: behind, at an easier pace, were sick and weak soldiers. They walked ten miles and spent the night in another schoolhouse.

The march finally ended on November 8 at the town of Chunggang-jin. The prisoners, including the exhausted Mother Eugénie, had completed a journey of more than a hundred miles over rugged terrain in the bitter cold and snow, leaving almost a hundred dead along the way. The long trek now had a name: The Death March.

CHAPTER 18

Mao Sets a Trap
(October 26–November 17)

1.

On October 26, the same day the civilian prisoners near the Yalu River had been moved to another camp, General MacArthur was celebrating the arrival of a patrol of the 7th Regiment, ROK 6th Division, at the Yalu. Reaching the border of Manchuria was truly a moment to savor, but MacArthur soon learned that disaster had just struck another regiment of the 6th Division, the 2nd, fifty air miles to the south. By dawn an entire battalion had been overwhelmed, disrupting the entire regiment, and survivors were scattering into the hills. This defeat and the overextension to the Yalu nullified the 6th Division as an effective fighting force.

The disintegration of the ROK 6th Division and the imminent collapse of the rest of the ROK II Corps placed Eighth Army's right flank in peril. Whitey Paik's ROK 1st Division would be a prime target of the Chinese and appeared to have little chance of survival. On Paik's right the remaining elements of the ROK II Corps were already falling back in disorder. On his left there was a gap of fifteen miles between his troops and the U.S. 24th Division.

General Gay's 8th Cavalry Regiment was ordered to go to Paik's aid, but because of clogged roads it took several days to reach Paik's lines just west of Unsan, fifteen air miles northwest of the Chongchon River. On the morning of October 31, First Lieutenant Harry Trollope, a platoon leader of G Company, set up an outpost with two rifle squads, a four-man weapons squad with a light machine gun and one BAR, and a bazooka squad. Including himself, there were twenty-seven men. They found the area littered with refuse left by the ROKs. Trollope sent out a four-man patrol and watched them through binoculars. When, after proceeding four hundred yards, they ran into small-arms fire, he telephoned his company commander, Captain Davis, for instructions. Told to hold the position, Trollope called his battalion commander and was informed he could have artillery fire in thirty minutes. If attacked, he was to hold until the rest of the battalion could set up.

About two P.M. Trollope saw a battalion-sized enemy unit heading towards him. His platoon fired and the opposition scattered. But an hour or so later Trollope was startled to see more enemy converging on him. Directly ahead, only three hundred yards away, was a column of twenty; and on the right flank, fifty others began moving in. This group was wearing quilted uniforms and soft caps and seemed well disciplined.

As they neared he called, "Open up!" Mortars and bazookas joined together, and all but five of the group of twenty enemy were killed. The group on the right broke for cover, and then began moving forward again.

Ammunition was running low, and Trollope requested further orders. He was told to fall back immediately to the company perimeter. The platoon pulled back, bringing with them one dead and five wounded. Trollope was ordered to set up a defense with two tanks. All was quiet until nine-thirty P.M. when the platoon received fire from seventy-five yards. The enemy then rushed to within twenty-five yards; but with the tanks firing point-blank, they were repulsed.

Next, fifty enemy soldiers came in with small arms and grenades. When two figures rushed toward the tanks, Trollope fired at them with the .50-caliber machine gun. He heard a woman scream and saw a kneeling figure, hands over face. During a lull he crept closer and could make out the woman. She had a soldier's haircut and wore a soldier's uniform. She possessed two hand grenades.

A messenger crawled to Trollope. The right flank of E Company was overrun, and enemy were infiltrating there and perhaps behind G Company, too. Someone yelled, "The enemy's over there!"

As the two tanks backed out, fire began coming from all sides. "Break out!" shouted Trollope. It was a rout. He fell back twenty-five yards, bringing two wounded. There were now eight or nine casualties piled on each tank. But they drew fire, and were taken off while the tankers and survivors of the platoon pulled back over an eight-foot-high bank.

Bugles began blowing on the left and right. They seemed to be coordinated. Trollope could see many enemy running up the road. As he led the way, heading south over a small ridge, he heard someone call,

"Lieutenant Trollope, Lieutenant Trollope! Captain Davis has been hit and wants you."

Trollope moved back to the ridge and found Davis with a second lieutenant leaning over him. "Try and get me out," said Davis. He said he was hit in the leg, but Trollope couldn't find the wound. Then he saw a hole in the captain's stomach. The bullet must have coursed down through his leg and lodged in his left knee. Paralysis had set in, but Davis felt no pain. "Stay with me," he said. "Assume command."

He was laid on a poncho. Trollope, the second lieutenant, and two enlisted men each took a corner of the poncho and started up the ridge. Near the top they saw enemy about fifty feet away. Just then the moon came out and a bugle began to blow. The enemy rushed down the hill. The second lieutenant and two enlisted men dropped Davis and jumped into an erosion ditch. Grabbing the poncho, Trollope managed to pull the captain after them. When the enemy was twenty feet away, the second lieutenant and enlisted men jumped out and ran. The enemy soldiers took off in pursuit, not noticing Davis and Trollope. There was a burst of fire, and one of the enlisted men dropped.

The second lieutenant escaped, but the other enlisted man was also mowed down. After fifteen minutes, Trollope crawled out. The enemy soldiers were milling around. He crept back and covered Davis with the poncho, then pulled up grass as camouflage. Carrying an M-1, he crawled to a gully, where he saw the enemy examining the two dead enlisted men. Trollope fired five rounds before scrambling to the top of the ridge to circle the enemy and lure them away from Davis. It was well past midnight by the time he circled back.

Several times Trollope crept up to the ridge looking for help. He found no one. About six A.M., on November 1, he saw that Davis was warm but had no pulse and wasn't breathing. To draw attention to the body, Trollope tied an OD (olive drab) handkerchief on a stick stuck in the ground, then moved toward the outpost position, still hoping to find aid. After about two hundred yards, he abruptly ran into two enemy. One was armed with an M-1, the other with a Russian carbine, bayonet attached. He halted and raised his hands as they covered him. No one spoke. The one with the bayonet poked his weapon at Trollope. Laughing, they patted Trollope's pockets, then, jabbering, pushed him down the path to a small hut. Before entering, one of them took Trollope's wedding ring.

In the hut, Trollope tried to communicate with them, but they couldn't understand English. Since they had better clothing than the North Koreans, he figured these must be the Manchurian soldiers he'd heard about. He could see that the man with the M-1 held it at the ready with the safety on. Obviously, he wasn't familiar with the rifle, and Trollope looked for a chance to clobber him. The guard motioned Trollope outside and gave him a pick to dig a grave for a dead American lying on a path nearby. Trollope scraped dirt over the body and placed a rock and stick on top.

The Chinese motioned Trollope to return to the hut. Trollope shifted the pick to his right hand and swung it. He struck the guard in the head three times. Grabbing the M-1, he hurried across the ridge, down into a small valley, and up another ridge, and hid in heavy brush. He was in good shape and had six rounds of ammunition. It was bitter cold and, come what may, he was determined to go south for the winter.

By November 1 there was at last convincing evidence of large Chinese troop movements throughout the Unsan area. During the afternoon, a spotter plane sighted two columns of enemy infantry moving southeast over trails not far from Trollope's outpost. "Our shells are landing right in their columns and they keep coming!"

General Gay requested permission to withdraw Trollope's regiment, the 8th Cavalry, but General Milburn, commander of I Corps, refused. Later in the day Milburn, a former West Point athlete, got a telephone call from Walker. The entire ROK II Corps had ceased to exist, and the right flank of I Corps was unprotected. With his dachshund, Ebbo, Milburn immediately set off for Kunu-ri, a town a few miles south of the Chongchon River, to organize a blocking force on the road leading to Pyongyang.

During the day the situation around Unsan deteriorated, and by nightfall the entire 8th Cavalry Regiment was under heavy attack. Milburn gave Gay permission to withdraw these beleaguered troops, and at 11:45 P.M. Gay issued a warning order alerting all battalions and regimental trains for withdrawal south.

Lieutenant Trollope, awakened the morning of November 2 by voices and digging noises, found he was in the midst of the enemy. He had good cover, though, and with the sun out it was so comfortable he went back to sleep. It was raining when he awoke the second time. He looked at his watch. It was six P.M.—fortunately he had slipped the watch up his arm just before the Chinese took his wedding ring. He waited for dark before moving out, then moved slowly for five hundred yards to a river. Chinese were digging in on both sides. He could hear bugles blowing, and two hours later heard 200 enemy singing as they marched in formation along a main road. Trollope lay in his bushy ridge observing the considerable activity and concluding that he must be beside a replacement depot of some sort. The initial attack, he figured, must have come from the northwest. Through the remainder of the night he took catnaps.

It had been a harrowing day for his regiment. By this time, all three battalions of the 8th Cavalry were shattered, with survivors fleeing southwest.

Behind enemy lines Lieutenant Trollope awoke the next morning to find mist. He moved through the brush halfway up a hill, halting every fifty yards to observe. About ten A.M. he noticed a lone soldier dressed in an American uniform about a hundred yards away. He was Oriental but appeared to be avoiding enemy troops in the area, so Trollope figured he was friendly. Covering him, Trollope called out, "Hey, soldier, are you a GI?" He was. "What company?" G Company—Trollope's outfit—but he hadn't seen the guy before. "What platoon?"

"Lieutenant Saksa's."

"Come over here and keep your weapon in your left hand pointed to the ground."

He did so, explaining he was Corporal Shigeru Katakawa. Trollope then recognized him and told him he planned escaping around the flank. He and Katakawa set out and soon came upon civilians scrounging in the area, two of whom were armed and firing shots, apparently into foxholes. Trollope and Katakawa decided to go west, cross the river ahead and then swing south. At the base of the hill, 200 Chinese, as well as Korean civilians, were carrying wounded to the north. Since it was midafternoon by the time the Americans reached the river, they waited until dark before crossing. But once night fell, bugles blew—it was the Chinese communication system, not a morale booster as Americans thought. Flashlights appeared on the other side of the river. As they started back to the hill, they heard talking and froze. Then they realized it was English. Katakawa crawled forward, hid behind a bush and called out, "Hey, you guys GIs?"

"Yes, I'm Lieutenant Lauber of G Company."

He came down with Private Jimmie Watson, also G Company, and a sick man from E Company. Trollope sent Watson out with the M-1 to act as security and spent the rest of the night making plans. They would move out about four or five A.M. when enemy watchfulness was at its lowest and proceed in single file, fifteen feet apart, tapping out signals for control. Trollope told them to use voice only in case of an attack. Among them they had four M-1's and one .45 pistol. Katakawa had a pocketful of ammo and four grenades, ten packets of sugar, five packets of coffee, and a canteen and a half of water. They hadn't eaten since noon of November 1st, but no one was hungry. They decided to save the coffee and sugar as a booster, then traded names and home addresses in case anyone got back safely. All were ready to break through the enemy lines—except the sick man. He would only say, "It doesn't make a damn bit of difference to me."

2.

In Peking, Chairman Mao was kept informed of the progress of the battle in the west and had telegraphed Peng on the night of November 2 that it was necessary to use the Thirty-eighth Army to prevent enemy troops from linking up on both sides of the Chongchon River. He must then wipe out the U.S. 2nd Division, which was coming northward. "This is of primary importance and all else is secondary."

While Walker was struggling to shore up his collapsing front, General Almond, confident and in high spirits, was finally ready to launch his attack from the east. He ordered the 7th Marines to head north from the port city of Hungnam and drive up to the Yalu. The GIs of the 7th Division would also head north to the right of the Marines. "When we have cleared this all out," said Almond, "the ROKs will take over, and we will pull our divisions out of Korea." He was not yet aware of the heavy losses to the west.

"We can expect to meet Communist troops," Colonel Homer Litzenberg, commander of the 7th Marines, told his officers and NCOs in an informal briefing. "And it is important that we win the first battle."

On November 1, while the Chinese were assaulting Lieutenant Trollope and the 8th Cavalry, the 7th Marines had trucked out of Hamhung just behind the ROK 26th Regiment. Late in the afternoon they secured for the night in a tight perimeter. During the day the ROKs had been hit by elements of the 124th Chinese Division. Almond's G2 officers concluded the attackers were probably flank security for the Chinese Fourth Field Army and didn't constitute a threat.

The 7th Marines moved forward next morning, November 2, receiving a few casualties from long-range Chinese fire. By afternoon the Marines had advanced thirty-six miles against slight enemy resistance and were less than a mile from Sudong. In twenty-seven more miles they would reach Hagaru-ri, a strategic village on the southern tip of the Chosin Reservoir.

They expected little trouble the next day, unaware that a Chinese regiment was massed to the north and west while another held the high ground east and a third reserve regiment was several miles in the rear. At eleven P.M. Litzenberg's 1st Battalion reported an attack on the right flank; an hour later the 2nd Battalion reported two NK battalions on the left flank. It was soon apparent that two battalions of the 7th Marines were being hit by a full-scale attack on both flanks.

That night the Chinese increased their pressure, holding up the Marines for two days. At last, on November 4, the Marines managed to break free and push forward six thousand yards.

*   *   *

The most important event the next day, November 5, was an order from MacArthur, without consulting Washington; to bomb the Korean end of the Yalu River bridges. By now he realized that the Chinese intervention was serious, for the Chinese had driven Eighth Army back across the Chungchon River and were threatening to overrun Walker's bridgehead at the main crossing.

To stop this great flow of Chinese troops into Korea, MacArthur had ordered the bombing without consulting the Joint Chiefs. This so concerned General Stratemeyer, the Far East Air Force commander, that he immediately alerted the Pentagon. An hour and twenty minutes before the planes were to lift off, the Joint Chiefs ordered MacArthur to postpone all bombing of targets within five miles of the Manchurian border until further notice.

At two A.M., November 6, a messenger woke MacArthur to give him this dispatch from Washington. He took it to his desk for better light. He was astounded. First he canceled the bombing order, then sat down to compose his reply. "Men and matériel in large force are pouring across all bridges over the Yalu from Manchuria," he cabled. Every hour the bombing was postponed would be paid for dearly with the blood of Americans and other UN force troops. "Under the gravest protest that I can make, I am suspending this strike and carrying out your instructions." He requested immediate reconsideration of the Joint Chiefs' order.

Bradley read the message from Tokyo over the telephone to the president, who had recently narrowly escaped assassination at Blair House by revolutionary Puerto Ricans. Apparently being in no mood to confront MacArthur, Truman bowed. "Give him the go-ahead," he replied to Bradley. After all, MacArthur was on the scene and felt strongly about the matter. And so once more MacArthur had his way. The Joint Chiefs authorized him to proceed with his planned bombing.

As if they were privy to everything going on in Tokyo and Washington, the Chinese, for no reason apparent to the Americans, broke contact with UN forces that same day. In the west, Australians, from their positions along the Chongchon River, saw the Chinese withdraw after a predawn attack. Throughout the day aerial spotters reported seeing Chinese troops moving back north. By nightfall they had disappeared into the mountains. In the east, the 7th Marines were still fighting the Chinese north of Chinhung-ni, but when they awoke the following morning, the enemy had mysteriously vanished.

Their evacuation renewed the debate over Chinese intervention. Was it really serious? Perhaps they had been hit so hard they were backing off. Others surmised they had withdrawn to give the UN time to reconsider the drive to the Yalu.

As for MacArthur, he was only encouraged to make plans for an all-out offensive from both east and west.

3.

In Peking, Mao was in high spirits. His analysis of MacArthur had been correct. Overweening self-confidence was luring the supreme commander into a trap. Since Walker had somehow succeeded in withdrawing the bulk of his troops safely across the Chungchon River, Mao realized it would be foolhardy to press his own attack. The Volunteers had already outrun supplies. And so the previous day he had ordered Peng to abruptly cease attacking in both west and east, thereby concluding the First Campaign.

Mao reasoned that although they had not achieved as much as first planned during the first thirteen days, 15,000 enemy *had been* annihilated and MacArthur's plan to occupy all of Korea by Thanksgiving had been foiled. The Korean situation had been stabilized, winning time for the readjustment and re-forming of Kim Il-sung's scattered troops. The campaign had also enabled the Chinese Volunteers to establish a firm position in Korea while gaining experience in fighting the heavily armed enemy.

By suddenly withdrawing, Mao guessed that MacArthur, assuming *he* had beaten the Chinese, would push his troops farther north, thus dangerously lengthening his own supply route. Then the Volunteers and North Koreans could come out of their hiding places in the wooded mountains and win the decisive battle.

Following Peng's suggestion, Mao ordered the Volunteers to combine a mobile horizontal defense with guerrilla warfare. "If resistance is of small scale, the Volunteers will surely annihilate the enemy; but if it is heavy, withdraw and suck the enemy into a trap. Then the enemy can be destroyed by our main forces."

With approval from the Joint Chiefs, MacArthur ordered the bombing of the Yalu bridges on November 8. The first bombs did little damage, and the flow of Chinese troops into Korea continued. The bombing did, however, involve the first all-jet air battle in history. Lieutenant Russell Brown, in an F-80, shot down a Russian-built MiG-15, perhaps piloted by a Chinese. The appearance of MiG's encouraged MacArthur in his belief that a serious Chinese intrusion could best be stopped at the Yalu. The fact that the Chinese—after destroying an ROK division and then battering one of Gay's regiments—had disappeared and were yet to be found led him to conceive of an immediate all-out attack to end the war promptly.

A message from the Joint Chiefs on that same day gave MacArthur the opening he needed. They asked for his latest views on bombing in light of the next move the Chinese might make. His response set off alarm bells in Washington. With his air power, he replied, he could prevent reinforcements from coming across the Yalu to support those Chinese forces now arrayed against him. "I plan to launch my attack for this purpose on or about November 15th with the mission of driving to the border and securing all of North Korea. Any program short of this would completely destroy the morale of my forces and the psychological consequences would be inestimable."

MacArthur then aimed a blow directly at Truman: "To give up any portion of North Korea to the aggression of the Chinese Communists would be the greatest defeat of the free world in recent times. Indeed to yield to so immoral a proposition would bankrupt our leadership and influence in Asia and render untenable our position both politically and militarily."

The Joint Chiefs bowed again. They recommended that Mac-Arthur's all-out offensive "should be kept under review but should not be changed." In other words, he should be allowed to go ahead as long as there appeared to be "a reasonable chance of success."

Acheson, Marshall and others adopted, word for word, the Joint Chiefs' cowardly reply. "All the President's advisers in this matter, civilian and military, knew that something was badly wrong, though what it was, how to find out, and what to do about it, they muffed." So confessed Acheson. If Truman had backed the Chiefs with an order to draw back to the narrow waist of Korea, as the British had suggested, and Walker wanted to do, common sense would have reigned. "But it would have meant a fight with MacArthur, charges by him that they had denied his victory. . . . So they hesitated, wavered, and the chance was lost. While everyone acted correctly, no one, I suspect, was ever quite satisfied with himself afterward."

On the western front, the Eighth Army would have at least seven divisions and a mass of artillery and tanks for the all-out offensive. What concerned Walker most was logistics. It would take four thousand tons of supplies a day to support such an offensive, and he was getting only half of that. He informed MacArthur that he could not start until November 24th.

On the eastern front, there was another problem. MacArthur's operations officer, Brigadier General Edwin Wright, felt that Almond had spread X Corps on too wide a front. He persuaded MacArthur to deemphasize Almond's eager attempts to reach the Yalu River at several points. Instead, X Corps should do everything to support the Eighth Army drive. Wright consequently advised Almond to be prepared to change his mission so he could coordinate with the all-out attack by Walker.

Although MacArthur had great faith in Almond, he agreed with Wright; and on November 15, the X Corps commander was ordered to reorient his attack. The race to the Yalu was to be subordinated to helping support General Walker, for whom Almond had little respect. Almond accepted MacArthur's decision without protest. Plans for mounting an attack to the west in support of Walker were left mainly to the Marines; but General Barr was allowed to continue the 7th Division drive to the Yalu. Almond was, in effect, pulling Barr away from any role of being able to support the Eighth Army.

The large gap between Walker and Almond still extended a minimum distance of twenty air miles from the northernmost right flank of the Eighth Army to the nearest left-flank position of X Corps. Farther south, the gap was about thirty-five air miles, and the road-mile distances over mountain trails were far greater.

Almond had arranged with Walker for a patrol system, but patrols rarely entered the gap. This omission did not appear to bother Almond, but concerned Walker deeply. MacArthur himself felt that the mountainous backbone of North Korea made it impossible for the Chinese to use the area for military operations. This showed how little he knew about his new enemy. Radio communication between X Corps and the Eighth Army and a daily air trip by a liaison officer appeared to Almond to be sufficient.

By November 17, Walker had solved his logistics problem, and he informed Tokyo he could start the all-out attack within a week. MacArthur passed on the tentative date to the Joint Chiefs, adding optimistically that air attacks had isolated the battlefield from Chinese reinforcements by radically reducing the flow of enemy supplies. The future, he reiterated, was bright.

4.

A week earlier Mao had ordered Peng to launch a combined attack on both east and west fronts within a month. Seven or eight enemy regiments were to be destroyed and the front advanced from Pyongyang to the east coast. "If this is achieved," he concluded, "we will have essentially won the war."

Four days later Peng assembled the Volunteers Communist Party Committee to decide what steps should be taken. It was agreed to continue the policy of integrated mobile, positional, and guerrilla tactics. By attacking on the front and harassing from the rear simultaneously, they should be able to destroy enemy troops in movement.

The committee also agreed that there were two ways they could destroy the enemy: surround a unit and then pick off those troops coming to their assistance; or thrust two or three armies—the equivalent of six to nine U.S. divisions—into enemy-controlled territory. "Chairman Mao's orders must be followed to push south from Pyongyang to the east coast, annihilate six or seven regiments and force the enemy to turn from offense to defense. This will pave the way for our general counteroffensive in the future."

To set up Mao's trap, the Volunteers in the east had suddenly withdrawn on November 7 from their attack on the Marines heading up to the Chosin Reservoir. Two days later the Volunteers on the west had also withdrawn as if beaten.

On November 10, Walker and Almond, following MacArthur's order, continued pushing north. By the end of a week both were approaching the area Peng was preparing for the crucial battles. Unfortunately, Eighth Army and X Corps intelligence sections had grossly underestimated Peng's strength—in fact, they were still under the illusion that Lin Piao was in charge of the Volunteers—and failed to identify the whereabouts of the invisible enemy that was secretly preparing for their annihilation.

CHAPTER 19

Even Victors Are by Victory Undone
(November 6–26)

1.

On the western front Lieutenant Harry Trollope was still frustrated in his attempt to lead his group to safety. Caught between two fires, they had little chance of success. On November 6, they had come upon abandoned foxholes where they found two barracks bags filled with six blankets, two sleeping bags, shorts, socks, shaving equipment, and toothbrushes. They also discovered a case of grenades and ammunition. By then Trollope had lost one man. The four remaining felt more secure after placing grenade booby traps around their position, but what really improved Trollope's morale was to be able to brush his teeth.

The next afternoon, while looking for food, they heard tanks and heavy small-arms fire and decided to sit tight and wait for friendly troops to break through. After dark, Trollope moved to the top of the ridge as lookout. At four A.M. on November 8 he heard another blast of tank fire and the movement of T-34's. Trollope started down the ridge to rejoin his comrades. He found a roll of toilet paper and spelled out "HELP" in five-foot letters on the ground, securing the paper with stones. A liaison plane circling overhead at dawn apparently didn't see them. Trollope took off his T-shirt and waved it. Again no luck.

They were hungry, and in midafternoon Trollope and Katakawa decided to examine the only Korean house in the area. When they were two hundred yards away, they came upon a boy of about eighteen.

Trollope signaled with his trigger finger. Should they shoot him? Katakawa signaled back to attempt a capture. They crawled to within thirty feet of the youngster and then jumped him.

"Me GI!" the Korean kept saying. Trollope asked what battalion. "2nd." What officers? The boy gave three names and described Captain Fields, then said he could get food after dark. Still suspicious, Trollope instructed him to meet them there at seven P.M.

Katakawa and Trollope returned an hour early to guard against any trickery. They saw the Korean move out of a cave a few minutes later with a large package. At exactly seven P.M. he called out, *"Oi!"* (Hey!) He had brought about ten pounds of millet mixed with kidney beans, along with a dark green paste, stringy and sour. The boy begged to come with them. "Bring more food tomorrow, same time," said Trollope, "and we'll think about it."

They ate in the dark, saving some rations for tomorrow. To Trollope the food tasted as good as sirloin steak. Early the next day they ate again and cleaned their weapons. That afternoon one of the grenade booby traps went off. They waited anxiously for half an hour but no enemy appeared. Curious, Trollope and one man crept up the hill and found a middle-aged Korean woman, dead. They dragged her off and buried her.

A C-47 flew overhead, circling the area. They could hear a woman's voice broadcasting in a foreign language, probably Chinese, then music, followed by more talk. An hour later a liaison plane flew back and forth overhead. The four came out of the brush and waved, but the pilot didn't see them. "We all expressed our opinion in flagrant terms about the plane and discussed the pilot's ancestry," wrote Trollope in his diary.

After dark, Katakawa and Trollope returned to meet the young Korean. Again he brought food, but said the people who gave it to him had no more. Trollope decided to let him join them. They shared equipment but didn't let him stand guard. For three days they constantly changed positions in vain attempts to break through to the south. On the night of November 12, about twenty air miles east of the Chungchon River's mouth, they crossed a stream, passed a village, then climbed a ridge where they came upon a lone hut. Inside they found potatoes and a barrel full of dried corn. They built a small fire, made coffee, and parched the corn. It tasted like popcorn hulls and was delicious.

Their continued ascent was so steep they had to rest every five minutes. At last they located a level spot and settled for the night. They could hear artillery close by, but were so tired they didn't bother observing where the sounds came from.

At dawn they reached the top. From there they could see the mouth of the Chongchon River and the Yellow Sea. The air had turned bitter cold, and there was frost on the ground. Trollope saw enemy troops in the north digging holes and building a tank trap. He figured friendly lines were about five miles to the south and decided to move down a ridge and up a valley so they could meet UN troops advancing north.

They were ready to leave at dawn when they saw a civilian leading eight NK soldiers up the trail. They approached to within thirty yards, then turned to another trail. Katakawa and Trollope cautiously moved over to a small saddle and saw six enemy moving down from the rear. Realizing they were again surrounded, they set up booby traps.

That night was so cold it was almost impossible to sleep, and by morning they had lost most of their initiative. Katakawa was the most active, and Trollope had come to rely on him. They went for water while Watson, Lauber and the young Korean, now nicknamed Charley, searched for food. The latter three returned several hours later with sweet potatoes and a small amount of millet. Lauber then revealed that they'd met four North Korean boys and brought them along.

Trollope was angry. Why? And where the devil were they? Below, in a cave. The oldest was about seventeen, the youngest fifteen. Trollope questioned them. They told him they'd been hiding from North Korean soldiers for fear of being conscripted. Noting that all were wearing army-type tennis shoes, Trollope guessed they had probably been in the North Korean Army. He asked if they had weapons. Yes, rifles—a dirty M-1, the bolt frozen, and two long Russian rifles, with only half a dozen rounds of ammunition. Trollope was beginning to trust them and from them learned that American tanks had approached the area but couldn't break through.

"What do you think about us moving out?" asked Trollope.

The answer was negative. The boys would have done so before if it had been possible. The next morning—it was November 16—Trollope went with two of the Koreans down the hill for water and to see if the enemy had moved. Fifty NK were moving east with two oxcarts. An hour later, as the three were moving back up the hill, they heard a booby-trap grenade explode. "Well, we got a couple," Katakawa told Trollope.

"Did you kill them?" asked Trollope.

"We didn't examine, but I believe so."

After that noise, Trollope knew they had to leave. As they were packing their gear, they heard voices approaching. Watson and Trollope grabbed their M-1's and grenades and lay on a rocky ledge to cover the others. To his amazement Trollope saw below an ordinary scene: half a dozen women in white clothing with packs on their heads were moving along the south side of the ridge down to a valley, where three children were playing around a house. Trollope returned and told the others they must wait to move until morning. That night snow fell.

They left at dawn, heading west, then worked down the side of the mountain. At night truck convoys began moving both north and south.

Ahead lay flat country providing no cover during the day. They were too exhausted to move at night. Even so, morale was good. The next morning, the enemy was spread out at fifty-yard intervals only half a mile away. Trollope's group remained in hiding all day and that evening decided to keep moving ahead.

It was still dark when they started out at four A.M. They came to a small river and waited for a safe chance to cross, but there was too much activity and they turned south. When it was getting light, they moved off the road toward several houses that looked abandoned, but decided it would be too dangerous to enter. All agreed they could go three more days without food. It was now November 19, and Trollope and his little group had been on the run for two and a half exhausting weeks.

2.

Walker had completed plans for the attack that would reach the Yalu. The British Commonwealth Brigade was already getting into position, even though many of the men still wore their tropical clothing from Hong Kong. Not one had any form of winter kit. Private Julian Tunstall found the wind literally blowing ice in his face. This was his first experience of a Korean winter, and he had never felt such cruel cold. The weather finally broke on November 19, and the British were delayed by a twelve-hour torrent of rain which turned the iron-hard earth into a morass.

In Tokyo there was euphoria when, on November 21, Task Force Cooper, the spearhead of the 7th Division on the eastern front, reached Hyesanjin, a village on the Yalu, without opposition. Almond drove up thirty miles to have his picture taken looking across the river. MacArthur was ecstatic and sent the X Corps commander a warm message: "Heartiest congratulations, Ned, and tell Dave Barr that the 7th Division hit the jackpot."

It was a field day for photographers, and a number of jubilant Americans imitated Churchill and Patton at the Rhine by urinating into the Yalu—a sight that must have puzzled any Chinese watching through field glasses from the other side.

The news made headlines. Acheson and other State Department officials meeting with Secretary of Defense George Marshall, the replacement of Louis Johnson, and generals at the Pentagon expressed pleasure at the achievement, but their main concern was the difficulty of getting the Chinese to agree to a neutral zone at the border. Deputy Secretary of State Lovett made a suggestion: MacArthur should create a de facto demilitarized zone at the Yalu by simply withdrawing to a defensible position south of the river. Almost everyone favored Lovett's idea, and General Collins even traced a possible line ten to twenty-five miles south of the Yalu.

This proposal showed that the Joint Chiefs had no concept of the critical damage Walker's Eighth Army had already suffered. What Lovett had suggested was totally unrealistic. That military as well as civilian experts could even consider such a proposition was a demonstration of the confusion among America's leaders sitting half a world away. The greater tragedy, however, was that MacArthur and others sitting close to the boiling pot of Korea were equally unable to face reality. The entire ROK II Corps was in disarray, yet the Joint Chiefs were under the impression the war was nearly over because a small American force had reached the Yalu. Hadn't they remembered what happened to the first UN troops who had reached this same illusory goal?

3.

Chairman Mao was planning the final steps of his trap in an ancient one-story structure just outside the walls of the Forbidden City. This modest office was where he had lived and worked in seclusion with his wife since China's entry into the war. He rarely left the building even to hold meetings in the headquarters of the Chinese Communist forces, several miles away. Instead he met privately with two bright young staff officers and Chou En-lai, whom he trusted for two reasons: Chou was a Confucian who had no ambition to be on top and was, therefore, utterly loyal. Second, he was a master administrator, capable of dealing with military, diplomatic, domestic, and even party problems on every level.

Orders to Peng were based on the decisions reached at these meetings. The group was so small and exclusive that no one could know who Mao's advisers were.

Mao would spend hours, half-sitting, half-lying on his bed, studying ancient Chinese history. He had never attended a military school and was a self-made tactical genius. Through the years he had learned from his own successes and failures. While Peng admired Mao, he had reservations. The chairman didn't seem knowledgeable about modern weapons and relied too heavily on the strategy of such ancient masters of warfare as Sun Tzu without putting their teachings in the correct context.

At the same time, Peng fully approved of Mao's trap, which he himself had inspired. The strategy was simple. The Chinese would open the door, as if retreating. Once the enemy rushed in, Peng's troops would pounce on thier weakest flank. When Mao learned that MacArthur had taken the bait by ordering a general offensive on November 24, he telegraphed Peng to launch their own counteroffensive at twilight of the 25th. It would surely take Walker by complete surprise.

4.

On November 22, the eve of Thanksgiving, Reginald Thompson, the British journalist, visited General Shrimp Milburn and got the impression that the I Corps commander was not happy about the coming all-out offensive. The unsatisfactory movement of supplies still had not prevented arrival in Korea of a multitude of turkeys, cans of cranberry sauce, and pumpkin pies, so that every mother's fighting son could enjoy a traditional Thanksgiving dinner.

Thompson spent the holiday traveling around the northwestern front. Regimental headquarters had printed elaborate menus, and tables were laid with white cloths and decorated with candles in the midst of the charred ruins of burned-out villages. Some units were given a ration of whiskey; others had the luxury of hot showers and a change of uniform.

Up on the Yalu, engineers of Task Force Cooper working at Hyesan-jin were treated to a full-scale Thanksgiving dinner along the side of the road paralleling the river. Afterwards they resumed their job of swinging picks. It was so cold that Private First Class Lenoise Bowman felt as if his hands would fall off after three swings. Every so often the Chinese across the river would lob mortar rounds at them. The men, ordered not to return fire, just ducked and continued working.

Far to the south, other X Corps troops were enjoying Thanksgiving dinner as well as the great news that Task Force Cooper had arrived at the Yalu without meeting any opposition. The 5th Marines were spread out on the east side of the Chosin Reservoir, with Taplett's 3rd Battalion in the lead. The 7th Marines, moving up the other side of the reservoir, got nothing but cold rations. They would have to wait until tomorrow for their turkey. It was a miserable day because of the intense cold. One youngster went to the head and a few minutes later his comrades heard him shouting for help. He was frozen to the seat, and it took a doctor to get him free.

At ten A.M., November 24, Walker's all-out offensive began with a tremendous artillery preparation. Forty minutes later MacArthur's plane touched down at an advance airstrip near the Chongsong River. He was met by Walker and General Milburn. MacArthur squatted down to pet Milburn's dachshund. After a briefing, he jeeped to IX Corps headquarters, where its commander, Major General John Coulter, told him that his troops were eager to reach the Yalu. The attackers were meeting little resistance all along the seventy-five-mile front. Earnest Hoberecht of UP heard MacArthur reply, "You can tell them when they get up to the Yalu River, Jack, they can all come home. I want to make good my statement that they will get Christmas dinner at home."

During the five-hour tour of the front, MacArthur appeared to be in a cheerful mood and, wrapped in a gaily checkered muffler, chatted informally with officers, undaunted by the bitter, windy weather. By midafternoon he was again airborne, and everyone aboard settled back for the three-hour return trip to Tokyo. Suddenly MacArthur surprised everyone by instructing the pilot to head for the mouth of the Yalu River. A correspondent jokingly asked, "Is this trip necessary?"

They flew south to pick up an additional jet escort coming from Kimpo Airfield, then turned and started north. At the mouth of the Yalu they turned right and flew along the river. They passed over Kanggye, believed to be enemy headquarters. It was burning.

They crossed snow-covered mountains so the general could see two large reservoirs where power-generating dams were located. Then MacArthur told the pilot to fly over Hyesanjin, which had recently been occupied by Task Force Cooper. "Flap the wings or something."

The passengers buckled up, and a few minutes later the plane dipped its wings to salute Task Force Cooper. Then the plane turned for home. As the jet escorts left them, MacArthur radioed, "Thanks for the grand ride."

It had been a heady day for MacArthur, but not for Walker. When the convoy of jeeps returned to the *SCAP*, Joe Tyner and Mike Lynch noted a strange look on their boss's face. They had come to know him as few would. Even during the most trying days, he seldom registered emotion. What they saw was a very different man. As they stood watching MacArthur's departure, Walker suddenly said, "Bullshit." Joe and Mike were surprised. They had never heard him use profanity in their presence before. Yet one look told them that whatever disturbed him had become too much to hide.

They began walking toward the L-17 for their flight back to Pyongyang. Suddenly, Walker asked Mike to stop one of the military police jeeps departing the airfield. He climbed in and told the driver to take him to the 24th Division CP. The visit was a brief one. He directed General Church to tell Dick Stephens, whose 21st Infantry was leading the western attack, that "if he smells Chinese chow, pull back immediately." By this one command he had taken it upon himself to change his orders from that of an all-out attack to one of reconnaissance in force. Once done, a look of calmness returned to his face.

To a layman, Walker's action may not seem important. But for a professional soldier, it was the most difficult decision of his military career. It comes when a commander is forced to choose between an irrational order by his superior and the safety of his men. Such a decision was called by General Matthew Ridgway the greatest challenge a combat leader must face. General George C. Marshall described it as "laying your commisison on the line." Walker had manufactured every excuse to delay the offensive until he could gain a better picture of the Chinese situation. Although finally forced to attack, he still had serious misgivings. During those five hours with MacArthur, he kept weighing their divergent views of the threat. He finally concluded that his own assesssment was the more accurate. Once he was convinced, there was no moral alternative. He had to countermand the order.

In Tokyo, MacArthur released a special communiqué to the UN and the world. Seldom before in the history of warfare had a senior commander ever divulged his attack plans to the enemy. But there was no one who could have stopped him. He had become an unchallenged Caesar answerable only to himself. "The giant pincer moved according to schedule today." There were advances on both wings. "Our losses were extraordinarily light." The prospects were bright, and in three days Almond was scheduled to launch his attack. He was now planning to switch the 5th Marines to the west side of the Chosin Reservoir and let Barr's 7th Division attack alone from the east. This would catch the enemy between pincers. That morning Lieutenant Colonel Don Faith, Commander of the 1st Battalion, 32nd Infantry, arrived at Hagaru-ri, the southern end of the reservoir. As he was starting up the eastern side of the reservoir, he met Colonel Raymond Murray coming towards him. The 5th Marine commander informed Faith that the new 32nd Regiment CP was about eight miles north and that Taplett's battalion was about four miles farther north. Murray was still in charge of the area, since Almond's new orders had not been issued. He assigned Faith an assembly area halfway up towards Taplett. Murray explained to the puzzled Faith that he had not yet received orders to transfer his regiment to the west side of the reservoir but expected to get those orders in the morning.

Taplett had already sent a platoon-size reconnaissance patrol north to a huge hydroelectric plant. They encountered Chinese, killed five, captured one, and destroyed an abandoned 75-mm gun. After proceeding to the northern tip of the reservoir without finding more Chinese, they turned back. All seemed quiet in the north.

During November 25, the Eighth Army continued to advance modestly. On the extreme left flank of the seventy-five-mile front, Lieutenant Trollope and his little group had no idea that a major battle was being waged to the east. They had managed to find their way back to their position overlooking the Yellow Sea, and Trollope sent the five young Koreans, whom he now trusted, to find a place to break through the enemy lines. After dark they all moved down a trail led by one of the Koreans. When they reached a village, Trollope ordered everyone to sling arms as if they were on patrol. The houses were burning and civilians were too busy saving possessions to notice them. Then several enemy soldiers approached. Increasing their pace, Trollope's little group pulled down their caps. The enemy soldiers, wearing various uniforms, politely stepped to one side to let them pass. No one spoke.

Ahead was a glow of fire. One Korean boy reported that the enemy, spread all around them in the woods, were coming into the village to wash and eat. Trollope's men continued to another village, also burning. Katakawa was now leading. They paralleled the river, moving fast. Suddenly they came upon two enemy at a curve in the trail. Katakawa killed them with his M-1.

Task Force Dolvin was the spear of the attack by the U.S. 25th Division. By dusk of the 25th of November, one of its components, Easy Company of the 27th Regiment, was on the high ground covering the valley—only about five miles east of Trollope's group. Lieutenant J. C. Burch, commander of the 3rd Platoon, spread his three squads evenly over the crowns of three cone-shaped peaks. The lieutenant's own group found themselves in a Korean graveyard, where the men reluctantly dug fox-holes in the frozen ground. In the dusk they had seen figures scuttling in the underbrush far away and thought they were civilians. But with darkness came the jabber of a machine gun on the right and a few rifle shots, followed by disturbing silence.

It was Mao's counteroffensive. Three Volunteer armies—equivalent to nine U.S. divisions—suddenly attacked the western front at twilight.

In minutes the squad on Burch's right was wiped out. Burch could hear foreign chattering nearby, but nothing was visible. He tried to radio for mortar and artillery fire but couldn't get through. After twenty minutes the talking ceased, and there was momentary quiet. Then half a dozen grenades exploded among the graves and monuments. Burch crouched, still working his radio. He saw two of his ROKs step out in the moonlight. They cried out as a dozen enemy came over the rise. A grenade landed beside a sergeant lying near Burch blowing the sergeant against him. Burch leaped up to see at least eighty Chinese half-surrounding him so close he could have hit any of them with a rock.

"Fall back on the company!" he shouted. The survivors ran while Burch held off the Chinese with his carbine. He killed two and then took off before the enemy could fire. They kept shouting, "Come on back, GI! Afraid, GI?"

Soon rifle and tommy-gun fire descended on Burch's men, who were outnumbered ten to one, but the last twenty yards of the cone were steep and the Chinese were visible in the moonlight. The Americans kept rolling down grenades and firing their M-1's.

By this time Burch was back at his CP and could get artillery-fire cover for his beleaguered 3rd Platoon, also getting help for the Ranger

Company. At his CP, Lieutenant Colonel Welborn "Tom" Dolvin, commander of the task force, was learning that his Ranger Company had been hit hard by a mass of Chinese, blowing bugles.

Trollope and his men were still looking for a place to break through the enemy lines. About an hour after midnight, his group moved on with Lauber leading. After a quarter of a mile Lauber stopped and said, "I hear something!" The men spread out. Trollope had started towards a cliff when he saw a flicker of light under a tree and crawled forward to bypass what he thought was another enemy outpost. But then he heard someone grumble, "Jesus Christ, my feet are cold!"

Trollope yelled, "Hey, GI!"

"Who's there?" a voice called out.

"Lieutenant Harry Trollope!" He stood up, keeping his weapon pointed to the ground. A guard appeared and began questioning him. What was Trollope's hometown? The capital of his state? His organization? How many were with him?

"One man come up," the guard finally said. As Trollope approached, the soldier said, "Okay, let the rest of them come." But he kept his BAR at the ready, examining each man.

The saga of Harry Trollope had come to an end after twenty-five grueling days. He was recovered a mile west of Yongbyong by elements of the 89th Tank Battalion. Ironically, he had reached the dubious safety of Task Force Dolvin.

Forty-five minutes later Tom Dolvin got a brief message that the Rangers had driven off the Chinese, even though their commander was wounded. This report was followed by ominous silence. The fighting in front of Easy Company lasted until just before dawn but continued to their right where the Rangers had been hit.

By now Dolvin knew that the Rangers had lost their hill, so he requested the artillery to concentrate fire against the crest, using plenty of white phosphorus. By the time the ridge was ablaze, Dolvin had reached the exhausted Ranger survivors. Once they were passed back to Division, Dolvin decided to put Baker Company of the 35th Regiment into the attack.

But the 35th had not yet come up abreast of the task force, and Dolvin had no contact with the 24th Regiment on the right. The ridge now held by the enemy within the 24th zone menaced Dolvin's own rear. During the night, Baker Company was also hit, though not badly. But the loss of the Rangers had created a hole Dolvin couldn't fill. He reluctantly concluded that unless the 24th Regiment came abreast, he was in bad shape. He didn't know that the 24th, battered in the night's battle, was heading straight into the heart of a massive Chinese buildup. To the east, the 9th Infantry of the 2nd Division had also been savaged, with two rifle companies, poorly supplied and out of contact with other units, overwhelmed.

At the extreme right of the Eighth Army line, there were still only fragmentary reports from Major General Yu Jae-hung, commander of the ROK II Corps; and Walker had no idea that both of its divisions had already collapsed under Peng's onslaught. Peng had sent small units to penetrate behind the UN troops in order to attack with grenades and bayonets, thus denying the enemy the use of their superior firepower. These tactics devised by Peng and Mao had taken the ROKs completely by surprise. In the resulting confusion, vehicles became entangled and all roads to the rear were hopelessly jammed.

That afternoon General Chung Il-kwon, the ROK chief of staff, and his adviser, Jim Hausman, now a major, jeeped up to Kunu-ri to find out from General Yu what was going on. Yu and his American adviser, just returned from the front, revealed that both their divisions had collapsed and desperately needed help. Yu, who had fought so well in the Bowling Alley, urged Chung to return to General Milburn's headquarters, and report what had happened. "You can give them an on-the-ground explanation—my casualties and my needs." Neither Chung nor Hausman was happy, since it was getting dark and Chinese had been reported in the rear.

After Yu offered to give them his best MP officer to guide them, Chung and Hausman left, sitting in the back of a jeep behind two men who had only side arms. The dark roads were jammed with trucks, assorted vehicles and refugees. When the MP lost the way, the ordinarily composed Chung angrily pulled out his pistol several times as if to shoot him. The half-hour trip took several hours, but they finally reached the I Corps commander.

Hausman reported that there were no Chinese near Kunu-ri. "We didn't see one. Chung and I reconnoitered the whole area." Then he told how Yu's two divisions had been shattered north of the Chongchon River. Reinforcements had to be sent up to protect the two American divisions on the ROK's left.

Far to the east, at the Chosin Reservoir, the Marines and the GIs of the 7th Division were just about ready to launch their own "Back home by Christmas" offensive—unaware of the debacle on their left.

PART VI

THE CHOSIN RESERVOIR

CHAPTER 20

Trapped
(November 27–28)

1.

The X Corps attack started as scheduled on November 27. At 8:10 A.M., two companies of the 3rd Battalion, 7th Marines, set out from the outskirts of Yudam-ni, a mountain village near the northwest end of the Chosin Reservoir, to secure the high ground on both sides of the road going west. About half an hour later the 2nd Battalion of the 5th Marines headed out of the same village to launch the main attack. They planned to follow the road as it swung north towards the Yalu, with the rest of the 1st Marine Division to follow. There was little opposition, but at 9:35 a Marine spotter plane reported Chinese positions all across the front.

The Marines were scheduled to join Walker's Eighth Army at the first objective, some forty miles northwest of Yudam-ni. Together they would race to the Yalu and end the war. This was pie in the sky! The elements of Walker's Army that were supposed to meet the Marines were already fleeing to the rear. Moreover, no word had come from General Almond of the disaster on the western front. The farther the Marines advanced, the more likely they were to be destroyed.

Early that morning, Almond left his headquarters and jeeped north so he could watch the Marines launch their offensive. On the way he had to pass many elements of the 31st Infantry Regiment heading for the right side of the reservoir. They would join the 7th Infantry Division attack which would begin the next morning. As the general neared

Hagaru-ri and headed up the left side of the reservoir towards Yudam-ni, he found the road jammed with convoys of the 1st Marine Division. This delay kept him from seeing the kickoff; and by the time he arrived at the 7th Marine regimental CP, he was told there were obviously a lot more Chinese in the area than expected, and they were not going to have an easy race to the Yalu.

Discounting such talk, Almond passed out medals to officers and several enlisted men; but, after further inspection of the area, he promptly reported to MacArthur that because the strength of the enemy was considerable, "a re-examination was needed of the disposition of the Marines."

On the other side of the reservoir, Colonel Taplett also had trouble getting his 3rd Battalion of the 5th Marines around to the west. Early that morning he had left his position on the east and trucked his people back south to Hagaru-ri, then up the western side of the reservoir to Yudam-ni. By the time he was in his assembly position northwest of the village in the midst of precipitous mountains, it was already noon. He found himself located near the junction of the main road going west and a smaller one leading directly north. He was supposed to follow the 2nd Battalion and join the attack to the Yalu, but word came that the 2nd had already run into heavy resistance and many roadblocks. Now he was ordered to remain in the assembly area and simply post local security for the night. After carrying out these orders, he undertook a personal reconnaissance and soon discovered that a long spur of land came down from the north—a tremendous mass, like a razorback, 1,450 meters high. West of the spur was the road that would eventually swing north, and a stream; to the east was a saddle and a valley floor that jutted back into the landmass. He placed his weapons company in that position, and soon got a disturbing report from the company commander that there were numerous holes like those they had seen on the other side of the reservoir. These were small Chinese foxholes—wide enough for only a small man to enter, but deep and hollowed out inside. Taplett and his executive, Major John Canney, found a number of these holes, all empty. There were no bodies, no equipment. By now it was getting dark. He returned to his CP and put one rifle company astride the road to the west, another across the road to the north. Both roads were mined. A third company was placed on the low ground to the south with outposts on high ground. He also put a platoon above the battalion CP, nestled against the slope of the spur.

Two days earlier Mao had learned that his favorite son, Mao Anoing, had been killed in a bombing raid on Pyongyang. He also received a distressing report from Peng, who had planned to start his surprise attack on the eastern front on November 26. First his Ninth Army would attack the west side of the Chosin Reservoir and then hit the east side. But the Volunteers had trouble getting across the mountains, and the attack could not get under way until twilight of the 27th. If it had come as scheduled, the Marines—without Taplett's battalion and an extra day to bring up supplies and reinforcements—would probably have been overrun.

At about nine P.M. Taplett got a call from the battalion surgeon: "I'm getting all these casualties, and they claim they're from the 7th Marines."

Taplett found them badly shot up, still in a state of shock. Some were barefoot. They were elements of the 3rd Battalion, 7th, and were supposed to be on Hill 1410, about a mile west of Taplett's CP. But they'd been surprised by Chinese on the back side of the little mountain and never reached the top. In the next hour, twenty or thirty more 7th Marines wandered in, some badly wounded, some victims of shock and the freezing weather. Taplett phoned the regimental commander, Colonel Ray Murray, who said, "Well, they're still on the top of the hill and you'd better get some wire up to them, because nobody has any communication with them."

Taplett's communication officer ran a wire to the hill, but it soon went dead. Then word came from Murray that a company of his 2nd Battalion was having a lot of trouble. They had infiltrators and a couple of fierce firefights were going on. The report caused Taplett concern, since he was supposed to be in an assembly area, resting up to pass through the 2nd Battalion in the morning.

At midnight Taplett received further disturbing news, this time from H Company, on a hill less than a mile away. The Chinese had hit How Company with considerable force and were sideslipping to their right, which meant enemy were coming down towards the battalion CP. George Company was also getting hit. Private First Class Fred Davidson, the Oklahoman who had utter faith in America and the Marines, felt he was undergoing a personal white-phosphorus barrage. The first round exploded fifty yards to his left, sending off white-hot shrapnel in every direction. The second hit twenty-five yards in front and the third landed twenty-five yards to the left. He figured the next shell would explode on top of him, so he jumped up and ran, just as the fourth round landed at his heels. He was slammed face-down into the snow, but it was several seconds before he realized his back was on fire. He tried to slap out the flames but couldn't reach them. He yelled for help. Two men tore off his clothes and packed the burns with snow. A corpsman appeared, did what he could and helped Davidson down the road to the battalion aid station.

No one seemed to know how to handle the burns. It was freezing weather, and the corpsman didn't want to take off all Davidson's clothes, but decided they had to put on a dressing to ward off infection. Davidson painfully removed parka, field jacket, sweater and wool shirt. Then he unbuttoned the top of his long johns to his waist. Davidson felt no pain as a doctor applied something to the burns and put on a dressing. As he started to dress, he had to rig a pair of suspenders to hold up his trousers, and finally did struggle back into his clothes. He was shivering so much it was almost impossible to put on his gloves. Then he was taken outside the unheated tent to where several Marines in sleeping bags were lying on straw covered by a large tarpaulin.

By this time, Taplett had learned that the roadblock to the north had been hit so hard that the defenders had to withdraw, and Item Company in the rear was also under heavy attack. Major Canney crawled into the CP tent. "I want you to know that we're here all by ourselves," said the exec. "All the H and S people have pulled back and the Weapons Company people are also back across the road." The battalion perimeter had collapsed. "What's left is about three hundred yards inland from the road."

The CP was completely exposed. Because a mortar round had knocked out the switchboard, Taplett could either stay where he had communications with his rifle companies or abandon the place and be without communications. He had to make a tough decision. "John," he told Canney, "you go back and tell those bastards to get back up here. We're under heavy pressure, but there's no reason for them to withdraw. Send them back to their area positions." As Canney left to carry out his order, a bullet smashed through his forehead. He died instantly.

Just across the road at the George Company CP, Captain Chester Hermanson, who had replaced Mize as commander, was briefing his three platoon leaders on next morning's patrol when a firefight broke out in the rear.

"What the hell's going on up there?" asked one of the platoon leaders, Second Lieutenant John "Blackie" Cahill.

"That's Item Company," said Hermanson. "A bunch of reserves and replacements. You know how new men are the first time in combat. They shoot at shadows."

The fire increased and several rounds came through the tent. "If that's Item Company," said Cahill, "then somebody better tell them they're shooting in the wrong direction."

A few feet behind them, Private First Class Preston Parks, who had been with Taplett since August, was at the field phone. He heard some-one from Taplett's CP report, "Item Company is under heavy attack and they need reinforcements right away." He passed this on to Hermanson, who turned to Blackie: "Take your platoon up there and help them."

By the time Cahill had run out of the tent, the field phone rang again. "Item Company is overrun!" said a voice. "The gooks are in the CP! The major is dead, and I can't find the colonel."

Parks relayed the bad news about Canney and Taplett.

"Break out all the men," said Hermanson to the three platoon leaders. "Form a skirmish line this side of the road. We're going to have to take that hill." He turned to Parks. "You stay with me." Everyone else scrambled out of the tent. In the confusion, Parks soon got separated from Hermanson. He grabbed his rifle and ran up the road where Sergeant Arnold was hollering to form a skirmish line.

"Say, Arnold," said Parks, "where is the captain? I can't find him."

"The hell with the captain. Get over here with Rafone's squad."

"The captain said for me to stay with him."

"They're all dead," was the reply. "We've got to take that hill and the high ground over there, so let's move."

No sooner had Taplett learned that Canney had been killed than Herb Kelly, his communications officer, informed him that the radio was not working, and Taplett could not contact the rifle companies except by wire.

Kelly borrowed a flashlight, and under heavy Chinese fire crawled back to repair the switchboard. In a few minutes he returned, mission accomplished. At last Taplett had communications! He decided to order George Company to attack and told Lieutenant Charles Mize, now his assistant S3, to get across the road and see that the assault was mounted properly. He and Mize had worked closely since the Pusan Perimeter days, and he knew George Company men liked the affable southerner. Mize found people milling around George's CP. Fortunately, he had two outstanding platoon commanders, Cahill and Second Lieutenant Dana Cashion, as leaders, but even so it would take a long time to get everyone off the outpost.

Taplett and his remaining staff had to sit tight, still under attack, for more than an hour. At last the colonel heard yelling as Cahill and Cashion and their two platoons swept across the low ground from the road to the slope. They were howling like a bunch of wild Indians. Since the noise scared the hell out of Taplett, he figured the Chinese would be scared all the way back to the Yalu.

Cahill reported that the two platoons were at last ready to charge up the hill. As they started forward, flares were lighting the sky like day, making funny, squeaking noises when they fell. Parks could see enemy darting every which way. He ran across the open ground for seventy-five yards. At the foot of the hill, Sergeant Arnold gathered the men milling around and formed them into a skirmish line. "We got to take this ground or we're all dead!" he exclaimed. "Let's go!"

They started up the steep slope. The whole thing, thought Parks, was like a riot with Marines dashing around shooting and shouting. The

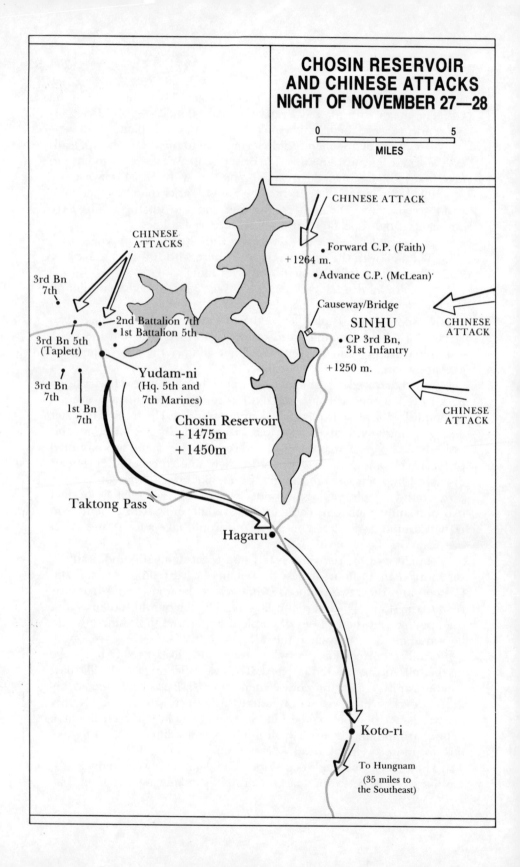

CHOSIN RESERVOIR AND CHINESE ATTACKS NIGHT OF NOVEMBER 27—28

0   5
MILES

CHINESE ATTACK

•Forward C.P. (Faith)
+1264 m.

•Advance C.P. (McLean)

CHINESE ATTACKS

3rd Bn 7th

Causeway/Bridge
SINHU

CHINESE ATTACK

2nd Battalion 7th
•1st Battalion 5th

•CP 3rd Bn, 31st Infantry

3rd Bn 5th (Taplett)

+1250 m.

Yudam-ni
(Hq. 5th and
7th Marines)

CHINESE ATTACK

3rd Bn 7th

1st Bn 7th

Chosin Reservoir
+1475m
+1450m

Taktong Pass

Hagaru •

Koto-ri •

To Hungnam
(35 miles to
the Southeast)

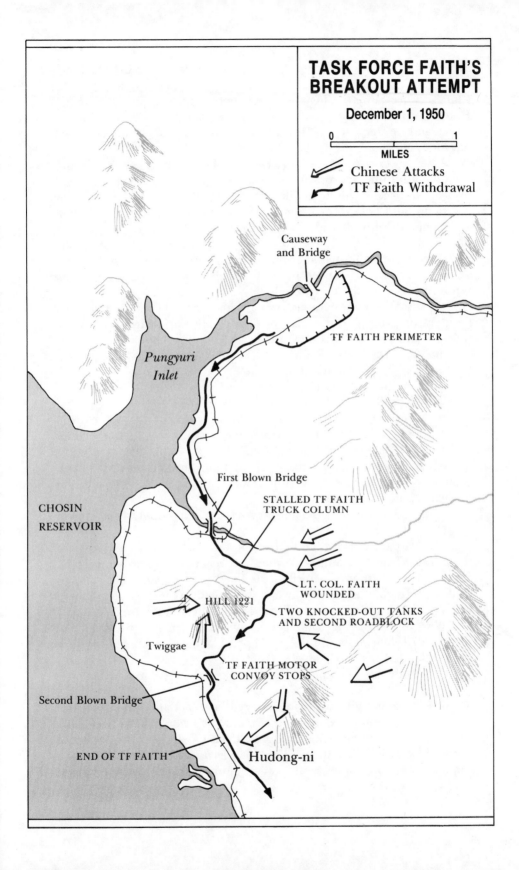

TASK FORCE FAITH'S BREAKOUT ATTEMPT

December 1, 1950

0 ─────────── 1
MILES

Chinese Attacks
TF Faith Withdrawal

Causeway
and Bridge

TF FAITH PERIMETER

*Pungyuri
Inlet*

First Blown Bridge

STALLED TF FAITH
TRUCK COLUMN

CHOSIN
RESERVOIR

LT. COL. FAITH
WOUNDED

HILL 1221

TWO KNOCKED-OUT TANKS
AND SECOND ROADBLOCK

Twiggae

TF FAITH MOTOR
CONVOY STOPS

Second Blown Bridge

END OF TF FAITH

Hudong-ni

Chinese were also running here and there, shooting and screaming. Halfway up the hill, there was suddenly a bright flash. Something hit Parks, and he went down. "Jesus Christ, what was that?" he exclaimed out loud. He shook his head.

It was a concussion grenade. He scrambled to his feet. Once more something hit him and down he went. He sat on the snow, then rolled over on his back, trying to get his senses back. Blood was coming out of his mouth and nose. He'd been hit in the throat. He wiped the blood off his mouth with his mitt glove because the blood was freezing on his lips when he tried to spit. He stood up, and something else hit his knee. This time he saw a flash and someone thirty yards down the hill aiming a rifle at him. Parks grabbed his M-1 and emptied the clip. The enemy tumbled back and slid down the hill.

Parks sat for a few minutes, trying to get the blood out of his mouth, then crawled down to the man he'd shot. He was wearing a Marine uniform and parka! Parks unwrapped the clothing. Thank God, he was a Chinese! Parks hollered for a corpsman. "Jesus Christ," he said to himself, "No one is coming to help me!"

Then he heard a voice say, "Who is it?"

"It's Parks."

"Which one?" There were two Parkses in the outfit.

"It don't make a goddamn which one it is. I'm the Parks that's hit and I need help. Get the hell up here."

The man arrived with a flashlight, and they hustled across the open ground to the aid station. Corpsmen were holding bottles of penicillin in their mouths to keep them thawed.

"Where are you hit?" asked the medic who had brought Parks down.

"I don't know. All over."

The corpsman put a battle dressing on his throat, wiped some of the blood off his face and neck, then made Parks drop his pants so he could give him a shot of penicillin. He filled out a tag and told Parks to sit down. His right leg gave way and he pulled up his pants' leg. There was blood on his knee. "Jesus Christ, doc, I've been hit in the knee too."

While he was being bandaged, a Marine burst into the tent. "I'm from the 7th Marines and I'm heading back! I have a jeep and can take three wounded with me."

"You only need two more," said Parks, "because I'm going."

The two Marine regiments being savaged near Yudam-ni realized they were fighting against superior forces, but they would have been horrified to know that elements of eight Chinese Volunteer divisions had been lying in wait for them. The 79th Division had been attacking Taplett from three sides, and it was a miracle that anyone remained alive at his CP.

Despite the odds, at 1:45 A.M. Colonel Murray ordered Colonel Roise, commander of the 2nd Battalion, to continue the attack west (which fortunately for the Marines had made only modest progress) so that Taplett could then move forward at dawn, deploy, and add his weight to Almond's great offensive. Colonel Roise was not yet aware of his own peril; and when Murray at last realized how desperate the situation was and changed the attack order to a withdrawal, the 2nd Battalion commander thought a mistake had been made in the map coordinates. Roise questioned Murray about the "error" which would force him to retreat and finally realized his own predicament.

2.

On the other side of the Chosin Reservoir, the Chinese 80th Division had already approached the American 7th Infantry Division positions without being observed. Also nearing the GI position from the south on the evening of November 27 was the 3rd Battalion, 31st Infantry Regiment. They were to replace Taplett's battalion, which was being sent to the other side of the reservoir. The GIs had been marching two full days and a night. By now they were frozen, hungry, and exhausted. Some had walked off the road in the dark; some fell off cliffs. Others had passed out on the road and were placed in jeeps until they came to. Private Ed Reeves was afraid to sit down during the breaks for fear he'd never be able to get up. Sick since Thanksgiving from an allergy to shrimps, he realized he couldn't go on much longer. To stay awake he counted his steps, praying he'd reach wherever they were going before he came to one thousand. He fell asleep but kept walking and when he wakened he feared he'd walk off a cliff. He unrolled his sleeping bag in a ditch, lay down and pulled his poncho over him for shelter from snow. He passed out, too far gone to remember that tanks put one track in the inner ditch to stay on the winding, narrow, icy road which was little more than a trail.

When he awoke the sun was up and he was completely covered by snow. He was all alone. Ed was one anxious farmboy from Illinois. He had left the farm at twelve and worked in factories in Joliet until he was sixteen. Two years later he enlisted and became an acting assistant platoon leader. Then war broke out and he volunteered to go to Korea; he wanted to know if he could take combat. Also there would be a bit of adventure.

Colonel Allan MacLean, formerly Walker's G3 and now commander of Reeves's regiment, had recently passed by. He was to lead the Army attack to the Yalu the following morning, reinforced by the 57th Field Artillery, eight AA vehicles, a tank company and the 1st Battalion of the 32nd Infantry, commanded by Colonel Faith.

After reaching Hagaru-ri, MacLean and his staff turned right and started up the east shore of the Chosin Reservoir. After eight miles they reached Faith's forward CP. MacLean was told Taplett's Marines had just pulled out, not waiting for the Army troops to relieve them on the spot. All was quiet out front. After breakfast with Faith, MacLean, eager to get the troops in position for tomorrow's offensive, started north with his exec, Captain Hugh Robbins, and Faith to make a reconnaissance of the outposts vacated by Taplett. They saw several dead Chinese but concluded that these had probably been lost and wandered into the Marine lines.

Robbins was ordered to establish a small forward regimental CP several miles south of Faith's CP. The position was near the village of Sinhung-ni, which the 4th Company of the Chinese 239th Regiment was secretly reconnoitering for a night attack. The 239th's objective was to wipe out the UN forces north of the village and block the escape route to the south.

That evening GIs of the 3rd Battalion, 31st Infantry, bedded down near the causeway bridge crossing the end of the Pungyuri Inlet and on the ridge overlooking the reservoir. Unlike the Marines across the reservoir, most of the GIs wore only field jackets with pile liner and thin cotton pants. They had leather dress gloves with wool inserts, which were useless in the cold. Their supposedly "waterproof" pants were worn and not waterproof. Fatigue hats with earlaps did help insulate the men's heat-sucking metal helmets. In short, the immediate enemy was the cold, not the Chinese. At seven P.M., Captain Robert Kitz, commander of K Company, went to the CP of the 3rd Battalion, located in a shack a few hundred feet south of the causeway bridge. Lieutenant Colonel William Reilly, the battalion commander, ordered Kitz to attack to the north in the morning. K Company would move along the ridgeline while L followed the road. Reilly wanted to start early, but had not yet received clearance from the task force commander, Colonel MacLean. Half an hour later MacLean told Reilly they'd have to wait a day. There was a report that several hundred enemy were in a village six miles to the northeast, and Reilly was to send up a small patrol at first light. Kitz arranged for the patrol and was preparing to hit the sack at ten P.M. when he received a red alert from battalion. He doubled the guards, but no one alerted the men up on the hill who were on normal fifty percent watch.

Several miles to the northwest, Marine Captain Edward Stamford was bedding down for the night in a bunker. Stamford, assigned to be Faith's forward air controller, was the only Marine officer on this side of the reservoir, and he occupied two bunkers with three enlisted Marines. One stood watch at the north end of Stamford's bunker while the south end was covered with a poncho to keep out falling snow. Just before midnight Stamford heard shots, then shouting from Captain Ed Scullion, the A Company commander. There was chattering outside, then the poncho was pulled aside and Stamford was startled to see a fur-rimmed face in the moonlight outside the bunker. He fired just as a grenade exploded on the foot of his sleeping bag. He was unharmed, but one of his men was wounded. All four Marines scrambled to a slit trench, where they hunkered down while a friendly machine gun cleaned off the top of the bunker. Stamford then began organizing his men for the defense of their position. This done, he moved to the 1st Platoon leader's position and learned that Captain Scullion, in his first action in Korea, had been killed. Stamford tried to locate the executive officer and was amazed to learn that he was directing troops in the bunker area instead of determining the situation in the other platoons.

"Well, Captain," said the mortar officer, First Lieutenant Carlos Ortenzi, "you are the next senior man. I guess you have the company."

Stamford, a cool veteran, took charge again. He sent one of his Marines for reports from the other platoons and appointed the exec as leader of the 1st Platoon. Stamford himself brought the 2nd Platoon down to strengthen the line and clean the Chinese out of the area.

Inside the 1st Battalion CP, Colonel Faith had been awakened by scattered rifle fire. He summoned Captain Bigger of D Company. "Do you suppose those ROKs are firing at each other again?" he said. The past few nights they had been shooting at imaginary enemies. "I have had a garbled report that something has happened to Ed Scullion—that he may have been killed." He ordered his assistant S3, Captain Robert Haynes, to go up to A Company and see what the situation was. Bigger offered to go with Haynes. "I know the troop situation up there, and I want to check on my heavy weapons with the company."

The two climbed the hill to A Company and were challenged by a man in a parka who was lying in the road. He spoke in a language that sounded like Korean and gave the countersign. As he turned, Bigger said, "We're American soldiers." The man—he was Chinese—raised his rifle and fired just as Bigger shouted to hit the ditch. Both he and Haynes dived. The Chinese was coming towards them, but the bolt on Bigger's carbine was frozen. Two grenades exploded nearby. Luckily no one was hit. Bigger and Haynes scrambled into the brush and made it back to Faith's CP.

Faith tried to piece together what had happened. One minute they had been planning an attack at dawn; the next, they were fighting for their lives without knowing who and where the enemy was.

Several miles to the rear, Captain Kitz of K Company was awakened by the commotion and asked the lieutenant at the roadblock, "Who's firing?"

"Someone behind our position."

Kitz figured someone had been trigger-happy. He put on his shoes and went out to investigate the shack that housed the regimental CP. There was a burst of shooting, and rounds thumped into the area. Cooks dashed out of their tents and streaked toward the rear. Kitz tried to get them to return fire, but things were so confused he couldn't tell who were friends and who were Chinese.

The firing increased, and the 4th Platoon pulled back to Kitz's position. "We can't stay out in the open field," said Kitz. "Pull back to the lake." As they started to move, fire came from the rear—from Battery A of the 57th Field Artillery, mistaking them for the enemy. With the help of an artillery officer, Kitz got his men under control and stopped Battery A's fire.

Bugle calls awakened mortarman Private Edward Farley, who was near the reservoir. He had no idea what they meant. Moments later, firing broke out. Farley had his two mortars set up—but what was he to shoot at? He and the other section and platoon leaders checked with their commander, who ordered them to douse all fires and prepare for an attack. By the time Farley returned to his mortars, gunfire was erupting ahead. Men began rushing back for refuge. He stopped a friend, Sergeant Harold Drews, who gasped out that his platoon had been overrun. "You'd better pull back to high ground!"

Farley ordered his gunners to fire at the position abandoned by Drews. Then he began leapfrogging the two guns to the rear. Now the Chinese were coming in waves, screaming and firing their burp guns. Someone in front prepared to shoot a recoilless rifle. "Don't fire that goddamn thing!" shouted Farley, too late. The next moment he was flung across the ice by the back blast from the recoilless rifle.

In the dark, the Americans and a few ROKs were trying to hold off more than three times that many Chinese. The 3rd Battalion CP near the causeway bridge was already under heavy attack. Inside the shack, Colonel Reilly sat facing the window when Chinese tried to climb in. He shot two of them with his pistol, and in the melee that followed, the battalion operations officer was wounded in the chest. As his assistant tried to remove his pistol from its holster, his right arm was blown off by a grenade—and he didn't even feel it.

When Lieutenant Oliver Robertson of Headquarters Company heard the bugles, he knew something unusual was going on, since there were no bugles in the battalion. Outside the CP, it looked as though the entire battalion perimeter, as well as the interior, was under attack. In the pale moonlight Robertson saw a Chinese running forty yards away. Robertson fired and the body fell forward. Then everything seemed to cave in around the hut, with Chinese screaming and shooting everywhere.

On the north ridge above, a series of "drunken" bugle calls alerted

Private Ed Reeves, who was lucky to be wearing a white parka. He stood up in his foxhole to check. Nothing to see. Then strange noises came from the next valley. From a foxhole some ten yards up the ridge he heard an ROK private shout, "Ed, someone she is nuts! I'm gonna go see what she is."

The ROK climbed to the top of the ridge and looked over. "Chinese!" he yelled and dashed back toward his foxhole. Enemy shots came from several directions. Chavez didn't make it. A long row of white-hooded heads bobbed above the ridge line. Ours or theirs? wondered Reeves. Other figures in white bounced through the snowy underbrush like ghosts. Us or them? A GI ran past Reeves yelling that someone was hit bad. Battle noise to his rear built in waves. The valley below was a mass of flames and tracers! Ours *and* theirs! Rounds cracked. Chicom voices and clanking equipment came from the foxholes on both sides. Reeves squatted, peering over the edge of his foxhole. Behind came a shout in Chinese. Reeves turned. A huge man in white was covering him with a rifle. The Chicom ordered Reeves to do something. "Do what? Boy, you've had it!" he thought. He glanced at his rifle lying on the edge of the foxhole. "Don't just let 'em shoot you," he told himself. "Do something." All he could think of was to count cadence. "Hut Four!" he shouted as the Chicom lowered his rifle a little and, puzzled, leaned forward. Reeves grabbed his own rifle. It slipped through his glove-covered hands. He snatched up the rifle, aimed it at the Chicom and pulled the trigger. The white figure crumbled like a potato sack.

Every time Reeves peered out, bursts of submachine-gun fire came from uphill foxholes on both sides. He popped up to snap a few shots at a dozen enemy running right past him in single file. "Holy cow!" he exclaimed out loud. Ignoring him, the enemy kept trotting past. Reeves squatted low, his mind racing fast. Then a wild-eyed ROK, Bak Ho-yah, exclaimed, "Eddie, Chinese! Eddie, Chinese!" Reeves tried to remember how to say, "I know," in Korean while tossing grenades in all directions. They couldn't reach enemy positions but the noise would keep the Chicoms back and, he hoped, give him time until help came.

From all sides Chinese were talking loudly as if they were alone. Reeves bobbed up, snapped off several rounds and got a glimpse into the valley leading to the reservoir. Rings of muzzle blasts and tracers indicated where friends were making their stand. Maybe he and Ho could roll out of the back of their foxhole and down the ridge before the enemy could react. "We're taking a long walk right now!" said Reeves in Korean, and motioned rolling down the hill. He threw his last grenade, then leaped out of the foxhole. After rolling twice, something brought him to a stop. Jumping to his feet, he started sprinting down the hill, but he felt something dragging him back, and his progress turned into a clumsy jog. He had to move to avoid hitting large lumps of snow. As he passed the lumps, he saw flashes coming from them. Chicoms in white! He turned, fired several rounds at the white lumps and then headed down the hill, tensing his back for the shock of a bullet. But no bullet came. The Chinese had ignored him and kept firing at targets downhill. Reeves guessed that the enemy must have thought he and Ho were Chicoms since they were wearing white parkas.

Reeves scrambled down the hill and into a draw. All at once a tree loomed up in the dark. Unable to slow down or dodge, he smashed into the tree. Reeves regained consciousness to see in the gun flashes a form leaning over him. It was Ho tightly clutching Reeves's parka tail. No wonder he hadn't been able to run; he had been dragging a passenger down the hill. Reeves knocked Ho's hand loose, rose up and jogged toward the reservoir, followed by Ho.

They slowed to a walk where the draw entered the valley. Groups and lines of Chinese were moving toward the rings of flashing U.S. weapons. A quad-50's tracers made a fifty-yard sweep. Ignoring rounds snapping past, Reeves forced his mind to work. "How'll our guys know me and Ho ain't Chicoms?" Easing cautiously across the valley, staying away from groups of Chinese, the two men moved with the attacking enemy toward the nearest ring of fire. When the quad-50 swept their area of the field, he and Ho hid behind a vibrating mound of dirt. Once clear they moved toward another mound closer to their friends. "GIs coming in!" he yelled when they were close enough to make a run for it.

"Hold your fire! GIs comin' in!" someone shouted from a farmhouse. Reeves and Ho jumped up and hurried forward. A half-track crew watched them carefully from behind their quad-50 as the two men in parkas passed at full jog and headed around the farmhouse, the M Company CP. A major pulled Reeves to a stop and yelled into his face, "Soldier, where's your position?"

Ho looked from the major to Reeves wondering what was going on. Reeves looked back at the ridge which was winking with pink Chinese flashes. He pointed. "Up there."

"Soldier, why'd you leave your position?" shouted the major as rounds snapped past.

All Reeves could think of to reply was, "Sir, you're nuts."

"Get over there and use a weapon," said the major pointing to the other end of the building. "The whole Chinese army's trying to come through here."

Reeves and Ho spend the rest of the night with a handful of GIs holding off the Chinese. After dawn the attacks slowed down. Enemy within the perimeter were being killed, captured or driven out. Reeves's clothing had bullet holes, rips and burns from mortar and grenade bursts, yet he had only received minor scratches. The ridge was littered with bodies and he told himself, "They can't kill you, Ed. You're too good a fighter."

The major emerged from the M Company CP and called to Reeves. "Soldier, come here." No sooner had Reeves taken two steps than a mortar exploded at his heels and threw him in the air. As he landed he didn't feel so invincible. Gasping for breath, he watched blood flowing from many holes in his arms and feet. He tried to get into a shed but couldn't make it. As he sat in the filthy snow, he yelled angrily, denouncing every officer he could think of. It had to be someone else's fault that he hurt so much. Mortar rounds whanged in a row across the middle of the farmyard. The major limped toward him with a sergeant. They pulled Reeves through the mortar fire and into a room of the farmhouse. He hurt all over and kept drifting into a daze but didn't want to trouble anyone with something that seemed trivial. The room was filled with wounded with big problems. When someone died he was taken out so another wounded outside could take his place.

The sergeant who had helped Reeves asked how he was doing. The cold had frozen the blood of Reeves's wounds. If he didn't move much, he explained, the blood flow stopped. By now he was sure his left foot was gone but the right one might make it. "The shrapnel that went through your legs hit the major," said the sergeant. "He just died from internal injuries."

CHAPTER 21

Chaos on Two Fronts
(November 28–29)

1.

By dawn of November 28, the X Corps situation on both sides of the reservoir was desperate. But General Almond, at his headquarters in Hamhung, regarded dispatches describing distress as a simple loss of nerve by the Marines and the GIs. Their reports of vast numbers of Chinese, he believed, were grossly exaggerated. If so many Chinese had suddenly sprung up, why hadn't air reconnaissance spotted them? The answer was simple. Mao and Peng had hidden their troops in the daytime, moving them only at night. It was a triumph of ancient Chinese cunning over modern technology.

Determined to get his own attack moving, Almond and his aide, First Lieutenant Alexander Haig, flew by helicopter to the 1st Marine Division CP in Hagaru-ri, arriving at eleven-thirty A.M. To Almond's dismay, General O. P. Smith strongly recommended that the drive to the Yalu be canceled. Two of his regiments, the 5th and 7th Marines, had been hit hard and should go on the defensive. Almond was irked by such conservatism. It was the same old story—the Marines were dragging their feet, as they had done on the drive to Seoul. But since he did not have total control of the Marines, Almond reluctantly let the cautious Smith have his way.

Disgruntled, Almond headed by helicopter for the east side of the reservoir, where he conferred with Colonels MacLean and Faith. Both

304

were still shaken by the night battle. Faith explained that his battalion CP at the northernmost point had been hard hit and he'd lost the high ground of his perimeter to the Chinese.

Unimpressed, Almond unfolded a map on the hood of a jeep. "The enemy who is delaying you for the moment," he said, "is nothing more than remnants of Chinese divisions fleeing north." These two officers, he felt, were as shaky as Smith and his Marines. "We're still attacking and we're going all the way to the Yalu. Don't let a bunch of Chinese laundrymen stop you." These words offended not only MacLean and Faith but the enlisted men within earshot. "Retake the high ground lost during the night," Almond ordered peremptorily. "And prepare to attack north, once the 2nd Battalion of the 31st arrives."

Almond remarked that he had three Silver Stars to award. He handed one to Faith, who selected a second medal for the wounded Lieutenant Everett Smalley, sitting nearby. Almond called over a mess sergeant and gave him the third citation.

The first two recipients were enraged. After Almond left, Smalley unpinned his medal and shoved it in his pocket. Faith muttered, "What a damned . . . !" He ripped off the Silver Star and threw it in the snow.

As Almond headed back for his headquarters, he left behind a deteriorating situation on both sides of the reservoir. But his own spirits were improved. Word had come that a small motorized task force had battered its way almost a hundred air miles northwest of the Chosin Reservoir and was about to seize Singalpajin, a village on the Yalu River. It was led by Robert Kingston, an aggressive, twenty-two-year-old Irish second lieutenant from Brookline, Massachusetts. With no maps or aerial photographs, he had beaten his way north in bitter weather through mountainous terrain and determined enemy attacks.

By the time he approached Singalpajin, Kingston had only seventeen infantrymen left. He sent Sergeant Vanretti and seven men to act as point. Kingston followed with several officers. In the rear were eight men under Sergeant King. The tiny attack force followed the road to the village. On the left side was a row of intact houses. Four men scouted the first one. Empty.

So were the next two. Then, without warning, the officer group was met by a volley of rifle fire. It looked as if the enemy were holed up in the third house. Kingston crawled down the ditch to get out of the line of fire of his own men. After about half an hour he leaped up and darted for the house, grenade in one hand, rifle in the other, whooping and yelling as loud as he could. At first the crusted snow held him, but then it broke and the faster he tried to go the deeper he floundered. Vanretti and two of his men were also struggling through the snow toward the house.

Kingston was breathing in gasping sobs. His eyes stung from tears caused by the cold, but he kept lunging forward, and with his last strength threw a grenade toward the house. As he watched it arch through the air, something hit him on the top of his head.

When he came to he saw Vanretti bending over him and heard him say imploringly, "You're all right. You got to be all right!"

Then Kingston saw the sergeant was holding a helmet creased on top by a bullet.

"We got them," said the sergeant. "The grenade came in perfect."

"Anybody hurt?"

"Not a one. Nobody."

"How many were in there?"

"Five. We got them. We thought they got you."

Just then about 200 GIs came marching around the curve in the road. It was a full company, and had finally caught up with Task Force Kingston. They cleared the village of the few North Korean soldiers left. The bulk of the enemy battalion had apparently crossed over the ice-covered Yalu to Manchuria.

By the time news of Kingston's achievement arrived at Almond's headquarters, the general had learned that Walker's Eighth Army was retreating. Like others at X Corps, Almond figured this was one more instance of Walker's loss of nerve. Still convinced that the Chinese assaults were not serious, Almond feared that any attack across the Yalu into Manchuria might not get MacArthur's approval. No publicity, therefore, was issued on Kingston's feat. The second lieutenant was instructed to withdraw.

2.

The situation on the western front was even worse than that in the east. The Eighth Army was staggering under much heavier Chinese assaults, and by dusk of November 28 the withdrawal of the 2nd Infantry Division down a single road had caused a horrendous traffic jam. Two regiments had already been nearly wiped out, and only Paul Freeman's 23rd Infantry Regiment was putting up any resistance.

The 25th Division had pulled back, and Task Force Dolvin had been hammered by almost constant attacks. But the rest of the division was in fairly good shape. During the day, the collapse of Walker's right flank forced him to withdraw the still-intact 24th Division as well as Whitey Paik's ROK 1st Division, which was getting hit hard.

In Tokyo MacArthur did not share Almond's disregard concerning the Chinese attacks. Earlier that day he had cabled the Pentagon: "We face an entirely new war." He estimated Chinese forces as approaching 200,000 and North Korean "fragments" as about 50,000. "This command has done everything possible within its capabilities but is now faced with conditions beyond its control and strength."

MacArthur's message was telephoned to the president at 6:15 A.M., November 28, Washington time. "We've got a terrific situation on our hands," he quietly told his staff. They were stunned by the news, but Truman remained calm. "This is the worst situation we have had yet. We'll just have to meet it as we've met all the rest."

That afternoon, Truman called an extraordinary expanded session of the National Security Council, where Bradley sketched in the military situation. No decisions were made, but all agreed with Acheson that, above all, war with the Soviets must be avoided. There should be no preemptive air attacks on Manchuria that might provoke the Soviets into intervening in Korea. "America is much closer to the danger of war with the Soviet Union," said Acheson. Peking would not have intervened in force in Korea unless Stalin had ordered or desired it. "We must consider Korea not in isolation but in the worldwide problem of confronting the Soviet Union as an antagonist." World War III might erupt tomorrow morning. "We want to achieve a termination of this involvement," continued Acheson. "We can't defeat the Chinese in Korea. They can put more in than we can."

Ever since the disastrous by-elections, Truman and the Joint Chiefs had allowed MacArthur to control the Korean War. Truman was facing a problem never encountered by an American president since the Civil War. The country was divided, and vilification was the order of the day on both sides. This undermined not only the morale of the troops but an all-out commitment to victory. As a result, most Americans wanted the war to end.

3.

While Bradley informed Truman of the "rather hysterical" cable from MacArthur, Walker and Almond were flying to Tokyo. Their conference with MacArthur and his commanders at the American embassy began at 9:50 P.M. on November 28 in a grim atmosphere, with MacArthur— as usual—dominating. The Chinese, he said, would probably push both the Eighth Army and X Corps back so as to be in a position for a massive spring offensive designed to throw the UN troops out of Korea.

He authorized Walker to go on the defensive and fall back farther if necessary. Where, he asked, could Eighth Army make a successful stand? Walker felt he could hold Pyongyang for some time by establishing a defense line north and east of the city. Almond was even more optimistic. He repeated what he had told MacLean that afternoon. He was confident that both the 1st Marine and 7th Infantry divisions could continue to the Yalu from both sides of the Chosin Reservoir.

MacArthur replied that he hoped Walker could hold Pyongyang but disagreed with Almond's desire to continue his attack. MacArthur wanted both X Corps and the Eighth Army to go on the defense, but during the meeting, which ended at one-thirty A.M., November 29, he gave neither commander specific orders. Before they left Tokyo, however, he asked Walker to hold the Pyongyang area if possible. If further withdrawal was necessary, he was to keep the Chinese from moving around his right flank and into the rear. Almond was ordered to withdraw his corps all the way back to the Hungnam area.

4.

At one A.M., the 29th, the forward perimeter was hit hard on the east side of the reservoir held by Army troops, a mortar round landing fifty yards from Colonel Faith's CP, the farmhouse. A light snow began to fall. Inside Colonels Faith and MacLean were listening to reports of savage attacks on all companies. It was apparent to Captain Hugh Robbins, MacLean's operations officer, that every weapon in the battalion was being fired as fast as it could be loaded. Robbins could see shadow forms going in and out of the CP, runners and men carrying wounded.

There was little for him to do except stand in place and look out on the eerie scene, half-expecting a white-clad Chinese to appear. The firing died down at two A.M. when Robbins was told that Colonel MacLean had ordered the battalion to prepare to withdraw and fight its way to the battalion CP at Pungyuri Inlet, several miles to the southeast. It took an hour and a half for the order to reach Major Crosby "Dick" Miller, Faith's exec, at C Company's CP. Their battalion, said Faith, would join the 3rd Battalion at the inlet, leaving at four-thirty A.M. Miller walked east to A Company and found it under attack. He ordered the company commander to take off at four-thirty so his men could enter the inlet perimeter at dawn.

In the meantime, Faith was talking to other unit commanders telling them to remove vital parts from any vehicle they had to leave behind, since abandoned positions would be reoccupied in twenty-four hours. Faith ordered all trucks near his CP to be loaded with wounded. It was snowing heavily, and Captain Robbins found the footing extremely slippery. Drivers began the arduous task of starting the frozen motors. Robbins had to crank his own jeep and thought his arm would give out before it started. All preparations were complete at the CP by four-thirty A.M. Columns of foot troops formed on each side of the crawling vehicles.

It was strangely quiet as the caravan of some sixty machines headed slowly towards the inlet. Just before dawn, they reached their former regimental CP and halted. Robbins dismounted and went up front to MacLean's jeep. The driver was there, but MacLean had gone around a bend down the road, out of sight. Robbins was told that the colonel was reconnoitering a roadblock. But no one knew exactly where MacLean was.

Then someone came down the line shouting that all vehicles were to disperse into an area on the left. Everyone went into defensive positions in case the Chinese caught up. They walked for what seemed to Robbins like hours. Suddenly a small group of enemy came trotting into their midst and then, in obvious surprise, took to their heels.

Robbins returned to MacLean's jeep. His bodyguard and radio operator told Robbins that the colonel had not gone forward to the roadblock but had headed boldly down the road to a long concrete bridge. Beyond this span, it was only two hundred yards to their goal—the 3rd Battalion perimeter—and safety. Robbins moved cautiously up the road. At the bend he could see, through glasses, troops along the bridge supports firing at targets beyond. While Robbins was wondering whether these were Chinese or American, Colonel Faith arrived with good news. His company had cleared the roadblock and the men holding the bridge were ours.

Robbins returned to his jeep so he could join the dash through the gauntlet. During the crossing, a few vehicles were hit, but Robbins's jeep didn't have a single hole. Dead and wounded lay around the Korean mud house that was the 3rd Battalion CP; Robbins counted twenty dead Chinese in their quilted jackets and tennis shoes a few yards beyond. Other Chinese bodies were strewn throughout the area.

Robbins found Colonel Reilly inside the hut propped up on a stretcher with a bullet hole and many grenade splinters in his leg. But he was in good spirits; and when Faith arrived, the two laid plans to consolidate their battalions and the field artillery into a tight circle of defense.

Robbins set out to find MacLean, who had started off earlier with Captain Bigger. Robbins was told that these two were approaching the southern end of the 3rd Battalion, 31st Regiment, perimeter when they saw a column of troops preparing to cross it. MacLean shouted, "Those are my boys!" Then firing broke out from both sides. MacLean thought his two battalions were shooting at each other, unaware that the Chinese were now holding the southern end. He ordered Captain Bigger to circle on the ice around the bridge and stop this firing. MacLean then went onto the ice himself and headed directly toward the bridge.

As Bigger headed out on the ice he saw MacLean fall several times but pick himself up and continue. He could be slipping on the ice or hit. As MacLean neared the far bank, Bigger saw Chinese come onto the ice and pull the colonel to brush-covered ground. No trace of MacLean was ever found.

Faith spent the rest of the morning finding what was left of I and

K companies of the 31st and tying them in with his own three companies. Task Force MacLean was now Task Force Faith.

Captain Stamford, the Marine forward air controller, relieved from temporary command of A Company, was back at his job of calling in Marine Corsair strikes. He also reported that the embattled troops were short of ammunition and supplies. In the afternoon, two Flying Boxcars dropped ammo and rations. One parachute failed to open, and the load hit ROK soldiers twenty feet from Captain Robbins, killing one man. Other drops landed in Chinese territory. When a helicopter landed to evacuate Colonel Reilly and the commander of the field artillery, the sight of two high-ranking officers being carried off to safety lowered the enlisted men's spirits. It was, recalled one observer, "a real morale-buster."

5.

In Washington, the Joint Chiefs of Staff were holding a morning meeting. Admiral Forrest Sherman was so concerned about his Marines at Chosin that he insisted MacArthur be ordered to withdraw X Corps to a consolidated defense line across the narrow waist of Korea; but Collins and Bradley were still reluctant to give MacArthur tactical orders. What utter confusion would have resulted, thought Bradley, if Marshall had sent Eisenhower such orders during the Battle of the Bulge! They did, however, agree to send MacArthur this message: "What are your plans regarding the coordination of the Eighth Army and X Corps and the positioning of X Corps, the units of which appear to us to be exposed?"

This would mean establishing a continuous line across the peninsula, and MacArthur cabled back that any such line was "quite impracticable" because of its length and the numerical weakness of his forces. Instead, he would withdraw X Corps into the Hamhung-Wonsan area. This out-of-hand rejection outraged Bradley, who felt MacArthur was treating the JCS "as if we were children."

As soon as Walker returned to the western front from the Tokyo conference on the 29th, he ordered a general withdrawal from the area. There were few good roads, and he directed the 2nd Division to hold just south of the Chongchon River until the 25th Division could cross.

At noon, the 2nd Division CP, located below Kunok, learned that a truck convoy had been ambushed by the Chinese. Assuming this was small-scale interference, General Keiser sent a recon company to clear the road. When the recon company was repulsed, Keiser then sent a platoon of tanks along with an infantry company. But the road was still blocked, and supply trains began backing up in a catastrophic jam.

By now there was common censure of Walker at X Corps for pulling back his troops so early in the battle. These critics did not know that he had done so in hopes of saving his men, who were caught in Mao's trap. The question was: Had his orders come in time?

CHAPTER 22

"You Don't Have the Chance
of a Snowball in Hell!"
(November 28–29)

1.

On the west side of the reservoir, the 5th and 7th Marines were still tied down near Yudam-ni in desperate need of supplies and reinforcements. In this emergency, General Smith ordered formation of a task force that would leave Koto-ri and fight its way north to Hagaru-ri, thus opening the supply route to his two beleaguered regiments and reinforcing the garrison at Hagaru-ri. The group would consist of George Company, 3rd Battalion, of Chesty Puller's 1st Marines, commanded by Captain Carl Sitter and supported by the 41st Commando, Royal Marines, and Baker Company of the 7th Division's 31st Infantry. These GIs would then turn right at Hagaru-ri and head up the east side of the reservoir to help their besieged comrades. This 922-man force was organized by Colonel Puller and placed under the leadership of Lieutenant Colonel Douglas Drysdale, commander of the British unit. Drysdale had requested service with the U.S. Marines, and General Smith had been glad to have his experienced unit of 14 officers and 221 enlisted men.

Because of irritating delays caused by strong Chinese resistance, it was not until 1:55 P.M., November 28, that Task Force Drysdale started off with seventeen tanks in the lead, followed by George Company of the 1st Marines, the Commandos, Company B of the 31st Regiment and Division Headquarters and Service troops, with a dozen tanks in the rear. It was a formidable array that, in addition to the tanks, included 141 other vehicles, but progress was slow because Captain Sitter's Marines were soon hit by small-arms fire from houses and dug-in positions on the right of the road.

The procession crept on, however, with slowdowns as tanks clambered around craters and roadblocks. Every so often the infantry had to leap out of trucks and clear away persistent Chinese, and Task Force Drysdale was only about four miles north of Koto-ri when it halted at 4:15.

Drysdale and Sitter met with tank officers, who felt that they could smash their way the remaining seven miles to Hagaru-ri, but that the trucks would have too tough a time because of road conditions and increasing Chinese resistance. Drysdale could see it was hopeless to continue north, and he ordered Sitter to turn the trucks around and return to Koto-ri. Drysdale radioed General Smith and was told to continue despite possible heavy losses. Reinforcements had to get to Hagaru-ri to relieve troops on both sides of the reservoir. As Sitter and Drysdale heard this coming over the air, they looked at each other, but neither spoke. Orders were orders.

During this arduous maneuver, small-arms fire came from the east. First Sergeant Rocco Zullo stood up in a truck firing a .50-caliber machine gun to help protect the convoy. Zullo was already a legend in the Marine Corps, and his men feared him more than they did the Chinese. And Rocky had assured his troops that no bullet could kill him. Then came a direct order by radio from Colonel Puller for everyone to proceed north to Hagaru-ri, as planned, at all costs. Drysdale realized he had to obey. Again the trucks were turned around. This time Drysdale ordered the tank commander to intersperse his tanks throughout the column to give covering fire for the trucks. He then ordered alternate drivers for each truck; any vehicle hit was to be pushed off the road so the column could keep moving. By now the infantry was mixed with headquarters troops, and command control was difficult. Conflicting orders brought the convoy to a halt.

After a long wait while the tanks were being refueled, they again moved forward, but at dusk firing came from both sides of the road. Sitter's jeep was destroyed. Fortunately Zullo, in the truck behind, slowed down and gave Sitter a chance to hop onto the running board. It was beginning to look as though they might break through when heavy fire started up again. Sitter leaped to the road. Zullo started after him, but caught a burst of machine-gun bullets in the stomach.

"Everyone off the trucks!" shouted Sitter. People nearby were being mowed down. It was as though he alone was protected by an invisible shield. "Face out and shoot!" he yelled. "Put your backs to the trucks and start shooting whether you see something or not!"

He went forward to find Drysdale. "I'm hit," said the Commando chief. "You now have command."

Sitter, awarded a Silver Star as a platoon leader in World War II, was scared as hell. "Okay," he managed to say. "I'm going to get this thing going. I'm going to use the tanks as covering fire."

Sitter started back on foot, looking for his first sergeant. He was told that Rocco had been killed and his clerk shot. He then gave orders to put all the wounded into trucks. Someone objected. "I don't give a damn," he said. "We are going to take everybody with us." He rushed to a tank and beat on it with his carbine until the turret opened and a face peeped out. "There's a railroad embankment to our right," he said. "I want you to fire along there. Do whatever you can. Give us some fire because I'm going to get this column moving."

He hopped on the side of a truck and ordered it to head north. Finally appeared the glow of Hagaru-ri. They came around a bend in the road and he saw large tents, American tents. "Hell, boy," he said to himself, "we've got it made." Then all hell broke loose as Chinese fire poured out of the tents onto the column, and several trucks were destroyed. Sitter directed that all trucks and men make an all-out effort to get into the perimeter.

He thought he was being followed by the entire column; but some sixty Royal Marines Commandos, most of the 31st Infantry and practically all of the Division Headquarters and Service troops had been left behind. This amalgamation was soon divided into one big and three small groups. The largest was closest to Hagaru-ri and consisted of about 135 men commanded by Major John McLaughlin, the X Corps liaison officer with the Marines. It was a mixed lot: 31st Infantry GIs, some Commandos, Marine MPs, service troops and an Associated Press photographer, Frank "Pappy" Noel. The trapped men had only one 75-mm recoilless rifle, plus a few carbines, M-1's and grenades.

Trucks were burning and Chinese mortar rounds were landing on all sides. Bugles were blowing, whistles screeching, men screaming. It would soon be known as Hell Fire Valley. McLaughlin's men were almost out of ammunition by two A.M. The recoilless rifle was useless, its GI crew killed or wounded. Twice the crews of the deadly Chinese mortars had been driven away from their weapons, but were back again and dishing out hell. The photographer, Noel, and two men volunteered to run the gauntlet for help but were captured after a hundred yards. Fortunately, the enemy fire slackened and abruptly, a little after three A.M., stopped.

About three hundred yards south of McLaughlin's group, Major Henry "Pop" Seeley, the division motor transport officer, was in a drainage ditch with the survivors of two GI platoons and a few Marines, planning to form a perimeter. About thirty yards farther down the ditch were about 15 Headquarters troops and Marine First Lieutenant John Buck, General Craig's aide. He could hear only the sound of flares and distant firing. Then a figure near a burning farmhouse started towards him. "All hands hold fire!" yelled Buck. Soon he could see that the figure was wearing a Marine parka. "Come in with your hands up!" he ordered.

As the man came over the top of the embankment, Buck saw he was a staff sergeant from the 1st Marine Division supply section. He revealed that his group had been captured about an hour earlier. Almost all were wounded but were being cared for by the Chinese. A Chinese officer who could speak English had instructed the sergeant to come over and get them to surrender.

"That's the one thing we can't do!" said Buck.

They were interrupted by a commotion to the south. Moments later Major Pop Seeley appeared with two men. Seeley's .45 had just been shot out of his right hand, which was now shaking. Buck hurriedly briefed Seeley. "You're senior officer now. It's a command decision. It's up to you."

"I'll go and talk to the Chinese to gain time," said Seeley. In the meantime Buck was to prepare to break out. As soon as Seeley left with the staff sergeant to parley with the Chinese, Buck and the division public information officer, Captain Michael Capraro, began to organize their men for the escape. Ten men were to help the wounded, and four others would form a point with Buck. Within fifteen minutes Seeley was back, alone. "You have ten minutes to surrender," he said. Then there would come an assault.

Buck led the way to the rear of their perimeter toward the frozen Changjin River, about sixty yards wide. Fearing the ice might be thin, Buck started across cautiously. But the surface was solid, and they made it to the other side without getting the machine-gun fire Buck thought might rake them. The rest of the party followed, and within minutes everybody had climbed several hundred feet up a steep ridge covered with pines. Then came mortar explosions on their ditch, followed by shouts and mortar flares. They watched the Chinese push through their old positions and start towards the river.

Redoubling their efforts, Buck's party scrambled up the ridge. When they paused to catch their breath, the lieutenant heard the sound of the Chinese moving through the brush on the lower slope. If they could only hold out until daylight, thought Buck, they could probably make it. But as they approached the crest, they heard more voices. Buck consulted the Royal Marine Commandos and they all decided to proceed along the ridge to the south at the same elevation.

Another Royal Marine Commando, Andrew Condron, had also been stuck in the ditch running along the east side of the road. His lieutenant had asked for volunteers to get back to Koto-ri for help. It was an out-of-the-frying-pan-into-the-fire situation; but Condron, a working-class Scotsman, thought he might as well have a crack at it. Eleven others joined him, and they crawled and half-ran down the ditch seeking a safe place to cross the road, which was illuminated by blazing trucks. Mortars and flares were coming in, and it looked almost like daylight. The snow was deep on the ground; fresh flurries lashed their faces. At last they decided to go across an open field one at a time. The first eight made it, but by Condron's turn heavy fire was coming in. He and the last two men huddled together and waited a long time. It was like being in a bee's nest. By the time they reached safety across the field, their comrades had taken off.

The three agreed to try to catch the others, heading south with an NCO in front and Condron in the rear. As they moved around a tree, there was a shot and the NCO fell, dead. Then they heard voices across the stream. American voices. The Yanks had shot the NCO.

Condron called out to explain they were friends. Angry, he shouted, "You shot my mate!" The Americans told them to show themselves. Condron yelled, "Don't fire now. I'm coming out!" Unlike the NCO, who wore a beret, Condron had on an American helmet he had taken from a dead Yank because he felt the beret was not much help against bullets. He warily came out of the brush and crossed the icy stream with his companion.

"Your best bet is just to stay with us," said an American captain. "In a few more hours it's going to be light, and they'll send trucks for us."

Condron and his companion agreed there was no point in trying to go on. They were soaking wet. Condron removed his boots and two pair of socks, hung them on a branch to dry, prayed his feet wouldn't freeze, and waited for dawn.

By this time Major McLaughlin realized his group would soon be overrun. Only about forty men were fit to fight. They had little choice but to surrender, and he asked for a volunteer to go out with a Korean interpreter and parley with the Chinese. When no one spoke up, Sergeant Guillarmo Tovar, son of a Mexican gold miner, volunteered, even though he had a .45 slug in his head and was still feeling the effects of morphine.

McLaughlin told him to ask the Chinese to surrender first. "They are going to laugh at you, but try to sell them the goods." Tovar and the interpreter walked south and after about 150 yards were met by several Chinese officers and an interpreter who could speak Korean. When Tovar repeated the message from McLaughlin, the Chinese in charge replied, "Go back and tell your commander that he has ten minutes to surrender."

Tovar returned with this ultimatum. McLaughlin told Tovar to say he needed until six-thirty to surrender so he could take care of his wounded. The major was playing for time in hopes that air cover would come over at dawn.

Tovar and his interpreter went back to the Chinese. The answer was "No." They had five minutes. McLaughlin decided to make his own pitch. While he and the Chinese were talking, Tovar had a chance to speak to James Eagan, a wounded Marine major, who lay on the ground. "What do you think of surrendering?" asked Tovar.

"You don't have the chance of a snowball in hell," said Eagan. There were at least three Chinese regiments out there.

Tovar could see that McLaughlin was still arguing and the Chinese were getting angry. Chinese soldiers started closing in on the Americans.

"Shit or get off the pot!" Tovar shouted to McLaughlin, who drew out his .45 and handed it to a Chinese officer.

Buck and his party were still free on the ridge west of the road. It was just beginning to get light. As they neared Koto-ri and were starting downhill, Buck spotted, less than two hundred yards ahead, a long column of Chinese crossing their path. He passed the word for silence and all hands watched about 500 enemy troops move rapidly towards the valley floor. They were carrying mortars and water-cooled machine guns. Suddenly, just ahead of the Chinese, appeared two Marines in dark parkas. They were about to run into the Chinese column! There was nothing to do but watch in fascination. As the Marines were about to bump into the Chinese, a hundred-yard break developed in the long enemy column. Miraculously the two Marines passed through the Chinese line with neither side noticing the other.

While Buck was watching the breathtaking escape of the two Marines, Commando Andrew Condron and his group had been hiding near the road. Once dawn came they could walk safely into nearby Koto-ri. The Scotsman was suffering from the cold, his clothing still frozen stiff. While he was bandaging a wounded British Royal Marine, he heard someone behind him grunt, "Huh!"

Condron turned to see what he thought was a South Korean, since he was wearing a snow cape. The man looked shell-shocked. Again he said, "Huh!" and leveled a tommy gun at Condron. This must be a Chinese!

Condron stood up and was about to have a go at him when an American shouted, "Hey, buddy, you throw that rifle down. We're surrendering."

Condron was disgusted. He flung his rifle aside. "Nobody tells us bugger-all around here!" And even more surprisingly, the Chinese with the tommy gun ran over and began shaking hands with him. Condron and the others were searched cursorily. The Chinese wanted weapons, not souvenirs. Then a Chinese officer arrived, gathered the prisoners, and gave a little speech of welcome. The real enemies, he said, were the American imperialists. "You have been sent thousands of miles to Korea to kill innocent men, women and children. But you are not to blame. My argument isn't with you. In fact, I'm a proletarian and you are all proletarians." Condron wasn't quite sure what either an imperialist or proletarian was.

A GI next to him said, "Prole-what? I thought they were fucking Commies."

They were marched to a hut, where a guard brought in a large gourd of steaming-hot water. The thirty or so prisoners washed up. By the time the guard came back, the water had become soapy and filthy. The guard looked in amazement at the water and glared angrily at them. He swung his bayonet menacingly until all the prisoners were pushed back against a wall.

Condron and the others had no idea what had set him off. He shouted what sounded like curses, kicked the gourd over and stomped out. A few minutes later the officer who had spoken so cordially before reappeared. He too was angry. The guard, he explained, had gone to much trouble to be kind. He had built a fire at considerable risk to himself because of American aircraft and had boiled the water so the prisoners could have a drink. To wash in it was a great insult. The prisoners tried to explain that it was not their custom to drink hot water. The officer continued to berate them, thinking they had deliberately slighted the guard and made him lose face by demeaning his gift. It was, thought Condron, an example of East meets West with total misunderstanding on each side.

In the meantime, a large group of American prisoners had been collected near a U.S. truck. They watched with tears in their eyes as Chinese soldiers began to rip open Christmas packages from home. The wind was blowing and holiday paper flew all over while the Chinese were pulling out watches, fountain pens, ski socks and other presents. Nearby, other Chinese had already looted a PX truck, and the wrappings from Tootsie Rolls, Hershey's bars and Dentyne littered the road.

The fifteen men of Buck's party descended from the ridge, since most of the Chinese seemed to be breaking off action. They crossed over the fast-flowing little river on a log and were heading for the road when Buck noticed several Chinese duck into a farmhouse. They ran up to the house, and Buck kicked open a door, only to find the Chinese had somehow disappeared. The Americans continued south. On each side of the road they passed many dead Chinese and Americans, all frozen stiff. Soon they heard a helicopter, and they all waved at the pilot, who touched down in a nearby field. Buck recognized the Marine pilot and was explaining their situation when a machine gun began to chatter. Buck gave a vigorously upward sign to the pilot, and as he took off vertically, the Marines zigzagged knee-deep through the snow to the safety of a drainage ditch. They proceeded cautiously towards Koto-ri, not knowing what lay ahead. By this time all the Chinese had melted into the heights on the east. Buck's group at last reached the 1st Marine CP in Koto-ri. After the lieutenant had related the entire action to Puller, the colonel gave him a cup of hot chocolate and a shot of whiskey. Did he need anything else? "Yes, sir. A toothbrush."

At the north end of the ambush there was also quiet. Hagaru-ri was totally destroyed except for a few houses. Captain Sitter, who was awarded the Medal of Honor for his actions, was mourning the death of his first sergeant, Rocco Zullo. At the improvised morgue, a corpsman was passing Zullo's body when he heard a cough and checked. Zullo was still alive! His men were not at all surprised. No bullet could kill Rocco Zullo.

CHAPTER 23

Bloody Retreat: Running the Gauntlets
(November 30–December 1)

1.

November 30 was another bad day for the Eighth Army. At dawn Keiser's 2nd Division was still held up by the roadblock south of Kunu-ri, and his combat elements had been reduced to 600 exhausted, frozen men. Keiser outlined to his commanders the final withdrawal to Pyongyang. By early afternoon the Chinese held six miles of the road with some forty machine guns, ten mortars and numerous infantrymen.

The 9th Infantry tried to smash through. Some managed to succeed. When Captain Harris Pope reported that only 37 men out of some 800 in the 3rd Battalion had made it, the commander, Colonel D.M. McMains—later awarded the DSC—threw his arms around Pope and broke down.

Those who survived the six-mile gauntlet had to go through a defile that had become a graveyard; by the time General Keiser, suffering from a severe chest cold, reached the pass at three-thirty P.M., it was clogged with trucks and tanks. The men were in such a state of shock that they seemed to see or hear nothing.

"Who's in command here?" shouted Keiser. "Can any of you do anything?"

No one answered. Occasionally someone whispered, "Water! Water!" Most did nothing except wander aimlessly, their faces masklike because of a heavy coating of dust. Keiser walked to the south end of

Kim's advance headquarters near the Iron Triangle destroyed by U.S. bombing. *James Lewellyn, United States Army*

Horrendous results of U.S. napalm bombing
National Archives

Wounded North Korean soldiers surrender to "come over to democracy." *National Archives*

Numerous United Nations soldiers were also surrendering. *People's Military Museum*

Major James Hausman (*far left*), father of the ROK Army and adviser to ROK Chief of Staff Chung Il-kwon, keeps a characteristically low profile. *James Hausman*

A grinning Lieutenant Colonel Robert Taplett points to Christmas wreath. The sign inside the wreath reads, "Merry Xmas, what the hell." This picture was taken on Thanksgiving eve, and Taplett's executive officer, Major John J. Canney (*right*), was killed at the Chosin Reservoir a week later. *United States Department of Defense (Marine Corps)*

Chosin Reservoir in late November 1950, just before the battle *National Archives*

Chinese mass attack at Chosin Reservoir *People's Military Museum*

The 1st Marine Division pulls out of the reservoir. *United States Department of Defense (Marine Corps)*

The broken bridge just below Funchilin Pass *National Archives*

Repaired bridge over which Marines and their vehicles head to safety *National Archives*

Wilfred Burchett, left-wing Australian correspondent, who was useful to his Western colleagues *National Archives*

Thousands of North Korean civilians boarding U.S. ships at Hungnam Harbor as they flee to safety in South Korea, thanks to Major General Edward Almond, commander of X Corps *National Archives*

April 1951. Lieutenant j.g. Eugene Clark (*with cigar*) on his secret mission with General Sams (*far left*) into North Korea. *Eugene Clark*

Civilians fleeing Seoul across the frozen Han River to escape approaching Chinese *National Archives*

Lieutenant General Matthew Ridgway, replacement for General Walker, who was killed in a jeep accident. *Photograph by Carl Mydens. Courtesy of General Matthew Ridgway and* Life *magazine.*

Alan Winnington of
the London *Daily
Worker,* reading *Time* to
other representatives
of the Communist
press *National Archives*

ROK Major General Paik Sun-yup
helps Admiral C. Turner Joy
descend as he arrives at Kaesong to
begin negotiations with the Chinese
and North Koreans.
National Archives

A year later Paik
became the Chief of
Staff of the Republic
of Korea Army and
the first four-star ROK
general. *General Paik*

the pass to see if it was blocked by the Chinese. Bullets were screeching down from American planes, chipping the rocks nearby. Napalm from friendly planes also bounced off the cliffs, spilling onto the road near the general.

Finally he saw an American operating an 81-mm mortar from a truck. He was the only man fighting, but others were helping the wounded. A soldier was trying to drag an injured man to cover. "Now get your goddamned leg around the corner of the jeep!" he yelled. "Do it, I say."

Keiser passed a mass of dead Americans, Turks and ROKs lying in the ditches and along the road. He started back, convinced that the air strikes had wiped out the Chinese machine guns so the wrecked vehicles could be cleared away. Exhausted, he tried to step across a body but struck his toe against a corpse's stomach. The indignant corpse sat up and yelled, "You damned son of a bitch!"

"My friend," said Keiser, "I'm sorry," and walked on.

2.

In Washington the bad news from Korea was raising havoc. At his press conference Truman said, "We hope that the Chinese people will not continue to be forced or deceived into serving the end of colonial policy in Asia." The newsmen were not impressed, and Truman was asked if any attacks in Manchuria would depend on action in the United Nations. "We will take whatever steps are necessary," he replied, "to meet the military situation, just as we always have."

"Will that include the atomic bomb?" asked an excited reporter.

"That includes every weapon that we have."

"Mr. President, you said, 'every weapon that we have,' " cut in Paul Leach of the Chicago *Daily News*. "Does that mean that there is active consideration of the atomic bomb?"

"There has always been active consideration of its use. I don't want to see it used. It is a terrible weapon, and it would not be used on innocent men, women and children who have nothing to do with this military aggression."

The UP correspondent would not let him off the hook.

"Mr. President, I wonder if we could retrace that reference to the atomic bomb? Do we understand you clearly that the use of the atomic bomb is under active consideration?"

"Always has been," snapped Truman impatiently. "It is one of our weapons." Caught off guard, he had violated the taboo against mentioning use of the atomic bomb. He floundered. "It's a matter that the military will have to decide. I'm not a military authority that passes on these things." This rash statement aggravated the error. Sole authority

on the use of the bomb was, by law, vested in the president's hands—
not in those of the field commander.

Frank Bourgholtzer tried to pin him down. "Mr. President, you said
this depends on United Nations' action. Does that mean that we wouldn't
use the atomic bomb except on a United Nations authorization?"

"No, it doesn't mean that at all!" he exclaimed. "The action against
Communist China depends on the action of the United Nations. The
military commander in the field will have charge of the use of the weapons, as he always has."

Within minutes UP announced: "President Truman said today the
United States has under consideration use of the atomic bomb in connection with the war in Korea." The AP bulletin reported: "The decision
of whether to drop atomic bombs was one for the commander in the
field." The afternoon papers carried scare headlines making it appear
as if Truman were sending A-bombs to MacArthur with carte blanche
to use them.

Truman's words went around the world, causing panic in London
and Paris. First reports turned a dull debate on foreign affairs in the
House of Commons into an uproar. Prime Minister Attlee announced
that he felt compelled to come to the United States and discuss the
situation in the East.

3.

At the Chosin Reservoir, General Smith had already issued orders to
the 5th and 7th Marines to adjust their positions, and both regiments
prepared to break off action on the morning of December 1 in order
to withdraw to Hagaru-ri. Litzenberg and Murray were acting under
separate orders from General Smith, but their units were so intertwined
that they had to work in close coordination. Out of necessity they pooled
resources, exchanging an east-to-west perimeter for one pointing from
north to south along the road to Hagaru-ri. Although this maneuver
was made in daylight, taking advantage of observation for air cover and
artillery, the Chinese for some reason did little to impede the operation.

Taplett's battalion had the mission of seizing the commanding
ground on both sides of the road part way to Hagaru-ri. *Darkhorse*, the
call sign of the 3rd Battalion, began to withdraw at 8 A.M. Taplett's last
unit, George Company, had to be pulled out from Hill 1282. For two
days they had been so close to the Chinese that grenades were the main
weapon for each side.

Withdrawal was ticklish but was accomplished without having the
Chinese swarm over the hill in pursuit. Once these last elements had
joined the rest of the battalion, Taplett began occupying the high ground
on both sides of the road. Moments later, Murray radioed Taplett to

report to the combined Marine CP at Yudam-ni. "We're going to change your orders," he said.

"We just moved into the position you gave us!"

"That's all been changed."

"What is my mission?"

"You're to pull your troops off the positions they just occupied. Your battalion is going to lead the attack!" Taplett was to make the breakout south to Hagaru-ri.

Taplett headed back to Yudam-ni to find numerous fires. PX supplies, chow, records—everything was being destroyed. Never had he seen such rattled people. In the confusion, someone threw a grenade in one fire, killing several men. Taplett was now ordered to proceed about four miles farther south to the highest land mass, Hill 1520. When it was secured, he was to continue leading the main attack to the south.

"Okay. What kind of support are you giving me?" Taplett asked Murray.

"We'll give you artillery support and air-on-station."

"That's great," said Taplett, who had his doubts. He still had two companies up on Hill 1282. "I'm going to have to get them both under control because they were assigned to take another peak. I'll have to start them reassembling."

"We want you to attack right away."

Taplett tried to curb his anger. "Christ! How can I attack right away? They're way up on the hill. It's going to take them a while to get down."

As he strode out of the CP toward his jeep, the battalion chaplain, Bernie Hickey, saw he was hot under the collar. "What's the problem?" he asked.

"We're attacking out of here!"

"Want to go to confession?"

Taplett nodded.

"I'll walk alongside of you while you talk." When Taplett had finished, Hickey said, "For your penance, when the going gets tough on that hill, you make the sign of the cross and say, 'Not my will but thy will be done.' And you'll be successful."

While Taplett was jeeping back, he radioed the commander of Item Company. "We'll need the line of attack and the order in which we're going to move down the road." Item was to lead, followed by G and H. By the time Item was off the high ground and on the road, Taplett had caught up. He could only edge forward, since the road was badly congested with traffic. He noticed that some troops were coming down the slope to the left. That was odd. There shouldn't be anyone over there. As he drew near, he could see they were 7th Marines.

"What the hell are you doing over here?" he called. He had not been informed of anyone operating on the left of the MLR. 3/7 was supposed to be attacking, south along the MLR to seize Hill 1520 at which time Taplett was to pass through 3/7 and continue the attack along the MLR. Taplett's job was to lead the Yudam-ni elements into Hagaru-ri.

"We're launching our attack," replied a lieutenant.

It was ridiculous. "I thought you people were attacking Hill 1520." This was farther down the road.

"We're just getting started, sir."

"Where's your other company?" asked Taplett.

"They're across the road, moving up that high ground."

Taplett couldn't believe what he'd heard. "Who's attacking 1520 then?"

"That's us."

"Where's your parent CO?" This would be the CO of the 3rd Battalion, 7th Marines. The lieutenant pointed to a little spur coming down towards the road. Taplett jumped out of the jeep and angrily stalked forward, accompanied by First Lieutenant Charlie Mize and chased by his radioman, Private First Class Swede Swenson, who had to backpack his heavy equipment.

Taplett and Mize found a lieutenant colonel standing nearby. "Are you the CO of this battalion?" He was. "My name is Taplett and I have orders to pass through you when you take Hill 1520. When are you going to take it?"

"You've got to be kidding."

Taplett was startled by the look in his eye. "What do you mean?"

"We're just getting started now. I've got one company over here and my reserve company is someplace back down the road."

"When do you expect to take off?"

"Hell only knows."

Mize could see that Tap couldn't tolerate such a hopeless situation and feared he'd lose his temper.

"Good Lord, man!" exclaimed Taplett and hurried back to his radioman. It was already midafternoon. "Swede, this is a horrible mess! Get Colonel Murray on the radio." But Murray was too busy to talk to Taplett. "Then let me talk to the S3."

"I don't know where the S3 is."

"Is there any officer in the Fifth Marine headquarters I can talk to?" insisted Taplett.

"Yeah, I think I can get ahold of Colonel Dowsett."

Soon the regimental exec of the 7th was on the radio. Taplett had never met him. "The 3rd Battalion, 7th, is nowhere near the objective," explained Taplett. "They're still milling around. I've already got Item Company about half a mile to three-quarters of a mile down the road, ready to relieve them on Hill 1520. And they haven't even started up yet!" He paused. "I'd like to know what my instructions are!" Mize feared what he knew was coming.

"Do what you damn well see fit."

Taplett cussed him. "You can tell Colonel Murray that I'm attacking, and if he doesn't like it, he can call me!" Taplett discussed the changed situation with Mize and his company commanders and decided to put How Company in the lead, followed by Item and then George. Engineers went forward to clear any roadblocks. The 3rd Battalion started down the road and after a mile caught some fire from the right. But there were few casualties; and after sending the infantry ahead, Taplett dismounted from his jeep to set up a CP some twenty yards off the road. It was dark by the time he started across the snow to find where the hell the rest of his Headquarters and Service Company was. The next thing he knew there was a loud explosion and snow began flying all around. When he came to, he was lying under Charlie Mize, with the radio operator on top of both of them. Taplett's first words were: "Charlie, Swede, are you all right?" By some fluke, no one was seriously wounded.

A call came in from How Company. "We couldn't reach you on the radio," said Captain Harold Williamson. "If it's okay with you, Item Company has taken the left side of the road and I'll take the right." Taplett agreed and the two companies started up the spurs on both sides of the road.

Murray called to ask what the situation was. Taplett explained his plan. "Good, carry on," said Murray. "I want you to keep going. The pressure is on back here, and we've got to get into Hagaru-ri. Attack all night long." This meant Taplett had to clear Hill 1520 so the 5th and 7th Marines could get through Toktong Pass and on to the safety of Hagaru-ri.

Late that evening Item took the first objective on Hill 1520, a big spur. "I'm going to have to attack across the plateau to another spur ahead of me," radioed I Company's commander, Captain Harold Schrier. Then Williamson radioed, "We've run into fifteen or twenty Chinks and cleaned them out, and then forty or fifty more." Taplett was concerned. The two companies were separated too damned far, and only the CP group was on the road.

About midnight Schrier called from the hill. "I'm running into a buzzsaw up here. It's going to be a disaster."

"Okay," said Taplett. "Pull back to the other position and set up for the night."

Then came another message from regimental headquarters: "Resume the attack."

"I am not going to resume any attack at night," replied Taplett. "Not over terrain I know nothing about."

"I said to resume the attack."

Taplett reluctantly called Schrier. "I've got pressure from the two combined commanders." He was referring to the coordinated command of Murray and Litzenberg. "Can you attack again?"

"I'll try," said Schrier. Item ran into another buzzsaw. The earth was frozen so that foxholes were barely below ground level and gave little protection from a shower of mortar rounds, grenades and small-arms fire. Veterans of World War II thought it was worse than Iwo Jima. After taking heavy casualties, Schrier called Taplett. "We're under very heavy attack, Tap. From the front and both sides."

"Can you withdraw?"

"We're trying to withdraw now."

There was no further word from Item, and Taplett radioed George Company in reserve. "I want you to go into defensive positions behind Item Company," said Taplett. They were to stay there for the rest of the night.

Once George got into position, Captain Hermanson radioed, "We can hear a lot of activity ahead. There's a lot of heavy firefighting."

H Company had run into strong resistance on the high ground on the right of the MLR. The situation was desperate. As a last resort, Taplett moved his engineer company behind Hermanson's position. Again and again Taplett tried in vain to reach Item, and hours later in the early light of dawn he found Schrier at the aid station. "What's going on?" Schrier had been shot through the neck. All he could say was, "Impossible. Everybody killed." Only about twenty men, one an officer, Second Lieutenant Willard Peterson, had come through the night alive. It was the most welcome daylight of the entire war for the 3rd Battalion, the longest night of all time.

Taplett called Murray. "Christ, Item Company has been chewed up. We're in a hell of a mess up here. I've just got H and S people on the road."

"We're going to renew the attack," said Murray. He promised to send help.

Only one tank arrived from Murray. When Taplett emerged from the aid tent, he saw Colonel Murray walking towards him. "What's happening?" Murray asked.

"We already filled you in on the radio," said the exhausted Taplett.

"Well, we're going to continue the attack."

"Then I'm going to need some additional people. I've just got two companies now, and one company is down. How Company has only about sixty people and G Company about eighty. Item Company is gone." He had to have somebody on the road. There were roadblocks ahead, all of them protected by fire. "I've been on the point up the road and it's pretty touchy. I'd like to get somebody out in front."

"All right," said Murray. I'll send up this one tank, and we're going to form a composite company out of some remnants from the 7th Marines and artillery and engineers."

Taplett sighed. It was going to be more of the same for at least another day and night.

4.

On the opposite side of the reservoir, Task Force Faith had spent a relatively quiet November 30th. Soon after dawn Captain Stamford had his Marine planes on station, and there was little sign of enemy activity. Just before noon a helicopter landed at a clearing near the battalion CP. The unexpected visitor was General Barr, the division commander, who had just come from meetings with Almond and Smith. He brusquely passed those greeting him and hurried in to see Faith.

After his return to Hagaru-ri, Barr told General Smith Faith's greatest problem was 500 wounded he must evacuate before he could try to make a breakout. But Barr believed that Faith could probably do it if he had strong Marine support.

At 2:10 P.M., Almond began a conference with his commanders in pyramidal tents set up on the airstrip. Obviously shaken by the disastrous Task Force Drysdale ambush and the precarious position of the two Marine regiments near Yudam-ni, he told them their situation had changed drastically. He was a far different man from the Almond who had told Faith not to fear a few Chinese laundrymen. X Corps, he said, was going to abandon the Chosin area. The very survival of the corps was at stake, he added, striking a note of alarm. Then came his order to withdraw the two Marine regiments; Almond ordered Barr to prepare a plan and time schedule for withdrawing Task Force Faith the following day, December 1.

The next morning, Colonel Faith prepared his breakout. Just before noon he ordered Captain Robbins to get the trucks warmed up and load the wounded aboard. Moments later a mortar round knocked Robbins sideways. He was hit by fragments in the arm and leg. Stunned, he saw that his carbine had been blown from his hand. Several rounds in the clip had exploded and the slide mechanism wouldn't work. He was soon bandaged and hoisted aboard a truck along with Private Ed Reeves and other wounded, while artillery gunners dropped phosphorus grenades down the muzzles of guns they would leave behind. Drivers were setting afire those vehicles to be abandoned. Leading the column was the 3rd Platoon of C Company with an M-19, a dual-40 antiaircraft full-track vehicle.

Then came a jeep mounting a .30-caliber machine gun, followed by the command group. Captain Stamford was stationed only twenty yards behind the point. He would control air strikes on Faith's orders. Major Dick Miller, Faith's exec, was also up front. Behind came some thirty-five trucks filled with hundreds of wounded. Troops marched on both sides of the truck column.

When the lead platoon passed through A Company's roadblock, enemy machine-gun and small-arms fire broke out. Although some men were hit, the column kept moving. Faith instructed Stamford to call in an air strike. Corporal John Durham saw a plane drop a napalm tank and watched aghast as it threw up a wall of fire over a group of GIs. It was the most horrible thing he'd ever seen. Men were screaming in agony, some begging to be put out of their misery, and Durham saw a sergeant shoot one pleading man in the head.

From his truck, Robbins also witnessed the terrible sight of men ablaze from head to foot, staggering back or rolling on the ground screaming for help. His own assistant sergeant major, blazing, was only ten yards away, yet Robbins was powerless to help. He had to turn his head. Then he saw officers and noncoms rallying their men, getting them to move forward again.

In the lead, Major Miller was horrified at the sight of some ten men of C Company ablaze from the flaming gobs of jellied gasoline, seriously burned before they could be rolled in the snow. Although a crushing blow to morale, the napalm caused the Chinese at the roadblock to flee in terror, allowing the 1st Battalion to inflict heavy casualties. Napalm had also hit the Chinese. At least forty lay dead in the ditch.

Faith helped stem the panic, rushing towards those retreating and threatening them with his drawn pistol until they turned to face the enemy. Then he led the charge against the fleeing Chinese, exhorting, ordering, threatening.

The advance continued, but many of the men were getting out of control. Officers and noncoms tried to herd them to the higher ground so they could protect the road-bound column, but most of them kept racing down the road toward safety.

During this pell-mell flight, planes directed by Stamford were having a heyday strafing and bombing in front of the advancing GIs. Antiaircraft guns were also placing direct withering fire on the Chinese. Nevertheless, the Chinese managed to inflict serious casualties on the Americans during this running fight.

The column had progressed about two miles when a jeep radio picked up a message: "To Colonel Faith: Secure your own exit to Hagaru-ri. Unable to assist you. Signed Smith, CG 1st Marine Division." The only help Task Force Faith might get would come from Marine planes.

By this time, Lieutenant James Mortrude and his point men had reached a blown bridge, a twenty-foot span broken in the middle and collapsed into the stream below. The infantrymen soon waded to the other side and rushed down the road, where they found cover in the ruins of a house.

By now the motor column had reached the blown bridge. A big M-19 descended the steep bank, crossed the stream and swamp grass, then clambered up the other side with no difficulty. Dick Miller was hopeful that the trucks could get across the stream as easily as the full-tracked vehicle, but the first one broke the crust ice of the stream and got stuck in the swampy water. Miller immediately ordered the M-19 turned around. A cable was attached to the mired truck and the M-19 winched it to the other side. As each truck, its wounded occupants screaming, was extracted from the stream, it had to cross a frozen swamp, to be met by mortar and small-arms fire. Progress was slow. If a driver was hit trying to run this gauntlet, the occupants of the truck became targets for the enemy until a new driver took over. About a hundred civilian men, women and children had been tagging along with the trucks, and many of these were gunned down.

The truck carrying Captain Robbins bounced and crashed over two-foot-high grass hummocks. He still wore his helmet, which protected his head as it banged against the front and sides of the truck. Then the vehicle came to a crashing stop. But eventually the M-19 pulled the truck to solid ground and it continued. Robbins could hear heavy fire coming from the heights, the continual smack of slugs slapping the sides of the truck. Word came back that a roadblock, heavily defended by the Chinese, was holding up the column.

Captain Stamford, realizing that these stalled vehicles were at the mercy of Chinese moving towards the road, brought in an air strike. The enemy scattered and fled back into the valley. Otherwise they would have wiped out the column and attacked from the rear those GIs heading towards Hill 1221.

The troops of the 32nd Infantry were moving toward the roadblock while men of the 31st were skirting the valley below the road to force the block. The 31st was under heavy fire from Chinese on the high ground as well as from the other side of the valley, but the 32nd looked as if it could break through. Then they ran into heavy fire and began falling back in disorder as if they had lost their leaders. Again the Chinese occupied the roadblock.

Most of the 32nd officers were casualties; and their men, clustered around the stalled vehicles, were drawing fire toward the wounded. Then Colonel Faith appeared, shouting and waving his pistol to force the troops back up the hill. Ignoring the increased rifle fire, Faith rallied the men with threats and encouragement. Seeing an ROK soldier tying himself to the underside of a truck, Faith exhorted him to get out and fight. The man kept shouting in Japanese, "I'm hurt." The ROK wouldn't come out and both Stamford and Private First Class Mitchell Heath saw

Faith kill him. "The son of a bitch is retreating!" shouted the colonel. "Shoot anyone who runs away!"

Heath had admired Faith, ever since hearing him tell off the general who had refused to take wounded in his helicopter. Again, he felt the colonel was doing the right thing.

Captain Kitz was also having trouble handling the men. He couldn't get them to move up the hill. Exhausted from four days of fighting, they huddled together, convinced their only safety lay near the trucks, even though they were drawing most of the fire.

Kitz, together with five junior officers, managed to get more than 200 men on the move. They charged a ridge and knocked out several roadblocks, then sent a runner back to prod the rest of the troops and get the vehicles moving. Some of the walking wounded joined the Kitz group, but the trucks were still stalled. Kitz sent two men back to urge the trucks to come around the bend and follow them to the west. But when none appeared, he took off toward the reservoir with about 210 men.

In the meantime Faith was trying to hit the roadblock from the rear. By sheer willpower he had managed to gather about 350 men. When the whole battalion seemed in disarray, Faith inspired the men to follow him up the hill. Near the top, pistol drawn, Faith declared, "We are going to charge the roadblock all together!" He shouted as he charged down the hill waving his pistol. He turned around and to his dismay saw only a few men with him. He ran back up the hill swearing and threatening the men so they would charge the roadblock.

Private Louis Joseph Grappo, a seventeen-year-old member of 32d's Heavy Mortar Company, inspired by Faith's bravery and leadership, joined the charge. As he approached the rear of the roadblock, Grappo could hear Chinese talking and thought they wanted to surrender since so many Americans were charging the roadblock. He could see three immobile U.S. tanks, one turned on its side on the road. These tanks were remnants of the attempt on November 28 to send help to the 31st and 32nd. Crawling on the ground, Grappo came upon one of the few survivors of this ill-fated attempt. He tried to talk to the tanker but he was badly wounded and in total shock.

Faith ordered a patrol down the road, but they soon came running back. When he tried to send another, nobody would go. He set out alone. The lead truck started after Faith with Grappo hanging on to the rear of a two-and-a-half-ton truck. The rest of the column followed. By now Grappo was so tired and with such frozen feet that he could hardly keep going. Then he heard a weak voice call out, "Help! Help!" One of the sergeants called out, "Who are you?" A reply came back. "I'm Colonel Faith! Help me!"

Two sergeants went forward and found Faith in a ditch, wounded.

They loaded him into the lead truck and the column headed south. By now the trucks were filled with casualties. Wounded alongside the road, screaming to be taken along, were strapped on the hoods and bumpers. When there was no room left on the vehicles, the remaining wounded were left along the roadside. They kept reaching out their hands and pleading for help. Grappo couldn't bear to look at them. There was nothing he could do for them. He himself was near the end of his endurance. His feet were frozen and snow had gotten into his boots. He still clung desperately to the rear of the lead truck knowing he'd be a goner if he let go.

The lead truck turned off a stretch of railroad tracks and advanced without waiting for the rest of the column. As it entered the village of Twiggae, it was suddenly hit by intense fire from mortars and machine guns. Grappo dropped from the tailgate and stumbled back toward the column. He bumped into the exec, who asked what was going on.

"They ambushed us, sir! Colonel Faith is in the first truck!"

"Form a skirmish line!" shouted the exec.

As Grappo and the others headed forward, followed by the trucks, he saw shadows near railroad tracks. Then he heard an explosion and dropped to the ground, hit by a bullet through the center of his right leg. It was his first wound, and it hurt like hell. He was weeping when his platoon leader, First Lieutenant Robert Reynolds, asked, "What happened?"

"I got shot," he said. Reynolds ordered two men from Grappo's platoon to load him into a truck. But by now all the trucks were filled, and there was no more room on the fenders or hoods. Grappo shouted to a friend in one truck who was not wounded and asked if he could have his place. The man refused.

Grappo yelled at the driver, another friend. "Bunny, I'm wounded and I need a space in your truck!"

Bunny spun out of his cab, leveling his .45 at the man who had refused Grappo. "Get your ass out of here or I'll give *you* a reason to be in the truck." The man instantly made room for Grappo, who landed among screaming men. At last the truck moved, and Grappo heard an explosion near his ear. His shoulder didn't hurt, but he finally realized shrapnel had pierced his helmet. The twang of the steel helmet made his ears ring and the concussion almost knocked him out. "My God!" he exclaimed. He had taken thirteen pieces of shrapnel and a large piece of flesh was missing from his right shoulder.

Inside his mittens was a rosary. "I'm a young kid," he prayed. "I don't even know what it is to have a girlfriend, or to go to a dance. If you will just let me live to experience life, I'll go to Mass and Communion every day for a year." But he knew he was lying. He thought about what he had just promised, then said, "God, I'm bullshitting you," he con-

fessed. "I'm not going to do it for a year. But I *will* do it for six months."
Then the youngster from Youngstown, Ohio, the baby of twelve children, passed out. He had prayed so hard his rosary had fallen to pieces.

A wild-eyed ROK soldier leaped into Robbins's truck and flung
himself on top of the wounded, who yelped in pain. Robbins saw he
wasn't injured, only terrified, and shoved the barrel of a carbine in his
face. "Get the hell out of the truck!" he yelled—so mad he would gladly
have blown the soldier's head off. The man hastily left and joined others
milling outside. Robbins decided to get the hell out of the truck, despite
his aching leg, rather than risk getting captured. He would try to make
it south on his own.

By now Captain Stamford, who had joined the stalled column,
learned that Faith was in the lead truck, badly wounded. The indomitable
Marine took over guiding the convoy down a hill. At the bottom he held
up the line to see if a bridge ahead was passable. On the way forward
he met a soldier who said he'd been set upon by a Chinese patrol but
managed to escape. There was an enemy machine gun in the area, he
said, but Stamford couldn't find it. He returned to Twiggae to confer
with a small group of Army officers there, and when Stamford lit a
cigarette, he recognized a lieutenant colonel. But neither he nor any of
the other officers who outranked Stamford attempted to take over command. Stamford was so annoyed that he walked up to Faith, sitting in
the cab of the lead truck. "Do you want me to try and continue into
Hagaru tonight?" he asked.

"Yes," Faith replied weakly. He was in pain and seemed on the verge
of losing consciousness.

Stamford placed himself in a jeep at the point, since there didn't
seem to be any other way to get the column moving. He led the convoy
in the dark down the hill to a railroad trestle, part of which was blown.
Stamford cautiously drove his jeep onto the tracks to see if it would fit.
The left wheel was against one rail and the other wheel on the ties.

"If I get across the trestle," he called, "you guys get the trucks up
here." All trailers had to be left behind. He had already shown the drivers
how to negotiate the railroad tracks and get back to the main road.

Stamford got the jeep safely across. Assured that his trucks could
follow, he cut across to the highway with three GIs. Upon reaching the
road, they left the jeep and started walking south to see if the way was
clear of roadblocks, but after half a mile they were suddenly surrounded
by the enemy. One Chinese motioned Stamford to lie down on the side
of the road. He reacted so slowly the guard fired his rifle, the shot barely
missing Stamford's head. Two Chinese with automatic weapons herded
the prisoners back up the road towards the trestle. One man was sent
ahead to reconnoiter, but several rounds of mortar fire were followed

by bursts of fire from the south. Stamford figured these had to come from the convoy following him.

Then he saw the lead truck from the column rumbling towards them, the one carrying Faith. The Chinese, apparently too surprised to fire, fled; and the truck broke through. Then a second truck sped past Stamford, but a few seconds later a rocket hit this vehicle and stopped it. Stamford turned to see Faith's truck halt just north of the village of Sasu-ri. Stamford figured that Faith's driver was waiting for the rest of the trucks.

But none of the others tried to run the gauntlet, and Faith's truck moved off toward Sasu-ri. Stamford sneaked through this village and onto the road without meeting any Chinese. He knew the place well and safely propelled himself across the icy surface of a small river, determined to find Faith's truck. But there was no sign of his commander, and he continued south. When a Chinese approached, he changed direction but the man kept following. In the dark Stamford hurried west into scrub pine and the roughest terrain he could find. As he scrambled down the far side of the saddle, he stumbled and sprained his ankle.

The trucks behind Stamford had managed to cross the trestle; but the jostling was painful, and the wounded cried out and moaned. Upon reaching the road, Major Wesley J. Curtis, 32nd Infantry, walked forward past stalled trucks and located Faith in one of the cabs. They were the same age, thirty-two. "Colonel," said Curtis, "this is Butch. How are you doing?"

"Let's get going," said Faith.

Curtis continued down the column, where he found Major Miller lying across the hood of Stamford's jeep. "Dick," he said, "you're going to have to walk if we get out of here."

"I'm hurting too bad to walk." One hand was shot up, the other frozen, and there were bullets in one leg. After talking to Curtis, Miller checked several soldiers; those with weapons had only one or two rounds left. He learned there was a roadblock ahead and they couldn't get through. At close to midnight, the long silence was broken by two mortar rounds bursting to the right of the road a hundred yards from Miller. Then two more rounds hit closer, and he knew they would soon be bracketed. He could visualize the wounded hit again; a truck set on fire would make them all sitting targets.

The leading truck driver asked him for permission to make a run for it. He'd been forward a hundred yards and seen no movement. It was a choice of the unknown against the known danger. "Move out," said Miller.

The column rolled forward two hundred yards to a bend. Then

came a terrific blast of rifle and machine-gun fire from a hill to the left. The lead truck, met by the hail of bullets, piled into the ditch, blocking the road. Miller watched in desperation. The column had been stopped cold and was now being punished unmercifully. Moments later Chinese began closing in on the other trucks, setting them afire with grenades. Miller watched a wounded soldier crawling across an open field to reach shelter. Silhouetted against the snow, he was promptly shot.

Miller knew his hands would freeze if he didn't protect them. He examined the downed soldier and made sure he was dead. But before he could take his gloves, machine-gun bullets rippled around Miller's head. He crawled to a pile of ties where two unarmed GIs were hiding. One started over the railroad embankment but quickly dropped back. "Chinks moving toward us," he said. All three started in the opposite direction, but the wounded Miller lagged far behind. One GI returned to help, but Miller said, "Go ahead while you have the chance."

Miller managed to inch around the bend, where he found a stick. Using it as a crutch, he started across a field to Sasu-ri but soon realized that his right hand was frozen stiff around the stick. As he attempted to ford a stream on ice and rocks, his left foot slipped and his shoe filled with water. He continued into the village, which seemed to be deserted, finally finding an empty house with comforters on the floor. He sat down and, after what seemed hours, managed to open his penknife with his teeth, cut the left bootlaces and pull off the soggy boot. The extra socks he carried under his shorts were still dry and he managed to get one on the bare left foot. Feeling no pain, just an overall numbness, he pulled a comforter over himself and was soon asleep.

Early in the breakout, the walking wounded fighting alongside the trucks to keep the Chinese back had been called forward to break roadblocks. The trucks of wounded back in the column were on their own. With several rifles to a truck they fought their way south. Trucks slamming together, bouncing through creek beds and bridge bypasses kept everyone's wounds open and hurting. All along the road constant incoming fire killed some on Private Ed Reeves's truck and rewounded others. They waited under fire till dead drivers were replaced by wounded volunteers from the back of the truck, then raced to catch up.

Reeves's truck now sat with a dead motor three hundred feet behind the end of the column. Sergeant Ben Dryden walked calmly back through enemy fire to tell them, "Column's stopped. If you can walk, drag another wounded man in his sleeping bag across the reservoir ice. Marines are on the other side." Reeves couldn't go. Once he moved his legs, he passed out from the pain. Those who could left, some crawling, some dragging others, some leaning together for support. Some apologized for not being able to help Reeves and the others who couldn't move and then headed across the fields. The wounded still on Reeves's truck had nothing left to fight with. After a while a group of Chinese walked up to the truck. Shouting and poking the GIs with bayonet points, they motioned for them to get up and go with them. Sleeping bags were unzipped and wounds shown to the Chinese who didn't want badly wounded prisoners. The Chicoms moved on.

Later a Chinese officer appeared at the tailgate of Reeves's truck. He was obviously important since he traveled alone without a political watchdog. He wore polished leather boots and a clean, long greatcoat. "Good day, gentlemen," he said with a clipped British accent. The wounded men reminded him of the Geneva Convention rules for POW treatment: shelter, doctors, food. "I am sorry I can give you none of those things," he replied regretfully. "If I am heard talking to you like this, I will be shot. I stopped to say, God bless you, the Lord be with you." He turned and walked away. The other wounded men were angry that this Chinese officer had not helped, but Reeves felt that God was telling him, "You're not alone. I know all about this."

North Korean families of old men, women and children came past the truck column. At each truck they looked in at the wounded GIs for a moment, then bowed slowly. Reeves felt honored they would do this right in front of Chicoms who might chop their heads off. Besides being physically miserable, Reeves felt the ache and helplessness of being a POW. Needing help and hope he took out his pocket New Testament, turned to the 23rd Psalm and read it aloud. His comrades listened quietly.

"Hey, driver," Reeves called to a badly wounded man up front. "Where's that smoke coming from?" A dark cloud was rising above the road. The driver called back that the trucks ahead were being burned with the wounded inside. Reeves had expected death many times but not being burned alive. He prayed that God would take his terrible fear away and let him die like a man. Then he told Jesus he'd see him soon. Amazed at the peace that followed, he sat up and watched, waiting to die and thinking about seeing Jesus.

The gas in Reeves's truck had drained through bullet holes in the tank. When three Chinese couldn't set the vehicle on fire, they divided their job. One started shooting wounded who had rolled under the truck for shelter. Another shot into the truck from the tailgate. The third Chicom climbed up on the side of the truck, leaned over and started killing the GIs, one shot in each head. He worked toward the front where Reeves sat. The man next to him went into eternity and the rifle barrel moved to Ed. "Jesus, here I come," he said. The muzzle blast knocked him flat. Opening his eyes, he looked at the Chicom, amazed that he wasn't dead. You don't miss at four feet! The amazed Chicom looked back, then climbed down from the truck. Once all the Chinese left, Reeves slid down in his sleeping bag, zipped it up, then checked his head; only a scalp wound.

Some Americans were escaping over the ice. At midnight a hundred GIs were challenged at a Marine outpost about a mile north of Hagaru-ri. Although no one knew the password, the Marines advised them not to move since they were on the edge of a minefield. The Marines later guided them to their defensive area, where they received a hot meal.

Major Robert E. Jones and Lieutenant Hugh May led one of the largest groups. They had picked up Captain Robbins, who had left his truck despite his pain rather than risk being captured. Near midnight flashes of machine-gun and artillery fire in the distance indicated they were approaching the Marine site near Hagaru-ri. They decided to risk moving straight ahead; staying overnight in the nearby hills would invite freezing and capture. As they cautiously came closer to the fireworks and clamor, they were startled by an unmistakably American, "Halt!" It was the sweetest word Robbins had ever heard. Reconnaissance pilots had alerted the Marines that Americans were coming during the night, so they were prepared. First they offered hot food and medical attention, then a cot. As Robbins drifted off to sleep, he said his prayers with the full assurance that he had received a lot of assistance from the good Lord that day.

The resourceful Captain Stamford had also worked his way south, careful to stay off the road, since it showed signs of being heavily traveled by troops on foot. From a hill near the reservoir he had seen the lights of Hagaru-ri. He infiltrated the Marine guards and was picked up by a rocket battery.

When Louis Grappo from Youngstown finally came to, it was just getting light. He'd been unconscious for ten hours and had no idea his truck was one of the few not on fire. He heard Chinese all over the place. Ammo was going off. It was hell. Next to him was a guy with a bullet through his temple. The bones were sticking out of his head. Grappo reached over and pulled the body over himself for protection and grabbed a grenade. "If they come for me," he told himself, "I'll pull the pin." Everyone else in the truck seemed to be dead. He passed out again, and when he awakened it was quiet. He held his breath, then finally pushed the body off him. His wounded leg hurt so much he had to get out. He peered cautiously through the slot of the truck. It looked like a campground with hundreds of people lying asleep, but they were all dead.

God! Task Force Faith was wiped out. He screamed for his buddy, "Jerry!" There was silence, then he heard a low voice. "Grappo . . . Grappo." To Grappo's amazement, Jerry Miller was lying on the other side of the truck! Jesus Christ! He panicked. Jerry was saying, "Grapp, Grapp, help me." What could he do? He grabbed a sleeping bag and threw it to his friend. Beyond, Grappo saw North Korean refugees melting snow and giving water to wounded Americans. He shouted to them and made motions toward Miller. The civilians wrapped Miller up while Grappo found strength enough to cover himself with two sleeping bags.

A little later, two fuzzy-faced Chinese, who looked about sixteen years old, approached carrying American carbines. They surveyed the truckload of dead and saw Grappo was the only one who seemed to be alive. Grappo, thinking they might feel sorry for him, showed them his wound. He marveled that the civilian NKs kept helping the wounded and wondered why the Chinese didn't shoot them. But the Chinese only stood guard. Grappo decided to wait until afternoon when he hoped to be strong enough to escape over the ice.

Nearby, Private Ed Reeves, the only one in his truck to survive, lay among the dead. When no enemy was around, he tried to get off the truck. Each time he'd start to faint, slide back into the sleeping bag, then faint. "God, why am I alive when everyone else is dead? If you want me off this truck, you do it. I can't." At night Chicoms would climb into the truck searching for combat boots. Reeves would watch them feel the GIs' feet through the sleeping bags. If they found leather boots, they pulled the body out, took the boots and put them on. Each time they felt Reeves's feet, he held himself stiff like a frozen body. They wanted leather combat boots and he only had shoepacks. They would leave and he'd try to get off the truck again. Then pray.

By afternoon Grappo decided he had to leave the truck, even though it seemed impossible to walk. He put a grenade in his pocket, grabbed two Russian rifles and crawled over to Jerry Miller. He was sure his friend was dead and began to cry. But there was still life in him. "I'll send them back for you," said Grappo and hobbled across the railroad tracks just as Corsairs swept over firing their machine guns. He saw a naked American crawling forward, then another, and one man without shoes. From behind came a volley, and bullets passed over his head from the Chinese behind him. He became hysterical. "I don't care if they kill me or not," he told himself. He was just going to keep his body moving. At last he reached the ice of the reservoir, and the next thing he knew he was looking up at a Marine colonel. Grappo fell into his arms and the man carried him as if he were a child to a jeep surrounded by Marines with submachine guns.

"Son," asked Lieutenant Colonel Olin Beall, "how many of our guys are alive over there?" The fifty-two-year-old Beall had been tirelessly directing rescue operations for hours.

"A few."

"Do you think we can attack and save them?"

"Yes, you can do it," said Grappo. But then he shook his head. "No, Colonel, those guys holding that hill will stop you." He was loaded into a jeep and taken to a Marine aid station. He was going into shock and began to scream, "You sons of bitches, help me!" He could see all those bodies lying on the open ground, freezing.

Then Grappo realized that medics were cutting off his clothes and he was naked with a blanket around him. "Couldn't you m-m-move me next to the fire?" he asked a doctor. He was trembling, and it took a long time before he warmed up. He discovered someone had taken his watch, wallet and the Russian rifle he wanted to take home. He complained to the doctor, and some time later the watch, wallet and gun were returned.

"That's a beautiful weapon, son," said the sympathetic doctor. "And I don't blame you for wanting to take it back with you."

In the cab of an abandoned, bullet-ridden truck several miles north of safety rested the body of Lieutenant Colonel Don Carlos Faith. After a harrowing day of battle, hardship and exhausting effort against impossible odds, he had reached the gate to freedom, only to die of his wounds. He had waged a gallant yet losing battle, but he ended where he would have wished—at the head of Task Force Faith. And it was fitting that President Truman posthumously awarded him the Medal of Honor.

Many of Faith's men had fled in terror; but many more were heroes, fighting through the freezing and terrifying day to the last of their resources. Few were ever honored except by comrades.

CHAPTER 24

"We're Going Out Like Marines"
(December 1–4)

1.

Military records reflect scant coverage of Walker's thoughts and actions during the period between the Chinese attack and Eighth Army's withdrawal. Walker was a changed man after the emergency meeting in Tokyo on November 28th," Mike Lynch remembered. "He became more reflective and remarkably candid in revealing his hidden frustrations."

He felt that too many decisions had been based on map studies done in remote offices. He was convinced his Kunsan plan would have destroyed Kim Il-sung's capability for years to come. Although the landing at Inchon was a technical success, subsequent actions were tactical and strategic failures. He thought the crossing of the 38th parallel was premature because the UN forces had not destroyed the enemy or secured the parallel. Had these things been done, regular NKPA units would not now be threatening his flanks in the north, while bypassed guerrillas harassed supply lines in the south. Above all, he wouldn't be facing massive Chinese forces.

There was no buffer to his front. Eighth Army and X Corps were widely separated and unable to support each other. MacArthur's peremptory pronouncements had brought China into the war. Then he had made a public disclosure of Eighth Army's offensive plan. Walker could not recall ever having faced greater odds in battle than on that fateful November 28.

What disturbed him most was the extent to which politics had dominated decisions. He was convinced that UN forces could have won the war had they been sent to fight months before. They had a chance to destroy the North Koreans in the south, and they could have secured a defensible line above the 38th parallel pending resolution of political questions. But, following Inchon, America had abandoned military objectives that were within her capability to achieve. Instead, she made the mistake of pursuing political objectives that were beyond her ability to control.

Despite these feelings, Walker fought like a man possessed. According to Lynch's flight records, the general averaged almost four hours a day in the air. When the ROKs collapsed on his right flank, he had kept the area under personal surveillance. When the 2nd Division was ambushed below Kunu-ri, he had flown over the site three different times, drawing intense fire on each occasion.

During the emergency Tokyo meeting, he had stated his intent to hold north of Pyongyang. This was based on assumptions that his right flank could be restored and he would suffer no major losses. But within hours of his return, the ROKs had disintegrated, the Turks had a major setback, and the 2nd Division was entrapped. At that point, his focus shifted to ensuring the survival of his army.

"He wanted to go everywhere at once," Lynch recalled. Operating from a road near his headquarters, Walker was now using his unheated L-5 to visit front line commanders. Shifting to his heated L-17, he made reconnaissance flights along his right flank, searching for enemy movement. Then he would fly south to study the terrain over which he might have to make an extended withdrawal. "He worked at a pace that would have exhausted a man half his age," said Lynch.

As he had done with the North Koreans, Walker began studying the characteristics, patterns and tactics of the Chinese. He was quick to recognize similarities. They, too, were disciplined, aggressive and tenacious. Envelopment was their favorite tactic, from battalion to army. And, once an advantage was attained, they were quick to exploit it. But, as with the NKPA, logistics was their Achilles heel. He would aim at that vulnerable target.

December 1 was a critical day for Walker. "He arrived at the airstrip with a map showing a perimeter around Pyongyang," Lynch recalled. As was his practice, posted on the map were essential elements that determined where he would have to defend, and critical indicators that would influence when and how. After take-off, they headed for the port of Chinnampo. If the enemy attempted an envelopment of Pyongyang, this would be the key objective. Its seizure would force Eighth Army to survive with supplies on hand. Ten minutes over its delta-type terrain convinced Walker that it would be impossible to defend.

Next they began to fly the defense line Walker had sketched. As was the case so often, the terrain they saw was not nearly as hospitable as that depicted on the map. While flying beyond the right flank of the 1st Cav, they encountered an enemy force moving along the road in plain view. Troops merely looked up and waved. Walker realized several disturbing things. They were Chinese. They were unopposed. They were much farther south than any units had been reported. And they were loaded with equipment captured from the ROKs. Lynch reversed course immediately. Walker had learned all he needed to know. Pyongyang could not be defended.

On the return flight, he vocally critiqued his own plan, concluding that Eighth Army was strong enough to conduct a defense. They had adequate logistics to hold out for a time. And the enemy's supply shortages would prevent them from attacking at once. But Chinnampo was vulnerable. Terrain favored the enemy in the long run. And supplies captured in the past days had improved the enemy's capability to carry out intentions.

He heeded Patton's advice. "Once you've decided, don't delay. The best is the enemy of the good . . . a good plan violently executed *now* is better than a perfect plan next week." He would order an immediate retirement of the bulk of his troops. Once begun, he would tailor a force to conduct delays on successive positions. He would destroy anything of help to the enemy. He would move back to the best defensible positions, regardless of distance. And he would get it done before the Chinese commander could envelop with his Thirty-eighth and Forty-second armies.

2.

Darkhorse, Taplett's battalion, was still leading the way to Toktong Pass on December 2 despite the previous day's casualties. They had to fight for every yard. George Company was on the left, along Hill 1520, while the composite company of Dog and Easy, called "Damnation," moved astride the road. The engineers had suffered many casualties, and there was only one bulldozer left to clear roadblocks.

By noon George Company secured its objective, but Damnation was stalled near a demolished bridge some three hundred yards past Hill 1520. After calling in Corsairs, which efficiently cleared the Chinese from the ravine, Taplett ordered How Company on the right to move through the high ground south of the bend in the road: but Captain Williamson's people were soon pinned down while trying to cross a stream.

Taplett was walking down the road with Swede Swenson, his radio operator, followed by the radio jeep, when machine-gun fire chattered from the right. Taplett realized it was coming from high ground above

Williamson. He heard a strange, gaspy sound but kept going and then, when more fire came in, he hit the deck. He turned and couldn't see his radioman. He found Swede in the snow at the side of the road. "What the hell's the matter with you?" Taplett asked. Swenson was indispensable and at his best in a crisis.

"I'm in bad shape," he mumbled. A round had gone through the radio on his back and into his lungs. Taplett looked for the jeep driver who had been right behind him. He too was bleeding. The colonel called for litters and medics. It was getting dark as the engineers ahead finished constructing a bypass around the blown bridge. Taplett sent his single tank forward. Minutes later he learned that it had slid off the road. "Get some people in the motor platoon," he radioed, "and see what you can do about getting this damn thing moving."

At last the tank was in place and the advance continued. Then Taplett heard that George Company was in trouble. Hermanson was wounded. Taplett pulled George off the hill and put Lieutenant Mize, his S3 and its former commander, in charge.

Spirits were sagging throughout the battalion, and the will to fight was fading. Their progress seemed slow to Colonel Murray, and he pressed Taplett to move faster. Taplett started up the road with a new radio operator and found the tank sitting near the ditch. Lolling nearby were several Marines. "Where's Dog-Easy's company commander?" asked Taplett.

"In the tank."

Machine-gun fire came from the hill on the right and bullets spattered in the snow. Taplett wiggled on his stomach to the far side of the tank and got on the phone at the back. No one would respond. Angrily he yelled at the commander.

"I'm not coming out," was the muted reply.

"If you don't, I'm going to get you court-martialed," shouted Taplett. There was no answer. "Okay, you lousy son of a bitch. You stay in the tank." As he turned to go back, his helmet flew off, creased by a bullet from the hill. Then he heard someone calling, "Taplett! Taplett!"

He turned and saw a man snaking through the snow.

"I'm Lieutenant Eddy!" he called. "I've got a message from Colonel Murray."

"You can tell him that he can wait and give it to me himself."

Eddy explained that after reaching the Toktong Pass, Taplett was to turn over the attack to the 1st Battalion of the 7th Marines. In the meantime, Colonel Litzenberg, the commander of the 7th Marines, wanted Taplett to continue his attack immediately. "Ray Davis and his people on Toktong Hill are attacking towards you and driving the Chinese right into your arms."

"Tell Colonel Litzenberg he's full of shit. We're chasing a lot of

Chinese in front of us but there's none running into our arms. If he doesn't believe it, he and Murray can come up here themselves."

No one came, and Taplett reorganized his H and S company and pulled George Company down off the hill on the left. Then Taplett got a secondhand message from his own regimental commander. "You tell Ray Murray," Taplett told the informant, "that as far as I'm concerned, I want to continue the attack into Hagaru-ri because I don't want to stop. My men's feet are going to freeze up if they stop. I think we've broken through all the resistance. We'll be able to walk all the way to Hagaru-ri without a shot fired."

Taplett had not exaggerated the condition of his men. Charlie Mize, for example, was facing an almost impossible task with the remnants of George Company. There were only about forty men, and he had never seen troops look so hopeless or care so little. They had not eaten much and were now too tired to stomach the frozen, unpalatable rations.

The men sprawled on the road, undisciplined and morose. Mize gathered his unit leaders. "The first thing we've got to do," said the low-key Mize, "is reorganize if we're going to be a fighting unit. So here's what I think we have to do. And we'll do it unless somebody disagrees." He put all the infantrymen and riflemen under Blackie Cahill, then formed one machine-gun section with two guns, and one mortar section also with two weapons. "Get all your people together and let me talk to them."

The disgruntled men gathered. "Men," said Mize, "this is Charlie. I'm back. I sense a great deal of discouragement, a great deal of worry, and we are in a hell of a mess. But you and I together have gone through many battles. We've always done the job, and I know we can do it again." It was the kind of talk that ordinarily would have been met with sarcasm. But the men who had fought with Charlie in the Pusan Perimeter responded. Mize felt the electricity between himself and the men. His patient appeal had done more than shouts and threats. "Now, we're going to get reorganized and you're going to be with people that you can trust and that you know are going to do the job for you. There's a tank out on the road that Tap told me we could have, and with that tank and this outfit, tomorrow morning we're going all the way to Hungnam!"

By dawn of December 3, six inches of new snow covered the ground, giving the road to the Toktong Pass a deceptively serene appearance. *Darkhorse* was again on the move, its mission to break through the Chinese that were blocking the pass so the 5th and 7th Marines could reach Hagaru-ri. Mize's reinvigorated George Company led the way with a tank. Then came Taplett's engineers. Forty-eight had started two days earlier; now there were only 17. Taplett was up front with them. How Company, which had been fighting all night on the heights, was doing its best to keep pace with Mize.

Darkhorse was doing so well that Taplett again requested Murray for permission to keep going rather than let Colonel Ray Davis take over at Toktong Pass. But his plea was denied, and by midmorning Davis and his 7th Marines had cleared the enemy from the ridge above the pass before leading the way to Hagaru-ri. Taplett stayed behind to herd the straggling column through the pass. He radioed Murray that it would take until after midnight. Then he would fight off any attacks from the rear.

3.

Three days earlier, Peng realized the number of enemy troops he was facing at the Chosin Reservoir was double that of the original estimate. He decided to concentrate the forces of the Ninth Army on the weakest link of the reservoir defense: Task Force MacLean. Heavy attacks resulted in MacLean's death and the crushing of Task Force Faith. Now Peng owned everything east of the reservoir and could concentrate on the other side—the Marines.

He was not as pleased by his results on the western front. Although his troops had scored substantial victories and the U.S. Eighth Army was in full retreat, the purpose of the campaign—to destroy Walker's main forces—had failed. On the morning of December 2, when the Central Committee of the CPC learned from intelligence that the unpredictable Walker might now set up a new defense with Pyongyang as the epicenter, it ordered Peng to rest all troops on the western front for four or five days "to regroup, and bring up supplies."

Upon resumption of the attack on Walker, they should use new tactics. The Eighth Army should be chased back to Pyongyang by numerous small units. And Peng also ordered the annihilation of the pesky Marines on the eastern front as soon as possible.

4.

By now General Walker had succeeded in withdrawing the bulk of his men to Pyongyang. Three ROK divisions and one American, Keiser's 2nd, had been smashed, and the Turkish Brigade dispersed. Other units, such as the 25th and 1st Cavalry divisions, had suffered heavy losses. With the survivors Walker encircled Pyongyang, but it soon became obvious that he would have to pull back. He asked MacArthur's approval to do so. Receiving no immediate reply, he told his staff, "I will give up any amount of real estate if necessary to prevent this army from being endangered." He ordered withdrawal to the Imjin River, fighting only a delaying action. Highway and railroad bridges and culverts would be blown behind the last troops. The most important was the trestle railroad bridge over the river at Pyongyang. The company surrounding this bridge was commanded by Lieutenant Sam Walker. On December 3, Walker jeeped to his father's van and knocked on the door. "Happy birthday, Dad," he said. General Walker was sixty-one.

The correspondents were prepared to get out of Pyongyang. As Homer Bigart and Tom Lambert, the last to leave, drove around the city before heading for the airfield just before dusk, the streets were empty. It was eerie. At last the two boarded their plane. As the plane flew low, large fires were visible in and around the city where U.S. supply dumps of food and clothing were being put to the torch. On the short trip to Seoul they saw headlights of trucks in great long columns, hauling men south. For Lambert the retreat from Pyongyang was melancholy. "We've been run out," he said.

That day, MacArthur cabled the Joint Chiefs that Almond's entire X Corps was being withdrawn to the east coast as rapidly as possible and that the Eighth Army situation had become critical. "General Walker reports, and I agree with his estimate, that he cannot hold the Pyongyang area and under enemy pressure, when exerted, will unquestionably be forced to withdraw to the Seoul area." He went on to state that his small command was "facing the entire Chinese nation in an undeclared war and unless some positive and immediate action is taken, hope for success cannot be justified and speedy attrition leading to final destruction can reasonably be contemplated." His men, after almost unending combat for five months, were mentally fatigued and physically battered.

After Truman read MacArthur's startling message, he approved an immediate reply by the Joint Chiefs. Men must not be sacrificed. The answer to MacArthur went out: "We consider that the preservation of your forces is now the primary consideration. Consolidation of forces into beachheads is concurred in." Truman then instructed General Collins to fly to Tokyo at once and find out, both there and in Korea, the latest facts. Then he began preparing himself for the arrival of Prime Minister Attlee the next day.

At daylight, December 4, Taplett arrived in Hagaru-ri, after a mean skirmish at a blown-out bridge. It had taken the head of the column sixty-nine hours to cover the fourteen rugged miles from Yudam-ni. Taplett and the rear units needed seventy-nine hours. In the best Marine tradition, they had hauled about 1,500 casualties to safety.

Taplett was astounded to find among ruins a tent city bustling with activity. Twin-engined planes were roaring in and out of a newly constructed airstrip, while overhead huge cargo planes dropped hundreds of colored parachutes carrying rations, fuel, and ammunition. In the daylight all seemed peaceful. There was no sign of the Chinese.

Air evacuation was now in full operation. Big Private First Class
Preston Parks, who had fought with Taplett since August, had managed
to survive the grueling trip despite his wounds. After taking a shot of
penicillin, swallowing a can of chow and getting a few hours' sleep, he
was loaded into a twin-engine plane with bucket seats. The engines
revved so violently that Parks thought the crate would fall apart. Before
long it landed in Japan and he was put in an ambulance and brought
to a hospital. For the first time in months he felt he was out of danger.

Back in Hagaru-ri, Keyes Beech and other correspondents who had
made that village a household name in America were listening to a tall,
rangy man with high cheekbones and almond-shaped eyes address his
officers. Colonel Ray Murray's lean Texas face took on a slightly Mon-
golian look and his words had an unreal quality as he talked of retreat.
Nothing like this, he told his men in wonderment, had ever happened
to the Marines before. "But, gentlemen, we are going out of here. And
we're going out like Marines. We are sticking together and we are taking
our dead and wounded and our equipment. Are there any questions?"
There were none, and the battalion commanders stumped out. As Beech
took off his tall fur hat from Peking, Murray recognized him. "Keyes!
What the hell are you doing here?"

"Damned if I know. I can think of lots of places I'd rather be."

Murray poured bourbon into canteen cups for both of them. Beech
hadn't seen him since the liberation of Seoul; the colonel had aged. His
face was gaunt, the cheekbones more prominent. "You should have been
with us at Yudam," said Murray. "You'd have gotten a story there!"

"I'm damned glad I wasn't," replied Beech, and asked how they
would get out of Hagaru-ri.

"We got out of Yudam, didn't we? If we got out of there we can
get out of here." He confessed he'd thought they wouldn't. "I never told
anybody." As he tried to talk about Yudam-ni, he began to weep. Wiping
the tears from his eyes with his parka sleeve, he tried again. Again he
choked up.

Beech walked into the bright sunlight, where only a few men were
moving over the snow-covered landscape. But he knew there were over
15,000 thousand men inside tents and dugouts trying to keep warm. He
walked to a building that served as an aid station for walking wounded
and frostbite.

"Hi, Beech," said Navy Captain Eugene Hering, the division surgeon. "Okay, son, you can walk out," he told a man with a pair of purplish
feet.

"But, doc! For Christ's sake, look at my feet!"

"You can walk, can't you? Now get out of here."

The Marine looked at the doctor with hurt eyes, then hobbled rapidly away.

"Jesus!" said Hering quietly. "This is the hardest thing I ever had to do in my life. They all want to fly out. Who the hell doesn't? I'd like to fly out myself!" Beech was shocked at the change in a once high-spirited, exuberant man. He was now a husk, his eyes were sunk deep, and the white stubble of beard added to his look of age. "You should have been at Yudam! By God, we brought out our wounded!" He told how men had been strapped across jeep radiators and tied onto towed guns. "Some of them lay there in the cold for as long as seventy-two hours without moving. When we got to Hagaru, the only way you could tell the dead from the living was whether their eyes moved. They were all frozen stiff as boards."

That afternoon General Almond arrived by plane to discuss the breakout plan with General Smith. He presented the Distinguished Service Cross to Smith, Litzenberg, and Murray, and to Lieutenant Colonel Olin Beall, who had personally rescued many GIs of Task Force Faith. The toll of the last few weeks could be seen on Almond's face; and he, like Murray earlier that morning, cried. "I don't know what he was weeping about," remembered Smith. "Whether from the cold or emotion, or what."

It was agreed that the 5th Marines would launch an attack on the hill east of Hagaru-ri, which was infested with Chinese. Then the 7th Marines, reinforced by GIs from the 31st Infantry, would attack towards Koto-ri.

5.

On December 4 the Chinese were boldly moving on the roads and ridges in daylight. Reeves knew help must be far away. He peeked out and watched them loot GI bodies, then pile them in the road behind his truck. After looting and stacking the bodies from his truck, they unzipped Reeves's bag. Holding stiff, he played dead while one searched his pockets. A fist hit his face. The Chicom had felt the warmth of a live body. They beat him, then threw him off the truck. His prayer to God was answered. He at last was on the ground. But he couldn't stand no matter how much the Chinese ordered, kicked and hit. Finally two lifted him by the hair and held him against the tailgate while a third went through his pockets. After pitching him onto the pile of corpses, they picked up their rifles. Reeves said, "Jesus, here I come." They pounded his head with rifle butts. He tried to protect his head with his hands but his broken fingers hurt too much. A Chinese lifted his head by the hair and looked into his face. "Don't blink or breathe," Reeves told himself.

"Just stare up the road." The Chinese let go of his hair. He and the other Chicoms left with their loot.

Reeves crawled from the corpse pile to a tree beside the road, Grasping the tree, he worked himself up to his feet and tried to walk. Three times he fell flat. Sitting against the tree, looking at the far shore of the reservoir, he prayed aloud in anger, "Lord, if the mortar didn't kill me, the shooting didn't kill me, and the beating didn't kill me, you must want me out of here. But I can't walk. How can I get outta here?" An answer came to mind. "You must crawl before you can walk."

He crept on elbows and wounded knees through snow-covered fields toward the reservoir. Chinese on the hills watched but didn't shoot or try to stop him. He crossed railroad tracks and more fields. Smooth hardness under the snow caused him to stop and clear snow away with an elbow. Thick ice! He was on the reservoir. He began to sing. Over and over he repeated, "Yes, Jesus loves me!" By now it was dark. He started crawling across the ice and doggedly kept moving until his strength was almost gone. His elbows and knees kept slipping out, dropping him to the ice. Each time it took longer to force the limbs back into position to crawl. Needing rest, he rolled into a ball with hands under his armpits inside the open jacket. Just starting to doze, he heard the squeak of feet in the snow. He rolled to his back to see, forty feet away, a Chinese with a submachine gun moving cautiously toward him. After all the pain and effort of escape, this Chinese would loose one burst and it would be all over. In disgust he threw out his hands and shouted, "Ahh, no!" The startled Chinese turned and ran away. Reeves watched in amazement till the enemy disappeared into the night. The Chinese had a gun. Ed had no weapons, yet the Chinese had run. Why? Wide awake now, he rolled over and crawled on. Cadence count didn't help him keep moving so he softly sang songs of boyhood faith over and over. "Yes, Jesus loves me, the Bible tells me so," and "Jesus loves the little children, all the children of the world. Red and yellow, black and white, all are precious in his sight . . ." Another mile of ice was covered.

Overwhelming exhaustion and numbing cold kept him from feeling much pain. He willed his limbs to move. They responded, one limb at a time. He didn't know when dawn of December 5 came. He'd covered about three miles and was moving southwest toward the shore. Something green moved in the shore's underbrush. A Chicom wearing GI clothes? If it was a GI, he could help. Reeves called, "Hey, GI, come here!" A wounded GI came out on the ice and walked to him. As he stood looking down at Reeves, three Marine Corsairs made a circling stack above them. The lowest plane dove, flew low past them and fired at the enemy in the rear. Ed shouted for the GI to write HELP in the snow. The GI started writing over the reservoir by dragging a foot. As the planes zipped past, Reeves and the GI waved to get the pilot's attention. A plane roared past, lifted and turned back. With lowered flaps, the plane circled them just above the ice. The pilot was signaling "OK." The three planes dropped low to fly a circle of protection.

A little later a Marine jeep driven by Private First Class Ralph Milton stopped beside them. He and Lieutenant Colonel Olin Beall surveyed the area fearing a trap. They knew that the Chinese would sometimes shove wounded GIs onto the ice, then wait to ambush rescuers. Milton eased the jeep up beside the two wounded men. Colonel Beall climbed out and helped the GI into the jeep, then squatted next to Reeves. "Where do you hurt, son?" he asked.

"Please watch the legs, sir."

Beall picked up Reeves and gently placed him in the jeep. His field pants had come undone in the long crawl so the colonel tucked them under Reeves's feet, then took off his own parka and wrapped it around Reeves. During the ride to an airstrip Reeves saw the colonel's name tag: "Beall." He must remember that name.

The colonel sat on the side of the jeep holding Reeves so he wouldn't fall out of the seat. Ed looked up at Beall's silver-gray hair. A simple thanks wasn't enough to say. He relaxed in the warm feeling of being back with friendly troops, then finally came out with, "Colonel Beall, sir, you sure look like Santa Claus to me."

Reeves wakened when the jeep bounced onto rough earth. Men at a tank roadblock watched them pass. He dozed again till Beall said, "Drive right up to the plane, Ralph." They stopped beside a C-47 that sat with props turning. The colonel gently retrieved his fur parka before Reeves was placed on a stretcher and carried to the plane. As the C-47 vibrated into the air Ed thought, "He answered. Every time I asked God, He answered." The prayers weren't always answered the way he expected, but they'd been answered. The plane leveled. A nurse came and asked if he hurt. She returned with a shot, his first medical treatment since being wounded a week earlier. They landed at Yonpo Field near Hamhung and Reeves's stretcher was carried to an aid tent. While Ed's clothes were cut off and wounds bandaged, Marine Private First Class George Graham, on the next stretcher, fed Ed his first meal in nine days—delicious, hot C-Ration soup. Another shot and onto another plane that gently rocked Reeves to sleep.

He was aroused by terrible pains in his head and feet. "It hurts. Knock it off," he yelled at his stretcher-bearers. They trotted on, bouncing him while the front pair of legs banged against his head and the rear pair hit his feet. A sergeant ran up beside them yelling, "Put him down!" They kept trotting; Reeves kept yelling. The sergeant grabbed the lead man, pulled him to a stop and forced them to lower the stretcher. The sergeant chewed out the bearers. They weren't impressed. He pulled out his .45 automatic and stuck it under the nose of the lead man.

He had their attention. He growled between clenched teeth, "If I ever see you treat a wounded man like that again, I'll blow your brains out."

Lifted gently, Reeves was taken into a tent. He noticed it had a floor. He'd reached a rear area somewhere in Korea. Another shot for pain and he slept. Burning eyes wakened him. "My eyes burn," he told the soft voices nearby. Nurses rinsed medical soap from his eyes and warned him not to move. He was under bright lights with mirrors above. One nurse held back large flaps of scalp while the other scrubbed his skull with a soapy brush.

He felt someone cutting his legs. Looking down he watched the doctor snip out pieces of dark flesh. Digging with long tweezers, the doctor would find a piece of metal, then clunk it into a basin on the floor. Ed had just turned nineteen and two pretty girls were working on his head. Gotta say something impressive, he thought. "Hey, Doc, will you save that shrapnel for me? I'm gonna need some souvenirs when I get outta here." The doctor told the nurses, "This one might make it." Might? Who did the doc think he was to say "might make it," after God had brought him so far? The doctor put the pieces of metal in a small bag and hung it on the stretcher. Reeves went back to sleep while they sewed his scalp together.

A Japanese ambulance driver gave Reeves and the other wounded men a wild drive through town to Tokyo General Army Hospital. Their stretchers were placed in metal racks in a large triage room, then carried into numbered examining rooms. Some came out with blankets over their faces. "They ain't putting me in no dying room," Reeves decided. A doctor took the medical records from under his pillow and flipped back the blankets, leaving him lying there wearing nothing but bandages. "Soldier, were you wounded?" the doctor asked, with pen ready to write. Reeves thought it was the dumbest question he'd heard. Why would he have so many red bandages if he wasn't wounded. Instead of the obvious answer, he replied, "No, sir, I tried to commit suicide and botched the job up."

"Take this man to Room Four," the doctor told two waiting aides.

"You're not putting me in one of your dying rooms! Get me upstairs for treatment or World War Three starts right here."

After checking his clipboard, the doctor sent Reeves upstairs. Whenever he woke and groaned he was given another shot. His food trays sat next to the bed untouched. Who wanted food when you were full of pain and morphine? He woke to doctors in the hall saying a Private Reeves was in the room dying. "Don't waste time on him. There are too many others to be treated." Ed needed to show them he wasn't dying, but how? He'd eat. Dead people don't eat. He called the nurse and demanded food. She was surprised but brought him a full tray. He ate and drank everything on the tray and demanded more food. The nurse ran for the doctor. A lieutenant, a captain and a colonel came in. The captain was the doctor who had told the others not to bother. Now he was drawing blue lines above Reeves's wrists and knees. "Don't cut on me!" exclaimed Ed. The captain asked the colonel if a private could tell a captain he couldn't operate and was assured a private could. The colonel told them to X-ray Reeves's head to see if there was any metal inside the skull. There wasn't, so they moved him to a room with two other "maybes." All were told that if they lived three more days, they'd be put on a plane to the States. They did, and were sent home.

6.

On the day Taplett got to Hagaru-ri, General Collins and a small staff arrived in Tokyo. After a brief meeting with MacArthur, the Collins group took off for Korea to get a firsthand view of the situation. That evening Lieutenant Colonel James H. Polk, one of MacArthur's keenest intelligence officers, was writing his wife:

> The whole of GHQ, and I guess the whole free world by now, has a bad case of the blues. I have been so down in the mouth that I haven't been able to write you for three days; the whole thing is such a psychological turnabout, a few days ago the whole thing was going to end with a great victorious flourish and now no one can see the end of it all, ever. It really is one hell of a note.
>
> The old man, MacA I mean, is really one hell of a gambler as I have told you many times while you were over here. Well, this time he gambled it a little too hard and really pressed his luck a bit too far and the whole house fell in on him. He had every reason to know what might happen and took a chance on staking it all on one big throw, and for once the great MacA's luck ran out on him. He just didn't believe that the whole CCF would be thrown against him. I really admire him in defeat but it sorta looks like the end of an era.

Earlier that day Mao Tse-tung told his subordinates in Peking that the Korean War might be settled quickly, but there was also a possibility the war could be a protracted one. China must be prepared for at least another year of war. When asked about armistice negotiations, he declared these could start only after the United States retreated south of the 38th parallel. At present, the Volunteers should concentrate on annihilating South Korean troops. This would expedite the withdrawal of the Americans. And once the United States agreed to pull out, Mao would accept a UN decision to let all the Korean people elect a single government. But both China and the USSR must participate in the supervision of this election. He warned that the United States was like Chiang Kai-shek in that its promises and agreements were not reliable. China should, therefore, be prepared for deception.

The Indian ambassador, Kavalam Panikkar, had already noticed that the Chinese seemed undisturbed by Truman's recent talk of using the atom bomb. Yet there was increased construction along the city walls of Peking, widely believed to be preparations for underground cells for protection against explosives of all kinds. Propaganda aimed at American aggression also increased, and "Aid Korea to Resist America" became the slogan for increased production, greater national integration, and more rigid control over antigovernment activities. All this, concluded Panikkar, indicated that Truman's atomic threat had become a tool useful to Mao rather than a threat to be feared.

PART VII

ATTACK AND COUNTERATTACK

CHAPTER 25

The Breakout
(December 5–11)

1.

While more correspondents came into Hagaru-ri on December 5, plans were completed for a withdrawal to Koto-ri the following morning. It hardly seemed like a battle area to the newly arrived Maggie Higgins. There were no signs of fighting, but the dire situation was brought to life by a briefing Colonel Murray gave to a dozen of his officers who were standing on a field lashed by hard snow. "At daylight," he told them, "we advance to the rear." While Murray talked, Maggie watched the faces of his officers. Their expressions were of pride deeply hurt. "This is not retreat," he repeated harshly. "This is an assault in another direction. There are more Chinese blocking our path to the sea than there are ahead of us. But we're going to get out of here. Any officer who doesn't think so will kindly go lame and be evacuated." He looked around. "I don't expect any takers."

Maggie spent the rest of the day and night interviewing survivors of the trek from Yudam-ni. The men were in a daze. They were ragged, their faces swollen and bleeding from the icy wind, their mittens torn and raveled. Some had no hats and their ears were blue. Men were walking into the doctor's tent barefoot, since they couldn't get into their frozen snow-pacs. She had not seen Murray since the triumphant days of the Inchon landing. Now he was haggard as he explained to her that the breakout from Yudam-ni had been possible only because of a basic

355

mistake. "If the Chinese had concentrated their troops at the point of exit, we could never have gotten out of the trap. By trying to keep us constantly encircled, they dispersed their strength."

"Do you think they'll make the same mistake again?"

"They've *got* to!"

She went over to men on stretchers waiting to be evacuated. Private First Class Win Scott watched her interviewing several of them and knew she was coming his way. But he didn't feel like talking. She bent down but he said, "Nope, I don't want to talk to you." When she didn't go away, he said, "Go to hell." As she left, he didn't know why he'd said that. He just didn't have anything he wanted to say.

Another enlisted man was also in no mood to talk. When asked how he endured the terrible cold in battle, he refused to answer. "What was the hardest thing you ever had to do?" she persisted. He thought, then grinned. "Get a three-inch prick out of six inches of clothing, lady."

2.

When Mao learned that Walker's Eighth Army was pulling out of Pyongyang and apparently had no intentions of defending it, he ordered Peng to attack at once without waiting for supplies or reinforcements. "If the enemy in Pyongyang has already retreated, then advance toward the 38th parallel."

Peng replied that he was using three divisions to advance southwards and converge on Pyongyang. Once it was taken, he would cross the 38th parallel and attack Seoul. Mao approved.

Chinese troops were soon approaching Pyongyang, met only by civilians waving North Korean flags. By nightfall of December 6, the city was occupied, and except for youths riding in jeeps and trucks and brandishing red flags and shouting, there was no commotion. To the gaunt, exhausted Chinese, the North Koreans looked well fed and relaxed.

The welcome to the capital was not particularly warm, and to overcome the apparent lack of enthusiasm, the Chinese soldiers were given receipts to pay for food and lodging. The amount of the receipt would be deducted from the next food levy imposed on the people by the North Korean government.

3.

In Hagaru-ri, final preparations were made for the 1st Battalion of the 7th Marines to move south at four-thirty A.M., December 6. They would clear the ground to the right of the river while the 2nd Battalion, supported by tanks, served as an advance guard, attacking along the road to Koto-ri. At daybreak the Marine 1st Division Headquarters in Hagaru-ri broke camp, and General Smith was preparing to fly in advance to Koto-ri. The gaps in Colonel Litzenberg's 7th Marines had been bolstered by 300 artillerymen from the 11th Marines, bringing Litzenberg's total strength to 2,200.

The advance guard of the 2nd Battalion of the 7th Marines took off at six-thirty. Within minutes the lead tank was taken under fire by a single bazooka. Twenty minutes later heavy fire from the high ground on the left delayed the advance until late morning. This battalion had been under heavy stress for ten days and its commander, Lieutenant Colonel Randolph Scott Dewey Lockwood, was so weakened by flu and bronchitis that a doctor determined that he was unable to continue in command. With Lockwood out of action, the next senior officer, Major James Lawrence, kept the battalion pushing south.

General Smith was so encouraged by a message from Litzenberg at two P.M. that he took off by helicopter from Hagaru-ri. Within ten minutes he and his aide landed at Koto-ri where the new command post had been opened. As the sun set on December 7, the last elements of the 1st Division train were moving into the Koto-ri defensive perimeter.

General Collins left Eighth Army that morning, reassured by yesterday's visit to I Corps headquarters and the 25th Division CP. Contrary to rumor, he had found no panic at Walker's headquarters. He flew back to Kimpo Airfield where correspondents asked whether the atomic bomb was going to be used as a tactical weapon against the Chinese. "Certainly not, from what I saw yesterday," he replied. Was there a possibility that Walker would be enveloped by the Chinese driving down his flank? "I think the Eighth Army can take care of itself," he said.

He was met by Almond at the airstrip just south of Hungnam. After a briefing and a flight to view the final defensive positions covering the beachhead, they flew over part of the escape route of the 1st Marine Division. Almond felt the Marines would get through without further heavy losses, and all the corps's troops could be evacuated south without great difficulty—if ordered to do so. Collins agreed, and went on to Tokyo, where he conferred with MacArthur and his staff for a thorough review of actions that might be taken in Korea. There were three possibilities. The first two assumed a continuation of all-out attacks by the Chinese; the third was based on a possible Chinese agreement not to advance south of the 38th parallel.

The first option assumed that existing restrictions against Allied bombing north of the Yalu meant no blockade of China, no reinforcements from Chiang Kai-shek, and no substantial reinforcements from the United States until April 1951. MacArthur vigorously protested. That option would be tantamount to surrender.

The second assumed an effective naval blockade of China, bombing of the China mainland, the acceptance of Chiang's Nationalist forces, and tactical use of the atomic bomb if necessary. To MacArthur this was the best solution, but if rejected, he would back the third possibility: if the Chinese agreed not to cross the 38th parallel, the UN should accept an armistice. But the North Korean forces should also remain above the parallel and all their guerrillas in the south should be withdrawn.

In any case, MacArthur added, U.S. troops should be increased to 75,000; and unless substantial reinforcements were sent quickly, the U.S. command should withdraw from Korea. Based on his visits to Walker and Almond, Collins agreed that, if the United States did not fully support MacArthur against the Chinese in Korea, the general should be ordered to prepare plans for evacuation of his troops.

After this meeting, MacArthur sent Almond and Walker new orders: "Current planning calls for a withdrawal in successive positions. Eighth Army will hold the Seoul area for the maximum time possible short of entailing such envelopments as would prevent its withdrawal to the south. Planning further envisions the early withdrawal of X Corps from the Hungnam area and junction with Eighth Army as practicable. At such time, X Corps will pass command to Eighth Army."

MacArthur's sudden reversal would come as welcome news to some of his subordinates, but others felt it was too late. Colonel James Polk wrote his wife on the 6th:

The last few days have been rugged with Joe Collins here and compounded by the fact that everyone is so short tempered and so down in the dumps and pessimistic about the outcome. . . . Honestly this Hq is in a terrible slump when there is plenty, and I mean plenty, to be done. After all, we are soldiers and do what we are told and by God, we better get about it. . . .
Why oh why oh why does MacA put up with some of the people that he does? Why does he keep people around him that will lead him into pitfalls? Why must we spend great gobs of valuable and crucial time feeding peoples' ego and distrusting others' motives and vying for the favor of the most high? Why in hell can't people do the best job they can under the circumstances and to hell with ulterior motives? I am disillusioned from this place and must get out. I simply must for the sake of my integrity and my immortal soul.
Darling, I have to pop off to you, there isn't anyone else. I just have to let go once in a while or blow my stack. All the above sounds like crazy rantings, but it is because I have to talk in generalities and not get down to definite cases because of security. So forgive me if I alarm you terribly by all this. I am

just in one of those wildly rebellious moods that hits me when I know things are being done wrong. And I can't stand it and yet feel so helpless.

4.

By dusk of December 6, the 2nd Battalion of the 7th Marines had advanced only five thousand yards, although losses had been light. Enemy resistance increased with the darkness. As the advance force entered Hell Fire Valley, where Task Force Drysdale had been ambushed, they were stopped at ten P.M. by a single machine gun. But an Army tank finally knocked out the Chinese weapon, and the 2nd Battalion continued half a mile before being temporarily halted by a blown bridge.

The 2nd Battalion pushed on but was slowed by a second blown bridge. To the rear, Division Train #1 was having trouble. Delayed by those ahead, it hadn't left Hagaru-ri until midafternoon, and progress was slow because of persistent Chinese fire. At one-thirty A.M., several trucks were hit by mortar shells and rockets. A little later, while stopping for road repairs, the convoy was again under attack.

Train #2 had not been able to start until after dark and by midnight had advanced only a short distance. The trouble ahead was tying up traffic, and in the emergency *Darkhorse* was again called on to help clear up the mess. Murray ordered Taplett to lead out Division Train #2. *Darkhorse* moved out with two rifle companies and headed up the road through the stalled vehicles. Enemy small-arms fire was coming across the road. It was hairy, but there were no casualties. *Darkhorse* crossed a rebuilt bridge and came to more stalled vehicles.

"I'm going up the road and find out what's holding up the column," Taplett told his S3, then started off with his radio operator. They came upon troops lying on both sides of the road doing nothing. Scattered rifle fire was coming from the north and south. Taplett tried in vain to reach Murray by radio to find out what the problem was, then set out on foot to investigate. He kept asking those in jeeps if they'd seen any 5th Marine headquarters people. Nobody had. After trudging a mile, he came upon an artillery unit.

"What's holding up the column?" he asked.

The 7th Marines had led the way and had apparently gotten through, but then the Chinese had hit the 1st Motor Transport Battalion. A few Chinese were some 150 yards off the road taking potshots at the column while the artillerymen just lay in the ditch without responding.

Taplett could not abide foul-ups. "What the hell's the matter with you?" he asked angrily. "Why don't you return the fire? There's only a few of them out there." He finally found a battery commander. "For God's sake, just fire your artillery piece!"

No one reacted until he encountered Colonel Beall, the middle-aged commander of the motor transport who had rescued Reeves and survivors of Task Force Faith. "What's the trouble?"

They were in an expanse of flat ground with hills on both sides. Beall pointed to shacks down the road. "The road narrows and goes between those two buildings. I'm going to try and run the ambush."

"Don't do anything!" warned Taplett. "Don't send anybody up the road until I come back with my two companies. We'll get the column moving again."

But Beall hustled forward, his two pearl-handled revolvers rising and falling jauntily from his hip holsters. He was obviously eager for action. There was a roar from the rear, and two of Beall's trucks suddenly appeared, following their commander. Before Taplett could stop them, the vehicles rumbled past to run the gauntlet. As they reached the shacks, Chinese dropped grenades into the trucks, killing or wounding those inside.

Taplett swore as he walked back. He found Murray's exec, Joseph Stewart, sitting in a covered jeep. "Joe, do you know what the hell is going on?" Stewart didn't. "Do you know where Ray Murray is?" No. The exec said he hadn't been able to reach him either.

"You tell Ray that I'm going to take G and H companies to the head of the column. We're going to attack down the road."

While rounding up his companies, he saw two more trucks heading towards him. Taplett yelled at them to stop, but they kept racing south. Taplett tried in vain to contact them by radio. Moments later both trucks were also destroyed at the ambush.

Just to the rear, two of Taplett's company commanders, Mize and Williamson, kept passing men huddled in their trucks. Then they came to a group of tanks. "What's going on?" asked Mize. "Why aren't you up there?" Didn't they have ammo? Yes, they had ammo. "Do you have the ability to fire?" Oh, yes. "Well, who the hell is in charge of this outfit?"

An officer came forward. "I am."

"Who the hell are you?" asked Williamson. The officer identified himself. "Why in hell aren't you doing something?"

"Who the hell are you?"

"It doesn't make a damn who we are," said Williamson. "We're in charge. Get those tanks on the road, get them ready to fire, and we'll be back. Tap will tell you what to do sooner or later."

Mize and Williamson went along the stalled column to rout men out of their trucks. Then the two met Taplett and told him what the situation was. He ordered Williamson to make a sweep while he called in air support. "Charlie Mize will leapfrog along the road, giving you flanking fire while you sweep through there and clean that area out."

The plan was perfectly executed, working like a textbook solution. Taplett watched in wonder. It was amazing to see the two companies go to work on the Chinese at the high ground. His Marines were actually pulling enemy out of their holes. He saw one Marine try to yank somebody out. No deal. The Marine reached down again, gave a great heave and, to Taplett's amazement, brought up the smallest Chinese he'd ever seen. Most of the enemy were killed, but a few were captured. These were obviously so cold they were comatose. They didn't appear to give a damn what happened to them.

Taplett finally got in touch with the regiment, told them what had been done, and reported that they were now going to move forward instead of remaining on the flanks. It was obvious, he reported, that the convoy column had been split; he himself would lead the forward column into Koto-ri.

At ten A.M., December 7, there was still a battalion of 5th Marines back in Hagaru-ri—Roise's 2nd Battalion. At last this battalion was ordered to leave the ravaged town, unknown in America a week earlier. Now millions were praying for those making the breakout.

Roise's battalion moved out at noon, followed by thousands of Korean refugees carrying their belongings, fleeing in panic. They had been warned by engineers that bridges would be blown on the trip, but their fear of the Chinese and North Korean officials was far greater than that of danger along the road. Roise's men met only scattered rifle fire all the way to Hell Fire Valley. Here, during a halt, several mortar shells landed. When the last man entered the Marine perimeter at Koto-ri, the epic first stage of the Marine breakout was over.

But trouble lay three and a half miles farther south. The Chinese had blown a crucial bridge just below Funchilin Pass for the third time. There was a sixteen-foot gap (twenty-four-foot, counting the abutments) to be spanned or the Marines would not be able to bring out their vehicles and guns. The bridge could not be bypassed because of the sheer drop down the mountainside. The only solution, it seemed, was to air-drop steel sections at Koto-ri and truck them to the pass. A test-drop had been made in Japan, but the parachutes failed to open. There was no time for another test, and that morning three 2,500-pound bridge sections, flown from Japan, were dropped safely, followed by five more sections at noon. One was damaged and one captured by the Chinese, but six sections were still intact. Only four would be needed to fill the gap. The next problem involved transporting everything to the bridge site by truck.

5.

Peng was not at all concerned about the eastern front where Almond's entire X Corps was in chaotic retreat. He telegraphed Mao that he would like to concentrate his main force on the western front, where the Eighth

Army had set up a line to defend the 38th parallel. He assured Mao he could annihilate many of Walker's troops, but added a warning: "If we go too far south it will increase the difficulties of further advances." He was also concerned about the weather. His troops were faced with a severe winter and needed time to shift their minds from warfare of movement to warfare of attack. "Therefore we intend to stop several dozen kilometers north of the 38th parallel and let the enemy hold that line. This will enable us to destroy the enemy's main forces when fighting resumes next year." He suggested sending a moderate force southward to cut off the enemy retreat "in a strategic sense." Mao approved this modest proposal.

In Washington, General Collins had just arrived from Tokyo and, with the aid of large maps, was showing Truman, almost battalion by battalion, the present position of the UN forces. General Walker, he explained, was convinced he could hold southern Korea, provided he didn't have to defend Seoul. Walker was also confident he could hold a sizable part of Korea indefinitely, using Pusan as his supply port. Collins added that MacArthur shared this confidence, but noted that the situation was still serious in X Corps. Withdrawal had been delayed. Collins had flown over the area where the Marines were fighting and witnessed the first part of their operation. A snowstorm had prevented his seeing the rest of it. He did know that the Marines had not yet started down the precipitous slope from the mountain to the valley. If they got a break in weather to permit air strikes, they had a good chance of getting out safely. But it was still touch and go. He concluded by expressing his personal judgment that, although the military situation in Korea remained serious, it was no longer critical.

6.

A swirling snowstorm slowed the retreat from Koto-ri, and little progress was made for a day. On December 9, the frozen men of Puller's 1st Regiment were cheered by sunlight. David Douglas Duncan, the *Life* photographer, noticed a Marine trying in vain to prod loose with his spoon a single, frost-coated bean from the others in his can. The cold had so cut into his eyes that even the look of animal survival was gone. At last he loosened the bean and slowly raised it to his mouth. Then he stood, unmoving, waiting for it to thaw.

"If I were God and it was Christmas," said Duncan, "what would you ask for?"

After several attempts to form words, the Marine's eyes went up into the graying sky, and he said, "Give me tomorrow."

Nearby two of Colonel Puller's companies were seizing high ground above the destroyed bridge. Lieutenant Colonel John Partridge, in charge of hauling the bridge sections to the pass, was informed his trucks could proceed. Once they reached the high point of the road, they were parked. Partridge and his men walked behind a dozer clearing the snow. There was no trouble until they reached the nose of the hill to the east above the bridge site. Small-arms fire broke out and several mortar rounds landed nearby. The shots were coming from a small observation house on the hill. Infantry soon cleared out the Chinese, and Partridge examined the gap. The abutment on the south side of the road had been blown, adding an additional five feet of damaged surface to the bridge, making a total gap of about twenty-nine feet.

But Partridge wasn't concerned. It would just take a little longer. Work started soon after noon. Some sixty prisoners were used to carry lumber from the trucks and handle the railroad ties. It was a beautiful day with the sun shining brightly and the air dominated by American planes. By three-thirty P.M. the bridge repairs had been completed.

Partridge jeeped to the top of the hill to announce that the division convoys could start. But they were not ready. By the time he returned to the bridge, it was five P.M. and starting to get dark; not until six P.M. did the first element of the convoy arrive. He sat down in one of the battalion jeeps, anticipating the pleasure of a ride down the hill. When no vehicles appeared, he walked back to discover a catastrophe. A tractor trying to cross with one track on the steel treadway and one on the plywood center panel had burst through the wood. Technical Sergeant Wilfred Prosser deftly backed the vehicle out of the wreck, but Partridge was faced with a problem: with the center panel destroyed and with the two steel treadways, each weighing about three tons, positioned as they were, the way was now closed to wheeled vehicles. Disheartened at first, Partridge then recalled from preliminary investigations that a total width of 136 inches would result if the treadways were placed as close together as possible. By manpower and the use of a dozer blade, the treadways were repositioned to give two spare inches for tanks on the treadways and half an inch for jeeps using the inside edges.

Soon the first jeep started across, its tires on both edges. It made it. Then trucks and tanks, guided by engineers with flashlights, followed successfully. The column moved in a series of stops and starts, slowed down by roadblocks and the slippery road, which descended steeply from an elevation of 4,500 feet to the coastal plain.

The column, led by engineer vehicles, was followed by Partridge's group on foot. Partridge heard mortar fire while bypassing the second roadblock. Hand grenades seemed to be going off in the hills. He was concerned about the engineers ahead, but welcome greetings met them as they walked into the lines of Puller's 1st Battalion.

"Don't worry, buddy," said a sergeant. "You're safe. Everything is okay. You've come through it alive."

All through the night the stream of men and troops poured across the span. "The sensation," Partridge reported, "was extremely eerie. There seemed to be a glow over everything. There was no illumination and yet you seemed to see quite well; there was the sound of many artillery pieces being discharged; there was the crunch of many feet and many vehicles on the crisp snow. There were many North Korean refugees on one side of our column and Marines walking on the other side. Every once in a while there would be a baby wailing. There were cattle on the road. Everything added to the general sensation of relief or expected relief."

In Tokyo, Colonel Polk was writing his wife in answer to two letters:

> The home folks are really upset from all that you say and they have a right to be, for this thing has been a real mess these last few days. As I told you earlier, I am extremely upset by the attitude of the Hq as they were so morbid and hopeless that they actually had adopted a "do nothing attitude" where all was going by emotions and nothing from the brain, a very bad state. However, I have the distinct impression that Joe Collins gave them a shot in the arm, and we are beginning to click again and do some smart things for a change.
>
> Almond will soon be under Walker, where he should have been all the time, but we couldn't do that because Walker might be nasty to the big "A" [Almond]. Anyway, Collins rammed it down someone's throat and that lash-up will soon be rectified. And I am not being optimistic when I say that we can give these Chinese one hell of a beating, 'cause we can. . . .
>
> I have often talked to you about how MacA gambles. He takes very long chances. We argued about it quite a bit and I often told you that it was all right with me if he gambled with his troops but I couldn't see him putting a gamble on with my family. Well, when a gambler pulls one off he is hailed as a genius, and when he fails, he is a bum. This time he failed and he has to take the consequences of failure as I see it. But as far as the G2 section of GHQ failing, it just isn't so; he just didn't care to take our advice. We had the dope but old CAW [Willoughby] bowed to the superior wisdom of his beloved boss and didn't fight him as a good staff officer should. But he is getting his lumps. . . .
>
> Baby, don't worry so about the situation over here so much and take the whole weight of the world on your shoulders; it is awful, and the poor old world, and the US in particular, is in a hell of a fix, but a lot of smart men are doing their best at

solving this thing. What you and I need to do is to learn from
it all so that when you and I are in the policy-making position
that the big brass are in now, we will have learned from all this
and won't make the same mistakes all over again. Maybe this is
just a training period for you and me to get us ready to carry
the ball about ten years from now.

That afternoon Chesty Puller was still at Koto-ri with the reconnaissance company, the last group to leave. Across the bumper of his
jeep lay a dead tank commander. Two other bodies were strapped to
the hood and several wounded men huddled in the rear. Sergeant Orville
Jones, Puller's jeep driver, was searching for other bodies.

"Just make sure they're Marines," called Puller. "Take our own
people."

The loaded jeep headed south at three P.M. with Puller walking at
its side. When the column was stalled by some obstruction, Jones noticed
that Puller's boots were freezing; he stripped them off and put Puller
in the jeep. The heater helped bring life back into the colonel, and as
soon as the column started up, Puller was again giving orders. "Whatever
you think of it, don't let the civilians come in on you from the perimeter,"
he said. "If they get close, you'll get hurt."

Despite Jones's protests, Puller walked most of the way down the
mountain, shouting to every passing unit until he was hoarse. "Don't
forget you're 1st Marines! Not all the Communists in hell can overrun
you!"

The next morning, December 11, the Marines of Puller's 1st Battalion
who had held the heights above the bridge finally heard the welcome
words, "Saddle up!" They were to form the rear of the division. When
they left their position, each man was carrying twice his share of equipment. No one wanted the Chinese to get anything. Gordon Greene, an
assistant BARman in Able Company, who was toting two M-1's as well
as machine-gun ammo, turned for a last look. Greene felt good. They
were leaving. The men slipped and skidded, and every so often someone
would take a look behind to see if the Chinese were following. Good-
bye, you sons of bitches! thought Greene. I hope you were worth it.

They reached the road and stopped while everyone had coffee and
gabbed. At last the end of the column arrived, trailed by five tanks, gun
barrels pointing to the rear. Greene and the others marched with the
tanks. There was a feeling of cohesion in the air. Greene's feet felt warm,
and the steady cadence brought him and his comrades back to life. His
original platoon now looked like a squad. They had started with 64 men;
now he counted only 18. If someone had said, "Turn around and go
back north," he would have been ready to go. "I feel that I've gone

through Hell and come through alive," he told himself. "We're the best and probably the luckiest."

As the last Marines reached the valley and safety at one P.M., December 11, they were loaded into trucks. When photographers shouted, "Wave and look happy!" they grinned obligingly. Why not? They were back where there were hot baths and hot meals; they were alive. And the pictures would relieve their folks back home.

Taplett's battalion, *Darkhorse*, was already at Hungnam; and Charlie Mize was writing his wife, telling her for the first time what had happened at the reservoir. "The misery and bravery that I saw, darling, I'll never forget. Neither can I forget the many Marines that were killed. We lost a lot of fine people in getting out. I hope not in vain. We know nothing of the big picture, just that we're going aboard ship to Pusan to reorganize. One thing I know is that only an outstanding Division would have gotten out of the mess the great Mac put us in. . . . Forever, your Charlie."

Mao's troops on both the eastern and western fronts had caused a sensational turn of events. Seventeen days earlier MacArthur had had dreams of taking all of Korea. Now he was in full retreat.

CHAPTER 26

"Your Dad Has Had an Accident"
(December 11–29)

1.

On the day the last Marine reached safety, Peng, the commander of the Chinese Volunteers, who had been touring the western battlefields despite heavy snowstorms, arrived in Pyongyang to learn that the liberation parade had not been as spectacular as promised. Fear of enemy air raids prevented the march that Kim Il-sung had called for. He had to settle for a brief speech from his balcony, followed by a hasty review of North Korean troops at the soccer stadium.

Two days later, December 13, Peng received new instructions from Mao. "If the enemy plans to give up Seoul without a fight, our armies on the western front should stop between Seoul and Pyongyang for a few days to give our exhausted troops the rest they need."

When Colonel General Terenty Shtykov, the Soviet ambassador, learned of this decision, he objected. The Volunteers, he said, should immediately drive into South Korea. Peng refused.

"Such hesitation in fighting a war," protested Shtykov, "has never been seen in the world."

"Chasing a modern army on foot would not be sensible," explained Peng. But he was so disturbed that he radioed Mao at his small quarters adjoining the Forbidden City: "After two victories the mood of quick victory and blind optimism has been growing out of proportion in all aspects. The Soviet ambassador insists the U.S. troops will flee quickly and demands that we move forward quickly. I am convinced that the war will be a protracted one and we should now go forward with calculation."

Mao agreed.

In Washington two days later, Truman told a bipartisan group of senior members of the committees on foreign relations, armed services, and appropriations that he was considering the issuance of a proclamation of national emergency. The great danger in Korea could be met, but speedy and determined action was necessary.

Senator Wherry of Nebraska, an outspoken foe of the president, asked Truman point-blank: "If you want more power, why not ask Congress for it?" Smarting, Truman retorted hotly that he thought everyone knew he was not interested in greater power.

There were other objections, but the majority backed Truman.

On Friday evening, December 15, Truman addressed the nation on radio. America, he said, would "continue to uphold and if necessary, to defend with arms, the principles of the United Nations—the principles of freedom and justice." The next morning, he announced he would issue a national emergency proclamation. "No nation has ever had a greater responsibility than ours at this moment. We must remember that we are the leaders of the free world."

Telegrams and letters flooded into the White House, with few dissenting.

In Peking, Ambassador Panikkar was depressed by Truman's call for mass mobilization. But to his surprise, the Chinese paid little attention to the challenging words. They seemed to enjoy the reaction they were arousing in America. "The strange thing is that neither the Soviets nor the Chinese have taken any public notice of these panicky actions," he wrote in his diary. "They go about their business as if nothing exceptional has happened and this lack of reaction is even more frightening than if they had blustered and threatened. The secrecy of the communist world gives you an uncanny feeling. Here in Peking there is an unnatural calm which is more deadly than all the shouting in America." The announcement in Washington that huge sums would be spent that year on defense did not frighten the Chinese. "The increase in the number of planes and in the weight of bombs seems to leave them cold, perhaps because they know that they have few industries to be destroyed and equally they know that the bombs the Americans may make for a hundred years will not be sufficient to destroy the manpower of China."

2.

By now Walker had withdrawn the bulk of his Eighth Army south of the 38th parallel. Strangely, there was no pursuit by the Chinese. Was it a political decision, he wondered, or were the Volunteers logistically incapable of pursuit? Or were they planning a vast encircling movement? Walker set up a defensive position at the Imjin River, some thirty air miles north of Seoul. It was manned from west to east by the 25th Division, the ROK 1st Division of Whitey Paik, the ROK 6th Division, the 24th Division, and on the right flank nine more ROK divisions.

On paper, the Eighth Army was at full strength and was combat-ready. Supplies from Pusan had replaced lost weapons and vehicles to all units. Ammunition was replenished, and all troops had received winter clothing. Mobile kitchens were providing three hot meals a day. But Walker was concerned. His G2 had told him that about 115,000 Communist Chinese troops were to the north "within one day's march." Some of his staff guessed the enemy would launch a frontal attack, but Walker feared another heavy assault on his right flank. Twice before the Chinese had done this, and both times the ROKs there had collapsed.

Walker was buying time so that Almond's X Corps could evacuate its troops by ship from the port of Hungnam. Since early December, Dr. Hyun Bong-hak, a young Korean civil affairs adviser, had been begging Almond to save the thousands of North Koreans who had been cooperating with the UN forces. If they didn't get out, the Communists would murder them. On the afternoon of December 14, Dr. Hyun was summoned to Almond's office. The area to the south, the general said, was in enemy hands, so evacuation over land was impossible. The only feasible route was by sea from Hungnam. All available ships were needed for the troops, but soon ships would be ready for the 4,000 to 5,000 civilians in Hamhung, ten air miles to the north. They should be brought to Hungnam by train, which would leave Hamhung at midnight.

When Hyun reached the Hamhung railroad station, it was jammed with more than 50,000 people. Sweating despite the freezing weather, MPs tried to control the crowd. Most of the Christians and all of the Korean political leaders boarded the train, but many others who should have been evacuated were left behind. Finally, at two A.M., the train pulled out, arriving at the port city three hours later. Many of those abandoned tried to walk through the rice fields and on mountain roads to Hungnam. More than half were turned back by MPs, but 50,000 civilians did succeed in reaching Hungnam. The refugees encircling Hungnam, from all parts of northeast Korea, swelled to over 100,000. Although Almond gave orders to feed and house them, most had to stay outdoors with no heat, water or cooking facilities.

At last, on December 19, the civilian evacuation began. LST's normally carrying a thousand passengers were jammed with at least five thousand, not counting babies on mothers' backs. As the hours passed, those waiting on the docks grew frantic. They could hear the roar of U.S. guns along the mountain ridges as the enemy drew closer.

Hyun boarded the *Sergeant Andrew Miller* on December 21 and was stricken by the sight of the multitude still waiting on the docks. Three days later the civilian evacuation was complete. When Hyun learned from Colonel Edward Forney how many fellow Koreans had been safely taken out of Hungnam, he was unable to speak. "I will never forget the look on your face when you knew that over 100,000 from your own part of the country had been saved," said Forney. "That look is sufficient thanks."

3.

Mao considered Walker's withdrawal of his troops behind the 38th parallel the end of the Second Campaign. He summarized its results. Although the Volunteers had been short of food and ammunition and the weather bitter cold, the outcome was more satisfactory than expected. The enemy had suffered decisive defeats. Not only had MacArthur failed to seize all of Korea, as promised, but the territory he had captured after Inchon had been retaken.

By mid-December, plans for the Third Campaign were being set up in Peking. Concerned about Walker's defense line along the Imjin River, Peng telegraphed Mao: "In view of the present developments, I believe the policy of advancing cautiously should continue." He feared that the war would be prolonged and difficult. "The enemy has turned from offense to defense, their lines have been shortened and their strength concentrated." The Eighth Army had far superior artillery and enjoyed almost complete air superiority. "Though their morale is weaker, the enemy has a strength of about 260,000 troops. It would be politically disadvantageous to the imperialists if their troops should surrender Korea quickly. Britain and France are not asking the U.S. to do this. But if the imperialists suffer one or two more defeats and lose two or three divisions, they may retreat to some bridgehead like Pusan or Inchon but not pull out of Korea completely. That is why our policy of advancing cautiously should continue." Peng then suggested that, in order to prevent unexpected setbacks, four armies should be concentrated to destroy the strong ROK Capital Division. "If this is successful and the battle develops smoothly, we should then strike at the puppet ROK III Corps. Otherwise we will have to halt the attack."

"Your estimate of the enemy is correct and long-term planning should be undertaken," replied Mao. "The view of quick victory *is* dangerous. The U.S. and U.K. are making use of the old concept of the 38th parallel in people's minds. This is political propaganda, an attempt to lure us into an armistice. It is therefore necessary to cross the 38th parallel, fight another battle, and then rest and consolidate our forces. We are in full accord with your suggestions, since the U.S.-U.K. troops are concentrating in the Seoul area and will be difficult to attack. We should, as you say, find and strike puppet ROK troops. If we can destroy all or most of these puppet troops, the U.S. troops will become isolated and will not be able to remain in Korea too long. The Korean question would be more properly settled if several U.S. divisions could be annihilated."

Walker's G2, James Tarkenton, had some inkling of Peng's plan and was doubtful that the defense line along the Imjin could be held against a frontal attack by an estimated 115,000 Chinese troops. He warned Walker that the Chinese would probably launch a minor thrust at the American units on the left flank while preparing the main assault on ROK units on the far right, a tactic they had so successfully adopted at the Chongchon River. Tarkenton predicted that this major attack would come on Christmas day. If the ROKs collapsed once more, the Chinese Volunteers could break through the American lines and rush into Seoul.

To prevent this, Walker ordered the 2nd Division to back up the ROKs on his right flank. Obviously such a small force wouldn't stop a major assault, but the presence of Americans might encourage the ROKs to fight well enough to prevent another disastrous withdrawal. On December 22, Walker ordered his engineer, Paschal Strong, a veteran of the war in Europe, to blow up every abandoned bridge and culvert on the railways and highways. Strong protested. He didn't have the resources to rebuild if the Eighth Army managed to come back. Shouldn't he just destroy key bridges and a single span of other bridges? The answer was negative. Walker's first job was to do everything possible to delay the Chinese.

The following morning, December 23, after the tactical briefing, General Walker decided to go by jeep to visit the units in the Uijongbu area about fourteen miles north of Seoul. Joe Tyner, Walker's aide, had been informed that the general's son, Sam, had been awarded a second Silver Star and suggested that the general make the presentation during the visit up front.

Tyner stuck the award scroll under the backseat of their jeep to keep it clean, and they set out. It was cold and hazy, the semi-paved road a sheet of ice. Usually Tyner rode behind Walker in a second jeep that always accompanied the first, but today Walker asked him to accompany him in the first jeep so they could talk. Walker was in front next to the driver, Master Sergeant George Belton. The windshield was raised, and the general had a robe tucked tightly around his legs. Tyner sat in the backseat with a machine gunner and had difficulty hearing Walker remark that the Chinese inactivity was merely preparation for a major offensive.

Belton, as usual, was going too fast for Tyner, who had frequently cautioned the general to slow him down. But Walker had gone safely through World War II with Belton and was convinced that nothing would ever happen.

A solid line of trucks and vehicles from the ROK 6th Division was coming south towards them. Suddenly, an ROK weapons-carrier pulled out in an attempt to pass and smashed into the left rear of Walker's vehicle. The jeep swung broadside on the icy road and rolled over. Tyner, the machine gunner and Belton were thrown clear, but Walker was pinned down by his lap robe. The windshield smashed into his skull. As the jeep continued rolling, Tyner went skidding down the ice into a snowbank.

"Give me a hand," he called to the machine gunner and the driver of the second jeep, which had stopped safely nearby. "Take me back to the general." Tyner knelt beside Walker and checked his pulse. No pulse. He checked his retinas. No reaction. The man who had been a father to him for two and half years was dead. A 3/4-ton truck rolled up and Tyner directed soldiers to put Walker in the back and cover him with blankets. They took the general to the nearby 8055th Mobile Army Surgical Hospital (MASH) unit.

Tyner ached all over but didn't realize he had a fracture of his right knee and that a hole had been torn into the back of the leg. At the aid station, Tyner learned the general had been killed instantly.

Lieutenant Sam Walker, unaware he was getting another award, was having lunch when Major General John Coulter, the IX Corps commander, told him, "Your dad has had an accident." Walker rushed to the aid station and went up to Tyner, who was lying on a stretcher. "Sir, what happened?"

Tyner told him, moved by the son's emotionally torn face. The last time young Walker had seen his father, he had warned Belton, "Sergeant, take it easy with Dad on these roads." His father's hero, George Patton, another advocate of speed, had been killed in a similar wreck.

When President Rhee learned of the accident, he was so distraught he ordered the driver of the weapons-carrier executed. Major Jim Hausman protested: "You can't do that, sir!" Moreover, it was Walker's fault for insisting on speed. Because of Hausman's intervention, the death penalty was rescinded, but the driver was sentenced to three years' imprisonment.

Within minutes MacArthur was informed of Walker's death. He immediately telephoned Collins in Washington. Both had already agreed that if anything happened to Walker, he should be succeeded by Matthew Ridgway. Collins telephoned Truman, Marshall and Secretary of the Army Pace. All agreed on Ridgway.

Collins located Ridgway at the home of friends. It was almost midnight, and the party was breaking up. "Matt," said Collins quietly, "I'm sorry to tell you that Johnny Walker has been killed in a jeep accident in Korea. I want you to get your things together and get out there as soon as you can." Across the room Ridgway could see his wife, Penny, looking at him with a question in her eyes. He smiled, shrugged and shook his head. He was determined not to trouble her sleep on their last night together.

The next morning during coffee, with their son, Matty, bouncing happily in his crib nearby, they talked of inconsequential things. Finally he told her of Joe Collins's call. There were no tears or questions, only an agonized, long-drawn-out, "O—h!"

Despite Walker's considerable accomplishments, many welcomed the advent of Ridgway, whose inspirational leadership had helped win the Battle of the Bulge. Some of Walker's enemies in X Corps did not mourn his demise but those who knew him best, such as Tyner and Mike Lynch, were convinced that his understanding of armor and mobile defense had saved the day in the Pusan Perimeter. They also agreed with MacArthur that his skillful withdrawal of Eighth Army in late November and December had been accomplished with such speed that it led to false conclusions by uninformed correspondents who had written that the troops were fleeing in panic. Thanks to Walker's early appreciation of Chinese power, he had managed to save the bulk of his army. Jim Hausman was another who appreciated Walker's performance before and during the Pusan Perimeter, as well as his ability to preserve the Eighth Army after the Chinese assault. Even ordinary leaders could look good during an offensive but it took a great leader to fare well on the defensive. Walker, he thought, was just such a leader.

Walker had saved his Army, but few appreciated the importance of his accomplishments. He never received credit for conducting one of the finest mobile defenses in military history. His successor, General Matthew B. Ridgway, identified one reason Walker never gained recognition. MacArthur, he wrote, hungered for praise and this "led him on some occasions to claim or accept credit for deeds he had not performed, or to disclaim responsibility for mistakes that were clearly his own."

Years later, a British author, Callum MacDonald, came to Walker's defense. "As for Walker, his crime was to be associated with an embarrassing defeat in an army with a cult of winning. It is difficult to believe that any other general could have done any better."

4.

On Christmas day, Almond landed near Pusan with the last evacuees. The operation reminded him of Dunkirk. He had successfully pulled out five South Korean divisions, three U.S. divisions, much of his corps headquarters, along with 100,000 Korean refugees, most of whom, he was convinced, would have been murdered by the Communists.

The Marines were recuperating at the Bean Patch, the Marine brigade bivouac area near Masan. Christmas trees and decorations were provided by the Navy. Headquarters units and the 5th Marines organized choirs. The weather was clear and crisp but not bitter, and the spirit of Christmas prevailed despite the men's exhaustion and their shock at losing so many comrades. General Smith held open house at his headquarters for the division staff and unit commanders. Liquor was plentiful for the officers. The enlisted men were treated to eggnog, sugar cookies and turkey with all the trimmings.

There was little peace, however, for Colonel Taplett. He and other officers of the 3rd Battalion had decided to send someone to Tokyo for liquor to enliven a celebration open to all ranks. An officer named Hap volunteered to go and had returned on Christmas eve with several cases. On the same plane returning to Korea with Hap was the Division G4, Colonel Francis McAlister, who was also bringing back a load of liquor for Division Headquarters.

In the morning Colonel Murray called Taplett and asked where Hap had been.

"Out with his company someplace."

But Murray had learned that Hap had gone to Tokyo for liquor. "He was absent without leave," accused Murray.

"No, he wasn't," retorted Taplett. "I knew where he was."

"Someone could be court-martialed for this," said Murray.

"You can do any goddamn thing you want, Ray, but if it wasn't for this battalion you wouldn't be here today and neither would any of the rest of us. What I did I did with the concurrence of all of my officers and NCOs. I don't see anything wrong in sending Hap over. There wasn't anybody that made any money on it, and nobody made off with a major share of the booze. It was shared by the whole battalion as a Christmas present—and a reward for the job they did up at the reservoir."

The matter was dropped.

5.

Many of those American and British troops captured at the Chosin Reservoir were arriving that Christmas day in Kanggye, a provincial

capital near the Yalu. They were marched eight miles to a camp, where
an officer lectured them on Chairman Mao's "Lenient Policy for Prisoners of War." The speech was ironic after the suffering and brutali-
zation to which they had been subjected on the long march to the north.
The officers were grouped into one squad but interned in the same area
as the enlisted men. Squads of from eight to twelve men were assigned
to a room. Each had a leader who was "progressive"—a man who would
cooperate and at least appear to accept the Communist viewpoint. A
"reactionary" was a prisoner who resisted the indoctrination.

At the first mass meeting, a Chinese indoctrinator assured the prisoners that he was not angry at them for being in Korea. He realized the
Americans and others had been duped by warmongers and Wall Street
imperialists. He assured the men that Chairman Mao had given orders
they should be treated with fairness. However, he warned, wrongdoers
would be publicly criticized and forced to stand at attention for long
periods.

The barn in which they were indoctrinated was decorated with two
Christmas trees, wreaths, candles, red paper bells and a sign: "MERRY
CHRISTMAS." There was also a large placard:

> If it were not for the Wall Street Imperialists
> you would be home with your wives and families
> on this Christmas night.

They were told that the daily routine would be pleasant if adhered
to strictly. They were to rise at seven A.M. and take a short walk or
perform light calisthenics. An hour later a representative of each squad
would draw rations from the kitchen. The food would be a healthy
combination of sorghum seed, bean curd, soya-bean flour, and cracked
corn. For a Christmas treat, they were to receive rice, boiled fatty pork,
candy and peanuts.

Each day, said the indoctrinator, the prisoners would be marched
to the barn for a communal lecture or informal political discussions.
Squad leaders would be responsible for assigned topics on Marxist dia-
lectical materialism.

Father Crosbie and the other noncombatant prisoners were nearby
at Manpo, a city on the Yalu. "The feast of Christmas had come," recalled
Father Crosbie. "We were at pains to appear bright and cheerful and
each one's 'Merry Christmas!' was given out with zest. But most of us, I
think, were sad at heart. There were few in camp who had not lost a
friend in the preceding month, and at such a time we were keenly
conscious of the gulf that separated us from friends at home, now exchanging presents and making merry."

Also in Manpo, the sole prisoner in a Korean house, was the highest ranking POW, General Dean, unable on this festive day to send a Christmas card to his family to let them know that he was still alive.

6.

The man who replaced Walker possessed an aura of determination which had an effect on officers and enlisted men alike. Matt Ridgway spoke quietly, making every word count. That he meant business was instantly understood. "The force that emanated from him was awesome," recalled Walter F. Winton, a fellow paratrooper who had accompanied him to Korea. "It reminded me of Superman. You had the impression he could knock over a building with a single blow, or stare a hole through a wall, if he wanted to. It was a powerful *presence*." In World War II he had proved to be one of the best—if not *the* best—combat corps commanders in the U.S. Army.

Ridgway landed in Tokyo at eleven-thirty Christmas evening. He was escorted to guest headquarters at the American embassy by his good friend Doyle Hickey, another stalwart of the Battle of the Bulge. Before going to sleep, he drafted a message for Hickey to transmit to Eighth Army. It eulogized the very man he had recommended be relieved in the summer of 1950, General Walton Walker.

He was up at seven and breakfasted alone before an open fire. At nine he met MacArthur, who greeted him warmly. He had known the general since his days at West Point as an instructor, when MacArthur was superintendent. Ridgway was still deeply impressed by the force of his personality.

MacArthur urged Ridgway not to underestimate the Chinese. "They constitute a dangerous foe." As Walker had reported, the Chinese avoided roads, using the ridges and hills as avenues of approach. "They attack in depth. Their firepower in the hands of their infantry is used more extensively than our own. The enemy moves and fights at night. The entire Chinese military is in the fight."

After MacArthur had covered all the points Ridgway had intended to ask about, Ridgway asked only one question. "General, if I get over there and find the situation warrants it, do I have your permission to attack?"

To Ridgway's astonishment, MacArthur grinned broadly. "Do what you think best, Matt. The Eighth Army is yours."

Ridgway was relieved to learn that the full responsibilities would be his own. They were the sort of orders, he thought, that put heart into a soldier. At four P.M., he stepped out of his plane in Taegu, poorly clad for the Korean weather. The cold struck to the bone. He was determined to make a personal inspection of his troops so he could determine how quickly they could return to the offensive. But the first task was to assure his ROK allies that America was not going to pull out suddenly and leave them open to wholesale slaughter.

He rose next morning when it was still dark and by dawn was aboard a B-17 Flying Fortress, now christened *Hi Penny!* He was sitting in the bombardier's seat in order to get a clear view of snowbound Korea. "The sight of this terrain," he wrote, "was of little comfort to a soldier commanding a mechanized army. The granite peaks rose to 6,000 feet, the ridges were knife-edged, the slopes steep, and the narrow valleys twisted and turned like snakes. The roads were trails, and the lower hills were covered with scrub oaks and stunted pines, fine cover for a single soldier who knew how to conceal himself. It was guerrilla country, an ideal battleground for the walking Chinese rifleman, but a miserable place for our road-bound troops who rode on wheels." The sight reinforced his determination to shift the Eighth Army from static defense to a limited offensive-defensive. Only then could he get a clear idea of Chinese power and deployment.

At 9:45 A.M. his plane landed at Kimpo Airfield, and he was escorted to Eighth Army advance headquarters in Seoul. The prevailing mood of depression that he found there gave him deep concern. "There was a definite air of nervousness, of gloomy foreboding, of uncertainty, a spirit of apprehension as to what the future held. There was much 'looking over the shoulder,' as the soldiers say."

Before visiting units for a firsthand view, he paid a courtesy call on the president in the company of Ambassador Muccio. Rhee greeted Ridgway rather impassively. The general extended his hand and said heartily, "I'm glad to see you, Mr. President, glad to be here, and I mean to stay."

Rhee's face broke into a warm smile, and his eyes grew moist as he took Ridgway's hand in both of his. He then led Ridgway to his wife; and while they shared a cordial cup of tea, the general did his best to impress the president with American determination not to be driven out of Korea, and assured him that an offensive would be launched as soon as possible.

But before such an offensive began, Ridgway was determined to restore the Eighth Army's fighting spirit. It must have pride in itself, feel confidence in its leadership, and have faith in its mission. He decided to make an immediate tour of the battlefield and talk with field commanders up front, traveling by light plane, helicopter and jeep. The men he met along the road seemed unsure of what they were doing in Korea. "Every command post I visited gave me the same sense of lost confidence and lack of spirit. The leaders, from sergeant on up, seemed unresponsive, reluctant to answer my questions."

Most of the correspondents were impressed by Ridgway's air of confidence, but some ridiculed his warlike appearance: parachute harness with a grenade taped to his right breast and a first-aid kit to the left. This outfit resulted in one of the myths of the Korean War—that he sported two live grenades. The GIs began to call him "Old Iron Tits," but they liked his flamboyance and assertiveness. To Ridgway the single grenade was not a symbol of bravado. Accustomed to being up front, a grenade could be "a very fine weapon" in close quarters.

Whenever Ridgway found leadership sadly lacking, he spoke out. He told field commanders that their infantry ancestors would roll over in their graves if they could see how roadbound this army had become. The Chinese, he told them, traveled light, at night, and knew the terrain far better than the Americans. "Nothing but your love of comfort binds you to the road," he said. They too could go into the hills. "Find the enemy and fix him in position. Find them! Fix them! Fight them! Finish them!"

Back in Washington, Ridgway had been exasperated with the Joint Chiefs' failure to control MacArthur even after they had the backing of Truman. "You must be ruthless with your general officers," he had warned Collins. "Be ruthless with them because everything depends on their leadership." Now, in Korea, he was carrying out his own dictum. When General Almond emerged from his first talk with Ridgway, Colonel William McCaffrey noted that the X Corps commander was a chastened man. It was obvious that he would never fiddle around with Ridgway as he had with Walker.

While Ridgway was building confidence among his troops, the Joint Chiefs, reflecting the general panic in Washington, were seriously considering the abandonment of Korea. On December 29 they cabled MacArthur that all available estimates indicated that the Chinese could drive the UN forces out of Korea if they chose. "It is not practicable to obtain significant additional forces for Korea from other members of the United Nations. We believe that Korea is not the place to fight a major war. Further, we believe that we should not commit our remaining available ground forces to action against Chinese Communist forces in Korea in face of the increased threat of general war." The Joint Chiefs instructed MacArthur to defend successive positions in Korea until the lines were forced back to the Kum River near Taejon. If the Chinese massed large forces at that point, "it then would be necessary . . . to direct you to commence a withdrawal to Japan."

MacArthur was astounded. The message seemed to indicate that the administration's "will to win" in Korea had deteriorated. He himself had never entertained the thought of defeat. If allowed to use his full military might without restrictions, "I could not only save Korea, but also inflict such a destructive blow upon Red China's capacity to wage aggressive war that it would remove her as a further threat to peace in

Asia for generations to come." Late in the evening of December 30, he began writing his reply. Never had Courtney Whitney seen him more distressed. Suppressing the bitterness welling up inside him, he recommended that they blockade the coast of China, destroy—through naval gunfire and air bombardment—China's industrial capacity to wage war, and secure reinforcements from Chiang Kai-shek.

The Joint Chiefs were dismayed and infuriated. Bradley felt certain that this explosive reply had partly come from MacArthur's legendary pride. "The only possible means left to MacArthur to regain his lost pride and military reputation," he recalled, "was to now inflict an overwhelming defeat on those Red Chinese generals who had made a fool of him."

Peng had already issued the final orders for the Third Chinese Campaign. The main assault would come at dusk on the last day of the year from 230,000 Volunteers with the help of 70,000 North Koreans.

On the night of the 29th, Chinese artillery positions were constructed. All guns were emplaced the following night, well camouflaged with branches and snow to blend with the surroundings. At the same time, advance echelons of regimental combat teams and command organizations took up their positions. The main assault would come across the Imjin River and strike directly at Seoul.

Division commanders personally inspected the state of their troops at dawn of December 31. Assured that personnel were taking cover in underground shelters, they ordered all defecation and urination be done in the trenches. Not a single man, horse, rifle or round of ammunition was exposed on that last day of the year, and Peng was confident that complete surprise had been achieved.

CHAPTER 27

The Third Chinese Campaign
(December 31, 1950–January 20, 1951)

1.

At 4:40 P.M., December 31, Peng's artillery began a covering barrage. When the enemy position had been softened up, they fired three rounds of flare shells—the signal to start mine clearing. Each regiment brought up twelve ladders for climbing the banks of the Imjin River. The soldiers of the river-crossing unit had already slit their padded pants so they could roll them up. Each soldier covered his feet with lard and suet to prevent frostbite. They began laying planks, to bridge holes in the ice made by enemy bombardment. These units were followed by shock companies carrying mine-clearing hooks fitted to twenty-foot poles.

At 5:03 the artillery fired five more flare shells, and the barrage was lifted. Light and heavy machine guns opened up as the infantry started across the river in the fading light. Straw strewn over the ice prevented the soldiers from sliding. Soon they were climbing the ladders.

Ridgway had placed the bulk of his defenses in the western and central sections of the peninsula, since he concluded the Chinese had concentrated their main forces just north of Seoul. I Corps held the Imjin River line with the 25th Division, the ROK 1st Division and the British 29th Independent Brigade, while IX Corps held the central sector with the 1st Cavalry Division, the 24th Division, the ROK 6th Division, the British 27th Brigade, and the recently arrived Greek and Philippine battalions. In the east, where Ridgway expected lighter attacks, he had placed ROK units.

Blowing bugles and horns, thousands of shouting Chinese struck along a forty-four-mile front. The hardest blow came against the ROK 1st Division. Ripped apart by the tremendous force, they fell back in the darkness. The ROK 6th Division held in the center for several hours, but long before midnight, desperation spread and three regiments retreated, enabling some Chinese to penetrate between two regiments of the 24th Division and force withdrawal of an entire company.

Just to the right of IX Corps, two regiments of the ROK 2nd Division also broke, but the third, the 17th, stubbornly held, even though six of twelve companies were ground up in the furious melee. Farther east, a strong Chinese force, aided by two recently reorganized North Korean corps, struck at the ROK II Corps, one of whose four divisions was soon overwhelmed.

"Enemy forces blocking our advance or encountered en route should be routed," Peng now ordered. "Complete annihilation is unnecessary. We should avoid 'losing much to gain little' by allowing small skirmishes to block the advance of the main body. Deploy swiftly on encountering enemy interception, assume the initiative, and launch an overwhelming fire against the enemy." Small units were to detour around hills and attack the enemy from the rear. "But the main force is not to deploy prematurely, since troops maneuvering across mountainous areas are not easily controlled. A frontal attack, launched when the enemy shows signs of weakening, will be most effective." Each attack was to go in waves, taking advantage of the enemy's confusion. "And once the enemy is routed, follow up their retreat, allowing them no time to rest."

Throughout most of the desperate night, Ridgway was at his headquarters trying to find out what was happening. He knew the collapse of the ROK 2nd Division endangered both I and IX corps of the American forces. He would probably have to withdraw his troops all the way to the line below Suwon. He was determined to make the Chinese pay for every advance by withdrawing cohesively.

In the morning, Ridgway dispatched a confident New Year's greeting to MacArthur and set off to inspect the situation in a jeep. Soon he ran into men of an ROK division. He was shocked by the panic flight. "I'd never had such an experience before, and I pray to God I never witness such a spectacle again. They were coming down the road in trucks, the men standing, packed so close together in those big carriers that another small boy could not have found space among them. They had abandoned their heavy artillery, their machine guns—all their crew-served weapons. Only a few had kept their rifles. Their only thought was to get away, to put miles between them and the fearful enemy that was at their heels."

Jumping down from the jeep, Ridgway stood in the middle of the road and waved them to halt. The first trucks dodged him without slowing, but he finally stopped a group carrying ROK officers, who listened without comprehending. "I might as well have tried to stop the flow of the Han. I spoke no Korean, and had no interpreter." They refused to obey his gestures, and the procession rolled on. The only solution, he concluded, was to set up roadblocks ahead to stop them.

When he saw American vehicles coming, he managed to halt six of them and ordered MPs to hold them in place. These men were from the 24th Division. He sent an order to General John H. Church to return his men to their units, but it was doubtful the order was carried out, since the entire division was preparing to withdraw.

Ridgway continued interviewing wounded from a battalion of Church's 19th Regiment. He found them "thoroughly dispirited, without the eagerness to rejoin the unit that American fighting men, when not too severely wounded, usually show. We were obviously a long way from building the will to fight that we needed."

Ridgway later skimmed over the front with Mike Lynch, who was now his personal pilot. Like Walker, the new commander insisted on flying dangerously low so he could see firsthand what had to be done. Most of the American units were either pulling back or preparing to do so because of the massive Chinese attack. Upon landing, Ridgway ordered a general withdrawal to the Seoul bridgehead.

Although almost everything was working as Peng planned, Walker's last order on December 22—to send the U.S. 2nd Division to back up the ROKs on the weak right flank—was giving Ridgway time to save the Eighth Army from destruction. By dawn of January 2, he had formed a perimeter around Seoul with ten infantry regiments, supported by several hundred tanks and considerable artillery. Offshore naval guns and close air support were called in. With all this strength, Ridgway might have been able to inflict heavy damage on the Chinese, but Peng's troops had already routed the ROK 2nd Division and threatened to outflank Seoul from the northeast. Since Ridgway had orders from MacArthur not to risk destruction of Eighth Army, he realized he had to make a general withdrawal.

It was also time, he decided, to confront Rhee with the problem of poor ROK performance. Accompanied by Ambassador Muccio, he saw the president. "We aren't going to get anywhere with your army until we get some leadership," he said. He added that unless the ROKs got rid of their incompetents and demonstrated that they had an officers' corps, he would not give them equipment or increase their strength.

He urged the president to come up front with him to put some heart back in his troops. Rhee was eager to go, and they flew to the central front in two unheated canvas-covered cubs. It was close to zero degrees Fahrenheit, and Ridgway almost froze in his heavy winter gear. The aged Rhee, clad only in a white cotton kimono and low shoes, didn't even have a scarf. His wrinkled face seemed to shrivel with the cold, but he didn't utter a word of complaint.

When they landed where MP roadblocks had stopped the retreating ROKs, Rhee addressed them with fiery eloquence. Ridgway couldn't understand a word, but the effect was obvious. As the two men started back to their planes, Rhee placed a hand on Ridgway's arm. "Do not be discouraged," he said. "They will fight again."

From Seoul, Ridgway wrote optimistic messages to both MacArthur and Joe Collins in Washington. To the first he said, "The Eighth Army will continue its present mission of inflicting maximum punishment and delaying in successive positions, maintaining its major forces intact." To the latter, "Everything is going fine. We shall be in for some difficult days, but I am completely confident of the ability of the Eighth Army to accomplish every mission assigned."

The next morning, January 3, Ridgway ordered a controlled withdrawal from the capital. "This retrograde movement," he told the commanders of I and IX corps, "will be executed with all necessary lateral coordination: with maximum losses inflicted on the enemy and with maximum delay consistent with the maintenance intact of major units." To ensure rigid control of traffic over the Han River bridges, he put Bridagier General Charles Palmer, Gay's impressive assistant division commander, in charge. Palmer was to use Ridgway's name to enforce whatever "measures were needed to keep Eighth Army traffic flowing."

Civilian refugees could use the bridges only until three P.M. If they persisted after that time, MPs were to fire warning shots, and then, "as a last resort, use their weapons directly against the offenders." Ridgway meant business.

At midafternoon, Ridgway left his command post to watch the stream of bumper-to-bumper military traffic cross the sagging, swaying bridges. Trucks followed by heavy eight-inch howitzers and tanks were spaced at seventy-five-yard intervals for safety.

"I stood there until dark, watching the pontoons sink and rise again, praying, as I know all of us were praying, that the bridges would hold. But my thoughts did not dwell alone on our own military problems. Off to the right and left of the bridges was being enacted one of the great human tragedies of our time. In a zero wind that seared the face like a blowtorch, hundreds of thousands of Koreans were running, stumbling, falling, as they fled across the ice . . . toward the frozen plain on the southern shore. Some pushed little two-wheeled carts piled high with goods and little children. Others prodded burdened oxen. Now and then an ox would go down, all four legs asprawl, and the river of humanity would break and flow around him, for in this terrible flight no man stopped to help his neighbor."

There was no weeping or wailing. "Without a sound, except the dry whisper of their slippers on the snow, and the deep pant of their hard-drawn breath, they moved in utter silence."

At eight-thirty P.M., a correspondent phoned a story of the evacuation to an agency colleague at Army headquarters south of Seoul. It told of long columns of vehicles jammed with soldiers and moving south over the bridge spanning the frozen Han. There were flames in the city as refugees set fire to their homes and other buildings. The agency submitted the story to Army censors. It was stamped DELAYED, since the release of such news would aid the enemy.

Keyes Beech had flown in from Tokyo that afternoon. With him were Maggie Higgins, Hal Boyle of AP, and Dwight Martin of *Time*. All Americans had been ordered to leave the city, but Beech felt bitterly that abandoning Seoul without a fight was a betrayal of those men who had died to retake it last September. He suggested they spend the night at his favorite hotel, the Chosun, but first they drove in a jeep, commandeered by the resourceful Higgins, through the downtown section. They stood in front of the city hall solemnly watching a building burning across the street. An occasional civilian could be seen silhouetted against the red glow of the flames. Only the crackle of fire and the far-off boom of artillery could be heard. Then close to them came a high, keening wail. A forlorn little boy stood abandoned in front of the city hall steps. What could they do? All over Korea children were crying.

"But we can't just leave him here," said Boyle.

"No," agreed Martin, "we can't just leave him."

They carried the child to the jeep and bundled him in a heavy quilt before continuing to the Chosun. This time there was no warm welcome. Guests and staff had long since left. They climbed upstairs, and went to sleep with the flickering shadows of the burning city on their walls. And the rescued child was safe for at least another day.

Back in his bleak room at Seoul, Ridgway was preparing to leave. He carefully put the picture of Penny and Matty in his briefcase. As he was packing personal belongings in his musette bag, he found the bottom half of an old pair of striped flannel pajamas. The garment was split beyond repair. His orderly affixed it on his office wall. Above it, in large block letters, he wrote

TO THE COMMANDING GENERAL
CHINESE COMMUNIST FORCES
WITH THE COMPLIMENTS OF

THE COMMANDING GENERAL

EIGHTH ARMY

As Ridgway left the room, he took a last look at the pajama bottoms "flapping derisively in the breeze."

2.

Northeast of the city, the 1st Royal Ulster Rifles were desperately trying to hold the line near Chaegunghyon. Private Francis Johnson, a rifleman, had been a policeman before volunteering to go to Korea. The unit had been hard pressed all day and that night they learned the ROKs on their right had bugged out. They were to withdraw.

It was every man for himself. Johnson and two others dashed across a field. They got lost in the dark, and Johnson returned to the road. He saw a Churchill tank and leaped on its back to join half a dozen others. Chinese were on both sides of the road, but the tank plunged through. When a mortar round hit the top of the tank, Johnson was thrown into the ditch with shrapnel wounds in the throat, arm and both legs.

Another tank stopped and two men jumped to the ditch. Johnson was cursing, but his vocal cords were cut, and no sound came out. "Pick me up!" he tried to shout; his rescuers thought he was saying, "Leave me behind. I'll carry on."

They hauled him to the top of the ditch, and the tank rumbled forward. A few minutes later a Chinese stuck a mine lashed to a bamboo pole between the tank treads. In the explosion, Johnson was hit again and thrown back into the ditch.

After a momentary quiet, he heard the Chinese coming towards him. He had to play dead. As they went through his pockets and took everything, he held his breath.

All night he lay as if dead. Occasionally he passed out, but forced himself to revive. Finally came the first light. He was still almost two miles behind enemy lines. He heard movement and figured it was the Chinese. But it turned out to be a comrade wounded in both legs. Another Royal Ulster man joined them. He'd been hit in the shoulder.

A small plane approached and flew low, wings flapping in recognition. The pilot threw out a wrench which landed nearby. The man with the shoulder wound retrieved it. A message was attached. "Make your way south along dry riverbed. Helicopters are on the way."

As the others were trying to pick up the helpless Johnson, they heard a *chop-chop-chop*. A helicopter! It managed to land nearby, and despite firing from the hills, the Yanks carried Johnson into the cabin. American jets swooped down, dropping napalm on the hills as the other two wounded were shoved aboard. The load was heavy, but the helicopter lifted and swung away from the firing. Johnson tapped the pilot on the shoulder and held up a thumb for thanks. He knew he never could have survived if captured. Soon they landed at Kimpo Airfield. The Royal Ulster men were unloaded, and the helicopter whipped off on another mission.

Johnson was brought to a hut. There was no time to put on dressings, since word had come that Kimpo was about to fall. Johnson was given morphine shots, which knocked him out, then rushed to the airstrip. He came to as his plane, under enemy fire, bounced down the runway. He passed out again, and the next he knew, he was in a hospital on an operating table.

Afterward he hurt all over. He'd been hit eleven times.

Early that morning of the 4th, Johnson's countrymen moved into Seoul, with the Chinese and North Koreans in hot pursuit. The city seemed deserted to Julian Tunstall of the Middlesex Regiment. His truck passed the buildings of the new medical school. The beautiful gardens were devastated, but the main part of the university seemed comparatively untouched. "The Capitol," he recalled, "still stood like a gaunt monster dominating the remainder of the city, but was already terribly defaced. Looters had already been hard at work when we came through, as if pledged to squeeze out of the city what little life there was left."

Among the last to leave Seoul, at the request of Rhee, were major Hausman and General Chung Il-kwon. The president told Chung and Hausman to study the mistakes of the first withdrawal from Seoul. Then most of the able-bodied civilians had been overrun by the enemy and were not available as soldiers. This time the civilians had been moved south ahead of the main withdrawal forces, so now there was a pool of men to draw upon. And no enemy tanks would be looking down their throats this time. Yes, they would eventually be back in Seoul.

While the Chinese were approaching the suburbs of Seoul, Ridgway learned from an intelligence report that a major Chinese force had already reached a village on the main road midway between Wonju and Suwon. If successful, this thrust would drive a wedge between Almond's X Corps and Eighth Army. Ridgway, therefore, decided to abandon his defense line immediately. At eight P.M., he ordered I and IX corps to withdraw, stopping temporarily at Suwon so that sixteen trainloads of supplies could be evacuated. Almond was ordered to shift from offense to defense, drawing together his two foremost elements, the 23rd and 38th RCT's.

There was chaos at the railroad yards just south of the Han River. Thousands of refugees were trying to jam into the last train bound southward. It was loaded with ammunition and explosives. Koreans crowded the tops of the box cars and hung from the ladders on the sides. Lieutenant Carroll LeTellier, son of a professor of engineering at the Citadel, had the task of blowing up the trains so the Chinese couldn't use them. LeTellier and his men did their utmost to get the civilians off each train until the last moment and then had to follow orders and set the cars on fire.

By early afternoon the Chinese began surging into Seoul. After raising red flags, they advanced to the Han River. But they needed to regroup before they could cross, and the lull that followed gave those being pursued a false sense of security.

The next day there was a triumphant celebration in Peking. The Volunteers were praised for retaking Seoul, but Peng, the conqueror of the capital, was disgusted. A celebration was premature. He had been forced to stop at the Han. Mines had to be cleared, roads needed repair, food and ammo were in short supply, and the troops were exhausted. He also believed that Ridgway's withdrawal was a trap to entice the Volunteers forward and then encircle them. Peng then revealed that he was again being pressed by Soviet ambassador Shtykov to liberate all of Korea. But he had "firmly refused to do so."

3.

By now North Korean troops were contributing substantially to the offensive with the II and V corps thrusting at Wonju on the central front. On January 8, the ROK units broke, leaving the U.S. 2nd Division exposed. There was a defile through which the 2nd Division main supply route passed. The new commander, Major General Robert McClure, was convinced the only solution was to fall back and cover Wonju with artillery fire. All day long he had been trying in vain to reach Almond. Finally he had to make the decision on his own. In a blinding snowstorm, the division pulled out of Wonju, moving back twelve miles to a position north of the defile so they could set up minefields and booby traps.

When Almond learned of the withdrawal, he was livid. This was direct disobedience of his orders and those of Ridgway. He ordered McClure to retake Wonju at once. McClure, in turn, ordered Colonel Paul Freeman, commander of the 23rd Infantry Regiment, to send a battalion to see if it was possible to recapture Wonju. But by this time the snow was so deep that the recently laid booby traps and mines were covered and couldn't be removed.

Freeman realized the entire division was confused and didn't have its normal teamwork. The artillery was mixed up—their position was far to the rear, and so was their commander. Nevertheless, that night

Freeman got a message to send two battalions to retake Wonju the following day. He would have to do this with men not equipped with real
winter clothing. "The battlefield was grotesque," recalled Freeman, "because the Chinese with their padded uniforms had gotten very damp in
the wet snow and then had just frozen all over the battlefield, so there
were corpses without any sign of an injury or wound." But he knew
there were many more live Chinese ahead of his troops.

That same day Ridgway wrote Collins,

> Again and again I personally instructed both Corps command-
> ers to so conduct their withdrawal as to leave strong forces so
> positioned as to permit powerful counterattacks with armored
> and infantry teams during each daylight period, withdrawing
> those forces about dark as necessary. [These orders had not
> been executed.] *There is a marked absence of [the] vaunted American
> resourcefulness.* We still cling to creature comforts which have to
> be carried by truck. We, therefore, stick to the roads. Our in-
> fantry has largely lost the capabilities of their honored fore-
> fathers in American military annals. . . . Unless you have seen
> this terrain, not only from the air, but from a jeep, it will be
> hard to visualize the difficulty of operations. Yet the other fellow
> manages and he seems never to lack ammunition, the heaviest
> load in his logistics stream, though, of course, he uses impressed
> human carriers and every local form of transportation—oxen,
> camels, ponies and two-wheel carts.
>
> The evil genius behind all this is some type of [E]astern mind
> and whether Russian or Chinese, we shall inevitably find many
> of the same methods applied on major scales, if and when we
> confront the S-1 in battle.
>
> I would say, let's go! Let's wake up the American people, lest
> it be too late!

But in America there was a growing demand for peace, particularly
from parents of sons fighting in this unpopular war.

4.

While leaders in Washington were trying to find a solution to the disaster in Korea, Peng was trying to find a solution to the problem that
his great advances had brought. The enemy's armored units were falling back about thirty kilometers a day, the limit his own troops could
march during the night. Peng guessed that Ridgway was forcing the
Volunteers to attack the UN strong points; then, when the Chinese

were totally exhausted, he would counterattack, simultaneously landing amphibious troops on the west coast to cut off the Volunteers from retreat.

Since entering the war, the Volunteers had fought three exhausting campaigns. For three months they had been ruthlessly bombed from the air and harassed by long-range artillery day and night. It was now the middle of winter, and they were suffering from the bitter cold, completely exhausted and at half strength from casualties. And the lines of supply were stretched to the limit.

Peng's troops needed rest and recuperation to prepare for the Fourth Campaign. They had successfully crossed the Han River and were approaching the 37th parallel. He decided he must withdraw his main force to the 38th parallel, where fortifications could be set up to stop any counteroffensive. Mao agreed and instructed Peng to brief Kim Il-sung on the situation.

The meeting was held at the combined headquarters of the Korean People's Army and the Chinese Volunteers Army. The offensive, began Peng, could not be continued because of the men's exhaustion and unreliable transportation. The Third Campaign, Peng admitted, had not achieved its objective, since Ridgway had managed to withdraw most of his troops safely. Ridgway could lose 70,000 to 80,000 more men before he would be forced to withdraw from Korea. After further discussion, Kim was obliged to accept Peng's assessment.

5.

Despite his disappointment over the withdrawal, Ridgway was by no means despondent. On January 11 he wrote Lieutenant General Wade Haislip, Collins's vice chief of staff, "The power is here. The strength and the means we have—short perhaps of Soviet military intervention. My one overriding problem, dominating all others, is to achieve the spiritual awakening of the latent capabilities of this command." Such optimism was not shared in Washington. The Joint Chiefs had finally answered MacArthur's call for all-out war against China. They cabled him that there was little possibility of sending more ground forces to Korea, nor could a military blockade of China be established. Further, naval and air attacks on China could be authorized only if the Chinese attacked U.S. forces outside of Korea. "Should it become evident that evacuation is essential to avoid severe losses of men and matériel, you will at that time withdraw from Korea to Japan."

This was dismal news to MacArthur. It also put the onus for evacuation on him. He dispatched another passionate plea for all-out war with China.

The issue really boils down to the question whether or not the United States intends to evacuate Korea, and involves a decision of highest national and international importance, far above the competence of a theater commander guided largely by incidents affecting the tactical situation developing upon a very limited field of action. Nor is it a decision which should be left to the initiative of enemy action, which in effect would be the determining criteria [sic] under a reasonable interpretation of your message. My query, therefore, amounts to this: is it the present objective of the United States political policy to maintain a military position in Korea indefinitely, for a limited time, or to minimize losses by the evacuation as soon as it can be accomplished?

General Whitney saw "puzzled exasperation on MacArthur's face" as he dispatched this message to Washington. "How on earth could he put the question any more clearly? Did Washington and the UN intend to stay in Korea or get out?"

The following day, the harried Joint Chiefs drew up a memorandum listing a sixteen-point program that could be put into effect if Korea was evacuated. This study was submitted to Secretary of Defense Marshall and a copy sent to MacArthur.

Official Washington believed almost universally that MacArthur was principally responsible for the critical situation, few realizing that a crucial factor had been Truman and Acheson's miscalculation in believing the war had been started as a Soviet-Chinese plot. These two still believed that China was only a puppet of a regime they distrusted and feared. Apparently Washington had also forgotten that it had authorized MacArthur to cross the 38th parallel. The Joint Chiefs were also far from blameless. They could have restrained MacArthur in his fiery determination to get to the Yalu and, if blocked, wage an all-out war against Red China. No individual in the government could be proud of his role.

The ones who had suffered most since June 1950 were the Korean people and the American troops who had been thrown into the war without proper training or equipment, along with leaders, Walker and Almond, who had faced almost impossible tasks.

MacArthur, who had been cheered throughout the nation as a military genius after the Inchon landing, was now blamed in some newspapers as the man responsible for one of the greatest military defeats in American history. In frustration, MacArthur used provocative words and tactics that threatened to lead to even more serious trouble. Truman was regretting his failure to fire him the previous October. The president sent the general a long, cautiously worded message, prepared principally by the State Department. A successful resistance in Korea, he said, would provide a rallying point around which the free world could be mobilized to meet the Soviet threat. "Our course of action at this time should be such as to consolidate the great majority of the United Nations." These nations would be desperately needed as allies if the Soviet Union moved against America.

Truman's message ended with an optimistic belief that the free world would combine in the defense of freedom, and with a reluctant pat on the general's back: "The entire nation is grateful for your splendid leadership in the difficult struggle in Korea and for the superb performance of your forces under the most difficult circumstances."

Realizing the message was not strong enough to conciliate MacArthur, Truman instructed Generals Collins and Vandenberg to fly to Tokyo for another personal visit.

6.

On January 14, Mao telegraphed Peng that MacArthur now had three options left. "Under pressure from Chinese and Korean troops, the UN forces would withdraw after marginal resistance. The second option would be to resist fiercely in the Pusan area but finally pull out of South Korea. Mao added that there was a third possibility; the Volunteers might be forced to fight a major battle in February. It was decided, therefore, to let the exhausted troops rest for two months before launching their spring offensive in March.

The next day, January 15, Ridgway launched a limited but coordinated counterattack, Operation Wolfhound. At dawn, seven infantry battalions and about 150 tanks, supported by three artillery battalions, attacked the Chinese in the west.

MacArthur explained to the newly arrived Collins and Vandenberg that he had been confused by the directives from Washington. How long and under what conditions was he expected to keep fighting in Korea? He read out the recent personal message Truman had sent. This, he said, removed all doubts as to his responsibilities and missions. He was to remain in Korea indefinitely. Didn't this contradict previous orders?

Collins hurriedly pointed out that the president's message was *not* a directive, then added that, just before he left Washington, Truman had declared that the decision to evacuate Korea should be delayed only as long as it didn't endanger the Eighth Army or the security of Japan. Truman's objective was to give the longest time for political action by the UN. Even if reinforcements were sent to Korea, Collins pointed out, they could not arrive for six weeks. In the meantime, MacArthur's basic mission of defending Japan remained unchanged.

Then Collins and Vandenberg flew to Korea. While the latter in-

spected the air forces, Collins reviewed the ground forces, escorted by
Ridgway. They had fought as equals in the Battle of the Bulge, but now
Collins had four stars, one more than Ridgway.

Both men were concerned at X Corps's predicament. The North
Koreans were apparently pulling out of Wonju; a patrol from the 38th
Infantry had discovered the town almost deserted. Almond told his
visitors that he had ordered the 2nd Division to retake Wonju, but to
pull back if heavily hit.

Ridgway and Collins moved on to IX Corps, where there was a
curious absence of enemy contact. The operations officer proposed a
force equal to that of Operation Wolfhound to retake the key highway
from Suwon to Wonju. Ridgway approved, and then suggested that I
Corps regroup after Operation Wolfhound and support the IX Corps
attack. By the following morning Michaelis's 27th Infantry was converging on Suwon. When other units closing the pincers around this key
town ran into heavy Chinese resistance, Ridgway ordered Michaelis to
break off his attack and pull back. During the day, Vandenberg flew
over enemy lines in the center of the peninsula. It had snowed a few
days earlier, but he saw no signs of life, no footprints, no wheelprints,
no movement whatever. Where were the enemy? Still inspecting on the
ground, Collins was impressed by the air of aggression he found not
only in high places but among the GIs. They were cold, but well fed
and cocky. The next morning he visited ROK troops with President
Rhee, then left with Vandenberg for Tokyo. On the flight, the two
discovered they'd both found renewed spirit in Korea. Contrary to
MacArthur's reports, Ridgway's men were neither tired nor embittered.

"Eighth Army in good shape and improving daily under Ridgway's
leadership," Collins cabled Bradley upon arrival in Tokyo. "Morale very
satisfactory considering conditions. . . . Ridgway confident he can obtain
two to three months' delay before having to initiate evacuation. . . . On
the whole Eighth Army now in position and prepared to punish severely
any mass attack."

As soon as he received this cheering message, Bradley took it to
Marshall, who telephoned Truman. "As the word spread through the
upper levels of government that day," recalled Bradley, "you could almost hear the sighs of relief." And when the Joint Chiefs met in the
afternoon, MacArthur's proposals to blockade and bomb China were
not approved.

MacArthur himself flew to Taegu to see Ridgway on January 20. They
talked briefly, then met with war correspondents. "There has been a lot
of loose talk," said MacArthur, "about the Chinese driving us into the
sea, just as in the early days there was a lot of nonsense about the North
Koreans driving us into the sea. This command intends to maintain a

military position in Korea just as long as the statesmen of the UN decide we should do so."

Without inspecting any units, the general left. The visit baffled Ridgway and others. MacArthur had come over for less than an hour and a half. Why? For the publicity?

CHAPTER 28

"The Old Man Will Get Us Out"
(January 24–February 20)

1.

Ridgway ordered Operation Thunderbolt, an offensive on the west by I and IX corps, to start on January 25. Determined to make a personal reconnaissance along the twenty-mile front, he took off on the eve of kickoff in a slow trainer. "For two hours we flew over that lonely, empty land, skimming the ridge tops, ducking into the valleys, circling over the little dead ridges." Despite the risks, they flew low, as usual. "Over all this snowy land, which covered our entire battle front, we saw no sign of life or movement." In one village at the head of a valley, they noticed a thin line of cart tracks. "It was clear that here, in this village, the enemy was taking shelter against the bitter cold by night, moving out before sun-up to hide in the woods; for with our bomber aircraft hunting targets like hungry hawks hunting mice, a village was no safe place by day."

At his headquarters, Ridgway reviewed what he had seen. He was now sure that he was not sending the Eighth Army into a death trap. In the morning his two corps—backed by close air support, massive artillery and heavy naval gunfire—advanced to the north. Tom Dolvin's 89th Tank Battalion, veterans since the Pusan Perimeter, had pushed up to the walls of Suwon by nightfall. After his harrowing experience north of Pyongyang in November, Dolvin expected a night attack. It began at two A.M., when a Chinese patrol crept through the wall so quietly and got so close that Dolvin's men had to use pistols and machine guns at point-blank range. He quickly moved the tanks back to a point from which they could fire. The Chinese chased the tanks, trying in vain to throw satchel charges on them. Soon firefights broke out. One lieutenant ran out of his CP in time to see two Chinese approaching with rifles. He waved his pistol, and surprisingly, they surrendered. Once in the CP, one Chinese tried to pull a grenade, but a guard hit him over the head with his rifle butt.

At daylight, Dolvin pushed ahead and, together with the infantry of the 35th Regiment, took the city, a key barrier to Seoul. Ridgway flew up to Suwon with Mike Lynch to examine the rubble. The advance continued relentlessly.

Two days later, MacArthur, who had recently turned seventy-one, landed at Suwon Airfield. As Ridgway greeted him, a British correspondent heard MacArthur say, "This is exactly where I came in seven months ago to start this crusade. The stake we fight for now, however, is more than Korea—it is a free Asia."

Ridgway hid his displeasure at the visit, which lasted less than two hours. "It had served no purpose except to get photographs of MacArthur with victorious troops; and it could have warned the Chinese that a large-scale offensive was just beginning."

Ridgway's fears were realized that night when the 7th Cavalry, struck hard by a strong Chinese attack, was forced to lose ground. The next night the Greek battalion on Hill 381 was hit by another Chinese regiment. Fierce fighting raged all night, but the Greeks managed to hold the strategic hill. An estimated 800 Chinese were killed, and Ridgway noted that "the blood which covered the hillside was mute evidence of the terrific struggle." Obviously the Chinese were prepared to put up stiff resistance; but Ridgway carried out his offensive as planned, and the slow advance on the west continued. To support this drive, Almond was to block a possible Chinese attack southeast down the Han River Valley.

During the night of January 29, a Chinese force occupied two strategic railway tunnels west of Wonju. Colonel Paul Freeman was sent with his 23rd Infantry Regiment to destroy the enemy at the Twin Tunnels, then occupy the high ground so that the road to Suwon could be defended. It was a tough assignment because of the speed required, the lack of transportation and the limited space for shuttling foot troops along the narrow, slippery mountain road. But the professional Freeman was ready to get into action. Late the next afternoon his forces assembled, and artillery was positioned to support the initial phase of the attack. At first light, the approach march began, with the French battalion assigned to him in advance-guard formation. Tanks, flak wagons and combat vehicles moved on the narrow, rough road that led to the high ridges west of the Twin Tunnels. The 3rd Battalion went up a streambed to

the hills east of the target. In coordination, the two forces began climbing
and ridge-running over the treacherous, snow-covered hills. Many of
the men had left behind rations so they could load up with cartridges
and grenades. But nobody had come without heavy coats and blankets.
Late in the afternoon, the objective area was outflanked by the two
battalions and Freeman directed them to converge. But no enemy! Freeman ordered the men to occupy the tunnels; next day they would find
and destroy the enemy. Not pleased with their hasty defenses and overextended position, the two battalions settled down for a night of uneasy
vigilance. It was an eerie place in the dark, but Freeman's men were
confident he would not lead them into a cul-de-sac. Despite his flares of
temper and insistence on perfection, most of them revered the crusty
Freeman. They also liked his spirit. He was a fighter and had shown his
combativeness. His exec, Frank Meszar, found him brusque at times but
considered this more of a facade. "He was a kind, gentle, caring person,
a brilliant commander, while still being a true gentleman."

During the night, Freeman had the embarrassing task of repri-
manding the commander of the French battalion, Lieutenant Colonel
Ralph Montclar. Wounded thirteen times in two previous wars and
plagued by perpetual hiccups, the fifty-nine-year-old Montclar (a *nom de
guerre*) arrived at his post after his men had already started small fires
to keep warm. When Freeman noticed them, he called the French CP.
"Tell your men to get those fires out!" he demanded.

"Yes, yes," Montclar replied. "In the morning I will tell them."

"Tell 'em now!" ordered the annoyed Freeman.

"But, *mon colonel*, they are such little fires."

"Big fires or little fires, get 'em out, damn it, and do it now! You've
already given away your positions to every Red within a hundred miles!"

There was a pause. "Ah, *mon colonel*," replied Montclar brightly. "It
is as you say, without doubt. But if they know where we are, they will
attack us. Then we will kill them."

Freeman hung up without retort, but within an hour all the French
fires had been extinguished.

At four-thirty the next morning, February 1, Freeman reported that
a long column of Chinese had courageously marched up to a roadblock
between a French company and his L Company, in the face of fire from
two armored vehicles. Many were felled, but they deployed on each side
of the road and began attacking the armored vehicles with bazookas and
grenades. One flak wagon, partially disabled by bazookas, limped back
to report.

Up front, firing was now pouring onto the east of the road against
L Company. Forward observers for artillery and mortar called in defensive fire, and soon the early-morning darkness was weirdly illumi-

nated by mortar shells and grenades. The impact so stunned the Chinese that they hastily pulled back to reorganize.

The attack resumed at six A.M., this time concentrating on the French company holding Hill 453, which dominated the area. Despite being blasted by heavy artillery and mortar fire, which took a terrific toll, wave after wave of Chinese continued to surge forward.

With little opportunity for armor in the restricted space, Freeman moved his tanks back several thousand yards to be used as artillery. To his relief, the French were still holding out against great odds. They were now engaged in hand-to-hand fighting, and when it looked as if they would be overrun, their commander ordered a counterattack with bayonets. With victory almost within Chinese grasp—a victory which would have jeopardized Freeman's entire force—the desperate French charge so frightened the Chinese, who had probably never seen such a bayonet attack, that they fell back.

The morning haze grew to a dark overcast, and the defenders could not hope for air support. But the French charge had turned the battle; although fighting continued throughout the day, the Chinese never launched another serious charge up that hill. Instead they concentrated on the weak point in the valley north of Hill 453 between two other French companies. Time and again waves of Chinese reached a group of destroyed houses within Freeman's perimeter. There the nucleus of defenders from the French heavy weapons company beat them back.

Fortunately, a section of Freeman's tank company arrived later that morning with nine vehicles. A platoon was placed in the hot-spot valley to thwart a breakthrough. The attack was now redeveloped against the 3rd Battalion on the east, with I Company absorbing most of the punishment. Like the French on Hill 453, they repulsed wave after wave, stacking up dead like cordwood in front of their position.

Toward noon the attacks against the French and 3rd Battalion intensified. The French 3rd Company was finally driven from its position, leaving L Company's left flank exposed. The Chinese, sweeping to the top of the ridge, directed murderous machine-gun fire into the interior of Freeman's position, blasting the aid station, the CP and vehicles. The French repeatedly tried to regain the height but were pushed back with heavy losses. Now the entire perimeter was furiously engaged. Freeman didn't have a single man to send the hard-pressed French.

In this desperate situation, he put into position two tanks and a twin-40 flak wagon, "the sweetest weapon possible for vacumn-cleaning a ridge." He ordered all available mortars and artillery to concentrate on the hill. By this time, the French enlisted men had replaced their helmets with kepis, and their officers had tied red scarves around their heads. With fixed bayonets they started running up the hill shouting

"*Camerone!*" the war cry of the French Foreign Legion defending a Mexican village of that name. There the Legionnaires had stood to the last man, and these troops were ready to do the same.

Just as Chinese victory was in sight, again the enemy turned and ran, pursued by the French and mortar fire. When the French reached the top of the hill, hundreds of enemy dead were piled there.

But the Chinese were not giving up. At two P.M. they pushed the French 2nd Company from its position. On the other side of the hill, I Company was in bad shape. One platoon had only twelve men. They had been fighting with grenades and bayonets for what seemed an eternity in their attempt to hang onto the razor-backed ridge; yet the Chinese had regained the high ground between I and L companies and again began pouring fire into the center of Freeman's perimeter. Furious fighting continued on Hill 453. Ammunition was running low as casualties mounted. At three o'clock Freeman feared the center of both battalions might cave in. He had already designated an inner perimeter to defend the east tunnel, if necessary. But that would be a last stand. "The crisis had arrived," he reported later. "Then, just like a Hollywood battle, the sun broke through!"

Fighter planes, waiting on nearby strips, could now sweep over the bloody battleground. Freeman watched four Marine Corsairs streak through the first hole in the clouds. On the ground, the Tactical Air Control Party directed the Corsairs to the Chinese attacking I Company. Friendly and enemy forces were so closely engaged that the planes had to circle four times to sort them out. Then they climbed for the dive. They started down, dropping daisy-cutters—five-hundred-pound bombs—right in the middle of the closely packed Chinese, then climbed and came in again, this time with "gook-goosers," as the GIs called rockets, and firing .50-calibers at the disintegrating enemy.

What beautiful air support! thought Freeman. The next flight concentrated on the destruction of the Chinese in front of the French position. The mass of enemy on the bare ridge went down "like prairie grass in a wind storm." After a total of twenty-four flights, what was left of the enemy tried to escape; but Freeman's tanks dashed up the road to cut them off. AAA vehicles with four .50-caliber machine guns, affectionately nicknamed "meat choppers" by the infantry, were rushed to vantage positions to mow down the frustrated Chinese. Spotter planes followed the fighters, giving the artillery eyes for the first time that day. The Chinese were caught behind their concealing hills and torn to pieces.

GIs and French now came charging out of their holes, shouting and shooting the stragglers. Thirteen hundred enemy bodies were counted in or near the perimeter, and total enemy casualties were estimated at 3,600. The Chinese 125th Division had probably been eliminated as an effective unit by Freeman, a master of tactics.

*   *   *

The Chinese high command took the defeat near Wonju and Suwon so seriously that the Army Political Propaganda Department issued a pamphlet on February 3. "What is the aim of the devilish tricks the American imperialists are plotting? Just at the time we were preparing to rest and regroup, the enemy started another attack." Why? Because the Americans had suffered such catastrophic defeats they needed a victory to bolster their fallen prestige. That was why MacArthur staged the all-out counterattack. "They occupied Suwon and Wonju, attacking us from two directions. It is a new conspiracy." The new conspiracy must be destroyed. "In the fourth phase of the war . . . we have confidence in victory, because we greatly outnumber the enemy and we have gained good experience in annihilating the enemy during the last three victorious phases of war." The next offensive would be easier, since they wouldn't have to break through strongly built fortifications. "Instead, we can freely practice our turning encirclement tactics so dreaded by the enemy. . . . In recompense for their desperate efforts to regain face we now have the best chance to further degrade the names of Truman, Acheson and MacArthur. . . . Let enemy continue to sacrifice their lives. . . . In the end they will save their lives instead of trying to save face."

2.

The UN prisoners of war at Kanggye were still undergoing the Chinese indoctrination course, with lectures day after day. They had been informed that the most "progressive" would be taken south of the front lines and released.

The Chinese selected a committee of prisoners and ordered them to write an appeal for universal peace that everyone would sign. A GI staff sergeant named Harrison drafted a document he felt would satisfy the Chinese yet not provide them with propaganda. It was turned down, as were four other drafts. Finally, the chief interpreter wrote a version. The committee refused to sign it but, after threats, agreed to do so if the other prisoners were exempt. The Chinese agreed, and the members scrawled illegible signatures or misspelled their names.

The failure of this program led to other strictures. The prisoners were forbidden to use the term "POW" and had to call themselves "newly liberated friends." The virtues of communism were expounded, even in informal conversations. Religion was denounced as a capitalist device for controlling people's minds, yet prisoners were allowed to keep Bibles and religious articles, and were even permitted to hold religious discussions and readings.

Although there was some military interrogation, more time was spent uncovering the prisoners' personal histories. The interrogators seemed to be satisfied only with answers that served their doctrinal purpose. When the prisoners were challenged about the income and social status of their parents, for example, and were persuaded to lower these figures, the Chinese were pleased and accepted the revised answers.

3.

The 137,000 North Korean prisoners of the UN were also being treated miserably. By early December, all of them were jammed into transit camps near Pusan. Men like Major Ju, who had surrendered to join democracy, were treated as harshly as those who were dedicated Communists. "Let's all fight for justice and for our true fatherland," Ju had first told fellow prisoners. But now he had almost given up hope.

Ju was housed in a special tent with some 500 North Korean majors and colonels. When rumors swept through the camps that the Chinese Communists had joined in the war, the Reds organized a League of Liberation. Major Park Ki-cheol, who also had come to democracy only to be abused, suggested they organize an anti-Communist group to fight for survival.

But Ju disagreed. "The world would laugh to see Red dogs fighting White dogs." Ju suggested they ask only to be separated from the Communists. When released, they could then fight against Kim Il-sung.

Their position seemed hopeless until the end of January, when the highest ranking North Korean prisoner arrived at their camp. Senior Colonel Lee Hak-ku was greeted as a hero by half of the officers and jeered as "Number One Traitor!" by the others. Even so he was asked to represent the entire camp as senior officer. He refused.

The next day the North Korean officers nominated Colonel Lee as representative and elected him by acclamation. To Ju's amazement, he swore he would once more be loyal to the invincible hero, Kim Il-sung. "If I repeat my mistake you may court-martial me."

A week later, on February 1, they were all transferred to Koje-do, a large island near Masan, just off the southern coast. Four enclosures, each subdivided into eight compounds, had been hastily erected. Each compound was intended to hold 1,200 men, but already the compounds on Koje were jammed with five times their capacity.

By the time Major Ju's group arrived, frantic improvisations were being made to house, guard and care for the inmates.

Space was at a premium, complicating the job controlling the crowded camp. Since only barbed wire separated the compounds, there was free communication among the civilian and POW internees. Koje was an ideal breeding ground for conspiracy and revolt.

The newly arrived North Korean officers soon took over, inciting the other prisoners to demand more humane treatment and better food and clothing. The American compound commander responded by demanding unconditional obedience to all camp rules. Colonel Lee protested in vain; but when the other NK officers insisted they all go on a hunger strike, he objected to such a drastic step. He was overridden, however, and the next morning the compound commander was handed a strike resolution.

For several days, the Red officers incited the prisoners to a frenzy of resistance, and on the morning of the strike not a single man touched his food. The compound commander was furious and announced that the POWs could eat rice or bullets. Instead of sending a representative to the front gate to negotiate, the officers encouraged the men to shout insults. At the height of the uproar, one prisoner flung a rock at the compound commander, who reached for his pistol and fired two shots. Moments later, heavy fire erupted from machine guns. Two prisoners were killed and at least three wounded; the compound commander had quickly brought the mob under control. To Major Ju's disgust, the POWs clustered around rice buckets eagerly extending their bowls. What a wretched, stupid bunch! he thought. They should have been holding a solemn memorial service for their dead comrades, not going crazy for a bowl of rice!

4.

By the beginning of February, the mood of depression in Washington was lifted by Ridgway's slow but steady progress north and by Freeman's unexpected victory on the central front at the Twin Tunnels. Optimism ended on February 11, when three Chinese divisions hit the ROK 8th Division only ten air miles north of Wonju in daylight. Taken completely by surprise, its three regiments were soon surrounded near Hoengsong. More than 7,000 men and most of the division's equipment were lost. The debacle also endangered supporting artillery and infantry units of the ROK 7th Division.

Unaware of the disaster, MacArthur was cabling Washington a bold new plan. First he would "clear the enemy rear all across the top of North Korea by massive air attacks." Next, "if I were still not permitted to attack the massed enemy reinforcements across the Yalu, or to destroy its bridges, I would sever Korea from Manchuria by laying a field of radioactive wastes—the by-products of atomic manufacture—across all the major lines of enemy supply. Then I would make simultaneous amphibious and airborne landings at the upper end of both coasts of North Korea, and close a gigantic trap. The Chinese would soon starve or surrender." The Joint Chiefs did not seriously consider this fantastic proposal. Out of the question, they replied.

* * *

Once Ridgway learned of the catastrophe at Hoengsong, he ordered the 38th Infantry and the 187th Airborne RCT to set up a strong defense at Wonju with as much artillery as could be found. If Chinese pressure was too great, they were to withdraw southeast and join up with the ROK 7th Division.

He ordered Freeman's seasoned 23rd Infantry to make a stand at Chipyong, some six air miles west of Wonju. It would be supported by the Commonwealth Brigade, now in IX Corps reserve. The outspoken Freeman was not pleased to learn he had to defend Chipyong. When Almond flew into his perimeter by helicopter at noon on February 12, Freeman recommended falling back to Yogu at once. Almond agreed, but Ridgway was convinced that Chipyong was the key to stopping the Chinese advance. It had to be held.

That night, Freeman gathered his unit commanders and told them they were probably being surrounded. "We'll stay here and fight it out," he said. The Commonwealth Brigade was on its way to help, as was the 5th Cav. When Freeman assured his commanders they were in a good defense position, they believed him. Not having enough troops to outpost the hills surrounding Chipyong, Freeman had set up a tight rectangular perimeter around the village. His three battalions, plus the doughty French battalion and the 1st Ranger Company, were supported by fourteen tanks, AA vehicles, heavy mortars, eighteen howitzers and six 155's. In the past few days, Freeman had managed to stockpile more ammunition than he'd ever had before in Korea. He was ready. And his men were confident despite the knowledge that they were almost surrounded. "Hell, the Old Man brought us here, and he'll get us out," was the consensus.

At ten P.M., a lookout reported figures in the rice paddies in front of G Company. Enemy rifle fire erupted, but Freeman's well-trained troops could not be lured into shooting at noises in the dark; they patiently waited until the attackers stumbled into the trip flares and booby traps in front of their lines. Since every piece of critical terrain outside the perimeter had been pinpointed, an artillery and mortar barrage descended on the Chinese. They withdrew in confusion but some came back only to be blasted again by a barrage. The stubborn Chinese tried again and again. The light of 155-mm illuminating shells made them perfect targets for the machine guns.

By midnight the entire perimeter was engaged, as the Chinese kept probing for a weak point. But defensive fire was terrific, and the attackers could never break through. There was a lull until two A.M. when the Chinese launched a platoon-sized attack against the French battalion just to the right of the machine-gun outpost. To the accompaniment of bugles and whistles, the Chinese, with fixed bayonets, ran screaming towards the French.

A hand siren was sounded and one squad dashed towards the Chinese, yelling and heaving grenades. The two forces were running headlong towards each other. When they were twenty yards apart, the Chinese suddenly turned and raced to the rear. The attack was over after one furious minute.

Dawn, February 14, revealed that only three Chinese had reached the front line. One was killed and the other two captured. The others had withdrawn behind the hills to the west and east. Almost all the buildings inside the U.S. perimeter were roofless, but the heavy tiles of the walls had saved most of Freeman's men. The tents were riddled with bullets.

Soon after first light, a mortar round exploded near Freeman's CP. He was sitting on the ground in his tent. In front of the next tent stood his S3, Harold Shoemaker, who was killed instantly by fragments. Another fragment shattered a bottle of whiskey, then struck Freeman's left calf. It was a jagged, painful wound, but Freeman hastily wrapped a rag around it and limped off to inspect the area. An hour earlier word had come that the roads to the south were cut and there was no escape route. It had been a rough night, but Freeman had committed no reserves, and his principal problems were ammo replenishment and the evacuation of some 200 wounded.

Division headquarters reported that the situation at Hoengsong was desperate and that Wonju itself was endangered. To the south of Wonju, infantry units were hard-pressed, but there was some good news for the surrounded 23rd. An armored column of the 5th Cav had crossed the Han and was making its way towards them up the west road. The British Commonwealth Brigade was also fighting its way up the east road, the 23rd's main supply route. Hang on, said division, and later, upon receiving word of Freeman's wound, called again. A plane would be sent up to evacuate him. "I brought them in here," Freeman replied brusquely. "And I'll take them out."

The troops were in good spirits and it was a quiet day. The artillerymen dug deeper holes and personnel trenches around the howitzers. Hot meals were served.

To the extreme annoyance of Freeman, a light plane landed on the nearby airstrip with Colonel Jack Chiles, Almond's G3. He had come to relieve Freeman but his plane was damaged on landing and Freeman returned to the task of preparing for the night attacks that were sure to come. Railroad ties and bags of rice found in the village were used to make revetments, aid stations, CPs, fire-direction centers, and supply dumps. Limping around energetically, he supervised distribution of ammunition and ordered routes reconnoitered by the reserve commanders so they could lead their units to any point in the coming darkness. He also sent out patrols to provide early warning of any daylight attack. The 23rd RCT was ready for the next move by the Chinese.

This time, the Chinese Volunteers had a plan. Officers of the 119th, 125th, and 126th divisions realized they had underestimated the enemy, expecting UN troops to flee after the first attacks, just as they had at Hoengsong. The stand of the 23rd had affected the battle plan of the whole area. Chinese unit commanders had thought the enemy had merely constructed fieldworks, whereas Freeman had astutely set up key points of defense—bunkers, wire entanglements, booby traps and trip flares. In addition, the Chinese strikes had not come from a centralized command, and regiments of the same division failed to coordinate their movements. Not only had the Volunteers failed to destroy the enemy, but they had also made a grievous mistake by withdrawing their main force in a disorderly manner. The new Chinese plan was to open up at dark with a heavy concentration of mortar and artillery fire. The firing continued for an hour, but Freeman's defense preparations kept the casualties low. Then came the unsettling sound of bugles and whistles.

The men of G Company waited tensely in their foxholes. One platoon was dug in on top of a small hill. At the bottom of the hill the Chinese began attacking a machine-gun position. Flares burst in front of G Company while tracers lit up the artillery position.

Time and again the Chinese hit G Company, only to be thrown back. Then came a savage assault at about ten P.M. Lieutenant Paul McGee, a platoon leader, looked down to see Chinese creeping out of the dry creekbed and starting up the hill towards his squad leader's hole. One tossed three grenades before McGee killed him with a BAR. The weapon was jamming every tenth round, and he was trying to extract the case with a knife but dropped it. When he couldn't find the knife in the dark, he grabbed a carbine and aimed at a Chinese ten feet away. McGee fired four times. The Chinese was dead, and so were three others in nearby holes.

McGee sent his runner for help. He soon returned, leading fifteen artillerymen up the hill. Then firing broke out. A mortar round killed one artilleryman and wounded another. The others retreated until stopped by the commander of G Company, Lieutenant Thomas Heath, at the bottom of the hill. He led them back up, but near the top, they turned and fled again. Shouting angrily, Heath charged after them and managed to grab several men. "Goddamn it!" he screamed, "Get back up on that hill! You'll die down here anyway. You might as well go up on the hill and die there." He kept yelling and yanking at the men and finally set up a line of resistance. A ferocious hand-to-hand struggle went on for three hours, with the Chinese battling for each foxhole. Heath was now using supporting fire from his own light mortars, H Company's 81-mm weapons, and some from the regimental heavy mortar company. But he could not stop the enemy from seizing the saddle. Three times he tried in vain to retake the lost ground with hesitant artillerymen. Still determined, he went back for reinforcements. He organized a group and roared, "We're going up that goddamn hill or bust!"

But the Chinese, gnawing away persistently at the hill, advanced relentlessly, foxhole by foxhole, until they reached the top. From an elevation they began firing into the bowl-shaped area on the positions of the artillery and mortars. By three A.M. G Company had lost the entire hill, and Freeman was forced to withdraw his armored vehicles at the roadblock, as well as those men to the left of the French position. During the confusion, the Chinese broke into the artillery perimeter. Part of B Battery abandoned its guns, falling back to the field-artillery position. The artillery commander rallied his men into making repeated attempts to drive out the enemy, but this was impossible, since G Company's hill was now in Chinese hands.

At dawn Freeman's exhausted troops expected the Chinese to withdraw as usual. Instead, they kept attacking all around the perimeter. Freeman had only 230 rounds of 81-mm and 4.2-inch mortar ammunition remaining. At eight, the situation was so grave he had to commit the regimental reserve, B Company, to help restore G Company's position. Several times B Company retook the hill but could not hold it.

Nevertheless, the Chinese were driven from ground gained during the night. Artillery—using direct fire, recoilless weapons, tanks and twin-40's—blasted the Chinese off the bare ridges. Once the haze had cleared, friendly fighter planes came in and worked the ridges over methodically. Unable to take such punishment, the Chinese withdrew from all points except G Company's hill. This was defended stubbornly by Volunteers determined to fight to the last man. Disdaining cover, they kept firing their rifles and machine guns at the attacking planes.

That morning, George Stewart, the 2nd Division assistant commander, radioed Freeman urging him to leave. Freeman protested vehemently. To be relieved from command while his regiment was in combat? That was the worst disgrace an officer could suffer. But Stewart insisted. The 5th Cav, he said, would soon arrive from the east. The battle of Chipyong was over. No one could possibly question his performance. He'd undoubtedly be decorated and promoted. Reluctantly, Freeman agreed and turned over his command to Chiles. He was taken by helicopter to a MASH unit at Chungju. Here he met Ridgway, who, after congratulating him, gave him the impression that he would be permitted to return to action in Korea after a brief R and R in the States.

Then Ridgway flew over the advancing 5th Cavalry armored column. It seemed to be making good progress towards Chipyong, and he radioed congratulations to its leader, Colonel Marcel Crombez. The cavalry arrived just as B Company finally fought its way to the top of G Company's hill. The die-hard enemy seemed to be faltering. Then B Company heard firing in the rear. The lead tanks of the 5th Cavalry came into view around the bend as the men on the hill waved and cheered. It was another Hollywood finish for Freeman's RCT.

The crusty colonel wrote a farewell letter to his troops: "Officers and men, I want to say to you that there is no grander fighting regiment in all the world than the 23rd RCT. . . . God bless you all."

On February 18, Ridgway received a report from IX Corps on the western front. The Chinese were pulling out of the terrain south of the Han River. The 5th Infantry Regiment had found 600 enemy dead in their foxholes along with abandoned weapons and cooking equipment. Ridgway passed the news to his other two corps commanders but cautioned them that "it might be a ruse." Later in the day, however, came another report of a mass withdrawal of Chinese and North Korean troops from Almond's central front. It was not a ruse. The Chinese and North Koreans were pulling back.

That evening, Ridgway met with his staff in the operations tent of advance Eighth Army headquarters. Intelligence sources, he said, had confirmed the Chinese withdrawal. To everyone's surprise, he announced they were going to counterattack the Chinese on the central front in three days. It would be called Operation Killer.

Later, standing before a floodlit relief map, Ridgway outlined his plans to correspondents in Taegu. "He spoke with a quiet eloquence which few military men, other than MacArthur, can equal," reported Rutherford Poats of UP. "What he had to say reflected a deep insight into the psychology of his own troops and of the enemy. What he had already done in helping Eighth Army regain faith in itself recommended him for a place in the select company of the great."

On the morning of the 20th, MacArthur flew to Korea to check the new offensive. He went over strategy with Ridgway, who emphasized that the situation had developed as a result of the heavy assault on Almond's front. The Eighth Army's strong counterattacks against the flanks of that dangerous penetration would have to wait until the Chinese attack was completely checked. "I told him," Ridgway wrote in his memo for record, "I was at the same time having my staff examine the possibility of a two-division attack north across the Han to cut the forces now attacking X Corps. General MacArthur expressed agreement, adding that I should hold strongly the line of the Han. I said I intended to do that."

MacArthur flew on to Wonju. "I am entirely satisfied with the situation at the front where the enemy has suffered a tactical reverse of immeasurable proportions," he told correspondents. "His losses have been among the bloodiest of modern times. . . . Our strategic plan—notwithstanding the enemy's great numerical superiority—is indeed working well and I have just directed a resumption of the initiative by our forces."

This statement made it appear as if Operation Killer had been MacArthur's idea, not Ridgway's. MacArthur clearly implied that he had flown in from Tokyo, discussed the situation with subordinates, and then ordered Ridgway to attack. Ridgway was not only surprised but amazed. His vanity had taken an unexpected roughing-up, but what struck him most forcibly was the "unwelcome reminder of a MacArthur that I had known but had almost forgotten." The Supreme Commander of the Allied Powers had to keep his public image always glowing.

CHAPTER 29

Ridgway in Action
(Late February–April 5)

1.

In mid-February, Peng was summoned to Peking to explain what had gone wrong with the Third Campaign and the first part of the Fourth. "I do not think we can win a quick victory," he told Mao.

"We'll take a quick victory if that is possible," replied the chairman. "But if we can't, we will take our time, think carefully, and win." He studied Peng's reports for several days, then concluded: "We must be prepared to fight in Korea for at least two more years." Obviously the Americans were planning a war of attrition. "Only about two thirds of our supplies are reaching the front because of UN bombing." In order to fight a protracted war, therefore, it was decided that Chinese troops would fight in Korea on a rotating basis.

A large contingent of fresh troops had already crossed the Yalu to support the spring offensive planned for April. Even more would follow soon. The first contingent had already suffered appalling losses. Mao's estimate of supplies reaching the front was far off the mark and in some units seventy-five percent of the men had died of starvation or bombings during the march to the front.

The day after Chin Hai-yon, a young farmer in the 32nd Division, crossed the Yalu, his unit was suddenly lit by flares from the sky. Napalm bombs fell "like raindrops" and many were burned alive. It was a horrible sight. Hundreds of comrades lay together in their own ashes. Survivors

408

rushed to nearby woods, where they hid until dark. Then they marched again, eating lightly of the rations each man toted in a long socklike container. Their few horses were packed with heavy weapons, but machine guns had to be dismantled and carried by the men.

Trudging over the snow-covered mountains was arduous and dangerous; every so often someone slipped and fell off a ledge. The long march to the front lines took from two to six weeks, depending on the load each man carried. Rations were gone after a week or so, and they had to eat whatever they could find. During the daytime, American planes bombed anything that moved so the troops stayed hidden. At night they lit no fires. But even these precautions did not prevent numerous casualties.

On the way south, they met many wounded coming from the front. Those too weak to move begged to be shot. Most of the men, like Chin, could not bear to kill a comrade, but the commissars were quick to comply. They also examined men on stretchers; those considered too maimed to recover and fight again were killed. Chin was horrified by this brutality, since he had fought with Chiang Kai-shek in the civil war until captured by the Reds. In that war, all Kuomintang casualties had been brought out, no matter how badly wounded.

Although Chin had gloves and a blanket, the cold nights were miserable. In the daytime, the troops usually just squatted, sometimes taking a nap. By the time they reached the front line, only 40 were left in Chin's company of 250.

Wei Tzu-liang had run a salt store before enrolling in the People's Liberation Army. His twelve-man heavy-machine-gun squad crossed the Yalu with the XII Corps. Their weapon, Russian-made, had a spare barrel, which Wei carried. Only a third of his squad ever reached the front.

Tzo Peng, a farmer's son, also had served in the Kuomintang. By the end of his unit's march, his heavy-machine-gun squad had only one rifle. They had been given fried flour and biscuits, which were supposed to last until they reached the front, but after a week there was nothing to eat. What distressed Tzo most was the sight of so many dead and wounded along the trail. When those still alive begged for help or food, he could do nothing. Almost every day enemy planes flew over the advancing soldiers, broadcasting pleas in Chinese to surrender, promising that they would be well fed and treated decently. Tzo talked secretly to two comrades about the broadcasts. They agreed to go over to freedom at the first opportunity.

2.

Operation Killer had not lived up to its name, and Ridgway, with MacArthur's approval, devised a new operation, Operation Ripper, designed to take the UN forces all the way to the 38th parallel. Concerned that MacArthur might appear in Korea on the eve of D-Day and again tip off the Chinese, Ridgway took direct action and sent the general a telex that few subordinates would have dared to dispatch. It started with fulsome tact: "Look forward with deepest pride and pleasure to your visits. Each brings so much of inspiration." Then he politely requested MacArthur not to come on D-Day.

> Not knowing reasons for your selection of date of visit, believe you would want to consider possibility of enemy deduction. He knows, as does all the world, of your fearless personal gallantry. He no doubt is fully aware that your intrepidity and tactical acumen reveal to you in advance where each crisis of battle will occur and take you there in person for that phase of action. . . . If this reasoning seems valid to you, would not your visit on D plus one or even later annul the value of his deductions, while still probably permitting you the opportunity of witnessing more tactical action than is likely to occur on D? You know, sir, your wishes are my only guide but I thought it possible this view may not have had your consideration. Faithfully."

Hoping this would delay MacArthur, Ridgway held an unprecedented press conference on the morning of March 6 to prevent another MacArthur statement that it was he who had personally ordered a resumption of the initiative. At the same time, Ridgway was careful to praise the general for the freedom of action and support he had given the Eighth Army.

The 25th Division would make the first attack, its objective the seizure of a nine-mile front across the Han east of Seoul. Operation Ripper began at two-thirty the next morning, March 7, with a heavy barrage, thousands of rounds landing on the north bank in an awesome display of firepower. An hour and a half later, the 24th Regiment began crossing, covered by fire from tanks of the 89th Tank Battalion and half-tracks of the 21st AAA (Antiaircraft Artillery) Battalion. First across in assault boats were E and F companies. Meeting little opposition—thanks to the previous barrage—they moved forward against small-arms fire.

John Groth, a combat artist-correspondent, was with an infantry company waiting its turn to cross. In the past few weeks he had interviewed Greeks, Turks, Australians and Canadians. Now he would have the chance to see his countrymen in action.

He felt like an orphan as he squatted next to a terrified GI who said, "My legs just won't move."

A mortar round landed near a row of tanks. "You've got company, bud," said Groth.

"What should I do, sir?" appealed the GI.

Groth remembered Henry Fleming in *The Red Badge of Courage*, who had first fled, then thought what his buddies would say about his loss of nerve. He told this story to the young soldier.

"The rest of your outfit is out there," he said. "If you don't go, they'll know you weren't with them. When night comes, you'll have to face them."

"Thanks a lot, sir," said the soldier and ran toward a boat.

Groth had intended to wait on the south bank until the other side was secured. Now responsible for sending the scared soldier across into danger, Groth sprinted to the edge of the river, where a group of soaked, shivering men, whose boat had capsized, were waiting to be evacuated. Groth asked a calm engineer of the 77th Combat Engineers Company, the black unit formerly commanded by Lieutenant Charles Bussey but now commanded by Lieutenant David Carlisle, if he could catch a ride across.

"You're damned right. I'm here to see that no one is left on this beach. Get in."

At midstream, a shell splashed fountains of water on Groth, who was already wet from frantic paddling. At last the men in the boat scrambled ashore and began climbing a steep hill. The soldier ahead jumped into an enemy foxhole, then popped out as if he had bounced on a trampoline. Groth peered into the hole and saw a decapitated corpse. Other enemy bodies, still smoldering from napalm, were scattered everywhere.

It was not like Normandy, where Americans and Germans alike had lain among scattered bits of letters, rations, cigarette packages, snapshots. Here all Groth saw were an occasional rice bowl, a pair of sandals, leaflets used as toilet paper. Groth fell into step with a lieutenant leading a platoon. They moved silently down the bank and along the river, where they met return traffic—wounded men on litters. A mortar round burst nearby, hitting two men. Groth saw one in the bushes, his legs scissoring in the air. The other GI grabbed his own right leg. "I've been hit!" he moaned.

Corpsmen crawled to the man in the bushes. Blood bubbled from his lips. The corpsmen girded infantry jackets around the wounded man, and Groth took off his trench coat and jacket for additional cover, then

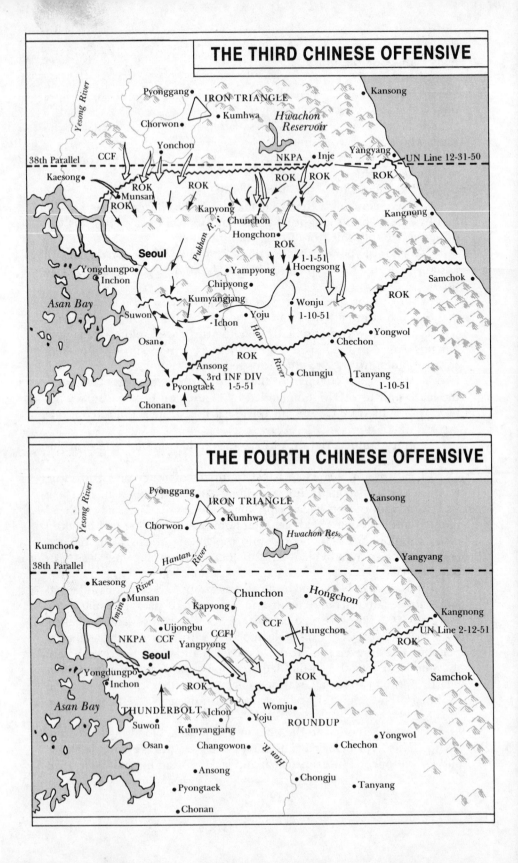

THE THIRD CHINESE OFFENSIVE

Yesong River
Pyonggang
IRON TRIANGLE
Kumhwa
Hwachon Reservoir
Kansong
Chorwon
Yonchon
38th Parallel
CCF
NKPA
Inje
Yangyang
UN Line 12-31-50
Kaesong
ROK
Munsan
ROK
ROK
ROK
ROK
ROK
Kapyong
Chunchon
Pukhan R.
Kangnong
Seoul
Hongchon
ROK
Yongdungpo
Inchon
Yampyong
1-1-51
Hoengsong
Samchok
Asan Bay
Chipyong
Kumyangjang
Suwon
Ichon
Yoju
Wonju
1-10-51
ROK
Osan
Han
River
Chechon
Yongwol
ROK
Ansong
3rd INF DIV
1-5-51
Chungju
Tanyang
1-10-51
Pyongtaek
Chonan

THE FOURTH CHINESE OFFENSIVE

Yesong River
Pyonggang
IRON TRIANGLE
Kumhwa
Chorwon
Hwachon Res.
Kansong
Kumchon
Hantan River
38th Parallel
Yangyang
Kaesong
Imjin River
Chunchon
Hongchon
Munsan
Kapyong
Kangnong
Uijongbu
CCF
CCF
Hungchon
UN Line 2-12-51
NKPA
CCF
Yangpyong
ROK
ROK
Seoul
Yongdungpo
Inchon
ROK
Womju
Samchok
Asan Bay
THUNDERBOLT
Ichon
Yoju
Suwon
Kumyangjang
ROUNDUP
Osan
Changowon
Yongwol
Han R.
Chechon
Ansong
Chongju
Tanyang
Pyongtaek
Chonan

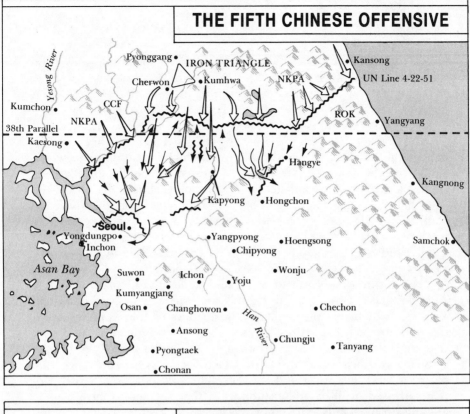

THE FIFTH CHINESE OFFENSIVE

Yesong River

Pyonggang
IRON TRIANGLE
Kansong
UN Line 4-22-51
Cherwon
Kumhwa
NKPA
Kumchon
CCF
ROK
Yangyang
NKPA
38th Parallel
Kaesong
Hangye
Kangnong
Kapyong
Hongchon
Seoul
Yangpyong
Samchok
Yongdungpo
Hoengsong
Inchon
Chipyong
Asan Bay
Suwon
Ichon
Wonju
Yoju
Kumyangjang
Osan
Changhowon
Chechon
Han River
Ansong
Chungju
Tanyang
Pyongtaek
Chonan

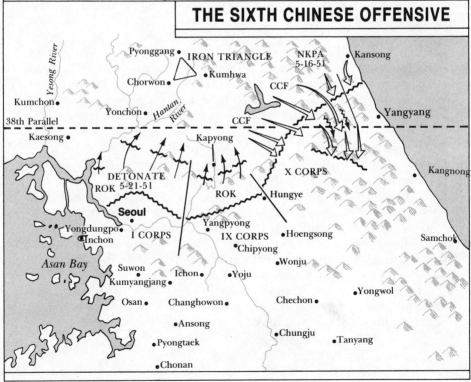

THE SIXTH CHINESE OFFENSIVE

Yesong River

Pyonggang
IRON TRIANGLE
NKPA
5-16-51
Kansong
Chorwon
Kumhwa
CCF
Kumchon
Yonchon
Hantan River
CCF
Yangyang
38th Parallel
Kaesong
Kapyong
X CORPS
Kangnong
DETONATE
ROK 5-21-51
ROK
Hungye
Seoul
Yongdungpo
Yangpyong
Hoengsong
Inchon
I CORPS
IX CORPS
Chipyong
Samchok
Asan Bay
Suwon
Wonju
Kumyangjang
Ichon
Yoju
Osan
Changhowon
Chechon
Yongwol
Ansong
Chungju
Tanyang
Pyongtaek
Chonan

talked with the second boy, who lay on his stomach in the snow. The soldier identified himself: Private Joe Henderson, Harrisburg, Arkansas.

The platoon was ready to proceed to its next objective. "Do you mind taking Private Henderson to the beach?" the lieutenant asked Groth. Groth agreed readily. He'd seen enough.

Supporting Henderson, Groth served as crutch on the slow trip back to the river. They were loaded into a duck (an amphibious truck) along with the dying man from the bushes. After Henderson's leg was treated at the battalion aid station, Groth helped him walk toward the jeep that would evacuate him. They passed a pile of bloody, discarded blankets and clothing. On top were Groth's trench coat and jacket. The soldier they had covered was dead. At the jeep Groth and Henderson shook hands and said good-bye. Then Groth, realizing how cold he was, went back to the bloody pile to retrieve his clothing.

He crossed the river again to make sketches on the battlefield. Only an occasional enemy shell fell. He followed the embankment to a small town, recently taken. Inside one of the abandoned houses he found an incongruous pair of pictures—a chromo of the Virgin and Child next to a portrait of Mao. Just beyond the town, he met an ROK private escorting two prisoners. Mistaking Groth for an American officer, he hastily turned them over and took off. The prisoners were North Koreans dressed in filthy quilted uniforms. One seemed to have trouble holding up his hands. The other was bleeding, his fingernails hanging by bits of cuticle.

Groth drew his .45 from its holster, the first time he had ever done so. He felt like the Lone Ranger. Motioning the prisoners to the road, he started walking them to the rear. He suddenly saw that he had *three* prisoners, not two. The third was a grim-looking, barefoot Chinese in rags. Where had he joined them? Apparently he had been hiding and decided to be Groth's prisoner because the artist was small and looked unmartial.

After watching the first crossings of the Han, Ridgway joined the commander of the 25th Division at his CP near the river. Word had come that MacArthur would be arriving later in the morning at Suwon. Expecting as much, Ridgway left in a light plane to meet the general, but once aloft he told Lynch, his pilot, to fly across the Han. He wanted a firsthand look at the operation. Spotting a landing place on the dry, gravel flood plain of the river, Lynch set down and the general walked among the men of the 25th Division who were leading the attack. All was going well, and they took off for Suwon.

Here Ridgway met MacArthur, who said, "If you succeed in the objectives you set on this operation, you will have done all that is humanly possible with the forces you have."

Ridgway admitted that he'd held a press conference the previous day, and had informed them about Operation Ripper. He added, tactfully, that he'd told the correspondents that never in his experience had he been more completely supported by his chief. This seemed to please MacArthur. "Don't let them give you the slightest concern," he added. "Matt, you do what you think is right every time, and never anything just because you think I may want it done. If you do that and make mistakes, I will back you one hundred percent."

MacArthur spent hours touring the 1st Cavalry Division. Upon returning to Suwon he held a press conference that he must have known would cause a storm in Washington. Exuding confidence, he said there were indications that a massive Chinese attack was coming in the spring. "Even under our existing conditions of restraint it should be clearly evident to the Communist foe now committed against us that they cannot hope to impose their will on Korea by force." The Communists had failed twice already. "Vital decisions have yet to be made—decisions far beyond the scope of the authority vested in me as the military commander, decisions which are neither solely political nor solely military, but which must provide on the highest international levels an answer to the obscurities which now becloud the unsolved problems raised by Red China's undeclared war in Korea."

Rutherford Poats and the other correspondents were stunned at the effect his words could have on the morale of the Eighth Army troops. Poats reported, "in effect he was telling the troops they were being called upon to ['die for a tie'] because their government had no policy except to muddle through. MacArthur's remarks, of course, were aimed at readers far from Korea."

They were aimed not only at Washington but at Peking. Since MacArthur's derogatory but challenging words about China had come just as the administration was trying to bring Mao to the negotiating table, Acheson was furious. While Washington was discussing this matter with their allies, trying to work out something, "these blasts come out of Korea, frightening everybody to death, showing that the commanding general is utterly out of sympathy with what the allies know to be the discussions they are having with officials of the United States, and stirring up popular opinion of the United States to be hostile to what the government is considering."

Two days later, as Operation Ripper relentlessly pushed north, MacArthur again pressed his campaign to gain a freer hand. When Hugh Baillie of UP asked about future strategy, MacArthur replied, "The problem involved requires much more fundamental decisions than are within my authority or responsibility to make as the military commander, decisions which must not ignore the heavy cost in Allied blood which a protracted and indecisive campaign would entail." In effect, he was demanding all-out war against China.

3.

As the battle raged along a fifty-mile front, an event of alarming potentialities was developing in the Tokyo office of Brigadier General Crawford F. Sams, MacArthur's public health and welfare chief. Several weeks earlier, a behind-the-lines agent near Wonsan, on the east coast of North Korea, radioed that enemy soldiers were dying of a disease characterized by high fever, backache, headache and running sores. General Sams feared this could be a new form of the plague, which was endemic in Manchuria. If the Chinese had brought this disease with them, it could wipe out UN troops who were not immunized against it. Sams reported to MacArthur that the plague could assume the pneumonic form and spread rapidly and broadly, like influenza. There was almost one hundred percent mortality from the Black Death, a third form of the disease, and the matter was as critical as any military operation.

Sams had canvassed all medical personnel in the theater for anyone familiar with the plague, without positive results, nor were there any medical agents in North Korea. The forty-eight-year-old Sams concluded that he must go to the area to determine whether or not there really was a plague. He had seen such an epidemic in Egypt and therefore knew the disease; moreover, he was familiar with the Wonsan area. He appealed to friends in Army Special Operations and the Navy to arrange for him to be put ashore, alone or with a small group, so that he might give MacArthur a clear yes or no.

The overall mission was assigned to a Navy lieutenant, Eugene Clark, who had spent two weeks spying at Inchon and who, also, was familiar with the Wonsan area. To Clark it was just another job; he didn't see anything difficult about it, but was very concerned indeed about the plague.

"Don't worry, Lieutenant," said Sams. "I'll give you and anyone else you have going a shot for the plague; however, you should know that it takes a series of three shots at spaced intervals, and we don't have time for them."

"Well, if you'll take the chance, so will I."

Clark suggested pointedly that Sams shave off his mustache and assume the rank of a sergeant since the North Koreans probably had a picture of him. Sams good-naturedly agreed. He didn't want to be another General Dean.

They set off for Pusan with Youn Joung, the young Korean who had been with Clark at Inchon. Sams had kept this mission secret from his own staff and got fake orders for a routine visit to the Eighth Army. At Pusan the group boarded the epidemic-control ship *LCIL 1091*, which contained the necessary laboratory equipment to diagnose smears from running sores and blood cultures.

On the morning of March 8, the ship left for Wonsan, arriving at a rendezvous point outside the harbor at noon the following day before being escorted through the minefield channel. The Sams team first visited Yodo, a nearby island, where they learned from civilians that there was much typhus and smallpox among the Chinese troops. An ROK Marine officer had already sent two separate parties of agents ashore to investigate. But none of the twenty-two agents returned and the ROKs were reluctant to risk sending another group since Chinese troops had moved into the area.

On March 10 the team returned to Yodo Island to interrogate other agents and civilian refugees. They reported widespread disease in and around Wonsan, principally typhus and smallpox. Clark learned that six airdrops of friendly Korean agents had been made along the coast and all but one of the agents had been captured by North Koreans or Chinese Reds. The agent who had originally reported symptoms of the plague was now twenty miles southwest in the mountains where Chinese troops were reported to be seriously afflicted. A field hospital located near Chilbo-ri was said to have had at one time fifteen hundred cases of serious diseases.

On March 12, the team boarded a destroyer, the USS *Wallace L. Lind*, Commander Carlson commanding, since it had been decided not to use the unwieldy laboratory vessel. The *Lind* was normally engaged in bombardment of coastal targets of opportunity. She proceeded south until they were offshore from Chilbo-ri. It was dark, and a sea was kicking up. The captain advised that it would be too dangerous to try a rubber-raft landing in that state of the sea. Clark conferred with Sams. There was no alternative but to delay the mission until a more auspicious time. The *Lind* up-anchored and plotted a course back to Wonsan. The seas having quieted significantly at five P.M. the next day, the team again boarded the *Lind* for Chilbo-ri. Shortly after arrival they boarded the ship's whaleboat, joined by an eager Navy correspondent with camera. When they were within several hundred yards of the beach, the team got into an inflated raft. The correspondent wanted to board, too, but Clark stopped him. It was ridiculous. The trio paddled toward shore, attached by a long line to the whaleboat, which was being tracked by ship's radar so they could be retrieved quickly.

As they approached the dark beach, they were greeted by an awesome sight. In the background high, rugged mountains, only a mile inland, were covered with snow. In the foreground, a convoy of trucks, headlights ablaze, was moving south along a road parallel to the shore.

Suddenly flares dropped from U.S. planes, the pilots unaware they were jeopardizing a secret operation. The bombs exploded and several trucks burst into flames. The planes began to strafe the convoy. Clark and Sams realized that survivors would scatter and the area would soon be crawling with military patrols, but both were determined to keep paddling to their rendezvous. Their contact on the beach warned them by walkie-talkie that they were approaching a mined area and should move farther south. By now their combat uniforms were drenched with icy spray. Although they wore no insignia, they carried pistols and grenades. Sams also had some culture tubes, syringes, and Syrettes containing morphine. The purpose of the last was twofold. "First," he recalled, "it might be necessary to put the patient into a comatose condition through the use of intravenous morphine, which reacts very quickly, so that we could get the patient out and take him aboard one of the ships. We could then, in his quiet state, make our laboratory determinations. The other purpose of the morphine syrettes was a little more drastic. We had agreed that if we fell into Communist hands, the fate that would await us would be such that it was better to not remain alive too long."

After about twenty minutes of heroic paddle splashing they safely grounded and met their contact, English-speaking Mr. Koh, a Korean CIA agent. As Koh led them through the beach minefield, he assured them that bombardments were common and only Chinese security troops were in the neighborhood. "So much for our apprehensions," Clark wryly commented. Near the back of the beach they came to the camouflaged mouth of a narrow tunnel. This led to a large cave, Koh's hideaway. Clark and Youn headed for the reported hospital located in the nearby village. They would try to secure a diseased patient and bring him to the cave—if not a live one, then a dead one. In the meantime, Sams would interrogate two agents who had closely viewed suspected plague patients. The general crawled down the tunnel, cocked pistol in hand, aware that he might be entering his own tomb.

While Sams was questioning the agents, Clark and Youn cautiously explored the seemingly abandoned bombarded village. Lolling outside a half-destroyed building, partly roofed over by canvas, were three Chinese soldiers. They carried rifles but seemed so lax that Clark took them for hospital attendants. He peered inside. Two patients lay on cots. The problem was to get rid of the three guards. Clark whispered to Youn to create a diversion. A minute later came a rustle and two of the soldiers hurried to investigate. Clark crept behind the third man and bayoneted him. A second guard came running toward the hospital. Clark knifed him, and as the third Chinese rushed out of the brush, Youn cut his throat. They dragged the three bodies into the brush and then went inside the building to see what it contained. Clark had hoped to find a dead Chinese to bring back to Sams but both patients were alive, although obviously terminal. Before killing them, he decided to report back to Sams. Perhaps it wouldn't be necessary.

By the time Clark had crawled back into the cave, Sams had finished his interrogations and was satisfied the disease was not the plague. Sams commented to Clark in obvious relief that the agents had indeed closely observed the suspected cases. Eruptions on the face, legs, arms and torso could be nothing but hemorrhagic smallpox. "There was no evidence of lesions or either bubonic or septicemic forms of plague. There was no respiratory symptom." The confusion, concluded Sams, was due to the "black" appearance of the victims, causing the North Korean doctors to believe it was plague, since the Korean word for *plague* meant "black pest." And these doctors had never seen a plague case.

In a few minutes, the Sams team was back in the rubber raft. Clark jerked on the line attached to the whaleboat and they were at once hauled to the whaleboat. Once they were aboard the destroyer, Commander Carlson offered each of them a shot of "medicinal" brandy, Clark having pointed to their icy-wet shoes and clothing. Sams dispatched a message to MacArthur that their fear of the plague was groundless. Unfortunately, public relations released the story to the press. Perhaps that Navy correspondent Clark had refused to take to the beach had got his story after all. The UP headline read US GENERAL RISKS LIFE BEHIND RED LINES TO PROBE DEADLY EPIDEMIC (UP). This was proof to the Chinese that America was waging germ warfare, and as a result, many prisoners of war would later suffer dire consequences. Clark and Youn breathed a sigh of thankfulness that they could skip the next two plague shots.

4.

On the Ides of March, Operation Ripper was proceeding on schedule. Eleven divisions—six American, five ROK—were attacking across the peninsula against relatively light resistance. To some, the advance—one or two miles—seemed painfully slow, but Ridgway demanded coordination in shoulder-to-shoulder progress.

Ridgway was surprised to learn that MacArthur was coming to Korea again, and would arrive in Suwon on the morning of the 17th. He was met by Ridgway. On the short plane trip to Wonju, they discussed the possibility of Russia entering the war. There had been reports from the FBI, Chiang Kai-shek and the British attaché in Moscow that the Soviets might soon join China and North Korea in a major attack. Ridgway said he was prepared and, if hard pressed, would immediately withdraw to the old Davidson Line near Pusan.

During this visit, MacArthur gave no signs of his growing discontent, but it erupted four days later when he read a dispatch from the Joint Chiefs that the UN was preparing to discuss conditions of a settlement in Korea. "Strong United Nations feeling persists that further diplomatic efforts towards settlement should be made before any advance with forces north of the 38th parallel. Time may be required to determine diplomatic reaction and permit new negotiations that may develop. Recognizing that 38th parallel has no military significance, State has asked Joint Chiefs of Staff what authority you should have to permit sufficient freedom of action for next few weeks to provide security for United Nations forces and maintain contact with the enemy. Your recommendations desired."

MacArthur wondered what he was supposed to recommend. Washington knew his opinion on how to bring the war to a close. He refused to discuss methods for weaseling on the original American pledge to restore Korea to the proper authorities. One thing he had to reiterate: too much restriction had already been placed on his freedom of action. He replied with an urgent request that "no further military restrictions be imposed upon the United Nations Command in Korea."

He instructed Ridgway not to cross the parallel without authority from him. "If press forces you to discuss questions," he added, "evade direct reply by saying matter is for my decisions."

From the moment Ridgway first conceived Operation Ripper, he had his eye on one key objective—the city of Chunchon. Capturing this vital road junction would accomplish three goals. It would force the enemy onto rugged trails to resupply his troops. It would give UN forces a logistical hub to support future operations in central Korea; and it would flank enemy forces concentrated around Seoul. Even so resistance against IX and X corps had been stiff. To relieve the pressure, Ridgway decided to use the 187th Airborne Regimental Combat Team, commanded by Brigadier General Frank Bowen. He planned to drop them just north of Chunchon, with the 1st Cavalry Division making the link-up. March 20 was the date for Operation Hawk.

By noon of the 19th, paratroopers and carriers had assembled at Taegu. Early that morning, the 1st Cavalry had begun a series of probes to gain better terrain from which to launch their attack. Then a strange thing happened. Except for mines in the roads, there was no opposition. Ridgway had just returned to his CP when he received word of their unopposed advance. He and Mike Lynch hurried back to the small strip and were airborne in less than five minutes. Captain Marcus Sullivan and Ridgway's senior aide, Lieutenant Colonel Walter Winton, Jr., followed in a second plane. They all headed for Chunchon.

Approaching the town, Ridgway could see an armored column from the 1st Cavalry entering the valley some ten miles to the south. He was both surprised and elated, but now faced a critical decision. Chunchon had been selected as an Army objective to be taken by a combined airborne assault and armor linkup. If the town was defended, he would continue with the scheduled drop. If not, he had to cancel it.

He and Lynch began circling the town out of small-arms range. Sullivan and Winton were just behind at a higher level. There was no movement below. The Ridgway plane kept dropping down until Lynch could look into the houses. Still no movement. Time was running out. A decision had to be made. By then, Cavalry units were a few miles away.

"Do you think we can get in?" asked Ridgway.

During the hectic days of December, when Chunchon had been surrounded, Lynch had landed in that town. It had been touch and go in a battle-worn L-5. Now he was flying a more powerful and maneuverable L-19. He made several passes over the site. "Yes, sir," he said. "I think we can make it. But it'll be a hairy landing."

Ridgway told him to let the other plane know that they were going to try to land.

"The Old Man wants to go in," radioed Lynch to Sullivan.

"Don't try it! We don't own the town!" was the reply.

"We gotta go, Sully," said Lynch, "because here comes the Cav, and if the town's not defended, we have to call off the drop." It would be a real challenge. They had to come in low under some wires, climb slightly to clear a stone bridge, and then drop down immediately to clear more wires before landing on a small dirt road leading to the railroad station. Once committed, there was no aborting. The brakes had to work.

"You're out of your mind," said Winton.

Lynch swept in under the wires, zoomed over the bridge, lowered just in time to get under other wires and came to a screeching stop in front of the railroad station. He could see no one. They were alone. Opening the door, he handed Ridgway a carbine.

"Cover me," said Lynch, and ran to the first building with his own carbine. He heard noises coming from the cellar and drew a bead on the doorway. A little boy with a big grin on his face stepped out. A dozen civilians followed. As Lynch and the general started towards the main street, more civilians poured out of every building. The two inspected the bridge for explosives. Nothing. No Chinese. A cavalry recon jeep, followed by two more jeeps and an armored car, approached, and the newcomers were startled to find themselves being welcomed by the Eighth Army commander and his pilot. Finally a tank rolled up, and down stepped Brigadier General Charles D. Palmer, commander of the 1st Cavalry Division. He had relieved Gay and had known Ridgway at West Point.

Palmer's original mission had been to link up with an airborne regimental combat team of some three thousand men. Instead, he found the two-man force of Lynch and Ridgway holding the town. Seizing the opportunity, Ridgway told Palmer to continue his advance beyond Chunchon. Ridgway wanted to gain as much terrain as possible while he had the momentum. In the meantime, he would issue new orders for continued operations once he reached his headquarters.

Lynch told the CAV to get off the road. They had to take off at once. He knew that getting out would be even hairier. They had to take off downhill and downwind. Ridgway was unperturbed as they reversed the tricky maneuver. Once airborne, they rejoined Winton and Sullivan for the return trip to their headquarters.

"You and the Old Man must have been scared as hell," Sully said as they pulled up alongside Lynch's plane at several thousand feet. Winton cut in and added, "I'll bet that shook the general." Mike turned and looked at Ridgway. He was calmly poring over his map, seeking a new site to drop the 187th now that Chunchon had fallen.

Back at their little headquarters in Yoju, Ridgway called off the Chunchon jump; the enemy had withdrawn too deeply. He changed the operation name to Tomahawk and the date to March 23. The new drop zone would be at a spot farther north at Munsan. Ridgway had planned to join the jump as he had in Normandy, but decided it would be a "damned fool thing to do." A broken ankle might force him to give up command of the Eighth Army. Instead, Mike Lynch would fly him up to observe the operation at first hand.

Ridgway was wakened early on March 23 with an order from MacArthur authorizing him to cross the 38th parallel. An amazing switch! "Am in complete accord with the plan you have outlined to advance to the phase line indicated in your message," continued MacArthur. "Make no announcements to this effect and allow the actual events to constitute sole press information. Further action beyond your suggested phase line will be determined by you in accordance with my previous message. Will see you at Seoul airfield Saturday."

Upon learning the 187th had become airborne at 7:30 A.M. Ridgway and Lynch took off from the small airstrip at Yoju. They flew north of Seoul until reaching I Corps's linkup forces. Just as they arrived, the first two American tanks struck mines. The column came to a halt. Although anxious to reach Munsan, Ridgway knew he could not afford delays in closing the gap. They dropped down to treetop level and circled the disabled tanks. When troops saw the plane's star plate and their Army commander, they began cheering. Ridgway knew they would do their best to make it. Having "shown the flag," Lynch climbed above small-arms range and turned toward Munsan, twenty-five miles behind enemy lines. It was fifteen minutes to H-hour.

The operation involved two drop zones, north and south of the village. The 2nd and 3rd Battalions, along with the 2nd and 4th Ranger companies, were to land in the north, the 1st Battalion in the south. Ridgway and Lynch headed for the northern drop. The Pathfinders came in. Lynch checked the plan on his leg pad. Three serials would arrive three minutes apart. He stayed above incoming aircraft as the 2nd and 3rd battalions landed. Ridgway suggested they get lower so he could see how the troops were performing. Down to five hundred feet. Mike knew what to expect. It wasn't long in coming. A voice from the backseat asked, "Can we land?"

Colonel Winton was flying with Sullivan in a second aircraft several miles to the rear. Mike notified Sully that he was going to try to land. "Don't do it," Winton cut in. "Tell the Old Man," said Lynch. "I'll put him on." Silence. Then, "Never mind. Roger out."

Mike spotted a road that looked long enough. He swooped low to take a look. Paratroopers were everywhere. Ridgway waved for them to get out of the way. They didn't move. Lynch made another pass. "We tried again," recalled Ridgway, "waving our arms and cussing them in every language we could think of. They merely waved back."

Then disaster! The lead aircraft of serials carrying the 1st Battalion to the southern drop zone had aborted. The second-in-command missed a checkpoint and headed for the northern area. Ridgway and Lynch were below one hundred feet at the time. Suddenly the air above them was filled with paratroopers. Lynch had no place to go.

"Hang on, General," he yelled. "We've got to go in!"

Spotting a dike at the edge of the drop zone, Mike lowered the flaps and started a tight turn. Rounding out, he got his first real look. The dike was less than three hundred feet long, not much wider than his landing gear, and fell off on both sides some eight feet. A burned tank marked its end. Going to full flaps, he tried to flare, but his tail wheel nicked a hut at the near end. They pitched forward and contacted the dike. Up in the air they shot. "Oh, God, please let me drop on that dike again!" he thought. They did. Mike hit full brakes and the plane skidded to a stop ten feet from the disabled tank.

They drew small-arms fire at once. "Go on down!" Lynch said. "I'll take care of the plane."

Ridgway stepped off the dike and, being a wary old soldier, peered into a culvert. He saw five Chinese, all dead, blood still oozing from head wounds. Hostile mortar fire began to come in, and Ridgway walked up the road. He heard the bang of an M-1 on the slope above, and a Chinese in padded uniform came rolling down the hill to hang on the bank above Ridgway. He didn't move and Ridgway assumed he was dead.

The general walked among the troopers. It was like Normandy revisited. Finding General Bowen, the 187th commander, he asked about the 1st Battalion. Nobody knew why they had been dropped in the main zone. Worse, neither Lieutenant Colonel Harry Wilson nor his command group in the lead aircraft could be found.

Ridgway was disturbed. He had not cut off the enemy as hoped and nobody could find Colonel Wilson, an old airborne friend. He decided to leave immediately so that he could divert one of the linkup columns to the west in search of the enemy. At the same time, he would try to find out what had happened to Wilson.

Up on the elevated dike Lynch had struggled in vain to turn the plane around so they could take off. He saw some troopers and yelled for help. Enemy machine-gun bullets ripped near him. He jumped to the safe side of the levee.

The troopers crept up to him and asked for directions to the road junction.

"Ten miles from here. You guys dropped in the wrong area." This was the main DZ. "My Old Man's down there," said Lynch, "and he'll get teed off as hell if I'm not ready to go." He pointed toward the machine-gun fire. "We've got to go up and take that machine gun."

Lynch organized three squads of troopers and they put up a base of fire. Maneuvering forward, they finally wiped out the machine-gun nest. As Lynch and several troopers were returning to the levee with four prisoners, one of the men exclaimed in amazement, "God! There's General Ridgway!"

"Oh, shit," said Lynch. "I'm in trouble. Come on, you guys, help me push the plane around."

Ridgway walked erectly as if no bullet would dare to hit him. "Mike," he complained, "we've got to get out of here in a hurry, and you don't even have the plane pushed out!" This was no time for his harried pilot to explain the reason why.

By the time Ridgway and Lynch were aboard, mortar rounds began falling around the dike. Lynch timed their impact. When a lull came, he "fire-walled" the throttle. The plane rumbled down the dike and took off as shells landed behind them.

Later that night at dinner, Ridgway got an after-action report on the airborne operation. Wilson and his headquarters staff had been dropped in the southern zone, coming under fire once they landed. The small group held off an enemy force until rescued by one of the armored columns.

The other bit of information the general learned was that eight prisoners were taken near the dike. Four of them by his own pilot. Turning to Lynch, he said, "Why didn't you tell me?"

"I didn't have time."

The next morning at eleven, as promised, MacArthur landed at Kimpo Airfield. Ridgway was on hand to escort him by jeep to Uijongbu, just north of Seoul, where the American 3rd Division, commanded by a paratrooper, Major General Robert "Shorty" Soule, was fighting.

During the visit Ridgway outlined the line of advance he wanted to take, "subject to the tactical situation and in accordance with the Army's unchanged basic objectives." MacArthur confirmed his approval, already given by radio. Had the general's estimate of Soviet intentions to intervene in the war changed? No, said MacArthur. Such a decision would be taken by the Soviets based on their realistic analysis of the world situation. But the complete collapse of the Chinese might bring them in.

"That would be the end of Russia," observed Ridgway.

"That would be the end of her," repeated MacArthur.

Just as MacArthur was leaving Kimpo at 2:40 P.M., Tokyo was releasing his communiqué embodying all his complaints and indignation. Despite its formal and bookish phrasing, it was another bombshell. MacArthur defied direct orders from his president by mixing military with foreign policy. "We have now substantially cleared South Korea of organized Communist forces," he said. Red China lacked the industrial capacity to wage modern war. Its military weaknesses had been clearly and definitely revealed. "The enemy therefore must by now be painfully aware that a decision of the United Nations to depart from its tolerant effort to contain the war to the area of Korea through expansion of our military operations to his coastal areas and interior bases would doom China to the risk of imminent military collapse." Korea and its people, he continued, should not be sacrificed. The fundamental questions continued to be political and must find their answer in the diplomatic sphere.

The communiqué was received in Washington at ten P.M., March 23. An hour later a group of senior government officials met in the living room of Acheson's Georgetown home. Everyone agreed MacArthur had to go. His message was a direct attempt to intimidate Peking. It mocked the Volunteer soldiers and intimated that the enemy would be wiped out unless they surrendered.

"Whom the gods destroy, they first make mad," commented Acheson. Someone suggested they phone Truman, but the secretary of state said they should break up and sleep on the problem.

Next morning Truman was stunned and irate at MacArthur's open defiance of his orders as president and as commander in chief under the Constitution. The general's communiqué not only was a challenge to the president but it also flouted the policy of the United Nations. By this act, MacArthur left Truman no choice: "I could no longer tolerate his insubordination."

Yet Truman hesitated. The last straw came on April 5 when Minority Leader Joe Martin read in the House the text of a letter MacArthur had sent him, implying that the general agreed with Martin's proposal that Chiang's Nationalist troops be used in an invasion of China. "It seems strangely difficult for some one to realize," continued MacArthur, "that here in Asia is where the Communist conspirators have elected to make their play for global conquest, and that we have joined the issue thus raised on the battlefield; that here we fight Europe's war with arms while the diplomats there still fight it with words; that if we lose this war to Communism in Asia the fall of Europe is inevitable; win it and Europe most probably would avoid war and yet preserve freedom. As you point out we must win. There is no substitute for victory."

To Truman that letter was the real clincher. MacArthur had to go.

PART VIII

"THE BATTLE IS JOINED"

CHAPTER 30

"Jeannie, We're Going Home at Last"
(April 6–25)

1.

The next day, Friday the 6th, Truman summoned Marshall, Bradley, Acheson and Harriman to the White House to discuss MacArthur. (Collins was out of town.) Giving no inkling that he had already decided to fire the general, he asked their opinion.

"Mr. President," said Harriman, "this was a problem which you faced last August and which you decided you would not deal with until later."

Marshall urged caution, particularly since firing MacArthur might have an adverse effect on the military appropriations being considered by Congress. Bradley agreed. There was considerable doubt in his mind whether "MacArthur had committed a clear-cut case of military insubordination as defined in Army regulations." Go slow, he said. He wanted "time to reflect and talk it over with the Joint Chiefs."

Although Acheson felt that MacArthur deserved to be fired, he agreed with Bradley. "If you relieve MacArthur," he said, "you will have the biggest fight of your administration."

"Think it over," said Truman.

That afternoon the four advisers met in Marshall's office for two hours. Marshall suggested they call MacArthur home for consultation. The others were strongly opposed, and Marshall withdrew his suggestion.

Truman was still seething that night. "MacArthur shoots another

429

political bomb through Joe Martin," he wrote in his diary. "This looks like the last straw. I've come to the conclusion that our Big General in the Far East must be recalled."

The next morning at 8:50, all four advisers met again with Truman. They advised the president to postpone any action until Monday, when Joe Collins would be on hand. Truman reluctantly went along, but soon Bradley had doubts. "As President and Commander-in-Chief, Truman had established our policy for the conduct of the Korean War. And MacArthur had openly and defiantly challenged him. It was not a question of who was right or who was wrong."

That afternoon Bradley called for a full Joint Chiefs meeting. He reported that the president was considering recalling MacArthur and wanted their views. It was agreed unanimously, if reluctantly, that MacArthur should be relieved. A sad and sober group reported to Defense Secretary Marshall in his office at four P.M. It was not easy to be a party to the dismissal of a distinguished soldier. Each man gave his opinion. Marshall simply noted that Bradley should present the JCS consensus to Truman the next day.

At the president's meeting with his chief advisers on Monday morning, Bradley conveyed the thinking of the Joint Chiefs. Harriman and Acheson had also had second thoughts and now agreed that the general should be relieved. Only then did Truman reveal what he had decided several days previously. MacArthur must be relieved. Who should replace him?

Bradley said that he and Collins had already selected Ridgway as the logical man for the job. They thought General James Van Fleet should become the next commander of the Eighth Army. Truman approved both choices.

While his fate was being decided, MacArthur was saying good-bye to Almond, who was taking a rare one-week vacation. The general looked disconsolate. "I may not see you any more, so goodbye, Ned. I have become politically involved and may be relieved by the president."

Almond, a true worshiper, was incredulous. "Well, General MacArthur, I consider that absurd and I don't believe the president has the intention of taking such drastic action."

At three the following afternoon, the four chief advisers again met with the president. Truman approved the suggestion that Secretary of the Army Frank Pace, now in Korea, return to Tokyo at once and deliver the order of relief to MacArthur in person. This would save the general the embarrassment of direct transmission through Army channels. Cable No. 8743 to Ambassador Muccio for delivery to Pace was composed and transmitted.

Unfortunately, a Chicago *Tribune* radio reporter in the Far East telephoned his paper saying he had an authoritative tip that MacArthur was about to be fired. Acheson gave no importance to the *Tribune*'s tip, but the other advisers did. Fearing MacArthur might beat Truman to the punch and resign, they decided to transmit an order to MacArthur immediately. It was also decided to call an unprecedented press conference for one o'clock Monday morning. A public release was hurriedly composed:

> With deep regret I have concluded that General of the Army Douglas MacArthur is unable to give his wholehearted support to the policies of the United States Government and of the United Nations in matters pertaining to his official duties. In view of the specific responsibilities imposed upon me by the Constitution of the United States and the added responsibilities entrusted to me by the United Nations, I have decided that I must make a change of command in the Far East. I have, therefore, relieved General MacArthur of his commands and have designated Lieutenant General Matthew B. Ridgway as his successor.

Soon the news was being publicly broadcast to Tokyo, where the MacArthurs were entertaining luncheon guests. The meal was proceeding quietly when Mrs. MacArthur noticed Colonel Sidney Huff, MacArthur's aide, in the doorway. Excusing herself, she went to him. There were tears in his eyes as he told her what he'd heard on the radio.

She returned to the table and touched her husband's shoulder. She delivered the news so softly that it could not be heard across the table. Momentarily his face froze, and he was briefly silent. Then he looked up at his wife, who still held a hand on his shoulder. "Jeannie," he said gently, "we're going home at last."

He continued the conversation as if nothing had happened. After the guests had left, he phoned Whitney. "Court, have you heard the news?" It sounded to Whitney as though he were talking about an important football game.

"Yes, General. I'll be right over." On the way to the embassy, he tried desperately to think of what he should or could say. When they met, all he could do was take MacArthur's hand and say, "I am sure, General, it will turn out all for the best."

But MacArthur, to his amazement, only wanted to discuss the problems Whitney would face when he left. "Why, General," he interrupted almost incredulously, "I accompanied you into Japan and I shall certainly accompany you out."

"But Court," was the calm reply, "I have served on active duty sufficient years to satisfy the statutory requirement to retirement, subject only to the approval of the Defense Department, and I am sure that when I submit my request for retirement this evening, it will encounter no opposition in Washington."

"I have just left the general," Whitney told the press, which had gathered like vultures. "He received the word magnificently. . . . I think this has been his finest hour."

The U.S. ambassador to Japan, William Sebald, heard the news at Prime Minister Yoshida Shigeru's garden party. Yoshida called him aside. "Can you confirm the report?" Sebald said he had no official information but would find out at his office. Upon receiving confirmation, he returned to Yoshida's residence and was received in the upstairs study. The prime minister had changed to a kimono, which, Sebald thought, added to his dignity and authenticity as head of the Japanese government.

Sebald said he hoped the prime minister and his cabinet would not resign in protest—the ambassador knew this would have been the traditional Japanese gesture, particularly in view of Yoshida's close relationship with MacArthur. Yoshida, visibly shaken, finally agreed not to resign.

Sebald proceeded to the Dai Ichi Building, where the general greeted Sebald with his customary smile. Sebald was so keyed up that he was unable to speak. A tear rolled down his cheek. There was an oppressive silence. Then, with some difficulty, the ambassador said, "General, you are a much better soldier in this business than I am."

"Publicly humiliated after fifty-two years of service in the Army," he replied somberly. He would have retired without protest, he added, if Truman had intimated he wished him to do so. It was obvious to Sebald that MacArthur was deeply hurt and, perhaps, momentarily defeated. "Watching and listening to him was the most painful interview I have had."

He asked if the general might ask the Japanese people to support and cooperate with Ridgway. When MacArthur said he would not, Sebald asked him to reconsider. "After all, the present state of Japan is a monument to you and I would hope that everything possible could be done to preserve it."

MacArthur made no comment, remarking instead that his dismissal was part of a plot in Washington that would eventually cause disintegration of the U.S. position in the Far East. He denied that he had disobeyed orders from Washington.

Ridgway was escorting Secretary of the Army Pace on a tour of the front when a correspondent asked if he was due for congratulations. Puzzled, Ridgway said, "I don't know what you're talking about."

Pace was equally puzzled when he was handed a cable from Washington:

"Disregard my cable No. 8743. You will advise General Matthew B. Ridgway that he is now the Supreme Commander of the Pacific; Vice General MacArthur relieved. You will proceed to Tokyo where you will assist General Ridgway in assuming the incidence of his command. Signed: Marshall."

But Pace had never received Marshall's cable No. 8743 because of a power failure in Pusan. It was an embarrassing situation and Pace led Ridgway outside, where it was hailing. "General Ridgway," he said, "it's my duty to advise you that you're now the Supreme Commander of the Pacific; Vice General MacArthur relieved."

The hail pounded on their heads. "I can't believe it, Mr. Secretary," the stunned Ridgway finally said.

ROK chief of staff, General Chung Il-kwon, was so troubled by the news that he hastened at once to Rhee's residence. Tears were running down the president's cheeks. "Truman has killed our hopes!" he exclaimed. Chung knew he was referring to the reunification of Korea. The chief of staff agreed.

In Peking, Ambassador Panikkar didn't learn what had happened until a BBC broadcast at seven P.M. No longer was MacArthur the super-Mikado, the man who thought he could defy anybody and get away with it. "Strange is the power of democracy," he observed. "The most powerful soldier in command of vast forces and exercising for the time supreme power over a great empire is dismissed by a single order, and he has no option but to surrender his authority and leave." To Panikkar's amazement, the Chinese showed no interest in the matter. There was no comment in their papers.

In Europe there was rejoicing. There were cheers in the Houses of Parliament in London. "MAC IS SACKED" exclaimed the London *Evening Standard*. French editorials approved, commenting that the Allies could not yield to "*un parleur de sa trempe*," a tall-talker like MacArthur. But Japan, where MacArthur was still revered as the Shogun, was distraught. "We feel as if we had lost a kind and loving father," reported *Asahi Shimbun*. "His recall is the greatest shock since the end of the war," declared *Mainichi Shimbun*. Only the Communists in Japan were openly jubilant. "One of Premier Stalin's great predictions, that 'all meddlers will no doubt meet with certain failure,' has come true."

In America there was more outrage than joy. The average citizen was on MacArthur's side. E. J. Kahn cabled *The New Yorker* from Korea that a terrific wind blew across the camp he was visiting at about the same time as word came of MacArthur's relief. "A few minutes later, a hailstorm lashed the countryside. A few hours after that there was a driving snowstorm. Since the weather has been fairly springlike for the previous couple of weeks, the off-climatic goings-on prompted one soldier to exclaim, 'Gee, do you suppose he is really God, after all?' "

In the wake of the flood of mail excoriating him, Truman made a mistake. On the evening of that devastating day, he spoke to the nation over the radio. The country was waiting to hear *why* he had suddenly fired MacArthur. Instead, following Acheson's advice, he concentrated on the administration's war policy. "In the simplest terms, what we are doing in Korea is this: we are trying to prevent a third world war." He talked on and on and finally mentioned that it was with great personal regret he had felt compelled to relieve MacArthur. To Bradley the speech was "a complete flop." Instead of specifically explaining the reasons for the dismissal, he chose the loftier and duller theme and failed to mobilize the country behind him.

Ridgway and Pace left Pusan the next afternoon, arriving in Tokyo at four-thirty. General Doyle Hickey, a comrade in the Battle of the Bulge, brought Ridgway to the embassy library, where MacArthur was waiting. Hickey was asked to remain for the hour-long conference. "He [MacArthur] was entirely himself—composed, quiet, temperate, friendly, and helpful to the man who was to succeed him," recalled Hickey. "He made some allusions to the fact that he had been summarily relieved, but there was not a trace of bitterness or anger in his voice. I thought it was a fine tribute to the resilience of this great man that he could accept so calmly what must have been a devastating blow to a professional soldier standing at the peak of his career."

MacArthur did tell them he'd been informed by an eminent medical man who had gotten it from General Graham, the president's physician, that Truman was suffering from malignant hypertension, an affliction characterized by bewilderment and confusion of thought. According to the medical men, Truman wouldn't live six months.

MacArthur also said he'd received an offer of $300,000 to write fifty lectures that would raise hell. In reply to Ridgway's queries, he said he saw no indication of a split between the Chinese and Soviets and still thought the latter would not precipitate a world war. He added that he hoped Ridgway would become chief of staff after leaving Tokyo and called his performance at Eighth Army brilliant. "If it had been up to me to pick my successor, I would have chosen you."

In his diary that night, Ridgway wrote: "He was as keen of mind as ever. His indomitable spirit seemed undiminished."

* * *

In Washington, the administration was shocked by the adverse reaction throughout the country. During the next Cabinet meeting, Truman asked Acheson to give his impression of the last few days. The dignified secretary of state said it was summed up by the story of the family with a beautiful daughter who lived near an Army camp. "The wife worried continually about the dangers to which this exposed their daughter. One afternoon the husband found his wife red-eyed and weeping on the doorstep. The worst had happened, she informed him: their daughter was pregnant! Wiping his brow, he said, 'Thank God, that's over!' "

Despite the calls to impeach "the Judas in the White House who sold us down the river to the left wingers," the great majority of the working press thought the president was justified. Although they felt the dismissal had been handled badly, the *Washington Post*, the New York *Herald Tribune*, and *The New York Times* agreed with Truman. The *Christian Science Monitor* editorialized that it had become necessary for MacArthur "to conform, to resign, or be removed." *Business Week* thought that talk of impeachment was irresponsible but pointed out that the president's "course of holding on in Korea and, like Micawber, hoping something will turn up, is alien to our national experience. . . . The General may not always be easy to deal with, but it is incredible that a policy could not have been worked out months ago." Why was not MacArthur simply ordered home to consult with the Joint Chiefs?

The conservative publishers—McCormick, Hearst, Luce, Scripps-Howard—supported MacArthur and attacked Truman.

2.

After meeting with MacArthur, Ridgway returned to Korea to oversee the latest operation, Operation Dauntless. It was going well, if slowly, with the same precision as his other operations. The Chinese were withdrawing into the Iron Triangle, an important communication and supply area encompassing Chorwon, Kumhwa and Pyonggang. He told his corps commanders at five P.M., April 13, that General Van Fleet would be arriving the next day to take command of the Eighth Army.

Soon after noon, on the 14th, Van Fleet landed at Taegu. Ridgway met him, and there was a formal change-of-command ceremony. Privately Ridgway told him, "To the extent you feel the situation warrants, please inform me prior to advancing in force beyond Utah." This was the next line to the north.

The correspondents took to Van Fleet, a big, commanding figure. *Time* described him as "a rugged combat soldier and crack commander." Correspondent Poats reported that the contrast between the two men was striking. "Ridgway was the suave, polished field marshal, clearly destined for higher station. Van Fleet was the fellow next door, good-natured, unaffected, strong but no world-beater at turning a phrase."

In his year book at West Point, Van Fleet was described as "a brusque, outspoken individual and not much of a mixer. He finds pleasure in the society of magazines and books, and is a frequenter of the gym. Perhaps this reticent attitude has kept some of us from knowing him as well as we should." He had fought in the first world war as a machine-gun-battalion commander. He had a brilliant combat record and was eligible to wear the combat infantryman's badge, which many soldiers thought preferable to any other medal. Poats felt that in the field with men, and maps, and tactical problems, Van Fleet would be at home—a cool, canny football coach with a head full of trick plays.

That evening, Ridgway flew back to Tokyo, settling in at the Imperial Hotel, where he met Ambassador Sebald to draft his arrival statement. Checking the final version, he crossed out the phrase, "with due humility." "I am not humble in this job or any other," he commented. "I am humble before God, but no one else."

The 15th of April was spent preparing for MacArthur's departure. Sebald arose at five A.M. so he could reach Haneda Airport before the MacArthurs were to arrive, two hours later. Already the road to the airport was lined with American troops and Tokyo municipal and rural police. Thousands of Japanese waited patiently for the man they called Makasa Gensui (literally, Field Marshal MacArthur). The buildings along the route were festooned with banners and signs; the one causing the most comment from Americans was stretched across the top floor of a building and expressed hopes that he would be the next president: "GOOD LUCK ON YOUR COMING ERECTION."

The motorcade left the embassy at 6:28 A.M. Despite the early hour, Japanese, standing ten deep, lined the twelve miles to the airport. The massive crowd obviously revered MacArthur as they did no other foreigner. They waved small American and Japanese flags. Some called out, "Sayonara!" Others held up banners such as: "We Love You, MacArthur" and "We are Grateful to the General."

Ridgway and Doyle Hickey formally greeted the MacArthurs at Haneda. Jean MacArthur, smiling, walked toward the wives of the occupation officials while her husband reviewed the guard of honor. MacArthur ended the brief ritual by shaking hands with the guards' commander. Then he strode toward his senior officers with a smile, to shake hands. To each man he gave a penetrating glance and to many a personal word. Sebald was moved by the painful scene. Many of the women were openly sobbing, and men who had seen battle with MacArthur were doing their utmost to suppress tears.

MacArthur's small staff, which would accompany him to America, boarded the plane. Just behind was the Chinese amah who chaperoned little Arthur. At last Mrs. MacArthur broke away from her weeping friends. The general helped her up the ramp and, at the top, turned to give a final wave as a nineteen-gun salute rumbled. Then they entered the plane and it taxied away. "Soon it was airborne," recalled Sebald. "Officers and their wives slowly trooped away, the flags were furled, the troops dismissed—and the working day began."

Ridgway held his first staff meeting at the Dai Ichi Building. Sebald found him firm, succinct, and forceful. "There was no doubt among those present about who was the boss of the Occupation at this point. For me, this was an impressive beginning."

MacArthur's homecoming was the greatest triumph any American hero had ever received. In San Francisco, he was greeted by a wildly enthusiastic crowd. The trip from the airport to his hotel took two hours because of 500,000 welcomers along the way. Two days later, on April 19, he entered the House of Representatives in Washington to thunderous applause. In a thirty-seven-minute televised oration, he made the speech of his life. The majority of the estimated twenty million viewers were enthralled by his manner, his rhetoric and his emotion. In a relatively brief time, he forcefully, dramatically and convincingly outlined his policy. "There are those," he said, "who claim our strength is inadequate to protect both Europe and Asia, that we could not divide our effort. I can think of no greater expression of defeat. The Communist threat is a global one. Its successful advance in one sector threatens the destruction of every sector. You cannot appease or otherwise surrender to Communism in Asia without simultaneously undermining our efforts to halt its advance in Europe."

He denied charges that he was a warmonger. "Nothing could be further from the truth." But the Korean War had been forced on America, and there was no alternative but to bring it to a swift end. "In war there is no substitute for victory. There are some who, for varying reasons, would appease Red China." They were blind to the lessons of history. Appeasement had always led only to a sham peace. He then praised the Korean people. "They have chosen to risk death rather than slavery. Their last words to me were: 'Don't scuttle the Pacific.' "

He concluded with words that would never be forgotten by his listeners. "The world has turned over many times since I took the oath on the plain at West Point, and the hope and dreams have long since vanished, but I still remember the refrain of one of the most popular barracks ballads of that day which proclaimed most proudly that old soldiers never die; they just fade away.

"And like the old soldier of that ballad, I now close my military career and just fade away, an old soldier who tried to do his duty as God gave him the light to see that duty. Good-bye."

He waved to his wife, then stepped into the crowd. Everyone wanted to touch him. "We heard God speak here today!" shouted Representative Dewey Short. Almost all those listening to the radio or watching television were moved. The phones of newspapers around the country began ringing with demands to "defy the bankrupt haberdasher" and the "traitorous" State Department. The White House was also being innundated with calls, most of them abusive.

The nation was enchanted, and when MacArthur drove through New York City the next day on a nineteen-mile parade, 2,852 tons of confetti, ticker tape and other pieces of paper were showered on him, surpassing the records of parades for Lindbergh and Howard Hughes. The crowds were estimated by the New York police to be the greatest ever—7.5 million. There was no doubt: General MacArthur was by far the most popular man in America, yet thoughtful observers wondered how popular he would be at the conclusion of the Senate hearings on the military situation in the Far East and the facts surrounding the relief of MacArthur. The hearings would start early in May.

3.

Just before Van Fleet arrived in Korea, Ridgway made it clear to his senior generals that, while he had confidence in their new commander, he was going to keep Van Fleet on a tight leash. A massive Chinese Communist offensive could begin any hour, and they must be prepared to withdraw as planned.

After listening to briefings by both Ridgway and the Eighth Army staff, Van Fleet was convinced that the Chinese "were ready for the biggest attack of all." When an uneasy quiet descended over the Eighth Army front on the morning of April 16, tension at Van Fleet's headquarters at Taegu increased. Then came reassuring reports. The Eighth Army advance was "practically unopposed." The Chinese Reds were withdrawing for no apparent reason. Even so, Van Fleet feared the enemy was going to attack. He let his troops advance cautiously for three days and then, on April 19, ordered a forty-eight-hour halt to prepare for a twin attack on the next objectives.

In Tokyo, Ridgway was concerned not only about the coming Chinese offensive but the defense of Japan in case of a Soviet invasion. He cabled, asking permission in the event of a major Chinese attack: "(A) to initiate withdrawal at my discretion of UN forces from Korea and (B) utilize redeployed UN forces in defense of the Far East Command." An answer from the Joint Chiefs came on April 19. While agreeing in principle, they did not give Ridgway the authority he wanted. A withdrawal could begin "only upon instructions furnished you."

On the morning of the 21st, Ridgway flew to Korea to watch the launching of Van Fleet's double attack: on the left flank to the Iron Triangle; and in the center to a line above the Hwachon Reservoir. Convinced that these would precipitate the Chinese onslaught, he instructed Van Fleet to be prepared to retire in orderly fashion and perform the main job—kill as many Communists as possible. Ridgway was not worried about losing real estate.

Van Fleet agreed, to a point, but was convinced that the Communists should not be allowed to recapture Seoul, which would ruin the morale of the South Koreans. He also felt that later in the summer, the Eighth Army should make an amphibious advance as far north as Wonsan on the east coast. Ridgway left Korea, unhappy with Van Fleet's Wonsan plan. It had the makings of the situation MacArthur blundered into when he separated X Corps. Ridgway sent Van Fleet a written directive. Acquisition of terrain, he said, was of little or no value. "Your mission is to repel aggression against so much of the territory (and the people therein) of the Republic of Korea as you now occupy and, in collaboration with the Government in the Republic of Korea, to establish and maintain order in that territory." He was to make no advances beyond the Iron Triangle. Under no circumstances was he to cross into Manchuria.

For more than a month, hundreds of thousands of Chinese reinforcements had been pouring over the Yalu, undergoing the same hardships as those who preceded them. Their food was gone before they were halfway to the front, and they too ate horses, shrubbery—anything edible. Along the trails, they came upon thousands of dead and dying, some of whom held socks of meal, which were appropriated. The reinforcements also came upon the thousands of walking wounded, for whom there was no transportation northward; few of these latter made it back to the Yalu. And now many of the frozen bodies that littered the North Korean countryside were thawing and giving off a sickening stench.

Wang Tsun-ming, who had undergone months of indoctrination, had finally been sent with his unit, the 31st Division, to a city on the north bank of the Yalu where they were told, at first, that they were to be used only on border defense. Then they were informed they would be sent across the Yalu "to guard prisoners of war." But when instructed to unload all excess equipment, they realized they were going to the front to fight. After the first night's march, their political commissar warned them, "There are a lot of South Korean bandits around this area who are robbing people. Everyone must stay with the unit or he might get killed."

Wang didn't believe him. The commissar was just trying to prevent desertions. Each succeeding night the commissar lectured on the cruelties of the Americans, who used napalm to burn the homes of peasants. The division was also instructed in military discipline. The penalty for disobedience was death. After ten days, all were weak from exhaustion and lack of food. Two of the men were shot because they couldn't keep up.

As Wang's unit neared the front, the commissar now encouraged them with stories of the great victories scored by other Volunteers troops. At this point Wang was suddenly struck down by diarrhea and had to be left behind with other sick troops. He hid his feeling of relief.

As the Volunteers moved into attack positions on April 21, Hsi Tzu-liang of the XII Corps had fallen out because of an infected foot. He had enlisted in the People's Liberation Army for fear he'd be liquidated, since his father was a merchant and, therefore, a capitalist. He was limping down a road when he suddenly came upon ten or so American soldiers. They were as surprised as he. When an interpreter wrote Chinese characters meaning, "Guarantee the safety of your life," Hsi breathed in relief. He was a prisoner of the Americans—a free man.

Another Chinese captured the next morning was Liu Chang, a company commander, a patriotic Volunteer. He felt disgraced for being taken alive and boasted to a fellow POW that he was going to escape to fight the corrupt capitalists again. His unit, the 2nd Artillery Division, was massing guns for a major attack tomorrow, but he refused to tell the interrogators anything except unimportant details.

"Are there any bad people in China?" he was asked.

"There are no longer any thieves or other criminals in the People's Republic of China, because everyone has plenty to eat since the Communists gained control."

"What about the morale of the men in your regiment?"

"High, because they want to help the Korean people in their struggle against the Americans, and because we must avenge the bombing of China by U.S. aircraft."

4.

The air was clear and crisp on the western front the morning of April 22. There was no movement along the entire sector held by the British 29th Independent Brigade. Brigadier Tom Brodie had deployed his three infantry battalions—the Royal Northumberland Fusiliers, 1st Glosters and 1st Royal Ulster Rifles—along the south bank of the Imjin River. The Glosters, in the middle, covered one of the classic invasion routes from the north to Seoul, thirty miles to the south. It was a peaceful Sunday, and the chaplain, Padre Sam Davies, was holding morning services at the neighboring Fusiliers' HQ to mark St. George's Day.

Late in the morning, reports came in of large-scale enemy movement north of the Imjin. That afternoon the Glosters prepared for battle. The first attack would obviously come at the river crossing. Originally, a small road had run down a cutting to the Imjin's edge. Incapable of carrying tracked or wheeled vehicles in wet weather, the road had been widened and strengthened by sappers. Steel-mesh matting had been laid upon a regraded surface in the cutting, and a series of marker buoys now showed the course of an underwater bridge.

Just before ten P.M., Bugler Tony Eagles of the 7th Platoon, who could fight as well as blow his bugle, saw something in the moonlight. "There's someone at the crossing, sir," he reported by telephone to Captain Anthony Farrar-Hockley, the adjutant. Eagles made out several figures wading across the river. When they neared the north bank, machine-gun fire wiped them out and their bodies were swept down the river. In moments a larger group started across, stumbling against the current's drag. This time fire from the north raked the defenders. More Chinese, supported by machine-gun fire and mortars, came forward, screaming as they fired their weapons.

When it seemed as if the invaders would succeed, the British ambuscade party opened up with light machine guns and Stens. Tony Eagles fired his rifle until the enemy got close, then heaved grenades. The Chinese were targets in the moonlight and their remaining numbers tried to rush back but were cut down by the Glosters. There was a lull, but soon a far larger group appeared. The Glosters' savage fire drove them back, but they returned a third and fourth time.

Lieutenant Temple sent a message to Colonel James Carne, commander of the Glosters: the Chinese were still trying to cross in hordes, and in another five minutes Temple's patrol would be out of ammunition.

"Tell Temple to start withdrawing in three minutes," said Carne. He ordered a final mortar concentration. "Then start dropping mortar rounds short of Gloster Crossing as soon as the patrol is back at the first cutting south of the river."

While Temple's men were holding Gloster Crossing, two battalions of the Chinese 187th Division crossed the river a mile and a half to the west. They headed towards Hill 148, already nicknamed Castle Hill. If they took it, they could overrun the Glosters.

Suddenly the Chinese charged. Clad in cotton khaki uniforms, the Chinese soldiers wore cotton bandoliers of ammunition crisscrossing their chests and shoulders. Behind, mules were drawing guns and ammo, and two-man teams were toting mortars and machine guns. As the Chinese came closer, they threw potato-masher hand grenades. Mortars sounded near the river, and flames spread east and went around Castle Hill. Hand-to-hand fighting broke out as the Chinese kept doggedly climbing the hill. They were also met by carefully planned defense fire. Vickers shells ripped across the cliffs and slopes into the mass of attackers. Mortars and machine guns found the range of the Chinese pressing up the hill. At midnight they began falling back, only to regroup and start again. The exhausted defenders, their ranks depleted, repulsed them, but the Chinese kept coming. One decimated Gloster platoon was forced to withdraw, and finally, after six hours of fighting, Castle Site, the highest point of the defense, was taken by the Chinese.

Pale dawn revealed a grim battlefield. The Glosters holding the rest of the hill were filthy with sweat and dust. Looking down the steep slope, they could see hundreds of Chinese discarding the bushes used for camouflage. By eight-thirty A.M. it was apparent to Colonel Carne that A and C companies were being swamped by the Chinese tidal waves. He ordered them to withdraw. The brigade commander informed Carne that he would try to send reinforcements the next day. But even if he were unsuccessful, the Glosters were to hold their position.

To the right of the British brigade, I Corps was also being pounded. The Puerto Rican 65th Infantry, reinforced by a Filipino battalion, was in bad shape. So were the Turks to their right; and once they had broken, the Puerto Ricans and Filipinos were also forced back, thus endangering the 25th Division farther east. On their right, IX Corps was being hit by a main thrust down the middle of the peninsula toward Seoul. Two Volunteers divisions had already crushed the poorly equipped ROK 6th Division on the left flank. During the night, two of its regiments had fallen back in disorder, one withdrawing six miles, the other twelve. The reserve regiment, ordered to counterattack, had also soon fallen back in confusion. All three discarded arms and equipment, with the ROK 27th Field Artillery Battalion abandoning thirteen howitzers. "The rout and dissolution of the regiments," reported the new corps commander, Major General William Hoge, himself a hero of the Battle of the Bulge, "was entirely uncalled for and disgraceful in all aspects."

The enraged Almond ordered Colonel William McCaffrey, commander of the 31st Infantry, to stop the stampeding ROKs. "Make them return to their position," he said. "Shoot them if you have to."

Reluctantly, McCaffrey—the youngest regimental commander in Korea—spread a rifle company across the streambed, backing them with several tanks. Then he came upon Almond arguing heatedly with an ROK lieutenant general. "Anyone who gets in my soldiers' way," said the ROK officer, "I'll shoot!"

"Anyone in your corps who doesn't stop," retorted Almond, "I'll shoot unless they return to their position."

A KMAG adviser, Brigadier General Frank Farrell, moved back and forth between the two angry men in an attempt to reason with them.

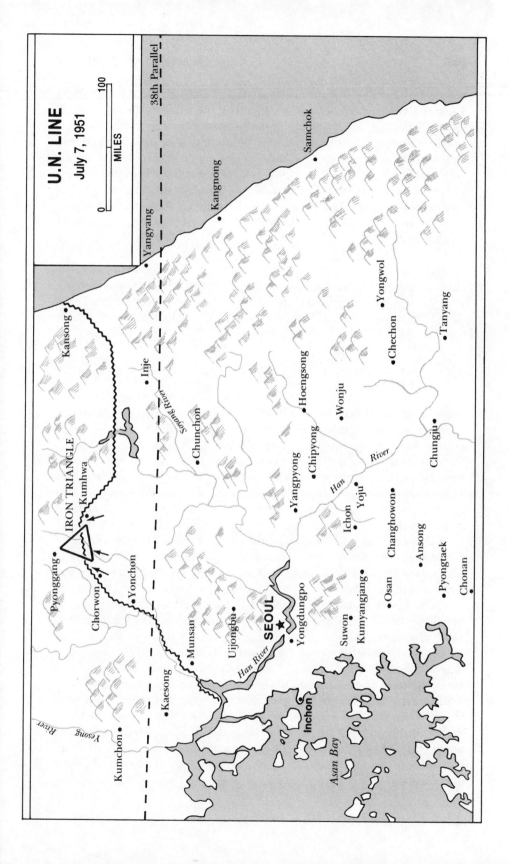

U.N. LINE
July 7, 1951

MILES
0   100

38th Parallel

McCaffrey watched this shuttle diplomacy. Was Almond going to shoot unarmed, friendly soldiers panicking down the stream? He didn't think so, yet he had an idea of what might happen if he didn't.

Fortunately, the diplomatic Farrell managed to convince Almond he should allow the ROKs to withdraw, reassemble in some sort of order, and then be reintroduced into combat. McCaffrey was eternally grateful to Farrell, for he knew nothing could have stopped the retreating ROKs except force, and he could imagine the headlines if these allies had been shot. In any case, the rout opened up a ten-mile hole in Van Fleet's central front.

At three A.M. April 24, the telephone at Carne's CP was momentarily quiet, but minutes later a report came that C Company was overrun. The Chinese now dominated the valley. "Pack up headquarters!" said Carne. He ordered the Glosters to pull back, dig in and wait for reinforcements.

5.

Ridgway flew to Korea to meet with Van Fleet and Robert "Shorty" Soule, commander of the 3rd Division. He was particularly concerned about Soule's left flank, held by the embattled British brigade. Soule briefed Ridgway on his plan to rescue the Glosters, not aware that the Filipinos and the Centurion tanks that were to go on this mission had already withdrawn. Both Van Fleet and Ridgway were angry. Why had Soule waited so long to launch his rescue mission? Soule explained that the Puerto Ricans hadn't been ready and Brigadier Brodie had been confident the Glosters could hold for another day.

Ridgway and Van Fleet agreed that the planned counterattack of the 1st Cav should be scrapped, and Eighth Army should begin a general withdrawal the next day, once the Glosters were rescued. Van Fleet still wanted to defend Seoul, pointing out that the Eighth Army was much better supplied and battle-hardened than those troops driven out of Seoul by the Chinese in January. Moreover, the weather was now so warm that even field jackets were not needed. Van Fleet also had far more artillery than Ridgway had possessed. Ridgway finally agreed to defend north of the Han and the capital. Perhaps the Chinese losses would be so great they would have to negotiate a cease-fire.

Ridgway issued a public statement. "It appears to me at this time that this attack is another major effort by our Communist enemy to drive United Nations forces from Korea, or destroy them, regardless of the further destruction of his own troops, and the continued criminal devastation of Korea. The battle is joined. It may well prove decisive."

*   *   *

It had been a long morning for the encircled Glosters, awaiting the attempt to resupply them. Just before dawn Carne had decided to concentrate his forces on Hill 235, renamed Gloster Hill. The heavy weapons were destroyed but all other arms were carried up the hill to prepare for a last stand. After several hours of darkness came the blare of Chinese bugles, followed by a fierce attack. The Chinese were driven back. Throughout the night the attacks continued, and each time the Glosters repulsed them.

By dawn of the 25th, the Glosters were almost out of ammunition. Again came the blare of bugles. Captain Farrar-Hockley suggested they confuse the Chinese by playing their own bugles. Carne instructed the drum major to play reveille, fire call—all the calls he knew. The only bugle in the drum corps belonged to Tony Eagles. "I'll play it," he offered.

"No, you bloody won't," said the drum major. "You stay here with your Bren gun."

The drum major started with the regimental call, then he played long reveille, a moving call. Never had Eagles heard it played so beautifully. Coming out of the darkness on a Korean hill in the middle of battle, it caused a sensation. The men cheered wildly. As the Chinese were coming over the ridge, the Glosters leaped out of their trenches shouting, bayonets thrust forward. Startled by the bugles and the desperate charge, the Chinese broke ranks. The drum major kept bugling through his entire repertoire: defaulters, cookhouse, officers dress for dinner, and company calls. Everything except retreat.

At dawn Eagles could see hundreds of Chinese advancing up the slopes. The remnants of A and B companies, battered all night, called urgently for air support. Within minutes two F-80's appeared, their silver wings shining in the sunlight. They circled, then came in dropping napalm tanks that burst into great orange flames. Eagles and his mates cheered as the deadly jellied gasoline descended on their enemies. By a miracle they still held Gloster Hill.

The brigade commander realized no help was coming to the Glosters and ordered Colonel Carne to pull out. Carne summoned Farrar-Hockley and other officers and took them to the edge of the ridge, pointing out the route south each should take. Then he told his medical officer, Dr. Hickey, "Bob, I'm afraid we shall have to leave the wounded behind."

Hickey paused. "Very well, sir. I quite understand the position."

A Company was first to withdraw, and at three minutes to ten Farrar-Hockley gave the sign to set off with the main body. Soon came word that there would be no gun support, since the artillery was also under attack. Carne revised his instructions. They were to break up—every man to make his own way back.

Farrar-Hockley met Captain Hickey. "Come on, Bob, we're about the last to go."

"I can't," said the doctor. "I must stay with the wounded."

Farrar-Hockley scrambled down Gloster Hill. All the way through the valley the captain heard machine guns. As his group approached the rise to the saddle, the walls of the valley narrowed, and he could feel the breath of the enemy's fire. No bullets hit them, but he knew they could now be mown down like grass before a scythe. "Exposed entirely to their weapons, we moved along the path under their very muzzles. The message they conveyed was quite plain: we are up here; you are down there; you are exposed; we are concealed, and you are in our sights."

He knew he had only one course if his men were to stay alive. Raising his voice, he called, "Stop!"

The men halted, faces expectant.

"Put down your arms!"

A few seconds later, at the foot of the saddle, he heard the support company commander call out the same thing. "The words rang in my ears like an echo, a shameful echo. After all the effort we had exerted in fulfilling our task, this was the end: surrender to the enemy!"

The whole valley was now silent. Numbers of Chinese ran toward them looking excited and pleased. They were not unfriendly but refused to let them carry the walking wounded. All continued down the hill, their pace slow because of the injured men.

When the order to withdraw came, Tony Eagles smashed his beloved bugle before joining a corporal named Cook and a lieutenant. "All we can do with what little we've got is pop off a few shots here and there," said the lieutenant. "Let them think we're all still here." The three men kept moving about, hiding behind boulders and trees, occasionally firing a shot. After half an hour the lieutenant told the two enlisted men to take off. He'd stay behind and cover their retreat. Eagles and Cook dashed down the hill, soon meeting three other men. At a narrow defile, Eagles said, "I'll have a look," and ran straight into three Chinese behind a machine gun. Not a shot was fired. All five Britons were marched down the hill to join a large group of prisoners. Marine planes few over, dipping their wings in salute as if to say, "Well, your war's over."

Private Sam Mercer, twenty-one years old, wounded earlier that morning, came to his senses. An ancestor of his had fought at Waterloo, and his father had served in India and World War I with the Gurkha Rifles. Sam had joined the Glosters three years earlier and was eager to do his bit. It was quiet. Was the battle over? From inside the aid tent he could hear the murmur of voices outside. He crawled out to find what was going on. Several men were sitting, talking quietly. It gradually sank into Mercer's dazed mind that all resistance was over. Then he saw Padre Davies, calm as usual, and felt better.

Suddenly three Chinese appeared on the slope above them. Shabby and tattered, they chattered excitedly as they gestured with their weapons. All the Glosters raised their arms. Through a captured South Korean interpreter, Davies asked a Chinese officer if they could carry the stretcher-wounded into the valley.

"No. Do not fear," was the answer. "We, the Chinese People's Volunteers, will bring your wounded down later."

Mercer couldn't get up, but painfully raised his hands. A Chinese poked him with his rifle until Mercer finally managed to stagger to his feet. He tried to walk and a medic helped him a few steps until the Chinese shouted and motioned the medic to move ahead. Without aid Mercer hobbled slowly as best as he could. The next thing he knew a shot rang out and he spun around and fell. A bullet had hit his left leg and gone straight through.

Mercer, glaring up at the Chinese who had shot him, shouted British barracks-room insults. "Why the hell he didn't pull the trigger again, I don't know. Fortunately he didn't understand English." The Chinese stared back a moment, then walked off. Mercer figured the hill would be an unhealthy place to stay, since the Americans would probably be back to cover it with napalm. He struggled upright and crawled off. He finally reached the bottom, where the Chinese were looting the battalion's transport. He watched as one Chinese pulled out a tin of Coleman's Mustard powder and stuck a spoonful into his mouth. Mercer knew what was going to happen and gloated. The spoon went one way and the Chinese went another, shouting and looking for water. "I can see him now, clear as day, and it was thirty-odd years ago. I won't say it completely obliterated what had happened to me, but it went a long way to redress the balance. Believe me, it made my day!"

Mercer hobbled up to an ambulance being loaded with the wounded of both sides. They were all taken to a nearby village, where Mercer and two others were pushed into a little Korean store. Hurt and hungry, Mercer felt lucky to be alive.

On the other side of the river the Chinese were so fearful of air attacks that they hid themselves and their captives throughout the afternoon. At dusk they brought more than three hundred Glosters to Gloster Crossing. The din of Chinese fire was terrific, and it seemed to the prisoners that every Volunteers division had earmarked this place for its own crossing. From the racket and the angry shouts, it sounded as though the Chinese would be at each other's throats at any minute. Every so often a mule-drawn artillery unit would take precedence over the infantry and simply storm through. Everyone seemed eager to move south and get into battle.

The prisoners waited for their turn to cross the river and head north. They stripped but kept their boots on because of sharp stones and barbed wire, making slow progress in the turbulent, chilly water while holding bundled clothing on their heads. Each man knew that at any moment he could be trodden down in the darkness and swept into the fast-flowing Imjin. And even if he made it safely across, what future lay on the other side?

CHAPTER 31

Prisoners of War
(April 25–Early May)

1.

On the morning of April 25, 1951, the British brigade was withdrawing as Chinese occupied the hills behind the scattered defenders and set up ambushes. Centurion tanks of the King's Royal Irish Hussars tried to break through to rescue the trapped Britons but were forced to fight with hatches down, since the Chinese boldly came to close quarters.

The Centurions finally managed to crash through and provide covering fire so that the Fusiliers and a company of the Ulster Rifles could break contact. It then became apparent that the Chinese were tightening their grip on the escape route to the rear, and all but one of the remaining Ulster Rifles companies struck out across the hills on a parallel route. With the tanks acting as rear guard, the last Ulster Rifles company and a unit of resolute Belgians conducted a fighting withdrawal through the valley. The Chinese were swarming all over the hills and, displaying insane courage, repeatedly tried to smother the Centurions with their human-wave tactics. Great swaths were cut through their ranks by the twenty-pounders and the coaxial machine guns, but still the Chinese clambered aboard and tried to pry open the hatches, to be shot off time and again by the fire of other tanks; one commander swept his vehicle clean of the enemy by driving straight through a house. When the Centurions reached safety, their tops were piled high with dead and wounded, their sides running scarlet with blood; there was blood on the tracks too, but none of it was British or Belgian.

The withdrawal of the British brigade left the U.S. 3rd Division to the east in a precarious position. Only one regiment, the 7th Infantry, was left to act as rear guard. It was holding the high ground on the Uijongbu–Seoul highway despite the loss of a battalion. Farther east, the reorganized 25th Division was pulling back without the loss of a single artillery gun. But the 24th Division on the right flank of I Corps was in danger because of the collapse of the ROK 6th Division. Two regiments of the 24th withdrew successfully, but the Chinese got behind the 5th Infantry and blasted the center of the column. In the darkness, the 555th Field Artillery Battalion, shattered in the Pusan Perimeter, had to abandon thirteen of its 105-mm howitzers and sixty vehicles. The rear of the column also took a beating. Seven Patton tanks were lost. In all, the 5th Infantry suffered 800 casualties that night.

To the right of the big gap caused by the ROK collapse, the 1st Marine Division was withdrawing in orderly fashion to the southeast. The next morning Corporal Don Hansen of the 1st Battalion, 7th Marines, a Marine since he was seventeen, was scanning the road below his ridge with glasses. He could see hundreds of bodies, smashed trucks, tanks, ambulances, and guns. On both sides of the road tents were torn down and there were more bodies than he could count. It was total devastation, a gruesome scene. He didn't know he was viewing the remnants of a regiment of the ROK 6th Division and the black 555th Artillery Battalion, the Triple Nickels.

The 3rd Platoon made it to the floor of the valley through a draw. No gooks. All gone. Someone got on the horn and radioed the company to come down. Coast was clear. Hansen and the others swung their BARs around, aiming towards a *clink-clink-clink* noise. They stripped the brush away and found a black soldier. "Thank God, you're Marines!" he exclaimed.

They pulled the man out of his hole. "Everybody just ran away and left me. They wouldn't fight."

"Were they all colored?" asked Hansen.

"Hell, no. White guys too. They's all the same. I love you Marines. I wish I could be a Marine. I can fight."

Lieutenant Paul Vanture, a white officer, later wrote a friend about the bugout. "I joined the general exodus, *black and white*, to the rear and in the ensuing days and nights had occasion to see troops of both 'persuasions,' *sans* weapons or helmets. On one of those nights we narrowly missed being cut off and ambushed and my platoon picked up some wounded stragglers who said their regimental CP had been overrun. They were white and had neither helmet nor weapon. If this was not the 24th's finest hour, neither was it anyone else's!"

2.

The Chinese had thrown some 350,000 men into the great attack. Most had fought fiercely, but some had "come over" to the UN side. Pamphlets had assured them they would be treated humanely and given plenty of food. Yao Chin-chung, son of a landowner, was a veteran of the Kuomintang. After his capture by the Communists in 1949, he was sent to a concentration camp, then placed in the LX Corps. When the offensive started, he looked for a chance to surrender. At last, on the afternoon of the 25th, he saw two Americans come up the hill towards him.

"Hello!" he shouted. Both Americans were unarmed. He laid down his own rifle, which he had never fired, and held up his hands. The GIs gave him bread and cigarettes. At last his war was over.

Lin Chin-chiang, a clerk in his local government, had been drafted into the People's Liberation Army and sent with no training to Korea. His job was to transport food and weapons on mules. He and two comrades planned to surrender at the first opportunity. Just before the start of the offensive, they left their unit and headed south over a mountain trail. Seeing a group of ROK soldiers eating, they held up their hands. Expecting fair treatment, they asked for food. Instead the Koreans took their possessions and shoes, then beat them with rifle butts.

North Korean soldiers were also "coming over to freedom." Corporal Han Chae-ung had not only read pamphlets offering good treatment but had also heard a plane broadcasting what sounded like the same offer. He freely answered all U.S. questions and revealed that the main reason he had deserted was discrimination. Although he was a platoon leader, his previous service in the Kuomintang, he said, "constituted a stigma in my relationship with other noncoms."

Private Kim Yong-chin had started out in the ROK Army, only to be captured in early July at Suwon. After five months' imprisonment he was assigned as a gunner in an antitank platoon. The spring offensive gave him his first chance to desert. He told interrogators that the morale of the majority of his comrades was high. One out of every three men was an ardent Communist, and almost all believed the Red forces would emerge victorious. Kim, however, found his antitank weapon ineffective against UN armor.

Another prisoner of war, Private Jing Ping-kuei, had been conscripted into the Chinese 193rd Division as a rifleman. He revealed that the men in his company feared the terrible firepower of the UN forces and had low morale because of the lack of food and rest. "None of them like to fight in Korea. All are homesick. All officers are party members and diehards. Discipline is very strict!"

Private Lee Pae-chun had been conscripted into the North Korean army with eleven other men a week after the war began. Most of the group belonged to the North Korean Blue Friend party, an anti-Communist organization. Escaping after four days on the march, they hid in the mountains but had been caught in January and assigned to the Railway Guard Corps. Lee, an ammo bearer, had fought in the battle against an ROK division but deserted during a withdrawal of his battalion on April 25.

Lieutenant Colonel Kim Tae-hun, assistant chief of the 8th KPA Division Political Section, wounded on April 25 at Munsan, also had read the leaflets promising humane treatment but did not believe them. Even so, he cooperated with the interrogators. "His answers were deliberative and consistent."

By April 26, both the Chinese and North Korean forces had been obviously weakened by lack of food and by the difficulty, because of UN air strength, of bringing ammunition and supplies to the front. But if they could keep up the pressure despite these difficulties, the Eighth Army would be in serious trouble.

3.

At midnight of the 26th, British prisoners who had crossed the Imjin were lined up and lectured by a Chinese officer in stilted English. "Officers and soldiers of the British army," he began, "you are now prisoners of the Chinese People's Volunteer Forces in Korea. You have been duped by the American imperialists. You are tools of the reactionary warmongers fighting against the righteous cause of the Korean people, supported by their brothers, the Chinese people. You are hirelings of the barbarous Rhee puppet-government, but you will be given the chance to learn the truth through study, and correct your mistakes. Do not be afraid—we shall not harm you. At home, your loved ones await you. Obey our rules and regulations, and then you shall not be shot."

The prisoners were crowded into stables and sheds. As they huddled in cramping positions, Padre Davies, the Glosters' chaplain, tried to sleep. In the river crossing the padre had lost his underpants, a spare pair of socks, and his clerical stock and collar. About two in the morning, he was led through the darkness by an interpreter and a guard to a small dugout. The military interrogator, an impassive man, sat cross-legged at a tiny table. Because of his scars he had already been nicknamed Napalm Face. In the light of a flickering candle, Davies (prounounced *Davis*) was asked to tell what he knew about the British 29th Brigade. He produced his Geneva Convention ticket, explaining that he could only give his name and number.

"We do not know about Geneva Convention," said the interrogater. "You must obey his orders." Raising his eyes devoutly, Davies made a sign of the cross and said, "I am chaplain, priest, religious man—Christian teacher."

"You are captain."

For an hour the padre was questioned about military matters. "I do not know any military information," he repeated over and over. "I do not carry any gun."

"You lie! We can punish unrighteous man!" Then, to the padre's surprise, Napalm Face suddenly fell silent and dismissed him with a wave of the hand.

The U.S. I Corps was slowly withdrawing towards Seoul and by noon of the 28th began occupying a defense position near Uijongbu called the Lincoln Line, a series of deep, interconnected trenches and bunkers replete with machine guns, recoilless rifles and flamethrowers. Out front were lines of coiled barbed wire peppered with antipersonnel mines, booby traps, and numerous gasoline drums filled with napalm and white phosphorus.

That night the North Korean 8th Division slammed into the ROK 1st Division. Whitey Paik's men gave up a hill but then counterattacked with Pattons from the 73rd Tank Battalion, killing an estimated 1,200 North Koreans. They fought so well that the youthful Paik was promoted to corps commander.

The next day, Sunday the 29th, the Chinese launched a thrust at Seoul with 6,000 men starting across the Han, west of the capital, in small boats. Once they reached the other side they could move down the Kimpo peninsula and outflank the capital's defenses. "It was here that our command of the air worked most tellingly," recalled Ridgway. "Our pilots swooped down upon the attackers while they were still waterborne and decimated them. The shattered remnants that succeeded in reaching the south bank were no match at all for the ROK 5th Marine Battalion, then defending the peninsula."

The Chinese and North Koreans redoubled their efforts and, although the outcome was still in doubt, Van Fleet replied emphatically, "No!" when correspondent E. J. Kahn asked if he would have to evacuate Seoul. He summoned his three corps commanders and told them, "Keep units intact. Small units must be kept within supporting distance." Every consideration should be given to the use of armor and infantry teams for a limited objective counterthrust. "For greater distances, have ready and use when appropriate, regiments of infantry protected by artillery and tanks." The Eighth Army had been pushed back to within striking distance of the capital but had inflicted some 70,000 casualties on the enemy. Even so, massive Chinese reserves had not been committed to battle. There would be, he predicted, a "second impulse" offensive in a few days, whose objective would be the capture of Seoul.

The estimate of enemy casualties may have been high, but there was no doubt that Van Fleet had seriously wounded the Chinese. At least one division, the Chinese 180th, was surrounded. The Americans had hit the machine-gun company of Tzo Peng so furiously that his team never got to fire a single shot. They had been told just the night before, "Now we are going to fight the Americans. We have five men against one American."

The Chinese fell back but couldn't get out of the trap, and for five days had nothing to eat. The situation was chaotic. Troops were moving back and forth. The shelling was horrifying. Tzo's team could neither fight nor escape. He and two others agreed to surrender at the first opportunity.

Another soldier of the 180th, Yu Tzeh-an, formerly in the Kuomintang, threw away his machine gun upon discovering his team was surrounded. He and three others moved up front so they could surrender. Then they'd surely get something to eat. Creeping up to a road, they waited until a truck appeared. They revealed themselves and five black soldiers, holding carbines, leaped out. The blacks searched them but took nothing and said they would send them to the rear. Then they gave the Chinese cigarettes. The prisoners were also given canned food. The taste was unfamiliar, but they were so hungry that anything edible was good.

Chang Se-ching's father was a salesman of medicinal herbs. Educated at a junior high school, Chang had studied Chinese classical literature. His job in the Army was to teach illiterate soldiers to read and the others to sing. Just before the great offensive, he had gone from man to man challenging each to perform a heroic act. When someone agreed, he would shout, for example, "Comrade Lin has accepted my challenge and will kill more capitalist enemies than anyone in his company!" Propaganda girls would join in, singing and banging pans. Once the battle started, Chang became a combat soldier. As soon as the division was surrounded, he and four others hid in a cave. Thinking the fighting was over, they sneaked out and were captured.

Other divisions besides the 180th had been badly mauled during the offensive, an offensive which Peking proclaimed a success because so much territory had been recaptured. While not underestimating the seriousness of the loss of men and matériel, Mao was determined to mount still another offensive that would surely take Seoul and—this time—completely rout the ROK divisions.

4.

The British prisoners' exhausting march to the north almost always took place at night to prevent strafing by UN planes. During the hot days, they lay in wooded hillsides or in shacks, fighting off swarms of insects and trying in vain to rid themselves of lice. Resuming the march was always agony. Overtaxed muscles had tightened, and the soles of their feet were indescribably tender.

Early in May, Tony Eagles, the bugler, decided to escape with Ron Allum from B Company and two GIs they had picked up. The four hid in the brush until their group left for the night march. Eagles was to give a signal, "Hoot! Hoot!" and they would head for the east coast. There they hoped to find a boat and be picked up by the U.S. or Royal Navy.

They made good progress for several days. But Allum got sunstroke, and Eagles couldn't bring himself to abandon his comrade. "I'll stick with him and see if I can get him some treatment," he told the GIs. "If you two want to go on, that's fine." The Americans insisted they all stick together, and the quartet started inland. An old Korean woman let them rest in her home, but after two days she said they must leave at once. Her grandson had seen them and was going to report them.

Soon the boy and his father appeared, armed with rifles. Allum was taken off by a Chinese soldier, but the others were left to the mercy of the NK police. Their wrists were tied with electric cord, and they were forced to squat while one of the police lit a cigarette, using it to burn the three prisoners on the lips. A little later an old man rushed in with a heavy stick. He had lost his family in a bombing and was bent on taking out revenge on Eagles. To protect himself, he kicked the old man in the crotch. To Eagles's surprise, the police did nothing, but one who could speak English said, "Come," to one GI, and took him away. Then Eagles heard shots. The police returned and grabbed the other GI. A minute later he heard more shots.

The English-speaking policeman returned, mumbling something about, "You Americans!"

"If you're going to shoot me," said Eagles, "shoot me as a British soldier, not as an American. I'm British."

"That's different," the policeman said and explained what Eagles had said to his comrades. Eagles had to go to the toilet—he didn't know if it was from fear. He was taken outside and to his amazement saw the two GIs—still alive. The mock shooting had been intended to terrorize them. Instead, both were mad as hell and called into question the lineage of Mao.

A Chinese patrol, drawn by the firing, came running into the village. When they found out what had happened they shouted that Mao would be unhappy to learn that his lenient policy was being ignored by his North Korean allies. The Chinese escorted the three prisoners to their headquarters where they found Ron Allum. All four were fed egg patties containing bean shoots, their first real food in many days. "It was like heaven to us."

Eagles never thought he'd be glad to see the Chinese again. They were marched off to join the other prisoners. Ron asked to be left behind, since he couldn't walk, but the others knew he'd die if abandoned. They half-carried, half-dragged him along the trail. At last they joined the column headed by Colonel Carne, and soon arrived at a village that was the halfway point to the Yalu River. At this village they rested for forty-eight hours. The four newcomers were interrogated by Napalm Face. He insisted that Eagles was the ringleader, since he was the oldest. He was actually the youngest, just twenty-two, but the others had claimed they were twenty. Napalm Face loaded his revolver and spun the barrel several times. Eagles didn't want to die just for the sake of being a bloody ringleader. He started to say something.

Napalm Face's eyes lit up. "Ah, I knew you were the ringleader!" he said and sentenced Eagles to fourteen days in the hole. The two GIs got the same sentence. One died of pneumonia soon afterward.

Private Sam Mercer and the other injured soldiers reached Pyongyang in a truck and were quartered that night in a wrecked warehouse. The next morning a Korean woman entered with a large bucket of wet rice. The single Chinese guard ignored her. By sign language she indicated she knew they were British and that the British had once helped her. She was repaying the debt.

As the group was preparing to start off at dark, a large number of angry Korean civilians crowded around the truck and were prevented from taking revenge on the enemy soldiers by the lone Chinese guard and his bayoneted rifle. He said nothing but made it clear he would shoot anyone who attacked a prisoner. It was a miracle, thought Mercer, as they moved safely out of the capital. In fact, he had experienced a number of miracles since being wounded at Gloster Hill. Almost every day they had a new guard, each one risking his life to keep civilians from lynching the prisoners. Mercer had a feeling that the Chinese high command didn't know about this truckload of wounded, and it was the lower echelons that kept passing it on. So far they had been treated well, but would the next guard show such concern for their safety?

CHAPTER 32

The Last Chinese Campaign
(May 1–30)

1.

At ten on the morning of May Day, Mao made his appearance on the balcony of Tienanmen Gate, the Gate of Heavenly Peace, to watch the May Day procession. There were huge portraits of the leaders of the proletariat in all countries and enormous cartoons ridiculing and condemning American action in the war. More than a million watched the seemingly endless procession of seven hundred thousand men, women, boys and girls, marching past. To the amazement of foreign diplomats, Mao remained standing until midafternoon without once relaxing. "For over two months," recalled Kavalam Panikkar, "the Hong Kong papers had been talking of Mao's illness, about his being put on the shelf by the Russians. In fact many among the Western diplomats even in Peking had begun to believe that Mao was seriously ill, as he had not appeared at any public function after the Indian National Day on the 26th of January. But there on the balcony he stood like a rock for five hours and a quarter, waving his hands every two minutes. The Swedish ambassador, Hammustrom, insisted that it could not be Mao but his double and repeated many stories of Hitler's days to prove his point. Moerch, the Danish minister, was equally convinced that Mao had been artificially propped up, and that he must have had numerous injections before coming to the ceremony. This was what the West liked to believe." Mao was actually in good health and in recent months had been confined in

457

his little house nearby, poring over maps and discussing the offensive in Korea with select advisers.

Panikkar hoped for a truce. Though he was pessimistic about the immediate prospects, he kept in touch with the Soviet bloc. The Polish ambassador, recently returned from North Korea, reported that conditions were horrendous. "According to him over eighty-five percent of the houses in North Korea had been destroyed and Pyongyang was a city of ruins and the people were living in holes and caves: but the morale of the North Koreans was high and their fighting spirit was higher than ever. This had been told me by others also; people who had been to Korea and come back. I was therefore satisfied that there was no possibility of the Americans gaining a military decision, especially as the Chinese air force had become a factor of importance."

This air force consisted of Russian MiG's, and the Americans were convinced that most of the pilots were Soviets. Whoever flew them, they had been a threat to the allies since late April, and the area they covered was nicknamed, with respect, "MiG Alley." Lately, however, the U.S. Air Force had regained control of the air, and the MiGs could not be a major factor in the offensive Mao was planning.

Despite the setback of the first spring offensive, Mao had already ordered the second step of his Fifth Campaign. During the first week of May, U.S. planes reported sighting almost four thousand vehicles behind enemy lines, more than half of them heading south. This news worried Van Fleet's G2, James Tarkenton, and on May 10, he told the general that an all-out Chinese attack on Seoul appeared imminent. The next day, Van Fleet canceled his own offensive, Operation Detonate, and informed Ridgway that the enemy would attack in the next seventy-two to ninety-six hours with nine Chinese divisions and three or four North Korean divisions. A secondary attack—of about ten Chinese and NK divisions—would probably follow in support of the main drive on Seoul. Van Fleet felt sure his new defense line would stand firm. Because he gave it no title, the men had dubbed it No Name Line.

Ridgway cabled the Joint Chiefs. The double attack seemed suicidal to the American. How could the Chinese launch a major offensive with such long supply lines over mountains? Mao had, in fact, a far different plan. He was going to wipe out Almond's X Corps on No Name Line, then continue south to Wonju before turning west to Suwon. This plan was bolder than the one Van Fleet and Ridgway had conceived, and if successful, it could open the way to Pusan.

By May 12, the Chinese divisions were assembling for the attack. Fang Hai-chin, formerly a lieutenant in the Kuomintang army, was now a transport man in the LX Corps. That morning he was ordered to bring his horse, carrying two hundred kilos of TNT, to the advance unit, the

540th Regiment. On the way, he picked up a leaflet dropped by an American plane. In English, Korean and Chinese it told how to surrender. He delivered his cargo and the next morning prepared to give up. He was about a hundred yards away from doing so when he saw nearly forty Chinese prisoners sitting on the ground, guarded by an ROK soldier with a machine gun. Suddenly the ROK began mowing down the prisoners. In protest an American captain rushed at the South Korean, kicking him, punching his face.

The terrified Fang found a hiding place near a road. Two hours later he heard a tank approaching. Seeing it was American, he stood up and raised his hands. The tank stopped and two black Americans emerged. Fang had never seen a black and was frightened. After searching him, the Americans handed him cigarettes and gum, then took him to the rear. Through an interpreter, one of the Americans praised him for surrendering. Fang was his first prisoner.

When Chen Huang, a platoon officer in the logistics section of the 34th Division, crossed the Yalu in March, he had been determined to prove he was a good soldier of Chairman Mao. But his experiences on the long march to the front had convinced him that the Volunteers were doomed to failure, since, having no air force, they couldn't fight in the daytime. They had no logistic support and hunger had made them weak. Their firepower and the quality of their weapons were far inferior to those of the UN. He decided to surrender.

He joined a group of deserters and wounded near the river. While he was there, four American jets swept down, strafing and dropping napalm bombs. A hut was set afire, and the wounded inside shrieked in agony. That night an artillery shell exploded nearby. Wounded by shrapnel, Chen lost consciousness. When he awoke he was lying on a stretcher in a jeep; he thanked God for leading the Americans to him. If the South Koreans had found him, he surely would have been killed.

In addition to attack orders, Chinese regiments were being issued top-secret information on the enemy's combat efficiency. Coordination among tanks and artillery was precise, and mobility of troops was good. "The infantry is equipped with many automatic weapons, while artillery is provided with strong, long-range firepower." On the other hand, the combat efficiency of the enemy infantry was low. "They are good neither in offensive nor in defensive action, but rely on support from planes, tanks and artillery." Since the enemy troops were heavily equipped, weather and terrain greatly impeded their movement. "The enemy is also afraid of both night combat and close combat. These conditions should, therefore, be exploited. The formation for attack should be wide in frontage and great in depth."

*   *   *

May 16 was dark, and the heavy overcast prevented observation planes from flying over the front lines. During the afternoon, Chinese forward units sent out probing patrols that were not detected. Nine Chinese divisions and four artillery regiments were secretly deployed east of the Hwachon Reservoir near Inje in preparation for the main attack on the ROK 5th, 7th and 9th divisions.

By dusk it was raining, and a few hours later the attack began. Some 175,000 Chinese and North Koreans rushed forward, blowing bugles and firing flares. Van Fleet was prepared for an attack, but not this far east. His main defenses were on the west in front of Seoul. To make matters worse, his two corps commanders on the east had become embroiled in an argument over territorial rights. The 5th and 7th ROK divisions held the right flank of Almond's X Corps. Their neighbor on the right, the ROK 9th, was in the ROK III Corps commanded by Brigadier General Yu Jai-hung. The only supply route for the 9th Division was a mountain road which swung for several miles into X Corps territory before swerving back to ROK III Corps lines. The commander of the ROK 7th Division had made no objection to this brief trespass, but Almond insisted on keeping control of this narrow territory despite Yu's pleas, and ordered a Yu battalion defending this bulge in the mountain road to get back into its own lines.

When the Chinese hit the seam between the ROK 7th and 9th divisions that night, they found few troops defending the critical bulge. Within hours, Chinese were behind Yu's division. Now he faced not only a cutoff of all supplies to his division but panic flight. There was little he could do, and by the end of the second day a huge hole existed to Almond's right, exposing the rear of No Name Line and threatening Almond's own 2nd Division. Only the division artillery and that of X Corps prevented a rout. A tremendous, never-ending barrage rained steadily on the six Chinese divisions, slowing their advance.

Exploiting the ROK cutoff, Peng's troops swarmed over the U.S. 2nd Division. The first target was a strategic hill defended by K Company, 3rd Battalion, of the 38th Infantry Regiment. In a classic two-day struggle, the stalwart men of K Company fended off persistent heavy Chinese attacks. Then at four o'clock on the morning of the 19th, there was abrupt quiet. The enemy had vanished.

A few hours later Almond met with General Clark Ruffner, who had replaced McClure as commander of the 2nd Division. Colonel Wallace Hanes's 3rd Battalion was holding a deep bulge in the front. They agreed that Hanes should withdraw to straighten out the corps's line. Convinced that his men could hold where they were, Hanes protested. But Ruffner ordered him to pull back to the south.

*   *   *

For two days General Yu Jai-hung had been trying to get supplies and reinforcements from the Eighth Army to his two beleaguered divisions. When nothing could be brought up, in desperation he flew to the CP of the ROK 7th Division, which was still trying to hold the eastern end of Almond's corps. Yu begged the commander, an old friend, for help. But his friend's troops were already out of control and the gap in No Name Line was deepening. Nothing could be done.

That morning, Ridgway arrived in Korea. He flew over the new 2nd Division front in a liaison plane, then returned to the X Corps CP to meet with Almond and Van Fleet.

"We are in a bad situation as I understand it," said Van Fleet. "General Almond, what is your opinion?"

"The Chinese are flowing like water around my right flank. The 2nd Division is holding in successive positions, but the ROK divisions on my right, the 5th and 7th, are disintegrating under this huge attack, and this will continue and be extended to the coast shortly, against the other ROK corps on the right flank. I think we are in a very serious situation." He urgently requested American reinforcement from Eighth Army reserve as well as more artillery. But Van Fleet was still concerned about Seoul. The Chinese attack could shift to the capital.

Almond insisted that the enemy must be stopped in his area. The Chinese could deal him a fatal blow if he didn't get immediate reinforcements. He requested the 187th Airborne Regiment, which was in Army reserve. He also wanted the 3rd Infantry Division. "I will arrange them by regimental combat-team deployment in general areas about fifteen miles apart. These I will use as islands so that the advancing Chinese Armies will have to bypass or eliminate them."

Van Fleet turned to Ridgway. "May I talk to you alone?"

Five minutes later Van Fleet told Almond, "We will give you the 187th Airborne tonight." And the 3rd Division would begin to arrive at midnight for Almond's disposition.

"That will allow me to strike the enemy's rear and cut his line of communication," said the relieved Almond.

Ridgway and Van Fleet had a broader concept. They were confident that Almond could hold back the Chinese and believed his plan to cut them off in the east was possible, paving the way for a potential all-out Eighth Army counterattack. Much territory could be retaken and, at worst, future Chinese offensives would be disrupted.

The two commanders decided to let Almond contain the Chinese while Bill Hoge's IX Corps started an offensive the next day. Hoge would drive north to Hwachon, where the Chinese would have to retreat when Almond counterattacked. If Hoge took Hwachon, most of the Chinese in the east would be trapped. To protect Hoge's left flank, I Corps was ordered to attack on the 20th. Three days later would come the major counteroffensive by all three corps.

Ridgway decided to stay another day to watch the two attacks. That night he cabled the Joint Chiefs outlining the new plan. "Morale excellent," he concluded.

On May 20, Hoge's attack was slowed by rain and mountainous terrain. During the day, Ridgway visited every corps and divisional CP in Eighth Army and toured the fronts. Distressed by the bugout of four ROK divisions, he ordered General Chung Il-kwon, the ROK chief of staff, to disband his III Corps. Ridgway left, wondering if Chung was capable of re-forming his troops. Fortunately, Chung had Major Hausman as his adviser.

That night Ridgway left for Tokyo and, upon arrival, cabled the Joint Chiefs. "Having visited all U.S. corps, all U.S. divisions and ROK 1st Division, I wish to cite all these units to you for superior spirit and conduct in battle." It was also clear that four ROK divisions had performed discreditably. "We are continuing our efforts to correct this lamentable situation."

In spite of the rain, the IX Corps's offensive advanced steadily but slowly over rough terrain. On the morning of May 23, Almond launched his counterattack. With three corps on the move, Van Fleet telexed Ridgway an encouraging report. "Eighth Army's counteroffensive now becoming effective, regaining much ground formerly occupied by 2nd Division."

The Americans were unaware that the Chinese Volunteers had overextended themselves and, while winning terrain and destroying thousands of ROKs, they had suffered severe casualties. The survivors were both exhausted and almost out of ammunition and food.

Although Peng had fooled the Americans by hitting No Name Line at its weakest point and opening a great gap in the UN lines, his triumph was short-lived. Many of the four ROK division troops had fled in panic. But others had not, and it was soon apparent to Peng that he could not break through to Wonju and then Pusan. He was stuck in the mountains, and his advance was slowing to a crawl. Therefore, he ordered the attack halted.

That same day, May 11, Van Fleet caught Peng by surprise with his two-corps counterattack in the west. And when Almond joined in with a third corps on the 23rd, Peng realized his advance had become a great disadvantage. The UN had also regained mastery of the air while controlling the sea on both sides of the peninsula.

2.

By the morning of May 26, the situation was critical for the Chinese, with troops surrendering in unprecedented numbers. Americans speculated that this was due to malnutrition and disease. But the majority of those surrendering were veterans of the Kuomintang who took advantage of the turn of the battle to "come over" to the side of democracy.

Many others, however, fought to the end for their country. Seventeen-year-old Zhang Da had enthusiastically joined the Chinese Volunteers and was sent to Korea in the 539th Regiment. The first victorious days of the spring offensive had been exciting. Then his regiment was surrounded by the U.S. 2nd Division. Many companies were down to twenty men and there was no ammunition left. On the night of May 24, the regimental commander gathered the survivors and ordered them to break out. All were near starvation and someone suggested killing their last horse. But the animal's tender burst into tears. "It is a revolutionary horse!" he pleaded. "It has followed me for years! You can't kill it."

It was agreed that the heroic horse should be set free. That matter settled, the breakout began. By morning Zhang found himself alone. He luckily came upon a small bag of rice. As he crept forward, he was seized by a Korean farmer. Zhang was so weak he couldn't get free, but he had an idea. In broken Korean he offered to give the farmer his rice. As the Korean was putting the rice into a bag, Zhang grabbed a rock, hit the man on the head, and retrieved the rice—it was his life!

He crept through an open field, only to be caught by an artillery barrage. When fragments of a shell hit his leg, he managed to tear off part of his uniform to bind the wound. He staggered for hours trying to get back to his own lines, then passed out. When he came to, he was near a Korean hut where he could see a woman cooking. He asked her if there were any American or Chinese soldiers nearby. All had left, she said, and agreed to cook his rice. Then she departed. Zhang assumed she was going to get wood, but she returned with three soldiers—two Americans and one South Korean.

They tied Zhang's hands and dragged him to a jeep before bringing him to a field hospital where he saw one of his own staff officers. The man winked at him. "I knew my duty then and refused to have any medical treatment. Because of this, I was beaten by an American soldier."

By May 26, the situation of the Volunteers was so serious that a Communist party committee of one division held a meeting close to the front. They conceded that the Americans controlled the air and sea, and that Chinese infantry was forced to walk while the U.S. troops rode on trucks and tanks. "The weakest part is supply," they concluded. Out of eight hundred Volunteer vehicles, six hundred had been destroyed by enemy bombing. Every time an offensive started, their troops could sustain it only a week. "When our troops start to move back, the enemy forces seize the opportunity and wage counterattacks." In this last offensive, the Volunteers had not expected the enemy to counterattack so quickly. The Americans had chased their division in tanks and motorized infantry, while paratroopers took over bridges, passes and ferrying points. "Our division is cut off," concluded the committee. "With transmitters lost by bombing, we have lost contact with headquarters."

The acting division commissar and chief of the political department, Wu Chengde, had served in revolutionary ranks for fourteen years. He stalked around the room, recalling the heroic history of his division. But they had run out of food three days earlier. Ammunition was almost gone.

"What is to be done?" he finally asked.

There was silence until someone whispered, "Disperse the division and break through." This action would be proper if they were in China, thought Wu, but not in these Korean mountains. They weren't familiar with the terrain and didn't understand the language. To his dismay, the committee accepted the suggestion.

Wu inspected the troops on horseback. In the light of incendiary blasts, he saw almost 400 men—injured comrades—crowded together in a mountain pass. He shot his own horse. "Comrades," he said, "I am with you!" Summoning party members and officers, he ordered them to re-form into teams of 40, each led by an officer. Their mission was to break through the line, but when Wu realized his team couldn't make it, he fired two shots and shouted, "Comrades, let's go guerrilla!" then led his survivors south.

In Peking that same May 26, Mao summarized the past five campaigns. He did not admit that the Fifth Campaign had failed completely; instead, he ordered Peng to shorten the line of battle and "crush the Americans a little at a time by eliminating isolated units." But Peng must first strengthen his own positions before waging a new type of warfare. Aboveground defense lines should be shifted to underground lines with an elaborate system of deep tunnels extending all along the 38th parallel.

At the same time, Mao launched a nationwide movement to "Resist America, Aid Korea, Protect Homes, and Defend the Nation." Young men eagerly signed up to serve in the Volunteers. People from all walks of life donated large amounts of money to buy MiG fighters. Chou En-lai supported the troops at the front by baking bread for the Volunteers. "We are totally dedicated to the fighting in Korea," announced Mao. "Whatever Korea asks, we shall supply."

3.

Upon learning that many enemy had escaped a trap laid by Almond on the central front, Van Fleet revived his plan of an amphibious landing of Marines on the east coast, sixty air miles north of the 38th parallel. This force could drive southwest and link up with Hoge's IX Corps, thereby trapping the escaping enemy troops. When Ridgway was informed, he was shocked. He had earlier emphatically rejected a Van Fleet plan to make an amphibious landing at Wonson. He immediately flew to Korea. He and Van Fleet soon came up with a far different plan. I Corps would attack north, its objective the Iron Triangle, while Hoge's IX Corps continued attacking north. The Marines would stay right of the Hwachon Reservoir and attack north to a dead volcanic crater, nicknamed the Punchbowl. The ROK I Corps, commanded by Whitey Paik, would take over the twenty miles from the Punchbowl to the east coast.

Ridgway stayed in Korea, touring corps and division CP's in the pouring rain until May 30, when he returned to Tokyo. "The enemy has suffered a severe major defeat," he cabled the Joint Chiefs. "Estimates of enemy killed in action submitted by field commanders come to total so high that I cannot accept it. Nevertheless, there has been inflicted a major personnel loss far exceeding, in my opinion, the loss suffered by the enemy in the April 21 offensive." The actual body count of enemy dead was 17,000, and some 10,000 had been captured. "All three U.S. corps commanders have reported a noticeable deterioration in the fighting spirit of the CCF forces." Great numbers of ammo dumps, mortars, machine guns, and automatic weapons had been abandoned, indicating that disorganization now existed among both CCF and KPA forces. "I therefore believe," he concluded, "that for the next 60 days the United States Government should be able to count with reasonable assurance upon a military situation in Korea offering optimum advantages in support of its diplomatic negotiations."

Despite the victory, some of the men who had won it were shocked at the cost. Earle Edson had fought in the southwest Pacific as an officer. Now he was a platoon sergeant in the 13th Engineers. "We crossed the parallel again yesterday," he wrote his wife and two children on May 28,

> and we have the Chinks on a wild retreat. . . . There's a hell of an air strike going on about 3 miles up the road . . . the Air Force and Artillery are giving us fits with their noise. And this place we are in now is a horrifying sight. We caught a bunch of Chinese in the open here (we are in a long valley along a river bed) and it certainly is a mess. Over a hundred vehicles, plenty of cannons, uncounted dead horses and of course,

Chinese. We caught them about day before yesterday and it really was a slaughter. The days are warm now and the sun is getting to them and the stink is terrific. No exaggeration this —we can't turn around without sighting dead men or horses. . . . We use bulldozers for the horses and mules, but naturally we have to pick the Chinese men up and place them in graves. A lot of people figure the more you bury the less you have to fight (I do too) but boy! When it comes to planting them I wish the Air Force and Artillery and our marksmanship weren't so thorough and precise. Boy! I wish I could see a little peace for awhile. I'm sick of the stench of the dead and dying and seeing torn bodies scattered like waste paper on a windy day.

With the Chinese no longer capable of mounting another major offensive, Mao ordered his troops to turn the war into one of sheer endurance.

PART IX

THE ROCKY ROAD TO PEACE

CHAPTER 33

The Negotiations Begin
(May 31–August 23)

1.

By the end of May, Monica Felton, a British leftist, and the other leftist delegates of an organization, supported by all the Communist nations and calling itself "The Women's International Commission for the Investigation of the Atrocities Committed by United States and Syngman Rhee's Troops in Korea," finished their lengthy interrogations.

Their official report told in vivid detail of the almost complete destruction of Pyongyang and other localities. In some towns, civilians were beaten by both the ROKs and American troops. The commission delegates could not believe that the latter, as Christians, could commit such barbaric acts. The delegates were shown by NK officials instruments used, such as a standard U.S. Army baseball bat. Streaks of blood stained the wooden floor of the corridors outside the cells where the victims were imprisoned.

One woman told how she had been tortured by having red-hot needles pushed under her fingernails and showed the marks of her disfigurement. She also recounted having seen people being thrown alive into a pit. The delegates examined the pit. "It appeared to be about 7 to 8 meters deep," said the report, "and in the strong morning light human remains could clearly be seen at the bottom." Dr. Felton noticed, near the surface of the pit, the body of a child dressed in a dark coat with shiny buttons. She and the others were taken to a burial site. "These graves had been opened to enable members to inspect the remains." The bodies were too mutilated to be identified. In addition to the remains, "the members could see children's shoes, tufts of women's hair, books and small personal possessions, and also the ropes with which people had been bound together." One witness, Huan Sin-ya, revealed that her mother had been buried alive but managed to dig herself out. "She was subsequently recaptured and buried again. In the same grave 450 people were said to be buried. There are twenty such graves on this hillside, and members were told that about twelve such hillsides had been put to similar use."

While Felton's group was listening aghast to these stories, other members were hearing similar ones from Pyongyang province. A third group, visiting the northern part of Korea, was told of six forest fires purposely set by UN planes, along with numerous accounts of torture and murder.

The conclusions of the delegates, attested by the signatures of every member, were as follows: "The people of Korea are subjected by American occupants to a merciless and methodical campaign of extermination which is in contradiction not only with the principles of humanity but also with the rules of warfare as laid down in the Hague and the Geneva Conventions."

While these conclusions were readily accepted by the Communist world, Westerners were not impressed by the litany of horrors, since the interviews had been set up by the North Korean government. No doubt, gross atrocities *had* been committed by South Koreans and some had probably been committed by a minority of Americans. Yet while the words of the witnesses had been taken as fact by the well-meaning members of the committee, they would not have been accepted in any democratic court of law, since there was no corroborating evidence or cross-examination—only the statements of distraught people who had lost loved ones and wanted vengeance.

But there was little doubt among objective Western experts that U.S. planes had killed hundreds of thousands of North Korean civilians. These atrocities were committed from the skies upon unseen multitudes and approved of by most Americans.

The words of Air Force general Emmett O'Donnell at the MacArthur hearings in Washington that spring vividly reflect this public attitude. He described the bombings of the five primary cities in North Korea. "We thought that the impact of taking those quickly, and getting—we could have gotten the five cities—I could have done that in ten days flat, and we think that maybe the terrific impact would so shock them that it might have pressed them into getting out." As a matter of fact, asked a senator, hadn't those cities been virtually destroyed? "Oh, yes, we did it all later anyhow. . . . I would say that the entire, almost the entire Korean peninsula is just a terrible mess. Everything is destroyed. There is nothing standing worthy of the name."

Senator Richard Russell of Georgia, chairman of the hearing, congratulated O'Donnell. "I think you have demonstrated [the] soldierly qualities that endeared you to the American people."

2.

On the last day of May, the Joint Chiefs cabled Tokyo rescinding all previous directives, and clarifying the ambiguities that had troubled Ridgway earlier. He was again denied authority to launch retaliatory attacks on China in the event of a Chinese breakthrough. If such a breakthrough occurred, he was to withdraw from Korea and defend Japan. For the present he was to "inflict maximum personnel and matériel losses on the forces of North Korea and Communist China operating within the geographical boundaries of Korea and the waters adjacent thereto." His principal aim now was to "create conditions favorable to a settlement of the Korean conflict."

He was allowed to continue air and naval operations within Korea, but prohibited from any such operations against Soviet territory, Manchuria, and the hydroelectric plants along the Yalu River. He was also to limit ground operations. These orders made it clear to Ridgway that Washington was preparing for a negotiated settlement of the war. On June 2, Van Fleet distributed a mimeographed statement to the press: "The Eighth Army's pursuit phase has now ended with the clearing, again, of enemy units from South Korea—less those in the former border areas west of the Imjin River."

Rewrite men in Tokyo and the States played up these words, setting off truce and peace rumors throughout the world. Correspondents on the spot deliberately aroused false hopes for the war's end, even though Van Fleet had confided in them that he intended to fight on. He was going to push northward in an attempt to drive the enemy from the vital Chorwon-Kumhwa-Pyonggang Iron Triangle.

Two days earlier, George Kennan had met informally with Jakob Malik, the Soviet representative at the UN. Kennan stated in Russian that he was calling on him not as a government official—since he had no official position—but as someone *near* the government. "I thought it might be worthwhile if we were to look at this situation of Korea and see whether there would be any possibility of conducting conversations looking toward a truce. I explained to him that I realized that neither of us could commit our government, that this was purely exploratory."

On June 5 they met again, and this time Malik said without hesitation that the Soviet government wanted a peaceful solution in Korea "and at the earliest possible moment." Malik added that the USSR "did not feel that it could take part in any discussion of the question of a cease-fire." The North Koreans and the Chinese Communists should be consulted in this matter.

Kennan reported the conversation to his superior in the State Department, assuring him that the words Malik used "did reflect a very carefully thought-over government decision in Moscow and that we could depend upon it; that if we were to proceed with conversations looking to a truce, they would not be exploited simply as a means of embarrassing us."

Kennan felt that Malik's advice to get in touch with the North Koreans and Chinese Communists meant that Soviet influence had already been brought to bear on them "to show themselves amenable to proposals for a cease-fire." He urged the State Department to "grasp the nettle of action."

During these first diplomatic maneuvers, men were still fighting and dying. The U.S. and Paik's ROK I Corps were struggling to take the Punchbowl, some twenty-five miles north of Inje. Its knife-sharp rim, rising several hundred feet from the crater floor, was solidly entrenched by the defenders. Casualties were heavy on both sides, and little territory was exchanged.

As that drive continued, the main offensive, Operation Piledriver, ground forward toward the Iron Triangle. Van Fleet, assured that the Chinese were beaten, expected rapid progress. Milburn's I Corps was to hold with two divisions on the left at the Imjin River while three divisions—the 1st Cavalry, the 3rd and the 25th—would cross the Hantan River and take the base of the Triangle. On the first day, June 3, the 3rd Division was hit by a vicious Chinese counterattack, and one battalion was driven back across the Hantan. The 25th Division was also held up by tenacious Chinese troops defending the high ground.

The next day, Almond's X Corps on the right flank resumed its attack toward the Punchbowl. For five days the battle raged; and so little progress was made that the 7th Marines, on reserve after their rugged battle on the ridge, were sent to the front with the 1st Marines on their right and the ROK Marines on their left.

At two A.M. on the 11th, the ROK Marines took their North Korean foes by complete surprise in a night attack, resulting in wholesale slaughter. This victory allowed them to advance toward the Punchbowl. By now, Operation Piledriver was also moving forward, and later in the day the allied forces took the town of Chorwon at the western foot of the triangle base, forcing the Chinese to abandon the eastern town, Kumhwa.

Three days later, Ridgway cabled the Joint Chiefs his concept of probable developments in Korea during the next sixty days. Despite their recent successes, both he and Van Fleet feared a major Chinese offensive. Ridgway felt that a general advance north would nullify Eighth Army's present logistic advantage over the enemy. Because of numerical superiority, the Reds could retain the overall initiative and launch at least one devastating attack.

3.

A week later, on June 23, Jakob Malik startled the world with a radio speech. Although he began with the usual charges of flagrant U.S. armed intervention in Korea and boasted of the Soviet program of strengthening peace throughout the world, he ended with a call for settlement of the Korean War. "The peoples of the Soviet Union believe that it is possible to defend the cause of peace. The Soviet peoples further believe that the most acute problem of the present day—the problem of the armed conflict in Korea—could also be settled. . . . The Soviet peoples believe that as a first step, discussions should be started between the belligerents for a cease-fire and armistice providing for the mutual withdrawal of forces from the 38th parallel. Can such a step be taken? I think it can, provided there is a sincere desire to put an end to the bloody fighting in Korea." The press asked for an expansion of these remarks, but Malik suddenly became "indisposed."

The U.S. State Department responded with a press-release later in the day: "If Mr. Malik's broadcast means that the Communists are now willing to end the aggression in Korea, we are, as we have always been, ready to play our part in bringing an end to the hostilities and assuring against their resumption."

Truman was in Tennessee, dedicating an aviation engineering development. Using the occasion to voice his reaction, he said, "We cannot be sure what the Soviet rulers will do." Although he believed the Kremlin was still trying to divide the free nations, he concluded that the free world must be ready to take any step in Korea which advanced world peace. "But we must avoid like the plague rash actions which would take unnecessary risks of world war, or weak actions which would reward aggression."

In the Soviet Union, the Malik proposal was given heavy play, but Peking Radio was silent for almost two days, the first comment coming from the *People's Daily*. After declaring that China wholeheartedly supported Malik's proposal, it complained about American "seizure of China's territory, Taiwan." That the Chinese were dissatisfied with the Soviets was indicated two days later in the publication *For a Lasting Peace, For a Lasting Democracy*. In an issue celebrating the thirtieth anniversary of the Chinese Communist party, the writers ignored the role of Stalin in the development of Chinese Communism. Success had come because of the theories and leadership of Mao. The Russian revolution, while important historically, was valid only for industrialized countries.

North Korea also responded with hesitation and apparent disapproval of the Soviet attitude toward armistice negotiations. Pyongyang Radio reminded its listeners their own fight for liberty would also serve to support the Soviet Union. Japan was being remilitarized by the United States "in order to carry on aggression against the Korean, Chinese, Vietnamese, and other peace-loving Asiatic peoples and against the Soviet Union and other nations of the peoples' democracies."

Such comments from both Peking and Pyongyang made it clear that the Chinese and North Koreans were dissatisfied with Soviet intervention in the war. Despite statements that both nations accepted Malik's proposal, each apparently suspected the goals and commitments of their big neighbor.

The day after Malik's speech, General Ridgway sent his commanders a warning to avoid any letdown among the troops. "Two things should be recalled. One is the well-earned reputation for duplicity and dishonesty possessed by the USSR; the other is the slowness with which deliberative bodies such as the [UN] Security Council produce positive action."

The next day, the first anniversary of the war, Ridgway received a message from the Joint Chiefs that cease-fire negotiations might soon be initiated. He promptly sent a member of his staff to confer with Van Fleet. Did the general think it was practicable and desirable for the Eighth Army to seize the high ground between its present frontline positions and the theoretical cease-fire line? Van Fleet replied that an advance on the eastern front would be costly in American lives and gain only real estate. The negotiations, he added, should take into account the area west of the Yedong River and south of the 38th parallel. He had no desire to occupy this land, but it could be traded at the bargaining table for desirable ground in the western zone.

On the 29th, Ridgway received instructions from the Joint Chiefs to approach the enemy on possible armistice negotiations. The next day, at the direction of Truman, he broadcast a message to the commander in chief of the Communist forces in Korea: "I am informed that you may wish a meeting to discuss armistice providing for the cessation of hostilities and all acts of armed force in Korea with adequate guarantee for the maintenance of such armistice. Upon receipt of word from you that such a meeting is desired I shall be prepared to name my representative. I would also at that time suggest a date at which he could meet with your representative. I propose that such a meeting could take place aboard a Danish hospital ship in Wonsan Harbor."

* * *

Late that night General Bradley brought the president a draft of new instructions to Ridgway from the Joint Chiefs. The JCS believed the best chance for a successful conclusion to the negotiation "may depend upon secrecy in at least the opening stages; it is not, therefore, intended to make these instructions public." The principal military interest lay in cessation of hostilities and the protection of UN forces. The discussions must be "severely restricted to military questions."

Truman approved the draft, and it was dispatched to Ridgway.

On July 1, in a broadcast sponsored jointly by Kim Il-sung and Peng Teh-huai, the two commanders agreed to meet with the UN representative but proposed the Kaesong area rather than the Danish ship. Although Ridgway felt it was typical Communist policy never to accept anything *in toto*, he notified them that he was prepared to meet their representative at Kaesong on July 10. He also proposed that three liaison officers from each side meet there five days earlier to organize details of the meeting. The Communists agreed but set the date at July 8.

By now the American press was rife with speculation. Some papers and magazines were using such phrases as "Let's Get the Boys Back Home," and "The War-Weary Troops." Ridgway was furious. On the 4th of July he cabled the Joint Chiefs his fear that public pressure for peace might force him to make military concessions. Any order to abandon his present line of defense would "vitally prejudice our entire military position in Korea."

At nine o'clock on the morning of July 8, Ridgway's three liaison officers flew over the Imjin River in a helicopter. Minutes later they were circling the ruins of Kaesong, scene of the unique North Korean attack by train on the first morning of the war. Searching for signs of the expected Red envoys, they saw little life except for a jeep driven crazily along the cratered streets. Had the enemy envoys been delayed? wondered Marine colonel James Murray, who had been selected to head the UNC staff group for determining the line of demarcation. Had there been some misunderstanding as to the time and place of the meeting?

Murray saw a white aircraft-marking panel laid on a field at the north end of Kaesong, not far from the 38th parallel. The helicopter landed and the three United Nations Command envoys found themselves surrounded by a ring of Red soldiers. Murray, air force colonel Jack Kinney, and ROK colonel Lee Soo-young dismounted from the helicopter. Once the sound of the motors died, an ominous silence fell. The enemies stared at each other. Then a North Korean officer and two

interpreters, one a young woman, approached the newcomers appre-
hensively and took them in two battered American jeeps to the meeting
place, a one-story structure, formerly a teahouse.

"As we entered the teahouse," recalled Murray, "the enemy group
rose." Following identification, both groups sat down. Colonel Chang
Chun-san, the North Korean liaison officer, led the way to an adjacent
room where a green-cloth-covered table had been set up. At 9:47 A.M.
they began to talk. After less than two hours the Communists requested
a recess for lunch. Biscuits, chocolate, beer, vodka and cider were served
in the anteroom.

The conversation in the afternoon revealed to Murray a great deal
about Communist and Oriental logic.

"Is your delegation agreeable to meeting on July 10?" asked Kinney.

"The time of the meeting," said Chang, the spokesman for the
Communists, "has been arranged by the commanders."

"No," said Kinney, "the commanders have agreed that the delegation should meet between the tenth and fifteenth of July. They have not
set the exact date."

"The date of meeting of the delegations," insisted Colonel Chang,
"shall be as the commanders have agreed."

"But when?" asked Kinney. "Shall it be the tenth, eleventh, twelfth?
What date?"

Murray quietly suggested to Kinney that he set the date unilaterally.
Apparently Colonel Chang did not have authority to do so.

"The United Nations Command delegation," announced Kinney
with authority, "will arrive in Kaesong at 1100 hours on July 10."

"The commanders have agreed," said Chang equably, "and it shall
be so."

An argument broke out when Kinney declined with thanks the use
of housing set up by the Communists for the UN delegation. He explained that Ridgway wanted the group brought back south every night.
Chang demurred, but Kinney said flatly, "Those are my instructions."
Truce headquarters, known as Base Camp, had already been constructed
for the UN group in an apple orchard on the outskirts of Munsan, the
village south of the Imjin River. Tents had been provided to house the
delegation.

On the morning of July 10, the UNC delegation headed for the
helicopter strip. Ridgway had explained his personal views on their
proper demeanor at the conference table. Lead from strength, not weakness, he advised, yet be prepared for lengthy propaganda speeches. Be
patient. Never cause them to lose face. At the same time, any opportunity
to intensify friction between China and the Soviets should be exploited.
In concluding, Ridgway had assured the delegates that if they handled
the negotiations skillfully, "history may record that Communist military

aggression reached its high-water mark in Korea, and that thereafter Communism itself began its recession in Asia."

The senior delegate, Vice Admiral C. Turner Joy, commander of Navy forces in the Far East, led the way to the helicopter. He was followed by Major General Laurence Craigie of the Air Force, Major General Henry Hodes of the Eighth Army, Rear Admiral Arleigh Burke, and Major General Whitey Paik, the ROK representative.

After they had posed near the helicopter for photographs, Admiral Joy spoke briefly. "We, the delegates from the United Nations Command, are leaving for Kaesong fully conscious of the importance of these meetings to the entire world." His manner was controlled, undramatic. "We are proceeding in good faith to do our part to bring about an honorable armistice, under terms that are satisfactory to the United Nations Command."

"Good luck to you, Admiral," called out the newsmen.

His helicopter took off, followed by two others carrying interpreters and liaison officers. Fifteen minutes later it landed on a field near the Kaesong Methodist Missionary compound, where the Reverend Larry Zellers had heard the first sounds of war.

The delegates were surrounded by Communist photographers. As they piled into jeeps flying white flags, a symbol of their mission, Burke noticed that one jeep bore the name *Wilma*. There were two bullet holes in the windshield. Burke figured the Communists had driven this vehicle to show their contempt for the visitors. They were taken to a stone house reserved for them. It was surrounded by guards with tommy guns. Suspecting that the house was wired, the delegates said little, and Admiral Joy soon led the way outside, explaining that they had headquarters in Munsan and did not need the stone house.

They met the Communist delegation in a small anteroom of the tea house. There was a moment of tension as the two groups faced each other. The Communists were stiff but polite, and both sides bowed almost imperceptibly. A tall North Korean officer said, "I am Nam Il." General Nam was the main delegate, the chief of staff of the Korean People's Army.

"I am Admiral Joy." The admiral nodded, noting that Nam Il appeared to be an intelligent young man.

There were two other North Koreans and two Chinese. The former were in Soviet-style uniforms with smart gray blouses decorated with red piping, and wide blue trousers. The Chinese wore simple khaki uniforms devoid of emblems designating rank.

At eleven A.M. both sides sat down at the green-baize-covered table, the Americans ensconced in low upholstered chairs, the Communists in high wooden chairs. Joy scored the first psychological victory by placing a UN flag on the table.

In an opening statement, translated into Korean and Chinese, Admiral Joy said, "Success or failure of the negotiations begun here today depends directly upon the good faith of the delegations here present."

He sat down. Nam Il rose. He was nervous and uneasy as he spoke in Korean, repeatedly forgetting to permit his interpreter to translate his remarks into Chinese. In trying to light one of his Russian cigarettes with Chinese matches, he struck a dozen without success. "Embarrassed and desperate, he brought out an American cigarette lighter. It clicked and flared brightly. He took one deep drag and then, apparently feeling that somehow he had been disloyal to things Communistic, he tossed the American lighter out the window behind him."

When Nam Il finally sat down, Joy could see that his own chair was far closer to the floor than Nam's. The North Korean was looking down on him. The admiral insisted that the chairs be the same height, then, calmly and with authority, declared that "the first item to be settled is the limitation of these discussions to military matters only." The meetings, he added, should also be restricted to Korean questions, and he proposed that they sign such an agreement now.

"This meeting was to begin arrangements to stop the fighting in Korea," protested Nam Il, apparently offended by Joy's manner of quiet command, "and I would like to know the reason for any such statement as this and the necessity for signing such a statement."

This objection suggested to Joy that the Communists intended to cover more than military matters. Nam Il presented the Communist position: a return of both sides to the 38th parallel, and the removal of all foreign troops from Korea. Once this was done, the question of prisoners of war could be discussed.

Refusing to discuss substantive matters now, Joy asked for the Communist agenda. The Communists responded by requesting a recess to prepare a copy and have lunch.

During the three-hour-and-thirty-five-minute recess the Communists countered Joy's first small victory. They placed a Korean flag on the table near the UN flag. It was several inches higher. While Nam was submitting his written agenda, four Communist reporters rushed in to take pictures.

Their appearance brought a sharp protest from Joy, who suggested that selected UN correspondents be allowed inside the compound. Of course, they would not be permitted to enter the conference room. Nam Il reluctantly agreed and then had second thoughts, saying he'd have to get confirmation from his commander.

The meeting ended with cool formality. The Communists had made it clear that their initial objectives were a return to the 38th parallel and the clearing of foreign troops from Korea, which would mean redressing the balance of military power in their favor. They could then proceed at their own pace and inclination.

That night newsmen at the Base Camp organized a pool on the length of the negotiations. Some optimists bet a week or two. The most pessimistic made it six weeks.

At the second meeting the following day, little was accomplished. What particularly irked Joy was that armed North Korean guards restricted the activities of the UNC delegates. He protested to Ridgway who responded by sending a message to Peng and Kim saying the UNC would not resume regotiations until he was assured the site was free of armed guards and the UN delegates and staff were allowed the same freedom of movement within the site as the Communists. Finally Ridgway received a reply from Peng and Kim, agreeing in essence to his demands.

On the afternoon of July 15, the UNC delegation returned to the teahouse. All were present, including General Paik. Joy opened the meeting by outlining details of Ridgway's proposals for neutralizing Kaesong. The road leading there from the Imjin River should be opened to unrestricted use by UNC vehicles. There should be a neutral area, five miles in radius, with only a minimum of armed personnel for MP duty. Nam Il agreed, and the conference resumed. The next afternoon, Ridgway met with President Rhee at Eighth Army HQ, in the presence of Muccio and Admiral Joy, to outline the basic ideas for creating a demilitarized zone, since both sides had agreed to include this topic in the agenda.

At Rhee's request, Ridgway pointed out the present location of the front lines. Rhee still wanted the UNC forces to push on to the Yalu River. Tremendous tonnage, replied Ridgway, would be necessary for further offensive action. The roads and railroads in their present condition could not support such weight. Rhee argued heatedly for half an hour. Ridgway was polite but inflexible. There was *not* going to be another major offensive. Rhee regained control of himself. "I'll tell the cabinet that they must accept UN actions," he said.

He must have spent a sleepless night. In the morning he wrote Ridgway: "The substance of the position of my government is that we cannot maintain our nation in half our country. A divided Korea is a ruined Korea, unstable economically, politically, and militarily." The only answer was reunification. Otherwise it would be impossible to prevent his people from feeling abandoned by their allies. To agree to continued division of his nation would be to accept inevitable loss of freedom. Koreans, both in the north and south, were convinced of the inevitability of reunification. "In every Korean heart and in every Korean mind the fact is clear that our nation would be plunged into irrevocable disaster by any acceptance of a continued dividing-line." The democracies were strong. "It is the Communist Empire which is rotten with internal weakness. Negotiations continued with this conviction should lead to success. In this spirit there is no need to settle short of the goal of re-unification and free elections."

This impassioned plea was signed by Rhee and six members of his government.

The wrangling continued in Kaesong over withdrawal of foreign troops. After a three-day recess, the delegates reconvened on July 25. Both sides finally agreed to discuss fixing a military demarcation line and make concrete plans for cease-fire and armistice. But the brief honeymoon came to an end on July 25 when Nam lost his temper. The UN proposal that the demilitarized zone be based on present battle lines was "incredible, naive and illogical, as well as absurd and arrogant." Joy, in his diary, called Nam's remarks "Inappropriate," "discourteous," and "groundless."

"Although it is too early to predict," Ridgway cabled the Joint Chiefs, "the possibility exists that discussions may deadlock on the issue of the 38th parallel."

In Seoul, the president was still seething. Ambassador Muccio was so concerned about the president's behavior that he cabled Acheson: "President Rhee, on blindly emotional ground, is attempting to sabotage armistice."

Discord ruled at Kaesong during the next week. On August 4, Joy noticed a company of Chinese soldiers marching along the road in the conference area. On return to Base Camp he reported this to Ridgway, who dispatched a strong note of protest on the neutrality violation to Kim Il-sung and Peng.

The next day was spent at Base Camp in a downpour of rain. On August 6, a reply came from the Communists, who gave assurances that the violation, a trivial accident, would not happen again. Talks were finally resumed on August 10. Nam Il opened the conference with a question: had the UNC given up its illogical proposal that the demilitarized zone be based on present battle lines? No, responded Joy forcefully. "We will not discuss further the 38th parallel as a military demarcation line." For two hours and eleven minutes not a word was spoken. It was as if everyone at the table was frozen. But the next morning vociferous quarreling broke out.

"It has been proved that your proposal is untenable and that our proposal is based on reason," declared Nam. "Therefore, whatever novel and ridiculous arguments you fabricate, they would never bolster your proposal. I can tell you frankly that as long as you do not abandon your unreasonable proposal, it will not be possible for our conference to make

General James Van
Fleet cuts the cake at
his farewell party,
assisted by Mrs.
Syngman Rhee.
National Archives

Korean boys help GIs.
National Archives

More Chinese
surrender.
National Archives

GIs solemnly survey a mass of dead Chinese. *National Archives*

A Chinese prisoner of war angrily assaults an International Red Cross representative. The North Koreans and Chinese refused to admit such IRC inspectors to their POW camps. *National Archives*

The Chinese and
North Korean
negotiating team at
Panmunjom. *From the
left:* Xie Fang, Deng
Hua, Nam Il, Lee
Song Cho, and Chang
Pyong-san. *Chinese
Museum of Revolutionary
History, Beijing*

The commander-in-chief of the
Chinese troops, Peng Teh-huai,
leading Chinese delegates to sign
the armistice agreement. *Chinese
Museum of Revolutionary History*

The signing
*Chinese Museum of
Revolutionary History*

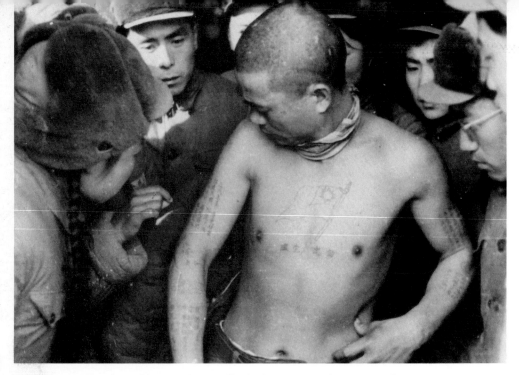

A returning Chinese prisoner displaying pro-Maoist tattoos *Chinese Museum of Revolutionary History*

Dissident Chinese are joyously welcomed in Taipei. *The Free China Relief Association*

Helicopter pilot Chief Duane Thorin (*left*) returns to freedom. *National Archives*

Civilian survivors of the infamous Death March in North Korea: the Reverend Larry Zellers (*far left*) and the indomitable Nell Dyer (*second from right*) arriving in West Berlin from Moscow, dressed in clothes provided by the Chinese. *Larry Zellers*

Zhang Ze-sin, a repatriated Chinese soldier, grossly mistreated and then imprisoned for fifteen years. *Toshiko Toland (1989)*

Ding Shang wing, another Chinese internee, was also mistreated and then imprisoned for thirteen years on return to his homeland. *Toshiko Toland (1989)*

Royal Marine Commando Andrew Condron was the only British POW who chose to go to China. He returned to England nine years later. Some of his comrades never forgave him, but others regarded him as a dissident Scotsman, not a traitor. *Andrew Condron*

Proud father General Walton Walker introduces his son Lieutenant Sam Walker to General Collins. United States *Eighth Army*

Mao with his favorite son, Anqing, killed on November 25, 1950, in a bombing raid on Pyongyang. *Chinese Museum of Revolutionary History*

President-elect Dwight D. Eisehower meets his son Lieutenant John Eisenhower up front in December 1952. The President-elect went to Korea to find a means to end the war. *John Eisenhower*

The sons of a number of American generals fought in Korea. General Van Fleet's son, James A. Van Fleet, Jr., was killed during a bombing raid in April 1952. General Mark Clark's son was wounded three times, so severely on Heartbreak Ridge that he was forced to retire.

any progress. As for our proposal, its reasons are irrefutable: therefore, it is unshakable. We insist on our proposal of making the 38th parallel the military demarcation line."

The whole performance was developing into a black comedy. The low-key Joy had been controlling his irritation. "Yesterday," he said, "you used the word 'arrogant' in connection with a proposal the United Nations Command delegation now has before this conference. The United Nations Command delegation has been in search of an expression which conveys the haughty stubbornness, the arbitrary inflexibility, and the unreasoning stubbornness of your attitude. 'Arrogance' is indeed the word for it. By your obdurate and unreasonable refusal to negotiate you have brought these meetings to a standstill. You have slammed every door leading to possible progress." Nam Il, he said, had tried to deceive the world into believing the Communists had defeated the UNC. "You refuse to negotiate except on your own terms, thus seeking to falsely portray yourself as a victor dictating to the vanquished."

"Your statement does not frighten us and cannot change our stand," retorted Nam Il.

Nothing was accomplished during the next ten days, which again featured diatribes larded with abusive words from both sides of the table. The following evening, August 22, Alan Winnington, correspondent for the London *Daily Worker*, was enjoying the summer night at the press camp near the Korean-Chinese headquarters when he heard a low-flying bomber.

"Put that bloody light out," he yelled at Wilfred Burchett, an Australian correspondent for the left-wing Paris newspaper *Ce Soir*, who was reading under a mosquito net. Winnington hit the ground as he heard the familiar whistle and whip crack of nearby bombs.

Burchett saw a rippling series of blinking white flashes. *Bang goes neutrality and the talks*, flashed through his mind as a Chinese guard guided him to a ditch.

Even though the U.S. Fifth Air Force admitted that an American plane had passed just west of Kaesong six minutes before the alleged attack, two U.S. officers reported, after investigating the area: "The incident was staged 100 per cent by the Communists." Burchett and other Communist reporters disagreed vociferously. No side had positive proof.

The next day, August 23, the Communists broke off the talks. Peng and Kim sent an angry protest about the "violation" to Ridgway and "awaited a satisfactory reply from your side." Ridgway replied just as angrily that the alleged incident was "so utterly false, so preposterous, and so obviously manufactured for your own questionable purposes," that it did not merit a reply. But he added that once the Communists were ready to terminate the suspension of the negotiations, "I will direct my representatives to meet with yours with a view to seeking a reasonable armistice agreement."

A certified copy of this message was sent to Kaesong by helicopter. Colonel Lee, General Paik's aide, handed the message to Colonel Chang, the North Korean liaison officer. In English, Lee said he had the honor to present this copy of General Ridgway's message to Kim Il-sung and Peng Teh-huai.

"Why don't you speak Korean?" said Chang contemptuously.

Lee drew himself up. "I will speak whatever language I please. That is what we are fighting for. Freedom of speech."

The talking was over. Negotiations were suspended indefinitely.

CHAPTER 34

"An Utterly Useless War"
(Early August–November 26)

1.

By early August, Peng's troops were operating, as Mao had ordered, from an underground labyrinth of caves and tunnels. This almost-static defense, he was convinced, would force the Americans to join the kind of positional warfare where bloody fights were waged with little exchange of land, as in the first world war.

Many of the men who had endured the huge losses and gains of territory in the past seesaw year were gone. General Walker was dead, and his rival, Ned Almond, had been replaced by General Clovis Byers. Also gone was Major James Hausman, the creator of the ROK Army. Of the first two ROK chiefs of staff Hausman had advised, one was dead and the other, Chung Il-kwon, was relieved of duty for reasons that did not include lack of ability. He was now on his way to America for study at Fort Leavenworth.

Most of those like Taplett and Mike Lynch, who had fought so desperately in the Pusan Perimeter, on the drive north, and in the dark, desperate days of winter, were also long gone. The front lines were manned principally by inexperienced replacements. Hausman, now in the Pentagon, complained to Major General Alexander R. Bolling of the situation in Korea. "You have an appointment with the Secretary of the Army, Frank Pace," said Bolling. "I want you to go in there and give him the same spiel you just gave me. And I want you to thump his desk as hard as you thumped mine, or I'll put my foot up your ass!"

Hausman told Pace what he thought should be done in Korea. First they should stop trying to discipline the Korean troops. "Let their officers do the job. They have their own form of discipline. Some of it is a little crude, but it's effective." He also recommended that Korean officer candidates be trained in American schools.

"We can't do that."

"Mr. Secretary, that is what's wrong with Korea today. We say we can't do this and we can't do that. I recommend, sir, that starting today we start doing *something*."

On August 24, four days after Almond had left Korea, the weather had improved sufficiently for Van Fleet to start a limited offensive designed to strengthen the UN position at the negotiating table. Progress was slow. Not until September 4 did General Byers finally seize his first objective, Bloody Ridge, after three weeks of bitter fighting—at the cost of over 2,700 casualties. The next target would be another ridge three miles to the south. It would soon be called Heartbreak Ridge.

The Eighth Army had reported erroneously that only ROK troops were being used. Now they released the fact that three U.S. divisions had carried out the limited offensive. "Until last night," David McConnell cabled the New York *Herald Tribune* on September 5, "censorship forbade mentioning other than South Koreans being in battle. Three weeks ago in Seoul, correspondents were told that the military did not want to disturb the American public with news that United States troops were taking part in an offensive while the peace talks were in progress." A trenchant critic of American policy, I. F. Stone, commented, "It would have been more precise to say that the American military had launched the offensive just when it looked as if the truce talks might succeed, and had kept the attack secret."

Although the Chinese and North Koreans were giving up little territory, their casualties were heavy. The shift to positional warfare created problems. The veteran Chinese cadres from revolutionary days, trained as guerrillas, had never before fought this kind of war on such a large scale. Mao was also concerned about production. The Chinese could supply only one tenth of the armament needed in Korea. The Soviets were providing large quantities without specifying payment. When asked how to settle the account, Stalin had merely replied, "Just sign a receipt." There were now indications that the price might be unusually high.

2.

Charges of two more alleged bombings further acerbated relations between the peace delegations, which were still not talking to each other. On September 2, Peking Radio transmitted a message to Ridgway from Peng and Kim. They demanded that Ridgway deal "conscientiously and responsibly" with the grave provocative incidents perpetrated by UNC forces. He must "thoroughly guarantee that there would be no recurrence of similar acts which violate the Kaesong neutralization agreement, so that the armistice meeting can be resumed."

On September 6, Ridgway's reply to Kim and Peng was dispatched. He denounced the Red charges as false. The good faith of the UN Command had again been impugned. He called on the Communists to cease their despicable practices and get on with the conference. "When you decide to terminate the suspension of armistice negotiations which you declared on August 23, I propose that our liaison officers meet at the bridge at Panmunjom to discuss selection of a new site where negotiations can be continued without interruptions."

At five o'clock on the morning of the 10th, Joy was awakened by a call alleging another strafing attack. Two officers were sent to Kaesong to investigate. They found no evidence of such an attack and *The New York Times* headline read: "KAESONG EVIDENCE HELD INCONCLUSIVE," while the *Herald Tribune* said, "UN LIAISON OFFICERS VISIT KAESONG TO INVESTIGATE, SAY CHARGE LOOKS FALSE." The Associated Press quoted Air Force colonel Don Darrow, a member of the UNC staff, as asking the Communists, "How do we know the plane was one of ours? Why not one of yours?"

Ridgway, irked at the Communists' failure to respond to his proposal for a new site, dispatched an angry message to the Joint Chiefs requesting authority to seize Kaesong by military force. Such an action would not only "remove one more basis for Communist stalling tactics" but "deprive the enemy of the distinct military advantage he now enjoys." Ridgway added that he would give the Communists twenty-four hours' advance notice and impose no conditions that would suspend or terminate the talks. The reply was negative.

Meantime, to the embarrassment of the Americans, a report from the Fifth Air Force confirmed the latest Communist charge. A B-26 *had been* over Kaesong at the time the Communists stated and *had* strafed some lights. Joy felt that they should acknowledge their responsibility. Ridgway did so, apologizing for an attack resulting "from the pilot's error of navigation." But Kim and Peng rejected the apology, demanding that the UNC put an end to its incessant acts of intentional violation.

The incident disturbed two Americans, David McConnell of the New York *Herald Tribune* and George Herman of CBS. They decided to learn what precautions were being taken to prevent a repetition of such a reckless attack. They asked a major, a lieutenant colonel, a colonel and finally a brigadier general—with no success. The brigadier general that the dogged correspondents approached was Frank A. Allen, chief Army public relations director. His answer was curt: "Don't forget which side you're on." This not-so-veiled threat deepened their growing discontent with Army public relations.

Ridgway was incensed at the Red rejection of his apology. He suggested sending a strong reply to Kim and Peng stating that only one violation was valid, but the Joint Chiefs persuaded him to dispatch a conciliatory message ending with an offer to send his liaison officers to the Panmunjom bridge for a consultation with the Communist liaison team.

The reply from Peng and Kim was a reiteration of charges of UNC treachery and deceit. They saw no reason for the liaison officers to meet, since they had no authority to negotiate. In turn, Ridgway requested permission to refuse categorically to send delegates back to Kaesong and insisted upon a new conference site. His proposed ultimatum alarmed the State Department. It would risk a definitive breakdown in the negotiations. Omar Bradley disagreed. "We feel that General Ridgway should not be made to go back to Kaesong unless he is satisfied with the conditions." He also shared Ridgway's fears that the Communists might take the UN delegates as hostages. But the State Department was so insistent that the Joint Chiefs went along. In a four-hour telecon on the 26th, General Collins and representatives from the State Department told Ridgway, Joy and Burke that both the State Department and the Joint Chiefs felt every effort should be made to arrange a meeting of principal negotiators as soon as possible in order that the real intention of the Communists could be revealed. The "single issue of our refusal to return to Kaesong would be disadvantageous to us as definitive breaking point of negotiations."

Distressed, Ridgway sent a personal message "FOR GENERAL COLLINS' EYES ONLY" complaining that the Joint Chiefs always acceded to Communist demands. "We have to tell them, 'Here we stand and here we stay!' " This was "the time and perhaps the last time, in the course of these negotiations, to take this course." In his official reply to the Joint Chiefs, he once more appealed for their support. "I shall continue to do my utmost to execute faithfully your instructions, whatever be your decision on this issue of renewing delegation matters to Kaesong." Then he dropped a bomb. "Unless, however, your decision should be to direct me to resume delegation meetings in Kaesong, I shall refrain from doing so."

Washington was shocked. The man who had turned things around in Korea and was regarded as such a welcome change from MacArthur was refusing to obey a direct order. The president had reason to fire him. But how could they fire a man so highly regarded throughout the Western world?

Bradley sympathized with Ridgway and offered to visit Tokyo to work things out peacefully. Chip Bohlen, experienced in negotiating with Communists, was to accompany him. They arrived on September 29. General Ridgway summarized the armistice negotiations, then covered in detail the military situation along with his conception of future ground operations. Bradley fully agreed with Ridgway's rejection of a general ground advance.

At ten-thirty, General Doyle Hickey joined the trio. After Ridgway gave his views on evacuation of Korea in the event of World War III, Bradley asked if he advocated pursuit by air across the Yalu. No, said Ridgway. Admiral Joy and General Craigie, the vice-commander of the Far East Air Force, were summoned, and they got down to the crucial point. "Everybody agrees we can't go back to Kaesong," said Bradley. Bohlen gave the State Department view. "We support you 100 percent," he said. Ridgway must have been amused at such ready compliance. It was as if there had been no uproar in Washington at all. The magical disappearance of all resistance was underlined by Bradley's declaration, just before the meeting broke up: "We have exchanged views, not come to transmit instructions nor to make decisions."

Eight days later the Communists proposed that the conference site be moved from Kaesong to the tiny village of Panmunjom, with both sides taking responsibility for immediate resumption of the talks. Ridgway concurred and instructed his liaison officers to meet their opposite numbers.

The fighting along the front continued to be bitter and inconclusive. On October 15, Heartbreak Ridge, just north of the Punchbowl, was finally secured—after 3,700 American casualties. On the Eighth Army left flank, Operation Commando reached its objective in four days but also with heavy losses. In the United States, the public responded in a poll, with two thirds describing the Korean conflict as "an utterly useless war."

While the liaison officers at Panmunjom were thrashing out an agreement, General Ridgway was attempting to pacify the correspondents. Hanson Baldwin of *The New York Times* protested that "embellished adjectives had replaced facts." The military communiqué of World War II had been simple, often terse. In this war it had become "a grab bag of service claims, so-called 'action' verbs and descriptive phrases." And the result was "all the more serious since censorship in Korea has been serious and often captious."

At a press conference on October 16, Ridgway acknowledged that "full and timely information" had not been supplied and promised "steps would be taken to correct the situation." At the same time, it would be "bad faith" to release certain kinds of information. As for the fighting, Ridgway acknowledged that the situation from some standpoints "could readily be construed as a military stalemate. It all depends on how you look at it."

A few days later the liaison officers came to an agreement. On the 22nd, Joy signed it and two days later Nam reciprocated. At last, on October 25, after sixty-three days of delays, the talks resumed at Panmunjom, a village of mud huts located on a barren plain. Nearby tents—installed with flooring, heating and lighting—had been set up to house the conferees, their staffs and the correspondents. Half a mile away mess, communications, security and engineer facilities were hastily erected.

The delegates convened in a large conference tent. Two thorny problems faced the negotiators: conclusion of an armistice and determination of the military demarcation line between the UN and Communist forces—the future border between North and South Korea. Nam proposed that these two items be referred to the subdelegates, since their previous meetings had been far more successful than those involving everyone. Major General Henry Hodes, an old cavalry man, and Admiral Burke met with the two Communist subdelegates, who, after several hours, traced a demilitarized zone on the map, a zone that included Kaesong. The Americans protested that UN troops would probably have taken the city if the site for the negotiations hadn't first been placed there. Instead, they offered to give up the offshore islands controlled by the UN. The Communists refused to barter. Kaesong was important politically and psychologically, since it lay south of the 38th parallel and President Rhee had been demanding its return. The argument went on day after day with neither side yielding, but unlike the larger meetings, there was no name-calling, only stiff bargaining.

Although Ridgway supported Joy and his two subdelegates, pressure from Washington to reach an agreement forced him to offer a compromise to the Communists: place Kaesong in the demilitarized zone with no side owning it. The Reds turned down the proposal and then made a surprising move: they refused even to begin discussion of an armistice until the demarcation line was settled to their satisfaction.

In America the press was upset by Ridgway's refusal to give up Kaesong. *The New York Times* editorialized that his delegates were "backing and filling over seeming trifles." Western correspondents at Panmunjom were also accusing Ridgway of issuing unsatisfactory communiqués and not allowing them to interview Hodes and Burke. How could they explain to their readers what was going on at the important subdelegate meetings? "At the noon recess in the truce negotiations," reported Maggie Higgins, "Allied officials—whom Allied newspapermen are not permitted to approach—stalk off to their helicopters, which fly them back to the Base Camp. This in turn is surrounded by barbed wire and military policemen, and no newspaperman is permitted to enter without being officially invited or under officer escort." A briefing to the correspondents was given every evening by a general officer not present at the liaison talks. She and her associates had been forced to depend on information from their Red colleagues, Burchett and Winnington. "The Communist briefings have been quite accurate and, until the last couple of days, more informative than the Allied evening briefings." She mentioned how helpful Wilfred Burchett in particular had been. She had been chatting with him one day as the truce meeting was breaking up. "Mr. Burchett excused himself to talk to the Communist liaison officers. 'I'll go find out what's happened so I can give you chaps a fill-in.' said Mr. Burchett. He produced the fill-in as promised, and it was through him that we learned the essence of the morning discussions."

Burchett had been equally helpful to other Western newsmen, and it was he who told them that the key figure in the talks was his old friend, Chiao Kuan-hua, one of Chou En-lai's closest associates. Winnington often met this mysterious figure strolling around the Kaesong compound. The Thin Man, as Chiao was nicknamed, had traveled widely, spoke excellent English and German and, like Chou, was aware of a world outside the Central Kingdom.

After Brigadier General William Nuckols, official spokesman for the UN delegation, warned the correspondents against accepting the Red newsmen's versions of the actual battle line, the correspondents invited Burchett and Winnington to their tent to see the map of the precise battle lines the U.S. military had drawn. Burchett was asked to check a tracing of this map at the Chinese–North Korean headquarters. He took it back to Kaesong and discovered that the U.S. map was inaccurate. The Western correspondents felt they had been tricked by Nuckols, and their resentment rose to outright anger on November 5, when Burchett and Winnington revealed that the Communist delegates had proposed a demarcation line along the exact existing battle line. This was news to the correspondents, who rushed to Nuckols, accusing him of withholding vital information. He denied that the Reds had made any new proposals. Burchett and Winnington gave their Western colleagues a copy of the official English text read in the conference tent the previous day. The Western correspondents returned to Nuckols, who read through it as if seeing it for the first time, then excused it as "a suggestion rather than a proposal." The hard-core group of Western correspondents were livid, and their reports next day made headlines.

By November 12, Washington was so disturbed by Ridgway's failure to reach a compromise that a joint meeting of Defense and State officials was convened to settle the matter. General Collins suggested they send Ridgway either a directive or an order to accept the Communist ultimatum concerning Kaesong in the name of the president. Bradley agreed it should be a directive but not to use Truman's name for fear Ridgway might take it to mean that the Joint Chiefs privately agreed with him but were overruled by the president.

The Joint Chiefs cabled Ridgway not long after midnight to "press for an early settlement." He was to make insignificant concessions, such as giving up Kaesong. Joy and all the delegates were confounded. Ridgway was indignant. "I feel there is substantial probability," he cabled Washington, "that announcement to Commies of the course you have directed will increase Communist intransigence on every substantive point. Having grown up with this developing situation, I have strong inner conviction that more steel and less silk, more forthright American insistence on the unchallengeable logic of our position, will yield the objectives for which we honorably contend. We have everything to lose through concession. With all my conscience I urge we stand firm."

That morning, Hodes and Burke were concerned to find the two Communist subdelegates acting "cocky as the devil." After a few minutes of discussion Hodes said, "Could we have a recess of about five minutes because I've got to go to the head?"

Once the two Americans were alone, Hodes said, "Those bastards have got something. They know something we don't know."

On their return to the Base Camp, they learned about the orders from Washington to accept the Communist proposal. They couldn't believe it and wrote a dispatch protesting their instructions. They could not accept them, because their whole negotiating position would collapse. "We had promised the Communists we would never lie to them, and we hadn't," recalled Burke. "We told them we would never accept the present battle line as the final line of demarcation, and now we had orders to do just that. We couldn't do it."

That night Joy wrote in his diary, "The $64 question at present is, will the JCS adhere to their expressed desire that we accept Commie proposal or will they be governed by R's [Ridgway's] splendid [message]? Hodes and Burke feel definitely that their usefulness is ended if we are forced to accept Commie terms. The same feeling is shared by me as to my own future usefulness."

The following cable arriving from Washington the next day came as no surprise to Ridgway. "JCS appreciate views expressed in [your message] and recognize that there are certain disadvantages involved in undertaking action directed by our [message]. However, from broader viewpoint, they feel these disadvantages are outweighed by desirability of early agreement on agenda Item 2." In plain words, Ridgway and Joy were to follow orders and give up Kaesong.

Burke and Hodes, reluctantly returning to Panmunjom, negotiated under protest. Admiral Joy shared their indignation. "I dislike these orders just as much as you do," said Ridgway, "but we are military people. We have stated as clearly as we know how our position. We have now been instructed to do something we believe to be wrong. But you are military people and you will carry out your orders."

Burke and Hodes said they would do so. "But that makes us liars and so we will not stay on this delegation." Moreover, Burke was confident that someone on our side was leaking information to the Communists. On November 17 they presented a new proposal agreeing substantially with that of the Communists. Four days later the UN offer was accepted in principle.

During the five months of talks, the UNC had suffered 60,000 battle casualties. Of them, 22,000 were American, and Truman's critics were convinced that war had been needlessly prolonged. The Communists' original demand, a line of demarcation on the 38th parallel, would have brought a quick armistice. Ridgway and Joy were convinced that Truman and the Joint Chiefs had made a grievous mistake by diminishing military pressure and giving in to the Communists.

On November 26, the delegates came to final agreement on the line of contact, which was drawn on two sets of maps initialed by both sides. The next day, all of the delegates met in the conference tent. After sixty-five meetings, at last agreement on the military line of demarcation was formally ratified by both sides.

Although the Communists had been forced to concede on the 38th parallel, they had won a considerable victory by establishing a definite line of demarcation. More important, their clever delaying tactics had given them time to construct a fairly impregnable defense line across Korea making it difficult for UN forces to keep exerting effective military pressure on the ground.

The delegates of both sides now were faced with setting up the machinery to administer an armistice, a problem that could be far knottier than the one just solved.

CHAPTER 35

"I Agree with Ridgway's Stand"
(Late November 1951–Early February 1952)

1.

The armistice negotiations resumed with tedious maneuvering on the question of military facilities. The UN wanted no increase on either side, particularly in airfields, since they enjoyed great air superiority; the Reds were determined to strengthen their air capability during the truce. After a week's fruitless debate, the Joint Chiefs ordered Admiral Joy to table the armistice talks and proceed with another important issue—the fate of the prisoners of war.

The subdelegates met on December 11. On the Communist side of the table was General Lee Sang-cho, KPA, and a Chinese officer, Cheng-wen, another able negotiator. Opposite were Colonel George Hickman, Jr., and Rear Admiral Ruthven Libby, the replacement for Burke, who was now in America. Libby, as salty as Burke, was quick-witted and blessed with common sense, a good partner for Hickman, an experienced staff officer. They inquired if the Communists were prepared to exchange POW data and invite the ICRC (International Committee of the Red Cross) to visit POW camps.

The important concern, replied Lee, wasn't data, but the immediate release of *all* prisoners. Why, responded the fiery Libby, do the Communists refuse to exchange POW data as required by the Geneva Convention? "What is your answer to our formal proposal?"

Lee protested that they were prepared to release all POWs thirty days after the signing of an armistice. Wasn't that more urgent than exchange of data or ICRC visits?

Using forceful language, Libby and Hickman kept pressing for the data and the Red Cross inspections. On the fourth day, the persistent Americans formally requested the Communists to fulfill their moral and legal obligations under the Geneva Convention. The people of the world awaited the answer which would clear the atmosphere and disperse apprehension about the well-being of the prisoners.

How, retorted Lee, can the UNC refer us to the Geneva Convention when we haven't signed it? "What is the reason for the UNC to retain prisoners of war after the armistice? Are we to believe the UNC is unwilling to pursue the armistice if we do not carry out your unreasonable demands?"

The arguments continued fruitlessly. Finally, at the end of the December 16 session, Libby and Hickman laid their own POW lists on the table, formally proposing an exchange then and there. The Communists declined.

Mao had given instructions that the negotiations should be flexible with no show of eagerness for an armistice. The negotiators were to try to reach agreement by the end of the year. "It would be good to have peace, but you should not be afraid of calculated procrastination." He had not thought the POW issue would be a big one; the venom erupting at Panmunjom, therefore, came as a surprise to him, and he realized that a new approach must be considered.

In Washington, Admiral Burke, who had refused to continue as a negotiator, was given fifteen minutes to tell Truman about Korea. The president asked questions and listened attentively to the answers. Suddenly the outspoken Burke exclaimed, "Mr. President, who the hell is —Are *you* giving these orders?"

"No, I accept what the Joint Chiefs agree to."

"Who originates it?"

"The State Department."

"Who in the State Department?"

"I don't know exactly."

"Mr. President, somebody in this government is leaking information because I know that the Communists got our orders before we did. I can't prove it, but I know it."

Fifteen minutes had passed. "My time is up, sir," he said and started to leave; but Truman kept him. "Mr. President," he continued, "General Ridgway is a wonderful man and he submits recommendations he feels are for the best interest of our country, but nobody pays any attention to those recommendations."

"Well, I agree with him but we've got to do the things that are best for the government as a whole, and he doesn't know all of it."

"That's right, sir."

"Well, I agree with Ridgway's stand."

2.

Since the middle of November the atmosphere in Panmunjom had been polluted with bitter charges and countercharges. It worsened when Colonel James Hanley, judge advocate general of the Eighth Army, summoned local Korean correspondents to Pusan and gave them a report that proved to be one of the biggest sensations of the war. Next morning, headlines declared: "U.S. REVEALS REDS KILLED 5,500 GI CAPTIVES IN KOREA." Two days later the total was raised to 6,270, causing AP to release another sensational headline: "REDS BUTCHERED MORE AMERICANS THAN FELL IN 1776." The AP story reported: "A highly-placed Allied officer said today the announcement that the Communists in Korea have murdered thousands of American prisoners has stripped the mystery from what has been holding up Korean armistice talks."

On the heels of this highly speculative story, Armed Forces Radio began broadcasting details, at intervals, to the troops, many of whom were already dissatisfied at the slow pace of the negotiations. The Hanley handout had been released without the knowledge of Ridgway, who made a formal statement to the press. "It may perhaps be well to note with deep reverence that in His inscrutable way God chose to bring home to our people and to the conscience of the world the moral principles of the leaders of the forces against which we fight in Korea. . . . It may well be that in no other way could all lingering doubts be dispelled from the minds of our people as to the methods which the leaders of Communism are willing to use, and actually do use, in their efforts to destroy free peoples and the principles for which they stand." He hoped the public realized that publication of the Hanley report "had of course, no connection whatever with the current armistice negotiations."

Some Western correspondents doubted the accuracy of the Hanley report. James Reston of *The New York Times* reported that the circumstances looked peculiar. "Several days ago it appeared that a compromise finally had been arranged on the cease-fire, at which time Secretary of State Dean Acheson, speaking in the United Nations meetings in Paris, attacked the Chinese Communists for conduct below the level of 'barbarians.' When this attack was followed—during the critical moment of the armistice negotiations—by the publication of Colonel Hanley's atrocities report, even officials here conceded that it might look to the world as if the United States was purposely trying to avoid a cease-fire in Korea."

At Panmunjom the Western newsmen again went to Wilfred Burchett, the correspondent for *Ce Soir*, for the facts. He assured them that the Hanley document was a provocation and a lie. On visits to the prison camps, Burchett had seen for himself that the Americans were in good shape. Bob Eunson, head of AP Tokyo Bureau, visited Burchett a day or so later. "If you say our prisoners are alive and well, then I believe you. But we have a veteran photographer, Pappy Noel, who was taken prisoner. Why not let us send a camera and film up the road to Pappy? Let him take pictures of the prisoners. We'll publish them in the hometown papers and people will start screaming to get them home again."

Since most of the POWs were now in camps run by the Chinese, Burchett put the proposal to Chiao Kuan-hua, the Thin Man, who was secretly helping to run the negotiations. "Why not," he replied, "if the AP wants to risk a camera." Several days later AP handed over a press camera and a generous supply of film, and these were soon on their way north to Pappy Noel. By the time discussion on the POWs began at Panmunjom, American newspapers were carrying front-page pictures of American prisoners playing volleyball, basketball and football, as well as a stream of individual portraits for local papers.

Burchett was approached again, this time by a UP executive, who complained that the AP pictures were scooping them. "The North Koreans say they are holding General Dean. Our people insist he's dead. Can you get us some pictures to prove he's alive?"

Burchett immediately began intricate negotiations for permission to interview Dean and take pictures.

At last progress was made at Panmunjom on December 18, when the Communists finally agreed to furnish POW data. A recess was declared to allow both sides to check their information.

This breaking of the logjam would have a dramatic effect on the life of the highest ranking UN prisoner of war. General Dean had spent the past year in two houses and two caves a hundred miles or so south of Manpo, almost completely ignored by his captors. "I had difficulty in remembering who or where I was, and maintaining any sort of sanity."

The next day, his prison life suddenly changed. A Korean major named Kim asked if he wanted to write to his wife. Dean penciled a letter but was horrified by his own script. "My *N*'s looked like *M*'s and my *M*'s like nothing legible. I struggled through a letter to Mildred, then tried to read it, but I couldn't even make it out myself, so I rewrote it twice more."

Dean also wrote his daughter, and had to make two copies to get one that was legible. Several photographs, taken shortly after his capture, were put in the letters. He slept very little that night from the excitement of having a pencil.

By this time Burchett had permission to see Dean and was speeding north up the road from Kaesong with a Chinese photographer.

The next morning, December 20, Dean had a visitor, a Major General Lee. He was friendly, asked a few questions through an interpreter and had the thin cotton pad on Dean's bed replaced by one much thicker. He also ordered a sheet, which turned out to be only about twenty inches wide and seven and a half feet long. More important, Dean's summer-weight suit was replaced by a pin-striped woolen affair made in East Germany, along with a new shirt. The latter turned out to be so small that Dean could not button the neck, and the sleeves were ridiculously short.

Lee suggested they have a drink, and an aide brought in butter in a tin, sliced bread, dried devilfish, black fish eggs, and *sake*. While they ate, Lee asked what Dean thought about the war. Did he really think the UN had any chance at all? Not possible, answered Lee himself: the UN had failed to win when the North Koreans were at their lowest point. But the NK's principal problem, transportation, had been solved. There was now only one ultimate victor: The Inmun Gun, the Korean People's Army.

Dean was too busy eating to add much to the conversation. "The butter was delicious, and this was the first *sliced* bread I had seen. The fish eggs and the devilfish also were wonderful. I don't care for *sake*, but I drank two small cups of that too."

The following day, a captain named Oh asked him to state that he had not been beaten. "It would be a great favor to the general, who wants to be your friend and to treat you kindly; also a favor to me. The general may be punished unless you do this for him."

Dean agreed. It was the truth. That evening, as Dean was getting ready for bed, he heard people outside the house. From his room he saw a group coming into the guards' quarters, many with cameras. At the head was an Occidental, who, grinning widely, extended a hand. "Hello, General Dean. I'm Wilfred Burchett." They shook hands. Dean was so glad to see another Caucasian that he felt like throwing his arms around him. "Are you American or British?"

"I'm an Australian, and I've come to get your story of how you were captured. Won't you come in and sit down?" He indicated a spot in the center of the floor in the guards' tiny quarters.

The two sat on the floor which was heated Korean style and were soon encircled by Chinese and Korean newsmen who had readied their notebooks. The floor became so hot that blankets were brought for the two to sit on. Even so, they sweated profusely.

"Now, to get started," said Burchett, "I'd like to ask you what you know about the war situation." Very little since July, 1950. "Then I'll bring you up to date. I'll brief you." Dean was amazed to learn how far the UN had driven north in 1950 and how far south they'd been driven back, and how far north they had pushed a second time. Since May of 1951 the line had been relatively stable along the 38th parallel.

Burchett told how a Russian spokesman had suggested the armistice and went into detail about the meetings at Kaesong where American aircraft had violated the truce area, almost ending the negotiations. The two sides were again negotiating, and the greatest stumbling blocks were construction of airfields and the POW question. There was trouble in getting proper lists of the prisoners' names, but this problem should be solved by the end of December and a truce could then be concluded— "if your Air Force doesn't violate it and your people are able to prevent Syngman Rhee from taking some overt action. Syngman Rhee is dead-set against any truce."

Burchett was certain the American people and the U.S. Army and Navy wanted peace. "But your Air Force and Syngman Rhee do not want any cease-fire." He took a bottle of Gordon's gin from his pocket. "Well, that's that. Now, I'd like to have your story of how you were captured. It's pretty warm in here, but I don't think a little of this would hurt us." There were no cups and Burchett passed the bottle to Dean. He reluctantly took a small drink. Burchett drank, as did Captain Oh and a Chinese photographer.

It took Dean three hours to tell his story, since everything had to be translated by Oh for the other newsmen.

By this time the bottle of gin was almost empty. "I have roughly copied notes on the letter you sent to your wife yesterday," said Burchett.

Dean was nettled. "Do you mean to say that letter was turned over to the newspapers?" The letters were personal and contained references to people other than his family.

"I won't mention the things you don't want mentioned," said Burchett and scratched out portions of his notes.

The two went into Dean's tiny room, where the general complained that he was allowed only fifteen minutes of exercise a day.

"Do you do any walking?"

"No. I've been trying to get regular walks and sun-baths, and I certainly would like permission for them. But I'm not even permitted to stand up. The only time I get to stand is when I go to the latrine."

Burchett was disturbed. "I'm certain that is not the will of the Supreme Command. That's not the policy of the Korean People's Republic. There must be some mistake."

"Up until yesterday I wasn't permitted to have a pencil, and I'm afraid they'll take away the one I have now."

Burchett handed him a book, Pastofsky's *Selected Short Stories*.

"Don't give me that, Mr. Burchett, because they won't permit me to have anything to read."

"You may have this book because I've already secured permission from the commanding general for you to have it; and I'm certain they won't take your pencil away from you. I also want you to know that your name went in to the prisoner of war list which was submitted two days ago. I've seen the news item telling of your wife's joy."

Burchett promised that the first thing he'd do when he returned to Panmunjom would be to write a letter to Dean's wife. "I'll tell her I've seen you, that you're well, and that she should learn to cook rice as the Orientals do, and to make kimchi, so that you'll have the food you desire when you return."

After the long interview the photographers took pictures of Dean and Burchett sitting on the floor and of the general demonstrating exercises. It was almost dawn when Burchett and the others left. A few hours later, Captain Oh arrived, all friendliness. General Lee had come to visit Dean on December 20, Oh explained, because it was Stalin's birthday, a day for celebration. There would be more festivities on the 23rd, Mrs. Dean's birthday, a fact Dean had mentioned to General Lee. In one big jump, Dean had gone from being ignored to being feted. If only the other prisoners of war could share this treatment, he thought.

About a hundred miles north of Dean, a dozen survivors among the civilian prisoners had recently been returned to Manpo. Larry Zellers, the Methodist minister, didn't recognize the place. Few buildings were left standing and landmarks were gone. On November 27, the prisoners were told that a cease-fire agreement had been reached and negotiations about a demarcation line and eventual truce were progressing. "The war will be over by Christmas," said their informant. Later a Korean general entertained the British and French diplomatic prisoners at a sumptuous luncheon. During the meal, the general asked Captain Vyvyan Holt, the British minister who had witnessed the atrocities on the death march, to write a letter to Kim Il-sung expressing his gratitude for the good treatment they had received.

Holt listened politely, then said icily, "My colleagues and I have been imprisoned and subjected to many inhumanities against all rules of international law and diplomatic convention and practise. Do you wish me to include the details of all this in my letter of thanks to His Excellency?"

"Please do not talk like this," said the embarrassed general. "You are hurting my feelings. Some mistakes were made, but now we are treating you properly, I hope." He left without getting a letter from Captain Holt.

By this time Burchett had turned over the negatives of his pictures to UP and given the details of his interview with Dean to the other journalists. The photos appeared in newspapers throughout America, showing Dean playing *chang-gi*, Korean chess, with his guards, eating with chopsticks, shadow-boxing, doing exercises, and strolling in a forest. They caused a sensation. What particularly irritated Ridgway was a double-page spread of Dean in *Stars and Stripes*! It looked as if Dean were in a damned R and R hotel. The editor was sacked.

3.

The Chinese provided the American and British POWs at Camp 2 with colored-paper boxes of children's paints to make decorations for Christmas. Placards were quickly produced announcing, "Peace on Earth, Good Will Toward Men," "Merry Christmas," "A Happy New Year," and "Peace in 1952." Every hut was gaily decorated inside and out in an effort to recapture the happier spirit of past holidays. "And to complete the Yuletide picture," recalled Lieutenant Dennis Lankford, a Royal Navy prisoner, "there was a fresh fall of snow on Christmas Eve so that the following morning it lay on the ground deep and crisp and even. As we emerged from our huts at dawn to gaze out at the landscape, there must have been a lump in many a throat, for our gaol nestling along the frosty firs now resembled so closely the scenes on Christmas cards that would not be reaching us—this year."

Lankford and other choristers toured the huts, and he would never forget the sight of grown men with tears trickling down their faces as they listened to "Silent Night." The unspoken welcome from the sick and wounded prisoners lying on the mud floor of the hospital shack would also be unforgettable. "Many of them, I know, were thinking how unlikely it was that they would see, ever again, a Christmas in their own homes and among their own folk."

There were religious services, followed by a Nativity play, enacted by the prisoners. "All this time our Chinese guards, most of whom had never had any first-hand contact with Western Christmas festivities, hung around watching, perfectly impassive, but obviously intrigued just the same. The better-educated among them tried to feign a certain disinterest, but the peasant types were hanging on every word and every movement." Lankford concluded with the observation that months of work on attempts to indoctrinate the prisoners in Communism went to the winds that Christmas Day.

The spirit of good fellowship ended for Lankford two days later. He was brought to an empty Korean house near the edge of town. "This," said his guard, "is to be your new home during interrogation."

He wondered why they chose him. Then an interrogator arrived with an interpreter. "You are a spy, saboteur, agent!" he exclaimed. "You must consider yourself to be not a prisoner of war, but a war criminal."

Lankford thought the man must be mad. The interrogator pushed a sheet of paper and a bottle of ink towards him. "You will now write your confession. You will sign what you write and then throw yourself on the mercy of the peace-loving peoples of the world." After a pause he added, "If you choose to be a peace-fighter and will study Communism seriously, with a view to embracing it, no harm will come to you."

Lankford started to explain that he was the fleet naval information officer and dealt only in providing newsreel and press pictures of the Navy, but he was cut short.

"Write," ordered the interrogator, then left the room with his interpreter. Both returned in the evening. The paper was blank. Refusal to cooperate would destroy Lankford's future, declared the interrogator over and over. The barrage continued throughout the night. Every time they said, "Write," he would reply, "I will not."

At dawn the paper was still blank. "I think you need some exercise," said the interpreter. As the two walked into the fir-clad hills, the Chinese worked quietly on Lankford, saying it was silly not to confess. When they returned, Lankford was given a hot meal of rice, and, to his amazement, scrambled eggs. He asked for more food and got it. Then the relentless interrogation continued. "If I stay here twenty years, I won't write a confession," Lankford said, "because it would not be true."

"If you don't cooperate, it's very likely that you *will* stay with us for twenty years."

For several days the two Chinese urged Lankford to write his confession. Finally the interrogator told him he had forty-eight hours to write a self-criticism. "You will end by writing that, if you are found to have been insincere, you will gladly accept any punishment that the Volunteers may decide to inflict on you."

The Chinese returned to discover that the paper was still a blank. He was warned that "if it becomes necessary to shoot you and your side accuses us of having murdered a prisoner, our reply will be that you were a spy and that according to the Geneva Convention we were within our rights disposing of you."

"I'll never know why," recalled Lankford, "but the threats had no effect on me whatever. I was not afraid. I felt nothing, except that perhaps I was becoming rather cocky."

The two Chinese ordered Lankford to sit down and face them. "Now we ask you to confess, sincerely and honestly. We suggest you write."

"I decided that as they had refused to let me tell them about my real job in the Navy, I would write it down. The Chinamen were delighted to see me scribbling away."

But once they read what he'd written, they were furious. The interrogator ripped the pages into pieces and threw them in Lankford's face. "You have wasted the people's ink and have worn the nib of the people's pen!"

As the interpreter left the room, the interrogator removed one heavy rubber boot and began jumping up and down. Swinging his boot like an Indian club, he bashed Lankford's head again and again. Then, like a machine switched off, he calmly put on his boot and stamped out.

After dark the two Chinese returned. "You understand," said the interpreter, "we of the Chinese People's Volunteers never mistreat prisoners. While you are with us, you will never be subjected to any physical violence."

"What about that sloshing with the boot?"

"You are lying. You have not been, as you say, 'sloshed.' You have committed a further crime by telling an untruth to the Chinese People's Volunteers. For this further act of treachery you will be punished. You will stand at attention through the remainder of the night."

At first the lieutenant was quite comfortable. But as time passed, with the eyes of the two inquisitors and two guards fixed steadily on him, the backs of his knees began to ache and he leaned against the wall. A guard promptly crashed a heavy timber beam against his calves. He fell to the floor writhing in agony, whereupon the other guard hit him with a club on his shoulder and the back of his neck until he scrambled to his feet.

Throughout the night, whenever Lankford wavered, a crack behind the knees would send him reeling to the ground. His legs lost their strength. Finally he crawled to a corner under a rain of blows and forced himself into a sitting position, propped against the wall, trying in vain to fend off the continuing assault. He stayed there until dawn. "You will crack before we do," said the interpreter over and over. All the next day, with brief intervals of squatting, he was forced to stand, and bludgeoned down if he faltered. At last he summoned the strength to make a signal. Explain what you want to say, the interpreter said. "Squatting on my haunches, bruised, bleeding, on the verge of collapse, I did so— in great detail and in words that are quite unprintable."

Lankford expected they would fly into a fury. Instead, he was told, "You have insulted the Chinese People's Volunteers, the representatives of the peace-loving peoples of the world. You will pay the price." Then the inquisitors and the guards departed, leaving Lankford to ponder what "price" he would have to pay. But that night he slept soundly.

4.

Relative calm had fallen on the battlefield. Van Fleet instructed his corps commanders "to keep the Army sharp through smell of gunpowder and the enemy" by instigating operations to capture prisoners through ambush. But there was little progress at Panmunjom. On New Year's Day, Admiral Joy made a special broadcast to America: "In six months," he reported, "we have made some progress toward an honorable, equitable, and stable armistice. That progress has been painfully slow to us here at the armistice camp, as it has to the men in the foxhole, to the men in the prisoner-of-war camps, and to you at home. But in dealing with the Communists there is no other way."

The next day, his subdelegates proposed that all POWs should be allowed to repatriate voluntarily—that none should be forced to return to his country. Such a concept was abhorrent to the Communists, and the next day General Lee replied that this was a shameful proposition. The UNC's absurd and unreasonable exchange on such a barbarous basis was intolerable. Colonel Tsai, the Chinese member, added that it would be dangerous to permit so-called voluntary repatriation of UNC-held Chinese POWs to Chiang Kai-shek's forces. Naturally, they should be returned to China. Day after day the Communists refused to recognize the principle of voluntary repatriation of prisoners, arguing, persistently and with considerable justice, that this was in conflict with the Geneva Convention. By the end of January the two sides were as far apart as ever on this issue.

At the plenary meetings on the cease-fire, there was equal belligerence. "With each passing day," Admiral Joy sadly noted in his diary, "there is less and less reason to think the Communists want a stable armistice. Certainly no one can accuse them of being in a hurry to demonstrate good faith." There was no end in sight.

The battle of the press had also reached a climax. In early February, Ridgway, still steaming over the newspaper coverage of General Dean and the other prisoners, banned fraternization between the UN and Communist correspondents. Certain Allied correspondents, he charged, "were abusing their news coverage facilities for the purpose of fraternization and were consorting and trafficking with the enemy."

When Alan Winnington arrived by jeep at Panmunjom the morning after Ridgway's dictum, the air crackled with tension. "An unusually large number of the 'UN' press people were herded together expectantly," reported Winnington. "They seemed to be waiting for some lead."

Dwight Martin, head of the *Time* Far Eastern Bureau, boldly challenged the fraternization ban. He stepped forward and came towards the *Daily Worker* correspondent. "How about a stroll, Alan?" he said loudly enough for Brigadier General Nuckols to hear. Everyone watched as Winnington and Martin walked off a hundred paces and came back. Martin brought out a fat flask, unstoppered it, and handed it to Winnington, who drank and wiped his mouth with the top of his sleeve. Then Martin took a slug and exclaimed, "That's to us and fuck the military!"

In the next issue of *Time* he wrote: "Since summer, UN newsmen have been faced with a dilemma. They have found the Communist newsmen, whom they see every day at Panmunjom, are often a better source of truce-talk than the sparse briefings by UN's own information officers. From such men as Alan Winnington of the London *Daily Worker* and Wilfred Burchett of Paris' pro-Communist *Ce Soir*, UN correspondents have extracted Red reaction to UN proposals even before the UN negotiators announced that the proposals had been made. And high-ranking UN officers have frequently asked correspondents what the Red reaction seemed to be."

The New York Times also wrote that the Communist journalists knew everything that was said at Panmunjom. "The Allied viewpoint, however, is that the UN correspondents cannot be allowed to send the same information for publication."

George and Ruth Barrett of the *Reporter* quoted a veteran AP reporter: "I hate to think of the half-baked stories we would all have written if Alan Winnington hadn't been around." The ban on fraternization was shelved.

In commenting on this situation to the Nevada Editors' Conference, Robert C. Miller of UP declared that the American public had often accused its newspapers of not printing the truth. Those charges had been right. "We are not giving them the true facts about Korea . . . and there will be little improvement in the war coverage unless radical changes are made in the military censorship policy. United Nations sources either denied or withheld comment on Communist-supplied information, then belatedly acknowledged its truth weeks later." The UN was fighting a deadly, costly battle against Communism called the Cold War. "Our most devastating weapon in this fight is the truth." Yet editors and publishers had printed certain stories from Korea that were pure fabrication. "Many of us who sent the stories knew they were false, but we had to write them because they were official releases from responsible military headquarters, and were released for publication even though the people responsible knew they were untrue."

PART X

WAR IN THE PRISON CAMPS

CHAPTER 36

Friend or Foe?
(February 7–Late February)

1.

In late January, a naval helicopter pilot, Chief Petty Officer Duane Thorin, won acclaim for his unorthodox and daring rescue of another Navy pilot downed in the icy waters off the east coast of North Korea. Using special equipment he had designed himself (after being unable to make a similar rescue two years before), Thorin and his number-one crewman, Ernie Crawford, had plucked the unconscious pilot from the open sea. In early February, what should have been a fairly simple pick-up from enemy territory of yet another Navy pilot turned into a fiasco. A captain, the commander of an Army intelligence unit on a nearby island, arrived aboard Thorin's ship, the *Rochester*, with news that his agents in North Korea had picked up a Navy pilot named Ettinger, shot down several weeks earlier, and surreptitiously moved him to the coast.

The original plan had been to bring him out of North Korea by boat, but his physical condition now required a helicopter. The Army captain had received approval of his mission from Admiral Martin, commander of the Seventh Fleet. The captain said his agents, under cover of darkness, would take Ettinger to a ridge in the low mountain area about ten miles inland where they would light three fires to guide the helicopter. It was to hover over the center fire. Thorin stopped the Army captain at that point because such a night operation was impossible in the present helicopters. "Tell me the circumstances," he told the captain, "and I'll tell you if and how we can pick him up."

There was a possibility the captain's agents might be compromised and were setting up a trap. But this would be checked further before a rescue attempt would actually be made. The captain wanted one of his men to go on the mission in place of Thorin's experienced crewman. This intelligence officer, First Lieutenant A.W.C. "Bill" Naylor-Foote, had worked with the Korean agents and knew the whereabouts of supply caches and safe areas behind the lines. He had been an experienced parachutist and a behind-the-lines operative in China in World War II.

An hour before dawn on February 7, Naylor-Foote appeared and informed Thorin that Ettinger was a stretcher case and could not be hoisted. He gave Thorin the map coordinates. The Korean agents would light a signal fire once they heard the covering aircraft from the carrier task force approaching. They would carry Ettinger onto an open area where the helicopter could land. Naylor-Foote left to suit up but did not return until moments before launch time. He was followed by two sailors, each carrying a large, heavy cardboard box. American cigarettes, whiskey and canned food for the agents, he explained.

"We can't haul all that stuff!" said the astounded Thorin.

"Can't I take one box along?"

"All right, but damn it, get in! We're late!" The covering planes were already roaring overhead. "When I tell you to get rid of that stuff, you dump it!"

The green flag was raised and they launched. Thorin called the flight leader of the covering aircraft and said he would cross the coastline at ten thousand feet, maintaining that altitude until directly over the pickup. Key landmarks were clearly in view and Thorin asked Naylor-Foote to locate the site. "Just beyond the farthest ridge," he replied.

"That's fifty miles ahead!" exclaimed Thorin. Their goal was actually only seven or eight miles away, and Thorin suddenly realized his companion didn't know the area.

A heavy column of black smoke rose from the valley and Thorin started his downward spiral. With only a few hundred feet of altitude to lose, he spotted the target, standing in the middle of the snow-covered paddy. "That's our man and he's standing up," he said. "Drop your box out! Right now!" He heard no response but assumed Naylor-Foote would comply. His concentration was required on a zigzag descent. There was no sign of a stretcher or blanket near the standing Ettinger. He was obviously in condition for hoist pickup and was probably expecting it. Thorin had to set the machine down on the terrace below the one Ettinger was standing on. Without the help of his experienced crewman, Thorin had to look for himself to make certain the right wheel was not extending over the lower edge of the terrace.

The night before, Ettinger had been informed by the agents that he would be picked up by hoist and assumed the device was broken. He was suffering from pneumonia, had no shoes and could hardly walk. He hobbled toward the helicopter but got no signal from Naylor-Foote, who sat motionless, carbine lying across his knee, staring out as if in a trance. Ettinger reached the vehicle and tried to climb in. Naylor-Foote grabbed his clothes and pulled him onto the floor. The addition of his weight brought down the nose sharply because Naylor-Foote hadn't thrown out his heavy box. Nor did he make a move to help Ettinger into the machine. Thorin had to pull up the helicopter to keep the rotor from striking the ledge of the higher terrace. This sudden movement caused loss of rotor RPM, and before Thorin could regain motor speed they drifted to the edge of a shallow ravine and settled in, the rotors smashing against the edge.

Thorin looked back to see Ettinger stretched in the rear of the cockpit across the excess cargo. Thorin radioed the strike leader cruising overhead and reported the crash. In the meantime Naylor-Foote had reached a knoll twenty yards away. He began excitedly shouting the radio code name of the team that had set up the mission. At a burst from a burp gun, Naylor-Foote dropped his carbine and raised his hands.

Three men in North Korean uniforms emerged from a nearby patch of woods. Since they had not fired on the helicopter, Thorin assumed they were part of the guerrilla team. He informed the strike leader what had happened. The Korean agents would probably lead them into the mountains. "If you spot anyone coming up our way from the populated area, I'd appreciate anything you might do to discourage or delay them." He signed off and joined Ettinger and Naylor-Foote, who was trying in vain to talk to the three Koreans. Two were teenagers, the third a man wearing sergeant's insignia.

"Are these the men who brought you here?" Thorin asked Ettinger. The pilot had never seen them before.

"Do you recognize them?" Thorin asked Naylor-Foote.

"How would I know them?" Naylor-Foote responded.

Thorin saw no point in mentioning that the Army intelligence captain had given assurance that his good man knew "all our people in the area." Thorin figured the three must be under orders of the Korean agents since they had relieved none of the Americans of their revolvers. Nor did the Korean "sergeant" seem bothered by the low-toned conversation among the trio. Instead he acted as a friend.

After a few minutes the sergeant motioned them to move. With him leading the way, they moved downslope in the woods alongside a winding stream. As they were about to emerge from the shelter of the woods onto a barren, snow-covered slope, Thorin called out to the sergeant, "Ho!" and indicated by hand signals that if they moved onto the open area, friendly planes overhead would strafe them. The sergeant quickly guided everyone back to the protection of an embankment in the woods alongside the stream. In a minute a Corsair pilot laced a burst of 20-mm across the landscape a few hundred yards downslope. The rounds sounded like popping corn.

A second Corsair appeared, and Thorin figured enemy troops were moving toward them. A short burst of a burp gun and several rifle shots confirmed this. Thorin peeked over the bank. No troops in sight. But shells from the Corsair were kicking up snow much closer to them than he expected. Thorin ducked his head just as shrapnel sizzled through the treetops above. After the sergeant motioned to keep his head down, Thorin was convinced this must be a friendly agent. He asked Ettinger where he'd been kept while waiting for the pickup.

"In a house down toward the village."

If the sergeant was working with the agents, he apparently had been given no instructions covering a crash of the helicopter and had no other place to take them. Thorin pointed toward the sounds of ground gunfire, wiggling his fingers to indicate the troops moving toward them. Then he pointed to the revolver in his own holster. The sergeant quickly relieved Thorin and Naylor-Foote of their weapons.

"What'd you remind him of that for?" asked the latter glumly. "Now he'll probably search me and find my grenades."

The sergeant promptly located the grenades in the lower leg pockets of Naylor-Foote's flight suit, then glanced at Thorin's pockets, which were similarly bulged. Thorin shook his head. The sergeant nodded and didn't bother to check.

It was to everyone's best interests, reasoned Thorin, that Naylor-Foote be disarmed. His overall performance indicated he was at least a borderline mental case. The two younger soldiers sat down close by the embankment with the three Americans. The sergeant seated himself on a log in the woods facing them. They would remain there until the planes were gone.

There was little talking as they waited. Naylor-Foote sat, head bowed, staring between his feet. Ettinger, weakened by a serious respiratory condition, rested his head on his arms folded across his knees. Once, lifting his head, he said sadly, "I'm sorry I got you guys into this mess."

"It isn't any fault of yours," said Thorin, who had remained standing. Ettinger asked if the hoist was broken. "No," Thorin replied. "We'll talk about that later." Still uncertain if the sergeant was friend or foe, it seemed unwise to discuss it in his presence. Naylor-Foote sat looking at the ground as though he didn't hear the exchange between Thorin and Ettinger. Thorin then knew for certain that Naylor-Foote had deliberately lied about Ettinger's physical condition in order to come on the mission in place of the experienced crewman.

Hours passed with the enemy troops taking shelter as the planes overhead maintained watch. Ettinger, Naylor-Foote, and the two young soldiers dozed now and again in the midday warmth. Thorin and the sergeant both remained alert. The sun was well behind the mountain when the last flight of covering aircraft started for their carrier. Then appeared a man wearing the uniform of a North Korean general, accompanied by another in civilian attire who spoke English quite fluently. These were the people who had arranged the rescue attempt. They expressed their regrets to Ettinger that the effort to get him out had failed. The general then gave instructions to the sergeant and the entire group began walking downslope toward the village.

Several irate civilians, brandishing clubs and pitchforks, shouted threateningly until a few words from the sergeant kept them from nearing the Americans. As they trudged, single file, down the path, Naylor-Foote moved alongside Thorin. He tossed his head back at Ettinger, who was having trouble walking. "That no good son-of-a-bitch lured us into a trap."

"What the hell you trying to pull," said Thorin quietly. "If you hadn't lied to me about his condition, even if you'd dumped that stuff out when I told you, he'd be in the *Rochester*'s sick bay right now getting some of the medical attention he needs."

He waited for Ettinger to see if he needed assistance. He didn't, but could not keep up the pace. The sergeant considerately slowed his own step. This gave Thorin and Ettinger time to get better acquainted. The latter said he'd never seen the three Koreans before, but felt sure they were acting under the orders of the two agents who had brought him to the pickup site—and they were now taking the Americans back to those men.

The sergeant left the Americans at a small building that appeared to be some sort of headquarters or town hall. There were no guards. A man at a desk wore no insignia. Some villagers came in to look at the Americans, but gave no indication of hostility.

Soon the sergeant returned and led the Americans to a nearby house. They were ushered into an upstairs room where the general and his interpreter-aide awaited. Food was brought—bowls of delicious fresh fish soup. Naylor-Foote refused to eat his ration. Thorin and Ettinger gladly shared it.

The general wanted to know what had gone wrong with the helicopter. Thorin knew he had to be careful how he answered. These two were obviously operating as double agents. But which side were they actually on? Nor could it be expected that Ettinger would know for certain. Possibly some bona fide pro-American agents had been captured and enough information extracted to effect a line into the U.S. intelligence network. Bringing out a downed pilot—Ettinger—might have been intended to convince the Americans that this was a reliable and competent team.

It was now obvious to Thorin that Naylor-Foote knew none of the agents and had never worked in the field. The two Koreans were behaving in a friendly manner but he still didn't know if they were friend or foe. It was imperative, therefore, not to tell them the real reason for the crash.

"Something went wrong with the engine," he said. "Perhaps a broken piston causing enough loss of power to prevent holding up the added weight."

From the expression on their faces, the two Koreans truly regretted this turn of events and were probably quite troubled by it. For whatever reason, they obviously had wanted Ettinger picked up and taken out. Thorin had the strong feeling that they wanted this done primarily for their own interests rather than Ettinger's.

The Koreans were on the spot. "They now had to figure out what to do with the three of us," recalled Thorin. "If they were, in fact, working for our side, while pretending to be loyal members of the North Korean forces, they would certainly need some good explanation for the presence of three Americans. If they were loyal to the North Korean regime, then I could find some solace in the fact that my own misfortune at least served to obstruct their plans to infiltrate and exploit our intelligence network."

After an extended conversation among the Koreans, the interpreter—a civilian named Chun—turned to Thorin. "Our sergeant tells us that you are a very good soldier."

"It is an honor to be so regarded by a soldier of his caliber." The interpreter translated that to the sergeant, who looked steadily at Thorin a few moments and then departed without further word. Thorin still couldn't tell which side the man was on, but he knew he had encountered someone who would be respectable as an enemy and dependable as a friend.

Ettinger was exhausted and dropped off to sleep but Thorin had too much to think about. One thing was certain. Escape would not include Naylor-Foote. Having him along would greatly lessen any chance of success. Ettinger, while obviously weakened by his illness, had plenty of guts.

In the morning there were no armed guards in sight. Someone brought them bowls of rice gruel, but they were otherwise left to themselves and could freely talk. Ettinger revealed that he had been captured on December 13 as soon as he landed by parachute from his stricken plane. For about three weeks he was kept in a bunker near the battle-front, where he acquired frostbitten feet, pneumonia and body lice. At the same time, he lost considerable weight due to meager and irregular rations. On January 9, he was taken to the main interrogation center near Pyongyang, called Pak's Palace by prisoners for the Colonel Pak who was in charge of it. On January 31, the general and Chun had taken him from there to Wonsan. Two days later he had been brought to the area where they now were and told he was going to be released.

Now Thorin knew for certain that his host was, in fact, a North Korean general, rather than a brash operative donning an enemy uni-form. How could an imposter extricate a POW from North Korea's primary interrogation center? The interpreter, Chun, also appeared to have greater intellect and perceptiveness than a regular field operative.

Later that morning Chun and the general took Ettinger to Wonsan in the jeep. Late that afternoon they returned and picked up Thorin. It was well after dark when they arrived at Wonsan and the three Amer-icans were reunited in a long building at the entrance of an underground headquarters on the west side of a ridge, sheltered from guns of Allied ships in the harbor. Bowls of soup were provided. Afterward, Chun called Thorin aside, told him that the general still wished to get Ettinger out so he might get proper medical treatment, and wondered if Thorin had any idea how that might be done.

Thorin suggested they could put Ettinger in the life raft which had been brought from the helicopter. Thorin and Naylor-Foote, both wear-ing frogmen suits, could swim alongside until they reached one of the U.S. ships in the harbor. Chun promised to pass the idea to the general and said, "We'll talk to you again in the morning."

Thorin reported that development to his two comrades as they all bedded down that night on crude mats at the end of a line of North Korean soldiers. Next morning, while Ettinger was being given a much-needed haircut, along with some of the soldiers, Chun appeared with the general and beckoned for Thorin to join them. Naylor-Foote fol-lowed and was standing alongside as Chun said to Thorin, "The general wishes to know, if only one of you can be allowed to take Ettinger in the raft, which one should it be?"

Before Thorin could answer, Naylor-Foote stepped forward and quickly said, "In that case it should be me because I'm an officer and can go directly to Admiral Martin and arrange your payment."

Chun translated Naylor-Foote's words to the general, who spoke but two or three words back to Chun, then turned and brusquely walked away.

Late that afternoon, Chun returned alone and approached Thorin. "I am sorry," he said, "there is nothing we can do now but send you to Pyongyang. A jeep will be here shortly to take you there. I cannot give you much in the way of positive assurance, except to say that I don't think any great harm will be done to you, and I have confidence in your ability to deal with the hardships you may have to endure."

Thorin realized there was no point in asking further about the life-raft idea. "May I ask what is in store now for Ettinger?"

"We will get for him as good medical treatment as our limited resources can provide. After that . . ." Chun's voice trailed away, and for several minutes he stood silently with Thorin as they waited for transportation.

A jeep arrived. As Thorin climbed into the back, Chun said, "Good-bye to you—and good luck." Whether he was friend or foe did not matter; it was a sincere personal message. Naylor-Foote asked Thorin if Chun had said where they were going. Thorin said only, "Pyongyang." He had the peculiar thought as the jeep moved out that in war a worthy foe was more desirable than an untrustworthy friend.

After arrival in Pyongyang, they were taken ten miles north to Pak's Palace. Here they were separated. It was dark by the time Thorin was brought to a windowless room. "There are others here," explained the guard, "so you will be kept warm, but you must not talk. They must not talk to you."

Dim figures shuffled to make space for him alongside a man at a back corner of the room. Under cover of conversations resumed between others, the figure in the corner whispered, "I'm Joe Green, Lieutenant USAF. Who are you?" After Thorin had identified himself, Green warned, "Anything you don't want the enemy to know about you, don't mention it in here. . . ." Green went on to explain that several of the other Americans were obsessive talkers, about anything and everything, in the enemy's presence and perhaps even directly to them. Also, in the opposite corner was an ROK soldier. Even if not basically disloyal, he would be under especially intense pressure for cooperation.

For the next several days and nights Thorin was isolated; interrogated throughout the day, alone but mostly sleepless at night because of the cold. He had decided in advance his course of behavior and response to interrogation. He would be, after all, "just an enlisted man who only followed orders and couldn't be expected to know much."

To Thorin's surprise, there were no questions at all about the mission. Either the interrogators had already been informed about it, or didn't care. It would be some time before he would realize he had just entered into a completely different kind of war—the psycho-political arena. The interrogators were not seeking information from the prisoners. They only sought to establish in their victim a willingness to give in to a request for cooperation in minor and even insignificant things. Then a progressive pattern could lead to the recording of ambiguously worded tapes for propaganda broadcasts, and eventually to such things as false confessions to germ warfare and other crimes, followed by public condemnation of their own government for ordering such atrocities.

During his interrogations Naylor-Foote was obsessed with the necessity to concoct a cover story for the fact that he was an intelligence agent. After one long session in Colonel Pak's office, where he'd been given a little rice wine, he said to Thorin, "I've told them that I know where our medicine caches are over on the east coast. I told them you could be helpful in helping locate these things and getting to these places. We've got whiskey and poisons in the caches and my whole idea is that we could slip some poison into their drinks and then we could escape. One thing you've got to understand. You've got to obey every one of my orders implicitly. I'm in charge."

Thorin let him keep talking. It appeared that Naylor-Foote didn't really comprehend the wrongness of many of his own actions. Finally Thorin said, "One thing that disturbs me. Your captain told me you were acquainted with all the agents in there, and yet when we arrived, you didn't know them."

Naylor-Foote answered with a question: "Why do you keep calling him captain? He's just a first lieutenant like me."

Thorin was appalled. Was this man a mental case? And who had dreamed up such an incredible operation? Who was responsible for the series of mishaps? Thorin was determined to escape so he could find out.

CHAPTER 37

"An Unholy Mess"
(February–April 28)

1.

The hunger strike in the UN prison camp at Koje Island in February 1951 had been only the first step in the growing Communist revolt. By now the NK officers' compound, to which the distraught Major Ju was assigned, was completely controlled by the Reds; and to survive, he was forced to lie low until he could escape to a White (anti-Red) compound. The camp leader was no longer the half-hearted Colonel Lee Hak-ku but a North Korean completely dedicated to Communism. Listed as Private Jeon Moon-il, his real name was Pak Sang-hyon. His parents had taken him as a boy to the Soviet Union, where he became a Red Army officer. Before the Korean War, he had worked with the commandant of Soviet Army headquarters in Pyongyang. When the invasion began, he was ordered to join the North Korean Army. After his capture, he received coded orders from Radio Pyongyang to perfect and command the Communist organization at Koje.

He was so effective that, although committed Communists were far outnumbered by those who had surrendered to get to freedom, he was virtually in control of most of the compounds. He passed specific instructions from North Korea to prepare for a mass breakout: "Whenever the time is appropriate for an uprising or break, the members dispatched to the outside will assist the fighting units to get out of the compound by occupying stationary firing posts and guard posts by surprise attack, ignite signal fires on the hills, capture weapons, and destroy United Nations ammunition and arms store-houses. This sub-section will be organized from Party members experienced in guerrilla fighting in China and South Korea, those who have a thorough knowledge of enemy weapons, and those who served in the Korean People's Army in engineering and reconnaissance."

Pak also received detailed instructions on procedures to be followed once the prisoners escaped. "Construct a partisan base and set fire to the camp headquarters, petroleum dump, food storage, and other supply areas and destroy the transportation route. After completion of this duty, go to the mainland and report to an officer higher than major and join the partisans. Extrication or escape will be accomplished before dawn, while on work details or during foggy weather."

While not as well organized or led, the non-Communists, particularly the former members of Chiang Kai-shek's Kuomintang, resisted bitterly. Thousands of them had already tattooed themselves (with the help of comrades) with anti-Communist and pro-Chiang slogans to show their fervent wish to be sent to Taiwan rather than China.

The result was civil war. Arguments usually turned into bloody clashes with fists, clubs and homemade weapons. Kangaroo courts on both sides tried opponents quickly, often handing out deadly sentences. This warfare grew more intense, since guards were not permitted to enter the compounds at night. In the morning, those beaten were either afraid or unwilling to talk; and even if the camp commander had evidence of beatings, the Joint Chiefs had forbidden him to take judicial action.

An information-and-education program set up to show the advantages of democracy and the fallacy of communism stirred up violent reactions among the Communist prisoners, even though attendance at the information lectures was voluntary. The Communists, in fact, managed to profit greatly from an education program designed to develop their vocational and technical skills after the war: the metalworking classes were turned into little factories for knives, spears, clubs and other weapons.

Unrest had reached a peak at Koje in the fall of 1951, when fifteen anti-Communist prisoners were sentenced to death by a "people's court." Three others were killed in rioting at Compound 78. Troops managed to restore order and remove two hundred prisoners who feared for their lives. Prison security was reinforced by Van Fleet; and Colonel Maurice Fitzgerald assumed command, the eighth officer to hold that unenviable position. The following month, Van Fleet sent three battalions and four escort guard companies of military police to Koje. In November, a battalion of the 23rd Infantry Regiment arrived, and by December more than 9,000 U.S. and ROK soldiers were stationed on the little island to control more than 100,000 prisoners.

Once the POW issue came under discussion at Panmunjom in December, the war between the two factions accelerated. On the 18th, a mass rock fight between compounds erupted, followed by riots and demonstrations. The guards, insufficient in number, many of them poorly trained and trigger-happy, responded forcefully. Fourteen prisoners died and twenty-four were wounded.

By early February, all compounds had been polled to determine their preference about their destination following release, except for the 5,600 inmates of Compound 62. Their leader declared that all members wished to return to North Korea, and there was no reason to screen. But the ROK teams insisted on doing their duty. At about four A.M., February 18, they arrived at Compound 62, backed up by the 3rd Battalion of the 27th Infantry. The soldiers passed through the gate with fixed bayonets as some 1,250 Communists streamed out of their barracks armed with pick handles, knives, axes, flails, and tent poles. Others, screaming defiance, hurled rocks. The soldiers threw a few grenades to stop the attackers, but they kept converging on the troops, who opened fire. Fifty-five inmates were killed. Twenty-two others died at the hospital and 140 were wounded. One American was killed, 38 wounded.

For fear the story might leak out in a distorted version, Ridgway was ordered by the Joint Chiefs to release an official account at once, putting the blame on the compound leaders while pointing out that only 1,500 inmates were involved, all of them civilian internees, not POWs. Two days later Van Fleet appointed Brigadier General Francis Dodd as the camp commandant.

2.

The deadlock over the cease-fire and POWs at Panmunjom continued into April. On the 4th, both sides agreed to recess in order to determine the round number of POWs to be repatriated by each side. The UNC also asked the Communists to issue a declaration of amnesty which could be presented to the POWs before a final screening. Two days later the declaration was delivered and hopes were high.

Interviewing began singly and in private. When the UNC delegate at Panmunjom announced on April 19 that approximately 70,000 of the 132,000 prisoners in UNC custody did not wish repatriation to the Communist side, the figure was frostily turned down by Nam Il.

What figure would the Communists accept? The answer was 132,000. All their men must be returned. The meeting ended with the two sides as far apart as ever.

Admiral Joy, accompanied by three delegates, left base camp on April 22 shortly before ten the next morning, arriving at Haneda Airport by midafternoon. The quartet held a conference with Ridgway, Hickey and three staff officers regarding a package proposal—an armistice document incorporating concessions to the enemy that had to be accepted within a stated time or the negotiations would be terminated and hostilities resumed. Ridgway liked the idea as the best way to get the cantankerous Reds to negotiate. He cabled Washington that he was authorizing the delegation to explore the package proposal in the POW executive sessions. "If Commies indicate interest in this exploratory suggestion, the continuation of the discussion will be suggested at level desired by them."

On April 26, Joy prepared the ground at a plenary meeting. "For more than nine months our two delegations have been negotiating for an armistice which will bring a cessation of hostilities in Korea," he began. "We have progressed to a point where only three issues remain between us and final agreement on an armistice." These were the restrictions on construction of military airfields, the exchange of POWs, and the selection of nations to compose the Neutral Nations Supervisory Commission.

"We believe that, because of the strong views already set forth by both sides in the respective meetings, we will only prolong the stalemate on each of the three differences if we attempt to discuss them further or to settle them separately. Therefore, we believe it absolutely essential that the three remaining issues be settled *together*. It is evident that if both sides remain adamant in their present position on the three issues, these negotiations will be deadlocked indefinitely."

The next morning, the proposal was presented at Panmunjom. The Communists requested a recess to study it. At two-thirty P.M. they returned. "Our side fails to see how your proposal this morning can really be of help to an overall statement of all remaining issues."

For a week, the Communists refused even to consider the American proposition. The outlook appeared hopeless to Joy. Richard Underwood, an interpreter, found the admiral in the conference tent alone, his head on the table. Underwood thought he was sick. "Admiral, can I help you?" Joy lifted up his head. He was not ill, just in deep grief. "Have you had bad news or something?"

"No, no. I wish to God that we didn't have radio," said Joy. "We are losing men at the front every day because I can't negotiate this damned truce."

3.

Although Ridgway had sent Van Fleet a sharp reminder of the need to maintain control of the Koje-do compounds, Van Fleet had instructed the camp commander, General Dodd, "to go easy" on the prisoners. Keep them quiet: an armistice was coming. Unlike his predecessors, the fifty-two-year-old Dodd often went unarmed to the sally ports of the compounds so he could talk to the leaders of the rebellious prisoners. While this practice kept him in close touch with his charges, it also inspired them to carry out the major uprising which the North Korean command had ordered. There were no locks on the compound gates, since work details were constantly passing through. Only guards carried guns, and security personnel were instructed never to shoot except in an emergency or in self-defense. Several UNC soldiers, including Lieutenant Colonel Wilber Raven, commander of the 94th Military Police Battalion, had already been captured and released. Now the Communist leader, Pak Sang-hyon, decided to kidnap Dodd on one of the general's trips to the sally ports. What world publicity! And what better time than during the present deadlock at Panmunjom over the POWs?

On the evening of May 6, final plans were made and the first steps taken. A Communist work detail refused to return to Compound 76 until they could see Raven. They complained that guards had beaten men of their compound while searching them for contraband.

Although Raven promised to investigate, the prisoners insisted on seeing General Dodd on matters of importance. Raven promised to pass along their request. The prisoners said they would be willing to be listed and fingerprinted if Dodd saw them, thereby enabling Dodd to complete a roster of his prisoners, something his superiors had been pressing him to do. Dodd swallowed the bait. He agreed to come to Compound 76 the following afternoon.

A few minutes after two o'clock on May 7, General Dodd joined Colonel Raven outside the unlocked main gate of Compound 76. They began conversing with the representatives of the compound, who had numerous questions about food and clothing. The two Americans were invited to come inside where they could discuss the situation in a more comfortable atmosphere. Raven refused; he wasn't going to be fly to their spider a second time.

A crowd of prisoners had massed around the sally port to listen. The representatives repeated their invitation and again were refused. There was a brief pause as a work detail arrived. Once the outer door was opened to let them pass through, the crowd, pretending to draw closer to listen, leaped out and grabbed the two Americans. Raven clung tenaciously to a post until guards with bayonets came to his rescue, but Dodd was dragged inside the compound and rushed into a tent already prepared for him. It was divided into five little rooms by blankets and sheets, giving the general a bedroom, office and toilet. He was treated as an honored guest, given two orderlies, and then informed this was a planned kidnapping.

Soon a large sign was raised at the sally port: "We capture Dodd. As long as our demand will be solved, his safety is secured. If there happen brutal act such as shooting, his life is danger."

A note was handed through the fence. It was in Dodd's handwriting. He was all right, and no troops should be sent in to get him until after 1700 hours. Brigadier General Paul Yount, the commander of the 2nd Logistical Command, passed the message on to Van Fleet, who ordered him to use no force to rescue Dodd until given permission. Yount instructed his chief of staff, Colonel William Craig, to fly at once to Koje and take charge. Craig was to get Dodd out by negotiation. "Obviously," said Yount, "if somebody makes a mass break, we most certainly will resist." But unless they attempted such a thing, under no circumstances should gunfire be used to rescue Dodd. "If we get them excited, only God knows what will happen!"

Motivated by the same reasons and hoping to localize the affair, Dodd decided to cooperate with the prisoners. He agreed to act as their go-between. After a telephone was installed in his tent, he ordered his subordinates to bring in prisoner representatives from all the other compounds so their demands could be submitted to the UNC.

That morning General Mark Clark, commander of U.S. forces in Italy during World War II, had landed at Haneda. He had been selected to replace Ridgway, who was preparing to leave for Paris to take over the prestigious post of head of NATO, since Eisenhower was departing to run for president. That night, Clark dined with the Ridgways at Maeda House, which he was to occupy shortly. After dinner they chatted, and Ridgway said they would fly to Korea in the morning so he could say good-bye to his field commanders and introduce Clark. Nothing was mentioned of Koje.

Dodd was still meeting with forty-three representatives of seventeen compounds. Pak insisted that Major Ju's friend, the confused Colonel Lee Hak-ku, take a prominent role because of his high rank. Lee, therefore, was elected head of the POW delegation. Dodd was told that he would be presented with the representatives' demands the next day. Now they were going to watch a show put on by the prisoners. Would General Dodd care to attend?

Later Dodd telephoned Colonel Craig that he was being treated well and urged again that no attempts be made to release him by force. The atmosphere was not at all hostile, and he was sure he would not be harmed. By now it was evident that the Communists had scored a re-markable victory. In addition to capturing Dodd, they were using him to open negotiations. They also had telephone communication among the compounds and the use of two vehicles for intra-compound travel. The following morning the representatives presented their demands to Dodd. While he had no authority to do so, he agreed to let them have most of the equipment they wanted, such as first-aid kits.

By this time Craig had sent for trained machine-gun crews, grenades and gas masks. A battalion from the 9th Infantry left Pusan on an LST bound for Koje, while ROK navy boats ringed the island in case of a major breakout. Army, Navy and Marine planes were placed on alert; a company of medium tanks started for Pusan; and Van Fleet sent Brigadier General Charles Colson, the fifty-five-year-old I Corps chief of staff, to take charge of the camp. Bring out Dodd, he was told.

Mark Clark woke up that morning eager to get on the job. He drove to the airport, met Ridgway, and they took off for Korea. Once they were airborne, Ridgway said, "We've got a little situation over in Korea where it's reported some prisoners have taken in one of the camp commanders, General Dodd, and are holding him as a hostage. We'll have to get into that situation when we arrive at Eighth Army headquarters and find out what the score is." Ridgway was determined to work out a solution to this prickly matter himself and not toss it, on such short notice, onto General Clark's dinner plate.

Clark was astounded by the news. "Although I had been briefed in Washington on every conceivable subject, this was the first time I had ever heard of Koje or the critical prisoner-of-war problem that existed behind our lines."

Upon arrival at Eighth Army headquarters, Ridgway ordered Van Fleet in writing "to establish order in the camp immediately and to maintain it thereafter, using whatever force was required, even tanks." If the Reds resisted, Ridgway was determined "to shoot and to shoot with maximum effect." Van Fleet at once ordered a battalion of tanks from the 3rd Division to move two hundred miles by road from their position and be transshipped by LST to Koje.

4.

At Koje, General Colson, a former combat leader, had taken over control without any knowledge of the conditions and with only a vague impression of the issues being debated at Panmunjom. He soon discovered that the Communists were treating Dodd well. They allowed American food to be sent in to him as well as medicine for his ulcers. No physical pressure had been applied, and his captors did everything possible to make him comfortable. At the same time Dodd felt sure that the Communists would kill him if Colson attempted a rescue by force. Aware of this and under orders to send in an official demand for Dodd's safe deliverance, Colson decided to wait until after dawn to present it.

Early that morning of May 9, Colson presented the official demand. Six hours passed without an answer and Colson issued a second order. Colonel Lee Hak-ku finally appeared at the sally port, claiming that Dodd had admitted carrying out "inhuman massacre and murderous barbarity" against the prisoners. Observing that Colson was now in command, Lee invited him to join Dodd at an important compound meeting.

Colson declined. Instead of giving Lee an ultimatum with a time limit, Colson felt he should wait. The tanks wouldn't arrive until late that evening, and it wouldn't be feasible to go into action until dawn. He checked with Yount and the chief of staff of the Eighth Army. Both agreed his was the proper course.

Deciding he should stop further concessions to the POWs, Colson ordered an end to circulating prisoners from one compound to another. This move upset the inmates. They requested Dodd to ask Colson if they could still visit each other without interruption. If so, they promised to free Dodd afterwards if everything went well. Colson agreed.

The meeting was an Oriental version of a French Revolution tribunal. Dodd was tried on nineteen counts of death or injury to compound inmates. Translating was so difficult that proceedings dragged on for hours. Outside the enclosure, Colson was reinforcing the guards of all compounds with men of the 38th Infantry. Automatic weapons were installed at all strategic points. Colson also ordered the commander of the 38th to draw up a plan to smash into Compound 76 with tanks, flamethrowers, armored cars, .30-caliber multiple mounts, tear gas, and riot guns.

Early that afternoon, Van Fleet flew into Koje. He informed Colson that he, Ridgway and Clark all agreed to ban press and photo coverage of the mess at Koje. Colson was to give the prisoners every chance to surrender peaceably. Nor should Colson break into the compound until firepower had forced the prisoners into small adjacent compounds. At the same time, Colson must realize that he had full authority to use any force necessary to free Dodd and control the rioters. Van Fleet left the timing of the operation up to Colson, insisting that negotiations end the next day by 1000 hours.

At dusk Dodd telephoned Colson. The trial was still going on and wouldn't finish during the night. Dodd asked for an extension until noon. Colson checked with Eighth Army. No deal. The deadline must be 1000 hours.

In a steady, heavy rain, twenty tanks, five equipped with flamethrowers, arrived and were emplaced. Sixteen small compounds were made ready to receive the prisoners of Compound 76. Gas masks were issued and the troops settled down for uneasy rest. In a final telephone conversation Dodd and Colson said good-bye, neither of them expecting Dodd to survive the operation.

At first light of May 10 the prisoners finally presented Colson with their latest demands, which had been hastily and poorly translated into sometimes incomprehensible English, to cease immediately "the barbarous behaviour, insults, torture, forcible protest with blood writing, threatening, confinement, mass murdering, gun and machine-gun shooting, using poison gas, germ weapons, experiment object of A-bomb, by your command. You should guarantee PWs human rights and individual life with the base on the International Law." Prisoners also must not be forced to be screened.

Colson was faced with a dilemma. Fearing heavy casualties and sure death for Dodd, Colson telephoned Yount. Most of the 'crimes' listed by the prisoners had not been committed by the UNC. "Why couldn't I inform Dodd the accusations were not true?" he asked. If Yount could get authority to renounce nominal screening, the prisoners could be persuaded to release Dodd. Yount checked with the chief of staff of Eighth Army who gave his approval.

Colson quickly wrote an answer to the prisoners. First, he said that the Americans had not committed the offenses alleged. Then he promised there would be no more forcible screening of POWs. He demanded that Dodd be freed at noon and no later.

For hours the prisoners argued about the wording of Colson's answer. Noon passed. Midafternoon passed. At last Dodd—with the leaders of the prisoners sitting beside him—phoned Colson that there *had* been POWs killed in the past. How could Colson deny such facts? Dodd offered to write in the changes demanded by the prisoners. Colson agreed and informed Yount.

When Ridgway finally learned about the prisoners' demands, he tried to stop Colson's reply, but was too late. Van Fleet assured him that Colson's answer didn't acknowledge any illegal or reprehensible acts. By the end of the afternoon, there was still no report of Colson's negotiations.

Because of translation difficulties and the length of the discussions, it was evening by the time the prisoners studied Colson's new version. At last they were satisfied. In it Colson admitted "that there have been instances of bloodshed where many PW have been killed and wounded by UN forces. I can assure in the future that PW can expect humane treatment in this camp according to the principles of International Law." It was a stunning victory for the prisoners.

After Colson signed the statement, Dodd was asked to affix his signature. Zhang Zeshi, the chief interpreter, noticed tiny drops of water on the general's face. One by one the POW representatives shook hands with him. As Zhang approached Dodd, he realized the tiny drops were tears. "I found something shared by mankind in the new wrinkles on the general's face. Tightly grasping both his hands, I hoped that he would understand a Chinese heart."

At nine-thirty P.M., a saddened Dodd slowly walked out of Compound 76, in pain from his ulcers and torn by his ordeal. It was the end of his army career.

Van Fleet somewhat discounted the damage done by Colson's letter, but the Joint Chiefs were stunned by the fact that after confessing to instances of killing prisoners, Colson had given assurance that in the future POWs could "expect humane treatment."

The next afternoon the Ridgways left Japan. It was a sentimental departure. Both felt deep regret at leaving their many Japanese friends. At the farewell dinner, Prime Minister Yoshida had seemed so deeply moved during a gracious speech that it was impossible for him to continue. As Ridgway rose to reply, he felt a great lump in his throat. "We had worked very closely together; we had handled very difficult problems of utmost gravity, and I had come to feel toward him a great warmth, an affection almost, like that which one feels for an old and honored friend." All the way to Haneda Ridgway had been greeted by waving throngs. "There was a palpable warmth of feeling, a sense of good will and friendliness in their presence, a happy memory to be treasured."

He was stepping from one hot controversy to another in his new role as head of NATO. In the past seventeen months he had tasted great success and bitter censure. He had been praised for turning a defeated army into a victorious one, and damned for his tough position at Panmunjom. The Joint Chiefs had been tempted to relieve him of his command yet were sending him to a post almost as prestigious as chief of staff. Was he being kicked upstairs so a more compliant successor in Tokyo could finally bring about an armistice? Whatever the case, he would try his best as he had done in Korea, for he was a man stubbornly determined to do what he thought right—regardless of the consequences.

That evening at Eighth Army headquarters in Seoul, General Dodd, still showing the effects of his imprisonment, read to the press an account of his capture and release, finishing with a statement that "the demands made by the POWs were inconsequential and the concessions granted by the camp authorities were of minor importance."

Astounded by such words, Clark was even more shocked to receive a message from Van Fleet expressing similar sentiments. On May 13, Clark selected a successor for General Colson, Brigadier General Haydon "Bull" Boatner. The stocky, capable assistant commander of the 2nd Division was an old China hand. As a young man, he had spent six years there as commander of a detachment of mounted scouts and as a Chinese language officer. During World War II, he had served eighteen months with General Joseph Stilwell, followed by six months as chief of staff in the Chinese Combat Command.

Boatner was in Tokyo on R and R leave when summoned by Clark, who spelled out the situation to him. Koje was in open rebellion—and had been for months. Then he gave Boatner orders so clear and concise they could not be misunderstood. "You are to regain control of the rebellious prisoners on Koje and maintain control thereafter."

Clark explained that Koje threatened to blow up the truce talks then under way at Panmunjom. What had happened at Koje, he added, had disgraced the U.S. Army and could no longer be tolerated.

"Cleaning up Koje might mean bloodshed," said Boatner.

"Do what you have to do. I'll support you."

Boatner flew at once to Pusan, spending the night with General Yount. They dined with Dodd, an old friend of Boatner's at West Point, who warned the new commander of what could happen. The burly Boatner enjoyed several advantages over his numerous predecessors. "First, I had clear instructions directly from General Clark—and his full support in my effort to regain control of the prisoners. More troops had been sent to Koje, and the operational priorities were high when compared to the low priorities under which Dodd and Colson had operated." Also, he had spent more than eight years in Asia. "I speak Chinese and I know something about the Oriental mind." With such a background, Bull Boatner felt confident he could break up the conspiracy on the island.

That morning, Boatner arrived at Colson's office. The latter appeared to be under no tension or pressure, acting like an old officer of the day passing on the special orders to the new. Having just come from the press storm in Pusan, Boatner was amazed. Setting out in a jeep so he could get a firsthand look at the camp, he was appalled at what he saw. The atmosphere was one of high-voltage tension and belligerence. "Within the compounds, the inmates were regularly holding mass demonstrations—marching and waving Communist flags, singing and shouting in unison. Inside were statues of Stalin and Kim Il-sung, along with tall flagpoles with Communist flags flying. The POWs would crowd against the perimeter fences and curse our Korean guards outside. In each compound, the prisoners had an observation post on a barracks rooftop from which semaphore messages were sent and received. Physically, the enclosures and compounds were in shambles. The prisoner fences were of twisted barbed wire strung on rotten sapling poles, and the corner perimeter guard towers had been built *inside* the perimeter fences. It was what any reasonable soldier would call an unholy mess."

There was also an unholy mess on the propaganda front. Throughout the Communist world, headlines proclaimed Dodd's confession. Pictures of the rioting, death, and massive Communist propaganda signs appeared in *Stars and Stripes*, the newspaper read by all UNC military personnel in Korea and Japan. At Panmunjom, Nam Il was having a field day, gloating over the confession of Dodd. The UNC package proposal, he said, only showed that "your side does not yet desire to reach an agreement on the question of the POWs, so as to bring about an armistice in Korea. The final unalterable and irrevocable facts are the determined resistance of our captured personnel against your inhuman treatment and the righteous struggle of our captured personnel against your forced screening; they are proof that your side will never be able to succeed in your attempt to retain our captured personnel as your cannon fodder."

Poor Joy could only reply that it was apparent the Communists were still not ready to accept the UNC equitable compromise proposal of April 28. He returned to Base Camp almost certain that his package proposal was doomed. If so, he would have to quit as senior delegate. That day's issue of *Stars and Stripes* was no consolation. A two-page spread of pictures supplied by the Communists showed smiling UNC prisoners playing games and relaxing, proving to the world how humanely the Communists treated *their* prisoners.

At 2nd Logistical Command headquarters that day an Eighth Army Board of Officers found Dodd and Colson blameless, but General Van Fleet recommended administrative action against Dodd and a reprimand for Colson. Deeply dissatisfied with the Eighth Army report, Clark appointed a new board of investigation, which broke both generals to colonel and reprimanded Yount for failing to eliminate the damaging phrases in Colson's statement. The Department of the Army concurred.

The next morning, Boatner lived up to his nickname upon receiving reports that a large demonstration was taking place in the Chinese compound. A GI had shot a prisoner to death. "Remembering Dodd's experience, I decided at first to stay away, but then realized the grave inadequacy of my staff on such matters, due to their inexperience with Chinese, and that I had had more than ten years previously with them as friend, ally and enemy, and *I was the commander* so bore the responsibility."

Not wanting to attract attention, he and his aide headed toward the Chinese compound in a jeep by a circuitous route. They came upon an incredible sight. Inside the compound some six thousand Chinese, each with a blue and yellow banner in hand, were chanting, singing and waving flags in unison. Watching outside were thousands of U.S. soldiers, who had flocked to the uproar as if it were a fire or sideshow. Waving fists, they shouted insults at the Chinese.

Boatner sent his aide, Warrant Officer Robert Mills, with instructions to bring back the U.S. officer in charge with the head Chinese and an interpreter. "Don't let anyone else come and don't let the mob see you."

Mills brought back a balding, mustached infantryman.

"Who's in command here?"

"I am," said Lieutenant Colonel Robert Garrett, commander of the 3rd Battalion, 9th Infantry.

"Then act like it, goddamn it! Run every damned American soldier who hasn't any duty around this compound out of here!"

In less than half an hour, Garrett reported that the demonstration was all over. Investigation had revealed that one POW had been killed and the Americans were not without blame. Boatner sent the Chinese twenty rolls of toilet paper and a quart of Mercurochrome to make funeral flowers. "I told them I would send a U.S. captain to the funeral as my representative. They demanded that some 7,000 inmates be permitted to march to the funeral. This I refused but arranged that one truck, with guards, be available to transport the body and party to the cemetery. Never after that did the Chinese compound give me trouble."

On May 17, Clark informed Admiral Joy that there would be no more individual screening on Koje. "As soon as practicable, inform Commies through liaison officers that approximately 80,000 individuals will be returned to their control, indicating that rosters containing at least this number will be available in a short period of time if the Commies agree in principle with the revised figure."

Joy and his delegates were alarmed. They replied to Clark, "Considered here absolutely essential that any new figure given Commies must be a firm, repeat firm, figure rather than an approximate figure such as planned in your message. The submitting of a new and larger approximate figure by UNC would encourage Commies to assume that a further period of denunciation and delay on their part would again cause UNC to revise this new figure upward; the giving of a new approximate figure would, in short, be fatal to the apparent firmness of UNC position."

*   *   *

To prevent future mass rioting or a mass escape, Boatner initiated a three-step plan: first, to progressively control overcrowded POW compounds; second, to demolish the inadequate existing compounds and refugee villages; third, to move rebellious prisoners into new and smaller compounds, each holding no more than five hundred men. The last step would take several weeks, but the first two were put into effect immediately. "I also played politics with the prisoners, in an effort to turn the North Koreans and Chinese against each other. I went to work on the Chinese. To bait them, I expressed bewilderment at the way they took orders from the North Koreans, who were nothing more than uncultured descendants of former slaves. When the Chinese Reds realized that I felt they had lost 'face,' a split developed between them and the North Koreans. On the other hand, the North Koreans tried to pressure me into meetings. But I needed time to establish control procedures, so I told my subordinates to take all messages addressed to me from the POWs. I recall that on one occasion when I felt that a message was too demanding, I startled one of my aides by exploding, 'Prisoners do not negotiate!' "

Tension increased so much each day that a number of observers protested Boatner's bulldozing tactics. UP reported that he was backing his policy "with sandbags, pillboxes and relocated fire-power." The pillboxes had been set up at key points. "Two or three United Nations soldiers man each of the pillboxes around the clock. Trucks carrying quadruple fifty-caliber machine guns stand guard outside the compounds, 22 tanks with their crews aboard stand ready for action at a moment's notice. Boatner ordered guard towers at corners of compounds to be moved back about 50 feet, giving gunners a wider range of fire." It was not explained that when Boatner had arrived the guard towers were *within* the compounds. He simply moved them outside of the POW enclosure so they couldn't be overrun. Within a week, he had weeded out incompetents in his command, put all his troops into combat fatigues, and kept them constantly armed. He issued orders to each compound to take down their flags and insulting signs, and destroy their Communist statues, but always gave them reasonable time for compliance.

"We never bluffed," Boatner recalled. "All orders were in writing and also broadcast so all the POWs, not just the leaders, knew the entire situation. Our troops rehearsed their roles piecemeal so as to conceal our intent; when the plan was put into effect, the POWs were surprised by the suddenness and clockwork precision of these small operations. The signalmen on rooftops were ordered off by a specified date. Again they did not comply, until the first shotgun load of No. 8 shot was fired into one man's legs from a reasonable distance. All then came down. The next order forbade the POWs to lean on the perimeter fences and established five yards as the closest they could be to the fence. They complied with that order."

At the same time, Boatner took positive steps to impress on American troops that humane treatment of their prisoners might bring better treatment for their own men being held in Korean prison camps. Those GIs using excess force were punished; and upon finding that the ROK guards were brutal with the prisoners, he relieved all their units from the close guarding of the compounds.

By May 22, the dejected Joy was convinced that it was hopeless to negotiate with the Communists. "It has been increasingly clear through these long-drawn-out conferences," he told them,

> that any hope that your side would bring good faith to these meetings was forlorn indeed. From the very start, you have cavilled over procedural details; you have manufactured spurious issues and placed them in controversy for bargaining purposes; you have denied the existence of agreements made between us when you found the fulfillment thereof not to your liking; you have made false charges based on crimes invented for your purposes; and you indulged in abuse and invective when all other tactics proved ineffective. Through a constant succession of delays, fraudulent arguments, and artificial attitudes you have obstructed the attainment of an armistice which easily lay within our grasp had there been equal honesty on both sides of this conference table. Nowhere in the record is there a single action of your side which indicates a real and sincere desire to attain the objective for which these conferences were designed. Instead, you have increasingly presented evidence before the world that you did not enter these negotiations with sincerity and high purpose, but rather that you entered into them to gain time to repair your shattered forces and to try to accomplish at the conference table what your armies could not accomplish in the field. It is an enormous misfortune that you are constitutionally incapable of understanding the fair and dignified attitude of the United Nations Command. Apparently you cannot comprehend that strong and proud and free nations can make costly sacrifices for principles because they are strong, can be dignified in the face of abuse and deceit because they are proud, and can speak honestly because they are free and do not fear the truth. Instead you impute to the United Nations Command the same suspicion, greed and deviousness which are your stock in trade. You search every word for a hidden meaning and every agreement for a hidden trap.

After months of conciliation, the UNC had told the Communists with firmness and finality that it could not recede from its position with respect to POWs.

> On the 28th of April we offered you an equitable and specific solution to the issues remaining before us. We told you then, and we tell you now, that we firmly adhere to the principles of humanity and the preservation of the rights of the individual. These are values which we will not barter, for they are one and the same with the principles which motivated the UNC to oppose you on the battlefield. No amount of argument and invective will move us. If you harbor the slightest desire to restore peace and to end the misery and suffering of millions of innocent people, you must bring to the solution of this issue the good faith which, as I said at our first meeting, would directly determine the success or failure of our negotiations. The decision is in your hands.
>
> After ten months and twelve days I feel that there is nothing more for me to do. There is nothing left to negotiate. I now turn over the unenviable job of further dealings with you to Major General William K. Harrison, who succeeds me as Senior Delegate of the United Nations Command Delegation. May God be with him.

CHAPTER 38

"I Was Forced to Be a Tool of These Warmongers, Made to Drop Germ Bombs"
(May 23–September 28)

1.

Upon arrival in Paris, Ridgway was greeted with signs painted on walls: "Ridgway Go Home." As he and his wife were escorted through the streets behind an impressive motorcycle escort of Metropolitan Police, a man broke through a police cordon, shouting something unintelligible. Ridgway did not feel that this inhospitable greeting, undoubtedly inspired by Communists still making capital of the trouble in Korea, represented the true sentiments of the French people.

General Eisenhower, suffering from painful eye trouble, received him in his darkened bedroom. They talked of the major problems at NATO. In a long informal session, Ridgway got Eisenhower's full views. He was leaving France to run for president, aware that Ridgway's problems in Korea were unresolved—with the petty haggling at Panmunjom giving off heat, not light. He was resolved, if elected, to end the war promptly.

Although Joy departed from Panmunjom dejected by his failure to reach a settlement, he had successfully negotiated all matters but the apparently insoluble one of repatriation. There had been much give-and-take; but in many instances he had attained more than Washington expected, and he had never surrendered any vital objectives. He had managed to suppress his own feelings no matter how bitterly he was attacked, always carrying on with patience and forbearance.

His replacement, Major General William K. Harrison, who had

served as a delegate at Panmunjom for four months, entered the fray on May 23 with vigor. A descendant of a famous family which included a signer of the Declaration of Independence and two presidents, he was an ardent reader of the Bible and was blessed with a happy disposition. He strode into the tent at Panmunjom humming, greeting all with a friendly smile. He was ready to negotiate—on his own terms. At the end of the first plenary session, for instance, he calmly postponed the next meeting four days despite the Joint Chiefs' desire that daily sessions be held for as long as the Communists wished.

He was convinced that the Communists were fighting a delaying action. "Fighting it with words and not with guns," he told an interviewer, "just trying to prevent us from getting an armistice which we wanted. And so we would give up and go home. Now if we are sensible people, we do the same thing. We should have a purpose for doing something, and if we don't have a purpose, maybe we had better not do it at all." The Reds had a purpose. They wanted world domination and weren't really bargaining. "When you negotiate with a fellow, you both try to get an answer." The Communists hadn't been doing that, and he wasn't going to take any nonsense from them.

Nam Il was not at all prepared for such a man. After several days of repetitious arguing, Harrison got to his feet and calmly said, "Apparently the only way I can convince you that I mean what I say is to get up and go out." He and his staff filed out of the tent, the confounded Communists staring after them in amazement. Harrison had taken a page from Mao's tactic of strategic prolongation.

Like Harrison, Boatner was a man of action. He had decided to construct new, smaller compounds where the rebellious prisoners could be segregated. His plan was to move the toughest compound first. At 5:15 on the morning of June 10, precisely one month after the release of General Dodd, loudspeakers outside of Compound 76 ordered the prisoners there to gather in groups of one hundred so they could be moved to a new compound in half an hour. None would be harmed if they cooperated. Nothing happened. Standing on a low hill nearby, Boatner surveyed the scene. Everything had been planned to the last detail and he was confident.

A signal flare shot lazily into the sky. The 187th RCT moved forward, their bayonet-tipped rifles at high post. Tear-gas grenades arched into Compound 76 as Patton tanks rumbled forward, battering down fence posts and crushing the barbed wire into the dust. Infantrymen with flamethrowers moved in behind the tanks. Then came the paratroopers, wearing gas masks. Only the magazines of their rifles were loaded, and they were forbidden to move the cartridges into the chambers of the barrels unless ordered to do so.

A scream of anger burst from the men of Compound 76, soon to be joined by men from adjoining compounds. Prisoners armed with knives, sharpened tent poles, and flails chanted ominously. The Americans advanced relentlessly against an increasing barrage of rocks and spears. Exploding tear-gas grenades set off puffs of stinging white fumes. Fiery tongues from flamethrowers ignited the buildings. Concussion grenades routed nests of diehards. Against stubborn resistance, the soldiers reached the first-phase line and halted.

"Move them up to phase line B," Boatner ordered.

The helmeted paratroopers began to move slowly forward against weakening resistance. By now most of the prisoners, stumbling and gasping from tear gas, began streaming to the central parade ground, hands clasped over their heads in surrender. Some of them were killed or wounded by prisoners who wanted to fight on. About 1,550 prisoners in the far corner of the compound attacked the paratroopers, who converged on them without firing a shot. The prisoners threw concussion grenades and then tear-gas bombs. Suddenly a group of about three hundred prisoners charged and repulsed the paratroopers. They stiffened, then moved forward again, using only bayonets and rifle butts. The hand-to-hand battle grew wild; and though some paratroopers were felled by spears or barbed-wire flails, still not a shot was fired by the disciplined troops. The arrival of half a dozen Patton tanks ended the battle. Forty-one prisoners lay dead and several hundred were wounded. One American paratrooper had died, and fourteen were wounded.

Boatner walked into the still-flaming compound. Inside one hut, he found the corpse of a prisoner hanging by his heels, apparently an example to those who were not eager to join the rebellion. Paratroopers found Senior Colonel Lee Hak-ku in a ditch and dragged him out roughly. They also found two sets of plans, one the defense for the resistance movement, the other details of a mass breakout set for June 20. It called for flight into the hills, killing everyone who got in the way.

Boatner's strike put an end to any breakout, nor did the 6,500 hard-core Communists of Compound 76 put up any resistance when they were separated into groups of five hundred and placed in new compounds. The men in Compound 77, also dedicated Communists, submitted without protest. Daily inspections and regular searches for contraband prevented the buildup of a new arsenal of weapons. Anti-Communists were moved to separate camps, safe from terrorism by their enemies. Soon the POW population of Koje was cut in half when pro-Communists were moved to new camps on other islands.

The Communist press was outraged by the Boatner tactics, and even many Westerners were shocked. The Canadians, through their ambassador in Washington, Hume Wrong, were particularly acerbic. Wrong berated the Americans constantly, charging that a few decent troops and officers could have righted the mess in short order.

Condemnatory stories were also coming from Burchett and Winnington. Their early reports of the negotiations and incidents at Kaesong had been more factual than those of the Western correspondents. But after the mutiny at Koje—apparently reflecting their horror at the bloodshed—their accounts echoed those coming from North Korean and Chinese reporters. Maggie Higgins was dismayed by the change in Burchett. She had appreciated his help earlier, regarding him as a misguided idealist. But now he was spouting the Communist line. Even so, she still liked him, as did many other Western correspondents. Winnington, on the other hand, was almost universally detested because of his arrogant manner. The Americans got their revenge by presenting him with a cake, topped by a penis in pink icing. The inscription read, "Happy Birthday, You Prick!"

It was apparent that no matter what the Americans did, no matter how violently provoked, their image throughout the world was besmirched by their inhuman treatment of prisoners. The only press coverage of UN prisoners was through pictures showing them enjoying life. The Communists were undoubtedly winning the battle of propaganda, largely because the International Red Cross teams were allowed to inspect the UN camps but were prohibited from entering those in North Korea.

2.

June was an uneventful month at Panmunjom. Harrison managed to keep Nam Il exasperated by resorting to three-day recesses. So little was accomplished that Harrison recommended a rescreening of POWs by neutral nations. If the Communists were still reluctant to conclude an armistice after such rescreening, the UNC should simply release on parole all prisoners except those opting for repatriation. He would continue his recess tactics until the Reds signed an armistice.

On July 26, he surprised Nam by announcing that staff meetings could resume but that there would be a seven-day recess of the plenary session. When Nam Il protested, Harrison observed sharply,

> In these meetings we have been restrained in our statements and have tried to be accurately factual. Your statements, on the other hand, have demonstrated utter hypocrisy. You have said we want to retain your personnel. What we know and what the world knows as a fact, is that those prisoners are afraid to be returned as slaves to the mercies of Communist control.

You have said we violate the Geneva Convention—a covenant intended to protect the rights of individual human beings, not the tyranny of totalitarian rulers. Probably no government or armies have more constantly ignored or violated the Geneva Convention than you have. You have no moral right to raise the issue or the question of the Geneva Convention. You have made utterly false statements about our actions. Such lies are recognized by everybody as typical of Communist propaganda."

He added that his delegation would return on August 3 and was on his way out of the tent, followed by his staff, before the astonished Nam had a chance to reply. A young member of Harrison's staff, William Vatcher, congratulated him on his bravura performance. "Vatcher," replied the general in his Tennessee drawl, "those weren't my words. It was the Lord that put those words in my mouth."

3.

Ever since the innocent expedition of General Sams and Lieutenant Clark to determine if stories of plague in North Korea were true, the Chinese had been charging that the Americans were waging biological warfare.

The American retort, that the United States would never use such weapons unless they were first used by the enemy, did not convince the suspicious Chinese. Against this background of deep distrust, the Chinese were now convinced that the United States was indeed waging germ warfare in Korea. On March 8, 1952, Chou En-lai indignantly announced that downed U.S. Air Force personnel using biological weapons would be treated as war criminals. A few days later the Soviets joined in the attack, bringing similar charges of American use of germ warfare before the UN Disarmament Commission.

On March 26, Chou En-lai sent a telegram to the Secretariat of the United Nations stating that his government and the Chinese people fully supported the "just position" of North Korea. "Everybody knows this was not the first time that American imperialism has used bacteriological weapons in its war of intervention in Korea." He listed numerous occasions.

"It must be pointed out that American imperialism was forced to hold armistice negotiations after sustaining, in the war of intervention which it launched in Korea, shattering blows at the hands of the heroic Korean People's Army and the Chinese People's Volunteers. Nevertheless, refusing to acquiesce in its own defeat, American imperialism, in the course of the negotiations, employs all kinds of shameless stalling tactics to obstruct the progress of the negotiations on the one hand and carries out callously brutal germ warfare on the other."

Chou claimed that the U.S. Air Force, in 448 sorties, had spread large quantities of germ-carrying insects over northeast China in an attempt to further American aims of "invading China and threatening the security of the Chinese people by the criminal and vicious device of mass slaughter of peaceful people."

Americans regarded these claims as utter nonsense, further proof that the Communists would stoop to the lowest kind of slander. But it was not illogical that the North Koreans, who had indeed suffered from epidemics, should truly believe the American devils had dropped poisoned insects. Hadn't they already shown their inhumanity by savaging the entire population with their bombings?

A week after Chou En-lai's report came apparent confirmation of the Chinese charges. An American flier, Lieutenant Kenneth Enoch, whose B-26 had been shot down three months earlier, finally confessed that he had dropped germ bombs. A few days later, his comrade, Lieutenant John Quinn, also confessed. "It is very clear," he stated, "that the capitalistic Wall Street warmongers, in their greed, their ruthless greed, have caused this horrible crime of bacteriological warfare in order to get more money for themselves in the hope of spreading the war. . . . I was forced to be a tool of these warmongers, made to drop germ bombs, and do this awful crime against the people of Korea and the Chinese Volunteers." The Chinese had been lenient, he said. "They issued me with warm clothing against the cold, gave me excellent food, bedding and a warm place to sleep. I am eternally grateful for their kind treatment. At last, after much patience on the part of the Volunteers, I realized my crime. My own conscience bothered me a great deal, and it is very good to be rid of this burden and to confess and repent. I have realized my terrible crime against the people." The stilted and ungrammatical language of this confession was obviously dictated by a Communist.

By July, germ warfare was a worldwide issue. Riots were staged by Communist supporters in many countries. The ensuing furor, combined with vivid stories of the horrors committed by the Americans at Koje, made Harrison's job at Panmunjom almost impossible. "Koje Island!" exclaimed *Pravda*: "We have learned that 'civilized' Americans can be yet even more inhuman, yet more infamous than the bloody Hitlerites. Dachau was a death camp. Maidanek was a death factory. Koje is a whole island of death."

Another *Pravda* article labeled American generals as "butchers in white gloves, the bloody bigots and traders in death who have unleashed the most inhuman carnage in history, warfare with the assistance of microbes, fleas, lice and spiders."

Dr. Hewlett Johnson, the dean of Canterbury, joined in the attacks. Returning to London from China that July, he told a meeting of the British-China Friendship Association that the "facts about germ warfare are conclusive and irrefutable." In Mukden he had seen, in a test tube, insects found on an ice rink. They were infected, he was told, with disease germs. In East Berlin, the World Peace Council was charging that the Americans were not only raining down infected organisms on Korea but had even succeeded in poisoning the fishing waters off the coast.

These attacks intensified the efforts of the Chinese and North Koreans to wring confessions from captured American fliers. "The use of bacteriological warfare is one of the detriments to world peace," admitted Lieutenant Floyd O'Neal. "The people of America must realize the seriousness of these terrible weapons and rise up together and stop this germ warfare. Only then can all mankind have peace."

"I want it known by whoever reads this statement," wrote Lieutenant Paul Kniss, "that it is my own sense of justice, my own ability to tell right from wrong, that has forced me to let everyone know the facts. I offer these facts to the world that an inhuman weapon is being used in Korea by the U.S. forces."

Except for these few men, the American fliers resisted extreme pressure from the Chinese, despite severe beatings.

For months, the Chinese had blocked investigation of the germ-warfare allegations by the International Red Cross and the World Health Organization, which they regarded as biased. They relied completely on the International Scientific Commission, which consisted of sympathetic Westerners, including such renowned men as Joseph Needham, the Cambridge University biochemist.

"The peoples of Korea and China have indeed been the objective of bacteriological weapons," reported the commission. "These have been employed by units of the U.S. armed forces, using a great variety of different methods for the purpose." These conclusions had been reached by the International Scientific Commission, but only reluctantly, because the members found it hard to believe that "such an inhuman technique could have been put into execution in the face of its universal condemnation by the peoples of the nations."

The Communist claims were bolstered by the confessions of three more American airmen shot down in the same B-26: the pilot, First Lieutenant James E. Gummo; the navigator, First Lieutenant David E. Penny; and First Lieutenant Bobby Hammett, the bombardier.

4.

Despite the stalemate on the fighting front, men on both sides were dying and suffering in bitter seesaw struggles for the desolate area near Chorwon, around a hill nicknamed Old Baldy. From June 6 to July 21, Clark's troops had suffered 351 casualties while inflicting an estimated 1,093 Chinese casualties. Then came six consecutive days of heavy rain, flooding streams and rivers. Bridges were swept away, and roads were blocked by landslides or washed out. At the end of the month, the 2nd Division again tried to secure control of Old Baldy, an action that was typical of the small but savage battles waged along the front.

Far to the west, near the Imjin River, was another bitterly contested hill called Kelly. On July 30 a new replacement, Major John Eisenhower, arrived at 15th Infantry headquarters and was told that his battalion, the 1st, was in the assembly area preparing to attack Kelly in the morning. Just before leaving for Korea, John had said good-bye to his father, who had been nominated for president by the Republican national convention in Chicago. "We talked of nothing very important, but in the course of conversation Dad gave me one admonition: never get captured. He shrugged off the fact that in infantry combat the chance of being hit by a mortar or artillery shell was always present; but as the son of a new nominee for President, my capture would not only subject me to special cruelties but would also put the Communists in a position to blackmail him."

"If you're captured," he said, "I suppose I would just have to drop out of the presidential race."

John assured his father this would never happen and told him not to worry. "Yet had I ever found myself surrounded by Chinese or North Koreans, I had every intention of keeping my promise and using my .45 pistol, taking, I hoped, some of them with me."

The next night Eisenhower was escorted to the front by the battalion operations officer, Major Red Allen. Beams from powerful searchlights directed at low clouds lit the areas in front of the trenches. "It gave one an eerie feeling," recalled Eisenhower, "to see the men struggling up the narrow dirt road sliced out of the side of a cliff, with the pencils of white light over their heads reflecting on the clouds to the front." Part way up the hill they came upon a soldier lying on the ground. Allen shook the man but was unable to get him to give his name. In a rage Allen beat and kicked the man, to no avail. Ignoring the revulsion and fear on the faces of the other GIs, he turned to Eisenhower, as teacher to a pupil. "If a man will give you his name," he said, "he'll fight; if he won't, you can't do anything with him."

Upon reaching the battalion observation post on top of the ridgeline, Eisenhower became oriented before the beginning of the attack. The

OP was higher than Kelly Hill, and its view over the area of action made it seem like a grandstand. Three companies were moving out through two lanes cut through the minefields. As the dark became gray, Eisenhower noticed to his astonishment that the dugouts in the OP were occupied not only by the battalion commander but the regimental commander, the division commander, and the corps commander. "All this brass was out to observe what was essentially a reinforced company attack on an isolated outpost!"

The intensified Chinese and North Korean interrogations caused many UN POWs to plan escape that summer. Even though all the escapes ended in recapture, helicopter pilot Duane Thorin was convinced that he could make it. Immediately after arriving at the annex near the British POW camp, he began conditioning himself for the venture. By late July he was finally ready.

He decided he should take a partner and selected a rugged private, John Shaw, a truck driver. Shaw was short on schooling but showed quickness of mind. He had picked up some Korean and was in good physical condition. Shaw insisted on bringing along another private. Thorin didn't have a compass but could use the North Star to guide them. They would wait until there was a storm at night to cover the noise of their departure.

At last a roaring night storm hit. With a sharpened piece of steel, Thorin cut through the wooden bars nailed across the windows on the back of the building.

In pitch darkness, Thorin led his companions over a ridge toward a mountain peak, their first objective. By daybreak they had reached the top. The rain had stopped. It took them a day to reach the Yalu. They tried to sleep in the woods despite occasional showers. But the next morning they were discovered by a Korean woman, captured, and brought back to the camp.

"You have been caught in the crime of trying to escape," said Lee, the camp commissar. "How do you think you should be treated?"

"You know it is not a crime for a prisoner of war to try to escape."

"Well, it was a crime," exclaimed Lee." Until then he had regarded Thorin as a placid prisoner. "China was not a signatory of the Geneva accord."

"You claim your lenient policy is better than the Geneva accord. So you know it is not a crime for a prisoner of war to escape."

Lee grew loud and angry. Suddenly he lashed out with his left hand, taking Thorin by surprise. Though he rolled with the punch, the blow broke a corner off a back molar and the ring on Lee's finger cut Thorin's face. "Now what do you say?" Lee said. "Do you still think it was legal for you to try to escape?"

Thorin came back to a watchful position and spat out the bit of tooth in disdain. "It's obvious you don't want me to say what I think. You want me to say what you think, so the only thing I can do is to say nothing."

The guard was ordered to take charge of Thorin. On the table were the bowl and spoon he'd been issued. "Shall I take my bowl with me or won't I be needing it?"

Angrily Lee grabbed the bowl and, without a word, shoved it at Thorin. In the darkness he was escorted to an old Korean house, now used as a solitary cell, and led into a dark room. The plank door was closed. A heavy log was placed against it. Thorin could hear the sounds of a board being nailed over the small window on the opposite side of the room. In the darkness he felt straw. He made a bed and stretched out on it. As he was drifting off to sleep, a rat bit his finger. Thorin slammed the rat against the wall, where it lay dead the next morning. Paper and pencil were shoved through the door with his rice ration. On one sheet was written, "You must realize your mistake." He spent most of the day meditating on the course of events, puzzled that the escape had worked so wonderfully at first and then suddenly had gone sour. "I wondered why God would be with me so much and then, here I am back. It occurred to me that I had learned a good deal in the time I'd been a prisoner but apparently I had yet more to learn."

A few days later Commissar Lee stuck his head in the door and asked why Thorin hadn't written anything. "I didn't see any reason to write anything. I didn't have anybody to write to."

"You must realize your mistake."

"I realize my mistake."

"You must write it."

When Lee picked up the paper the following day he read, "I realize I made a mistake."

"You must explain your mistake," said Lee.

It became a game. Thorin wrote, "I started out and didn't have a map to see where I was going, and didn't have a compass for direction." The next day he admitted he hadn't conditioned himself properly. Lee urged him to write more and more. Thorin now saw the enemy's purpose and wrote in a style unlike his own as if he were under duress, yet never admitted doing anything wrong. Lee pointed to a promise Thorin had written never to make the same mistakes again. "You must write explicitly that you promise not to escape again."

"If you want that in there, you'll have to write it in yourself."

Lee did so, making it evident he had practiced forging Thorin's handwriting. Then Thorin was sentenced to six months in solitary confinement.

5.

The rainy season continued through August, limiting activity along the front. Even so, Marine casualties at Bunker Hill had been so high during August that an emergency airlift had to bring in reinforcements. During this deadly struggle, Maggie Higgins had jeeped up to a forward observation post to find a Marine colonel kneeling at the side of the shell-gutted road. "He was holding a wounded Marine officer in his arms. The wounded man had stepped on a diabolic Communist box mine." The effects were ghastly; his legs were blown off at the knee. "The jagged metal had bitten into his face and head, his arms, his torso. He was so bloodied, it was hard to see what part if any, of his body remained whole."

She watched the man die. As a poncho was laid over him, the colonel turned to her. "You have just returned from the States," he said bitterly. "Will you please tell me what kind of a war the American people expect us to fight? See that ridge over there? Behind it the Chinese have dug in artillery emplacements. Their shells are making life hell over here. We could clean it up with a couple of tactical atomic bombs." Last night the division had lost more than a hundred men trying to hold onto Bunker Hill. "How do you think we feel, ordering men to take a hill when we know many will die unnecessarily because some politician under pressure from somebody decided not to use the weapons that could save their lives? After seeing Bill here, you can't tell me that one weapon is more horrible than another. These goddam box mines kill you just as dead as an atomic bomb. Only the dying usually takes longer." Tears began to flow down his cheeks. Maggie wept too.

While the casualties continued to mount little happened at Panmunjom during the first three weeks of September, with each side refusing to accept the other's proposal. It appeared to Harrison that the Communists were prepared to sit it out in hopes that the UNC delegation would concede from sheer fatigue. The invectives reached a climax on September 20. "When your outrageous proposition of forceful retention of war prisoners has gone bankrupt," charged Nam Il, "and you can no longer use it as a camouflage to play deceit, you cannot but resort to vituperation and distortion in these conferences. This only shows how desperate and disreputable—how childish and ridiculous—your side has become!" He went on and on.

Truman steadfastly backed the military. Voluntary repatriation of POWs must be settled within the armistice, not at some dangerously open-ended political conference. Four days after the Communist outburst at Panmunjom, he told a White House meeting, "Unless we wipe the slate clean, an armistice will do no good." He sent a personal word of encouragement to General Clark on September 27, urging that the UNC proposal be made "with utmost firmness and without subsequent debate."

The next morning, five months after the original package had been delivered, General Harrison briefly restated the previous plans which the UNC had brought forward to break the POW deadlock, only to be turned down. He urged that the Communists "give mature and careful consideration to our proposals. For that purpose I propose a recess of ten days and that we meet again here at 1100 hours on 9 October."

But Nam Il kept insisting that captured personnel of the Chinese People's Volunteers "must all be repatriated home." That alone, he said, would bring "a speedy termination of the Korean War."

"The United Nations Command has no further proposals to make," replied Harrison. "The proposals we have made remain open. The UNC delegation will not come here merely to listen to abuse and false propaganda. The UNC is, therefore, calling a recess. We are not terminating these armistice negotiations, we are merely recessing them. We are willing to meet with you again at any time that you are ready to accept one of our proposals or to make a constructive proposal of your own, in writing, which could lead to an honorable armistice." The UNC had gone as far as it could go. "I have nothing more to say. Since you have nothing constructive, we stand in recess."

The talks, which had begun on July 10, 1951, were definitely over at last, with prospects for an armistice as remote as ever. Harrison and his delegates returned to their base camp and packed for departure to Tokyo. The front lines were also deadlocked; each side had grown stronger. Clark now faced a dilemma: how much military pressure could he apply to bring concessions from the enemy without provoking large-scale warfare?

PART XI

WAR AND PEACE

CHAPTER 39

"Can Ike Win the War?"
(October 3, 1952–April 1, 1953)

1.

On October 3, Eighth Army learned from a Chinese deserter that an attack was planned on White Horse Hill, five miles northwest of Chorwon. Its loss would force IX Corps to withdraw to the high ground, thereby opening up the entire Iron Triangle to enemy penetration. The attack began on October 6 with diversionary forays and opening the floodgates of a reservoir. Then the Chinese assaulted White Horse Hill itself but were thrown back by the ROK 9th Division. Despite heavy losses, the Chinese persisted, only to be battered by artillery and air power. By mid-October the battle was over. Some 23,000 Communist troops had failed to dislodge the stubborn, disciplined ROKs, who lost over 3,500 men. The victory was evidence of the success of the intensive ROK training program instituted by Ridgway and continued by Van Fleet.

After the abrupt end of talks at Panmunjom, there were indications that China was anxious to reach some sort of accord. During the Peace Conference of the Asian and Pacific Region in Peking ending on October 12, Chinese rhetoric was markedly less militant. The accent was on "peaceful coexistence," and the speeches showed greater fear of Japanese resurgence than of the war in Korea.

Even in Moscow the Korean War seemed of less importance than other matters. Stalin's remarks to the Nineteenth Party Congress three days after the ending of the Peking peace conference implied a cautious attitude toward foreign adventures.

When Harrison and his staff walked out of the tent at Panmunjom, the war entered a new phase. The Communist charge that the UNC had broken off negotiations caused Washington to send Clark an order not to use the term "indefinite recess."

At the UN General Assembly, the United States was doing its best to bring both sides back to the conference tent. But the Soviets accused America of unilaterally ending the peace talks, then repeated the charges of UNC atrocities in prison camps. To counter this attack, Secretary of State Acheson addressed the UN Political Committee on October 24. He presented a resolution that called upon the Chinese and North Koreans to "agree to an armistice which recognizes the rights of all prisoners of war to an unrestricted opportunity to be repatriated and avoid the use of force in their repatriation."

He then pointed out the inconsistencies of the Soviet's position in opposing the concept of UN nonforced repatriation in Korea, since the USSR had previously upheld the right of POWs to choose or refuse repatriation. The UNC, he said in conclusion, was ready to reconvene at Panmunjom whenever the Communists accepted the fundamental principle of nonforcible return. Afterwards, the foreign minister of Pakistan exclaimed to him, "I had no idea our case was so powerful."

"I think it is fair to report," Acheson wrote Truman, "that things are moving for us far better than we might have expected." He described his proposition for repatriation. "Twenty other governments have joined with us in sponsoring this resolution. This includes virtually all the governments with troops in Korea. I believe we stand a good chance of presenting a firm majority on Korea, which may have an effect on the Communist expectations."

In Tokyo, however, General Clark was so frustrated that he cabled the Pentagon on October 16: "I consider it necessary that plans be made for the use of atomic weapons." Manchuria and North China should be bombed.

The Joint Chiefs and Truman promptly rejected his proposal, although the president himself had threatened to use this ultimate weapon.

By now most Americans were completely fed up with the Korean War and the fruitless negotiations for peace that had been strung out over fourteen and a half months. Many were going to vote for Eisenhower because he had promised that, if elected, he would go to Korea to determine what the conditions were in that unhappy country. Many felt he was just the man of action who could put an end to this tragic mess.

On November 4, the Eisenhowers cast their votes in New York City and that evening attended a party at the Commodore Hotel. General Eisenhower's doctor induced him to go to bed about ten-thirty. "I arose before midnight, after sleeping while the news came in. The verdict: we had taken about 55 percent of the popular vote and 422 of the 531 electoral votes, winning by a landslide margin of more than six and a half million votes."

When Eisenhower paid his formal visit to Truman on November 18, the briefings were necessarily general and official. "Eisenhower was unsmiling," remembered Truman. "I thought he looked tense." After twenty minutes, Acheson and others joined them. "I want to make available to General Eisenhower and his associates," said Truman, "the information that will be helpful to them in taking over the operation of the Government." The debate at the UN over Acheson's resolution would start the next day, and Truman suggested that Ike publicly support it. He read a statement prepared for the president-elect, but Eisenhower had his own ideas on what he would say. He then went over a draft of a joint statement Truman had written. Eisenhower requested two changes, and the joint statement was issued to the press. The conference ended at 3:15 P.M.

Once Truman was alone, he was troubled.

> I had the feeling that up to this meeting in the White House, General Eisenhower had not grasped the immense job ahead of him. There was something about his attitude during the meeting that I did not understand. It may have been that this meeting made him realize for the first time what the presidency and the responsibilities of the President were. He may have been awestruck by the long array of problems and decisions the President has to face. If that is so, then I almost understand his frozen grimness throughout the meeting. But it may have been something else. He may have failed to grasp the true picture of what the administration had been doing because, in the heat of partisan politics, he had gotten a badly distorted version of the true facts. Whatever it was, I kept thinking about it.

Later he wrote a blunt memorandum of the advice he had given Eisenhower. "I think," he concluded, "all this went into one ear and out the other."

Eisenhower would have been insulted by Truman's conjectures. As head of NATO, he was well aware of the awesome task of national security ahead of him, and of what he considered the mistakes in Korea made by his predecessor.

2.

When Rhee learned that Eisenhower was coming to Korea, he announced that the president-elect would be given a rousing reception in Seoul—parades, dinners, mass rallies. Clark alerted the Joint Chiefs to how far Rhee was going in making elaborate preparations. "I also wanted Washington to realize fully just how much of a shock it would be to Rhee when he learned that, because of security considerations, the President-elect would be unable to appear at these public demonstrations. I knew that there would be repercussions and that Rhee's feelings would be hurt."

Another major problem was press coverage. Six top-flight correspondents would accompany Ike. In addition, the forty or fifty war correspondents on the scene would be joined by planeloads of others from Tokyo.

Since the trip entailed risk, Clark had to make detailed plans to safeguard Eisenhower's life while helping the press corps tell the world about his crucial visit. The Joint Chiefs were also deeply concerned. "Should his itinerary be known in advance," wrote Bradley, "the Chinese Communists could launch an air attack on airports where Ike landed or took off or attempt to assassinate him with undercover teams."

The official party was purposely kept small. It landed in Korea on December 2. Van Fleet and Clark greeted Eisenhower, whose first words were, "Where's John?"

"John will be here first thing in the morning," said Clark, and explained that his son's every action was being watched. If they'd moved him down to Seoul in advance, it would have given away the show.

The next day Eisenhower was given a series of briefings by the senior commanders in Seoul and later taken on a tour of air and ground combat headquarters. On the 4th, there was another round of inspections and briefings. First came a visit to the British Commonwealth Brigade. The high point of the day for father and son was an outdoor lunch with enlisted men of John's battalion. Twelve years earlier, the father had commanded the same outfit, the 1st Battalion, 15th Infantry, 3rd Division.

During the long day, Ike witnessed a demonstration of the ROK Capital Division whose men were attaining an admirable proficiency. He was accompanied by President Rhee, who, despite the biting cold, remained until the end.

The hours flew on December 5, the final day of the visit, and it wasn't until late afternoon that Clark telephoned Rhee to ask if he could see him immediately. Clark arrived after dark; he said that General Eisenhower would be there at exactly 5:45 P.M. for a few minutes to say good-bye. Rhee beamed. A visit from Ike would be important politically, since it would demonstrate to the people how well Rhee stood with the Americans.

At the appointed minute, Eisenhower, his son, and some members of the official party appeared. Rhee and the president-elect spoke briefly and, as the latter prepared to leave, Rhee said, "I would like you to meet my cabinet." The doors were thrown open to reveal a multitude of Koreans dressed in their best, all eager to meet the president-elect.

At Eighth Army headquarters, the military commanders said farewell to Eisenhower and watched as he drove off to the airfield. Clark wondered what Ike's conclusions would be. There were now about 350,000 Chinese and 140,000 North Koreans manning the front. Facing them were 350,000 UNC troops. With the approach of winter had come a sudden decline of action. The Chinese and North Koreans hibernated in their caves and deep bunkers, sending out patrols and small raids, while Van Fleet was content to settle back and wait for new developments in the negotiations.

But in the prison camps the war continued. On the last day of November, the Communists claimed that 542 of their POWs had been killed or wounded during the past sixty-one days.

Meanwhile, some of the UN POWs were waging their own war by refusing to confess to crimes they had not committed or by courageously standing up for their human rights. Unlike the Communist prisoners, they neither staged demonstrations nor used any weapons in attacks on guards.

Most of the men who had tried to escape since the previous summer were still in solitary confinement or crowded into a small room, serving out sentences ranging from three months to three years. With them were men sentenced for refusing to study or making trouble for those prisoners, known as "progressives," who showed sympathy with the Communist way of life.

Among the prisoners spending a most miserable Christmas holiday were two Marine officers: Colonel Frank Schwable, chief of staff of the 1st Marine Aircraft Wing, and Major Roy Bley, ordnance officer of the wing. In July, they had been inadvertently flown over enemy lines on an administrative flight in a Beechcraft and were hit by fighters. Their motor quit and they parachuted to safety.

The Chinese knew they had captured a prize because Schwable, a veteran of sixty-five night missions in World War II and winner of four Distinguished Flying Crosses, was in uniform and carried his armed services identification card, a Virginia driver's license, a flight instrument ticket, pictures of his family, and a copy of his flight plan. For months he was kept in solitary confinement in a filthy lean-to under the eaves of a Korean house. The forty-four-year-old Schwable was harried, accused of being a war criminal, fed little, denied proper latrine privileges, refused medical attention, and subjected to extremes of heat and cold. Except for a "two-week thinking period," he was intensely interrogated, although he was never beaten. Finally, at the end of December, after intimidation and dire threats, the senior UN prisoner after General Dean finally submitted a confession that suited the Communists.

"In making my most difficult decision to seek the only way out," Schwable later wrote, "my primary consideration was that I would be of greater value to my country in exposing this hideous means of slanderous propaganda than I would be by sacrificing my life through non-submission or remaining a prisoner of the Chinese Communists for life, a matter over which they left me no doubt."

His companion, Bley, was also undergoing intense interrogations but was treated more harshly and periodically beaten. Early in January 1953, he was placed in an unheated mud hut. "With the light POW uniform I had on, I was unable to keep warm at any time, was required to stand at attention almost every day, and was not permitted to lie down at night. Anyway, it was necessary for me to keep moving around in the cell or I would have frozen, as the temperature was then below zero degrees Fahrenheit. I believe this treatment lasted for six or seven days; I'm not sure. Half frozen and without sleep for many nights, I was worn both physically and mentally."

Around midnight one night he was brought to the camp commander's office and told they had concrete evidence he had participated in germ warfare. He was shown a forty-eight-hour ultimatum written in English. "It stated, in effect, that I knew about germ warfare and that for the part I had played in it I would be considered a war criminal. I would be shipped to China and given a trial by a civil court on the charge of participating in germ warfare against the Chinese Volunteers and People of the Democratic North Korean Republic. However, it further stated that if I made a full confession, I would be treated as a regular POW and repatriated after the end of the war. I was taken back to my cell, not fed at all for the forty-eight-hour period, and again required to remain awake at night."

At the end of the ultimatum period the interrogation team returned, and Bley agreed to go along with the lie. It took several hours to rewrite the deposition until it was exactly as his captors wanted it. "They had great difficulty in deciding just what they wanted me to say and how I wrote it. I was in no condition to resist or even argue with them."

It had taken even more time for Schwable to write a confession that suited the Communists. He was photographed reading the final copy. His confession cleverly combined battle data and technical-sounding terminology that gave it authenticity. On January 21, 1953, he signed it. Together with Bley's confession, it was a masterly coup for the Communists, since the General Assembly of the United Nations was scheduled to reconvene two days later; these two important confessions were then circulated among the delegates.

3.

Two weeks earlier, Major John Eisenhower had received a telegram ordering him to proceed at once to K-14 airfield for transportation to the States. Obviously he was being called back to attend his father's inauguration. It was unwelcome news. "I had just been appointed to a position I prized, and if I were away too long, the division might have to find a replacement." He sent a message of protest to his father by the quickest possible means. But he got no answer and was soon on his way to America. He was surprised to be met at LaGuardia Airport in New York by the president-elect.

Inauguration Day, January 20, was chilly politically as well as meteorologically. Truman had sharply criticized Ike's trip to Korea, calling it "a piece of demagoguery." The Eisenhowers had declined Truman's invitation to a luncheon earlier in the week, but they set out that morning for the White House to pick up the Trumans.

The two men entered Ike's limousine while their wives took a second car. As Truman and Eisenhower drove down Pennsylvania Avenue, Ike asked Truman who had ordered John back from the combat zone to be present at the inauguration. "The President replied, 'I did,' and I thanked him sincerely for his thoughtfulness." It was the only conversation Eisenhower could later recall they had shared.

In his inaugural address, he said that the people of the free world were not helpless prisoners of history and had to be willing to accept sacrifices, since the people who value their privileges above their principles soon lose both. "The peace we seek, then," he concluded, is "more than the stilling of guns, easing the sorrow of war. More than escape from death, it is a way of life. More than a haven for the weary, it is a hope for the brave."

At Union Station, the Trumans found a cheering crowd of about five thousand faithful admirers waiting for them. Truman made his way through the throng, many of whom wanted to kiss him or shake his hand. He soon had lipstick all over his face. Truman and his wife finally reached the train, and he went out to the familiar rear platform to give the crowd a salute. "This is the greatest demonstration that any man could have, because I'm just Mr. Truman, private citizen, now. This is the first time you have sent me home in a blaze of glory. I can't adequately express my appreciation for what you are doing. I'll never forget it if I live to be a hundred. And that's just what I expect to do!"

It was a fitting farewell for a man who had stood by his principles in fair weather and foul. He had made mistakes, as had all presidents;

but even when wrong, he remained Harry S. Truman of Independence, Missouri. He had been battered by the Korean War, partially because of faulty intelligence from the CIA and the armed services, partially because he had steadfastly refused to force enemy POWs to return to their native lands, and partially because all the great powers of the world were not yet ready to understand that war between major powers possessing nuclear weapons was no longer practical.

The world was now asking: "Can Ike end the war?" The parade after the inauguration ceremony was joyous—and long. So were the ceremonies and balls that followed. Eisenhower was exhausted. The tasks ahead were momumental. "But at last—sometime around one in the morning—the long day was over, and I went to bed as President of the United States."

4.

In Korea, the war was still dragging on with no major operations, only a steady series of small, deadly actions that profited neither side. In 1952, during air strikes, Air Force and Navy aviators had hit the wrong targets sixty-three times. Van Fleet's distress at this statistic led to Operation Smack, a test of recent Air Force bombing techniques and Army ground tactics. The objective selected for the operation was Spud Hill near Chorwan, an enemy strongpoint east of T-Bone Hill and less than a mile north of Eerie Outpost. First would come numerous fighter-bomber and radar-controlled light- and medium-bomber sorties on targets in the T-Bone area, followed by extensive field artillery fire in direct and general support of a raiding party of the 7th Division.

Beginning on Inauguration Day the 57th Field Artillery Battalion, in support of the 312th Regiment, 7th Division, poured thousands of rounds of 105-mm fire into the T-Bone complex. On D-Day minus one, January 24, the Air Force dumped 136,000 pounds of bombs and fourteen napalm tanks on T-Bone Hill, while operations were being observed by Fifth Air Force, I Corps and 7th Division generals, and about a dozen correspondents. The visitors had been handed a six-page, three-color description of the experiment along with a "scenario" outlining the main events. The booklet reminded some correspondents of a program for a Broadway musical.

The next day the big show began with an overture of a strike by eight F-84 Thunderjets, carrying two 1,000-pound bombs apiece. They swept over T-Bone and unloaded their bombs as infantry and tankers gathered in assembly areas. Three more flights of eight had hit the enemy target by midmorning, followed by a mass strike of twenty-four Thunderjets.

The first act was over, and the second began with diversionary tank

movements to confuse the enemy. As the assault troops made final preparations, fifteen supporting tanks rumbled across the line of departure.
According to the program, two flights of four Thunderjets were to bomb
Spud Hill, but the first missed and the second dropped only one napalm
bomb on its target. What was supposed to be an imposing air finale by
eight Marine Corsairs—a smoke screen in front of the tanks and
infantry—was a fiasco. Some released their bombs too soon, and the
others failed to hit their targets.

The air phase completed, artillery, mortars, antiaircraft artillery and
automatic-weapon fire blasted the main line of resistance. The supporting tanks also joined the bombardment once they had come in range
of Spud Hill. Now was the big moment for the 2nd Platoon of E Company, commanded by Second Lieutenant John Arbogast, Jr., which was
to assault the hill. Nine times Arbogast's platoon had rehearsed on similar
terrain. Everyone knew his task. Two flamethrower teams had been
added to ensure success.

No time was specified for the attack to begin, since the platoon had
to wait until the air strikes were completed. The word was supposed to
come from the 2nd Battalion commander. But his radio failed, and
Arbogast's men were fifteen minutes late in crossing the line of departure. Two squads began climbing the northern finger of Spud; the other
two started up the southern finger.

Lieutenant Arbogast shot a green cluster, the signal for the tanks
to lift their fire up to Hill 299. The 2nd Platoon rushed up the hill. As
they neared the first knoll, the Chinese above began showering them
with grenades.

Arbogast was hit but scrambled to his feet and called for flamethrowers. "I want to go over the top!" he shouted. "Who's going with
me?" Then he got hit a second time in the right arm. A man went to
help him, but Arbogast said he just wanted to rest. Nevertheless, he was
out of action and Sergeant Robert Coffey took command. More grenades
poured down, and Coffey was hit in the legs.

The 1st Platoon started up the hill. But they were soon hit so hard
they had to seek cover. Thunderjets tried to help, dropping bombs every
half hour; but the 2nd Platoon on the hill was trapped. The 3rd Platoon
assaulted the hill, but was driven back with numerous casualties. The
regimental commander called off the attack.

The big show ended with a whimper despite the delivery of 224,000
pounds of bombs, eight tanks of napalm, plus more than 150,000 rounds
of ammunition from supporting artillery, tanks, heavy mortars, and
machine guns and rifles. Fewer than sixty-five Chinese were lost, and
the casualties of the three American platoons were seventy-seven. Operation Smack was a colossal flop that probably would have gone un-
noticed except for one newly arrived correspondent, whose story of high-

ranking Army and Air Force officers watching an experiment while clutching a three-color program vividly described this "scenario."

No serious enemy attacks developed, and Van Fleet's tenure ended soon thereafter. On February 11, he was replaced by Lieutenant General Maxwell Taylor, who was aware of Eisenhower's desire for an end to heavy casualties and a quick but honorable peace. Van Fleet's stay had been marked by controversy and the frustration of fighting a limited war. Despite this, he had somehow managed to keep his Eighth Army well prepared for serious battle in case either the Communists or Washington decided to mount an all-out attack to win the war. He left Korea in disgust, convinced that his troops could have beaten the Reds in the spring of 1951. His counterattack had caught the Chinese by complete surprise, he wrote in *Life*. "Though we could readily have followed up our success, that was not the intention in Washington; our State Department had already let the Reds know that we were willing to settle on the 38th Parallel. Instead of getting directives for offensive action, we found our activities more and more proscribed as the time went on. Even in the matter of straightening out our lines for greater protection, we were limited by orders from the Far East Command in Japan, presumably acting on directives from Washington." The opportunity was still there today. "General Maxwell Taylor, the new Eighth Army commander, can seize it as easily as I might have, if only our policy-makers give him the chance."

There was no possible basis for a genuine political settlement in the Far East. "I have looked the Chinese Red in the eye and this is my verdict: If ever I should be called back to fight him again, I would go with a confident heart.

"If we retreat from the Communists in Asia, we are lost anyway. What are we afraid of?"

5.

There was little action either on the battlefield or at the almost completely abandoned tents in Panmunjom throughout February. Then on March 5 came a dramatic change: Joseph Stalin died. Not one of the *Pravda* editorials on his death mentioned the Korean War. Some experts felt that Stalin's successors were not of the same mettle, and, having less confidence in gauging American reactions, would be diffident about pushing the Americans too hard. Stalin's successor, Georgi Malenkov, would need time to establish himself and his associates in power. At the Peking memorial for Stalin four days later, the Russian ambassador made only brief mention of the war which had been holding the world's attention for almost three years.

Although both Peking and Pyongyang were congratulating Malenkov, an article in *Pravda* that same day quoted a statement by Kim Il-sung that implied that North Korea's only hope for continuing the war in Korea depended on massive Chinese support. "Our people are not alone in their selfless and valiant fight," insisted Kim Il-sung. "Mighty People's China has sent its volunteers to our assistance. This aid is a good example of Stalin's friendship for the peoples of the mighty socialist camp." Such ironic words were a clear reminder to both Peking and Moscow that Stalin had given little military help to either North Korea or China in the bitter winter of 1950, and it was China which had saved the day.

Further evidence of a big breakthrough in the stalled negotiations for peace in Korea came on March 15, when Malenkov told the Fourth Session of the Supreme Soviet that "at present there is no disputed or unsettled question that could not be settled peacefully on the basis of mutual agreement between the countries concerned. This applies to our relations with all countries, including our relations with the United States. States that are interested in preserving peace can be assured both now and in the future of the Soviet Union's firm policy of peace."

Six days later, Moscow radio reported that the Soviets had agreed to use their good offices to release the nine British diplomats and missionaries held captive in North Korea since the outbreak of war. Such a gesture raised hopes in diplomatic circles throughout the non-Communist world that this was the beginning of a genuine Communist peace move.

On March 26, Chou En-lai and the Chinese delegation representing Mao at Stalin's funeral returned to Peking; and two days later Peng and Kim Il-sung, in reply to General Clark's request for the exchange of sick and wounded prisoners, said they would be willing to carry out the provisions of the Geneva Convention in this respect, and went on to propose a resumption of peace negotiations.

Clark cabled the Joint Chiefs that he would proceed with arrangements for the sick and wounded through the liaison officers at Panmunjom but would not agree to resume plenary sessions until the Communists presented a constructive package or were willing to accept one of the UNC's proposals. While Washington pondered, Chou En-lai issued a conciliatory statement opening the way to a rapid solution of the problem of repatriation of POWs, proposing that "both parties to the negotiations should undertake to repatriate, immediately after the cessation of hostilities, all those prisoners of war in their custody who insist upon repatriation, and to hand over the remaining POWs to a neutral state so as to ensure a just solution to the question of their repatriation."

It appeared as if the way was now open for an armistice. But the reaction in Washington was cautious. Admittedly, the Chinese had come forward with a detailed plan for carrying out their repatriation proposal. But what did Chou mean by "neutral," and who would determine the final disposition of the nonrepatriates?

Support for the Chinese offer came from Moscow on April Fool's Day. "I am authorized to state," announced Malenkov, "that the Soviet government expresses its full solidarity with this noble act of the government of the People's Republic of China and the government of the Korean People's Democratic Republic." The Soviet government, he added, "also expresses confidence that this proposal will be correctly understood by the government of the United States."

Malenkov's words gave further proof that it was now China which was determining Communist policy on the Korean War. The armistice seemed only a step away. For two years, both sides had bickered over matters that could have been solved in two months except for mutual distrust, procrastination, fear, and misunderstanding. Would the new proposal also end in a series of mutual insults and needlessly cause more blood to be spilled?

CHAPTER 40

The Rhee Rebellion
(February–June 20)

1.

Just before the Dodd Incident, Major Ju had escaped from Compound 66, dominated by the Communists, and was sent to a security compound in Pusan. For five months in late 1952 and early 1953, he was interrogated by U.S. intelligence officers. He told all he knew about the North Korean Army, particularly the preparations for the attack on South Korea. Then the CIA sent a civilian who spoke Russian to learn about the Soviet military advisers. In gratitude, the civilian gave Ju five books for the study of English. These were confiscated by an ROK MP who saw no reason for an NK prisoner to study English. A few days later Ju was put in a jail for prisoners who resisted authority.

2.

In early March, 1953, the 28,000 Marines of the 1st Division on the western front were expecting a major Chinese attack on their thirty-three-mile line of jagged peaks and steep draws. Rising temperatures had melted tons of snow, and the thawing Imjin River was turning their supply roads into quagmires. A Chinese assault of any size would end the five-month stalemate. Although "stalemate" probably meant—to those in the States—that nothing was happening, there had been many casualties on the western front during the past few months.

559

Ever since entering the service, Martin Russ had tried by every possible method to join an infantry outfit. He wanted to fight and had at last become the automatic rifleman of the second fire team of Able Company, 1st Battalion, 1st Marine Regiment.

In the second week of March the 1st Marines were abruptly pulled out of reserve and sent to Bunker Hill outpost. "The difference between the terrain south of the Main Line of Resistant in this sector and the terrain north of it is fantastic," Corporal Russ recorded in his memoirs. "There seems to be no connection between the two. No Man's Land here is a vast piece of ground; one can see for miles. Bunker Hill looks like a city dump, but spooky as hell." The spiderlike trenches were visible from Russ's vantage point. Early in the morning, an enemy loudspeaker began blaring forth, "Welcome, Marines of the 1st Battalion." How in hell, thought Russ, had they found out the designation of their unit?

An hour later, a Chinese mortar tube began pooping out a series of rounds. In less than a minute, the Marines fired back a reply, and five white-phosphorus rounds exploded out front. End of one Chinese mortar. "It is fascinating to spot the muzzle-blast of an enemy mortar; to know that a group of Chinese are close by it, and for us to be in a position to direct a counterbarrage."

Early on the fifth day Russ peered out of the bunker as sun rays began filtering through the fog. He heard a cough somewhere in front of the bunker on the other side of the little knoll. "I had a very strange reaction to that sound. Got deathly cold all of a sudden, and seemed to catch a severe chill. The cough was abrupt but distinct. It was no different than the kind of cough one might hear in the audience of a theater, but I nearly dropped my load. I sat as rigid as an axle spring. My damned imagination conjured up the picture of a Chinaman or two lying not twenty feet from the bunker. Despite the violent cold fit, I took a ferret-look through the aperture and huddled quickly down in the hole, having seen nearby what I imagined—the head and shoulders of a man." He was at least seventy yards away. "You couldn't miss him—a dark silhouette against the light sandy shale of the surrounding terrain, which is entirely devoid of vegetation due to months of intermittent bombardment. The excitement of seeing a Chinese soldier for the first time was enormous, and that is an understatement. . . . Excited as hell, more excited than I can remember having been, I made the mistake of firing a long burst at him, without really aiming. It would have been simple to have picked him off with a single aimed shot, but I think I was afraid he would disappear."

Although the attacks on Bunker Hill continued throughout March, the Chinese attempt to regain the initiative on the battlefield failed, and the Communists made another offer to resume the negotiations. The offer roused President Rhee to write Eisenhower a letter of protest criticizing the Communists' proposal to return to Panmunjom. A peace agreement, he said, would enable the Chinese to remain in Korea. In that case, South Korea would feel justified in asking all her allies to leave the country except those willing to join in a drive northward to the Yalu. The United States could then support and cover the frontline troops with planes, long-range artillery, and naval guns on both sides of the peninsula.

Eisenhower found the Rhee letter drastic in tone and extreme in its terms. "I answered promptly, in an effort to restrain and reassure him." While expressing sympathy with Rhee's position, he said that both sides must be willing to make every reasonable effort to reach agreement on an honorable basis. Eisenhower concluded by stating that America would seek a settlement, but such an effort would be nullified if the Rhee government took actions that could not be supported by the United States and the UN.

On April 11, the liaison officers at Panmunjom finally completed arrangements for an orderly exchange of sick and wounded POWs and signed a paper stating that "repatriation shall commence at Panmunjom not later than ten days after the signing of this agreement." After twenty-one months of haggling, a significant goal had been realized, offering hope that an accord might finally be reached on the exchange of all prisoners of war.

Operation Little Switch, as it was named, was scheduled to begin on the morning of April 29. In it, 149 Americans, 64 other UN troops, and 471 ROKs were to be released. A U.S. medical team waited at Panmunjom with three ambulance companies to evacuate the first POWs to Freedom Village near Munsan fifteen miles to the south. At six A.M. the first fifty wounded and sick UN prisoners arrived.

At the same time, almost ten times as many Communist prisoners were being released a few miles to the north. As newsreels ground and cameras clicked, the prisoners shouted defiance. Many turned down new clothing offered by the Americans. Others refused to be dusted with DDT powder. Some even went on hunger strikes, claiming their food had been poisoned.

The UN prisoners, on the contrary, were subdued. As the press converged on them to ask about their experiences, many were reluctant to talk and others would only speak of sick and wounded comrades still in the enemy camps. The ROKs were transferred to base hospitals in South Korea while some Americans were flown to Japan for rest and treatment. "American soldiers returning from the Communist prison camps," reported AP, "told a story today of generally good treatment." One prisoner praised his medical treatment, another said that there was no barbed wire around the camp he was in, that each man had been issued a quilt and blanket, and that he had never seen a prisoner ill-treated. The stories were so tame that the UP Tokyo office received an urgent interoffice message from New York: "Need only limited coverage on returning POWs except for tales of atrocities and sensations."

The *Time* correspondent reported that "under press interrogation at Munsan, prisoners talked of cruelty only when pressed by leading, insistent questions. Most of the prisoners said they had not seen their comrades murdered or subjected to deliberate cruelty. And when successive prisoners talked of death in the prison camps, some newsmen piled statistic onto statistic of 'atrocity deaths' without checking how much they overlapped."

"Not all of the prisoners," wrote *Newsweek*, "came home to banners and trumpets. One U.S.-bound plane from Tokyo traveled in nearly complete secrecy." Its passenger list was confidential. "The reason: some of the passengers, after 'limited' screening in Tokyo, had been tentatively listed as 'victims of Communist propaganda'—brainwashing." They were to be given psychiatric and medical treatment at Valley Forge Army Hospital.

On the morning Little Switch began, the door of Larry Zellers's hut in the prison camp near the Yalu River was thrown open and someone shouted in Korean, "Let's move!" The seven American civilians were told to get ready to leave. The stateless Russian and Turk civilians, having no government representative to inquire about them, were in tears. "Please tell everyone you see that we are here!" they pleaded.

On arriving in Pyongyang, the Americans were quartered in two rooms in a tunnel dug into a mountain. Their hosts were headquarters personnel of the Korean People's Army. Like seven British prisoners who had preceded them, they were measured for new clothing, given hot baths every day, and served nourishing food.

Just before Zellers's group left Pyongyang, they were addressed by a general in Korean. "In accordance with the very humane policy of the government of the Korean People's Democratic Republic, you are being released to your homeland today." Once this was translated, he looked directly at the Americans. The battery of cameras turned from the general to focus on the prisoners. They stood motionless, as if they had heard nothing.

The cameras stopped whirring and the general tried again. All cameras swung to him and then turned to the uncooperative prisoners. "You Americans are going home. Don't you understand? You will be seeing your families soon. Aren't you happy that you are going home?" The cameras whirred, but no sound came from the stubborn Americans. The general turned on his heels and stormed off, his departure so sudden that even the interpreter had to suppress a nervous laugh.

The press from the Soviet bloc surrounded the Americans. "You do not seem to be happy that you are going home," one said to Zellers.

"Oh, I'm happy all right. I'm just not going to celebrate until I am out of this country."

"Aren't you grateful to the Korean People's government for your very humane treatment?"

No American said a word. Several civilians wearing Red Crosses approached them. "We are from the Red Cross of the Korean People's government. Is there anything we can do to help you?"

"We are all right now, thank you," said Dr. Kristian Jensen, the Methodist missionary, sardonically. "We have never seen you before. Where were you when we really needed you?"

One Red Cross man smiled weakly. Another asked, "What do you think about your very good treatment?" Again, there was no reply. The correspondents began to show signs of embarrassment. "Isn't there anything for which you can thank the Korean People's government?" asked one in desperation.

"Yes, as a matter of fact, there is," said Nell Dyer, who had shown such courage during the death march. Still spunky after almost three years of hell, she said, "I thank the North Korean government that I am still alive. Knowing how little they value life in this country, I feel fortunate that I still have mine."

"Have you been treated badly?"

"Yes," she said tersely.

"We found out about that major who did some bad things to you in 1950, and we punished him severely," a North Korean officer shouted. "He was given Korean money worth $67,000 to provide transportation and food for you but he took it. He is a very bad man! He stole it from you and from us!"

"We didn't know all these bad things were happening to you," another Korean officer said.

"You didn't know, and you didn't care," said Louis Dans, summing it up for all the prisoners.

There was another embarrassed silence. Then the correspondents moved slowly toward their bus. The next day, Peking Radio reported that the seven Americans being released from North Korea had thanked their captors for their humane treatment.

The seven were transported to Mukden, then across Siberia to Moscow. The following day, May 12, a U.S. Air Force C-54 flew the group to Tempelhof Airport in West Germany. From here, a Pan American Stratocruiser took them to Frankfurt where they were to remain for an hour before departure for home.

It took Father Crosbie, the Australian priest, another three weeks before he finally reached freedom. He had lost his diary, but almost every word was still burned in his mind, and he began to re-create it. "I have returned to begin life again. I have come back to houses where the light enters, but the wind does not; where there is an abundance of hot water and soap and clean linen; where there is food so good that even people who are not hungry can eat it. I have returned to a thousand and one such simple things that others take for granted, but which to me are unbelievably fine. Yet these things were nowhere as important as returning to laws that respected an individual's freedom while providing for the good of the State. All this I prize; but I have gained a still greater and more precious freedom. It is the freedom to believe in God, and openly profess my faith; and the freedom to tell those who travel with me in life's marches of the City of God that lies ahead, and of Him whose love awaits us, to give our hearts their rest."

3.

Not until April 26, a Sunday afternoon, were the plenary sessions at Panmunjom finally resumed, the first full-scale meeting of the senior delegations since the previous October. The atmosphere was tense but not combative. Nam Il presented a six-point proposal for ending the POW impasse. Harrison agreed with some issues but objected strenuously to others, and the talks bogged down again.

Finally, on May 10, the U.S. Air Force launched one of the most concentrated attacks of the war. Three days later, Harrison returned to Panmunjom with a counterproposal that was categorically rejected the next day as "absolutely unacceptable."

In the meantime, the heavy bombings of North Korea continued. This time, numerous dikes were destroyed as well as an earthen dam at Toksan, twenty air miles north of Pyongyang. Air Force planners had long realized that the destruction of irrigation dams would seriously affect the rice crop of North Korea and, "for humanitarian reasons" had until now held off. On May 15, reported the U.S. Air Force official history, "Floodwaters poured forth, leaving a trail of havoc. . . . Buildings, crops, and irrigation canals were all swept away in the devastating torrent." Elated by the results at Toksan, the Air Force struck at other dikes, but the Communists had learned their lesson and had quickly drained the reservoirs under attack. "The water was lost but flood damage was averted."

By this time the American stand at Panmunjom had thrown the talks into an impasse that was escalating into a crisis. Despite the rising criticism of U.S. militarism throughout the world, Secretary of State Dulles told Prime Minister Nehru on May 22, for transmission to Peking, that America would bomb military sanctuaries north of the Yalu if the two sides did not come to terms quickly.

By the time the talks resumed at Panmunjom three days later, the Communists realized that the Eisenhower administration was not going to capitulate on voluntary repatriation. The war was costing both North Korea and China money and lives. How long could they afford to continue?

Harrison returned to Panmunjom with instructions from the Joint Chiefs not to insist upon immediate release of the Korean repatriates when the armistice became effective. Instead, these prisoners would be turned over to the Neutral Nations Repatriation Committee—India, Poland, Czechoslovakia, Sweden and Switzerland. With this exception, the most recent UNC proposal must be accepted. If the Communists failed to agree or provide a basis for further discussion, the negotiations would be terminated.

Obviously, Rhee would be distressed at turning over the Korean non-Communist prisoners to the neutral nations' committee. On the morning of the 25th, therefore, General Clark met with Rhee to give him the bad news and to attempt to soften the blow.

At the same time, Harrison was asking that the plenary meeting be conducted as a closed session. After the Communists consented, Harrison presented the new plan. After an hour and a half break, Nam Il returned, made several objections, and suggested meeting again in four days. Harrison thought they should have a longer time to study the proposal thoroughly and suggested an extra two days. Nam agreed. Things seemed to be clearing up.

To back up the plan, General Clark sent a strong letter to Kim and Peng on the 27th urging them to accept the new terms. "If your Government's stated desire for an armistice is in good faith, you are urged to take advantage of the present opportunity."

4.

Although Communist propagandists still insisted on referring to Syngman Rhee as an American puppet, those American officials who worked with him only wished this were true. Independence was his religion. From the start of the truce talks, Rhee had publicly predicted their failure; he regarded the projected armistice as the final—and totally unsatisfactory—outcome of the war. He was bent on blocking the armistice at all costs.

On May 30, Rhee wrote Eisenhower that the acceptance of any armistice arrangements which would allow the Chinese to remain in Korea would mean "a death-sentence for Korea without protest."

The concerned Eisenhower assured Rhee that the United States would not renounce its efforts to effect the unification of Korea by all peaceful means and would promptly, at the conclusion of an acceptable armistice, negotiate a mutual defense treaty with him.

When the delegates returned to Panmunjom on June 4, Nam submitted a counterproposal indicating acceptance of the UNC's proposal with one minor change. The counterproposal "seemed highly favorable" to Eisenhower, and he informed Rhee that the proposed items were acceptable, that Rhee's republic would retain all its prewar territory, and that the United States was committed to the eventual reunification of Korea—but only by peaceful means.

Rhee remained adamant. In an official government announcement, he outlined the minimum terms for a truce which he had earlier communicated to Eisenhower: simultaneous withdrawal of UN and Communist forces throughout North and South Korea. Adding action to words, on June 7 he declared martial law in South Korea, recalled his new Army chief of staff, Whitey Paik, from Washington, rescinded the trips of fifteen other ROK generals scheduled to leave for America, canceled military leaves for all officers and men, and issued a proclamation to the people asking for support for his "life or death" decision.

To Rhee's dismay, agreement finally came at Panmunjom the following day, June 8. After a year and half of bitter wrangling, the chief delegates on both sides signed an agreement on the repatriation of prisoners of war. The last barrier to an armistice was eliminated and peace seemed imminent. Such a peace, thought Rhee, would doom his dream of a truly free Korea. He decided he must act at once and summoned to his office Lieutenant General Won Yong-duk, one of the few generals he could trust. "The UN negotiators at Panmunjom," Rhee said, "are in dead earnest to conclude the armistice terms contrary to the view of our government." In his opinion all the North Korean prisoners should be released, free to go wherever they pleased, and not forced to return to their country of origin. "Do you have any good ideas?"

It took two days for Won to secretly work out a plan to release these Communist prisoners. It was approved by the home minister, the ROK delegate at Panmunjom and the government spokesman. Only these four men and Rhee were privy to this plot.

On June 8, General Clark called on Rhee to find the president alternating between despair and defiance. Clark and Rhee went over the same ground again. "I will never accept the armistice terms as they stand," Rhee said. "The Republic of Korea will fight on, even if it means a suicide, and I will lead them."

Clark tried to reassure him that Washington would always support Korea's legitimate aims but was determined to have an armistice on the present terms. He suggested the possibility of moving the nonrepatriates to an island like Koje or Cheju. Rhee's only answer was to announce that hereafter he would feel free to take any action he deemed appropriate.

"Does this mean the withdrawal of ROK troops from my command?"

"Not today, not tomorrow," said Rhee, "but if it comes to that, I will discuss it with you in advance."

In Washington, James Hausman, now a lieutenant colonel and executive officer of the section dealing with strategic intelligence in Japan and Korea, was awakened in the early hours of Sunday morning and ordered to write a white paper on what actions Rhee might take in the event of four imminent possibilities. He had threatened to shoot Indian troops if they arrived in Korea to supervise the armistice. "No," wrote Hausman, who probably understood the president better than any other foreigner. "He'll never do that." Second, Rhee had threatened to have his troops stand firm if ordered to pull back to a predetermined demarcation line. "No," wrote Hausman, "that would risk annihilation of his entire army." Third, will Rhee sign the armistice? "He will never sign it," concluded Hausman. "He wants to go down in history as opposing it, emphasizing his oft-stated remark, 'You can't do business with Communists or cowards.'" Fourth, would Rhee dare to set free the North Korean POWs? "Yes," he wrote. "He is sure the Americans really want him to do it."

But Hausman's conclusions were not taken seriously, and his paper was shelved.

The next day, General Won Yong-duk summoned the ROK provost marshal, Brigadier General Suk Chu-am, his executive officer, and his operations officer, Colonel Song Hyo-soon. First, they had to swear that "they would not, under any circumstances, give any person information of whatsoever would be discussed at the conference." The plan, said Won, was to be executed in top secrecy and not even the defense minister and Chief of Staff Paik were to be consulted or involved. No one, himself included, he added, could be certain of the outcome of the mass release.

General Suk said he could not take the responsibility for the grave consequences that would surely follow, and asked permission to leave the room. But he was first made to swear again to keep the secret. Colonel Song, as deputy commander, was put in charge of the operation. He made no protest, even though it seemed likely to him that there would be clashes between the Eighth Army and provost marshal troops when the latter unilaterally released the North Korean prisoners.

The following morning the Chinese unexpectedly emerged from their underground caves to assault three ROK divisions. Casualties were high and the ROKs fell back slowly to prepared positions. Four days later, the Volunteers struck again, this time with full force, advancing behind one of the war's greatest barrages. They smashed into the ROK 5th and 8th divisions. "Intense and almost ceaseless artillery barrages rained down on the ROKs as they fell back under the attack," reported Poats. The next day, AP reported, "The ROK 5th and 8th Divisions today buckled under a crushing attack by great waves of Chinese troops who rolled back the Korean line of demarcation as much as two miles in places along a blazing 30-mile stretch of the East Central Front. Censorship was tightened at US 8th Army HQ."

Mao and Peng had caught their enemy by surprise and had gained valuable territory. In the crisis, the Fifth Air Force and FEAF Bomber Command mounted its most intensive air effort of the war against the Red supply lines and frontline troops. Despite rumors that Rhee was planning a raid on POW camps near Pusan, Clark dared not pull out any U.S. troops from the combat area for fear the Chinese might make further advances.

He took the calculated risk, with Pentagon approval, that Rhee was bluffing. Clark still had Rhee's written assignment of full control of all ROK forces to the UNC. He had also just received new assurances from Rhee that Rhee would withdraw ROK forces from the UNC only after advance notice and full discussion. Without outside help and the collusion of ROK guards, a mass prison break was impossible.

General Taylor shared Clark's conclusion. By the 15th, pressure against the ROKs slackened because of heavy casualties, and Taylor felt that this was the last hurrah of the enemy. Now both Taylor and Clark were primarily concerned with working out the last detail of the armistice—the fixing of the final demarcation line on which a buffer zone between the two armies would be drawn. By the 17th, every correspondent at Panmunjom was aware that agreement had been reached, despite the secrecy of the staff officers' meetings. General Clark predicted privately that the armistice would be signed on the war's third anniversary.

But there was deep concern at the U.S. embassy in Seoul. During the day, Rhee had summoned Ambassador Ellis O. Briggs to give him an answer to Eisenhower's letter, in which Eisenhower had reminded Rhee of the necessity for a settlement. First Rhee expressed appreciation of the U.S. offers of assistance and a mutual security pact, but then he expressed doubt that such offers could be accepted if they meant the Republic of Korea would be forced to consent to an armistice.

That night Rhee faced the dilemma of his life. He owed much to America and was personally friendly with Americans. But how could he alter his outspoken and implacable opposition to the armistice without losing face in his homeland? On the other hand, freeing the North Korean POWs was bound to strain relations with the United States, even though he was sure that secretly most Americans would applaud him.

But the die was cast. Under the direction of Colonel Song, secret preparation had already been made in camps holding some 36,000 Korean prisoners at the southern end of the peninsula. Camps 9 and 2 near Pusan held 7,097. At zero hour, midnight, a task force of ROK MPs commanded by Lieutenant Colonel Sun Yong-chang sneaked into Camp 9 and cut four twenty-meter-wide breaks in the barbed-wire fences. Simultaneously, six MPs were disarming two American guards at the detention house. At fifteen minutes past midnight, June 18, Colonel Sun led his men into the POW compound where the prisoners had already gathered. "I have been ordered," he said solemnly, "by the Commanding General of the Provost Marshal Command to occupy this POW camp temporarily and release all of you anti-Communist prisoners!"

All lights within the camp were extinguished, and some 4,000 prisoners quietly marched out to freedom. Not until one A.M. did the Americans learn of the breakout, and in the darkness they were helpless. At nearby Camp 2, the prisoners weren't released until 2:40 A.M. By then the Americans knew what was happening, and only relatively few got out.

In the Kwangju area to the west, there were three camps—1, 2, and 3—comprising 10,610 prisoners. Zero hour was two A.M. The anti-Communist leaders of all three camps had been notified of the release earlier in the evening by a deputy of General Won. They were to read the following instructions to their men: "The day for our liberation has come at last. President Syngman Rhee has ordered Lieutenant General Won to release us at two A.M., June 18. All you have to do is get out of the barbed-wire fences through breakouts our Korean MPs have already prepared. One thing you should not forget is that you will have to get at least twelve kilometers from the compounds before dawn under the guidance of our Korean MPs. After that the Korean national police will take care of you."

Near midnight, Lieutenant Colonel Han Keun-ho, commander of the prisoners in all three Kwanzwana camps, began cutting the inside barbed-wire fences. At the same time, Korean MPs were quietly clipping the outside fences. At two A.M., a flashlight from the hill signaled zero hour. Earlier, Colonel Han had ordered his guards to let out two thirds of the prisoners and then release harassment fire pretending to prevent the breakthrough. But this fire started prematurely, alarming and alerting the American guards. A Korean guard and five fugitive prisoners were shot to death. Even so, by the time the American camp commander arrived at the scene at four A.M., he found only 165 out of 10,160 in his camp. These few had been recaptured.

To the north at Nonsan, zero hour at Camp 6, interning 11,038 Koreans, was also two A.M. Two of the three compounds were ready, but the men in Compound 1 learned of the plan too late. Only a third of them escaped, but more than 8,000 in Compounds 2 and 3 broke free in the dark. As the shocked American commander reported, "They simply disappeared into the town of Nonsan within thirty minutes of their escape." GIs chasing them reported, "They must have wings."

The shock and bewilderment of the American commander at Nonsan turned into rage. He correctly believed that he had been deceived by the ROKs, particularly by Lieutenant Colonel Hong Sung-jong, commander of the 3rd Security Battalion. "I'll take full responsibility for whatever has been done by my officers and men, for it constitutes my negligence of duty," said Colonel Hong, without blinking an eye. "But I can assure you that there have been no instructions from the High Command." He then added, "I'm not speaking as a battalion commander in charge of guarding the prisoners, but as a citizen of the Republic of Korea. You must remember that the prisoners who regained freedom early this morning and my officers and men who failed to prevent them from the mass escape are my fellow Koreans. If you understand this point, I don't think you can blame me for my sympathy towards them."

Other prisoners at smaller camps in Masan, Yongchon, Pupyong, and Taegu also escaped. In all, more than 27,000 not only broke free but managed to find refuge in friendly homes. Less than a thousand were recaptured. Sixty-one lost their lives.

General Clark was awakened at six A.M. His first step was to order the South Korean prison-camp guards to be replaced by American troops. Half an hour later, General Won announced to the public over the radio that he had directed the ROK guards under his command to release the prisoners. He called on the people to "help protect these patriotic youths." Later in the morning, Rhee announced, "According to the Geneva Convention, and also to the principle of human rights, the anti-Communist Korean prisoners should have been released long before this. Most of the United Nations authorities with whom I have spoken about our desire to release these prisoners are with us in sympathy and principle. But due to the international complications, we have been holding these people too long." He had, therefore, ordered their release on his own responsibility. "The reason why I did this, without full consultation with the United Nations Command and other authorities concerned, is too obvious to explain."

President Eisenhower was furious. He cabled Rhee that this release constituted a clear violation of his recent assurance to Clark and Taylor that he would take no action without prior consultation. "Unless you are prepared immediately and irrevocably to accept the authority of the UN Command to conduct the present hostilities and to bring them to a close, it will be necessary to effect another arrangement." As a friend, Eisenhower hoped Rhee would immediately correct the situation. "Accordingly I am making this message public."

The UNC press release briefly announced that approximately 25,000 militantly anti-Communist North Korean POWs had broken out of their camps, but it was clear, after statements by high ROK officials, including President Rhee, that it had been secretly planned and carefully coordinated at top levels. U.S. personnel had exerted every effort to prevent the mass breakout.

It was the truth; but throughout the world, even among the Allies, it was suspected that the sensational escape must have been carried out with the connivance of Mark Clark and other American leaders. Poats of UP described the action as the "boldest move to block an armistice." In a dispatch a few hours later, Poats was even more outspoken. "General Mark Clark took a calculated risk in leaving South Korean guards on duty at the anti-Communist POW camps. He knew from Rhee's own lips and from the South Korean government's statements that Rhee did not intend to allow 'patriotic' North Korean POWs to be interned by the proposed neutral-nations commission and submitted to reindoctrination lectures by Communist agents."

Poats was correct. Clark *had* feared a mass break and, like Hausman, had warned the Pentagon. But the general had known nothing definite of the plot and was profoundly shocked by its success. Harrison immediately informed Nam Il of the releases, putting all the responsibility on the Rhee government. But Nam and his associates were certain the plot had been "deliberately connived at" between Rhee and the UNC.

Although Peking agreed with Nam, their verbal attack on the Americans was perfunctory. What they really feared was that Rhee's action might endanger the truce negotiations, and they called for an early agreement before Seoul could abort the armistice.

American soldiers were still trying to round up escaped North Korean prisoners, but only a handful were recovered, since the South Korean people absorbed them into their families. Searches were fruitless, because all Koreans looked alike to the Americans and the prisoners were now wearing civilian clothes.

Denunciation of Rhee's act continued to come from everywhere. Winston Churchill called it "treachery" and stated flatly that the UN had no intention of conquering Korea on Rhee's behalf. Washington was in a state of consternation and anger. The matter was discussed at great length at the White House. America had been put in an embarrassing position. "We were now in a place," recalled Eisenhower, "where we could really not vouch that we could keep our end of any bargain we might make with our opponents."

Eisenhower was, nevertheless, convinced that the situation could be salvaged; and he was supported by Secretary of State John Foster Dulles, who vigorously expressed his opinion that, if the Communists wanted a truce as much as he thought they did, they would overlook Rhee's impetuosity and would soon sign an agreement, provided they were given the proper assurances.

The next day, Peng and Kim wrote General Clark a letter presenting the following questions: "Is the UNC able to control the South Korean government and Army? If not, does the armistice in Korea include the Syngman Rhee clique? If it is not included, what assurance is there for the implementation of the Armistice Agreement on the part of South Korea?" If the Rhee clique was included, concluded the message, "then your side must be responsible for recovering immediately all prisoners of war who are now at liberty—that is, those who are released and retained under coercion and to be press-ganged into the South Korean Army."

Believing that Mao still wanted an armistice very much, American diplomats hoped this statement was only a ploy to make a better deal. Yet even some of them were secretly applauding Rhee for saving a lot of time and tedious paperwork by his bold maneuver.

CHAPTER 41

A Time of Peace
(July 8–September 6, 1953)

1.

The problems caused by Rhee's rebellion impelled Eisenhower to send a special envoy to Korea to control the impetuous president. Assistant Secretary of State Walter Robertson was chosen, since he was both earthy and urbane. His soothing, rich voice, it was felt, could tame even the crotchety Rhee.

As the two men sparred at the Seoul presidential mansion, the impasse at Panmunjom continued; but on July 8, there appeared to be a break. In reply to a letter from Clark, the Communists agreed to reopen talks.

At last, on July 10, the second anniversary of the peace negotiations, the plenary sessions at Panmunjom resumed. General Harrison said that the UNC stood ready to sign an armistice at once but would withdraw all support of South Korea if the ROK Army took any aggressive action following an armistice. This meeting ended without wrangling.

The following day, the persuasive Robertson finally got Rhee to promise not to obstruct the implementation of the armistice. In return, Rhee was given assurance of a mutual security pact and long-term economic aid. He also won an extra dividend. His stature in Asia rose through the fact that an envoy of the president of the United States had consulted with him for more than two weeks.

Rhee had proved to the world that South Korea was no puppet

state. He also brought down on his troops one of the heaviest attacks of
the war when, the following evening, July 13, Peng launched the second
stage of the operation designed to demonstrate to the Americans that
the Chinese Volunteers were still strong enough to continue the war
indefinitely. The Chinese smashed into four ROK divisions.

"The rugged zig-zag battle-line exploded thunderously throughout
the night," reported the UP correspondent. "In some places the ROKs
stood firm. In others they buckled or were surrounded."

Outpost after outpost crumbled and melted away. During the morning of the 14th, the Communist offensive was enlarged by a six-division
assault, the brunt of resistance being borne by six ROK divisions and
the U.S. 3rd Division, hastily thrown into the battle.

The UP correspondent wrote that reports of the renewed offensive
were sketchy because of a security blackout and the confused nature of
the fighting. "But the UN infantrymen barely had time to get set when
the Communists struck again this afternoon, staggering the Allied line
across all but one small sector of the 20-mile bulge. Many units lost their
communications and their transport in the first withdrawal when four
South Korean divisions pulled back after abandoning thousands of
trucks, tanks, and guns."

By now Clark was convinced that "one of the principal reasons, if
not the only reason, for the savage offensive, was to give the ROKs 'a
bloody nose' and show them and the world that 'puk chin'—'go north'—
was easier said than done."

Mao had indeed made his point. During June and July, the UN had
suffered more than 50,000 casualties, most of them ROKs. Although
the Communists had lost twice as many troops, their supply of manpower
remained inexhaustible.

At Panmunjom the Communists were awaiting the outcome of the
battle, with Nam unprepared to accept UNC guarantees that the ROK
forces would be made to observe the cease-fire. Harrison urged that the
UNC unilaterally recess the conferences until the Communists realized
they would be given no more pledges or promises. The massive Communist attack showed they were not sincere in reaching an armistice.
Harrison now had authority to walk out, but the Communist delegation
beat him to the punch the next day by suggesting a recess until July 19.

When Harrison and his associates returned to Panmunjom on the
19th, their opponents were ready to proceed. The battle line was again
stabilized, the great offensive having concluded with heavy casualties on
both sides.

Nam still had a few reservations about such matters as negotiating
the demarcation line. But the task of resolving these final differences
fell on the shoulders of the staff officers, and even the most pessimistic
on Harrison's staff felt that the prospects were "most encouraging."

The following day the subdelegates set to work on revising the demarcation line. Each side claimed more territory than either deserved. After three days of horse-trading, both sides initialed copies of maps of the demarcation line, and by July 25, all details had been worked out. Interpreters were instructed to proceed with the final copy of the armistice agreement, which would be signed two days later. There were, however, other sticky matters to be settled. By now the Communists had finished constructing a special building for the ceremonies. When Clark learned that they had nailed two giant blue and white "peace doves," copied from Picasso's famous painting, over the entrance to the straw-mat building, he telephoned Harrison that the UNC would not meet under any conditions unless the doves were removed. They were symbols of international Communist propaganda. The Picasso doves were painted over.

After more dickering, it was finally agreed that the documents would first be signed at Panmunjom by Generals Harrison and Nam. Several hours later the supreme commanders—Peng, Kim and Clark—would affix their signatures at their respective headquarters.

A little before ten A.M. on Monday, July 27, the UNC and Communist delegations filed into the new T-shaped Peace Pagoda. Keyes Beech watched as the UNC men occupied seats on one side of the building. Across the room sat the Communists, stiff and unsmiling. "The [North] Koreans wore gold shoulder-boards and blue trousers with red stripes down their trouser legs. By contrast the Chinese, in unadorned brown uniforms, looked severe."

At precisely ten o'clock, Generals Harrison and Nam entered from opposite sides. They sat down at the table with the green baize cloth and signed their names. "A casting director," recalled Beech, "couldn't have selected two more striking opposites than these two. Harrison was short, undistinguished looking. He might have been a Baptist preacher. His shirt collar was open, his chest undecorated. Nam Il was younger, tall, a fine figure of a man, impassive of countenance."

Each man signed his name eighteen times on the armistice papers. Not a word was exchanged between the two men. "In the distance I could hear the *boom-boom-boom* of artillery as the Marines who manned the Panmunjom sector sought to have the last word," Beech recalled. The cease-fire would not come for twelve hours, to give the Communists, whose communications were not good, time to pass the word to all their units. "Then the ritual was over. Again, like wooden actors, Harrison and Nam Il rose and strode out of the building. The war had died, officially at least, as it had ended, on a note of shabby indecision."

At one P.M., Mark Clark entered the camp theater at the Munsan apple orchard. The place was packed with officers and men. Clark sat at a long table in front of the stage. The heat from the lights which flooded the scene for the newsreel and TV cameras was unbearable. After signing his name eighteen times, he read a statement: "I cannot find it in me to exult in this hour. Rather, it is time for prayer, that we may succeed in our difficult endeavor to turn this armistice to the advantage of mankind. If we extract hope from this occasion, it must be diluted with recognition that our salvation requires unrelaxing vigilance and effort."

He was thankful that the killing was over, but he was sure the struggle against communism would not end in his lifetime. The Korean War had only been a bloody, costly skirmish, fought on the perimeter of the free world. The enemy remained undefeated.

As Peng was signing the armistice, he was thinking, "Because we have done this once, it means that we will do it again and again in the future. This is a happy day for our people." The Chinese People's Volunteer Army and the Korean People's Army had stood shoulder to shoulder against the strongest armies of the West. "Through three years of fighting together the Volunteers had forged a comradeship in blood with the North Korean people and their army—a friendship which further deepened and strengthened our internationalist feelings."

As darkness approached that evening, Captain George S. Patton—son of the famed World War II commander, and commander of Company A, 140th Tank Battalion—noticed a definite slackening of incoming artillery. Action was quieting down all along the Punchbowl. But he and everyone nearby were on their toes. They didn't trust the Chinese. "We were sure there was going to be a big attack all along the front. By 1900 hours it was as if the entire world had ceased to exist. You could hear a pin drop." The silence lasted for two hours. Then a green flare went off over the enemy lines. Before the flare reached its apex, its ghostlike light spreading over the shell-torn battlefield, shells started coming over. The entire northern rim of the Punchbowl erupted with vicious explosions. Everything was coming in—white phosphorus, high explosives, small arms. Thousands of rounds of artillery and mortar. Patton called his people and instructed them to fire only on definitely located targets. "I told them to stay in their tanks. This last order wasn't necessary. But during all this time there was practically no fire coming from our positions."

At about nine-thirty, a red star cluster went up. "As if you had turned off the gas in the kitchen stove, the firing stopped. For a split second there was again that awful silence of uncertainty broken only by the wails of the wounded ROK infantry and the magnificent monkeylike chatter of the small-unit commanders." A white flare went up from the American side of the hill, and a huge artillery barrage hit the Chinese positions. "You could not hear yourself think."

*   *   *

Keyes Beech was out front at a Marine company CP. Mortar rounds and artillery were coming in; men were crouching in their trenches. It looked more like the beginning of a war than the ending. The nearest Chinese were thirty-five yards from an outpost named after Hedy Lamarr. "The Gooneys are walking on top of Hedy," a platoon leader reported to Captain Kenneth McLennan, the company commander. He ordered a searchlight turned on Outpost Hedy, and Beech went out to look. Hedy was lighted up like a Christmas tree, but Beech couldn't see anything but the black hulk of a ruined tank.

"Only half an hour before the cease-fire," somebody said. "It's too late for them to start anything."

"A helluva way to fight a war, by the clock," someone else remarked.

Beech heard an unknown voice from the sound phone. "The Chinks are walking up 'Boulder City.' They're not shooting or doing anything. What do we do?"

"Why don't we open up on them?" asked a corpsman. "We got twenty-five minutes left."

"I repeat, there will be no firing," Captain McLennan was saying over the phone. "Get that. No firing after 21:45 unless they crawl in the apertures. If they do, use your blades."

"Use blades, my ass!" someone muttered.

At 9:45 P.M., everyone went outside to stand in the trench line. They looked at Outpost Hedy, still lighted up by the searchlight's glare. A bewildered bird, his night turned into day, flew through the beams of the searchlight. A shattering quiet fell over the front. The guns were silent. Marines streamed out of their holes in the moonlight and stood trustingly on the skyline—an act that five minutes earlier would have meant certain death.

"A cool mist that rose through the valley bathed our faces. A mosquito hummed in my ear. The clouds passed and revealed a full moon."

At exactly ten o'clock, Gunnery Sergeant Dick Williams, a veteran of the frozen Chosin, set off a flare in the form of a white cluster. The sky was lit by other flares to the right and left. But all was dark on the Chinese side.

Sergeant Ernest McFarland was ordered to pick up the brass and prepare to pull back two thousand yards.

"It just don't seem right," grumbled McFarland. "It just don't seem right it should end this way."

Not far away, Marine corporal Martin Russ could see the hills illuminated by many flares: white star, red, yellow. A beautiful full moon hung low in the sky like a Chinese lantern. He saw men pop up along the trench. Some had shed helmets and flak jackets. "The first sound we heard was a shrill group of voices, calling from the Chinese positions behind the cemetery on Chogun-ni. The Chinese were singing. A hundred yards or so down the trench someone began singing the Marine Corps hymn at the top of his lungs. Others joined in, bellowing the words. Everyone was singing in a different key, and phrases apart. Across the wide paddy, in Goonyland, matches were lit up." Later, Chinese strolled over to the base of the hill to leave candy and handkerchiefs as gifts. The Americans above stared. They had been ordered not to fraternize with the enemy.

Captain George Patton listened at his position for sounds of the wounded ROKs. All he could hear on that beautiful summer night was the clinking of the rice-wine bottles and sounds of revelry—yelling and raucous laughter.

2.

Far to the south, near the 38th parallel, North Korean peasants just behind the front lines first became aware of the cease-fire news after dawn. They started moving to Kaesong, the men in their best, spotless white, the women wearing traditional flowing, colored silks. The roads to the town were filled with gay processions of people accompanied by drummers, gong beaters and pipe players dancing and rejoicing. Once in Kaesong, just before noon, they mixed with the townspeople in a vastness of white, blue, and red silk, under a sea of banners, in the town's main square.

At noon, the voice of Kim Il-sung boomed over the speakers from the victory celebration in Pyongyang: "Dear Fellow-countrymen, brothers, sisters, officers and men of the heroic Chinese People's Volunteers, dear comrades. Although the American imperialists mobilized not only their land, air and naval forces armed with most modern techniques, together with those of their allies, they were defeated with very great losses in men and matériel."

There were tempestuous cheers when Kim added that he believed international support and help would be available for reconstruction. "Korea belongs to the Korean people," he concluded. "It shall continue to belong to the Korean people."

There was little celebration in the south. AP reported from Pusan that the cease-fire had been greeted by the people of this provisional capital with surprising apathy. "There was no jubilant cheering, nor was there any anti-truce shouting. Speaker of the ROK National Assembly, Cho Pong-am, just looked irritated when asked to comment."

The atmosphere in America was also muted. "The nation received the news quietly," reported UP from Washington. "No public demonstrations. No exultation. No celebrations in the street. This was not the victory won by General Dwight D. Eisenhower and the Allied forces in the great Crusade of Europe." Some influential Congressmen criticized the truce terms, and Senator Joseph McCarthy voiced the feelings of many when he said, "The United States has suffered a great defeat."

Eisenhower and John Foster Dulles viewed the end of the war with a measure of satisfaction that was tempered by Eisenhower's haunting doubt that any peaceful negotiation could unite Korea until the basic conflict between the free world and the communistic one would one day be resolved. But three years of heroism, frustration and bloodshed were over.

3.

Mark Clark had solid evidence that the Communists still held 3,404 UNC prisoners, including 944 Americans. He was in a quandary. "How do you get these people back," he asked himself, "without pointing a gun at the Communists?"

The preparations for this final exchange of POWs, "Operation Big Switch," were elaborate. Several days before the exchange was scheduled to begin on August 5, it was evident that the old site of the Gate to Freedom, used in Little Switch, was inadequate for handling the approximately four hundred prisoners a day during a month-long process. The new site, Freedom Village near Munsan, contained an old Army warehouse, which was transformed into the 11th Evacuation Hospital staffed by one of the mobile Army surgical hospitals, better known as a MASH.

On the morning of August 5, Marine colonel Albert Metze, processing unit commander, made a final inspection of the center. The efficiency of the camp was his responsibility, and his being there was not unfitting, since he had been a POW in World War II.

Fifteen miles to the north, across the Imjin River, U.S. Marines assigned to the Provisional Command Receipt and Control Section were waiting near the famous Peace Pagoda at Panmunjom. The exchange agreement had specified that the repatriation would begin at nine A.M. Five minutes before that deadline, three Russian-made jeeps, each carrying one Chinese and two North Korean officers, moved out of the Communist side of the peace corridor, followed by trucks and ambulances.

"Marines, man your stations!" bellowed an officer. The convoy stopped; and, as Marine team captains called out names, haggard but smiling men shuffled from trucks to the medical tents. Litter cases were loaded on helicopters and taken to the MASH unit. Prisoners who needed no immediate medical attention were transferred by ambulance to Freedom Village for processing.

After medical screening, the able-bodied men were checked by the personnel data section and their military records brought up to date. Then they were cleared for press interviews. A crowd of correspondents and photographers was waiting eagerly. Two Marine combat correspondents were also on hand. Technical Sergeant Richard E. Arnold found all of the returnees relieved, but some a little afraid. "It's their first hour of freedom, and most tell you that they can still hardly believe it's true. Some are visibly shaken, some are confused—and all are overwhelmed at the thought of being free men once again." They didn't talk much.

The prisoners coming south were orderly. Those going north were riotous. Theodore Conant, son of the Harvard president, filmed many of the latter shouting insults at the guards as they were loaded into trucks. They tore off their American clothing, leaving behind on the road tunics, trousers and boots. Many retained only a towel wrapped around their loins. They cheered and lustily sang patriotic songs.

The first ambulance arriving in the Communist zone contained ten North Korean returnees. The door opened to reveal each emaciated man holding a small flag of his fatherland. In croaking voices they began singing the "Song of Kim Il-sung," their eyes blazing with hatred at the sight of the Americans who had brought them there. As trucks and more ambulances arrived, similar scenes took place. Chinese and North Korean correspondents interviewed the returnees as soon as they descended and were escorted into reception tents to get their first cigarettes and cups of tea.

4.

Duane Thorin, the helicopter pilot, was in the last car of the train carrying UN POWs for exchange at Panmunjom. Before the train started, he could hear shouts from a car some distance ahead. Some may have been of joy, but others were clearly of anger toward those "progressives" who had worked for the Communists and had been overlords in prison camp. Now they found themselves surrounded by a resentful crowd of former subjects who had waited long for vengeance.

Even after the train was rolling, the ominous shouts could be heard over the rattle of wheels on the rails. In his own car quiet talk went well into the night until all were comfortably asleep. Thorin awakened as the sun was just rising. There was a sensation of side-to-side motion as on a ship. When he looked out he saw the train was on a high trestle above a large expanse of water. "The entire train made it across but not quite all of its passengers. Word came back along that long line of cars, through heads sticking out of the windows, that two well-known 'progressives' had departed the train while it was creeping across the high trestle." They had been thrown out, of course. By the time the report reached

Thorin in the last car, "there was uncertainty as to whether or not the two were conscious when they left the train and might have some time for reflection before they hit the water."

The train stopped at Pyongyang for about an hour. There a large crowd of citizens was kept about a hundred yards distant by a solid line of North Korean soldiers. One soldier suddenly broke from the line, flung away his red-starred cap, and ran toward the train. A shout sent eight or ten other NKs in pursuit. About twenty yards short of arms outstretched to help him aboard, the fleeing soldier looked back, stumbled and fell. The pursuers kicked and stomped him to unconsciousness or death, and dragged him back for exhibit to the crowd.

A few miles south of Pyongyang, the train was halted at a bombed-out bridge. The prisoners piled into waiting trucks and were soon in the staging area near Kaesong. Somewhat surprising to Thorin was the luxury within his tent. Here were double-deck bunks with springs and mattresses! They didn't have to sleep on the ground!

Thorin's happiness over the nearness of freedom was dampened by thoughts of the unpleasant duty before him as soon as he crossed the line. Army Intelligence must be informed at once of the misdeeds of Lieutenant Naylor-Foote and his superior, the deliberate lies and misrepresentations made by them to Thorin and his Navy seniors. Thorin felt no desire for vengence toward Naylor-Foote. Army would surely now recognize that he was psychotic and deal with him accordingly. But his superior had to be called to account. He it was who had assured Thorin that Naylor-Foote was much-experienced, dependable, and eminently qualified by purported firsthand knowledge of people, territory and circumstances of which he proved to know nothing.

On the morning of August 30, Thorin and about fifty others sat on the ground ignoring a final lecture by one of their captors. Then in three small trucks they were taken south. Along the way they met a cavalcade of large U.S. Army trucks, jampacked with Communist soldiers headed north. On order from one of their number in each truck, the Red soldiers shouted and cast off items of clothing as they passed the trucks carrying the Americans. After a few more miles, the three small trucks swung about and backed near to a simple archway proclaiming in large letters: WELCOME! GATE TO FREEDOM!

Tsai, a diminutive Chinese who'd been number-one interpreter at Thorin's camp, hopped out quickly and attempted to somewhat formally present the list of returnees to a U.S. Marine captain. The captain deftly snatched the paper from Tsai's hand, stepped past the little fellow and began calling out the names.

As each prisoner came out of the truck, a young Marine was there to grasp his hand and escort him through the gate. "Welcome home, chief," Thorin's escort said. "How you doin'?"

"Doin' all right, Corporal. And glad to be here." It was good to feel the firmness of the young Marine's shoulder, though it made Thorin suddenly aware of his own thinness.

After a preliminary check by a doctor, and identification from the "missing" files, Thorin and several other navy and Marine flyers were assembled in a reception room and being welcomed by U.S. Marine general Randolph Pate. Cookies and ice cream were brought as refreshments.

General Pate then opened a slightly tattered cigar box. It contained a dozen or more pairs of golden naval aviator wings removed from their own uniforms by pilots in a Marine squadron to be presented to any navy and Marine pilots returning from prison. Arrangements had been made for the presentation to be televised. But as the general started to lead the way to the studio an aide said that could not be done, as planned, because all of this new group had said they did not want to meet with the press.

After a brief uncertain silence, Thorin spoke for the group. "We all agreed, along with other Navy and Marines while awaiting release, that we wouldn't meet with the press here at the exchange point, because the enemy brought copies of *Stars and Stripes* to the staging area and we saw the kind of ridiculous stuff that was being put out based on interviews with some who had already returned. Now, having the general pin those wings on us in front of a camera isn't anything the same as giving reporters the chance to misquote or exaggerate something we might say. The men who pulled those wings off their own chests so the general could pin them on ours deserve to see it done. It's also the kind of thing I think the folks back home ought to see and hear, instead of some of the tripe they're otherwise getting."

Without further word the general beckoned the men to follow him into the studio. After that ceremony, each man had the chance to privately tell the general anything he thought should be reported at once. Thorin had two things to tell him. First, that a well-known collaborator had crossed to freedom that day, who had survived to this point only because a Marine captain had dissuaded two soldiers whom he had betrayed from killing him while at the staging area. It was unlikely that he would make it all the way across the Pacific. Neither Thorin nor the Marine captain was concerned about the collaborator's fate, but about the possibility that good men might later suffer for doing him in.

Next, Thorin simply told the general that his own capture and failure of his mission had been caused by two officers of Army Intelligence, and that he felt their command should be informed of the details at once. Without pause or further question, the general directed that Thorin should go home via Tokyo so he could report those details to Army's Far East Command directly.

5.

For the past two years, "reactionary" UN prisoners had thwarted attempts by North Koreans and Chinese interrogators to indoctrinate them. No prisoner had shown more obstinacy than Captain Theodore R. Harris, the pilot of a B-29. He would not confess that he had dropped germ bombs. His steadfast refusal to cooperate for more than ten months had led to frequent severe beatings, which only made Harris more stubborn. Finally he was put before a firing squad and offered a blindfold, which he refused. He heard the command, "Fire!" then the click of hammers and silence. "This," he was told, "is only a sample of what you can expect if you don't confess."

In late January 1953, he had been blindfolded, shoved into a truck, and taken to Mukden, China, unaware that his entire crew was also there. The Chinese were no more successful than the North Koreans, despite renewed efforts to degrade and humiliate him. But he once did lose his temper when a Chinese officer wiped his dirty boots on Harris's shirt. In a blind rage he swung at the Chinese, who left only to return with a large wooden boxlike device. Its four sides and top were hinged to resemble a cross. Harris was ordered to sit in the center of this cross. The sides were folded up, the top snapped into place, and bolted. With knees drawn up against his chest, and only a half-inch hole for air, he was crammed inside this for more than ten hours with no food, drink or opportunity to relieve himself. After ten months of this daily ten-hour punishment, he was blindfolded and transported to another prison in Mukden. The floor of his small cell was perpetually covered with an inch of water. Here he was subjected to endless interrogations, which also failed to bring any confession. His "noncooperation" brought another torture-box treatment for a period of fourteen hours. This time something new was added; guards constantly beat a rhythmic tattoo on the box with wooden sticks. When released, he was temporarily paralyzed from the waist down. For ten days his head rang with the echo of the sticks striking the box.

For the next six weeks, he was brought every day to a military court. By whose authority, he kept asking, were they trying him for war crimes? Never was there an answer, nor did they respond to his repeated requests for a lawyer to represent him. Instead, they only said, "Are you ready now to confess?" "I will confess to nothing," he always said. "Now or ever!"

Finally, in May 1953, the indomitable Harris was told, "You have been found guilty as a war criminal, and your punishment will be forthcoming." He was blindfolded and taken back to his first prison in Mukden. What next, he wondered?

On September 1, four days after the cease-fire, Captain Harris was brought out of his murky Mukden cell and told, "Even though you have been found guilty of war crimes, you are to be returned to the UN Command." Harris had no idea what trick they were up to. He was hustled into a waiting weapons carrier, where, for the first time in fourteen months, he met his five crewmen. They were not allowed to speak, but their eyes told Harris they had experienced hardships similar to his own. All were transferred to a train, blinds drawn, and taken to Kaesong.

Shortly before dinner time on September 3, Wilfred Burchett arrived at the museum in Kaesong where General Dean was still held as a prisoner. Burchett was accompanied by a massive retinue of Chinese and North Korean reporters and photographers. "I have bad news," he said to Dean. "This is the last time I'll have the opportunity to eat with you. Bad news for me but good for you. Tomorrow you're going home."

After an orgy of picture taking, Dean was presented with two gift packages from the UN Red Cross and a larger one from a Communist Red Cross organization. The most wonderful gift was an American safety razor. As he shaved that night, he thought that maybe he really was going home.

The next morning he shaved again and then set out with two North Koreans in a pristine Russian jeep, clad in new blue denim trousers, a pink shirt, tennis shoes, and a coat from a tailor-made suit. At the outskirts of Kaesong, the jeep came alongside a column of parked vehicles. Some of the gaunt American prisoners crowded inside the trucks recognized Dean and began to yell, "Hey, General Dean! We didn't know we were waiting for you."

The jeep stopped at the head of the column, and Dean's Korean escort was replaced by an English-speaking Chinese officer and a Chinese guard with a submachine gun. During the next few minutes of waiting, he thought of the three long years of imprisonment and the North Korean and Chinese officers he had met. "But mostly I thought about the guards, those sergeants who would hold a blanket for hours around the shoulders of a chilling man, yet laugh when they saw a dog being tortured to death; gorge themselves one week and share with you their last bowls of rice the next; steal from each other and give away their precious pens or buttons; enforce the most rigorous regulations or walk ten miles through the bitter cold for a letter because they knew you wanted it."

In those few minutes, he tried to assess what he had learned from three years of imprisonment. "Perhaps I'm naturally naive, but the most important discovery to me was that the ordinary Communists who guarded me and lived with me really believed that they were following a route toward a better life for themselves and their children."

The column of trucks with Dean's jeep at its head moved slowly toward Panmunjom, past discarded piles of clothing. They passed north-bound truckloads of repatriated Communist prisoners nearly naked, shouting and screaming as they waved tiny North Korean flags. "Now, when we get there," the Chinese officer told Dean in clipped English, "a Chinese officer will come down the line and read off the names. But don't you get out of the jeep until your name is called."

As they pulled up to the exchange point, a large American colonel stepped up to the jeep and saluted. "Welcome back, General Dean. Will you step out, sir?"

"No, no!" spluttered the Chinese officer. "Not until his name is called!"

The colonel swung toward the Chinese, suddenly looking twice his size. "Your authority is finished here," he said. "We'll take over, right now." He took a step toward the Chinese.

"Never mind, Colonel," said Dean. "Let them call off the names. A few more minutes won't matter now."

On September 6, the final day of Big Switch, the last of the Americans who had signed confessions of waging germ warfare arrived at Freedom Village. Colonel Frank Schwable, the second highest-ranking UN prisoner, was in a jeep with two other fliers at the head of a truck convoy. Thank God! he thought. After a shower and a physical examination, he was interviewed by the press. "I think slow mental torture over a long period of time is worse than quick physical torture," he told correspondents. "You sit there day in and day out, day in and day out. Your choices are very limited. You either confess or you stay there."

Others who had confessed were avoiding direct questions. They were an uneasy lot, noticed Keyes Beech, and reluctant to talk until assured by security officers that it was all right. Even then their stories came out in fits and starts. "They had done a shameful thing and they knew it," recalled Beech. "Their problem was to make us understand *why* they had done this thing. They acted like men with cancer of the soul."

The most forthright was Colonel Walker Mahurin, one of the last to confess. Beech knew he had destroyed twenty-one German planes in World War II; and there was no doubt of his personal courage. He faced Beech and the other correspondents, chin up. Beside him sat Colonel Andrew Evans, Jr., a deputy wing commander. They were both thirty-four, but Evans looked years older. He was emaciated, his chin quivered uncontrollably, and he seemed on the verge of bursting into tears. Only three days earlier he had finally signed his confession.

"We all think we are traitors to our country," admitted Mahurin calmly. "Some of us confessed and some of us didn't. Those who didn't ought to get the Medal of Honor." He shot anxious looks at Evans, who began to shake like a man with a chill. When the reporters started asking his friend questions, Mahurin adroitly fielded them.

As the press took notes, as photographers popped flashbulbs, as television lights glared and cameras ground, Mahurin continued talking into a tape recorder. "They were just about as cruel as you can think, while you can tell by looking at Andy that he had a tough experience." He explained how interrogations had lasted until September 2. By then the Communists had gotten enough confessions. Burchett and Winnington, he added, were writing them. "They were bringing the confessions and making us copy them and sign them. And of course, in their society, those confessions are going to jibe with each other because by that time they had all kind of information so they could make them interrelate. The nature of the confessions are so ridiculous that a child would not believe [them] if he had any intelligence whatsoever." He and the others used names of officers who were dead, or of officers who had retired from the service years ago. "Things like that. They bought it. They thought that was good stuff."

Beech found it difficult to pass judgment on these men. "What would I have done under the same circumstances? Would I have cracked or confessed? How can I know, when I wasn't there?" Of one thing, however, there was no doubt. Whatever the findings of the investigating boards, the men who had confessed were finished as career soldiers. "And that was the saddest thing of all."

That same morning, a man who had refused to confess after many cruel interrogations was finally told he could board a lorry in Kaesong. Lankford, the stubborn British naval officer, could hardly believe his luck. His heart leaped with excitement. But instead of going south, they drove to a building on the outskirts of Kaesong. His group was taken into a Buddhist temple. His dejection was complete. Was he going to be cheated of freedom at the last moment because he had refused to confess?

At dawn, a Chinese appeared with a sheet of paper. They were to be handed over to the United Nations in two groups. The Chinese read off the names in the first group. Lankford was not on it. He looked around and counted seven other prisoners. Two hours passed. Then another lorry appeared. Was he really leaving or was it going to be another letdown? "I looked at the lorry. Its engine was idling. I toyed with the idea that, if my name was not called out now, I would wait until the others were aboard and then leap into the driving seat to make a dash for it."

The Chinese read out five names with great deliberation. Then he stopped. Lankford and a lieutenant named Costello waited tensely to hear their names. The Chinese looked calmly at them. Finally he spoke.

"Lieutenant Lankford, British Navy ... Lieutenant Costello, British Army." The two jumped into the lorry. Soon they came to a bridge. "At one end there stood a Chinese soldier, at the other a giant American military policeman. There was a wide grin on his weather-beaten face as he waved a welcome. I doubt whether I smiled back at him. I think I just stared."

They went around two bends in the road and there it was—a brightly colored arch bearing in huge letters the three wonderful words: WELCOME TO FREEDOM.

Those men and women prisoners heading north also told stories of hardship and torture. They were never given enough rice; their women had been mistreated and raped by the ROKs. Some Americans were equally brutal. One girl, Kim Kyong-suk, told how they had forced a group of women prisoners into a large room. Here they were stripped. Then nude male North Korean prisoners were shoved in. "We heard you Communists like to dance," an American shouted. "Go on! Dance!" They pointed bayonets and revolvers at the prisoners, who began to dance, while drunken, cigar-chewing, guffawing American officers stubbed out cigars on the girls' breasts and committed indecencies.

"No one was safe from their bestialities," said a former college student. "They even violated one 14-year-old servant girl whom they had rounded up as a prisoner of war." At the Inchon camp, two mothers with babies were repeatedly dragged off at bayonet-point. The children had their mouths gagged while the mothers were taken into the American guards' quarters and raped.

On September 6, the last day of Big Switch, Pak Sang-hyon, organizer of the Dodd kidnapping, finally arrived in an ambulance. When the door opened to reveal his wizened face and shrunken body, he didn't resemble a human being. "I only wanted to die honorably," he cried as he was tenderly carried into the reception tent. "I knew the end was coming. All I wanted was to fight to the last." Someone asked what happened after the Dodd Incident. "You know, it was difficult for me to believe that in the twentieth century such barbarians as the Americans proved themselves to be could exist." He told about the forcible screenings, the tortures and massacres, and then the nonstop interrogations after his capture. He had been kept in solitary confinement, beaten and half-starved until that morning.

6.

The previous day, Captain Harris and his five crewmen had been taken to a tent near Kaesong. A document was read in Korean and then in

English. It stated that Harris and his B-29 crew had been taken north to Mukden for interrogation concerning biological warfare crimes. Harris and the crew had volunteered their guilt.

Harris shouted, "That's a damn lie!" He demanded that his name be stricken from the list of those who had confessed. When the Chinese refused, the captain exclaimed that he declined to be repatriated. He had not fought off North Korean and Chinese interrogators for more than a year to give in now.

On the morning of the 6th, Harris and his crew were told to get ready to leave. The stubborn captain sat motionless in front of his tent, smoking. An interpreter asked why he wasn't packing. "I absolutely refuse repatriation under false and disgraceful assumption." he said. His five men were loaded into a truck, which started toward Panmunjom. They waved at Harris, who was still sitting on the ground smoking. He waved back.

An hour later, the interpreter and three soldiers tried in vain to load Harris into a jeep. The interpreter returned in a truck with more soldiers. They surrounded Harris, but he would not leave until he got a copy of the document in English showing that the paragraph in which he admitted that other USAF units had waged germ warfare was stricken. Half a dozen soldiers closed in on the indignant captain, and he was carted off to Freedom Village, handcuffed but still protesting, one of the last Americans to find freedom, and one the Communists must have been extremely relieved to get rid of.

The war that was not a war but a "police action" was over, and a peace that was not a peace finally descended on Korea. Almost two million Chinese, North Korean, South Korean, and American and other UN-country soldiers died in battle. More than two million Korean civilians were killed by bombings and atrocities committed by both sides. A beautiful peninsula was left in ruins, its surviving inhabitants left to mourn their dead and attempt to start a new life from the smoking ruins which still stank of death.

The fighting had started on June 25, 1950, at the 38th parallel. It ended in almost the same place more than three years later. The North Korean prisoners had gone home jubilant at having survived the on-slaught of the most powerful nation on earth. The South Korean prisoners had returned depressed at the inconclusive end of their civil war despite the support of the mighty United States. Kim Il-sung was jubilant despite ending where he had started; Syngman Rhee was depressed at the failure of achieving his great aim—the uniting of all Korea into one republic, his republic.

The atrocities committed by South Koreans, Americans, North Koreans and Chinese had been kindled by the unique nature of the Korean

War. This deadly ideological struggle between East and West could have broken out into World War III and could also have led to civil wars in both Korea and China. History has shown that nothing is deadlier than a war that pits brother against brother. Yet the atrocities had borne strange fruit—a noble spirit of dogged resistance to oppression, such as the selfless acts of Father Crosbie and Reverend Zeller, the indomitable refusal to bow down to captors by the Communist prisoners at Koje-do, and the courage of UN prisoners such as Theodore Harris.

EPILOGUE

1.

As the last of the Big Switch prisoners were being released, far to the south in the prison islands, 22,604 North Korean and Chinese POWs, the great majority of them anti-Communists, were being loaded into a flotilla of LSTs. They had been told they would be taken north to the Demilitarized Zone, where they must make up their minds within ninety days whether to go home or find other refuge.

The first group of four hundred arrived at the DMZ on September 12 and was taken to the southern end of this narrow no-man's-land, where ten compounds had been set up for them. This was South Camp. A little to the north a much smaller camp housed the thirty-five South Korean and twenty-four UN prisoners who had chosen to remain with the Communists. Twenty-three were American, one British. "Explainers" from both sides would endeavor to persuade each prisoner to go north to communism or south to democracy.

The first group of 491 anti-Communist Chinese scheduled to go through the specially erected explainer tents refused to leave the compounds. These people were fearful that the Communists would seize them and force them back to China.

Lieutenant General Thimaya of India, now in charge of all the prisoners in the DMZ, pleaded with the dogged Chinese. "If you are as anti-Communist as you say, you should go in and make this clear to the

590

explainers." In desperation he loaded their leaders into several trucks so they could examine the explainer area for themselves. They saw no mass of Communist troops nearby to kidnap them. The only soldiers were Indians, who vowed to protect them. The leaders returned to assure their comrades that it was safe to come out.

After several hours, they were persuaded and began filing to the sixteen explanation tents, each escorted by an Indian trooper. "It was like trying to watch 16 plays, all going at once," observed Paul Garvey, a U.S. Information Service reporter. As soon as a prisoner entered the tent, the three Communist explainers would stand, bow and smile. "Almost always the prisoner would spit at them, curse them, and on this first morning, immediately leave. The explainer would, with his coat-cuff, wipe the spit off his face and pull his expression back to normal. Once in the explaining tent, the prisoners felt free to show the Communists what they thought of them."

As the process continued, the Chinese explainers, who sat across a small green table facing a prisoner on a folding chair, managed to get across their message while dodging thrown objects. In a persuasive, friendly manner they assured those Chinese prisoners who would listen that if they came back to China all previous sins would be forgiven. Soon China would rule all Asia, so they should come over to the winning side. A wonderful new way of life was being built. Please come home, for the motherland needs her sons.

Violence continued throughout that first day. One prisoner suddenly stood and picked up his folding chair. The three terrified explainers flattened themselves against the tent wall while the prisoner called them filthy turtle eggs, the most insulting expression the Chinese possess. Then he flung the chair across the green table.

The Chinese explainers were sweating and embarrassed, and the obvious delight shown by the UNC personnel at the anti-Communist testimonials made it worse. On that memorable day, all but ten men went through the door to Taiwan. Four had listened patiently to the UNC explainers before passing through the China door. The other six had greeted the Communist explainers with enthusiasm, then spat at the UN representatives. They departed through the door to the People's Republic of China to the cheers of all the Communists in the tent.

In desperation at the miserable results with the Chinese prisoners, the Communists now demanded that Koreans go through the process, but the Koreans adamantly refused to come out of their compound.

It took so long to persuade the other prisoners to enter the tents that, after three months, only 3,100 men had talked to the explainers. Only 137 asked to be repatriated. Not before the end of the year had the great majority of Korean and Chinese prisoners made their choice. There remained only a handful like Majors Ju and Park who refused to enter either North or South Korea but insisted on going to a neutral country.

By now almost every compound was controlled by anti-Communists, and the neutralists had to defend themselves from attacks that called them "yesterday's friends, today's enemies."

When a major escaped from Ju's compound, the secretary of the anti-Communist party put his group under kangaroo martial law. The first man seized was Ju. He was not only terrified but overwhelmed with disappointment and bitterness.

"How many of you neutralists are there?" asked the secretary, gesturing with a baseball bat. "If you speak out, we'll be lenient. Otherwise, you'll be dead!"

"I don't know about any list," said Ju.

"You think you can get off by saying, 'I don't know'?" Someone smashed Ju over the head with a club. Others pounded him on his shoulders, hips and rear. He couldn't even scream and before losing consciousness heard someone say, "We may as well kill him." The secretary replied, "We'll interrogate him once more tomorrow, so just break his leg."

When Ju came to in a tent, his body ached all over. One rib seemed to be broken, since he couldn't touch it without acute pain. Both legs were numb and swollen. He heard screams and soon a prisoner, limp as cotton, was carried into the tent. Within an hour ten more groaning men were brought in. They too were neutralists who believed President Rhee and his government were worse criminals than members of the South Korean Communist Party.

For weeks afterward, Ju could not walk unaided, but he was massaging his legs every night so he could be in shape to escape. On January 10, he decided to make a break at any cost. After dark, he eluded his guards and dashed toward the barbed-wire fence. The sentries were shouting at him, but he managed to scramble over to the other side. Two Indian soldiers ran to help him. "Are you okay?" one shouted.

Okay? His hands were stained with blood, his clothes were torn into shreds and he had left a trail of red footprints in the snow. "Yes, I am okay!" he said. As the soldiers led him to the Indian hospital, he burst into tears.

Ten days later, on January 20, 1954, Indian soldiers massed at each compound. As the prisoners marched out of the camp, they were given their final chance to go north. None hesitated: 21,805 men, cheering and waving handmade banners of Nationalist China and South Korea, kept heading south, carrying neatly folded bedrolls. Of them, 14,343 were Chinese. Some were playing on horns and bugles hammered from food containers. The big parade took fifteen hours and forty-three minutes to pass the checkpoint. Major Ju and other neutralists watched in relief as they departed. Grinning and overjoyed, they crossed Freedom Bridge to the other side of the Imjin River to be greeted by an American military band and a huge welcome sign in Chinese.

The North Korean prisoners were met by the South Koreans and cheered lustily by high-ranking officers in the Nationalist Army and government officials from Taiwan before loading into trucks for the trip to Inchon. They pulled down the canvas sides of their trucks so they could return the roaring cheers of the throngs lining the roads. "At Inchon," reported Paul Garvey, "the Chinese colony was alerted, and the streets rang with the clang of cymbals and Chinese music—paper dragons fluttered overhead, and pretty girls in the traditional costume greeted them on stilts. What homesick Chinese could ask more?"

If they had gone back to China, they would have led the lives of slaves and few would have survived. The solemn promises of the Chinese explainers, that the prisoners' past crimes would be forgiven and they would live as welcome brothers in a brave new world, had been mere verbiage.

Those heroic prisoners who had fought so doggedly in the prison camps and remained true Communists had been welcomed as heroes by five high-ranking Chinese officers as they passed through the door to China. But they were then taken to a concentration camp in Manchuria for reeducation, on the premise that anyone who had dealt with the West—even in prison—could not be trusted. After several years, these gallant men were released and sent home, where they were shunned by their own families as traitors. They returned to their places of work but were given minor jobs. Zhang Ze-shi, a former high school principal, was demoted to teacher. Almost every day he had to stand on a table and confess his sins. After a year of this, he was demoted further, to janitor. He complained and was sentenced to ten years in prison. When Ding Shang-wing got home, his wife was forced to divorce him. One daughter died for lack of medical treatment and the other was so scorned as "a traitor's daughter" that she disappeared. Ding was imprisoned several times for a total of twelve years and was not released until 1983. Peng, the commander of the Volunteers, who had fought loyally for Mao in Korea, was ousted from his post as defense minister in 1959 and a decade later was tortured to death during the Cultural Revolution.

If these true believers were discredited and punished, one can imagine what would have happened to the former Kuomintang soldiers who had been assured they would be treated well in the People's Republic of China.

2.

Since the end of this bloody conflict, millions of words have been written describing it as a war that should be forgotten. The lives of four million people had been sacrificed and the border between North and South Korea remained about where it had been three years earlier. It was said that little or nothing had been accomplished, and that the 54,246 American servicemen killed had died in vain.

There is no doubt that many mistakes were made, not only by the Truman administration but also by the American military leaders. The commanders in the field won many tactical victories, but the strategic failures were primarily the creation of MacArthur and the Joint Chiefs.

From the beginning of the war, the U.S. leaders had focused on threats of their intentions, such as use of the atomic bomb, that might force political decisions by the Chinese and Russians rather than on sensible tactical action needed to counter the massive numbers of enemy ground troops. "In the process," concluded Mike Lynch, Walker's and Ridgway's pilot, who later became a general, "we made the worst mistake in warfare. We began by underestimating enemy capabilities and overestimating our own. Ironically, by the time we got around to cease-fire negotiations, these same people overestimated the enemy's capabilities and underestimated ours, thus forcing us to accept compromises that were not necessary."

Much also has been written about the winners and losers of the war. Syngman Rhee and his administration were undoubtedly saved. Chiang Kai-shek was similarly fortunate; the war foiled plans of the People's Republic of China to take over Taiwan in 1950. Although not an active participant, Japan was another winner. Acting as the service, supply and recreational base for the American and other UN troops, Japan accumulated much wealth. It was also producing many weapons for the war and had taken a giant step towards its economic recovery.

The Chinese today feel the greatest winner was the USSR, which watched the war from afar, delighted to see that America was concentrating its forces in the Orient rather than in Europe. The Soviets, moreover, sacrificed no lives and had not been generous in supplying armaments to either the North Koreans or the Chinese, humiliating the latter by making them pay a premium for what they did get. But the biggest gain for the Soviets, according to one Chinese historian, "was that this war killed the possibility of any rapprochement between the U.S. and mainland China."

At the same time, the war in Korea had made credible the American claim that the United States was protecting the free world against communism. Truman's success in making it a United Nations war was also a major blow to Stalin. Furthermore, it turned NATO from a paper power to a real force and proved that America had the will to stand up against the Communists.

Although the war was never popular with the American public, it provided an enormous stimulus to the national economy, a stimulus that raised prosperity to a new high. The war had given the United States such an overabundance of economic and military power that no lasting postwar settlement was possible without United States' involvement. The war created a Pax Americana, with the United States, powerful and erratically assertive, emerging as a reluctant giant with whom the world would have to deal.

The Chinese allegation of biological warfare is complicated and perplexing. Western historians generally treat the charges as a transparent Chinese propaganda ploy. Nevertheless, revelations and research in Japan and the United States have subsequently confirmed many of the essentials of the Chinese charges. The prominent British biochemist and sinologist, Joseph Needham, stated in 1952 that he was "97.5% certain" that BW had been used. In 1979, he categorically announced that "methods of biological warfare . . . were attempted by the American side in the Korean War."

Recently declassified JCS and Department of Defense documents reveal that the U.S. military took a keen interest in the use of BW during the Korean War. Deleted sections dealing with BW have often been withheld from researchers. Despite this evidence, Mark Ryan, author of an exhaustive study of the matter, concluded that if the United States had employed bacteriological warfare, it would have required a vast covert operation and almost surely would "have been revealed at some future point, especially given the range of other governmental and military behavior exposed over the decade since the Korean War." At the same time, Ryan concluded that it was possible that "the Chinese, up to and including the highest leadership, believed that the United States was using BW even in the absence of such attacks."

After numerous interviews with American and British POWs, as well as with Chinese officers and historians, it is difficult for me to believe that BW was waged by the United States, or that, conversely, the Chinese leadership did not sincerely believe they were the victims of BW.

It was a war that ended with a whimper not a bang—the only major war in American history unhonored by a national monument for almost forty years. But if one regards the wars of the twentieth century as a chain of events, its importance becomes obvious. World War I, with the crushing defeat of Germany and its allies, left Europe in a state of chaos, leading to the rise of nazism, fascism and communism. The inequities of the peace and the violent struggle for power in Europe, together with the dramatic emergence of a modern, aggressive nation in Asia, spawned World War II. Hitler and his evil cohorts were smashed, but no sooner was this danger eliminated than another arose—the Cold War and the constant threat of nuclear disaster.

The offspring of these evolutionary events was the Korean War, a kind of crisis never before faced by the great powers. The first two world wars had been fought ruthlessly. But in Korea it was impossible to wage an all-out conflict without loosing an atomic hell. The war in Korea, therefore, should have been the cautionary tale to end all cautionary tales. It proved—or should have proved—that total war was now impossible. The great powers failed to learn this lesson, however, and paid an even more costly price in Vietnam.

Was the Korean War worth fighting? It was a war of cruelty, stupidity, error, misjudgment, racism, prejudice, and atrocities on both sides committed by people in high, middle, and low ranks. Only the numerous instances of humanity on all levels—heroism in battle, self-sacrifice, kindness and sympathy to an enemy—make writing about war bearable.

Yet recent events in both Asia and Europe call a negative view of the Korean War into question. The forgotten war may eventually turn out to have been the decisive conflict that started the collapse of communism. In any case, those who fought and died in that war did not fight and die in vain.

I have attempted to approach history as a nonpartisan, ignoring nationality and ideology; and to portray the horrors of war in harrowing detail through the sufferings of ordinary people, as well as through those of the mighty.

After writing seven histories of twentieth-century wars, I have come to a number of conclusions. It is human nature that repeats itself, not history. We often learn more about the past from the present than the reverse. I also discovered that a vile person can occasionally tell the truth and a noble person tell a lie; and that men don't make history as often as history makes men; and that the course of history is unpredictable. Finally, that the history of war can never be definitive.

Acknowledgments

This book could not have been written without the cooperation of hundreds of people in Asia, Europe and the United States, particularly those who permitted themselves to be interviewed. Libraries and archives contributed immeasurably to the book; the National Archives, Washington, D.C. (John E. Taylor, Amy Schmidt, Jill Brett, and Lorraine Herbert); the Danbury (Connecticut) Public Library; the Harry S. Truman Library (Elizabeth Safly and Benedict Zobrist); the U.S. Marine Corps Historical Center, Washington, D.C. (Brig. Gen. Edwin H. Simmons); the Library of the U.S. Embassy Annex, Seoul; the Imperial War Museum, London; the Franklin D. Roosevelt Library (William Emerson and Raymond Teichman); the MacArthur Memorial (Col. Lynn H. Hammond, Jr., Edward Boon, Jr., and John Leeds, Jr.); the U.S. Army Military History Institute, Carlisle Barracks, Pa. (Col. Rod Paschall and Dr. Richard J. Sommers); the U.S. Army Center of Military History, Washington, D.C. (Hannah Zeidlik and Albert E. Cowdrey); the Institute of World History, Beijing (Prof. Zhang Haitao and Zhu Tingguang); the Department of Military History, People's Liberation Army Academy of Military Science, Beijing (Maj. Gen. Wang Daoping); National Defense University, People's Liberation Army Beijing; and the Tianjin Academy of Social Sciences, Center of American Studies, Tianjin.

Numerous agencies, organizations and individuals made substantial contributions:

The United States: Agnes Peterson, Hoover Institution, Stanford University; Elena S. Danielson, Associate Archivist, Stanford University; Lt. Gen. Donald E. Rosenblum; Col. Robert E. Jones; Lt. Gen. E. A. Craig; An Hong-kyoun, my first Korean contact; John T. Carrig, Jr.; Paul N. McCloskey, Jr.; Jerry Williams, State Adjutant, Veterans of Foreign Wars, Dept. of California; Lt. Col. Barney Dobbs; Warren G. Avery; Jerry Francois; Ann Urband, Office of the Assistant Secretary of Defense; Martin Blumenson; Carl Marzani; Col. George Rasula; Theodore Conant; Norm Strickbine; Col. Herbert Trattner; M. Sgt. William Cleveland; Paul Martin; James Ford; Gen. Richard G. Stilwell; and Harvey Ginsberg, Frank Mount and E. A. of William Morrow and Co.; Col. Layton Tyner (General Walker's aide) and Brig. Gen. E. M. Lynch (Walker's private pilot) both contributed invaluable material on the character and day-by-day activities of Gen. Walker.

England: British Korean Veterans Association (Donald Clarke and Peter Farrar; Sam Mercer; Mr. and Mrs. Tony Eagles; Maj. Peter Westrope); and Isobel Hinshelwood, Thames Television PLC.

Korea: Col. Thomas G. Fergusson; Andrew F. Antippas, U.S. Consulate General to Korea; Lt. Col. Ahn Kyoo-tek, Korean Veterans Association; Park Jae Chang, Cho Man Sik Memorial Association; Susan J. Metcalf, American Embassy, U.S. Information Service; Lt. Gen. Burton D. Patrick, Commander, Combined Field Army (ROK-USA); Insoo Rhee; Col. Peter Pace; Col. Lee Chang-rok, Gen. Chung Il-kwon's assistant; Horace and Richard Underwood; Thomas Ryan, U.S. Command Historian. Two men made major contributions: General Paik Sun-Yup, who not only conducted several field trips but opened numerous doors; and Frank Lee, our chief interpreter, who arranged many interviews.

Taiwan: Paul W. C. Kung, Department of Information and Protocol; Michael L. J. Chang, Director of Department of Information and Protocol; Rev. Wu Cheng-chiang, Gospel Baptist Association; Rev. Jack Bateman; Liang Yung-chang, National Policy Adviser to the President; Chung Chen-hung, Government Information Office; Maj. Gen. Fann She-ij, Director, Chicom (Chinese Communist) Defectors' Assistance Center, San Shia Village; James Hung, Ministry of Foreign Affairs; and our chief interpreter, Liu Wang-ping, who also translated the texts of forty-two interviews into English.

People's Republic of China: Tang Chun, Director, United Front Work Department, Communist Party, China, Yangzhou; Wang Changfu, Director, Guengling District Education Bureau, Yangzhou; Lt. Col. Xu Yan and Col. Yao Xua, National Defense University, Beijing; Meng

Qinglong, Beijing, who collected numerous official photographs; and Professor Hua Quingzhao, Tianjin Academy of Social Sciences, whom we consulted numerous times during his stay in the United States as a Fulbright Scholar at the Harry S. Truman Library. He also was guide and interpreter during our PRC research in 1989.

Finally, I would like to thank six people who contributed most outstandingly to the book: my chief assistant and interpreter, my wife, Toshiko; my tireless research assistant, Marine 1st Sgt. Lewis Michelony, a veteran of the Korean War; my secretary, Helen Collischonn; and three who waded through three drafts of the manuscript: my friend Prof. Fred Stocking; my agent, Carl Brandt; and my editor, Carolyn Blakemore.

Notes

The main sources for each chapter are listed below. The books and papers which proved of overall value and which will not be referred to again are: *South to the Naktong, North to the Yalu* by Roy Appleman (Washington, D.C.: Center of Military History, U.S. Army, 1986); *Korea, the First War We Lost* by Bevin Alexander (New York: Hippocrene Books, 1986); *The Forgotten War* by Clay Blair (New York: Times Books, 1987); *Memoirs* by Harry S. Truman, Volume II, *Years of Trial and Hope* (Garden City, N.Y.: Doubleday, 1956); *In Two Chinas* by Kavalam Panikkar (London: George Allen, 1955); *Reminiscences* by Douglas MacArthur (New York: McGraw-Hill, 1964); *War in Peacetime* by J. Lawton Collins (Boston: Houghton Mifflin, 1969); *The Korean War* by Dean Acheson (New York: W. W. Norton, 1971); *Princeton Seminars* (Dean Acheson et al.) Feb. 13–14, 1959; *A General's Life* by Omar Bradley and Clay Blair (New York: Simon & Schuster, 1983).

Prologue: Tools of History

Interviews: Gen. Paik Sun-yup, Gen. Chung Il-kwon, Kim Chang-soon, Maj. Ju Yeong-bok. *Child of Conflict*, edited by Bruce Cumings (Seattle: University of Washington Press, 1985); *The Origins of the Korean War* by Bruce Cumings (Princeton, N.J.: Princeton University Press, 1981); *The Politics of the Vortex* by Gregory Henderson (Cambridge, Mass.: Harvard University Press, 1968); unpublished *Memoirs of Maj. Ju Yeong-bok, 1990–91*; letters from Maj. Ju to author.

1: A Time of War

Interviews: Gregory Henderson, Gen. Paik, Gen. Yu Jai-hung, Rhee Dai-yung, Will Jorden, Keyes Beech. Letters to author: Larry Zellers, Maj. Ju. "Oral History Interview with Frank Pace, Jr." by Jerry Hess, Jan. 17, 1972, Harry S. Truman Library; "Oral History Interview with John J. Muccio" by Richard McKenzie, Dec. 27, 1973 Harry S. Truman Library; *Embassy at War* by Harold Noble (Seattle: University of Washington Press, 1974); *Vortex*, Henderson; *The Korean Decision* by Glenn D. Paige (New York: Free Press, 1968).

2: "We've Got to Stop the Sons-of-Bitches No Matter What!"

Interviews with Mrs. Syngman Rhee, James Hausman, Keyes Beech, James Lee, Gen. Chung Dong-hua. *Embassy at War*, Noble; *The Korean War* by Kim Chum-kon (Seoul: Kwangynyang, 1973); *Korean Decision*, Paige. Letters to author: Larry Zellers. "Oral History, Interview with John J. Muccio" by Jerry Hess, Feb. 10 and 18, 1971, Harry S. Truman Library.

3: "There Goes the Bridge!"

Interviews with Mrs. Rhee, James Hausman, Keyes Beech, Gregory Henderson. *The First Casualty* by Phillip Knightly (New York: Harcourt Brace, Jovanovich, 1975); *The Paper: The Life and Death of the New York Herald Tribune* by Richard Kluger (New York: Knopf, 1980); *War in Korea* by Marguerite Higgins (Garden City, N.Y.: Doubleday, 1951); *Witness to War: A Biography of Marguerite Higgins* by Antoinette May (New York: Beaufort Books, 1983); *Tokyo and Points East* by Keyes Beech (Garden City, N.Y.: Doubleday, 1954); *Korean Decision*, Paige: "Oral History, Muccio," Hess; *Embassy at War*, Noble; *Ambassador in Chains* by Raymond A. Lane (New York: P. J. Kennedy and Sons, 1955) (on Bishop Patrick Byrne); *Korean Decision*, Paige; *The Korean War and Syngman Rhee* by Mrs. Syngman Rhee (Seoul: *Joong-An Daily News*, June 24, 1983 to April 19, 1984).

4: "Our Forces Will Not Last a Day"

Interviews with Col. Park Ki-byung, Gen. Paik, Gen. Chung Il-kwon, Keyes Beech. *Ambassador in Chains*, Lane; *Winter Roads* by Larry Zellers (Lexington, Ky.: University Press of Kentucky, 1991); *Embassy at War*, Noble; *War in Korea*, Higgins; *Witness*, May: *The Paper*, Kluger; *First Casualty*, Knightly; *Korean War*, Mrs. Rhee; *Korean Decision*, Paige; *Asia Is My Beat* by Earnest Hoberecht (Rutland, Vt.: Tuttle, 1961); *Korean War*, Kim; "*American Caesar*" by William Manchester (Boston: Little, Brown, 1975).

5: "Here, Have Some Earth to Eat"

Interviews: Gen. Chung Il-kwon, Gregory Henderson, Homer Bigart, Carl Mydans, Carl Bernard, Eugene Jones, Col. Layton Tyner, Col. Xu Yan, Professor Hua Qingzhao. Thames TV interview of Lt. Oak Hyung-uk for *Korea: The Unknown War*. *Soldier* by Matthew Ridgway (Garden City, N.Y.: Doubleday,

1967); *General Walton Walker in Korea*, unpublished treatise by Brig. Gen. E. M. Lynch, 1991; *Memoirs*, Vol. II, by George Kennan (Boston: Little, Brown, 1972); *A War History of the Chinese Volunteers in the Anti-U.S., Aid-Korea War* by the Department of Military Science, People's Liberation Army Academy of Military Science (Peking: Military Science Press, 1988); *War from the Yalu to Panmunjom* by Colonel Yao Xu (Beijing: People's Liberation Army Press, 1981); *Communism in Korea* by Robert Scalapino and Chong-sik Lee (Berkeley: University of California Press, 1972); *The Strange Alliance* by Robert Simmons (New York: Free Press, 1975); *Embassy at War*, Noble; *War in Korea*, Higgins; *General Dean's Story* by William L. Worden (New York: Viking, 1954); "7 Bloody Hours That Saved Korea" by Major Walter Pennino, *REAL Magazine*, October 1952; *Korean War* by Mrs. Rhee.

6: The Fall of Taejon

Interviews with Col. Layton Tyner, James Hausman, Martin Blumenson. *War As I Knew It* by George S. Patton (Boston: Houghton Mifflin, 1947); *Operation Grasshopper* by Dario Politella (Wichita: Robert Longo, 1958); *War in Korea*, Higgins; *Korean War*, Kim; *Witness*, May; *The Paper*, Kluger; *General Dean's Story*, Worden; *Embassy at War*, Noble; "Kum River Defense, 16 July 1950" by Capt. Martin Blumenson, Military History Section, U.S. Eighth Army, and "Withdrawal from Taejon, 20 July 1950" by Capt. Martin Blumenson, Military History Section, Eighth Army, U.S. Army, Center of Military History, Washington, D.C.; *Walker in Korea*, Lynch.

7: A Private Takes Command

Interviews with Lt. Charles Bussey, Thomas Lambert, Eugene Jones, Col. Tyner, Maj. Park Ki-cheol, Pvt. Charles Dawson, Pvt. Frank Myers, Pvt. James Yeager; Letters to author: Pvt. Myers. *The Face of War* by Charles Jones and Eugene Jones (New York: Prentice-Hall, 1950); *War in Korea*, Higgins: *Interviews with General E. M. Almond* by Capt. Thomas Fergusson.

Fergusson, the grandson of General Almond, conducted six personal interviews in March, 1975. Upon learning that I was in Korea in 1987, Fergusson, a colonel on active duty, gave me a copy of his extensive interviews.

8: "General, This Is Complete Chaos and Desolation!"

Interviews: An Hong-kyoun, Lee Yun-sook, Father Philip Crosbie, Brig. Gen. E. M. Lynch, Col. Tyner, Col. Robert Taplett, Dr. Robert Harvey, Lt. Chester Lenon. Letters to author: Pfc. Fred Davidson, Pfc. H. R. Luster. *Ambassador in Chains*, Lane; *Pencilling Prisoners* by Philip Crosbie (Melbourne, Australia: Hawthorn Press, 1954); *Bert Hardy: My Life* by Bert Hardy (London: Lawrence and Wishart, 1986); *War in Korea*, Higgins; *Winters*, May; *Korean War*, Kim; *Walker in Korea*, Lynch.

Lt. Lenon finally recovered and was awarded the Distinguished Service Cross for extraordinary heroism.

In 1987, Taplett's interpreter, Capt. Ko Bong-chul, guided Sgt. Michelony and me over the battle areas of the 3rd Battalion, 5th Marines, in the Pusan Perimeter.

9: The Battle of the Naktong River

Interviews: James Hausman, Gen. Paik, Col. Taplett. Letters to author: Col. Francis Fenton, Pfc. Fred Davidson. *The Pusan Perimeter*, Vol. I, *U.S. Marine Operations in Korea* by Lynn Montross and Capt. Nicholas A. Canzona (Washington, D.C.: USMC, 1954); *Murrow: His Life and Times* by Ann M. Sperber (New York: Freundlich Books, 1987); *Embassy at War*, Noble; *Interviews with Almond*, Fergusson; "Interview of Captain F. I. Fenton, Jr.—Korean Campaign" by Historical Division, U.S. Marine Corps; *Walker in Korea*, Lynch.

In 1987 General Paik guided Sgt. Michelony and me throughout the Bowling Alley area.

10: "This Is an Impossible Situation"

Interviews: Gen. Lynch, Col. Taplett, Maj. Gen. Robert Bohn, Eugene Jones. "Interview of Fenton"; Letters to author: Col. Fenton, Pfc. Davidson, David Douglas Duncan. *Face of War*, Jones and Jones; *Pusan Perimeter*, Montross and Canzona.

11: Inchon

Interviews: Cdr. Eugene Clark, Gen. Chung Il-kwon, Col. Yao Xu. *Interviews with Almond*, Fergusson; *General Dean's Story*, Worden; *MacArthur: His Rendezvous with History* by Courtney Whitney (New York: Knopf, 1956); *Walker in Korea*, Lynch.

The inhabitants who stayed behind on Lt. Clark's island were killed by the North Koreans.

12. "It's a Piece of Cake!"

Interviews: Col. Taplett, Dr. Harvey, Gen. Bohn, Cdr. Clark, Eugene Jones, Pvt. Ray Walker, Keyes Beech. Letters to author: Pfc. Davidson, Maj. Ju. *Interviews with Almond*, Fergusson; *The Inchon-Seoul Operation*, Vol. II of *U.S. Marine Operations in Korea* by Lynn Montross and Capt. Nicholas A. Canzona (Washington, D.C.: USMC, 1955); *MacArthur*, Whitney; *Tokyo and Points East*, Beech; *War in Korea*, Higgins; *Witness*, May; *Face of War*, Jones and Jones; *Memoirs*, Ju.

In 1988, Taplett's interpreter, Capt. Ko Bong-chul guided Sgt. Michelony and the author throughout the Wolmi-do–Inchon area and the attack routes to Seoul.

13: Crossing Two Rivers

Interviews: Col. Taplett, Horace Underwood, Gen. Paik, Gen. Bohn. Letters to author on Col. Lee Hak-ku from Majors Ju and Park. *Memoirs*, Ju; *Interviews with Almond*, Fergusson; *MacArthur*, Whitney; *Walker in Korea*, Lynch; *Operation Grasshopper*, Politella; *War As I Knew It*, Patton.

14: The Fall of Seoul

Interviews: Keyes Beech, Pfc. Preston Parks, Col. Taplett, Maj. Gen. Charles Mize, Brig. Gen. Edwin Simmons, Col. Tyner, Brig. Gen. Lynch, Lt. Gen. Edward Rowny, Sgt. Ted Sell. Letter to author: Pfc. Davidson. *"Marine!"* by Burke Davis (Boston: Little, Brown, 1962); *Cry Korea* by Reginald Thompson (London: Macdonald, 1958); *Embassy at War*, Noble; *MacArthur*, Whitney; *Pusan Perimeter*, Montross and Canzona; *Victory at High Tide* by Robert Debs Heinl (New York: Lippincott, 1958); *Hell or High Water* by Walt Sheldon (New York: Macmillan, 1968); *Interviews with Almond*, Fergusson; *American Caesar*, Manchester; *Walker in Korea*, Lynch.

15: Across the 38th Parallel

Interview: Gen. Chung. *Self Accounts* by Peng Teh-huai, (Beijing: The People's Press, 1981); *War History of Chinese Volunteers*; *Interviews with Almond*, Fergusson; *Strange Alliance*, Simmons; *Communism in Korea*, Scalapino and Lee; *A Factual Record of the Korean War* by Choi Chenwen and Zhao Yongtian (Beijing: Chinese Communist Party History Material Press, 1987).

16: "Many, Many Chinese Are Coming!"

Interviews: Eugene Jones, Cdr. Clark, James Hausman, Gen. Lynch. *Walker in Korea*, Lynch; *U.S. Army in the Korean War: Policy and Direction: The First Year* by James F. Schnabel (Washington, D.C.: Center of Military History, 1970); *American Caesar*, Manchester; *Face of War*, Jones and Jones; *War History of Chinese Volunteers*; *Self Accounts*, Peng; *I Fought in Korea* by Julian Tunstall (London: Lawrence and Wishart, 1953).

17: The Death March

Interviews: Father Crosbie, Father Celestine Coyos, Shaucat Salahutdin, Marsara Vorosoff, Pfc. Wilber Ray Estabrook. "Thoughts and Incidents," privately printed pamphlet by Nell Dyer; "Internment in North Korea," privately printed pamphlet by A. Kristian Jensen, D.D.; *General Dean's Story*, Worden; *Ambassador in Chains*, Lane; *Winter Roads*, Zellers; *Pencilling Prisoners*, Crosbie; *Traitor Betrayed* by E. H. Cookridge (London: Pan Books, 1962); *The Climate of Treason* by Andres Boyle (London: Coronet, Hodder and Stoughton, 1980).

British minister George Blake was a spy for the Russians but had not as yet sent any information on the Korean War to Moscow. This was being done by three other British diplomats: Guy Burgess, Kim Philby and Donald Maclean. Now that the Commonwealth Brigade was fighting with the Eighth Army, copies of all messages between the Pentagon and MacArthur were passed along to the British through the British embassy in Washington and the American department in Whitehall. The latter was headed by Maclean. Both Philby and Burgess served on the Inter-Allied Board, the former as liaison officer between the CIA and the UK secret service.

18: Mao Sets a Trap

Interviews: Gen. W. G. Dolvin, James Hausman, Maj. Gen. Yu Jae-hung. *Interrogation Report #2, Far East Command, Military Intelligence Section, Evasion and Escape Division: 1st Lt. Harry B. Trollope, 18 July 1951*, U.S. Army Center of Military History, Washington, D.C.; *Self Accounts*, Peng; *War History of Chinese Volunteers*; *Strange Alliance*, Simmons; *Communism in Korea*, Scalapino and Lee; *Policy and Direction*, Schnabel; *Combat Actions in Korea* by Russell A. Gugeler (Washington, D.C.: Office of the Chief of Military History, U.S. Army, 1970); *The River and the Gauntlet* by S.L.A. Marshall (New York: William Morrow, 1953); *Factual Record Korean War*, Chenwen and Yongtian.

19: Even Victors Are by Victory Undone

Interview: Col. Taplett. *Interrogation Report #2*, Trollope; *War History of Chinese Volunteers*; *Cry Korea*, Thompson; *Asia Is My Beat*, Hoberecht; *East of Chosin* by Roy Appleman (College Station, Tex.: Texas A&M University Press, 1987); *Combat Actions*, Gugeler; *Walker in Korea*, Lynch.

20: Trapped

Interviews: Pfc. Preston Parks, Col. Taplett, Pfc. Ed Reeves, Pvt. Edward Farley. *East of Chosin*, Appleman; *War History of Chinese Volunteers*; *Self Accounts*, Peng; *Factual Record Korean War*, Chenwen and Yongtian; "Statement on Action East of Chosin" by Capt. Edward P. Stamford, Historical Division, HQ, U.S. Marine Corps, March 16, 1951; *Breakout*, report by Capt. Hugh Robbins; 31st Infantry Command Report, Enclosure 2 by Capt. Robert Ritz, 10 March 1951; accounts by Maj. Oliver W. Robertson, 1986. Ritz and Robertson reports at U.S. Army Center of Military History, Washington.

21: Chaos on Two Fronts

Interview: Gen. Robert Kingston. *Master of the Art of Command* by Martin Blumenson and James L. Stokesbury (Boston: Houghton Mifflin, 1975); *Interviews with Almond*, Fergusson; *Breakout*, Robbins; "Action East of Chosin," Stamford; *Combat Actions*, Gugeler.

Kingston and his men were never acclaimed for their remarkable feat. The trip back was equally dangerous but only one man was killed—by a mountain tiger. Kingston became a four-star general.

22: "You Don't Have the Chance of a Snowball in Hell!"

Interviews: Col. Carl Sitter, John Buck, Royal Marine Commando Andrew Condron, Sgt. Guillarmo Tovar. *The Chosin Reservoir Campaign*, by Lynn Montross and Capt. Nicholas Canzona, (Nashville, Tenn.: Battery Press, 1987.)

23: Bloody Retreat: Running the Gauntlets

Interviews: Col. Taplett, Gen. Charles Mize, Pfc. Louis Grappo, Pfc. Ed Reeves. *River and Gauntlet*, Marshall; *Breakout*, Robbins; *East of Chosin*, Appleman; "Action East of Chosin," Stamford; *Interviews with Almond*, Fergusson; *Combat Actions*, Gugeler.

24: "We're Going Out Like Marines"

Interviews: Col. Taplett, Gen. Mize, Pfc. Parks, Pfc. Reeves, Homer Bigart, Thomas Lambert, Gen. James Polk. *Chosin Reservoir Campaign*, Montross and Canzona; *Tokyo and Points East*, Beech; *War History of Chinese Volunteers; Walker in Korea*, Lynch; *Operation Grasshopper*, Politella; *War As I Knew It*, Patton.

After Reeves's weight fell from 165 pounds to 85 and the gangrene spread, he finally decided he was ready for amputation. It left him with neither feet nor fingers; but the faith that had sent him crawling across the ice later kept up his spirits. He and his wife have five children of their own and two adopted from Korea. Both are active in door-to-door evangelism, and they are now wondering if God wants them to go into full-time work as missionaries.

25: The Breakout

Interviews: Pfc. Win Scott, Brig. Gen. James Lawrence, Col. Taplett, Gen. Mize, Gordon Greene. "USMC interview with Lt. Col. John H. Partridge" by Historical Section, June 25, 1950 U.S. Marine Corps Historical Center, Washington, D.C. Letters: Gen. Polk, David Douglas Duncan. *Chosin Reservoir Campaign*, Montross and Canzona; *War in Korea*, Higgins; *Witness*, May; *Interviews with Almond*, Fergusson; *Marine!*, Davis; *War History of Chinese Volunteers; Self Accounts*, Peng; *Strange Alliance*, Simmons; *Combat Actions*, Gugeler.

Colonel James Polk eventually became a four-star general.

26: "Your Dad Has Had an Accident"

Interviews: Dr. Hyun Bong-hak, Col. Tyner, Gen. Lynch, Gen. Sam Walker, James Hausman, Col. Taplett, Gen. Ridgway. Winton comment on Ridgway: interview by Clay Blair, Nov. 6, 1982. *Interviews with Almond*, Fergusson; *The Korean War* by Matthew Ridgway (Garden City, N.Y.: Doubleday, 1967); *Soldier*, Ridgway; *War History of Chinese Volunteers; Self Accounts*, Peng; *Walker in Korea*, Lynch; *Korea, the War Before Victory* by Callum MacDonald (London: Macmillan, 1956).

27: The Third Chinese Campaign

Interviews: Gen. Ridgway, Gen. Lynch, Keyes Beech, Francis Johnson, James Hausman, Maj. Gen. Carroll LeTellier, Gen. Paul Freeman. Letter to author: Gen. Freeman. *Soldier*, Ridgway; *Tokyo and Points East*, Beech; *War in Korea*, Higgins; *MacArthur*, Whitney; *Interviews with Almond*, Fergusson; *War History of*

Chinese Volunteers; Self Accounts, Peng; *Policy and Direction*, Schnabel; *I Fought in Korea*, Tunstall; *Combat Action*, Gugeler; *Chinese New Years Offensive, 3 Jan. 1951* by Capt. Martin Blumenson, 4th Historical Detachment, Eighth Army, U.S. Army Military History Institute, Washington, D.C.; *Army Political Propaganda Department* pamphlets issued by Chinese, Feb. 3, 1950, Captured Enemy Documents, Korean War, National Archives, Washington D.C.; *Walker in Korea*, Lynch.

28: "The Old Man Will Get Us Out"

Interviews: Gen. Dolvin, Gen. Freeman, Majors Ju and Park, *Wonju thru Chipyong*, report by Col. Paul Freeman; *Decision in Korea* by Rutherford Poats (New York: McBride, 1964); *Present at the Creation* by Dean Acheson (New York: Norton, 1969); *Soldier*, Ridgway; *The Korean War*, Ridgway; *Memoirs*, Ju. Interviews with General Freeman by Lt. Col. James Ellis, Nov. 30, 1973, and April 16, 1974; Letter to author re Freeman from Brig. Gen. Frank Meszar; "Memorandum for Record, 19 Feb. 1951" by General Ridgway, U.S. Army Military History Institute, Carlisle Barracks, Pa.

Colonel Freeman expected to be returned to Korea after his R and R in the States. Instead he became a public information officer and was sent around the country to tell people what a great job their boys were doing. He felt he was being deprived of an opportunity for further glory and perhaps promotion, but he did become a four-star general.

29: Ridgway in Action

Interviews: Chin Hai-yon, Wei Tzu-liang, Tzo Peng, John Groth, Gen. Ridgway, Cdr. Clark, Gen. Crawford Sams, Gen. Lynch. *Studio Asia* by John Groth (New York: World, 1952); *Soldier*, Ridgway; *Korean War*, Ridgway; *Decision in Korea*, Poats; *Chronicles of Chinese Volunteers Prisoners of War* by Jing Dajin (Peking: Kumbun Publishing House, 1987).

General Sams was awarded the Distinguished Service Cross for this mission and Lieutenant Youn got his third Silver Star, but the Navy Awards Board held up the recommendation for Lieutenant Clark's Navy Cross on a technicality.

30: "Jeannie, We're Going Home at Last"

Interviews: Gen. Ridgway, Gen. Chung Il-kwon, Bugler Tony Eagles, Pvt. Sam Mercer, Wang Tsun-ming, Hsi Tzu-liang, Liu Chang, Lt. Gen. William Mc-Caffrey. *MacArthur*, Whitney; *American Caesar*, Manchester; *Policy and Direction*, Schnabel; *With MacArthur in Japan* by Russell Brines and William Sebald (New York: W. W. Norton, 1965); *Soldier*, Ridgway; *Korean War*, Ridgway; *The Edge of the Sword* by Anthony Farrar-Hockley (London: Companion Book Club, 1955); *The Glorious Glosters* by Tim Carew (London: Leo Cooper, 1970); *Decision in Korea*, Poats; *The Imjin Roll* by Col. E. D. Harding (Chilton, Glos., U.K.: Mayfield House, 1976); *Mass Behavior in Battle and Captivity* by Samuel Meyers and Albert Biderman (Chicago: University of Chicago Press, 1968).

31: Prisoners of War

Interviews: Cpl. Don Hansen, Paul Vanture, Lin Chin-chiang, Jing Ping-kuei, Yu Tzeh-an, Tzo Peng, Chang Se-ching, Lin Nanping, Meng Yen, Pvt. Mercer. Interrogation Reports, Eighth Army on North Korean POWs, National Archives, Washington, D.C.; *The Korean War: History and Tactics* by Bryan Perrett; *In Spite of Dungeons* by S. J. Davies (London: Hodder and Stoughton, 1954); *War History of Chinese Volunteers; Mass Behavior*, Meyers and Biderman. *Chronicles of Chinese Volunteers POWs*, Jing; *Korean War*, Ridgway; *The Peculiar War* by E. J. Kahn (New York: Random House, 1952); *EUSAK Command Report 15 April 1952*, U.S. Army Center of Military History, Washington, D.C.; *Strange Alliance*, Simmons.

32: The Last Chinese Campaign

Interviews: Fang Hai-chin, Chen Chuang, General Yu Jai-hung, Zhang Da. *Soldier*, Ridgway; *Korean War*, Ridgway; *Interviews with Almond*, Fergusson; *Mass Behavior*, Meyers and Biderman; "Communist Party Committee Report," Captured Enemy Documents, U.S. Eighth Army, Captured Enemy Materials, Korean War, National Archives, Washington, D.C.; *War History of Chinese Volunteers; Chronicles of Chinese Volunteers POWs*, Jing.

33: The Negotiations Begin

Interview: Gen. Paik. *That's Why I Went* by Monica Felton (London: Lawrence and Wishart, 1953); *Memoirs*, Kennan; *Breakfast with Mao*, Winnington; *At the Barricades* by Wilfred Burchett (New York: Times Books, 1983); *Again Korea* by Wilfred Burchett (New York: International Publishers, 1965); *Strange Alliance*, Simmons; *Truce Tent and Fighting Front* by Walter G. Hermes (Washington, D.C.: Office Chief of Military History, U.S. Army in Korea, 1966); *Report of the Women's International Commission for the Investigation of the Atrocities Committed by United States and Syngman Rhee Troops in Korea*, Harry S. Truman Library. This report was signed by all members of the commission, including Dr. Monica Felton, on May 27, 1951; *Panmunjom* by William H. Vatcher (New York: Praeger, 1968); *How Communists Negotiate* by Admiral C. Turner Joy (New York: Macmillan, 1955); *Negotiating While Fighting* by Allen E. Goodman (New York: McGraw-Hill, 1968).

34: "An Utterly Useless War"

Interview: James Hausman. *Breakfast with Mao*, Winnington; *At the Barricades*, Burchett; *Again Korea*, Burchett; *Panmunjom*, Vatcher; *How Communists Negotiate*, Joy; *Negotiating*, Goodman; *War in Korea*, Higgins; *Witness*, May; *Truce Tent*, Hermes; *Korean War*, Ridgway; *The Hidden History of the Korean War* by I. F. Stone (New York; Monthly Review Press, 1952). "U.S. Navy Oral History of Adm. Arleigh Burke," U.S. Naval Institute, Annapolis, Md.

35: "I Agree with Ridgway's Stand"

Letter to author: Larry Zellers. *How Communists Negotiate*, Joy; *Negotiating*, Goodman; *Winter Roads*, Zellers; *Panmunjom*, Vatcher; *Truce Tent*, Hermes; "Oral History, Burke"; *General Dean's Story*, Worden; *I Defy* by Dennis Lankford (London: Wingate, 1954); *Hidden History*, Stone; *First Casualty*, Knightly; *Korean Tales* by Lt. Col. Melvin B. Voorhees (New York: Simon & Schuster, 1952).

36: Friend or Foe?

Six interviews with Chief Warrant Officer Duane Thorin. Letters to author: CWO Thorin, Capt. Harry Ettinger.

37: "An Unholy Mess"

Interview: Richard Underwood. Letter to author: Maj. Ju. *Memoirs*, Ju; *The Medics' War* by Albert E. Cowdrey (Washington, D.C.: Center of Military History, U.S. Army, 1987); *How Communists Negotiate*, Joy; *Negotiating*, Goodman; *Panmunjom*, Vatcher; *Truce Tent*, Hermes; *From the Danube to the Yalu* by Mark Clark (London: George G. Harrup, 1954); *Strange Alliance*, Simmons; *Koje Unscreened* by Wilfred Burchett and Alan Winnington (London: British-China Friendship Association, 1954); *Plain Perfidy* by Wilfred Burchett and Alan Winnington (London: British-China Friendship Association, 1954); *Hidden History*, Stone; *Korean Tales*, Voorhees; *First Casualty*, Knightly; *Korean War*, Ridgway; *The Fight for Freedom* by Song Hyo-soon (Seoul: Korean Library Association, 1980). "Major General Haydon L. Boatner Tells How He Crushed the P.O.W. Riots on Koje," *ARMY*, Aug. 1963; "Asian Teeth Are Needed for Geneva Convention" by Major General Haydon L. Boatner, *ARMY*, Jan. 1954; Boatner Papers, Hoover Institution, Stanford University, Stanford, Cal.

38: "I Was Forced to Be a Tool of These Warmongers, Made to Drop Germ Bombs"

Interview: CWO Thorin. Boatner material in Chapter 37. Letter to author: John S.D. Eisenhower. *Strictly Personal* by John S. D. Eisenhower (Garden City, N.Y.: Doubleday, 1974); *Panmunjom*, Vatcher; *Truce Tent*, Hermes; *Plain Perfidy*, Burchett and Winnington; *War in Korea*, Higgins; *Witness*, May; *Korean War*, Ridgway; *Heroes Behind Barbed Wire* by Col. Kenneth K. Hansen (Princeton, N.J.: Van Nostrand, 1957); *Chinese Attitudes Toward Nuclear Weapons* by Mark A. Ryan (Armonk, N.Y.: M. E. Sharpe, 1984); "What Happened in Korea" by Jon Halliday in *Bulletin of Concerned Asian Scientists*, Nov. 1, 1973, Vol. 5, No. 3.

Because of an article by James Michener, "The Forgotten Heroes of Korea," which appeared in *The Saturday Evening Post*, Thorin's wife was mourning his death. Michener wrote at length about Thorin's helicopter-rescue exploits. "Out here it is not known what Duane Thorin has earned in the way of medals," concluded Michener. "But one and all hope he will be recognized for what he was, the bravest of the brave. He is not among the living—he volunteered for a rescue mission more hazardous than the one described, and lost his life."

Thorin became the model for the helicopter pilot in Michener's novel and in the movie *The Bridges at Toko-Ri*.

39: "Can Ike Win the War?"

Letter to author: John Eisenhower. *Strictly Personal*, J. Eisenhower; *Mandate for Change* by Dwight D. Eisenhower (Garden City, N.Y.: Doubleday 1963); *Panmunjom*, Vatcher; *Truce Tent*, Hermes; *Heroes Behind Barbed Wire*, Hansen; *Plain Perfidy*, Burchett and Winnington; *Danube to Yalu*, Clark; *Harry S. Truman* by Margaret Truman (New York: William Morrow, 1977); *Operation SMACK* by Military History Detachment, Eighth Army, U.S. Army Center of Military History, Washington, D.C.

40: The Rhee Rebellion

Interviews: Father Crosbie, James Hausman, Col. Song Hyou-soon. *Memoirs*, Ju; *The Last Parallel* by Martin Russ (New York: Rinehart, 1957); *Truce Tent*, Hermes; *Panmunjom*, Vatcher; *Heroes Behind Barbed Wire*, Hansen; *Mandate*, Eisenhower; *Winter Roads*, Zellers; *Pencilling Prisoners*, Crosbie; "Thoughts and Incidents," Dyer; *Traitor Betrayed*, Cookridge; *Climate of Treason*, Boyle; *Fight for Freedom*, Song Hyo-soon; *Decision in Korea*, Poats; *Danube to Yalu*, Clark.

41: A Time of Peace

Interviews: Keyes Beech, CWO Thorin, Theodore Conant, Maj. Gen. George S. Patton. Letter to author: Gen. Patton. *Truce Tent*, Hermes; *Panmunjom*, Vatcher; *Heroes Behind Barbed Wire*, Hansen; *Plain Perfidy*, Burchett and Winnington; *Last Parallel*, Russ; *Tokyo and Points East*, Beech; *War History of Chinese Volunteers; Memoirs*, Ju; *General Dean's Story*, Worden; *I Defy*, Lankford; Capt. Theodore Harris documents, National Archives, Washington, D.C.; Col. Frank Schwable documents, U.S. Marine Corps Historical Center, Washington, D.C.; *Chronicles of Chinese Volunteers POWs*, Jing.

Soon after arrival at a Tokyo hospital, Thorin was debriefed. Further investigation on the rescue fiasco continued in the United States, but no action was ever taken, since it was declared a matter of national security.

Epilogue

Interviews: Ding Shang-wing, Zhang Ze-shi, Gen. Lynch. *Heroes Behind Barbed Wire*, Hansen; *Panmunjom*, Vatcher; *Captives of Korea* by William White (Westport, Conn.: Greenwood Press, 1979); *Panmunjom*, Vatcher; *Memoirs*, Ju; *Chronicles of Chinese Volunteers POWs*, Jing; *Chinese Attitudes Toward Nuclear Weapons*, Ryan.

INDEX

Acheson, Dean, 20, 32, 34, 37, 38, 41, 53,
  59, 63, 68, 73, 250, 273, 279, 307,
  390, 399, 415, 425, 480, 548, 549
  China's threats discounted by, 235
  MacArthur's firing and, 429, 430, 431,
    434, 435
  MacArthur's Formosa mission and, 134
  peace talks and, 494
  rearmament favored by, 72
  Truman contrasted with, 42
Alexander, Bevin, 17
Allen, Frank A., Jr., 244, 245, 486
Allen, Red, 539
Allum, Ron, 455
Almond, Edward, 29, 40, 61, 92, 131, 176,
  195, 207, 210, 211, 224, 226, 238,
  239, 246, 250, 251, 252, 270, 273–
  274, 275, 279, 283, 289–290, 306,
  327, 347, 357, 358, 390, 392, 395,
  402, 430, 460, 461–462, 465, 484
  Byers's replacement of, 483
  Chinese troop presence discounted by,
    304–305
  civilian evacuees and, 369
  at MacArthur's emergency conference,
    307–308
  overconfidence of, 220
  personality of, 175
  in Polk's correspondence, 364
  Puller and, 212
  retreating ROK troops and, 442–444
  Silver Star awarded to, 228
  Smith's conflict with, 215–217
  Walker's perception of, 205–206
Alsop, Joseph, 31

Andrewes, William G., 183
An Hong-Kyoon, 125
Arbogast, John, Jr., 555
Armed Forces Radio, 494
Army Department, U.S., 527
Army Political Propaganda Department,
  Chinese, 399
Arnold, Richard E., 580
Arnold, Sergeant, 293
Asahi Shimbun, 433
Associated Press, 30, 37, 65, 109, 185, 187,
  314, 322, 384, 485, 494, 495, 503,
  561, 568, 578
atomic weapons, 8, 72, 93, 321–322, 352,
  542, 548
atrocities, 127–129, 152–153, 494, 562, 588–
  589
  Soviet allegations of, 548
  Women's International Commission and,
    469–471
  see also Death March
Attlee, Clement, 54, 322
Ayres, Harold "Red," 80, 81, 85, 102

Baillie, Hugh, 415
Baker, Robert, 224–225
Bak Ho Yah, 301–302
Baldwin, Hanson, 487
Barr, David G., 216, 224, 274, 279, 283, 327
Barrett, George, 503
Barrett, Ruth, 503
Barth, George, 79, 81, 82, 85, 86, 144
Bataan, 59, 60, 63
Beall, Olin, 338, 347, 349, 360

611

Béatrix, Mother, 126, 256, 257, 261–262, 264
Beauchamp, Charles, 102, 105, 216
Beech, Keyes, 30–31, 34, 48, 50–53, 60, 65–66, 79, 93, 202, 346–347, 384, 577, 585, 586
Belton, George, 129, 206, 371–372
Berlin Blockade, 36
Bernadette, Sister, 263
Bernard, Carl, 82
Bigart, Homer, 79, 345
Bigger, Captain, 299, 309
Biggs, Bradley, 109
biological warfare, 536, 537–538, 595
Blake, George, 256
Bley, Roy, 551–553
Bloody Ridge, 484
Blue Friend party, North Korean, 452
Boatner, Haydon "Bull," 526, 527–529, 533–534
Bohlen, Charles "Chip," 54, 72, 487
Bohn, Robert, 139, 140, 144, 156, 157, 168, 172, 173–174, 192–193, 212, 223
Bolling, Alexander R., 483–484
Booth, William, 45
Bourgholtzer, Frank, 322
Bowen, Frank, 420, 423
Bowling Alley, Battle of the, 159–160, 161
Bowman, Lenoise, 281
Bowser, Alpha, 220
Boyle, Hal, 384
Bradley, Omar, 29, 32, 64, 162, 240, 271, 307, 310, 379, 392, 429, 550
    MacArthur's dismissal and, 430, 434
    peace negotiations and, 475, 486–487
Bridges, Styles, 41, 54
Briggs, Ellis O., 568
Brines, Barbara, 76
Brodie, Tom, 440, 444
Brown, Russell, 272
Browning, Jack, 258
Brush, Charlie, 209
Buck, John, 315, 317, 318–319
Bunker Hill, 542, 560
Burch, J. C., 284
Burchett, Wilfred, 481, 489, 495, 496–499, 503, 535, 584, 586
Burke, Arleigh, 477, 486, 488, 490, 492, 493–494
Business Week, 435
Bussey, Charles, 109–110, 145, 411
Byers, Clovis, 483
Byrne, Patrick, 45, 55–56, 126–127, 256, 260

Cable No. 8743, 430, 433
Cahill, John "Blackie," 292, 343
Cairo Declaration (1943), 16
Canada, 72, 534–535
Canney, John, 143–145, 172, 191, 208, 290, 293–294
Capraro, Michael, 315
Carlisle, David, 411
Carlson, Commander, 417, 419
Carne, James, 441, 442, 444, 445, 456

Carroll, Monsignor, 45
Cashion, Dana, 208, 293
Castle Hill, 441–442
casualties, 408–409, 465, 539, 574, 588
CBS, 150, 485
Central Intelligence Agency (CIA), 182, 243, 253, 418, 554, 559
Ce Soir, 481, 495, 503
Chae Byong-duk "Fat," 26, 27, 33, 39, 45–46, 50, 51, 55, 60–61, 64, 76, 77, 112
    Chung's replacement of, 66–67
    death of, 114
Chambers, Loran, 81
Chang, John, 35
Chang Chun-san, 476, 482
Chang Se-ching, 454
Chen Chia-kang, 235
Cheng-wen, 492
Chen Huang, 459
Chester, Ed, 150
Chiang Kai-shek, 16, 18, 36, 41, 72, 108, 181, 352, 357, 379, 419, 426, 517, 594
    MacArthur's meeting with, 134–135
    Sino-American communiqué of, 134
    troops offered by, 67–68
Chiang Kai-shek, Madame, 134
Chiao Kuan-hua, 489, 495
Chicago Daily News, 30, 48, 321
Chicago Tribune, 54, 74, 430–431
Chiles, Jack, 403, 405
China, Nationalist, *see* Formosa
China, People's Republic of, 7, 8, 58–59, 93, 351–352, 358, 458, 594
    establishment of, 18
    Korean conflict entered by, 236–238, 240
    Malik's proposal as seen by, 474
    North Korea and, 72–73, 557
    Soviet Union and, 73–74, 238, 557
    U.S. germ warfare alleged by, 536–537
China, People's Republic of, military units of:
    38th Army, 341
    39th Army, 243
    40th Army, 243, 251
    42nd Army, 243, 341
    First Field Army, 236
    Fourth Field Army, 236, 270
    Ninth Field Army, 290–291, 344
    XII Corps, 409, 440
    LX Corps, 451
    2nd Artillery Division, 440
    31st Infantry Division, 439
    32nd Infantry Division, 408
    79th Infantry Division, 296
    80th Infantry Division, 297
    119th Infantry Division, 404
    124th Infantry Division, 270
    125th Infantry Division, 398, 404
    126th Infantry Division, 404
    180th Infantry Division, 454
    187th Infantry Division, 441
    193rd Infantry Division, 451
    239th Infantry Regiment, 298
    539th Infantry Regiment, 463
    see also Chinese Volunteers Army

Chinese Volunteers Army (CVA), 236, 240, 243, 248–249, 272, 274–275, 408–409, 465
see also China, People's Republic of, military units of
Chin Hai-yon, 408–409
Chipyong, Battle of, 402–406
Choe Yong-gun, 19, 25
Choi Yong-jin, 211
Cho Pong-am, 578
Chou En-lai, 58–59, 73, 188, 235–236, 240, 280, 464, 489, 536–537, 557, 558
Christenson, Jerry, 87
Christian Science Monitor, 54, 435
Chun (interpreter), 512–514
Chung Dong-hya, 39
Chung Il-kwon, 64, 65, 75, 76, 77, 129, 152, 185, 186, 286, 386, 433, 462, 483
  Chae replaced by, 66–67
  and crossing of 38th parallel, 233–234
Church, John H., 47–48, 56, 60, 66, 74, 75–77, 78, 79, 112, 281, 382
Churchill, Winston, 16, 279, 571
Clark, Eugene Franklin, 182–183, 185–187, 193–195, 252–254
Clark, Mark, 565, 571, 579
  Eisenhower's Korea visit and, 550–551
  peace agreement signed by, 575–576
  peace talks and, 543, 548, 557, 572, 573
  POW unrest and, 522, 523, 525–528
  Rhee and, 566–568
  Ridgway replaced by, 521
  Sams's secret mission and, 416–419, 536
  use of atomic bomb proposed by, 548
Clarke, Arthur, 102, 105, 106, 107, 111
Clymer, 134
Coffey, Robert, 555
Collins, Corporal, 221, 222
Collins, J. Lawton "Joe," 38, 64–65, 68, 92–93, 94, 175, 180–181, 206, 254, 280, 310, 364, 372–373, 391–392
  fact-finding mission of, 345, 351, 357–358
  MacArthur's firing and, 430
  peace talks and, 486, 490
  Ridgway and, 378, 379, 383, 388, 392–393
  Truman briefed by, 362
  Walker and, 176–178
Colson, Charles, 522–527
Communications Ministry, ROK, 29
Communist Party, South Korean, 592
Communist Party of China (CPC), 72–73, 236, 240, 344
Conant, Theodore, 580
Condron, Andrew, 315–316, 317–318
Coneter, John, 372
Congress, U.S., 35, 36, 41, 67–68, 368, 429
Connally, Tom, 40–41, 43
Connors, W. Bradley, 31, 32
Cook, Corporal, 446
Cory, Tom, 46
Costello, Lieutenant, 586–587
Coulter, John, 281
Counselman, John, 193
Craig, Edward, 134, 137, 138, 141, 142, 143–144, 145, 153, 229, 315

Craig, William, 521–522
Craigie, Laurence, 477, 487
Crane, Burton, 48, 50–53
Crawford, Ernie, 507
critical combat indicators (CCI), 130, 131
Crombez, Marcel, 406
Crosbie, Philip, 126, 256, 257, 258, 259, 260, 261, 262, 263–264, 375, 563–564, 589
Curtis, Major, 333

Dans, Louis, 260
Darrigo, Joseph, 25, 26, 27
Darrow, Don, 485
Dave, Louis, 563
Davidson, Fred F., 140–141, 157, 191, 193, 223, 225–226, 291–292
Davidson, Garrison H., 170
Davidson Line, 170, 419
Davies, Sam, 440, 447, 452–453
Davis, Captain, 266–267
Davis, Ray, 342, 344
Dawson, Charles, 114
Dean, Mildred, 495, 498
Dean, William, 79, 85, 87–88, 89, 93, 96, 97, 99, 100, 105, 224, 552
  Burchett's interview of, 496–499
  capture of, 179–180
  as lost, 107, 112, 138
  as POW, 255, 375–376, 495–499, 502
  release of, 584–585
  Taejon defense and, 91–92, 101, 106–107
  tanks hunted by, 102–104, 106
Death March, 255–264
de Fazio, Sergeant, 208
Defense Department, U.S., 31, 63, 64–65, 71, 91, 124, 181, 271, 306–307, 431, 490, 568, 595
Diachenko, 191
Ding Shang-wing, 593
Dodd, Francis, 518, 520–527, 587
Dolvin, Welborn "Tom," 285, 394–395
Dorquinn, Colonel, 19
Dosher, Richard, 82
Dowcett, Colonel, 324–325
Doyle, James, 178–179, 191, 195
Drews, Harold, 300
Drumright, Ernest, 48
Dryden, Ben, 334
Drysdale, Douglas, 312–314
Dulles, John Foster, 20, 27, 34, 48, 564, 572, 579
Duncan, David Douglas, 214–215, 362–363
Dunn, John, 257, 261
Durham, John, 328
Dyer, Nell, 256, 257, 261, 563

Eagan, James, 317
Eagles, Tony, 441, 445, 446, 455–456
Eddy, Lieutenant, 342
Edson, Earle, 465–466
Eisenhower, Dwight D., 162, 242, 310, 521, 532, 556, 573, 578–579
  election of, 548–549
  inauguration of, 553
  Korea visit of, 550–551

Eisenhower, Dwight D. (*cont.*)
  Rhee Rebellion denounced by, 570–572
  Rhee's correspondence with, 560–561,
    565–566
  Truman on, 549
Eisenhower, John, 539–540, 550, 551, 553
Ellis, Dale, 135
Emsley, Al, 47
Enoch, Kenneth, 537
essential elements of information (EEI), 130
Estabrook, Wilber Ray, 258
Ettinger (navy pilot), 507–514
Eugénie, Mother, 257, 261–262, 264
Eunson, Bob, 495
Evans, Andrew, Jr., 585–586

Faith, Don Carlos, 283, 297–299, 304–305,
    308, 309–310, 327, 328, 329–333, 338
Fang Hai-chin, 458–459
Farley, Edward, 300
Farrar-Hockley, Anthony, 441, 445–446
Farrell, Frank, 442–444
Federal Bureau of Investigation (FBI), 419
Fegan, Joe, 139, 140, 144, 156, 157
Felton, Monica, 469–470
Fenton, Francis "Ike," 153–156, 168–169,
    171–174, 214–215
Fields, Captain, 277
Fitzgerald, Maurice, 517
For a Lasting Peace, For a Lasting Democracy,
    473–474
Foreign Ministry, Chinese, 235, 240
Formosa, 18, 36, 42, 54, 68, 72, 181, 241
  MacArthur's mission to, 133–134
Forney, Edward, 370
Forrestal, James, 71–72
Freeman, Paul, 306, 387–388, 395–398, 401,
    402–403, 405–406
Funderat, Madame, 260, 262

Garrett, Robert, 528
Garvey, Paul, 591, 593
Gay, Robert "Hap," 99, 111, 121, 151, 167,
    204, 210, 224, 239, 243, 244, 246,
    248, 265, 268, 272, 383, 421
Gibney, Frank, 48–50, 50–51, 53
Gloster Crossing, 441, 447
Gloster Hill, 445–446
Graham, George, 349
Grappo, Louis Joseph, 330–332, 336–338
Green, Joe, 514
Greene, Daniel, 139–140
Greene, Gordon, 365–366
Gross, Ernest, 36, 54
Groth, John, 410–411, 414
Gummo, James E., 538

Haig, Alexander, 304
Haislip, Wade, 389
Hammett, Bobby, 538
Han Chae-ung, 451
Hanes, Wallace, 460
Han Keun-ho, 569
Hanley, James, 494
Han River line, 63, 67

Hansen, Don, 450
Hardy, Bert, 158
Harriman, Averell, 134, 240, 429, 430
Harris, Theodore R., 583–584, 587–589
Harrison, Sergeant, 399
Harrison, William K., 531, 533, 535–536,
    537, 542, 543, 548, 564, 565, 571,
    573, 574, 575
Harsch, Joseph, 54
Harvey, Robert, 136–137, 174, 191–192,
    193, 196
Hausman, James, 26, 35, 39, 40, 45–46, 50,
    51, 60, 61–62, 67, 98, 112, 152, 286,
    372, 373, 386, 462, 483, 484, 571
  background of, 24–25
  Rhee assessed by, 567
  at Seoul victory ceremony, 229
Haynes, Robert, 299
Hayworth, Leonard, 214–215
Heartbreak Ridge, 484, 487
Heath, Mitchell, 329–330
Heath, Thomas, 404–405
Hell Fire Alley, 314, 359, 361
Henderson, Gregory, 78
Henderson, Joe, 414
Henrico, 134
Herbert, Robert, 101–102, 104–107
Hering, Eugene, 346–347
Herman, George, 485–486
Hermanson, Chester, 292, 293, 326, 342
Hickerson, John D., 32
Hickey, Bernard, 144, 323
Hickey, Bob, 445–446
Hickey, Doyle, 210, 239, 376, 434, 436, 487,
    519
Hickman, George, Jr., 492–493
Higgins, Marguerite, 31, 48, 50–52, 57, 62–
    63, 65–66, 75–76, 79–83, 85, 86, 87,
    93, 98–99, 132–133, 135, 136, 198,
    230, 355–356, 384, 489, 535, 542
Hill, John, 153
Hill 106, 214
Hill 117, 167
Hill 148 (Castle Hill), 441–442
Hill 207, 156–157
Hill 208, 204
Hill 235 (Gloster Hill), 445–446
Hill 299, 555
Hill 303, 151, 152, 153
Hill 311, 157
Hill 342, 137
Hill 381, 395
Hill 453, 397–398
Hill 1221, 329
Hill 1282, 322–323
Hill 1410, 291
Hill 1520, 323–324, 325, 341
Hi Penny!, 377
HLKA radio station, 40, 44, 46
Hoberecht, Earnest, 60, 281
Hodes, Henry, 488, 490
Hoge, William, 442, 461, 462
Holt, Vyvyan, 45, 256, 498
Hong Sung-jong, 570
Hoover, Herbert, 58

Hope, Bob, 251
Ho Tzu-chien, 74
Houghton, Kenneth, 208, 209
House of Commons, British, 54, 322
House of Representatives, U.S., 426
  MacArthur's speech to, 437–438
Hsi Tzu-liang, 440
Huan Sin-ya, 470
Huff, Sidney, 431
Hughes, Howard, 438
Hyun Bong-hak, 369–370

Inchon landings, 7, 169, 170, 192, 195–196,
    198, 339, 340
  JCS opposition to, 175–176, 178, 181
  Mao's prediction of, 187–188, 198–199
  preliminary bombardments for, 181–182,
    185, 196
  secret intelligence team and, 182–188
  tides and, 183–184
  Walker's alternative to, 176–178
Independence, 32, 241, 242
Information Service, U.S., 76, 591
International Committee of the Red Cross
    (ICRC), 492, 535, 538, 584
International Scientific Commission, 538
Iron Triangle, 435, 439, 472

Jaffe, Sam, 227–228, 229
James, Jack, 29, 31
Japan, 15, 16, 91, 474, 594
Jensen, Kristian, 260, 563
Jeon Moon-il, 516
Jing Ping-kuei, 451
Johnson, Francis, 385–386
Johnson, Hewlett, 538
Johnson, Louis, 29, 31, 32, 35–36, 38, 42,
    63, 279
  Forrestal replaced by, 71–72
Joint Chiefs of Staff (JCS), U.S., 30, 63, 65,
    187, 237, 280, 458, 480, 517, 518,
    525, 550, 594, 595
  abandonment of Korea considered by,
    378–379
  Clark's atomic bomb proposal rejected by,
    548
  Inchon landings opposed by, 175–176,
    178, 181
  MacArthur and, 90, 227, 233, 235, 238,
    239, 250, 253–254, 272–274, 307,
    310, 345, 378–379, 389–390, 392,
    401, 419–420
  MacArthur's dismissal and, 429, 430
  peace negotiations and, 474–475, 485,
    486, 490–491, 492, 493, 557
  Ridgway and, 438–439, 462, 471–473,
    474, 480, 485–486, 490–491
Jones, Charles, 86, 110, 169–170, 222, 244–
    245, 254
Jones, Eugene, 86, 110–111, 169–170, 196–
    197, 198, 244–245, 254
Jones, Orville, 229, 365
Jones, Robert E., 336
Jorden, Bill, 30

Joy, C. Turner, 178, 195, 477–481, 485–
    488, 490–491, 492, 501–502, 519,
    527, 528, 530–531, 532
Ju Young-bok, 19–20, 28, 199–201, 202–
    203, 207, 213, 400–401, 516, 521,
    559, 592, 593

Kahn, E. J., 433–434, 453
Katakawa, Shigeru, 269, 276–277, 278, 284
Kean, William, 89, 99, 109, 110, 121, 133,
    135, 136, 137, 142, 143, 164, 207
Ke In-ju, 182
Keiser, Lawrence, 162, 163, 164, 165, 166,
    204, 310, 320–321
Kelly, Hercules "Herb," 141, 293
Kelly Hill, 539–540
Kennan, George, 54, 63, 72, 471–472
Kim, Major, 495
Kim Chong-kop, 62
Kim Hong-il, 56, 57, 60
Kim Il-sung, 18, 19, 29, 72, 90, 108, 113,
    125, 126, 129, 130, 146, 151, 161–
    162, 177, 186, 202, 237, 238, 239,
    240, 367, 400, 565
  background of, 17
  on China's aid, 557
  Inchon landing warnings to, 187–188,
    198–199
  peace negotiations and, 475, 479, 480,
    481–482, 485, 557, 572, 575
  Peng's briefing of, 388–389
  Peng's meeting with, 248–249
  radio speech of, 38–39
  UN mission refused by, 25–26
  victory speech of, 578
Kim Kun-bae, 185–186
Kim Kyong-suk, 587
Kim Sin-gyu, 77
Kim Tae-hun, 452
Kim Yong-chin, 451
King, O.H.P., 30
Kingston, Robert, 305–306
Kinney, Jack, 475, 476
Kitz, Robert, 298, 299–300, 330
Kniss, Paul, 538
Knowland, William, 41, 43
Koh (CIA agent), 418
Korea, prewar history of, 15–17
Korea, Democratic People's Republic of
    (North), 7, 17, 54, 58, 74, 557
  China and, 72–73, 557
  Malik's peace proposal and, 474
  propaganda of, 124–125
  Soviet aid to, 484, 557
  UN condemnation of, 45
  UN observers rejected by, 17, 25–26
Korea, Democratic People's Republic of
    (North), military units of:
  II Corps, 19, 387
  V Corps, 387
  1st Infantry Division, 18, 158, 164, 210
  2nd Infantry Division, 28, 164, 165
  3rd Infantry Division, 27, 96, 164
  4th Infantry Division, 18, 27, 92, 94, 102,
    149, 157, 163

Korea, Democratic People's Republic of
    (North), military units of (*cont.*)
  5th Infantry Division, 164
  6th Infantry Division, 108, 111–112, 129,
    131, 135, 146, 162, 164
  7th Infantry Division, 164, 165, 174
  8th Infantry Division, 164, 452, 453
  9th Infantry Division, 164, 199–200
  10th Infantry Division, 151, 164, 165
  12th Infantry Division, 164
  13th Infantry Division, 158, 159, 160, 164,
    204–205, 210–211
  15th Infantry Division, 164, 185
  18th Infantry Division, 156, 199
  105th Tank Division, 199–200
  105th Armored Brigade, 27
  Border Constabulary Brigade, 25
  87th Infantry Regiment, 199–200
  see also Korean People's Army
Korea, Republic of (South) (ROK), 58, 71
  Eisenhower's visit to, 550–551
  North Korean occupation of, 124–127
  UN support of, 72
  U.S. occupation of, 17
Korea, Republic of (South) (ROK), military
    units of:
  I Corps, 238, 239, 252, 465, 472
  II Corps, 252, 265, 268, 280, 286, 382
  III Corps, 370, 460, 462
  Capital Division, 238, 370, 550
  1st Infantry Division, 26, 27, 56, 57, 77,
    151, 158, 163, 164, 205, 210, 239,
    243–244, 246, 248, 251, 265, 306,
    369, 380, 381, 453, 462
  2nd Infantry Division, 26, 39, 381, 382
  3rd Infantry Division, 234, 235, 238
  5th Infantry Division, 460, 461, 568
  6th Infantry Division, 28, 56, 238, 249,
    250, 252, 253, 265, 369, 372, 442, 450
  7th Infantry Division, 20, 26, 27–28, 39,
    56, 77, 239, 249, 401, 402, 460, 461
  8th Infantry Division, 56, 249, 401, 568
  9th Infantry Division, ROK, 460, 547
  1st Infantry Regiment, 27–28
  2nd Infantry Regiment, 252, 265
  4th Infantry Regiment, 55
  7th Infantry Regiment, 252, 265
  11th Infantry Regiment, 27, 246, 248
  12th Infantry Regiment, 27, 246
  13th Infantry Regiment, 27, 28
  17th Infantry Regiment, 381
  26th Infantry Regiment, 270
  27th Field Artillery Battalion, 442
  5th Marine Battalion, 453
  73rd Tank Battalion, 453
Korean Military Advisory Group (KMAG),
    17, 46, 47
Korean People's Army (KPA), 23, 46
  Chinese cadres in, 18
  guerrilla fighting style of, 146
  prewar strength of, 18
  Soviet advisers to, 19–20, 26
  tactics of, 162–163
  U.S. prisoners executed by, 152–153
  Walker's analysis of, 131–132, 161–164

Korean People's Army (KPA) (*cont.*)
  see also Korea, Democratic People's
    Republic of, military units of
Korean War:
  assessment of, 594–596
  border clashes prior to, 18
  China's entry into, 236–238, 240
  first all-jet air battle in, 272
  first American ground victory in, 108–110
  NATO and, 38
  as police action, 63
  rumored plague epidemic in, 416–419
  U.S. as affected by, 8, 594–595
  see also atrocities; casualties; *specific events
    and individuals*
Korean Workers' Party, 19
Krock, Arthur, 41
Kum River line, 88, 90, 94–97

Lamb (assistant gunner), 217–219
Lambert, Tom, 65, 76, 109, 110, 345
Lankford, Dennis, 499–501, 586–587
Lantron, Newton, 263
Lauber, Lieutenant, 269, 278, 285
Lawrence, James, 357
Leach, Paul, 321
League of Liberation, 400
Lee, General, 496, 498, 502
Lee, James, 34
Lee Hak-ku, 210–211, 400–401, 516, 521,
    523, 534
Lee Hyung-koon, 39
Lee Pae-vhun, 451–452
Lee Sang-gook, 114
Lee Song-cho, 492–493
Lee Soo-young, 475, 482
Lee Yun-sook, 125–126
Leerkamp, Henry, 259
Lenon, Chester, 135–136, 138, 145–146,
    161
LeTellier, Carroll, 387
Libby, Ruthven, 492
Lie, Trygve, 36, 54
Life, 79, 214, 362, 556
Limb, Ben, 43–44
Lim Rae, 19
Lin Chin-chiang, 451
Lincoln Line, 453
Lindbergh, Charles, 438
Lin Piao, 236, 275
Litzenberg, Homer, 270, 322, 326, 342–343,
    347
Liu Chang, 440
Lockwood, Randolph Scott Dewey, 357
London *Daily Telegraph,* 223
London *Daily Worker,* 58, 127, 481, 502, 503
London *Evening Standard,* 433
Lord, Herbert A., 255–256, 257, 258, 260,
    261, 262, 264
Lovett, Robert A., 279–280
Lovless, Jay, 85, 87
Luster, H. R., 134–135
Lynch, Eugene Michael, 94, 96, 99, 100–
    101, 120–121, 129, 130, 158, 164,
    165–167, 170–171, 176, 179, 206–

Lynch, Eugene Michael (*cont.*)
207, 224, 282, 339, 373, 382, 414,
420–424, 483, 594

McAlister, Francis, 374
MacArthur, Arthur, 437
MacArthur, Douglas, 7, 25, 35, 38, 45, 46,
47, 48, 58, 60, 68, 88, 89, 99, 108,
114, 151–153, 162, 169, 170, 175–
177, 182, 183, 184–185, 191, 249,
265, 279, 280, 290, 344, 362, 366,
370, 372–373, 381, 382, 383, 399,
486–487, 594
all-out war sought by, 357–358, 389–391,
414–415, 419–420
bombing of Yalu River bridges ordered
by, 271, 272
Chiang's meeting with, 134–135
Collins's conference with, 92–93
and crossing of 38th parallel, 233, 234–
235, 422
in departure from Japan, 436–437
"die for a tie" press conference of, 415
divided command created by, 239, 246,
274
emergency conference held by, 307–308
Han River crossing observed by, 211–212
homecoming of, 437–438
Inchon battlefield visited by, 201–202
Inchon landings observed by, 133–195
Inchon site advocated by, 179
on invasion of South Korea, 29–30, 34
JCS and, 90, 227, 233, 235, 238, 239, 250,
253–254, 272–274, 307, 310, 345,
378–389, 389–390, 392, 401, 419–420
liberation of Seoul announced by, 223
Mao's trap and, 272
Martin letter of, 426
Murrow's criticism of, 150
named Commander-in-Chief, UN forces,
90
"new war" cable of, 306–307
"old soldiers" speech of, 437–438
Operation Killer and, 406–407
Operation Order 4 issued by, 246
in Polk's correspondence, 351, 358, 364
Rhee's meeting with, 62
Ridgway and, 373, 376–377, 392–393,
395, 406–407, 410, 414–415, 419
Ridgway as replacement of, 430–433
risk of China's intervention minimized by,
243, 252
Seoul burning observed by, 61–62
at Seoul victory ceremony, 228–230
special UN communiqué of, 283
State Department message to, 250
Truman's conflict with, 180–181, 273, 307,
390–391
Truman's firing of, 425–426, 429–435
U.S. combat team requested by, 64–65
Wake Conference and, 240–242
Walker and, 117, 210, 282–283
Whitney and, 186–187
Yalu River reconnoitered by, 281–282
MacArthur, Jean, 431, 436–437

McCaffrey, William, 378, 442–444
McCarthy, Joseph, 579
McClure, Robert, 387, 460
McConnell, David, 484, 485–486
MacDonald, Callum, 373
McFarland, Ernest, 577
McGee, Paul, 404
McGill, Henry, 97
McGrail, Thomas, 97, 101, 102
McLaughlin, John, 314, 316–317
MacLean, Allan D., 96, 100–101, 130, 166,
206, 297–298, 304–305, 308–309
McLennan, Kenneth, 577
McMains, D. M., 320
McNeely, Morgan, 139
Maher, Thomas, 97
Mahurin, Walker, 585–586
Mainichi Shimbun, 433
Makarounis, Lieutenant, 114–118
Malenkov, Georgy, 556–558
Malik, Jacob, 36, 54, 471–472, 473, 474
Manring, Roy, 153
Mao Anoing, 290
Mao Tse-tung, 59, 68, 72–73, 134, 236, 243,
248–249, 286, 290, 304, 351–352,
389, 454, 466, 474, 483, 484, 557,
568, 572, 574, 593
Inchon landings predicted by, 187–188,
198–199
May Day appearance of, 457
peace talks and, 493
Peng and, 237, 251, 270, 274–275, 280,
356, 362, 370–371, 391, 408, 464
personality of, 73
Soviet strategy rejected by, 367–368, 387
Stalin's meeting with, 73–74
Marie-Madeleine, Sister, 257, 263
Marshall, George C., 16, 250, 273, 279, 282,
390, 429, 430, 433
Martel, Madame, 260, 261, 262
Martin, Admiral, 507, 513
Martin, Dwight, 384, 502–503
Martin, Harold, 133
Martin, Joe, 426, 430
Martin, Robert, 87–88
Mary Clare, Sister, 256, 257, 263
Mauldin, Bill, 86
May, Hugh, 336
May, Ray, 60
Meloy, Guy, Jr., 92, 97
Mercer, Sam, 446–447, 456
Meszar, Frank, 396
Metze, Albert, 579
Michaelis, John "Mike," 121, 131–133, 137,
158, 392
Paik and, 159–160
"MiG Alley," 458
Milburn, Frank "Shrimp," 252, 268, 281, 286
Miller, Crosby "Dick," 308, 328, 329, 332,
336
Miller, Jerry, 337
Miller, Pop, 217–219
Miller, Robert C., 503
Mills, Robert, 528
Milton, Ralph, 349

Mize, Charles, 223, 292, 293, 324, 325, 342, 343, 360–361, 366
Montclar, Ralph, 396
Mortrude, James, 328
Mott, Harold, 112, 113, 114
Mount McKinley, 185, 186, 187, 193, 195, 201, 202, 210
Muccio, John J., 28–29, 31, 32, 38, 45, 47–48, 56, 74, 77, 78, 129, 227, 229, 377, 382, 430, 480
  Limb and, 43–44
  Rhee and, 24, 34–35, 40, 57–58, 59, 62, 149–152
  State Department instructions to, 57
  at Wake Conference, 241
Murray, James, 475–476
Murray, Raymond, 138, 146, 172, 173, 219, 220, 229, 283, 290, 297, 359, 360
  "advance to the rear" talk of, 355–356
  Hagaru-ri attack and, 322–327, 342–343, 346, 347
  Han River Crossings and, 207–208, 209, 211, 213, 216, 217
  at Inchon landings, 195–196
  liquor incident and, 374
  Obong-ni Ridge fighting and, 167–169
Murrow, Edward R., 150
Mydans, Carl, 79–80, 93
Myers, Baldwin Frank, 114–120, 121, 122–123

Naktong River, Battle of, 150–151, 153–157, 161–162, 163, 164–166, 169
Nam Il, 477–478, 480–481, 488, 518, 527, 533, 535–536, 542, 543, 564, 565, 566, 571, 574, 575, 588
Napalm Face (Chinese interrogator), 452–453, 456
National Defense Ministry, ROK, 23, 34
National Security Council, U.S., 63, 134–135, 307
NATO, *see* North Atlantic Treaty Organization
Naylor-Foote, Lieutenant, 508–515, 581
NBC-TV, 86, 110–111, 244
Needham, Joseph, 538, 595
Nehru, Jawaharlal, 235, 564
Neutral National Repatriation Committee, 565
Neutral Nations Supervisory Commission, 519
Newsweek, 150, 562
New Times, 98
Newton, George, 153, 155, 156, 168, 171
New Yorker, 433
New York *Herald Tribune*, 31, 48, 79, 87, 93, 435, 484, 485
New York Times, 35, 40, 41, 48, 54, 58, 63, 152, 238, 435, 485, 487, 488, 494, 503
Nieh Yen-jung, 219–220
Noble, Harold, 24, 46–47, 56–57, 60, 74–79, 97, 129, 151, 228
Noel, Frank "Pappy," 314, 495
No Name Line, 458, 460, 461

North Atlantic Treaty Organization (NATO), 25, 38, 521, 525, 532, 549, 594–595
North Korea, *see* Korea, Democratic People's Republic of
Nuckols, William, 489, 502

Oak Hyung-uk, 82
Obong-ni Ridge, 153, 156, 158, 162, 168, 171
Observation Hill, 173
O'Donnell, Emmett, 470–471
Oh, Captain, 496, 497, 498
O'Neal, Floyd, 538
Operation Big Switch, 579–587, 590
Operation Commando, 487
Operation Dauntless, 435
Operation Detonate, 458
Operation Hawk, 420
Operation Killer, 406, 410
Operation Little Switch, 561, 579
Operation Piledriver, 472
Operation Ripper, 410–415, 419, 420
Operation Smack, 554–556
Operation Thunderbolt, 394
Operation Tomahawk, 422–423
Operation Wolfhound, 391, 392
Organization of American States, 58
Ortenzi, Carlos, 299
Outpost Hedy, 577
Overseas Press Club, 150
Owen, Norman, 256

Pace, Frank, Jr., 31–32, 65, 240, 430, 432–433, 434, 483–484
Paik Sun-yup "Whitey," 27, 28, 57, 59–60, 151, 152, 158, 205, 210, 239, 243, 246–248, 254, 265, 453, 465, 567
  Chinese intervention discovered by, 251–252
  heroism of, 159–160
  Michaelis and, 159–160
  peace talks and, 477, 479, 482
Pak, Colonel, 513, 515
Pak Sang-hyon, 516–517, 520, 521, 587
Pak Sung-chol, 185
Palmer, Charles D., 383, 421–422
Pang Ho-san, 112
Panikkar, Kavalam, 219, 235, 352, 368, 433, 457–458
Park, Colonel, 199, 200, 202
Park Ki-byung, 55
Park Ki-cheol, 112–113, 400, 592
Parks, Preston, Jr., 217–219, 292–293, 296, 346
Parrott, Lindesay, 63
Partridge, Earle, 129, 164, 177, 206, 224
Partridge, John, 363–364
Pate, Randolph, 582
Patton, George S., 88, 99, 111, 129, 130, 246, 279, 341, 372
  on speed vs. haste, 205
Patton, George S. (son), 576, 578
Payne, Charlie, 83
PC-703, 183

Peace Conference of the Asian and Pacific
    Region, 547–548
peace negotiations, 469–503, 533, 535–536
    Acheson and, 494
    agreement reached in, 566, 568
    armistice signed in, 574–576
    Bradley and, 475, 486–487
    Chou's conciliatory statement and, 557–
        558
    Clark and, 543, 548, 557, 572, 573
    Collins and, 486, 490
    Dean interview and, 496–499
    demilitarized zone issue in, 473, 475–481,
        485–491
    germ warfare allegations and, 537–538
    Hanley report and, 494
    JCS and, 474–475, 485, 486, 490–491,
        492, 493, 557
    Kim and, 479, 480, 481–482, 485, 557,
        572, 575
    Malik's proposal for, 471–472
    Mao and, 493
    media and, 481, 485–489, 494, 502–503
    Paik and, 477, 479, 482
    Peng and, 479, 480, 481–482, 485, 557,
        572, 574, 575
    POW issue and, 492–495, 501–502,
        518–519, 528, 530–531, 532, 542–
        543, 561, 564
    Rhee's opposition to, 479–480, 497
    Ridgway and, 475, 476, 479, 480, 481–
        482, 485–491, 492, 494, 519
    Stalin's death and, 556–557
    State Department and, 472, 473, 486, 487,
        490, 493
    38th parallel in, 473, 474, 478, 480–481
    Truman and, 474, 475, 542–543
Peach, Major, 127–129
Peking Radio, 473
Peng Teh-huai, 236, 243, 272, 286, 290, 304,
    344, 379, 381, 382, 462, 483, 565, 568
    fate of, 593
    Kim briefed by, 388–389
    Kim's meeting with, 248–249
    Mao as strategic partner of, 251, 270,
        274–275, 280, 356, 362, 370–371,
        391, 408, 464
    Mao's appointment of, 237
    peace agreement signed by, 576
    peace negotiations and, 475, 479, 480,
        481–482, 485, 557, 572, 574, 575
    Shtykov's strategy rejected by, 367–368,
        387
Penny, David E., 538
People's Daily, 473
People's Liberation Army, Chinese, 72–73
Perry, Miller, 85
Peterson, Willard, 326
Pierce, Eddie, 182
Poats, Rutherford, 406, 415, 435–436, 568,
    571
Poland, 74, 565
Politella, Dario, 131
Polk, James H., 351, 358–359, 364–365
Pope, Harris, 320

Pravda, 37, 58, 537–538, 556–557
Printup, Carter, 193
prisoners-of-war (POWs), 318, 463, 498, 532,
    540
    anti-Communist, 590–593
    atrocities alleged by, 587
    biological warfare and, 595
    British, 447–448, 452–455
    Chou's conciliatory statement on, 557–558
    Clark and, 522, 523, 525–528
    Dean as, 255, 375–376, 495–499, 502
    in Death March, 255–264
    Dodd Incident and, 520–525
    exchanges of, 561–562, 579–587
    false confessions by, 551–552
    indoctrination of, 374–375, 399–400
    North Korean, 400–401
    peace talks and, 492–495, 501–502,
        518–519, 528, 530–531, 532, 542–
        543, 561, 564
    Rhee's mass release of, 566–571
    Ridgway and, 518, 520, 522–524
    unrest among, 516–517, 526–529, 533–
        534
    Van Fleet and, 517, 518, 520, 522–526
Prosser, Wilfred, 363
Puller, Lewis "Chesty," 201, 207, 216, 217,
    219, 220, 222, 225, 312, 313, 319,
    363, 365
    Almond and, 212
    Seoul victory ceremony and, 228–230
Punchbowl, 465, 472, 576
Pusan Perimeter, 124, 132, 149–157, 161
    Battle of Naktong Ridge and, 150–157
    size of, 129–130
    Taegu's importance to, 150–151
    U.S. breakout from, 204, 224–225
    Walker's aerial reconnaissances and, 164–
        167, 170–171
    Walker's defensive dispositions in, 163–
        164
Pyle, Ernie, 86

Quinlan, Monsignor, 256, 257, 262, 264
Quinn, John, 537

Radio Pyongyang, 223, 474, 516
Radio Seoul (HLKA), 40
Raven, Wilber, 520
Rayburn, Sam, 68
Red Badge of Courage, The (Crane), 411
Reeves, Ed, 297, 301–303, 327, 334–336,
    337, 347–351, 360
Reilly, William, 298, 300, 309, 310
Reinholt, 40
Reston, James, 41, 54, 494
Reuters, 37, 80
Reynolds, Robert, 331
Rhee, Madame Syngman, 35, 43–44, 48, 57,
    59, 62, 75, 122, 150, 229, 377
Rhee, Syngman, 20, 25, 28, 31, 33, 35, 39,
    48, 65, 71, 73, 74–75, 77, 78–79, 113,
    122, 124, 125, 186, 200, 227, 392,
    573–574, 588, 592, 594

Rhee, Syngman (*cont.*)
  atrocities and, 129
  background of, 17
  Chung appointed chief of staff by, 67
  Clark and, 566–568
  Eisenhower's correspondence with,
      560–561, 565–566
  Eisenhower's Korea visit and, 550–551
  election of, 17
  Hausman's assessment of, 567
  MacArthur's dismissal and, 433
  MacArthur's meeting with, 62
  martial law declared by, 566
  mass release of POWs by, 566–571
  Muccio and, 24, 34–35, 40, 57–58, 59, 62,
      149–162
  peace negotiations opposed by, 479–480,
      497
  retreating troops confronted by, 382–383
  Ridgway and, 382–383
  Ridgway's first meeting with, 377
  Seoul evacuated by, 43–45, 386
  at Seoul victory ceremony, 228–230
  38th parallel ordered crossed by, 233–234
  Walker's death and, 372
  Walker's meeting with, 98
Rhee Dai-yong, 28
Ridge, Thomas, 220, 221, 222
Ridgway, Matthew, 72, 282, 380–381, 385,
    386, 434, 444, 458, 461, 465, 532,
    547, 594
  aerial reconnaissances by, 382, 394–395
  Chipyong battlefield reconnoitered by,
      405–406
  Clark's replacement of, 521
  Collins and, 378, 379, 383, 388, 392–393
  in departure from Japan, 525
  JCS and, 438–439, 462, 471–473, 474,
      480, 485–486, 490–491
  on MacArthur, 373
  MacArthur and, 376–377, 392–393, 395,
      406–407, 410, 414–415, 419
  MacArthur replaced by, 430–433
  on Malik's peace proposal, 474
  media and, 410, 487–488, 502–503
  nickname of, 378
  Operation Thunderbolt ordered by, 394
  Operation Wolfhound launched by, 391
  peace negotiations and, 475, 476, 479,
      480, 481–482, 485–491, 492, 494, 519
  personality of, 376, 377–378
  POW unrest and, 518, 520, 522–524
  Rhee and, 377, 382–383
  Sebald on, 437
  UN retreat described by, 381–384
  Van Fleet contrasted with, 435–436
  Walker replaced by, 372
Ridgway, Matty, 373, 384
Ridgway, Penny, 373, 384
Robbins, Hugh, 298, 308–309, 327, 329,
    332, 336
Roberts, William, 24
Robertson, Oliver, 300
Robertson, Walter, 573
Rochester, 195, 507, 511

Rockwell, Lloyd, 27
Roise, Harold, 138–139, 297, 361
ROK, *see* Korea, Republic of
Roosevelt, Franklin D., 16, 37
Rowny, Edward, 228
Ruffner, Clark, 460
Rusk, Dean, 31, 32, 34, 240
Russ, Martin, 560, 577–578
Russell, Richard, 471
Ryan, Mark, 595

Saksa, Lieutenant, 269
Salahutdin, Shaucat, 259
Salisbury, Harrison, 238
Sams, Crawford S., 416–419, 536
Sanders, Cecil, 221
Sanders, Private, 138, 145
Saturday Evening Post, 133
Schreier, Harold, 325, 326
Schryver, Nick, 156
Schwable, Frank, 551–553, 585
Scott, Win, 356
Scullion, Ed, 299
Sebald, William, 432, 436
  on Ridgway, 437
Security Council, UN, 32, 54, 227
  emergency meeting of, 36–37
  Korean Command established by, 90
Seeley, Henry "Pop," 314–315
Selected Short Stories (Pastofsky), 497
Sell, Ted, 227–228, 229
Senate, U.S., 41, 43, 438
Senate Foreign Relations Committee, 40
Sergeant Andrew Miller, 370
Shadrick (U.S. infantryman), 83
Sharra, George, 113–114
Shaw, John, 540
Shening, R. J., 198
Shepherd, Lemuel, Jr., 195, 202
Sherman, Forrest, 38, 175–176, 178, 179,
    180, 310
Shin (defense minister), 43, 44, 45, 75, 114
Shin Sga-bong, 185–186
Shoemaker, Harold, 403
Short, Dewey, 68, 438
Shtykov, Terenty F., 26, 199, 367, 387
Siegal, Judah, 208–209
Simmons, Edwin, 220–222
Simmons, Walter, 74
Sitter, Carl, 312–314, 319
Smalley, Everett, 305
Smith, Archie, 94
Smith, Charles Bradley, 78, 80, 81–82, 83
Smith, H. Alexander, 54
Smith, Lawrence, 208
Smith, Lynn, 181, 187
Smith, Oliver P., 176, 201, 212, 219, 220,
    226, 229, 304, 305, 312, 313, 322,
    327, 328, 347, 357, 374
  Almond's conflict with, 215–217
Song Hyo-soon, 567, 569
Song Jeung-taik, 30
Soule, Robert "Shorty," 425, 444
South Korea, *see* Korea, Republic of

Soviet Union, 8, 32, 35–36, 37, 54, 63, 307,
    352, 391, 419, 473, 474, 594
  atomic bomb produced by, 72
  China and, 73–74, 238, 557
  North Korea aided by, 484, 557
  North Korea recognized by, 17
  UN boycotted by, 36
  U.S. atrocities alleged by, 548
Spud Hill, 554–555
Stalin, Joseph, 16, 36, 38, 72, 199, 202, 307,
    433, 473–474, 484, 594
  on China's entry into Korean War, 238
  death of, 556–557
  Mao's meeting with, 73–74
  Nineteenth Party Congress remarks of,
    547–548
Stamford, Edward, 298–299, 310, 327–330,
    332–333, 336
Stars and Stripes, 499, 527, 582
State Department, U.S., 31, 32, 35, 44, 279,
    390, 420, 438
  MacArthur's message from, 250
  Muccio instructed by, 57
  peace negotiations and, 472, 473, 486,
    487, 490, 493
Stephens, Richard, 92, 93, 97, 282
Stewart, George, 405
Stewart, Joseph, 142–143, 220, 360
Stilwell, Joseph, 526
Stone, I. F., 484
Stratemeyer, George, 60, 271
Strong, Paschal, 371
Struble, Arthur, 178, 195, 202
Suk Chu-am, 567
Sullivan, Marcus, 420, 421, 422, 423
Sun Tzu, 280
Sun Yong-chang, 569
Sweden, 565
Swenson, Swede, 324, 341

Taegu, 129, 149, 150–151, 159, 169
Taejon, 90, 91–107, 111, 177, 178
Taft, Robert, 59
Taplett, Robert, 136–145, 153, 156, 157,
    181, 186, 213, 281, 283, 296, 297,
    374, 483
  Chosin Reservoir fighting and, 290–293
  fall of Seoul and, 220–221, 223, 225, 226
  Hagaru-ri attack and, 322–327, 341–345,
    351
  Han River crossing and, 207–212
  in Inchon landings, 191–193, 195–196
  Obong-ni Ridge fighting and, 167–169,
    172–174
  retreat to Koto-ri and, 359–361
  Seoul victory ceremony and, 226–227
Tarkenton, James, 371, 458
Task Force Cooper, 279, 281, 286
Task Force Dolvin, 284–285, 306
Task Force Drysdale, 312–313, 327, 359
Task Force Faith, 310, 327, 328, 336, 338,
    344, 347, 360
Task Force Kean, 135, 139–140, 146, 149,
    150
Task Force Kingston, 306

Task Force Lynch, 224–225
Task Force McGrail, 97
Task Force MacLean, 310, 344
Task Force Smith, 77–78, 80–82, 85
TASS, 58
Taylor, Maxwell, 568
  Van Fleet replaced by, 556
Temple, Lieutenant, 441
Teng Hsiao-ping, 73
Thérèse, Mother, 256, 260, 261, 263
Thimaya, General, 590–591
38th parallel, 200, 233–234, 238, 339, 340,
    369, 389, 390, 422, 464, 588
  in peace negotiations, 473, 474, 478, 480–
    481
  Truman on crossing of, 235
Thompson, Reginald, 223, 281
Thorin, Duane, 507–515, 580–582
Thornton, Cordus, 258–259
"Tiger," Major, 256–260, 262
Tighe, Larry, 31
Tihinoff, Ivan, 260
Time, 50, 79, 246, 384, 502, 503, 562
  Van Fleet described by, 435
  Walker on cover of, 123
Tito (Josip Broz), 36
Tobin, John, 153
Tofte, Hans, 182
Tolman, Lieutenant, 143
Tovar, Guillarmo, 316–317
Trollope, Harry, 265–270, 276–279, 283–
    284, 285
Truman, Harry S., 7–8, 17, 25, 35, 41, 45,
    48, 59, 64, 71, 75, 250, 253, 254, 345,
    378, 399, 491, 594
  Acheson contrasted with, 42
  aid to South Korea announced by, 58
  atomic bomb news conference of, 321–
    322
  bombing of Yalu River bridges authorized
    by, 271
  Burke's briefing of, 493–494
  Chiang's troop offer declined by, 68
  Clark's atomic bomb proposal rejected by,
    548
  Collins's briefing of, 362
  Collins's report to, 180–181
  combat team authorized by, 65
  congressional leaders briefed by, 53–54,
    67–68
  Connally and, 40–41
  and crossing of 38th parallel, 235
  on decision to commit U.S. troops, 42
  domestic support for, 58
  on Eisenhower, 549
  Eisenhower's inauguration and, 553–554
  first formal statement on Korea by, 41
  international support for, 58
  on invasion of South Korea, 32
  Korean War termed police action by, 63
  MacArthur and, 273
  MacArthur-Chiang meeting and, 133–134
  MacArthur fired by, 425–426, 429–435
  MacArthur's conflict with, 180–181, 273,
    307, 390–391

Truman, Harry S. (*cont.*)
  MacArthur's Formosa statement and, 180–
    181
  on Malik's peace proposal, 473
  military commitment made by, 37–38
  national emergency proclaimed by, 368
  and partition of Korea, 16
  peace negotiations and, 474, 475, 542–543
  Soviet policy misunderstood by, 72–74
  Wake Conference and, 240–242
  Wherry's confrontation with, 368
Truman, Margaret, 37
Truman Doctrine, 36
Tsai, Colonel, 502
Tunstall, Julian, 248, 279, 386
Twin Tunnels, Battle of, 395–399, 401
Tyner, Layton "Joe," 87, 111, 121, 129, 130,
    158, 164, 170, 206, 224, 282, 371–373
Tzo Peng, 409, 454

Underwood, Horace, 208
Underwood, Richard, 519
United Kingdom, 54, 72, 370–371
United Kingdom, military units of:
  Commonwealth Brigade, 279, 402, 550
  29th Independent Brigade, 380, 440, 452
  27th Infantry Brigade, 162, 239, 380
  Middlesex Regiment, 248, 386
  41st Commando Battalion, 312, 314
  1st Gloster Battalion, 440–442, 445–447
  1st Royal Ulster Rifle Battalion, 385, 440,
    449
  King's Royal Irish Hussars, 449
  Royal Northumberland Fusilier Battalion,
    440
United Nations, 7, 16–17, 37, 41, 42, 54, 63,
    76, 127–129, 321–322, 352, 391, 425,
    494, 503, 552–553, 561, 594
  Disarmament Commission of, 536
  MacArthur's special communiqué to, 283
  North Korea condemned by, 45
  Political Committee of, 548
  POW issue in, 548
  resolution supporting occupation of North
    Korea passed by, 238–239
  South Korea supported by, 72
  Soviet boycott of, 36
  Soviet cease-fire plan in, 235
  see also Security Council, UN
United Nations Communiqué 9, 223
United Nations Temporary Commission on
    Korea (UNTCOK), 16–17
United Press, 29, 30, 31, 60, 281, 321–322,
    406, 415, 419, 495, 498, 503, 529,
    562, 571, 574, 578
United States, 16, 351–352, 371
  antiwar feeling in, 487, 548
  and invasion of South Korea, 35–36,
    40–41
  Korean War outcome and, 8, 594–595
  military unreadiness of, 71–72
United States, military units of:
  Fifth Air Force, 94, 164, 481, 554, 568
  1st Marine Aircraft Wing, 551
  Marine Air Group, 33, 156

United States, military units of (*cont.*)
  Seventh Fleet, 38, 42, 72, 178, 507
  Third Army, 130, 132
  Eighth Army, 87, 91, 93, 96, 100, 111,
    117, 120, 129–132, 162–164, 170–
    171, 173, 185, 199, 205, 210, 224,
    233, 250, 252–253, 265, 271, 273–
    275, 280, 283, 286, 289, 306–308,
    320, 339, 341, 344–345, 357, 358,
    362, 369–371, 373, 377, 382–383,
    386, 391, 392, 394, 406, 430, 434–
    435, 438–439, 444, 452–453, 461–
    462, 473–474, 484, 487, 522–524,
    527, 547, 551, 556, 567
  I Corps, 268, 281, 286, 357, 380, 381, 383,
    386, 392, 394, 422, 442, 453, 461–
    462, 465, 472, 522, 554
  IX Corps, 238, 281, 372, 380, 381, 383,
    386, 392, 394, 402, 406, 420, 442,
    461, 462, 465, 547
  X Corps, 176, 205, 210, 212, 215, 217,
    220, 224, 226, 233, 238, 239, 250,
    251, 273, 274, 275, 279, 281, 289,
    304, 306, 307–308, 310, 314, 327,
    339, 345, 358, 362, 369, 373, 386,
    392, 420, 439, 458, 460, 461, 472
  1st Cavalry Division, 99, 104, 111, 120,
    121, 151, 163, 164, 167, 171, 204,
    224, 243–244, 248, 341, 344, 415,
    420, 421, 444, 472
  2nd Infantry Division, 162, 163, 164, 166–
    167, 170, 171, 204, 210, 270, 286,
    306, 310, 320, 340, 344, 371, 382,
    387, 392, 405, 460, 461, 462, 463,
    526, 539
  3rd Infantry Division, 425, 444, 450, 461,
    472, 522, 550, 574
  7th Infantry Division, 212, 216, 219, 223,
    224, 225, 227, 270, 274, 279, 283,
    286, 289, 297, 307, 554
  24th Infantry Division, 75, 77, 86, 92, 96,
    99–101, 112, 131, 163, 164, 204, 210,
    224, 239, 265, 281, 306, 369, 380,
    382, 450
  25th Infantry Division, 89, 108, 120, 121,
    129, 131, 135, 142–144, 158, 160,
    161, 162, 163, 164, 171, 238, 284,
    306, 310, 344, 357, 369, 380, 410,
    414, 442, 450, 472
  1st Marine Division, 174, 201, 220, 223,
    289, 290, 304, 307, 315, 328, 357,
    450, 559
  1st Provisional Marine Brigade, 134, 312–
    313, 319
  5th Cavalry Regiment, 248, 402, 403, 405
  7th Cavalry Regiment, 224, 246, 395
  8th Cavalry Regiment, 204, 210, 265, 268–
    269, 270
  5th Infantry Regiment, 406, 450
  7th Infantry Regiment, 450
  9th Infantry Regiment, 162, 165, 166, 286,
    320, 522, 528
  15th Infantry Regiment, 539, 550
  19th Infantry Regiment, 88, 89, 92, 96,
    97, 99, 101, 105, 163, 382

United States, military units of (*cont.*)
  21st Infantry Regiment, 77, 86, 88, 92, 97,
    99–100, 163, 282
  23rd Infantry Regiment, 163, 306, 387,
    395–398, 402–405, 518
  24th Infantry Regiment, 285, 410
  27th Infantry Regiment, 89, 121, 137, 158,
    159, 163, 164, 284, 392, 518
  29th Infantry Regiment, 112
  31st Infantry Regiment, 289, 297, 298,
    305, 309–310, 312–313, 314, 329,
    330, 347, 442
  32nd Infantry Regiment, 212, 216, 283,
    297, 329, 330, 333
  34th Infantry Regiment, 80, 85, 87–88,
    89, 92, 94–96, 97, 100, 101, 102, 104,
    105, 216, 258
  35th Infantry Regiment, 137, 142, 162,
    165–166
  38th Infantry Regiment, 210, 392, 402,
    460, 523
  65th Infantry Regiment, 238, 442
  312th Infantry Regiment, 554
  1st Marine Regiment, 195, 196, 201, 207,
    212, 215, 219, 222, 227, 362, 365,
    472, 560
  5th Marine Regiment, 134–135, 136, 138–
    140, 142, 146, 150, 153, 163, 167,
    174, 181, 195, 196, 197, 198, 200,
    202, 204, 207, 211, 213, 214, 217,
    219, 281, 283, 289, 290, 304, 312,
    322, 325, 343, 347, 359, 361, 374
  7th Marine Regiment, 227, 270, 271, 281,
    289, 290, 291, 304, 312, 322, 323–
    324, 325, 327, 342, 343, 344, 347,
    356–357, 359, 450, 472
  11th Marine Regiment, 357
  187th Airborne Regimental Combat Team,
    402, 420, 422, 423, 461, 533
  5th Regimental Combat Team, 135, 137,
    142, 167
  9th Regimental Combat Team, 153
  23rd Regimental Combat Team, 386, 404,
    406
  24th Regimental Combat Team, 109
  38th Regimental Combat Team, 386
  21st AAA (Antiaircraft Artillery) Battalion,
    410
  57th Field Artillery Battalion, 297, 300,
    554
  90th Field Artillery Battalion, 142
  555th Field Artillery Battalion, 142, 143,
    144, 450
  94th Military Police Battalion, 520
  89th Tank Battalion, 285, 394, 410
  140th Tank Battalion, 576
  77th Combat Engineers Company, 109,
    135, 411
  2nd Logistical Command, 521, 527
  11th Evacuation Hospital, 579
  8055th Mobile Army Surgical Hospital
    (MASH), 372

Vandenberg, Hoyt, 38, 92–93, 94, 391–392
Van Fleet, James, 430, 444, 453–454, 458,

Van Fleet, James (*cont.*)
    460, 461–462, 472, 473, 474, 484,
    501, 547, 554
  amphibious landing proposed by, 438–
    439, 465
  POW unrest and, 517, 518, 520, 522–526
  Ridgway contrasted with, 435–436
  Taylor's replacement of, 556
  Time's description of, 435
Vanretti, Sergeant, 305, 306
Vanture, Paul, 450
Vargas (radio operator), 221
Vatcher, William, 536
Veterans of Foreign Wars (VFW), 181, 241
Villemot, Paul, 126, 256, 257, 262
Voice of America, 58

Wadlington, Robert "Pappy," 92, 94, 96, 97,
    102, 105–106
Wake Conference, 240–242
Walker, Ray, 197–198
Walker, Sam, 224, 345, 371, 372
Walker, Walton, 87, 91, 92, 93, 99, 108–109,
    111, 124, 129, 135, 142, 149, 151–
    152, 153, 159, 160, 161, 185, 186,
    199, 246, 249, 250, 252, 253, 268,
    270, 271, 273, 274, 275, 280, 281,
    297, 344–345, 358, 362, 369, 370,
    376, 390, 483, 594
  aerial reconnaissances by, 100, 107, 120,
    164–167, 170–171, 206–207
  Almond as perceived by, 205–206
  on ammunition usage, 205
  assessment of, 373
  as censured by X Corps, 310–311
  Collins and, 176–178
  correspondent reprimanded by, 158
  Dean's briefing of, 89
  death of, 371–373
  enemy forces as analyzed by, 131–132,
    162–164
  Hausman's first meeting with, 98
  hidden frustrations of, 339–340
  "hold this line" speech of, 121
  Inchon alternate of, 176–178
  Kum River battle viewed by, 104–106
  leadership style of, 130
  MacArthur and, 117, 210, 282–283
  at MacArthur's emergency conference,
    307–308, 339
  Naktong Bulge reconnoitered by, 164–167
  Patton as model for, 88, 89–90, 130–131,
    162, 205, 341
  in Polk's correspondence, 364
  Pusan Perimeter breakout and, 204–205,
    210, 224
  Pusan Perimeter conceived by, 96
  Pyongyang area reconnoitered by, 340–
    341
  Pyongyang offensive and, 238–239
  Rhee's meeting with, 98
  Ridgway as replacement of, 372
  Silver Star awarded to, 228
  Taejon reconnoitered by, 206–207
  on *Time* cover, 123

Wallace L. Lind, 417
Wang Tsun-ming, 439–440
War As I Knew It (Patton), 130
Washington Post, 40, 435
Watson, Jimmie, 269, 278
Wei Tzu Liang, 409
Westerman, Jack, 225–226
Weston, Logan, 133
Wherry, Kenneth S., 68, 368
White, Horton, 109
White Horse Hill, 547
Whitney, Courtney, 60, 186–187, 241, 379,
    390, 431–432
Williams, Dick, 577
Williamson, Harold, 325, 341–342, 360
Willoughby, Charles A., 61, 364–365
Wilson, Harry, 424
Winnington, Alan, 127, 481, 489, 502–503,
    535, 586
Winstead, Otho, 97
Winton, Walter F., Jr., 376, 420, 421, 422,
    423
Won Yong-duk, 566, 567, 569, 570
World Health Organization, 538
World Peace Council, 538

Wright, Edwin, 273–274
Wright, W.H.S., 48, 50, 51, 52
Wrong, Hume, 535
Wu Chengde, 464
WVTP radio station, 33–34

Yao Chin-chung, 451
Yeager, Jim, 115
Yechon, Battle of, 108–110
Yoshida Shigeru, 432, 525
Youn Joung, 182, 183, 184, 416, 418
Yount, Paul, 521, 523, 524, 526, 527
Yugoslavia, 32, 36, 37, 54
Yu Jae-hung, 286
Yu Jai-hyung, 20, 26, 56–57, 76, 460, 461
Yu Suncheol, 19
Yu Tzeh-an, 454

Zellers, Larry, 25, 40, 45, 256, 257,
    259–260, 262, 263–264, 477, 498,
    562–563, 589
Zhang Da, 463
Zhang Zeshi, 524–525, 593
Zullo, Rocco, 221, 313–314, 319

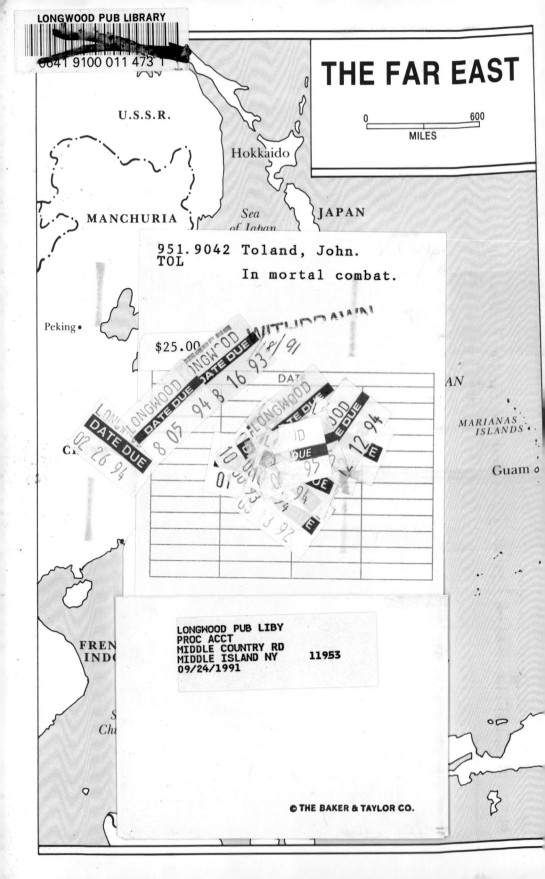

THE FAR EAST

0   600
MILES

U.S.S.R.

Hokkaido

MANCHURIA

Sea
of Japan

JAPAN

Peking •

951.9042   Toland, John.
TOL
     In mortal combat.

$25.00

MARIANAS
ISLANDS

Guam

WITHDRAWN

DATE DUE

02 26 94

FREN
INDO

© THE BAKER & TAYLOR CO.